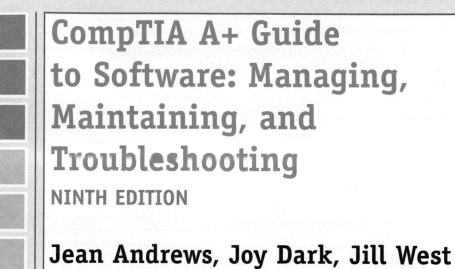

CompTIA A+ Guide to Software: Managing, Maintaining, and Troubleshooting

NINTH EDITION

Jean Andrews, Joy Dark, Jill West

CENGAGE
Learning·

Australia • Canada • Mexico • Singapore • Spain • United Kingdom • United States

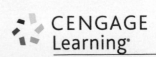

CompTIA A+ Guide to Software: Managing, Maintaining, and Troubleshooting, Ninth Edition, Jean Andrews, Joy Dark, Jill West

SVP, GM Skills & Global Product Management: Dawn Gerrain

Product Director: Kathleen McMahon

Product Team Manager: Kristin McNary

Senior Director, Development: Marah Bellegarde

Product Development Manager: Leigh Hefferon

Senior Content Developer: Michelle Ruelos Cannistraci

Product Assistant: Abigail Pufpaff

Vice President, Marketing Services: Jennifer Ann Baker

Marketing Director: Michele McTighe

Senior Production Director: Wendy Troeger

Production Director: Patty Stephan

Senior Content Project Manager: Brooke Greenhouse

Managing Art Director: Jack Pendleton

Cover image(s):

©iStockphoto.com/traffic_analyzer

©iStockphoto.com/simon2579

All screenshots, unless otherwise noted, are used with permission from Microsoft Corporation. Microsoft® is a registered trademark of the Microsoft Corporation.

For product information and technology assistance, contact us at **Cengage Learning Customer & Sales Support, 1-800-354-9706**

For permission to use material from this text or product, submit all requests online at **www.cengage.com/permissions** Further permissions questions can be e-mailed to **permissionrequest@cengage.com**

Library of Congress Control Number: 2015957525

ISBN: 978-1-305-26650-6

Cengage Learning
20 Channel Center Street
Boston, MA 02210
USA

Cengage Learning is a leading provider of customized learning solutions with employees residing in nearly 40 different countries and sales in more than 125 countries around the world. Find your local representative at **www.cengage.com.**

Cengage Learning products are represented in Canada by Nelson Education, Ltd.

To learn more about Cengage Learning, visit **www.cengage.com** Purchase any of our products at your local college store or at our preferred online store **www.cengagebrain.com**

Notice to the Reader

Publisher does not warrant or guarantee any of the products described herein or perform any independent analysis in connection with any of the product information contained herein. Publisher does not assume, and expressly disclaims, any obligation to obtain and include information other than that provided to it by the manufacturer. The reader is expressly warned to consider and adopt all safety precautions that might be indicated by the activities described herein and to avoid all potential hazards. By following the instructions contained herein, the reader willingly assumes all risks in connection with such instructions. The publisher makes no representations or warranties of any kind, including but not limited to, the warranties of fitness for particular purpose or merchantability, nor are any such representations implied with respect to the material set forth herein, and the publisher takes no responsibility with respect to such material. The publisher shall not be liable for any special, consequential, or exemplary damages resulting, in whole or part, from the readers' use of, or reliance upon, this material.

Printed in the United States of America
Print Number: 02   Print Year: 2017

Table of Contents

CHAPTER 8

Supporting Mobile Operating Systems........................359

CHAPTER 9

Windows Resources on a Network.... 417

CHAPTER 10

Security Strategies...............467

CHAPTER 11

Virtualization, Linux, and Mac OS X . . 523

APPENDIX A

Safety Procedures and Environmental Concerns 579

APPENDIX B

Entry Points for Startup Processes . . . 595

APPENDIX C

CompTIA A+ Acronyms 599

Glossary. 607

Index. 637

CompTIA A+ 220-902 Exam Mapped to Chapters

CompTIA A+ Guide to Software, Ninth Edition fully meets all of CompTIA's A+ 220-902 Exam Objectives.

DOMAIN 1.0 WINDOWS OPERATING SYSTEMS

1.1 **Compare and contrast various features and requirements of Microsoft Operating Systems (Windows Vista, Windows 7, Windows 8, Windows 8.1).**

OBJECTIVES	CHAPTER	SECTION
◢ Features:		
• 32-bit vs. 64-bit	1	System Window
• Aero, gadgets, user account control,	1	Windows Interfaces
bit-locker, shadow copy,	2	Windows Tools for Users and Technicians
system restore, ready boost,	2	Verify Your System Qualifies for Windows
sidebar, compatibility mode,	2	Installations with Special Considerations
virtual XP mode, easy transfer,	2	Set Up User Accounts and Transfer User Data
administrative tools, defender,	3	Backup Proceures
Windows firewall, security	3	Clean Up the Hard Drive
center, event viewer, file struc-	3	Back Up Windows System Files
ture and paths, category view	4	Step 5: Consider Using ReadyBoost
vs. classic view.	4	Administrative Tools
	4	Event Viewer
	10	Use BitLocker Encryption
	10	Step-by-Step Attack Plan
	10	Windows Firewall Settings
	10	Dealing with Malicious Software on Personal Computers
• Side by side apps, Metro UI,	1	Windows Interface
Pinning, One Drive, Windows store,	1	Windows Tools for Users and Technicians
Multimonitor task bars, Charms, Start	1	Windows User Accounts
Screen, Power Shell, Live sign in,	3	Display Settings and Graphics Software
Action Center.	4	Commands to Manage Files and Folders
◢ Upgrade paths – differences between	2	Choose the Type of Installation: In-Place Upgrade,
in place upgrades, compatibility tools,		Clean Install, or Dual Boot
Windows upgrade OS advisor		

1.2 **Given a scenario, install Windows PC operating systems using appropriate methods.**

OBJECTIVES	CHAPTER	SECTION
◢ Boot methods	2	How to Plan a Windows Installation
• USB	2	How to Plan a Windows Installation
• CD-ROM	2	How to Plan a Windows Installation
• DVD	2	How to Plan a Windows Installation
• PXE	2	Deployment Strategies for Windows
• Solid state/flash drives	2	How to Plan a Windows Installation
• Netboot	11	Troubleshoot OS X Startup
• External/hot swappable drive	2	How to Plan a Windows Installation
• Internal hard drive (partition)	2	How to Plan a Windows Installation
◢ Type of installations	2	How to Plan a Windows Installation
• Unattended installation	2	Deployment Strategies for Windows
• Upgrade	2	How to Plan a Windows Installation
• Clean install	2	How to Plan a Windows Installation

• Repair installation	2	How to Plan a Windows Installation
• Multiboot	2	How to Plan a Windows Installation
• Remote network installation	2	Deployment Strategies for Windows
• Image deployment	2	Deployment Strategies for Windows
• Recovery partition	2	Installations with Special Considerations
	6	Tools for Reinstalling Windows
• Refresh/restore	6	Tools for Reinstalling Windows
◢ Partitioning	3	Managing Files, Folders, and Storage Devices
• Dynamic	3	Managing Files, Folders, and Storage Devices
• Basic	3	Managing Files, Folders, and Storage Devices
• Primary	3	Managing Files, Folders, and Storage Devices
• Extended	3	Managing Files, Folders, and Storage Devices
• Logical	3	Managing Files, Folders, and Storage Devices
• GPT	3	Managing Files, Folders, and Storage Devices
◢ File system types/formatting		
• ExFAT	3	Managing Files, Folders, and Storage Devices
• FAT32	3	Managing Files, Folders, and Storage Devices
• NTFS	3	Managing Files, Folders, and Storage Devices
• CDFS	3	Managing Files, Folders, and Storage Devices
• NFS	9	How to Map a Network Drive or Network Printer
• ext3, ext4	11	Linux Commands
• Quick format vs. full format	3	Managing Files, Folders, and Storage Devices
◢ Load alternate third party drivers when necessary	2	Installations with Special Considerations
◢ Workgroup vs. Domain setup	1	Windows Network Connections
◢ Time/date/region/language settings	1	Control Panel
	2	Installing Windows 8.1 and Windows 7
◢ Driver installation, software and windows updates	2	What to Do After a Windows Installation
◢ Factory recovery partition	2	Installations with Special Considerations
◢ Properly formatted boot drive with the correct partitions/format	2	Installing Windows 8.1 and Windows 7

1.3   Given a scenario, apply appropriate Microsoft command line tools.

OBJECTIVES	CHAPTER	SECTION
◢ TASKKILL	5	Responding to Specific Error Messages
◢ BOOTREC	6	Error Messages and Problems
◢ SHUTDOWN	3	Commands to Manage Files and Folders
◢ TASKLIST	5	Responding to Specific Error Messages
◢ MD	3	Commands to Manage Files and Folders
◢ RD	3	Commands to Manage Files and Folders
◢ CD	3	Commands to Manage Files and Folders
◢ DEL	3	Commands to Manage Files and Folders
◢ FORMAT	3	Commands to Manage Files and Folders
◢ COPY	3	Commands to Manage Files and Folders
◢ XCOPY	3	Commands to Manage Files and Folders
◢ ROBOCOPY	3	Commands to Manage Files and Folders
◢ DISKPART	6	Tools That Can Affect Windows System Files and Settings
◢ SFC	5	System File Checker
◢ CHKDSK	3	Commands to Manage Files and Folders
◢ GPUPDATE	9	Use Group Policy to Improve QoS for Applications
◢ GPRESULT	9	How to Share Folders and Files

▲ System utilities

• REGEDIT	4	The Registry Editor
• COMMAND	3	Commands to Manage Files and Folders
• SERVICES.MSC	4	Services Console
• MMC	4	Microsoft Management Console (MMC)
• MSTSC	9	Remote Desktop Connection (RDC)
• NOTEPAD	1	Windows Tools for Users and Technicians
• EXPLORER	1	Windows 8 File Explorer and Windows 7 Windows Explorer
• MSINFO32	1	System Information Window
• DXDIAG	4	Display Settings and Graphics Software
• DEFRAG	3	Schedule Preventive Maintenance
• System restore	3	Back Up Windows System Files
• Windows Update	3	Schedule Preventive Maintenance

1.5   **Given a scenario, use Windows Control Panel utilities.**

OBJECTIVES	CHAPTER	SECTION
▲ Internet options	9	Internet Explorer
• Connections	9	Internet Explorer
• Security	9	Internet Explorer
• General	9	Internet Explorer
• Privacy	9	Internet Explorer
• Programs	9	Internet Explorer
• Advanced	9	Internet Explorer
▲ Display/Display Settings	4	Display Settings and Graphics Software
• Resolution	4	Display Settings and Graphics Software
• Color depth	4	Display Settings and Graphics Software
• Refresh rate	4	Display Settings and Graphics Software
▲ User accounts	1	Windows User Accounts
▲ Folder options	1	Folder Options
• View hidden files	1	Folder Options
• Hide extensions	1	Folder Options
• General options	1	Folder Options
• View options	1	Folder Options
▲ System		
• Performance (virtual memory)	3	Schedule Preventive Maintenance
• Remote settings	9	Remote Desktop Connection (RDC)
• System protection	3	Back Up Windows System Files
▲ Windows firewall	10	Windows Firewall Settings
▲ Power options	1	Power Options
• Hibernate	1	Power Options
• Power plans	1	Power Options
• Sleep/suspend	1	Power Options
• Standby	1	Power Options
▲ Programs and features	2	Install Applications
▲ HomeGroup	1	Windows Network Connections
▲ Devices and Printers	2	Install Hardware
▲ Sound	1	Control Panel
▲ Troubleshooting	9	How to Share Folders and Files
▲ Network and Sharing Center	1	Windows Network Connections
▲ Device Manager	2	Install Hardware

1.6 Given a scenario, install and configure Windows networking on a client/desktop.

OBJECTIVES	CHAPTER	SECTION
◢ HomeGroup vs. WorkGroup	1	Windows Network Connections
◢ Domain setup	1	Windows Network Connections
◢ Network shares/administrative shares/ mapping drives	9	Controlling Access to Folders and Files
◢ Printer sharing vs. network printer mapping	9	How to Map a Network Drive or Network Printer
◢ Establish networking connections	7	Connecting a Computer to a Network
• VPN	7	Create a VPN Connection
• Dialups	7	Create a Dial-Up Connection
• Wireless	7	Connect to an Ethernet Wired or Wireless Wi-Fi Local Network
• Wired	7	Connect to an Ethernet Wired or Wireless Wi-Fi Local Network
• WWAN (Cellular)	7	Connect to a Wireless WAN (Cellular) Network
◢ Proxy settings	9	Internet Explorer
◢ Remote Desktop Connection	9	Remote Desktop Connection (RDC)
◢ Remote Assistance	9	Remote Assistance
◢ Home vs. Work vs. Public network settings	1	Windows Network Connections
◢ Firewall settings	10	Windows Firewall Settings
• Exceptions	10	Windows Firewall Settings
• Configuration	10	Windows Firewall Settings
• Enabling/disabling Windows firewall	10	Windows Firewall Settings
◢ Configuring an alternative IP address in Windows	7	Alternate IP Address Configuration
• IP addressing	7	Dynamic and Static Configuration
• Subnet mask	7	How IPv4 IP Addresses Are Used
• DNS	7	Dynamic and Static Configuration
• Gateway	7	Dynamic and Static Configuration
◢ Network card properties		
• Half duplex/full duplex/auto	7	Manage Network Adapters
• Speed	7	Manage Network Adapters
• Wake-on-LAN	7	Manage Network Adapters
• QoS	7	Manage Network Adapters
	9	Use Group Policy to Improve QoS for Applications
• BIOS (on-board NIC)	7	Manage Network Adapters

1.7 Perform common preventive maintenance procedures using the appropriate Windows OS tools.

OBJECTIVES	CHAPTER	SECTION
◢ Best practices	3	
• Scheduled backups	3	Backup Procedures
• Scheduled disk maintenance	3	Schedule Preventive Maintenance
• Windows updates	3	Schedule Preventive Maintenance
• Patch management	3	Schedule Preventive Maintenance
• Driver/firmware updates	3	Schedule Preventive Maintenance
• Antivirus/ Antimalware updates	3	Schedule Preventive Maintenance
◢ Tools		
• Backup	3	Backup Procedures
• System restore	3	Backup Procedures
• Recovery image	6	Tools for Troubleshooting Windows Startup Problems
• Disk maintenance utilities	3	Schedule Preventive Maintenance

DOMAIN 2.0 OTHER OPERATING SYSTEMS AND TECHNOLOGIES

2.1   Identify common features and functionality of the Mac OS and Linux operating systems.

OBJECTIVES	CHAPTER	SECTION
◢ Best practices	11	
• Scheduled backups	11	Backups and Updates Maintain and Support a Mac
• Scheduled disk maintenance	11	Backups and Updates Maintain and Support a Mac
• System updates/App store	11	Backups and Updates Maintain and Support a Mac
• Patch management	11	Backups and Updates Maintain and Support a Mac
• Driver/firmware updates	11	Backups and Updates Maintain and Support a Mac
• Antivirus/ Antimalware updates	11	Backups and Updates Maintain and Support a Mac
◢ Tools	11	
• Backup/Time Machine	11	Maintain and Support a Mac
• Restore/snapshot	11	Maintain and Support a Mac
• Image recovery	11	Troubleshoot OS X Startup
• Disk maintenance utilities	11	Maintain and Support a Mac
• Shell/Terminal	11	Linux Commands Use the Mac
• Screen sharing	11	Use the Mac
• Force Quit	11	Use the Mac
◢ Features	11	
• Multiple desktops/Mission Control	11	Use the Mac
• Key Chain	11	Use the Mac
• Spot Light	11	Use the Mac
• iCloud	11	Use the Mac
• Gestures	11	Use the Mac
• Finder	11	Use the Mac
• Remote Disc	11	Use the Mac
• Dock	11	Use the Mac
• Boot Camp	11	Boot Camp
◢ Basic Linux commands		
• ls	11	Linux Commands Use the Mac
• grep	11	Linux Commands Hands-On Project 20-4: Install FTP Server in Ubuntu
• cd	11	Linux Commands Use the Mac
• shutdown	11	Linux Commands
• pwd vs. passwd	11	Linux Commands Use the Mac
• mv	11	Linux Commands
• cp	11	Linux Commands
• rm	11	Linux Commands
• chmod	11	Linux Commands
• mkdir	11	Linux Commands Use the Mac
• chown	11	Linux Commands

• App source (play store, app store and store)	8	Operating Systems Used on Mobile Devices
• Screen orientation (accelerometer/gyroscope)	8	Operating Systems Used on Mobile Devices
• Screen calibration	8	Operating Systems Used on Mobile Devices
• GPS and geotracking	8	Operating Systems Used on Mobile Devices
• WiFi calling	8	Operating Systems Used on Mobile Devices
• Launcher/GUI	8	Operating Systems Used on Mobile Devices
• Virtual assistant	8	Operating Systems Used on Mobile Devices
• SDK/APK	8	Operating Systems Used on Mobile Devices
• Emergency notification	8	Operating Systems Used on Mobile Devices
• Mobile payment service	8	Operating Systems Used on Mobile Devices

2.6   Install and configure basic mobile device network connectivity and email.

OBJECTIVES	CHAPTER	SECTION
◢ Wireless / cellular data network (enable/disable)	8	Configure iOS Network Connections Configure Android Network Connections Configure Windows Phone Network Connections
• Hotspot	8	Configure iOS Network Connections Configure Android Network Connections Configure Windows Phone Network Connections
• Tethering	8	Configure iOS Network Connections Configure Android Network Connections Configure Windows Phone Network Connections
• Airplane mode	8	Configure iOS Network Connections Configure Android Network Connections Configure Windows Phone Network Connections
◢ Bluetooth	8	Configure iOS Network Connections Configure Android Network Connections Configure Windows Phone Network Connections
• Enable Bluetooth	8	Configure iOS Network Connections Configure Android Network Connections Configure Windows Phone Network Connections
• Enable pairing	8	Configure iOS Network Connections Configure Android Network Connections Configure Windows Phone Network Connections
• Find device for pairing	8	Configure iOS Network Connections Configure Android Network Connections Configure Windows Phone Network Connections
• Enter appropriate pin code	8	Configure iOS Network Connections Configure Android Network Connections Configure Windows Phone Network Connections
• Test connectivity	8	Configure iOS Network Connections Configure Android Network Connections Configure Windows Phone Network Connections
◢ Corporate and ISP email configuration	8	Configure iOS Email Configure Android Email Configure Windows Phone Email, Sync, and Backup
• POP3	8	Configure iOS Email Configure Android Email Configure Windows Phone Email, Sync, and Backup
• IMAP	8	Configure iOS Email Configure Android Email Configure Windows Phone Email, Sync, and Backup

• Documents	8	Sync, Back Up, and Restore from Backup in iOS Sync, Update, Back Up, and Restore from Backup with Android Configure Windows Phone Email, Sync, and Backup
• Location data	8	Sync, Back Up, and Restore from Backup in iOS Sync, Update, Back Up, and Restore from Backup with Android Configure Windows Phone Email, Sync, and Backup
• Social media data	8	Sync, Back Up, and Restore from Backup in iOS Sync, Update, Back Up, and Restore from Backup with Android Configure Windows Phone Email, Sync, and Backup
• eBooks	8	Sync, Back Up, and Restore from Backup in iOS Sync, Update, Back Up, and Restore from Backup with Android Configure Windows Phone Email, Sync, and Backup
◢ Synchronization methods		
• Synchronize to the Cloud	8	Sync, Back Up, and Restore from Backup in iOS Sync, Update, Back Up, and Restore from Backup with Android Configure Windows Phone Email, Sync, and Backup
• Synchronize to the Desktop	8	Sync, Back Up, and Restore from Backup in iOS Sync, Update, Back Up, and Restore from Backup with Android Configure Windows Phone Email, Sync, and Backup
◢ Mutual authentication for multiple services	10	Authenticate Users for Large Networks
◢ Software requirements to install the application on the PC	8	Sync, Back Up, and Restore from Backup in iOS
◢ Connection types to enable synchronization	8	Sync, Back Up, and Restore from Backup in iOS Sync, Update, Back Up, and Restore from Backup with Android Configure Windows Phone Email, Sync, and Backup

DOMAIN 3.0 SECURITY

3.1 Identify common security threats and vulnerabilities.

OBJECTIVES	CHAPTER	SECTION
◢ Malware	10	Dealing with Malicious Software on Personal Computers Dealing with Malicious Software on Mobile Devices
• Spyware	10	Dealing with Malicious Software on Personal Computers Dealing with Malicious Software on Mobile Devices
• Viruses	10	Dealing with Malicious Software on Personal Computers Dealing with Malicious Software on Mobile Devices
• Worms	10	Dealing with Malicious Software on Personal Computers Dealing with Malicious Software on Mobile Devices
• Trojans	10	Dealing with Malicious Software on Personal Computers Dealing with Malicious Software on Mobile Devices
• Rootkits	10	Dealing with Malicious Software on Personal Computers
• Ransomware	10	Dealing with Malicious Software on Personal Computers
◢ Phishing	10	Dealing with Malicious Software on Personal Computers Dealing with Malicious Software on Mobile Devices
◢ Spear phishing	10	Dealing with Malicious Software on Personal Computers Dealing with Malicious Software on Mobile Devices
◢ Spoofing	10	Dealing with Malicious Software on Personal Computers Dealing with Malicious Software on Mobile Devices
◢ Social engineering	10	Dealing with Malicious Software on Personal Computers Dealing with Malicious Software on Mobile Devices
◢ Shoulder surfing	10	Dealing with Malicious Software on Personal Computers Dealing with Malicious Software on Mobile Devices

3.3 Compare and contrast differences of basic Windows OS security settings.

OBJECTIVES	CHAPTER	SECTION
◢ User and groups	9	Classify User Accounts and User Groups
• Administrator	9	Classify User Accounts and User Groups
• Power user	9	Classify User Accounts and User Groups
• Guest	9	Classify User Accounts and User Groups
• Standard user	9	Classify User Accounts and User Groups
◢ NTFS vs. Share permissions	9	Controlling Access to Folders and Files
• Allow vs. deny	9	Controlling Access to Folders and Files
• Moving vs. copying folders and files	9	Controlling Access to Folders and Files
• File attributes	9	Controlling Access to Folders and Files
◢ Shared files and folders	9	Controlling Access to Folders and Files
• Administrative shares vs. local shares	9	Hidden Network Resources and Administrative Shares
• Permission propagation	9	Controlling Access to Folders and Files
• Inheritance	9	Controlling Access to Folders and Files
◢ System files and folders	3	Backup Procedures
◢ User authentication	10	Securing a Windows Personal Computer
• Single sign-on	1	Windows User Accounts
◢ Run as administrator vs. standard user	1	Windows User Accounts
◢ Bitlocker	10	Use BitLocker Encryption
◢ Bitlocker-To-Go	10	Use BitLocker Encryption
◢ EFS	10	File and Folder Encryption

3.4   Given a scenario, deploy and enforce security best practices to secure a workstation.

OBJECTIVES	CHAPTER	SECTION
◢ Password best practices	10	
• Setting strong passwords	10	Securing a Windows Personal Computer
• Password expiration	10	Local Security Policies Using Group Policy
• Changing default user names/passwords	10	Securing a Windows Personal Computer
• Screensaver required password	10	Securing a Windows Personal Computer
• BIOS/UEFI passwords	10	Use UEFI/BIOS Features to Protect the System
• Requiring passwords	10	Local Security Policies Using Group Policy
◢ Account management		
• Restricting user permissions	9	Controlling Access to Folders and Files
• Login time restrictions	10	Local Security Policies Using Group Policy
• Disabling guest account	10	Use Windows to Authenticate Users
• Failed attempts lockout	10	Local Security Policies Using Group Policy
• Timeout/screen lock	10	Use Windows to Authenticate Users
◢ Disable autorun	10	Local Security Policies Using Group Policy
◢ Data encryption	10	File and Folder Encryption
◢ Patch/update management	3	Schedule Preventive Maintenance

3.5   Compare and contrast various methods for securing mobile devices.

OBJECTIVES	CHAPTER	SECTION
◢ Screen locks	10	Securing a Mobile Device
• Fingerprint lock	10	Securing a Mobile Device
• Face lock	10	Securing a Mobile Device
• Swipe lock	10	Securing a Mobile Device
• Passcode lock	10	Securing a Mobile Device

3.6   Given a scenario, use appropriate data destruction and disposal methods.

3.7   Given a scenario, secure SOHO wireless and wired networks.

DOMAIN 4.0 SOFTWARE TROUBLESHOOTING

4.1 Given a scenario, troubleshoot PC operating system problems with appropriate tools.

OBJECTIVES	CHAPTER	SECTION
◢ Common symptoms		
• Proprietary crash screens (BSOD/pin wheel)	6	Troubleshooting Windows Startup
• Failure to boot	6	Troubleshooting Windows Startup
• Improper shutdown	6	Troubleshooting Windows Startup
• Spontaneous shutdown/restart	6	Troubleshooting Windows Startup
• Device fails to start/detected	6	Troubleshooting Windows Startup
• Missing dll message	5	Responding to Specific Error Messages
• Services fails to start	5	Responding to Specific Error Messages
• Compatibility error	5	Responding to Specific Error Messages
• Slow system performance	4	Improving Windows Performance
• Boots to safe mode	6	Troubleshooting Windows Startup
• File fails to open	5	Responding to Specific Error Messages
• Missing NTLDR	6	Error Messages and Problems
• Missing Boot Configuration Data	6	Troubleshooting Windows Startup
• Missing operating system	6	Troubleshooting Windows Startup
• Missing Graphical Interface	6	Troubleshooting Windows Startup
• Missing GRUB/LILO	11	Hands-On Project 20-2: Install Ubuntu Server in a VM
• Kernel panic	11	Backups and Updates
• Graphical Interface fails to load	6	Troubleshooting Windows Startup
• Multiple monitor misalignment/orientation	4	Display Settings and Graphics Software
◢ Tools		
• BIOS/UEFI	3	How Partitions and File Systems Work
• SFC	5	System File Checker
• Logs	4	Event Viewer
• System Recovery Options	6	Tools for Troubleshooting Windows Startup Problems
• Repair disks	6	Tools for Troubleshooting Windows Startup Problems
• Pre-installation environments	6	Tools for Troubleshooting Windows Startup Problems
• MSCONFIG	4	Manually Removing Software
• DEFRAG	3	Schedule Preventive Maintenance
• REGSRV32	5	Responding to Specific Error Messages
• REGEDIT	4	Manually Removing Software
• Event viewer	4	Event Viewer
• Safe mode	6	Tools for Troubleshooting Windows Startup Problems
• Command prompt	3	Commands to Manage Files and Folders
	6	Tools for Troubleshooting Windows Startup Problems
• Uninstall/reinstall/repair	6	Tools for Troubleshooting Windows Startup Problems

4.2   Given a scenario, troubleshoot common PC security issues with appropriate tools and best practices.

OBJECTIVES	CHAPTER	SECTION
◢ Common symptoms	10	What Are We Up Against?
• Pop-ups	10	What Are We Up Against?
• Browser redirection	10	What Are We Up Against?
• Security alerts	10	What Are We Up Against?
• Slow performance	10	What Are We Up Against?
• Internet connectivity issues	10	What Are We Up Against?
• PC/OS lock up	10	What Are We Up Against?
• Application crash	10	What Are We Up Against?
• OS updates failures	10	What Are We Up Against?
• Rogue antivirus	10	What Are We Up Against?
• Spam	10	What Are We Up Against?
• Renamed system files	10	What Are We Up Against?
• Files disappearing	10	What Are We Up Against?
• File permission changes	10	What Are We Up Against?
• Hijacked email	10	What Are We Up Against?
○ Responses from users regarding email	10	What Are We Up Against?
○ Automated replies from unknown sent email	10	What Are We Up Against?
• Access denied	10	What Are We Up Against?
• Invalid certificate (trusted root CA)	10	Step-by-Step Attack Plan
◢ Tools		
• Antivirus software	10	Step-by-Step Attack Plan
• Antimalware software	10	Step-by-Step Attack Plan
• Recovery console	6	Error Messages and Problems
• Terminal	11	Linux Operating System Drive Maintenance Tools
• System restore/Snapshot	10	Step-by-Step Attack Plan
• Pre-installation environments	10	Step-by-Step Attack Plan
• Event viewer	10	Step-by-Step Attack Plan
• Refresh/restore	10	Step-by-Step Attack Plan
• MSCONFIG/Safe boot	10	Step-by-Step Attack Plan
◢ Best practice procedure for malware removal	10	Step-by-Step Attack Plan
1. Identify malware symptoms	10	Step-by-Step Attack Plan
2. Quarantine infected system	10	Step-by-Step Attack Plan
3. Disable system restore (in Windows)	10	Step-by-Step Attack Plan
4. Remediate infected systems	10	Step-by-Step Attack Plan
a. Update antimalware software	10	Step-by-Step Attack Plan
b. Scan and removal techniques (safe mode, pre-installation environment)	10	Step-by-Step Attack Plan
5. Schedule scans and run updates	10	Step-by-Step Attack Plan
6. Enable system restore and create restore point (in Windows)	10	Step-by-Step Attack Plan
7. Educate end user	10	Step-by-Step Attack Plan

4.3 **Given a scenario, troubleshoot common mobile OS and application issues with appropriate tools.**

OBJECTIVES	CHAPTER	SECTION
▲ Common symptoms		
• Dim display	8	Troubleshoot iOS Devices Troubleshoot Android Devices Troubleshoot Windows Mobile Devices
• Intermittent wireless	8	Troubleshoot iOS Devices Troubleshoot Android Devices Troubleshoot Windows Mobile Devices
• No wireless connectivity	8	Troubleshoot iOS Devices Troubleshoot Android Devices Troubleshoot Windows Mobile Devices
• No bluetooth connectivity	8	Troubleshoot iOS Devices Troubleshoot Android Devices Troubleshoot Windows Mobile Devices
• Cannot broadcast to external monitor	8	Troubleshoot iOS Devices Troubleshoot Android Devices Troubleshoot Windows Mobile Devices
• Touchscreen non-responsive	8	Troubleshoot iOS Devices Troubleshoot Android Devices Troubleshoot Windows Mobile Devices
• Apps not loading	8	Troubleshoot iOS Devices Troubleshoot Android Devices Troubleshoot Windows Mobile Devices
• Slow performance	8	Troubleshoot iOS Devices Troubleshoot Android Devices Troubleshoot Windows Mobile Devices
• Unable to decrypt email	10	Common Mobile Device Malware Symptoms
• Extremely short battery life	8	Troubleshoot iOS Devices Troubleshoot Android Devices Troubleshoot Windows Mobile Devices
• Overheating	8	Troubleshoot iOS Devices Troubleshoot Android Devices Troubleshoot Windows Mobile Devices
• Frozen system	8	Troubleshoot iOS Devices Troubleshoot Android Devices Troubleshoot Windows Mobile Devices
• No sound from speakers	8	Troubleshoot iOS Devices Troubleshoot Android Devices Troubleshoot Windows Mobile Devices
• Inaccurate touch screen response	8	Troubleshoot iOS Devices Troubleshoot Android Devices Troubleshoot Windows Mobile Devices
• System lockout	10	Device Access Controls
▲ Tools	8	Troubleshoot iOS Devices Troubleshoot Android Devices Troubleshoot Windows Mobile Devices
• Hard reset	8	Troubleshoot iOS Devices Troubleshoot Android Devices Troubleshoot Windows Mobile Devices
• Soft reset	8	Troubleshoot iOS Devices Troubleshoot Android Devices Troubleshoot Windows Mobile Devices

4.4   **Given a scenario, troubleshoot common mobile OS and application security issues with appropriate tools.**

DOMAIN 5.0 OPERATIONAL PROCEDURES

5.1 **Given a scenario, use appropriate safety procedures.**

OBJECTIVES	CHAPTER	SECTION
◢ Equipment grounding	A	Protecting the Equipment
◢ Proper component handling and storage	A	Protecting the Equipment
• Antistatic bags	A	Protecting the Equipment
• ESD straps	A	Protecting the Equipment
• ESD mats	A	Protecting the Equipment
• Self-grounding	A	Protecting the Equipment
◢ Toxic waste handling	A	Protecting the Environment
• Batteries	A	Protecting the Environment
• Toner	A	Protecting the Environment
• CRT	A	Protecting the Environment
◢ Personal safety	A	Protecting Yourself
• Disconnect power before repairing PC	A	Protecting Yourself
• Remove jewelry	A	Protecting Yourself
• Lifting techniques	A	Protecting Yourself
• Weight limitations	A	Protecting Yourself
• Electrical fire safety	A	Protecting Yourself
• Cable management	A	Protecting Yourself
• Safety goggles	A	Protecting Yourself
• Air filter mask	A	Protecting Yourself
◢ Compliance with local government regulations	A	Protecting the Environment

5.2 **Given a scenario with potential environmental impacts, apply the appropriate controls.**

OBJECTIVES	CHAPTER	SECTION
◢ MSDS documentation for handling and disposal	A	Protecting the Environment
◢ Temperature, humidity level awareness and proper ventilation	A	Protecting the Equipment
◢ Power surges, brownouts, blackouts	A	Protecting the Equipment
• Battery backup	A	Protecting the Equipment
• Surge suppressor	A	Protecting the Equipment
◢ Protection from airborne particles	A	Protecting the Equipment
• Enclosures	A	Protecting the Equipment
• Air filters/Mask	A	Protecting Yourself
◢ Dust and debris	A	Protecting the Equipment
• Compressed air	A	Protecting the Equipment
• Vacuums	A	Protecting the Equipment
◢ Compliance to local government regulations	A	Protecting the Equipment

5.3 **Summarize the process of addressing prohibited content/activity, and explain privacy, licensing, and policy concepts.**

OBJECTIVES	CHAPTER	SECTION
◢ Incident Response	10	
• First response	10	Corporate Policies for Dealing with Prohibited Content or Activity
○ Identify	10	Corporate Policies for Dealing with Prohibited Content or Activity
○ Report through proper channels	10	Corporate Policies for Dealing with Prohibited Content or Activity
○ Data/device preservation	10	Corporate Policies for Dealing with Prohibited Content or Activity

5.4 **Demonstrate proper communication techniques and professionalism.**

5.5   **Given a scenario, explain the troubleshooting theory.**

OBJECTIVES	CHAPTER	SECTION
▲ Always consider corporate policies, procedures and impacts before implementing changes.	5	
1. Identify the problem	5	Strategies to Troubleshoot Any Computer Problem
○ Question the user and identify user changes to computer and perform backups before making changes	5	Strategies to Troubleshoot Any Computer Problem
2. Establish a theory of probable cause (question the obvious)	5	Strategies to Troubleshoot Any Computer Problem
○ If necessary, conduct external or internal research based on symptoms	5	Strategies to Troubleshoot Any Computer Problem
3. Test the theory to determine cause	5	Strategies to Troubleshoot Any Computer Problem
○ Once theory is confirmed determine next steps to resolve problem	5	Strategies to Troubleshoot Any Computer Problem
○ If theory is not confirmed re-establish new theory or escalate	5	Strategies to Troubleshoot Any Computer Problem
4. Establish a plan of action to resolve the problem and implement the solution	5	Strategies to Troubleshoot Any Computer Problem
5. Verify full system functionality and if applicable implement preventive measures	5	Strategies to Troubleshoot Any Computer Problem
6. Document findings, actions and outcomes	5	Strategies to Troubleshoot Any Computer Problem

Introduction: CompTIA A+ Guide to Software

CompTIA A+ Guide to Software: Managing, Maintaining, and Troubleshooting, Ninth Edition was written to be the very best tool on the market today to prepare you to support desktop and laptop computers as well as mobile devices. The text has been updated to include the most current software technologies and takes you from the just-a-user level to the I-can-fix-this level for software matters. It achieves its goals with an unusually effective combination of tools that powerfully reinforce both concepts and hands-on, real-world experiences. It also provides thorough preparation for the content on the new CompTIA A+ 220-902 Certification exam. Competency in using a computer is a prerequisite to using this book. No background knowledge of electronics is assumed. An appropriate prerequisite course for this book would be a general course in computer applications.

This book includes:

- *Several in-depth, hands-on projects* are spaced throughout each chapter that invite you to immediately apply and reinforce critical thinking and troubleshooting skills and are designed to make certain that you not only understand the material, but also execute procedures and make decisions on your own.
- *Comprehensive review and practice end-of-chapter material*, including a chapter summary, key terms, review questions that focus on A+ content, critical thinking questions, and real-world problems to solve.
- *Step-by-step instructions* on installation, maintenance, optimization of system performance, and troubleshooting.
- A *wide array of photos, drawings, and screen shots* support the text, displaying in detail the exact software and hardware features you will need to understand to set up, maintain, and troubleshoot personal computers and small networks.

In addition, the carefully structured, clearly written text is accompanied by graphics that provide the visual input essential to learning and to help students master difficult subject matter. For instructors using the book in a classroom, instructor resources are available online.

Coverage is balanced—while focusing on new software, the text also covers the real work of an IT support technician, where some older technology remains in widespread use and still needs support. For example, the book covers how to use a 64-bit operating system to support the latest processors, but also addresses how to get the most out of a 32-bit OS with limited hardware resources. At the time of writing this text, Windows 8 and Windows 7 are the most popular Microsoft operating systems used on desktop and laptop computers. The text focuses on supporting Windows 8/7 systems, while also including light coverage of Windows Vista where knowledge of Vista is necessary for the CompTIA A+ 900 series exams. The text also has light coverage of Linux and Mac OS X operating systems for desktops and laptops and Android, iOS, and Windows Phone operating systems for mobile devices. Other new technologies covered include virtualization, cloud computing, UEFI firmware, and GPT partitioning systems.

This book provides thorough preparation for CompTIA's A+ 220-902 Certification examination. This certification credential's popularity among employers is growing exponentially, and obtaining certification increases your ability to gain employment and improve your salary. To get more information on CompTIA's A+ certification and its sponsoring organization, the Computing Technology Industry Association, see their website at *www.comptia.org*.

FEATURES

To ensure a successful learning experience, this book includes the following pedagogical features:

▲ *Learning Objectives.* Every chapter opens with a list of learning objectives that sets the stage for you to absorb the lessons of the text.

▲ *Comprehensive Step-by-Step Troubleshooting Guidance.* Troubleshooting guidelines are included in almost every chapter. The chapters, "Supporting Customers and Troubleshooting Windows" and "Troubleshooting Windows Startup," also focus on general strategies that work when troubleshooting applications and Windows.

▲ *Step-by-Step Procedures.* The book is chock-full of step-by-step procedures covering subjects from hardware and operating system installations and maintenance to troubleshooting the boot process or a failed network connection and optimizing system performance.

▲ *Art Program.* Numerous visually detailed photographs, three-dimensional art, and screen shots support the text, displaying hardware and software features exactly as you will see them in your work.

▲ *CompTIA A+ Table of Contents.* This table of contents gives the chapter and section that provides the primary content for each certification objective on the A+ exam. This is a valuable tool for quick reference.

▲ *Hands-On Projects.* These sections give you practice using the skills you have just studied so that you can learn by doing and know you have mastered a skill.

▲ *Applying Concepts.* These sections offer real-life, practical applications for the material being discussed. Whether outlining a task, developing a scenario, or providing pointers, the Applying Concepts sections give you a chance to apply what you've learned to a typical computer or network problem, so you can understand how you will use the material in your professional life.

A+
220-902

A+ Icons. All of the content that relates to CompTIA's A+ 220-902 Certification exam is highlighted with an A+ icon. The icon notes the exam name and the objective number. This unique feature highlights the relevant content at a glance, so that you can pay extra attention to the material.

 Notes. Note icons highlight additional helpful information related to the subject being discussed.

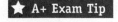 *A+ Exam Tip Boxes.* These boxes highlight additional insights and tips to remember if you are planning to take the CompTIA A+ exams.

 Caution Icons. These icons highlight critical safety information. Follow these instructions carefully to protect the computer and its data and to ensure your own safety.

OS Differences *OS Differences.* These boxes point you to the differences among Windows 8, Windows 7, and Vista.

▲ *End-of-Chapter Material.* Each chapter closes with the following features, which reinforce the material covered in the chapter and provide real-world, hands-on testing:

- *Chapter Summary*: This bulleted list of concise statements summarizes all major points of the chapter.

- *Key Terms*: The content of each chapter is further reinforced by an end-of-chapter key term list. The definitions of all terms are included with this text in a full-length glossary.

- *Review Questions*: You can test your understanding of each chapter with a comprehensive set of review questions. The "Reviewing the Basics" questions check your understanding of fundamental concepts focused on A+ content, while the "Thinking Critically" questions help you synthesize and apply what you've learned and also focus on A+ content.

- *Real Problems, Real Solutions*: Each comprehensive problem allows you to find out if you can apply what you've learned in the chapter to a real-life situation.

▲ *Student Companion Site.* The companion website includes older content and additional resources that still might be important in some repair situations. The content includes the following historical and older content that might still be important in some computer repair situations. The content: The Hexadecimal Number System and Memory Addressing, Supporting Windows XP, Electricity and Multimeters, Facts About Legacy Motherboards, How an OS Uses System Resources, Facts About Legacy Processors, All About SCSI, Behind the Scenes with DEBUG, FAT Details, and Selecting and Installing Hard Drives Using Legacy Motherboards. Other helpful online references include Frequently Asked Questions, Sample Reports, Computer Inventory and Maintenance form, and Troubleshooting Flowcharts. A video archive of clips that feature Jean Andrews illustrating concepts and providing advice on the real world of computer repair is also included.

WHAT'S NEW IN THE NINTH EDITION

Here's a summary of what's new in the *Ninth Edition*:

▲ Content maps to all of CompTIA's A+ 220-902 exam.

▲ There is now **more** focus on A+, with non-A+ content moved online to the companion website or eliminated.

▲ The chapters focus on Windows 8 and Windows 7 with slight content about Windows Vista.

▲ New content is added (all new content was also new to the A+ 220-902 exam).

- Windows 8 is added. Operating systems covered are now Windows 8, Windows 7, and Vista. New content on Linux, Mac OS X, and mobile operating systems (Android, iOS, and Windows Phone) is added.

- Enhanced content on supporting UEFI firmware is now included.

- Enhanced content on supporting mobile devices (including the Android OS, iOS, and Windows Phone) is covered in the chapter, "Supporting Mobile Operating Systems."

- Hands-On Projects in several chapters use virtual machines so that you get plenty of practice using this up-and-coming technology.
- New content on virtualization and supporting the Linux and Mac OS X operating systems is covered in the chapter, "Virtualization, Linux, and Mac OS X."
- Supporting GPT hard drives and Storage Spaces is covered in the chapter, "Maintaining Windows."
- Supporting and troubleshooting laptops is integrated throughout the text.

FEATURES OF THE NEW EDITION

Chapter **objectives** appear at the beginning of each chapter, so you know exactly what topics and skills are covered.

A+ **Exam Tips** include key points pertinent to the A+ exams. The icons identify the sections that cover information you will need to know for the A+ certification exams.

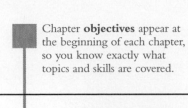

CHAPTER 7

Connecting To and Setting Up a Network

After completing this chapter, you will be able to:

• Explain the TCP/IP protocols and standards Windows uses for networking

• Connect a computer to a wired or wireless network

• Configure and secure a multifunction router on a local network

In this chapter, you learn how Windows uses TCP/IP protocols and standards to create and manage network connections, including how computers are identified and addressed on a network. You also learn to connect a computer to a network and how to set up and secure a small wired or wireless network.

This chapter prepares you to assume total responsibility for supporting both wired and wireless networks in a small-office/home-office (SOHO) environment. So let's get started by looking at how TCP/IP works in the world of Windows networking.

★ **A+ Exam Tip** Much of the content in this chapter applies to both the A+ 220-901 exam and the A+ 220-902 exam. This text includes icons for the A+ 220-902 (software) exam only. For markup of content relating to the A+ 220-901 (hardware) exam, see the companion volume to this text, *A+ Guide to Hardware, 9th ed.*

Hands-On | Project 1-2 Create Shortcuts

A+ 220-902 1.4

Do the following to practice creating shortcuts on the Windows desktop:

1. Open Windows 8 File Explorer or Windows 7 Windows Explorer and create a folder under the root directory of the hard drive called **\Temp**. List the steps you took.

2. Add a subfolder to \Temp called **\MyFiles**. List the steps you took.

3. Create a text file in the MyFiles folder named **Text1.txt**. List the steps you took.

4. Create a shortcut to the MyFiles folder on the Windows desktop. List the steps you took.

5. Rename the file **Text2.txt**.

6. Double-click the shortcut on the desktop. What error did you get?

7. The program file for Microsoft Paint is mspaint.exe. Use Windows Explorer to locate the program file and launch the Microsoft Paint program.

8. Create a shortcut to Microsoft Paint on the Windows desktop. Launch Microsoft Paint using the shortcut.

9. To clean up after yourself, delete the \Temp folder and the shortcuts. Close the two Paint windows.

Cautions identify critical safety information.

Hands-On Projects provide practical exercises throughout each chapter so that you can practice the skills as they are learned.

Notes indicate additional content that might be of student interest or information about how best to study.

> ✎ **Notes** Be aware that a laptop might show the Bluetooth icon in the taskbar even when the laptop does not support Bluetooth.

APPLYING | CONCEPTS USE AN APP TO EXPORT A DOCUMENT TO iCLOUD DRIVE

A+
220-902
2.6, 2.7

The Documents Free app on an iPad can interface with iCloud Drive. Follow these steps to create a document in the app and save it to iCloud Drive:

1. To use the app to create a new document file, open the app, tap **iCloud** in the left pane to select the location where the file will be saved, then tap the "+" sign at the bottom of the screen. Select the type of document to create, as shown in Figure 8-19a.

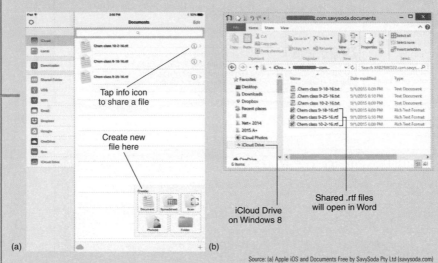

(a)   (b)

Source: (a) Apple iOS and Documents Free by SavySoda Pty Ltd (savysoda.com)

Figure 8-19   (a) Access iCloud Drive through compatible apps on your device; (b) iCloud Drive files are automatically synced to all devices where it is installed, including Windows computers

2. After you're finished creating the document, to save it, tap **File** in the upper-left corner of the app and tap **Save** (to use the app's default name for the file) or **Save As** (to rename the file). To return to your Documents list, tap **File** and tap **Don't Save**. The file is now available inside the app's own folder in iCloud Drive at *icloud.com* and also on any device or computer that syncs with your iCloud Drive account.

In Windows 8 on a personal computer, iCloud Drive is listed under Favorites in File Explorer, and there you can find the document file uploaded from your iPad, as shown in Figure 8-19b. (The app saves two copies of each file, one is an .rtf, or rich text format, file associated by default with Word, and one is a .txt, or text, file associated by default with WordPad.)

3. To download a document from iCloud Drive to the Documents Free app, on the Documents list screen, tap the **menu icon** in the upper-left corner. In the menu list that appears on the left side of the screen (see Figure 8-19a), tap **iCloud Drive**. You can then drill down into folders on your iCloud Drive and tap a file you want to download. The file can then be viewed and edited in the app.

Visual full-color graphics, photos, and screen shots accurately depict computer hardware and software components.

Applying Concepts sections provide practical advice or pointers by illustrating basic principles, identifying common problems, providing steps to practice skills, and encouraging creating solutions.

Chapter Summary bulleted lists of concise statements summarize all major points of the chapter, organized by primary headings.

>> CHAPTER SUMMARY

Operating Systems Used on Mobile Devices

◢ The most popular operating systems used on mobile devices include Android by Google, iOS by Apple, and Windows and Windows Phone by Microsoft.

◢ Android is an open source OS, and anyone can develop and sell Android apps or variations in the Android OS. Google is the major distributor of Android and Android apps from its Google Play website.

>> KEY TERMS

For explanations of key terms, see the Glossary for this text.

accelerometer	geotracking	iOS	PRL (Preferred Roaming List)
Action bar	Gmail	iPad	
AirDrop	Google account	iPhone	Product Release Instructions (PRI)
Airplane mode	Google Play	iPod touch	
Android	GPS (Global Positioning System)	iTunes Store	rooting
APK (Android Application Package)	gyroscope	iTunes U	screen orientation
		jailbreaking	SDK (Software Development Kit)
App Store	Handoff	launcher	
Apple ID	hard reset	location data	S/MIME (Secure/ Multipurpose Internet Mail Extensions)
Apps Drawer	hotspot	Microsoft Exchange	
Bluetooth PIN code	iCloud Backup	Microsoft Store	
closed source	iCloud Drive	Miracast	soft reset
emergency notifications	IMEI (International Mobile Equipment Identity)	mobile payment service	tethering
factory default		notifications	virtual assistant
Favorites tray	IMSI (International Mobile Subscriber Identity)	open source	Wi-Fi calling
force stop		pairing	Windows Phone (WP)

>> REVIEWING THE BASICS

1. List four types of antennas a smart phone might contain. Which three antennas are disabled in Airplane mode?

2. What company provides and oversees the Android Play Store? What is the website of this store?

3. List three Apple devices that use iOS.

4. Who is the sole distributor of apps for iOS?

Key Terms are defined as they are introduced and listed at the end of each chapter. Definitions can be found in the Glossary.

Reviewing the Basics sections check understanding of fundamental concepts.

Thinking Critically sections require you to analyze and apply what you've learned.

>> THINKING CRITICALLY

1. Suppose you find an app that cost you $4.99 is missing from your Android. What is the best way to restore the missing app?

   a. Go to backup storage and perform a restore to recover the lost app.

   b. Purchase the app again.

   c. Go to the Play Store where you bought the app and install it again.

   d. Go to the Settings app and perform an application restore.

>> REAL PROBLEMS, REAL SOLUTIONS

REAL PROBLEM 2-1 Recovering Data from a Corrupted Windows Installation

As an IT support technician for a small organization, it's your job to support the computers, the small network, and the users. One of your coworkers, Jason, comes to you in a panic. His Windows 8.1 system won't boot, and he has lots of important data files in several locations on the drive. He has no idea in which folder some of the files are located. Besides the application data he's currently working on, he's especially concerned about losing email addresses, email, and his Internet Explorer Favorites links.

After trying everything you know about recovering Windows 8.1, you conclude the OS is corrupted beyond repair. You decide there might be a way to remove the hard drive from Jason's computer and connect it to another computer so that you can recover the data. Search the Internet and find a device that you can use to connect Jason's hard drive to another computer using a USB port on that computer. The hard drive uses a SATA hard drive interface. Print the webpage showing the device and its price.

REAL PROBLEM 2-2 Troubleshooting an Upgrade

Your friend, Thomas, has upgraded his Windows 7 desktop to Windows 8.1. After the installation, he discovers his media card reader does not work. He calls you on the phone asking you what to do. Do the following to plan your troubleshooting approach:

1. List the questions you should ask Thomas to help diagnose the problem.

2. List the steps you would take if you were sitting at the computer solving the problem.

3. What do you think is the source of the problem? Explain your answer.

Real Problems, Real Solutions allow you to apply what you've learned in the chapter to a real-life situation.

WHAT'S NEW WITH CompTIA® A+ CERTIFICATION

The CompTIA A+ exams include two exams, and you must pass both to become CompTIA A+ certified. The two exams are 220-901 and 220-902.

Here is a breakdown of the domain content covered on the two A+ exams. This text covers content on the 220-902 exam. Content on the 220-901 exam is covered in the companion text, *A+ Guide to Hardware*.

CompTIA A+ 220-901 Exam	
Domain	**Percentage of Examination**
1.0 Hardware	34%
2.0 Networking	21%
3.0 Mobile Devices	17%
4.0 Hardware & Network Troubleshooting	28%
Total	100%

CompTIA A+ 220-902 Exam	
Domain	**Percentage of Examination**
1.0 Windows Operating Systems	29%
2.0 Other Operating Systems & Technologies	12%
3.0 Security	22%
4.0 Software Troubleshooting	24%
5.0 Operational Procedures	13%
Total	100%

CompTIA.

Becoming a CompTIA Certified IT Professional is Easy

It's also the best way to reach greater professional opportunities and rewards.

Why Get CompTIA Certified?

Growing Demand

Labor estimates predict some technology fields will experience growth of over 20% by the year 2020.* CompTIA certification qualifies the skills required to join this workforce.

Higher Salaries

IT professionals with certifications on their resume command better jobs, earn higher salaries and have more doors open to new multi-industry opportunities.

Verified Strengths

91% of hiring managers indicate CompTIA certifications are valuable in validating IT expertise, making certification the best way to demonstrate your competency and knowledge to employers.**

Universal Skills

CompTIA certifications are vendor neutral—which means that certified professionals can proficiently work with an extensive variety of hardware and software found in most organizations.

Learn	Certify	Work
Learn more about what the exam covers by reviewing the following:	Purchase a voucher at a Pearson VUE testing center or at CompTIAstore.com.	Congratulations on your CompTIA certification!
• Exam objectives for key study points.	• Register for your exam at a Pearson VUE testing center:	• Make sure to add your certification to your resume.
• Sample questions for a general overview of what to expect on the exam and examples of question format.	• Visit pearsonvue.com/CompTIA to find the closest testing center to you.	• Check out the CompTIA Certification Roadmap to plan your next career move.
• Visit online forums, like LinkedIn, to see what other IT professionals say about CompTIA exams.	• Schedule the exam online. You will be required to enter your voucher number or provide payment information at registration.	
	• Take your certification exam.	

Learn more: Certification.CompTIA.org/aplus

* Source: CompTIA 9th Annual Information Security Trends study: 500 U.S. IT and Business Executives Responsible for Security
** Source: CompTIA Employer Perceptions of IT Training and Certification

CompTIA AUTHORIZED QUALITY CONTENT

 CompTIA A+ Guide to Software, Ninth Edition has earned CompTIA's Authorized Quality Content approval. The text has been reviewed and approved by ProCert Labs, a CompTIA appointed third party. CAQC approval indicates the textbook material meets CompTIA's comprehensive coverage of the exam objectives, instructional design standards and high quality criteria.

DISCOUNTED CompTIA CERTIFICATION EXAM VOUCHERS

As a CompTIA Authorized Partner, Cengage Learning is able to provide you with a promo code that saves you 10% off the non-member price of a CompTIA Exam voucher when purchased through the CompTIA Marketplace.

Save 10% when you use coupon code **CL10Percent** during checkout. Redeeming the coupon code is easy:

1. Go to **www.comptiastore.com**.
2. Select the CompTIA Certification you want.
3. Add the voucher to the cart (note that for A+ you will need a separate voucher for each exam).
4. Enter the code **CL10Percent** on the purchase screen and click **Apply**.

INSTRUCTOR'S MATERIALS

Please visit *login.cengage.com* and log in to access instructor-specific resources on the Instructor Companion Site, which includes the Instructor's Manual, Solutions Manual, Test creation tools, PowerPoint Presentation, Syllabus, and figure files.

Instructor's Manual: The Instructor's Manual that accompanies this textbook includes additional instructional material to assist in class preparation, including suggestions for classroom activities, discussion topics, and additional projects.

Solutions: Answers to the end-of-chapter material are provided. These include the answers to the Review Questions, Thinking Critically, and to the Hands-On Projects (when applicable), as well as Lab Manual Solutions.

Cengage Learning Testing Powered by Cognero: This flexible, online system allows you to do the following:

- Author, edit, and manage test bank content from multiple Cengage Learning solutions.
- Create multiple test versions in an instant.
- Deliver tests from your LMS, your classroom, or wherever you want.

PowerPoint Presentations: This book comes with Microsoft PowerPoint slides for each chapter. These are included as a teaching aid for classroom presentation, to make available to students on the network for chapter review, or to be printed for classroom distribution. Instructors, please feel at liberty to add your own slides for additional topics you introduce to the class.

Figure Files: All of the figures in the book are reproduced on the Instructor Companion Site. Similar to the PowerPoint presentations, these are included as a teaching aid for classroom presentation, to make available to students for review, or to be printed for classroom distribution.

TOTAL SOLUTIONS FOR CompTIA A+

MINDTAP FOR A+ GUIDE TO IT TECHNICAL SUPPORT, NINTH EDITION

MindTap is an online learning solution designed to help students master the skills they need in today's workforce. Research shows employers need critical thinkers, troubleshooters and creative problem-solvers to stay relevant in our fast paced technology-driven world. MindTap helps you achieve this with assignments and activities that provides hands-practice, real life relevance and certification test prep. Students are guided through assignments that help them master basic knowledge and understanding before moving on to more challenging problems.

MindTap activities and assignments are tied to CompTIA A+ certification exam objectives. The hands-on labs provide real-life application and practice. The IQ certification test prep engine allows students to quiz themselves on specific exam domains, and the pre- and post- course assessments are mock exams that measure exactly how much they have learned. Readings and "whiteboard shorts" support the lecture, while "In The News" assignments encourage students to stay current. MindTap is designed around learning objectives and provides the analytics and reporting to easily see where the class stands in terms of progress, engagement and completion rates. Use the content and learning path as-is or pick-and-choose how our materials will wrap around yours. You control what the students see and when they see it. Learn more at *http://www.cengage.com/mindtap/*.

- Instant Access Code: (ISBN: 9781305944657)
- Printed Access Code: (ISBN: 9781305944664)

LAB MANUAL FOR A+ GUIDE TO SOFTWARE, NINTH EDITION

This Lab Manual contains over 70 labs to provide students with additional hands-on experience and to help prepare for the A+ exam. The *Lab Manual* includes lab activities, objectives, materials lists, step-by-step procedures, illustrations, and review questions.

- Lab Manual (ISBN: 9781305266568)

COURSENOTES

This laminated quick reference card reinforces critical knowledge for CompTIA's A+ exam in a visual and user-friendly format. CourseNotes will serve as a useful study aid, supplement to the textbook, or as a quick reference tool during the course and afterward.

- A+ Exam # 220-901 CourseNotes (ISBN: 9781305269248)
- A+ Exam # 220-902 CourseNotes (ISBN: 9781305269255)

PC TROUBLESHOOTING POCKET GUIDE, NINTH EDITION

This compact and portable volume is designed to help students and technicians diagnose any computer problem quickly and efficiently. This guide is up to date and current for today's technologies (ISBN: 9781305266537).

ACKNOWLEDGMENTS

Thank you to the wonderful people at Cengage who continue to give their best and to go the extra mile to make the books what they are: Kristin McNary, Amy Savino, Michelle Ruelos Cannistraci, and Brooke Greenhouse. I'm grateful for all you've done. Thank you, Deb Kaufmann, our Developmental Editor extraordinaire, for your careful attention to detail and your awesome commitment to excellence, and to Karen Annett, our excellent copyeditor/proofreader. Thank you, Serge Palladino, for your careful attention to the technical accuracy of the book.

Thank you to all the people who took the time to voluntarily send encouragement and suggestions for improvements to the previous editions. Your input and help is very much appreciated. The reviewers of this edition all provided invaluable insights and showed a genuine interest in the book's success. Thank you to:

>Susan Booth – Cape Fear Community College
>Ron Cannon – Wichita Technical Institute
>Steve Ebben – Fox Valley Technical College, Appleton
>Glenn Goe – Stark State College
>Abigale Trimble – Wichita Technical Institute

To the instructors and learners who use this book, we invite and encourage you to send suggestions or corrections for future editions. Please write to the author team at *jean.andrews@cengage.com*. We never ignore a good idea! And to instructors, if you have ideas for how to make a class in A+ Preparation a success, please share your ideas with other instructors! You can find us on Facebook at *http://www.facebook.com/JeanKnows*, where you can interact with the authors and other instructors.

This book is dedicated to the covenant of God with man on earth.

Jean Andrews, Ph.D.
Joy Dark
Jill West

ABOUT THE AUTHORS

Jean Andrews has more than 30 years of experience in the computer industry, including more than 13 years in the college classroom. She has worked in a variety of businesses and corporations designing, writing, and supporting application software; managing a PC repair help desk; and troubleshooting wide area networks. She has written numerous books on software, hardware, and the Internet, including the best-selling *A+ Guide to Hardware, Ninth Edition* and *A+ Guide to IT Technical Support, Ninth Edition*. She lives in northern Georgia.

Joy Dark is CompTIA A+ and HIT certified. She has worked in the IT field as a help-desk technician providing first-level support for a company with presence in 29 states, a second-tier technician in healthcare IT, and an operations specialist designing support protocols and structures. As a teacher, Joy has taught online courses in IT with the Stride Center in California and has taught English as a Second Language in the United States and South America. She has helped write several technical textbooks with Jean Andrews, her mother, and Jill West, her sister. Joy lives in Dalton, Georgia, with her two daughters and Doberman dog.

Jill West brings a unique variety of experience in writing, business, and education to the development of her innovative educational materials. She has taught multiple ages and content areas using a flipped classroom approach, distance learning, and educational counseling. Jill's résumé includes service with a nonprofit agency to inner-city disadvantaged populations, on-the-job training with a law firm, ten years working with Jean Andrews in textbook development, multiple entrepreneurial ventures, and CompTIA A+ and Network+ certifications. Her insights into the art of self-teaching provide students with effective tools for taking ownership of their own learning. Jill and her husband Mike live in the hills of northwest Georgia where they homeschool their four children.

READ THIS BEFORE YOU BEGIN

The following hardware, software, and other equipment are needed to do the Hands-On Projects in each chapter:

- You need a working desktop computer and laptop that can be taken apart and reassembled. You also need a working computer on which you can install an operating system. These computers can be the same or different computers. Use a Pentium or higher computer.
- Troubleshooting skills can better be practiced with an assortment of nonworking expansion cards that can be used to simulate problems.
- Windows 8 Professional and Windows 7 Professional are needed for most chapters. In addition, the Mac OS X is used in the chapter, "Virtualization, Linux, and Mac OS X."
- Internet access is needed for most chapters.
- An iOS or Android smart phone or tablet is needed for the chapter, "Supporting Mobile Operating Systems."
- A SOHO router that includes a wireless access point is needed for the chapter, "Connecting To and Setting Up a Network."

⚡ **Caution**   Before undertaking any of the lab exercises, please review the safety guidelines in the appendix, "Safety Procedures and Environmental Concerns."

Survey of Windows Features and Support Tools

After completing this chapter, you will be able to:

- Use Windows to interface with users, files and folders, applications, and hardware
- Use Windows tools to explore, examine, and support the system
- Make network connections using Windows
- Manage local user accounts and Microsoft accounts in Windows

This text takes you from being an end user of your computer to becoming an information technology (IT) support technician able to support all types of personal computers. The only assumption made here is that you are a computer user—that is, you can turn on your machine, load a software package, and use that software to accomplish a task. No experience in electronics is assumed. This text prepares you to pass the A+ 220-902 exam by CompTIA *(www.comptia.org)*. This exam is primarily about software. The A+ 220-901 exam and the A+ 220-902 exam are required by CompTIA for A+ certification. The A+ 220-901 exam is primarily about hardware, and content on this exam is covered in the companion book, *A+ Guide to Hardware: Managing, Maintaining, and Troubleshooting, Ninth Edition*. This text and the *A+ Guide to Hardware* fully prepare you for both exams.

In this chapter, you learn about Microsoft Windows and how this operating system provides the interface between users and applications and between applications and hardware devices. You learn to use several Windows tools and utilities that are useful to view and manage storage devices, examine a system, and troubleshoot simple problems with hardware and applications. You also learn how Windows connects to a network and accesses resources on a network. Finally, you learn about user accounts, including how to create and manage them.

★ **A+ Exam Tip** In this text, you learn about Windows 8.1, Windows 8.0, Windows 7, and a little about Windows Vista. All these operating systems are covered on the A+ 220-902 exam. (Windows 10 is not on the exam.) In the text, we use Windows 8 to refer to Windows 8.0 and Windows 8.1.

★ **A+ Exam Tip** As you work your way through a chapter, notice the blue A+ mapping icons underneath headings. These page elements help you know to which objectives on the exam the content applies. After studying each chapter, take a look at the grid at the beginning of this text and make sure you understand each objective listed in the grid that is covered in the chapter..

WINDOWS INTERFACES

An operating system (OS) is software that controls a computer. In general, you can think of an operating system as the middleman between applications and hardware, between the user and hardware, and between the user and applications (see Figure 1-1).

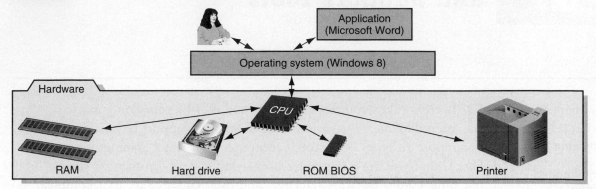

Figure 1-1   Users and applications depend on the OS to relate to all applications and hardware components

Several applications might be installed on a computer to meet various user needs, but a computer really needs only one operating system. Although there are important differences among them, all operating systems share the following four main functions:

▲ *Function 1*: Provide a user interface

   ▲ Performing housekeeping procedures requested by the user, often concerning storage devices, such as reorganizing a hard drive, deleting files, copying files, and changing the system date

   ▲ Providing a way for the user to manage the desktop, hardware, applications, and data

▲ *Function 2*: Manage files

   ▲ Managing files on hard drives, DVD drives, CD drives, USB flash drives, and other drives

   ▲ Creating, storing, retrieving, deleting, and moving files

▲ *Function 3*: Manage hardware

   ▲ Managing the UEFI/BIOS (programs permanently stored on hardware devices)

   ▲ Managing memory, which is a temporary place to store data and instructions as they are being processed

   ▲ Diagnosing problems with software and hardware

   ▲ Interfacing between hardware and software (that is, interpreting application software needs to the hardware and interpreting hardware needs to application software)

▲ *Function 4*: Manage applications

   ▲ Installing and uninstalling applications

   ▲ Running applications and managing the interface to the hardware on behalf of an application

Windows 8 is an upgrade to Windows 7, which was preceded by Windows Vista. Every IT support technician needs to be a power user of Windows 8 and also be familiar with Windows 7.

> ✏ **Notes** This chapter assumes Windows 8 or Windows 7 is already installed on your computer, and it would be great if you have access to both operating systems as you work your way through this chapter. If Windows is not yet installed, read the chapter, "Installing Windows," and install Windows 8 or 7. Then you can return to this chapter to learn how to use the OS.

The editions of Windows 8 include Windows 8, Windows 8 Professional, Windows 8 Enterprise, and Windows RT. Windows 8.1 is a free update or release of the original Windows 8. Editions of Windows 7 include Windows 7 Ultimate, Windows 7 Enterprise, Windows 7 Professional, Windows 7 Home Premium, Windows 7 Home Basic, and Windows 7 Starter.

> ★ **A+ Exam Tip** The A+ 220-902 exam covers Windows 8.1, Windows 8, Windows 7, and Windows Vista. For the most part, Windows 7 and Vista work alike. Important information about Vista where it differs from Windows 7 is presented in OS Differences boxes. Although Windows 10 is currently the latest Microsoft operating system, Windows 10 is not covered on the exam and is not covered in this text.

Every Windows OS offers a graphical user interface (GUI; pronounced "GOO-ee") that uses graphics instead of with a command-driven interface. Windows 8 has two graphical user interfaces, the modern interface and the desktop. Windows 7 offers one graphical user interface, the desktop. We next examine all three interfaces.

WINDOWS 8 MODERN INTERFACE

A+
220-902
1.1

The Windows 8 modern interface, also called the Windows 8 interface and formerly called the Metro User Interface or Metro UI, presents the Start screen to the user. The Start screen contains tiles that represent lean apps, which use few system resources and are designed for social media, social networking, and the novice end user (see Figure 1-2). Click a tile to open its app. Some apps use live tiles, which offer continuous real-time updates. For example, the People app has a live tile to make it easy to keep up with updates on Facebook, LinkedIn, and Twitter.

> ✎ **Notes** In this text, we use Windows 8 as an umbrella term to cover Windows 8.0 (the first release of Windows 8) and Windows 8.1 (the free update to Windows 8.0).

Figure 1-2 The Windows 8 Start screen is used to view app tiles and to open apps

The modern interface uses pages in comparison to the windows used on the desktop. The interface is specifically designed for touch screens.

> ✎ **Notes** To conserve system resources, you can turn off a live tile. To do so, right-click the tile on the Start screen and then click **Turn live tile off** in the shortcut menu that appears. You can also use Task Manager to find out how the app is affecting overall system performance. You learn to use Task Manager in a later chapter.

> ✎ **Notes** The figures and steps in this text use Windows 8.1 Professional and Windows 7 Professional. If you are using a different edition of Windows 8 or 7, your screens and steps may differ slightly from those presented here.

THE CHARMS BAR AND THE SETTINGS CHARM

The charms bar appears on the right side of any Windows 8 screen when you move your pointer to a right corner (see Figure 1-3a). It gives handy access to common tasks such as returning to the Start screen, searching for content, connecting to a wireless network, personalizing the Start screen, or changing other Windows settings. In the charms bar, click a charm to select it. The Settings charm can be particularly useful, and items at the top of the Settings pane can change depending on the situation. Figure 1-3b shows the Settings pane from the Start screen, and Figure 1-3c shows the Settings pane from the desktop.

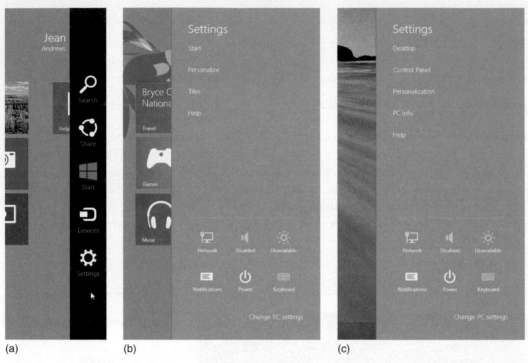

(a)   (b)   (c)

Figure 1-3   (a) The charms bar, (b) the Settings pane on the Start screen, and (c) the Settings pane on the desktop

> ✎ **Notes** With the first release of Windows 8, many users complained that important items like the charms bar were difficult to find and not at all intuitive to use. As a result, beginning with Windows 8.1, Microsoft added tips that randomly appear on screen to help users learn how to use the new interface.

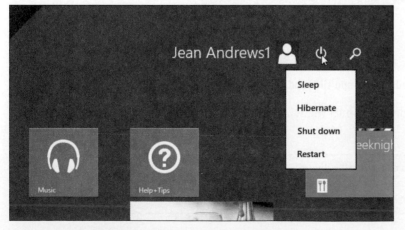

Figure 1-4   Use the Power icon at the top of the Start screen to shut down or restart the system

THE SETTINGS CHARM AND THE POWER ICON

The Power icon in the upper-right corner of the Start screen can be used to shut down or restart the computer. Click the **Power** icon, and then click an item in the menu that appears (see Figure 1-4). The items on this menu always include Shut down and Restart, and, depending on the configuration, might also include Sleep and Hibernate.

APPLYING | CONCEPTS SIGN IN TO WINDOWS 8 AND USE THE WINDOWS 8 INTERFACE

**A+
220-902
1.1**
Although the Windows 8 interface is designed to work best with a touch screen, you can also use a mouse and keyboard. Follow these steps to learn how to sign in to Windows 8 and manage apps using the Windows 8 interface:

1. When you first start up a Windows 8 computer, you see the lock screen shown in Figure 1-5a. Click anywhere on the screen and the sign-in screen appears (see Figure 1-5b). To sign in, select a user account and enter the account password. The Start screen appears.

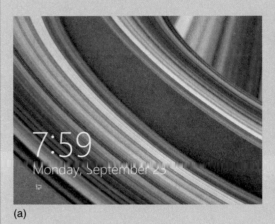
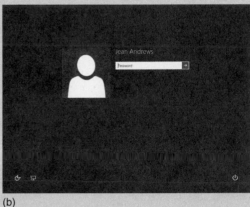

(a)   (b)

Figure 1-5   (a) The Windows lock screen, and (b) the Windows sign-in screen

Notes These instructions assume you are using a mouse and keyboard. If you're using a touch screen, simply tap instead of click; press and hold instead of right-click; double-tap instead of double-click; and swipe to scroll the screen to the right or left.

2. To open an app, click the app tile on the Start screen. If the app works in the Windows 8 modern interface, the app page opens. (If the app works on the Windows desktop, the desktop appears and the application window opens.)

3. To return to the Start screen, press the **Win** key. Open a second app, which fills the entire screen.

Notes In Windows, there are multiple ways to do the same thing. For example, to return to the Start screen (a) press the **Win** key, (b) move your pointer to the lower left of the screen and click the **Start** (Windows logo) button that appears, or (c) move your pointer to a right corner of the screen and click the **Start** (Windows logo) charm in the charms bar that appears.

4. You can snap a page to the left or right side of the screen so a second page can share the screen, which is called side-by-side apps. To snap a page, first move your pointer to the top of the screen—the pointer changes to a hand. Then press and drag the page down and to the left or right side of the screen. The page snaps to the side, and the second app takes up the other side of the screen. You can press and drag the vertical bar between the two pages to adjust the page sizes (see Figure 1-6).

Notes To snap pages, your screen resolution must be at least 1366 × 768.

(continues)

Figure 1-6   Two app pages show on the screen with other open apps shown as thumbnails in the left pane

5. Open three other apps using each of these three methods:

◢ If the app tile isn't showing, move your pointer to the bottom of the screen. You can then use the scroll bar that appears to scroll the screen to the right or left to see more apps on the Start screen. (You can also move your pointer to the far left or right side of the screen to scroll the screen.)

◢ Some apps are not on the Start screen. Move your pointer to the bottom of the Start screen and a down arrow appears. Click the **arrow** to see the Apps screen, which shows all installed apps. Click one to open it.

> ✎ **Notes** Right-click a tile on the Start screen or Apps screen to select it and view its shortcut menu (see Figure 1-7). To uninstall the app, click **Uninstall** in the menu.

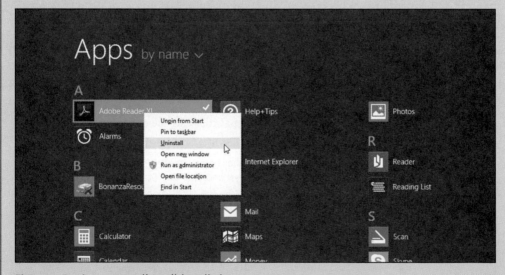

Figure 1-7   Apps screen lists all installed apps

◢ You can also use the Search feature to open an app. On the Start screen, start typing the name of the app. As you type, the Search pane appears. For example, in Figure 1-8, you can see the top of the pane when *no* is typed. The remaining letters in *notepad* automatically appear in the Search box, and other possibilities are listed in the pane. If you want to open the Notepad app, click it. By default, the Search app searches for apps, Windows settings, files, web images, and web videos. If you click an item at the bottom of the pane, Internet Explorer opens to find it on the web.

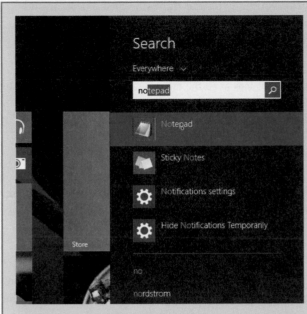

6. Only two apps can use the screen at one time. To see thumbnails of open apps that are not on the screen, move your pointer to the upper-left corner of the screen (refer to Figure 1-6).

7. To close a selected app, move your pointer to the top of the screen. A menu bar appears. Click the red **X** on the far right of the menu bar. Close all open apps.

Figure 1-8 Use Search to search for apps, settings, files, and content within other apps and on the web

WINDOWS 8 DESKTOP

A+
220-902
1.1, 1.5

Tools used by technicians to support, secure, and troubleshoot Windows, as well as productivity software, such as Microsoft Office, QuickBooks, and Dreamweaver, are primarily accessed from the desktop. To access the desktop, click the Desktop tile on the Start screen. When you move your pointer to a right corner of the desktop screen, the charms bar appears, as shown in Figure 1-9. Click the **Start** charm in the charms bar to return to the Start screen. Alternately, you can click the Start button in the taskbar to return to the Start screen.

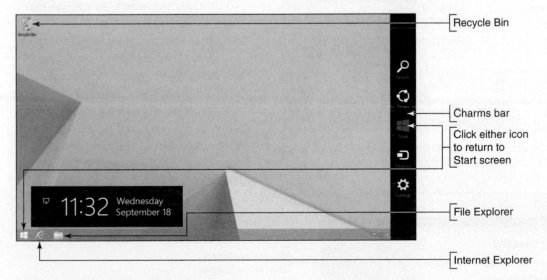

Figure 1-9 Windows 8 desktop with charms bar in view

The taskbar is normally located at the bottom of the Windows desktop, displaying information about open programs and providing quick access to others. By default, Windows 8 places the Internet Explorer and File Explorer icons in the Quick Launch toolbar, which is on the left side of the taskbar. Click an icon to open the program. An open application displays a program icon in the taskbar to the right of the toolbar.

The notification area, also called the system tray or systray, is usually on the right side of the taskbar and displays open services. A service is a program that runs in the background to support or serve Windows or an application. The services in the notification area include the volume or sound control and network connectivity.

> ✎ **Notes** If you have a sluggish Windows system, one thing you can do is look at all the running services in the notification area and try to disable the services that are taking up system resources. How to do that is covered in the chapter, "Optimizing Windows."

To launch a program from the desktop, use one of these methods:

◢ *Start screen.* Click the **Start** button to return to the Start screen and use the Start screen to open a program. For example, on the Start screen, start typing the name of an application, and then click it when it appears in the search list. If it's a desktop application, the program window launches on the desktop.

◢ *Quick Launch menu.* To launch most Windows support tools, right-click the **Start** button and select an item from the Quick Launch menu that appears (see Figure 1-10). Click an item to open it. You can also press **Win+X** to launch the menu from anywhere in Windows 8, including the Start screen.

Notice the *Shut down or sign out* item near the bottom of the menu. When you point to it, you see submenu items that always include Shut down, Sign out, and Restart. Depending on your system configuration, you might also see Sleep or Hibernate.

◢ *Pin to taskbar.* For a desktop program you use often, you can add its icon to the taskbar on the desktop, which is called pinning to the taskbar. To do that, right-click an app on the Start screen or Apps screen to see the app's shortcut menu (refer back to Figure 1-7). If the app works on the desktop, the menu includes the item *Pin to taskbar*. Another way to add a program icon to the taskbar is to open the program, right-click the program's icon in the taskbar, and then click **Pin this program to taskbar** (see Figure 1-11).

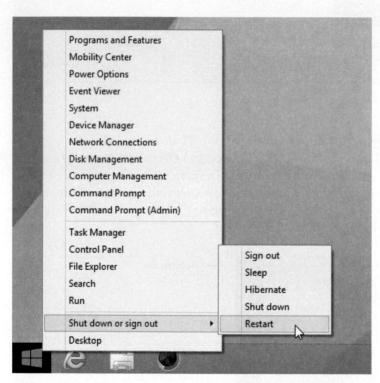

Figure 1-10 Use the Quick Launch menu from anywhere in Windows to access useful Windows utilities and screens

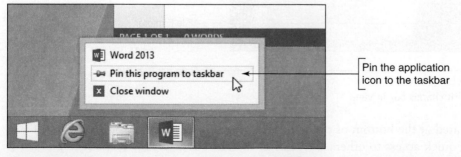

Figure 1-11 Pin an open program to the taskbar on the Windows desktop

▲ *Double-click the program file name in File Explorer.* File Explorer allows you to view and manage files and folders on your computer or the network. To open File Explorer, click the **File Explorer icon** in the taskbar. You can launch a program by double-clicking the program file name in File Explorer. You learn to use File Explorer later in this chapter.

▲ *Shortcut on desktop.* You can place a shortcut to a program on the desktop. How to do that is coming up later in this chapter.

▲ *Run box.* If you know the name of the program file, you can open the Quick Launch menu and click **Run**. The Run box appears. Type the name of the program file and press **Enter**. For example, the program file name of the Notepad text editor is notepad. exe. When you type **notepad** in the Run box and press **Enter**, the Notepad window appears. See Figure 1-12. (Windows assumes the file extension for a program is .exe, so it's not necessary to type the extension.)

Figure 1-12 Use the Run box to launch a program

Here are a few tips about managing windows on the desktop:

▲ Drag the title bar of a window to move the window. Use the buttons in the upper-right corner to resize, maximize, minimize, and close a window.

▲ Drag a window to the top of the screen to maximize it. Drag the window downward on the screen to return it to its original size. Drag a window to the right or left of the screen so that it snaps to the side of the screen to fill half the screen.

▲ Press and shake (drag back and forth quickly) the title bar of a window to minimize all other windows except the one you shake. Shake again to restore the size of the other windows.

Hands-On | Project 1-1 Practice Using the Charms Bar and Quick Launch Menu

A+
220-902
1.1, 1.5

Do the following to practice using the charms bar and Quick Launch menu:

1. Click the **Power** icon on the Start screen. What are the options on the Power icon menu?

2. Open the **Quick Launch** menu, and practice using several options on the menu. What are the submenu items that appear when you point to *Shut down or sign out*?

3. Click **Power Options** on the Quick Launch menu. Find the settings in the Power Options window that allow you to change the options available in the *Shut down or sign out* menu.

4. Go to the **Start** screen. Click your user name in the upper-right corner of the Start screen. What options appear in the dropdown menu? Use the Lock and Sign out options, and describe what each option does.

Now, onward to the Windows 7 desktop.

WINDOWS | 7   THE WINDOWS 7 DESKTOP

> **A+**
> **220-902**
> **1.1**

In Windows 7 (and Vista), the desktop is the initial screen that is displayed after the user logs on and Windows is loaded. Just as with Windows 8, you can move, maximize, resize, minimize, shake, and close windows on the desktop. The Windows 7/Vista desktop provides a 3D user interface called the Aero user interface that gives a glassy appearance and is sometimes called Aero glass (see Figure 1-13). (TheAero interface is not available for the Windows 7 Starter and Home Basic editions.) For Windows 7 to support Aero, the system must have at least 1 GB of RAM and the video adapter must support Aero.

> **✎ Notes** According to Microsoft terminology, you *sign in* to Windows 8 and *log on* to Windows 7/Vista.

Figure 1-13   The Windows 7 desktop using the Aero interface has a glassy transparent look

> **✎ Notes** If you are using the Aero interface, you can get a flip 3D view of applications by pressing **Win+Tab** (the Windows key and the Tab key). Then use the Tab key to move from one open application to another.

The Windows 7/Vista desktop can have gadgets on it, such as the clock gadget shown in Figure 1-13. A gadget is a mini-app that provides information such as the time, date, news headlines, or weather. To control Windows 7 gadgets, right-click the desktop and select **Gadgets** from the shortcut menu that appears.

> **↻ OS Differences** Windows 7 gadgets can appear anywhere on the desktop, but Vista gadgets appear in the Vista sidebar on the right side of the Vista desktop.

To start a program, click the **Start** button to access the Start menu, click an icon pinned to the taskbar, double-click a shortcut on the desktop, click the **Start** button and enter the program file name in the Search box, or double-click the program file name in Windows Explorer. Windows Explorer is the Windows 7/Vista utility used to view and manage files and folders.

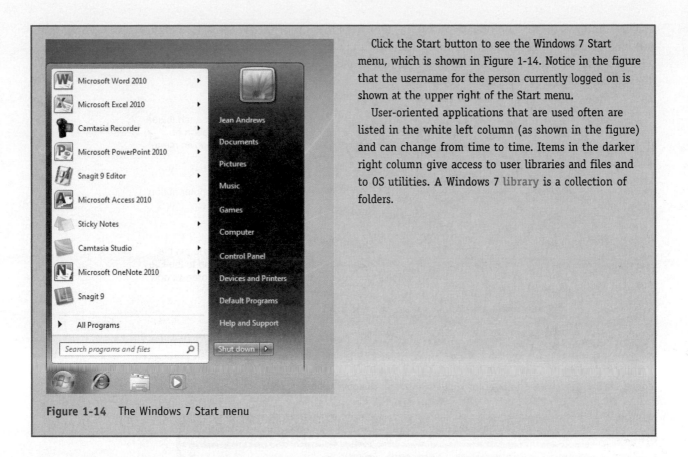

Click the Start button to see the Windows 7 Start menu, which is shown in Figure 1-14. Notice in the figure that the username for the person currently logged on is shown at the upper right of the Start menu.

User-oriented applications that are used often are listed in the white left column (as shown in the figure) and can change from time to time. Items in the darker right column give access to user libraries and files and to OS utilities. A Windows 7 library is a collection of folders.

Figure 1-14   The Windows 7 Start menu

Now that you're familiar with the Windows interfaces, let's learn to use several tools that are helpful to both users and technicians.

WINDOWS TOOLS FOR USERS AND TECHNICIANS

All users need to know how to use File Explorer or Windows Explorer. In addition, a technician needs to know how to use the Control Panel, Power Options, System window, System Information window, and Action Center. All these tools are covered in this part of the chapter.

WINDOWS 8 FILE EXPLORER AND WINDOWS 7 WINDOWS EXPLORER

Windows 8 File Explorer or Windows 7 Windows Explorer is opened in these ways:

◢ Click the yellow File Explorer or Windows Explorer icon in the taskbar. If an Explorer window is already open, it becomes the active window.

◢ From the Windows 8 desktop, open the Quick Launch menu (press **Win+X**) and click **File Explorer** in the menu. For Windows 7, right-click **Start** and select **Open Windows Explorer** from the menu that appears. If an Explorer instance is already open, a new instance of Explorer is created. Having two instances of Explorer open makes it easy to drag and drop files and folders from one location to another.

◢ Open the Windows 8 Quick Launch menu, click **Run**, type **explorer** in the Run box, and press **Enter**. For Windows 7, click **Start**, type **explorer** in the Search box, and press **Enter**. You can use this method to open multiple instances of Explorer.

The Windows 8 File Explorer window has tabs near the top of the window (see Figure 1-15). These tabs can change depending on the situation. You click a tab to see its ribbon or a dropdown menu that appears with more tools. The Computer ribbon is shown in the figure. The Windows 7 Windows Explorer window doesn't use ribbons (see Figure 1-16).

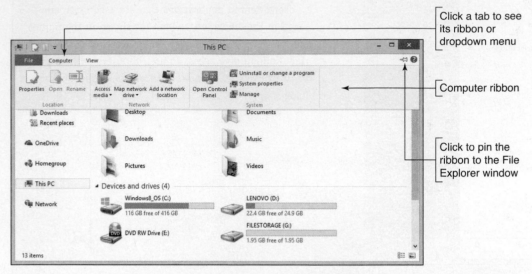

Figure 1-15   Windows 8 File Explorer window with the Computer ribbon shown

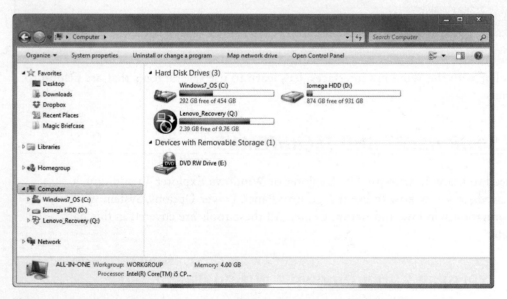

Figure 1-16   Windows 7 Windows Explorer window with the Computer item in the left pane selected

Let's see how to use the Explorer windows to manage files and folders and other system resources.

FILES AND DIRECTORIES

Every OS manages a hard drive, optical drive, USB drive, or other type of drive by using directories (also called folders), subdirectories, and files. The drive is organized with a single root directory at the top of the top-down hierarchical structure of subdirectories, as shown in Figure 1-17. The exception to this rule is a hard drive because it can be divided into partitions that can have more than one volume such as drive C: and drive D: on the same physical hard drive (see Figure 1-18). For a volume, such as drive C:, the root directory is written as C:. Each volume has its own root directory and hierarchical structure of subdirectories. You can think of volumes as logical drives within the one physical drive.

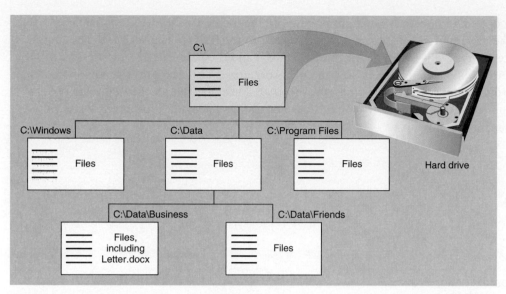

Figure 1-17 Storage devices such as a USB drive, DVD, or hard drive are organized into directories and subdirectories that contain files

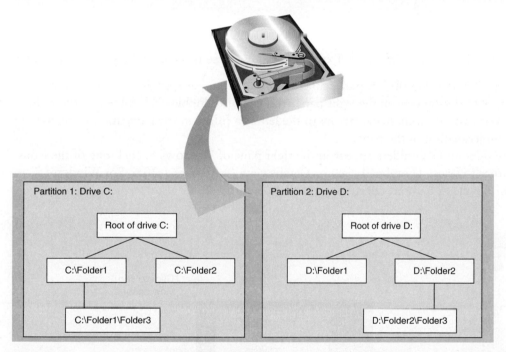

Figure 1-18 A hard drive can be divided into one or more partitions that can each contain a volume such as drive C: or drive D:

As shown in Figure 1-17, the root directory can hold files or other directories, which can have names such as C:\Data. These directories, called subdirectories, child directories, folders, or subfolders can, in turn, have other directories listed in them. Any directory can have files and other subdirectories listed in it; for example, Figure 1-17 shows that one file on drive C: is C:\Data\Business\Letter.docx. In this path to the file, the C: identifies the volume and is called the drive letter. Drive letters used for a hard drive, CD, USB drive, or DVD are C:, D:, E:, and so forth.

> ✎ **Notes** Technicians tend to call a directory a folder when working in File Explorer or Windows Explorer, but when working with a command-line interface, they call a directory a directory.

When you refer to a drive and directories that are pointing to the location of a file, as in C:\Data\Business\Letter.docx, the drive and directories are called the path to the file (see Figure 1-19). The first part of the name before the period is called the file name (Letter), and the part after the period is called the file extension (.docx). A file extension indicates how the file is organized or formatted, the type of content in the file, and what program uses the file. For example, the .docx file extension identifies the file type as a Microsoft Word document file. By default, Windows does not display file extensions in Explorer. How to display these extensions is coming up.

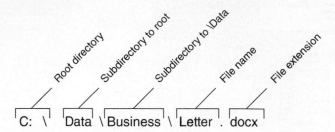

Figure 1-19   The complete path to a file includes the volume letter, directories, file name, and file extension; the colon, backslashes, and period are required to separate items in the path

NAVIGATE THE FOLDER STRUCTURE

When working with the File Explorer or Windows Explorer window, these tips can make your work easier:

▲ ***Tip 1***: Click or double-click items in the left pane, called the navigation pane, to drill down into these items. The folders or subfolders appear in the right pane. You can also double-click folders in the right pane to drill down. When you click the white arrow to the left of a folder in the navigation pane, its subfolders are listed underneath it in the pane.

▲ ***Tip 2***: To control how files and subfolders appear in the right pane of Windows 8, click one of the icons in the lower-right corner to select Thumbnail view or Details view (see Figure 1-20a). For Windows 7, click the View icon in the menu bar and select your view (see Figure 1-20b).

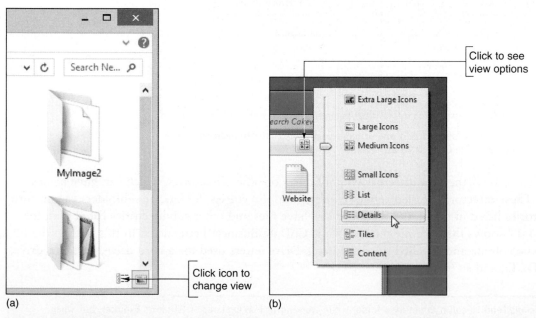

Figure 1-20   Click the View icon to change how files and folders display in the right pane of (a) Windows 8 File Explorer or (b) Windows 7 Windows Explorer

▲ *Tip 3*: To control the column headings that appear in Details view, right-click a column heading and select the headings that you want to appear (see Figure 1-21). To control which column is used to sort items in Details view, click a column heading.

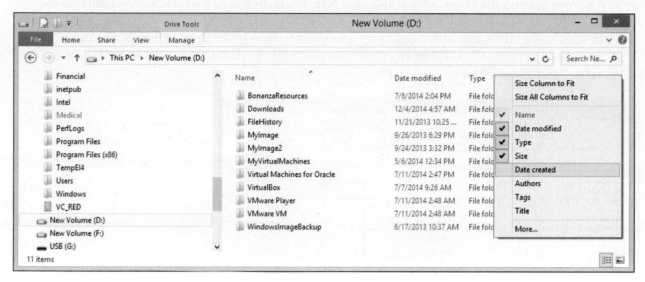

Figure 1-21 Right-click a column heading to select columns to display in Details view

▲ *Tip 4*: To search for a folder or file, use the Search box in the upper-right corner of the window.
▲ *Tip 5*: Use the forward and back arrows in the upper-left corner to move forward and backward to previous views.
▲ *Tip 6*: Click a right arrow in the path displayed in the address bar at the top of the Explorer window to see a drop-down list of subfolders (see Figure 1-22). Click one to move to this subfolder.

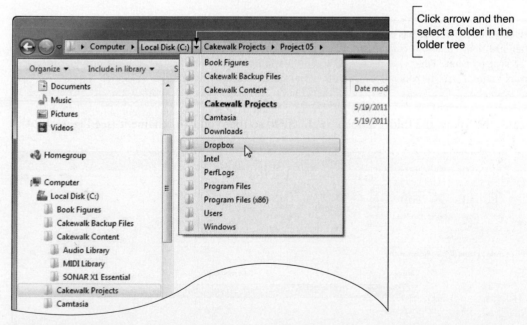

Figure 1-22 Click a right arrow in the address bar to move up the folder tree and down to a new folder

CREATE A FOLDER

To create a folder, first select the folder you want to be the parent folder. (Remember that a parent folder is the folder that contains the child folder.) Next, use one of these methods to create the new folder:

- In Windows 8, select the **Home** ribbon and click **New folder**. In Windows 7, click **New folder** on the menu bar.
- Right-click in the white area of the right pane and point to **New** in the shortcut menu. The menu in Figure 1-23 appears. Click **Folder** to create a regular folder or click **Compressed (zipped) Folder** to create a compressed folder.

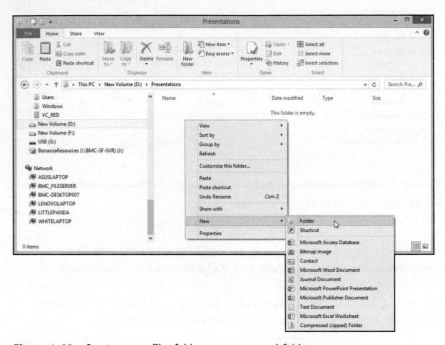

Figure 1-23 Create a new file, folder, or compressed folder

> ✎ **Notes** A compressed (zipped) folder has a .zip extension. Any file or folder that you put in this folder will be compressed to a smaller size than normal. A compressed folder is often used to compress files to a smaller size so they can more easily be sent by email. When you remove a file or folder from a compressed folder, the file or folder is uncompressed back to its original size. In general, Windows treats a compressed folder more like a file than a folder.

After Windows creates the folder, the folder name is highlighted so that you can rename it (see Figure 1-24).

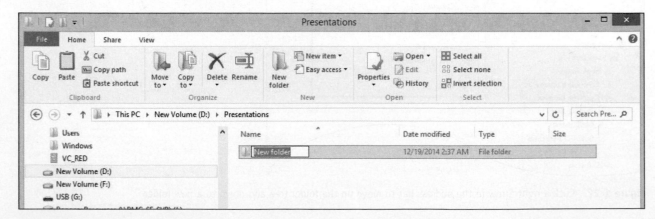

Figure 1-24 Edit the new folder's name

1

✎ Notes The Windows desktop is itself a folder and is located at C:\Users*username*\Desktop. For example, if the user, Anne, creates a folder on her desktop named Downloads, this folder is located at C:\Users\Anne\Desktop\Downloads.

CREATE A FILE

You can create a file using a particular application, or you can create a file using File Explorer or Windows Explorer. In Explorer, right-click in the unused white area in the right pane of the window and point to **New** in the shortcut menu. The menu lists applications you can use to create a file in the current folder (see Figure 1-23). Click the application and the file is created. You can then rename the file. However, to keep the proper file association, don't change the file extension.

COPY, MOVE, RENAME, OR DELETE FILES OR FOLDERS

Use these handy tips to copy, move, rename, and delete files or folders using File Explorer or Windows Explorer:

▲ To copy a file or folder, right-click it and select **Copy** from the shortcut menu. Then right-click in the white area of the folder where the copied item is to go and select **Paste** from the shortcut menu. You can also use the Cut and Paste commands to move an item to a new location.

▲ Drag and drop an item to move or copy it to a new location. If the location is on the same drive as the original location, the file or folder will be automatically deleted from its original location. If you don't want it deleted, hold down the **Ctrl** key while you drag and drop the item.

▲ To rename a file or folder, right-click it and select **Rename** from the shortcut menu. Change the name and click off the file or folder to deselect it. You cannot rename a data file when an application has the file open; first close the data file and then rename it.

▲ To delete a file or folder, select the item and press the **Delete** key. Or you can right-click the item and select **Delete** from the shortcut menu. Either way, a confirmation dialog box asks if you are sure you want to delete the item. If you click **Yes**, you send the file or folder and all its contents, including subfolders, to the Recycle Bin.

✎ Notes In Windows, the difference between a window and a dialog box is that a window can be resized, but a dialog box cannot be resized.

▲ To select multiple items to delete, copy, or move at the same time, hold down the **Shift** or **Ctrl** key as you click. To select several adjacent items in a list, click the first item and **Shift-click** the last item. To select nonadjacent items in a list, hold down the **Ctrl** key as you click each item.

Files deleted from the hard drive are stored in the Recycle Bin on the desktop. Emptying the Recycle Bin will free up your disk space. To empty the Recycle Bin, right-click the bin and select **Empty Recycle Bin** from the shortcut menu.

✎ Notes In this chapter, you learn how to use File Explorer or Windows Explorer to create, copy, move, delete, and rename files and folders. In the chapter, "Maintaining Windows," you will learn that you can do these same tasks using commands from a command prompt.

CREATE A SHORTCUT

To create a shortcut on the Windows desktop to a data file or program, use File Explorer or Windows Explorer to locate the data file or program file, right-click it, and click **Create shortcut** in the menu that appears. For example, in Figure 1-25, you can see a shortcut to the C:\Windows\System32\notepad.exe program is about to be placed on the Windows desktop.

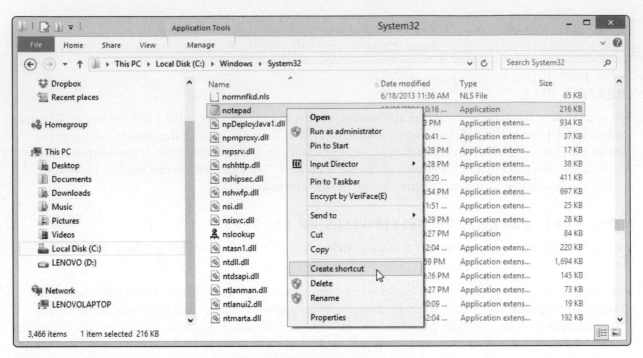

Figure 1-25   Place a shortcut to a program file on the Windows desktop

Hands-On | Project 1-2   Create Shortcuts

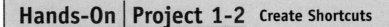

A+
220-902
1.4

Do the following to practice creating shortcuts on the Windows desktop:

1. Open Windows 8 File Explorer or Windows 7 Windows Explorer and create a folder under the root directory of the hard drive called **\Temp**. List the steps you took.

2. Add a subfolder to \Temp called **\MyFiles**. List the steps you took.

3. Create a text file in the MyFiles folder named **Text1.txt**. List the steps you took.

4. Create a shortcut to the MyFiles folder on the Windows desktop. List the steps you took.

5. Rename the file **Text2.txt**.

6. Double-click the shortcut on the desktop. What error did you get?

7. The program file for Microsoft Paint is mspaint.exe. Use Windows Explorer to locate the program file and launch the Microsoft Paint program.

8. Create a shortcut to Microsoft Paint on the Windows desktop. Launch Microsoft Paint using the shortcut.

9. To clean up after yourself, delete the \Temp folder and the shortcuts. Close the two Paint windows.

CONTROL PANEL

A+
220-902
1.1, 1.2

Control Panel is a window containing several small utility programs called applets that are used to manage hardware, software, users, and the system. (In general, a utility program is a program used to maintain a system or fix a computer problem.) To access Control Panel in Windows 8, right-click **Start** and click **Control Panel**. In Windows 7, click **Start** and click **Control Panel**.

By default, Control Panel appears in Category view where utilities are grouped by category. To switch to Classic view, click **Category** and select either Large icons or Small icons. Figure 1-26 shows the Windows 8 Control Panel in Small icons view. Use the Search box in the title bar to help find information and utilities in Control Panel.

Click to switch
to a different view

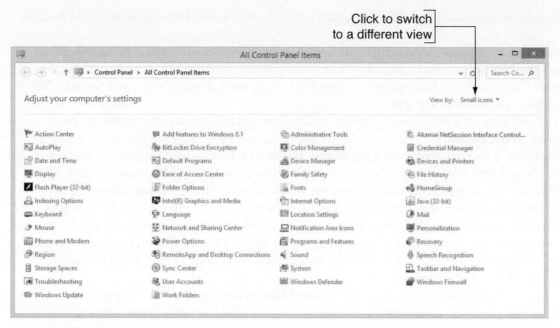

Figure 1-26 Many technicians prefer to use Control Panel in Classic view to more easily access utilities

⭐ **A+ Exam Tip** The A+ 220-902 exam expects you to contrast Control Panel Category view and Classic view and to know how to use Classic view, which generally presents more options to a technician than does Category view.

Here is a short list of some of the applets in Control Panel. Later in the text, you learn to use these and other Control Panel applets:

◢ The Date and Time applet is used to set the date and time in Windows. The Date and Time tab is shown in Figure 1-27a where you can change the date, time, and time zone. Windows can pick up the date and time from UEFI/BIOS firmware on the motherboard. Alternately, on the Internet Time tab (see Figure 1-27b), you can allow Windows to automatically synchronize the date and time with the *time.windows.com* website.

(a)

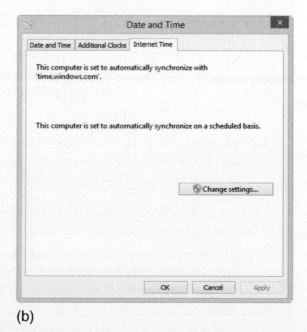

(b)

Figure 1-27 Use the Date and Time applet (a) to manually adjust the date and time, or (b) to automatically synchronize Windows date and time to *time.windows.com* or to a different Internet time server

▲ The Sound applet is used to select a default speaker and microphone and adjust how Windows handles sounds.

▲ Administrative Tools is a console rather than an applet. A console in Control Panel is a collection of support tools used by technicians to support Windows, hardware, applications, and users. Examples of Administrative Tools are Print Management, Computer Management, Event Viewer, and Services. You'll learn to use these tools later in the text.

▲ Windows Firewall puts up a shield to protect the system from outside attacks and to enforce security policies applied to the system.

▲ Windows Defender is antivirus software embedded in Windows 8 that can detect, prevent, and clean up a system infected with viruses and other malware. Defender is included in Windows 7 but is not antivirus software and only protects against spyware, which is out to steal personal information on a computer. You'll learn more about protection against malware in the chapter, "Security Strategies."

▲ BitLocker Drive Encryption is a Windows utility that works with the motherboard and hard drive to encrypt a drive so that, in the event a computer is lost or stolen, data on the drive cannot be read.

▲ Action Center is an easy-to-use tool that can help nontechnical users solve simple problems with Windows, hardware, and applications.

▲ The Folder Options applet lets you change how files and folders are displayed in File Explorer or Windows Explorer.

FOLDER OPTIONS

The Folder Options applet in Control Panel can be used to view and change options assigned to folders. These options control how users view the files in the folder and what they can do with these files. In File Explorer or Windows Explorer, Windows has an annoying habit of hiding file extensions if it knows which application is associated with a file extension. For example, just after installation, it hides .exe, .com, .sys, and .txt file extensions, but does not hide .docx, .pptx, or .xlsx file extensions until the software to open these files has been installed. Also, Windows really doesn't want you to see its own system files, and it hides these files from view until you force it to show them.

APPLYING CONCEPTS   CHANGE FOLDER OPTIONS

A technician is responsible for solving problems with system files (files that belong to the Windows operating system) and file extensions. To fix problems with these files and extensions, you need to see them. To change folder options so you can view system files and file extensions in Windows 8/7, do the following:

1. **Open Control Panel** and, if necessary, change the view to **Small icons** view. Then click **Folder Options**. The Folder Options dialog box appears with the General tab selected (see Figure 1-28a). On the General tab, you can change settings for how Explorer browses folders and handles the navigation pane.

2. Click the **View** tab. Scroll down in the Advanced settings group and make these selections to show hidden information about files, folders, and drives, as shown in Figure 1-28b:

   ▲ Select **Show hidden files, folders, and drives**.
   ▲ Uncheck **Hide extensions for known file types**.
   ▲ Uncheck **Hide protected operating system files (Recommended)** and respond to the Warning box.

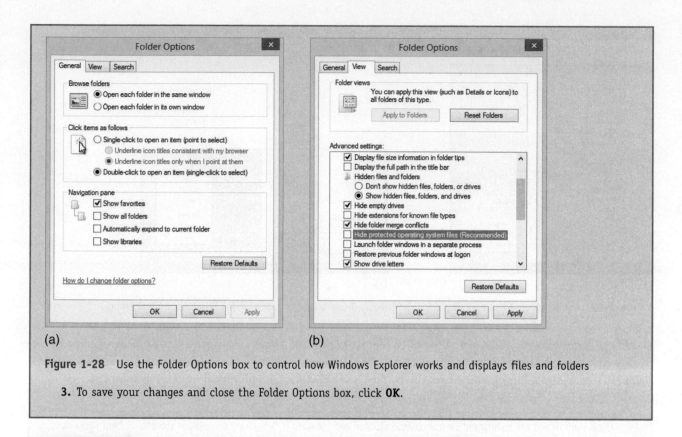

(a)   (b)

Figure 1-28   Use the Folder Options box to control how Windows Explorer works and displays files and folders

3. To save your changes and close the Folder Options box, click **OK**.

> ⭐ **A+ Exam Tip**   The A+ 220-902 exam expects you to know how to view hidden files and file extensions in File Explorer and Windows Explorer.

POWER OPTIONS

**A+
220-902
1.5**

The Power Options applet of Control Panel can help you conserve power and increase the time before a battery pack on a laptop needs recharging. Power is managed by putting the computer into varying degrees of suspend or sleep modes.

> ⭐ **A+ Exam Tip**   The A+ 220–902 exam expects you to know how to manage power, including using power plans, sleep (suspend), hibernate, and standby modes.

Here are the different power-saving states:

◢ *Sleep mode.* Using Windows 8/7/Vista, you can put the computer into sleep mode, also called suspend mode, to save power when you're not using the computer. If applications are open or other work is in progress, Windows first saves the current state, including open files, to memory and saves some of the work to the hard drive. Then everything is shut down except memory and enough of the system to respond to a wake-up. In sleep mode, the power light on the laptop might blink from time to time. (A laptop generally uses about 1 to 2 percent of battery power for each hour in sleep mode.) To wake up the computer, press the power button or, for some computers, press a key or touch the touch pad. Windows wakes up in about two seconds. When Windows is in sleep mode, it can still perform Windows updates and scheduled tasks. Windows can be configured to go to sleep after a period of inactivity, or you can manually put it to sleep. To put the system to sleep manually in Windows 8, you can use the charms bar as you learned to do earlier in the chapter. You can also open the **Quick Launch** menu, point to **Shut down or sign out,** and click **Sleep** (see Figure 1-29a). For Windows 7, click **Start**, click the arrow to the right of Shut down, and then click **Sleep** (see Figure 1-29b). A laptop might also be configured to go to sleep when you close the lid.

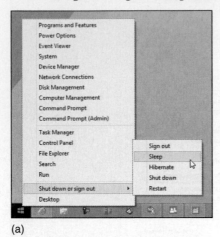

(a)

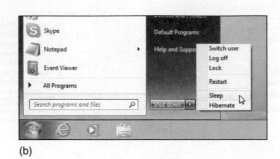

(b)

Figure 1-29 Put Windows to sleep using the (a) Windows 8 Quick Launch menu or (b) Windows 7 Start menu

◢ **Hibernation.** Hibernation saves all work to the hard drive and powers down the system. When you press the power button, Windows reloads its state, including all open applications and documents. When Windows is in sleep mode on a laptop and senses the battery is critically low, it will put the system into hibernation.

> **Notes** Hard drives are permanent or nonvolatile storage and memory is temporary or volatile storage. A hard drive does not require power to hold its contents, but memory, on the other hand, is volatile and loses its contents when it has no power. In hibernation, the computer has no power and everything must, therefore, be stored on the hard drive.

APPLYING | CONCEPTS CONFIGURE WINDOWS POWER-MANAGEMENT SETTINGS

A+
220-902
1.5

Follow these steps to configure power in Windows 8/7:

1. In Control Panel in Classic view, click **Power Options**. The Power Options window opens. Figure 1-30 shows the window for one laptop. The plans might be different for other laptops.

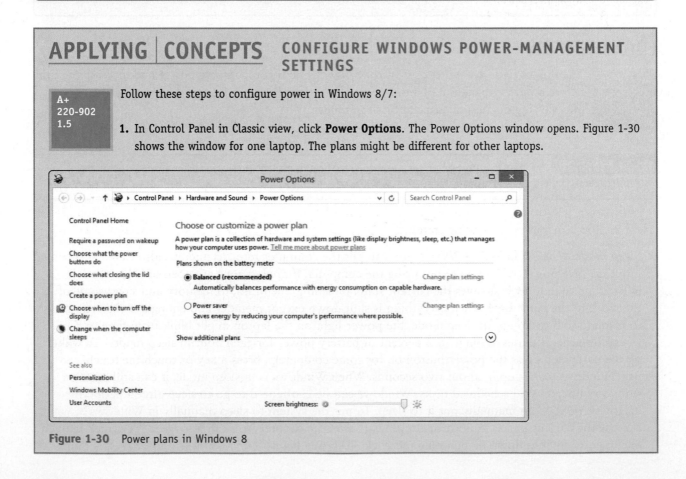

Figure 1-30 Power plans in Windows 8

2. You can customize each plan. For example, under Balanced (recommended), click **Change plan settings**. The Edit Plan Settings window appears (see the left side of Figure 1-31). Notice in the figure the various times of inactivity before the computer goes into sleep mode, which are called sleep timers.

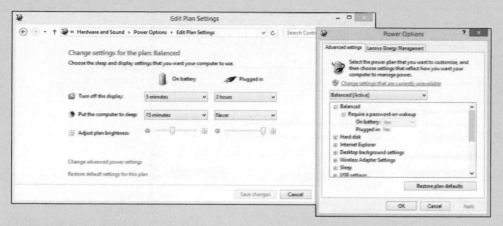

Figure 1-31 Customize a power plan

3. To see other changes you can make, click **Change advanced power settings**. Using this Power Options box (see the right side of Figure 1-31), you can do such things as control the minutes before the hard drive turns off; control what happens when you close the lid, press the sleep button, or press the power button; or set the brightness level of the LCD panel to conserve power. You can also use this box to set what happens when the battery gets low or critically low. Make your changes and click **OK** to close the box.

4. If you made changes, click **Save changes** in the Edit Plan Settings window. Close the Power Options window.

As an IT support technician, you need to be able to sit down at a working computer and within 5 or 10 minutes find the details about what software and hardware is installed on the system and the general health of the system. Within 20 minutes, you should be able to solve any minor problems the computer might have such as a broken network connection. Some quick-and-easy support tools that can help you are the System window, System Information window, and Action Center. All these tools are discussed next.

★ **A+ Exam Tip** The A+ 220-902 exam expects you to know how to use File Explorer, Windows Explorer, the System window, the System Information window, and the Action Center. If the utility can be accessed by more than one method, you are expected to know all of the methods.

SYSTEM WINDOW

A+
220-902
1.1

The System window is your friend. It can give you a quick look at what hardware and software are installed and can get you to other useful Windows tools. To open the System window in Windows 8, open the Quick Launch menu (press **Win+X**) and click **System**. In Windows 7, click **Start**, right-click **Computer**, and select **Properties** from the shortcut menu. (Alternately, you can open **Control Panel** and click **System**.) Figure 1-32 shows the resulting System window for one Windows 8 laptop.

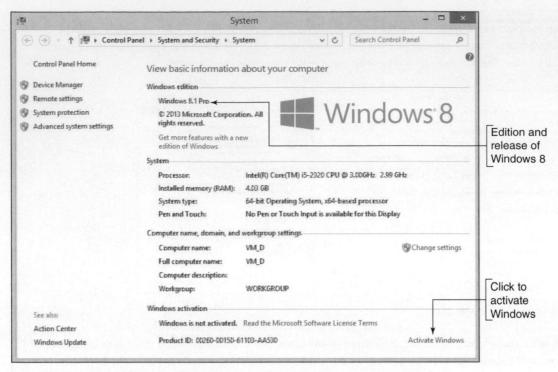

Figure 1-32   System window reports Windows 8.1 Pro is installed but not yet activated

So what technical information are you looking at? Here is the rundown:

- Windows 8/7 comes in several editions and you can see this system has the Windows 8.1 Professional edition installed.
- The type of OS installed is a 64-bit OS. A 32-bit operating system processes 32 bits at a time, and a 64-bit operating system processes 64 bits at a time. Most editions of Windows 8/7 come in either 32-bit or 64-bit versions. A 64-bit OS performs better than a 32-bit OS, but requires more memory. A 32-bit OS can support up to 4 GB of memory, and a 64-bit OS can support much more. The details of how much memory each edition of Windows can support are covered in the chapter, "Installing Windows."
- The processor installed is the Intel Core i5-2320 and about 4 GB of RAM is installed.
- You can also see that Windows 8.1 is not activated. To activate Windows, make sure you're connected to the Internet and click **Activate Windows**. The product key used during the installation will be verified during activation.

◇ OS Differences Recall that Windows 8 offers free major updates and the only one Microsoft has published to date is Windows 8.1. However, Windows 7 handles major updates differently. A major update to Windows 7 is called a service pack, and the Windows 7 System window reports which service packs, if any, have been installed. See Figure 1-33. Minor updates or fixes that are released more frequently for Windows 8 or 7 are called patches and are not reported on the System window.

1

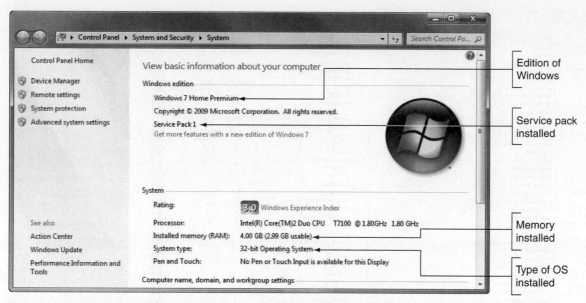

Figure 1-33 A 32-bit version of Windows 7 Home Premium with Service Pack 1 installed

That's a lot of useful information for a first look at a computer.

SYSTEM INFORMATION WINDOW

A+
220-902
1.1, 1.4

Turn to the System Information (msinfo32.exe) window for more details about a system, including installed hardware and software, the current system configuration, and currently running programs. For example, you can use it to find out what BIOS version is installed on the motherboard, how much RAM is installed, the directory where the OS is installed, the size of the hard drive, the names of currently running drivers, a list of startup programs, print jobs in progress, currently running tasks, and much more. Because the System Information window gives so much useful information, help desk technicians often ask a user on the phone to open it and read to the technician information about the computer.

When strange error messages appear during startup, use the System Information window to get a list of drivers that loaded successfully. Device drivers are small programs stored on the hard drive that tell the computer how to communicate with a specific hardware device such as a printer, network card, or scanner. If you have saved the System Information report when the system was starting successfully, comparing the two reports can help identify the problem device.

To run System Information in Windows 8, open the **Quick Launch** menu, click **Run**, enter **msinfo32.exe** in the Run box, and press **Enter**. In Windows 7, click **Start**, and enter **msinfo32.exe** in the Search box and press **Enter**. The System Information window for one computer is shown in Figure 1-34. To drill down to more information in the window, click items in the left pane.

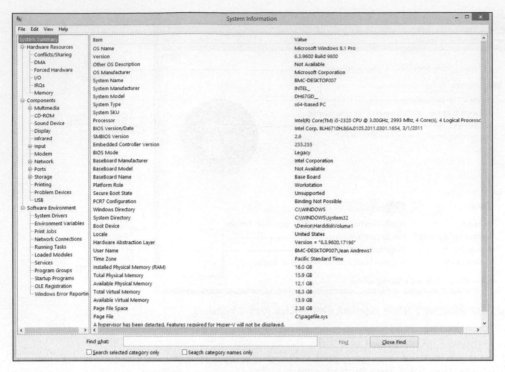

Figure 1-34   Use the System Information utility to examine details about a system

Hands-On | Project 1-3   Use the System Information Utility

A+
220-902
1.1, 1.4

Do the following to run the System Information utility and gather information about your system:

1. Use the **msinfo32.exe** command to launch the System Information window.

2. Browse through the different levels of information in this window and answer the following questions:

   a. What OS and OS version are you using?

   b. What is your CPU speed?

   c. What is your BIOS manufacturer and version?

   d. How much video RAM is available to your video adapter card? Explain how you got this information.

   e. What is the name of the driver file that manages your network adapter? Your optical drive?

ACTION CENTER

A+
220-902
1.1

The Action Center is the tool to use when you want to make a quick jab at solving a computer problem. If a hardware or application problem is easy to solve, the Action Center can probably do it in a matter of minutes because it lists errors and issues that need attention and proposed solutions. The Action Center flag appears in the notification area of the taskbar. If the flag has a red X beside it, as shown in Figure 1-35, Windows considers the system has an important issue that needs resolving immediately. When you click the flag, you can see a brief report of issues, as shown in the figure.

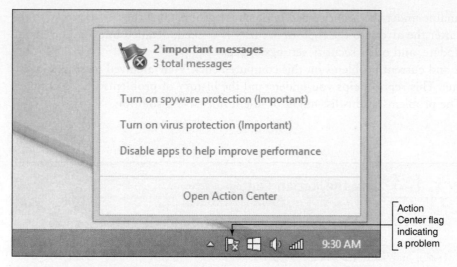

Action Center flag indicating a problem

Figure 1-35 A red X on the Action Center flag in the taskbar indicates a critical issue needs resolving

⭐ **A+ Exam Tip** The A+ 220-902 exam expects you to know about the Windows Vista Security Center. It was the predecessor to the Windows 8/7 Action Center and gave quick-and-easy access to several Windows tools, including Windows Firewall, Windows Update, anti-malware settings, including that of Windows Defender, and other security settings.

To open the Action Center, you can click the red flag in the taskbar and then click **Open Action Center**. Alternately, you can open **Control Panel** and click **Action Center**. The Action Center window for one Windows 8 computer is shown in Figure 1-36. (The Windows 7 Action Center is similar.) Notice the colored bar to the left of a problem. The red color indicates a critical problem that needs immediate attention. In this example, antivirus software is not running on the system. The orange color indicates a less critical problem, such as apps running in the background that might be slowing down the system or no backups are scheduled. Click the button to the right of a problem to find a recommended solution.

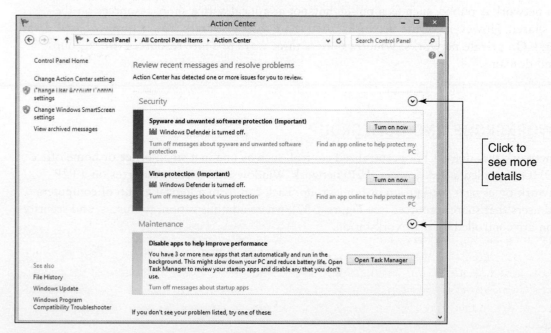

Click to see more details

Figure 1-36 The Action Center shows a critical problem that needs a resolution

To see other information available under the Security or Maintenance group, click the down arrow to the right of a group. For example, after the arrow to the right of Security is clicked, detailed information about Windows Firewall, Windows Update, and other security settings appears.

To see a complete list of past and current problems on this computer, click **View archived messages** in the left pane of the Action Center. This report helps you understand the history of problems on a computer that you are troubleshooting. The problems in this list might or might not have a solution.

Hands-On | Project 1-4   Use the Action Center

> A+
> 220-902
> 1.1

Using Windows 8/7, follow these steps to explore and use the Action Center:

1. Open the Action Center and list any problems it reports.

2. If a problem is listed, follow the links in Action Center to investigate possible solutions to the problem. If appropriate for your system, apply any solutions not yet applied. Make notes regarding the solutions you applied and the results of applying these solutions.

3. In the left pane of the Action Center, click **View archived messages**. Do you find a previous problem with this computer that already has a solution applied? If so, double-click the problem to read about the solution. Describe the problem and the solution that was applied.

WINDOWS NETWORK CONNECTIONS

> A+
> 220-902
> 1.5, 1.6

An essential task of IT technicians is to connect computers to a wired or wireless network and support these connections. Before we get into the Windows networking tools to help you, let's start by looking at the ways Windows accesses resources on a network. If a network is public, such as a public hotspot at a local coffee shop, resources on the network aren't shared. However, private networks often share their resources (for example, shared data files and printers). On private networks, Windows offers three ways to share resources: workgroups, homegroups, and domains.

WINDOWS WORKGROUP AND HOMEGROUP

> A+
> 220-902
> 1.5, 1.6

A network that doesn't have centralized control, such as one in a small office or home office (SOHO), is called a peer-to-peer (P2P) network. Windows can access resources on a P2P network by using a workgroup or homegroup. Each can form a logical group of computers and users that share resources (see Figure 1-37), where administration, resources, and security on a workstation are controlled by that workstation.

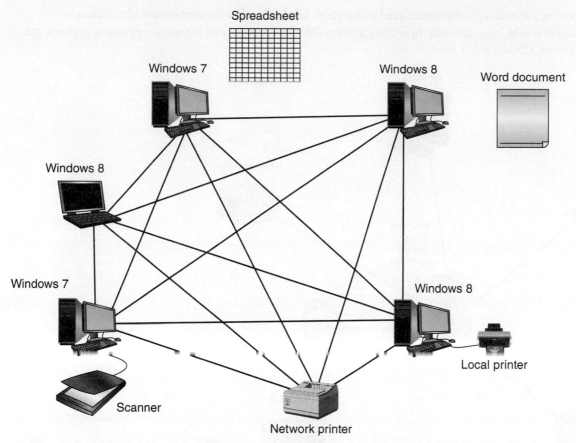

Figure 1-37 A Windows workgroup or homegroup is a type of peer-to-peer network where no single computer controls the network and each computer controls its own resources

---

Notes When looking at the diagrams in Figure 1-37 and later in Figure 1-38, know that the connecting lines describe the logical connections between computers and not the physical connections. Both networks might be physically connected the same way, but logically, resources are controlled by each computer on the network or by using a centralized database. In network terminology, the arrangement of physical connections between computers is called the physical topology. The logical way the computers connect on a network is called the logical topology.

In a Windows workgroup, each computer maintains a list of users and their rights on that particular computer. The computer allows a user on the network to access local resources based on the rights she has been given. In a homegroup, each computer shares files, folders, libraries, and printers with other computers in the homegroup. A homegroup provides less security than a workgroup because any user of any computer in the homegroup can access homegroup resources.

★ A+ Exam Tip The A+ 220-902 exam expects you to contrast a workgroup, homegroup, and domain. You also need to know that homegroups only apply to Windows 8/7, but not to Windows Vista, which does not support homegroups.

WINDOWS DOMAIN

A+
220-902
1.5, 1.6

A Windows domain is implemented on a larger, private network, such as a corporate or college network. The domain forms a logical group of networked computers that share a centralized directory database of user account information and security for the entire group of computers (see Figure 1-38). A Windows domain is a type of client/server network, which is a network where resources are managed by centralized computers. Using the client/server model, the directory database is controlled by a network operating system (NOS). Examples of network operating systems are Windows Server, UNIX, and Linux.

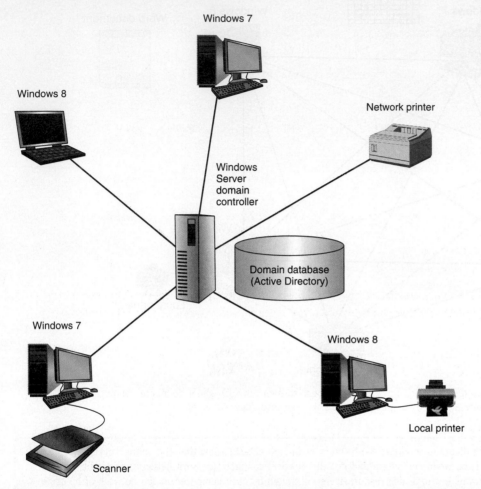

Figure 1-38   A Windows domain is a type of client/server network where security on each computer or other device is controlled by a centralized database on a domain controller

> **Notes** Windows Home Editions do not support joining a domain. If you plan to join a domain on your network, install Windows 8.1 Professional or Enterprise, or Windows 7 Professional, Enterprise, or Ultimate editions.

Windows Server controls a network using the directory database called Active Directory. Each user on the network must have his own domain-level account called a global account, network ID, domain account, or global username, which is kept in Active Directory and assigned by the network or system administrator. If you are connecting a computer to a domain, the administrator will tell you the network ID and password to the domain that you can use to sign in to the network.

> **Notes** If your computer is part of a domain, when Windows starts up, press **Ctrl+Alt+Del** to display a sign-in screen, and then enter your network ID and password.

PUBLIC AND PRIVATE NETWORKS

A+
220-902
1.5, 1.6

When you connect to a public network, such as when you connect your laptop to a public wireless network at a local airport, you always want to ensure that your computer is protected from outside hackers and malware. Windows 8 offers two types of network security:

▲ *Public network.* When using Public network security, Windows configures strong firewall settings and you cannot join a homegroup or domain.

▲ *Private network.* When using Private network security, you can join a homegroup or domain and share files and printers.

Windows 7 offers three network security options, which are managed by Network Discovery settings that allow this computer to see other computers on the network and other computers can see this computer:

▲ *Public network.* Network Discovery is turned off and you cannot join a homegroup or domain. This option is the most secure.

▲ *Home network.* Network Discovery is turned on and you can join a homegroup.

▲ *Work network.* Network Discovery is turned on, you can join a domain, but you cannot join a homegroup.

MAKE A WINDOWS 8 NETWORK CONNECTION

To make a wired connection to a network, unless you have an unusual network setup, simply plug in the network cable and Windows does the rest.

To create a wireless connection in Windows 8, you can use the charms bar or the Network icon in the taskbar on the Windows 8 desktop. Here are directions when using the charms bar:

1. On the charms bar, click the Settings charm, and then click the Network icon. A list of available wireless networks appears (see Figure 1-39a). Click one to select it, and then click **Connect** (see Figure 1-39b).

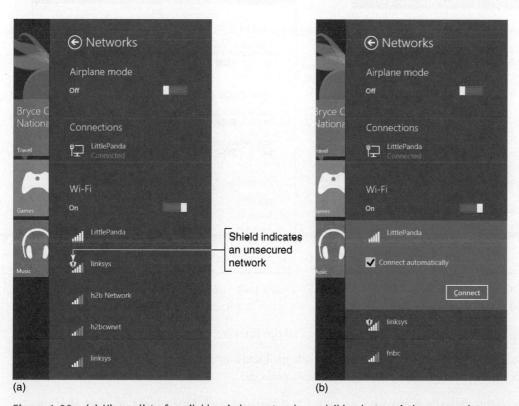

(a)   (b)

Figure 1-39 (a) View a list of available wireless networks, and (b) select a wireless network to connect

2. If the network is secured, you must enter the security key to the wireless network to connect.

To view and change network security settings, click the **Settings** charm and click **Change PC settings**. On the PC settings screen, click **Network**. On the Network screen, if necessary, click **Connections** (see Figure 1-40).

Figure 1-40   Use the Network screen to manage the security of network connections

Notes When you click **HomeGroup** on the Network screen shown in Figure 1-40, you can use the HomeGroup page that appears to join or leave a homegroup, view the homegroup password, and decide whether libraries and printers are shared with the homegroup. These homegroup settings can also be managed from the Network and Sharing Center.

When you click a connection in the right pane, you can view and change some of the properties for the connection. For example, Figure 1-41 shows a wired connection and Figure 1-42 shows a wireless connection. To set the network security to Private, turn on **Find devices and content**. To set the network security to Public, turn this setting off.

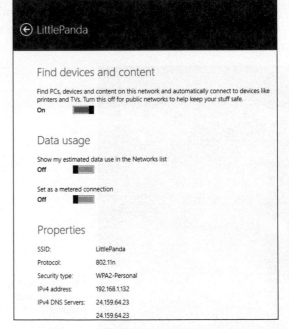

Figure 1-41   View and manage a wired network connection

Figure 1-42   View and manage a wireless network connection

3. Open your browser window and verify you have access to the Internet.

To view network information and to troubleshoot network problems, use the Network and Sharing Center. To open the Network and Sharing Center, use one of these methods:

◢ On the desktop, right-click the **Network** icon in the taskbar, and click **Open Network and Sharing Center** in the shortcut menu that appears.

◢ Open **Control Panel** in Classic view and click **Network and Sharing Center**.

The Network and Sharing Center is shown in Figure 1-43. Notice you can see the active connections and network security setting. In later chapters, you'll learn to use the Network and Sharing Center to troubleshoot network problems.

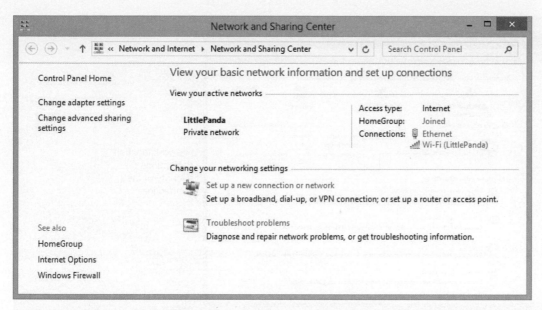

Figure 1-43 Windows 8 Network and Sharing Center reports network information and gives access to network troubleshooting tools

WINDOWS | 7   MAKE A WINDOWS 7 NETWORK CONNECTION

A+
220-902
1.5, 1.6

In Windows 7, to connect to a wireless network and secure the connection, do the following:

1. Click the Network icon in the taskbar. A list of available networks appears. Click a network and click **Connect** (see Figure 1-44). If the network is secured, enter the security key the first time you connect and click **OK**.

2. To verify or change the security setting, open the **Network and Sharing Center** window (see Figure 1-45). For example, to change the security to Public network (the highest level of security), if the network location says Home network or Work network, click it. The Set Network Location box appears (see Figure 1-46). Click **Public network** and click **Close**.

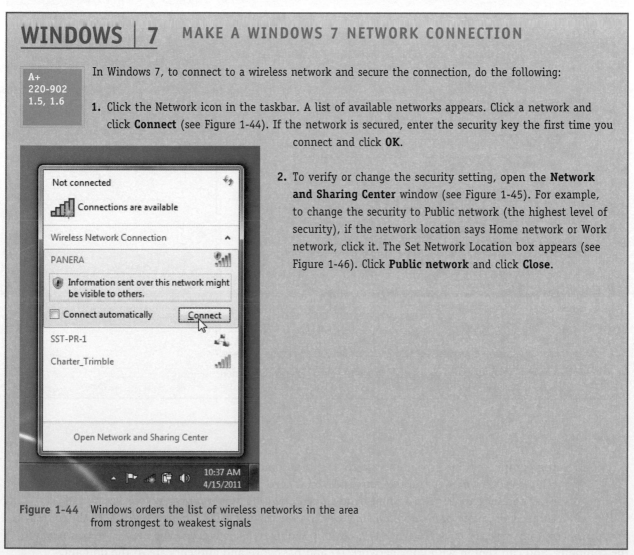

Figure 1-44 Windows orders the list of wireless networks in the area from strongest to weakest signals

(continues)

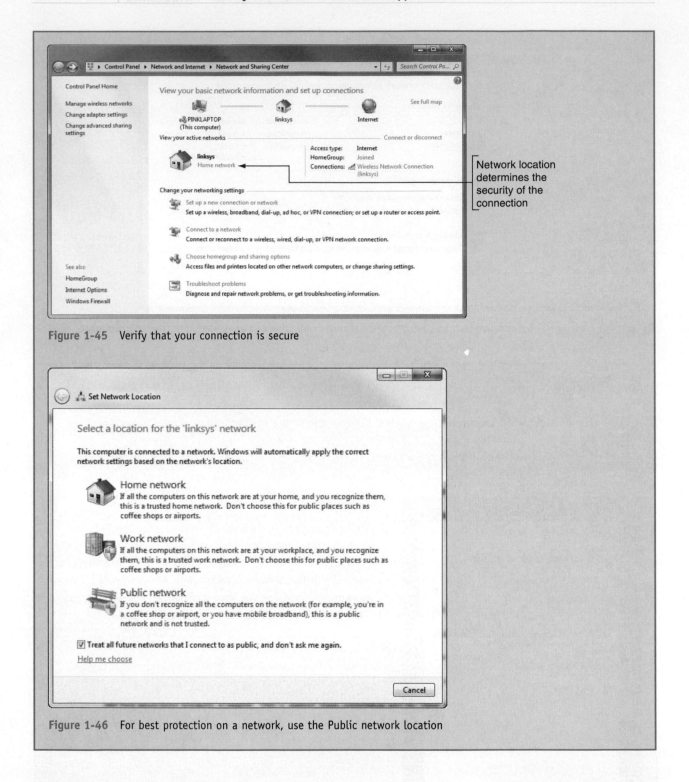

Figure 1-45 Verify that your connection is secure

Figure 1-46 For best protection on a network, use the Public network location

DOMAIN SETUP

**A+
220-902
1.5, 1.6**

If a computer is already connected to a network and you want to access resources controlled by a Windows domain on the network, you'll need the network ID and password to the domain provided by the network administrator. Then open the System window (see Figure 1-47).

Under *Computer name, domain, and workgroup settings*, click **Change settings**. In the System Properties box that appears, click **Network ID** and follow directions on screen. The next time you restart the computer, you can sign in with your network ID and password and authenticate to the domain.

Figure 1-47 Set up Windows to join a domain

The details of securing and managing shared resources on a network and connecting to and setting up a network are covered later in the text.

We now turn our attention to the various types of user accounts supported by Windows.

WINDOWS USER ACCOUNTS

**A+
220-902
1.1, 1.5,
3.3**

A user must sign in to Windows with a valid user account to gain access to the OS. Windows supports various types and privileges for user accounts. Here's a brief overview:

▲ **The scope of the account.** A local account is created on the local computer and is recognized only on the local computer. As you have already learned, a network ID is created by a network administrator in a centralized database that manages an entire corporate network. When you sign in to Windows using a network ID, you are authenticated to the local computer and also to the Windows domain or network.

▲ **Privileges for the account.** In Windows, there are two types of privileges assigned to a user account: an administrator account and a standard account. An administrator account has more privileges than a standard account and is used by those responsible for maintaining and securing the system. In addition, Windows 8 offers a third type of privilege: a child account that parents can set up for their children, which has very limited privileges.

▲ **A Microsoft account.** For Windows 8, a Microsoft account is an email address, which allows you to access several types of online accounts, including Microsoft OneDrive, Facebook, LinkedIn, Twitter, Skype, *Outlook.com*, and others. A Microsoft account is an example of a single sign-on (SSO) account, which accesses multiple, independent resources, systems, or applications after signing in one time to one account. To set up a Microsoft account, go to the *live.com* website and link an email address to the Microsoft account. The account is assigned a OneDrive, which is 15 GB of free storage space in the cloud. You can pay for additional storage, and you can also use Microsoft's free cloud apps to manage data files stored on your OneDrive. A Microsoft account can be linked to a local account or a network ID and can be assigned the privileges of a standard account or an administrative account.

APPLYING | CONCEPTS   CREATE A LOCAL ACCOUNT

A+
220-902
1.5

To create a local account, you must first sign in to Windows with an administrative account. In Windows 8, you can then create a new local account using the Settings charm, or you can create accounts using the Computer Management console, which is one of the Administrative Tools in Control Panel. In Windows 7, you can create accounts through the User Accounts applet in Control Panel or the Computer Management console.

In Windows 8, to use the Settings charm to create an account, do the following:

1. Sign in to Windows 8 using an administrator account. Open the **Settings** charm, and click **Change PC settings**. On the PC settings screen, click **Accounts**. On the Accounts screen, click **Other accounts** (see Figure 1-48).

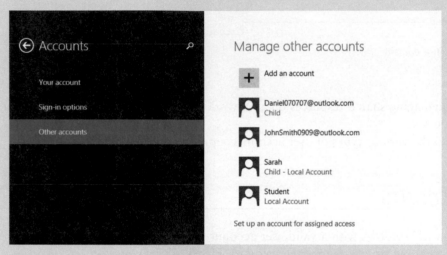

Figure 1-48   Set up a new user account

2. Click **Add an account**. The *How will this person sign in?* screen appears (see Figure 1-49) where you have four options:

    ◢ To set up an existing Microsoft account on this computer, enter the email address for the account, and click **Next**.

    ◢ To sign up for a new email address that will also be a Microsoft account, click **Sign up for a new email address**.

    ◢ To set up a child account, click **Add a child's account**.

    ◢ To set up a regular local account (not a Microsoft account), click **Sign in without a Microsoft account (not recommended)**, and click **Next**. Follow directions on screen to set up the account.

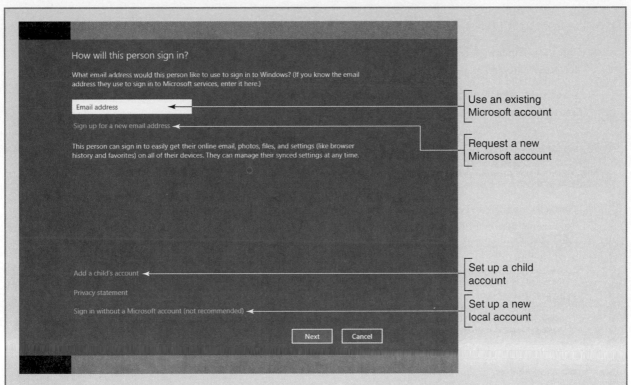

Figure 1-49 Four ways to set up a new user account

The first time a user signs in to Windows with the account, user files and folders (called the user profile) are created in the C:\Users folder.

By default, a new account is a Standard user account. Later, if you want to remove an account or change the account type (for example, to make a standard user account an administrator account), return to the Accounts screen, and click **Other accounts**.

To remove an account, click the account, and click **Remove**. To edit the account type, select the account, and click **Edit**. In the Edit account pane, you can change the account type to an Administrator, Standard User, or Child account (see Figure 1-50).

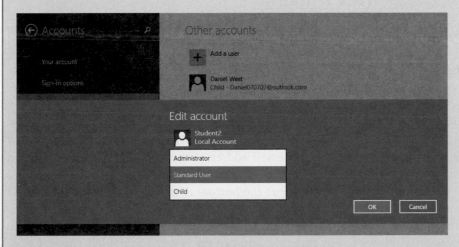

Figure 1-50 Use the Settings charm to change an account type

(continues)

Follow these steps to create a local user account in Windows 7:

1. Sign in to Windows 7 using an administrator account. Open Control Panel in Classic view and click **User Accounts**. Click **Manage another account**. Click **Create a new account**.

2. In the next window, enter the username (see Figure 1-51). Select Standard user or Administrator. Click **Create Account**.

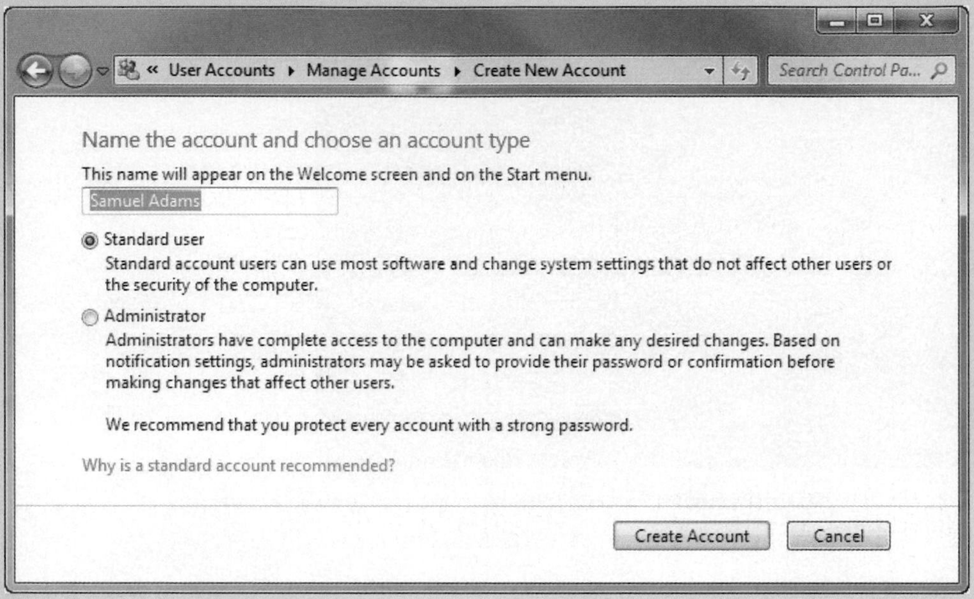

Figure 1-51   Enter the username and decide the privilege level for the new account

You can also use the User Accounts applet in Windows 7 Control Panel to create a password for an account and remove an account.

USING A MICROSOFT ACCOUNT WITH WINDOWS 8

A+
220-902
1.1, 1.5,
3.3

There are advantages and disadvantages of signing in to Windows using a Microsoft account, including:

▲ *Personal settings across several devices.* When you use the same Microsoft account to sign in to multiple computers connected to the Internet, your personal settings follow you to each computer, including your themes, Internet Explorer favorites, and language preferences.

▲ *OneDrive storage in the cloud.* When you sign in to Windows 8 using your Microsoft account, which is called a live sign in, Windows automatically signs you in to your OneDrive, Facebook, LinkedIn, Mail, or other online accounts that are set up with this email address. When you open the OneDrive app on the Start screen, you see the folders at the root level of your OneDrive (see Figure 1-52). Right-click white space on the page to see the status bar at the bottom of the screen where you can create new folders. Click a folder to see its contents, and right-click a folder or file to see options to manage the item, such as delete, copy, cut, or rename a folder or file or add files to a folder. OneDrive is embedded in many features of Windows 8. For example, you can see it listed in the left pane of File Explorer (refer back to Figure 1-15).

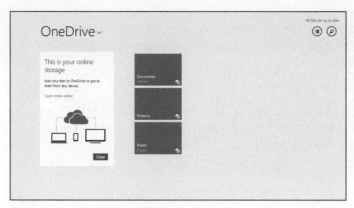

Figure 1-52 OneDrive app page shows folders stored on a OneDrive

◢ *Windows Store.* When you are signed in to Windows with a Microsoft account, you can access the online Windows Store where you can purchase and download apps that use the Windows 8 interface, similar to the way apps on smart phones and tablets are purchased. Apps purchased from the Windows Store can be synced with up to five computers that use your Microsoft account.

◢ *Private settings stored on the local computer.* A disadvantage of using your Microsoft account to sign in to Windows is that your private settings and access to your apps and online accounts are stored on the local computer. Therefore, you would only want to set up your Microsoft account on a computer where you trust those with administrative access to the computer. For many, this means using a Microsoft account only on your own personal computers that are under your complete control. When you are not signed in to Windows with your Microsoft account, you can still use a browser to access online accounts, including your OneDrive. See Figure 1-53.

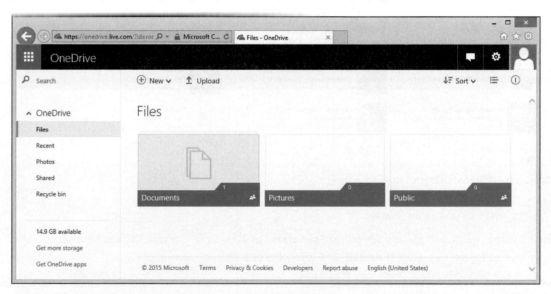

Figure 1-53 Use a browser to access your OneDrive storage area at *live.com* without signing in to Windows with your Microsoft account

Hands-On | Project 1-5 Install and Uninstall Windows 8 Apps

A+
220-902
1.1

Windows 8 apps are installed from the Windows Store, and you must have a Microsoft account to do so. If you don't already have an account, you can get one free at *live.com*. Follow these steps to use a Microsoft account to install an app and then uninstall it:

1. If you don't already have a Microsoft account, go to the Windows desktop, open Internet Explorer, and go to **signup.live.com**. To create the account, you can use an existing email address (for example, someone@ sample.edu) or request a new email address, which will be an *outlook.com*, *hotmail.com*, or *live.com* address.

(continues)

You'll need to enter your name, gender, and birth date, and, for security purposes, you'll need to associate a cell phone number and/or an alternate email address with the account. Be sure you write down your email address and password for your Microsoft account.

2. After you have created your account, close your browser, and return to the Start screen.

3. To install an app, click the **Store** tile. Next, scroll through the apps in the Store or use its Search box to find an app (see Figure 1-54). Click a free one, and follow the directions on screen to install it. If you did not sign in to Windows using a Microsoft account, you are asked to sign in.

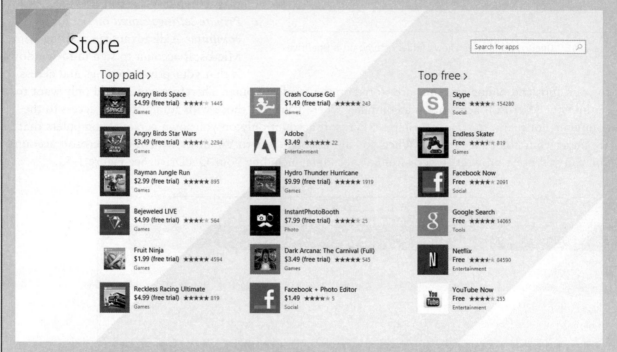

Figure 1-54   Search the Windows Store for apps to install

4. Practice using the app to make sure it works.

5. To uninstall the app, right-click the app tile on the Start screen or Apps screen to view the app's shortcut menu (refer back to Figure 1-7). Click **Uninstall**, and follow the directions on screen.

CONNECTING A MICROSOFT ACCOUNT TO A LOCAL ACCOUNT OR NETWORK ID

You can connect an existing local account or network ID to a Microsoft account. To do so, open the **charms** bar, select the **Settings** charm, select **Change PC settings**, and click **Accounts**. Select **Your account** and then click **Connect to a Microsoft account**. Follow directions on screen.

> **✎ Notes**   To connect a network ID on a domain to a Microsoft account, Group Policies controlling the Windows domain must allow it. After the connection, the Microsoft account is used to authenticate to the domain.

If you want to switch the user account on a Windows 8 computer from a Microsoft account back to a local account or network ID, open the **charms** bar and go to the **PC settings** screen, click **Accounts**, and then click **Disconnect** (see Figure 1-55).

1

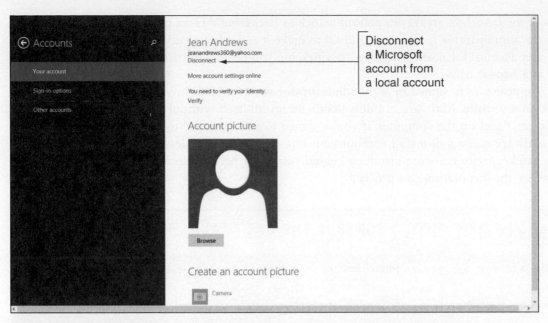

Disconnect
a Microsoft
account from
a local account

Figure 1-55 The Windows user account can be converted from a Microsoft account to a local user account

Recall that you can sign in to Windows using a local account, network ID, or Microsoft account. As you ponder the differences among these accounts, consider where the account is authenticated:

◢ A local account is authenticated on the local computer and gives access to the local computer. An administrator local account has more access than a standard local account.
◢ A network ID is authenticated by a computer on the network, which gives you access to the local computer and other resources on the network.
◢ A Microsoft account is authenticated on the *live.com* website, which gives access to the local computer and online resources, such as OneDrive and Facebook.com. A Microsoft account can also be associated with a network ID so that you can sign in with the Microsoft account and be authenticated to the network as well as to *live.com*.

USER ACCOUNT CONTROL DIALOG BOX

| A+ |
| 220-902 |
| 1.1 |

At some point while working with a computer to maintain or troubleshoot it, the User Account Control (UAC) dialog box, shown in Figure 1-56, will pop up. When the UAC box appears, if you are signed in as an administrator, all you have to do is click Yes to close the box and move on, as shown in Figure 1-56a. If the user account does not have administrative privileges, you'll have the opportunity to enter the password of an administrative account to continue, as shown in Figure 1-56b.

(a)   (b)

Figure 1-56 (a) The User Account Control box of an administrator does not require an administrative password; (b) the UAC box of a standard user requires an administrative password

The purposes of the UAC box are: (1) to prevent malicious background tasks from gaining administrative privileges when the administrator is signed in, and (2) to make it easier for an administrator to sign in using a less powerful user account for normal desktop activities, but still be able to perform administrative tasks while signed in as a regular user.

For example, suppose you're signed in as an administrator with the UAC box turned off and click a malicious link on a website. Malware can download and install itself without your knowledge and might get admin privileges on the computer. If you're signed in as a standard user and the UAC box is turned off, the malware might still install without your knowledge but with lesser privileges. The UAC box stands as a gatekeeper to malware installing behind your back because someone has to click the UAC box before the installation can proceed.

APPLYING | CONCEPTS   CONTROL THE UAC DIALOG BOX

A+
220-902
1.1

Using Windows 8/7, you can control how the UAC box works. Do the following:

1. Open the Control Panel and click **User Accounts**.

2. In the User Accounts window, click **Change User Account Control settings**. The User Account Control Settings window appears (see Figure 1-57).

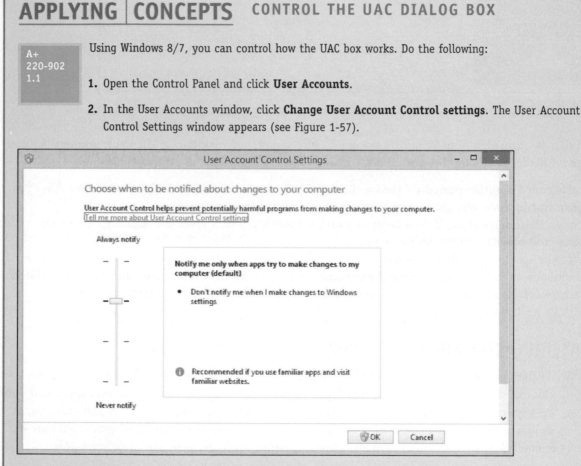

Figure 1-57   Windows provides options to control the UAC box

3. Change when the UAC box appears. Here is a description of the four options shown in Figure 1-57:

   ◢ Always notify me when apps try to install software or make other changes to the computer and when I make changes to Windows settings.

   ◢ Notify me when apps try to make changes, but don't notify me when I make changes to Windows settings. (This is the default setting.)

   ◢ Same as the second option above but, in addition, do not dim the Windows desktop. Dimming the Windows desktop can alarm a user and take up resources.

   ◢ Never notify me when apps try to install software or make changes to my computer or I make changes to Windows settings.

4. Click **OK** and respond to the UAC box.

> ★ **A+ Exam Tip** The A+ 220-902 exam expects you to know how to change the settings that control when the UAC box appears.

>> CHAPTER SUMMARY

Windows Interfaces

◢ An operating system manages hardware; runs applications; provides an interface for users; and stores, retrieves, and manipulates files.

◢ Windows 8 offers two GUIs: the modern interface and the Windows 8 desktop. The Windows 7/Vista desktop offers the Aero user interface.

◢ Ways to launch a program from the Windows 8 desktop include using the Start screen, the Quick Launch menu, an icon pinned to the taskbar, File Explorer, a shortcut on the desktop, and the Run option on the Quick Launch menu.

◢ Ways to launch a program from the Windows 7 desktop include using the Start menu, the Search box, an icon pinned to the taskbar, Windows Explorer, or a shortcut on the desktop.

Windows Tools for Users and Technicians

◢ Windows 8 File Explorer and Windows 7 Windows Explorer are used to manage files and folders on storage devices. Folders are organized in a top-down hierarchical structure of subfolders.

◢ The file extension indicates how the file contents are organized and formatted and what program uses the file.

◢ Control Panel gives access to a group of utility programs used to manage the system. Technicians generally prefer the Classic view for Control Panel.

◢ The Folder Options applet in Control Panel changes the way files and folders are displayed in Explorer.

◢ The Power Options applet in Control Panel manages power settings on a computer.

◢ The System window gives a quick overview of the system, including which edition and version of Windows is installed and the amount of installed memory.

◢ The System Information window gives much information about the computer, including hardware, device drivers, the OS, and applications.

◢ The Action Center is a centralized location used to solve problems with security and computer maintenance.

Windows Network Connections

◢ Windows 8/7 supports workgroups, homegroups, and domains to manage resources on a private network. Vista supports workgroups and domains.

◢ A network ID and password are used to authenticate to a Windows domain, which gives access to resources on the network.

◢ Windows 8 supports public and private settings for network security, and Windows 7 supports public, home, and work settings for network security.

◢ To connect to a wireless network in Windows 8, use the Settings charm or the Network icon in the taskbar on the desktop. Windows 7 uses the Network icon in the taskbar to connect to a wireless network.

◢ Use the Network and Sharing Center to view information about network connections and solve network problems.

◢ Use the System window to set up a computer to connect to a Windows domain.

Windows User Accounts

◢ Windows supports local accounts that are recognized only on the local computer and network IDs that are recognized on a Windows domain.

◢ Two main types of privileges can be assigned to a Windows account: An administrator account has more privileges than a standard account and is required when maintaining and securing a system.

◢ Windows 8 offers a Microsoft account that is authenticated online at the *live.com* website. The account is assigned a OneDrive, which is storage in the cloud.

◢ Use the Settings charm to manage Windows 8 user accounts. In Windows 7, use the User Accounts applet in Control Panel. For Windows 8/7, the Computer Management console in the Administrative Tools group in Control Panel can be used for advanced management of user accounts.

◢ You can associate a Microsoft account with a local account or network ID on a domain.

◢ The User Account Control box helps prevent malware from installing itself on a system. The UAC box settings are controlled in the User Accounts applet in Control Panel.

>> KEY TERMS

For explanations of key terms, see the Glossary for this text.

32-bit operating system	domain account	Network and Sharing Center	sleep mode
64-bit operating system	File Explorer	network ID	sleep timer
Action Center	file extension	Notepad	Sound applet
Active Directory	file name	notification area	standard account
Administrative Tools	folder	OneDrive	Start screen
administrator account	Folder Options applet	operating system (OS)	subdirectory
Aero user interface	gadget	patch	suspend mode
BitLocker Drive Encryption	global account	path	System Information
Category view	graphical user interface (GUI)	peer-to-peer (P2P)	system tray
charm	hibernation	physical topology	System window
charms bar	homegroup	pinning	systray
child directory	library	Power Options applet	taskbar
Classic view	live sign in	Quick Launch menu	User Account Control (UAC) dialog box
client/server	live tiles	Recycle Bin	volume
compressed (zipped) folder	local account	root directory	Windows 8.1
console	logical topology	Security Center	Windows Defender
Control Panel	Metro User Interface (Metro UI)	service	Windows Explorer
Date and Time applet	Microsoft account	service pack	Windows Firewall
device driver	modern interface	sidebar	Windows Store
domain	navigation pane	side-by-side apps	workgroup
		single sign-on (SSO)	

>> REVIEWING THE BASICS

1. List four major functions of an OS.

2. Which app do you use on the Windows 8 Start screen to install new apps?

3. What might happen to the Windows system if too many services are running as indicated by multiple icons in the notification area of the taskbar?

4. What part of a file name does Windows use to know which application to open to manage the file?

5. What is the program file name and extension of File Explorer?

6. When you use File Explorer or Windows Explorer to delete a file from the hard drive, where does Windows put the file?

7. Which keys do you press to open the Windows 8 Quick Launch menu?

8. What file extension is used to name a compressed folder?

9. What is the program name for the System Information utility?

10. By default, when does Windows hide file extensions in File Explorer?

11. Which Windows 7 window can be used to get a report of the history of problems on a computer?

12. What are the two basic Windows 8 settings for network security?

13. List three types of user accounts available in Windows 8.

14. Which Windows 8 charm can you use to set up a new user account?

15. When does a user need to enter a password into the UAC box in order to continue?

>> THINKING CRITICALLY

1. Suppose you have purchased and installed apps from the Windows Store on your Windows 8 home computer using your Microsoft account. At work, you connect your Microsoft account to your network ID to sign in to your work computer. Will the apps installed on your home computer now be installed on your work computer? Select the best answer.

   a. No, because apps from the Windows Store are only installed on the device where they were originally purchased.

   b. Yes, because apps purchased with your Microsoft account are installed on up to five computers you sign in to using this account.

   c. No, because syncing apps to all computers that use your Microsoft account is disabled by default.

   d. Yes, because when you purchase an app from the Windows Store, you can designate that app be synced with all computers that use your Microsoft account.

   e. No, because apps can never be synced on work computers that belong to a Windows domain.

2. A user clicks the OneDrive app on the Windows 8 Start screen and Windows requests her Microsoft account and password. Which of the following statements are true?

   a. Another user has used the OneDrive app on this computer.

   b. This is the first time the user has opened the OneDrive app.

   c. The user doesn't have a Microsoft account.

   d. The user did not sign in to Windows using a Microsoft account.

3. What two Windows tools can you use to know how much RAM is installed on your system?

4. Mary wants her 32-bit installation of Windows 7 Professional to run faster. She has 4 GB of memory installed on the motherboard. She decides more memory will help. She installs an additional 2 GB of memory for a total of 6 GB, but does not see any performance improvement. What is the problem and what should you tell Mary?

   a. She should use Control Panel to install the memory in Windows 7. After it is installed, performance should improve. Tell Mary how to open the Control Panel.

   b. A 32-bit OS cannot use more than 4 GB of memory. Tell Mary she has wasted her money.

   c. A 32-bit OS cannot use more than 4 GB of memory. Tell Mary to upgrade her system to the 64-bit version of Windows 7 Professional.

   d. A 32-bit OS cannot use more than 4 GB of memory. Explain to Mary the problem and discuss with her the possible solutions.

5. Jack needs to email two documents to a friend but the files are so large his email server bounced them back as undeliverable. What is your advice?

   a. Tell Jack to open the documents and break each of them into two documents and then email the four documents separately.

   b. Tell Jack to put the two documents in a compressed folder and email the folder.

   c. Tell Jack to put each document in a different compressed folder and email each folder separately.

   d. Tell Jack to put the documents on a USB drive and snail mail the drive to his friend.

>> REAL PROBLEMS, REAL SOLUTIONS

REAL PROBLEM 1-1 Using Windows Help and Support

The best IT support technicians are the ones continually teaching themselves new skills. You can teach yourself to use and support Windows by using the web and the Windows Help and Support utility. To start the utility in Windows 8, type Help and Support on the Start screen. In Windows 7, click Start and click Help and Support. If you are connected to the Internet, clicking links can take you to the Microsoft website where you can find information and watch videos about Windows.

   Do the following to learn to research a topic so you can become an independent learner about Windows:

1. The Windows 8/7 Snipping Tool can help you take screen shots of the Windows desktop. These screen shots are useful when documenting computer problems and solutions. Use Windows Help and Support to find out how to use the Snipping Tool. Use it to take a screen shot of your Windows desktop. Save the screen shot into a file on a USB flash drive or on the hard drive. Print the file contents.

2. Windows 7 Home Premium, Professional, Enterprise, and Ultimate editions all support the Aero interface. If you are using one of these editions, find out how to turn the Aero interface off and on. Describe the difference in the appearance of Windows when using Aero and not using it.

3. Access the *support.microsoft.com* website for Windows 8/7 support. Save or print one article from the Knowledge Base that addresses a problem when installing Windows 8/7.

4. Search the web for the purpose of the Pagefile.sys file. What website did you use to find your answer? Why is the Microsoft.com website considered the best source for information about the Pagefile.sys file?

REAL PROBLEM 1-2 Documenting How to Use Windows 8

This real problem requires a microphone, and a webcam would also be useful. Make a screen recording with voice-over to teach end users how to use Windows 8. Do the following:

1. Screencast-O-Matic offers free software to make a screen recording with voice and video. Go to **screencast-o-matic.com** and launch the online video recording software. You might be required to download and install the software.

2. Select a Windows 8 feature to explain. For example, you can explain how to open and close an app, install or uninstall an app, create a new user account, empty the Recycle Bin, or use the charms bar or search feature. You or your instructor might have other ideas.

3. Use the Screencast-O-Matic software to make a screen recording to show how to use the Windows 8 feature you selected. The recording should be no longer than three minutes. Explain the steps as you go. The software records your screen movements, your voice (if a microphone is detected), and video (if a webcam is detected).

4. View the video. If you see a problem, record it again. When you're satisfied with your video, save it as an MP4 file.

REAL PROBLEM 1-3 Launching the Windows 8 Desktop at Startup

Some users prefer to go directly to the Windows 8 desktop rather than to the Start screen at Windows startup. To make this change, you'll need Windows 8.1 installed. Go to the Windows desktop, right-click the taskbar, and click Properties. In the Taskbar and Navigation properties box, click the Navigation tab. Then check When I sign in or close all apps on a screen, go to the desktop instead of Start. See Figure 1-58. Apply your changes. When you next sign in to Windows, you are taken directly to the desktop.

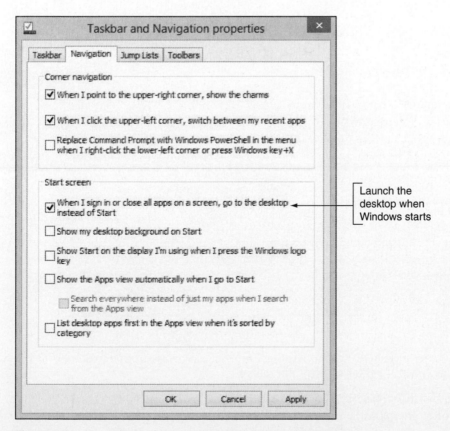

Figure 1-58   Control what happens when you navigate Windows 8

CHAPTER 2

Installing Windows

After completing this chapter, you will be able to:

- Plan a Windows installation

- Install Windows 8.1 and Windows 7

- Configure Windows settings after the installation

- Discuss special concerns when installing Windows in a large enterprise

Windows 8, 7, and Vista all share the same basic Windows architecture, and all have similar characteristics. Windows 8 includes a free upgrade to Windows 8.1 via the Windows Store. Windows 8.1 and Windows 7 are available for purchase directly from Microsoft, but you can no longer purchase Windows 8.0 or Vista. (However, Windows 8.0 and Vista can be purchased from other vendors.) Mainstream support of Windows Vista by Microsoft ended in 2012, and extended support is slated to end in 2017. Because many individual users and corporations still rely on Vista, you still need to know how to support it.

By the time this text is published, Windows 10 should be available. How to install and support Windows 10 is not covered in this text.

This chapter discusses how to plan a Windows installation and the steps to perform a Windows 8.1 or Windows 7 installation in various scenarios, including what to do after the OS is installed. You also learn about what to expect when installing Windows on computers in a large enterprise.

> ✎ **Notes** In the text, we use Windows 8 to refer to Windows 8.0 and Windows 8.1.

HOW TO PLAN A WINDOWS INSTALLATION

As an IT support technician, you can expect to be called on to install Windows in a variety of situations. You might need to install Windows on a new hard drive, after an existing Windows installation has become corrupted, or to upgrade from one OS to another. Many decisions need to be made before the installation, and most of these decisions apply to any Windows operating system.

CHOOSE THE EDITION, LICENSE, AND VERSION OF WINDOWS

When buying a Windows operating system, know that the price is affected by the Windows edition and type of license you purchase. You also need to decide between 32-bit and 64-bit architecture. In this part of the chapter, you learn about your options when purchasing Windows and how to make sure your computer qualifies for the version and edition you've selected.

EDITIONS OF WINDOWS

Windows 8 provides a choice of these editions designed to satisfy a variety of consumer needs:

- Windows 8.1 is the edition of choice for a laptop or desktop computer used in a home or small office. This edition supports homegroups, but it doesn't support joining a domain or BitLocker Encryption.
- Windows 8.1 Professional (Windows 8.1 Pro) includes additional features at a higher price, while Windows 8.1 Pro for Students is available for a lower price to students, faculty, and staff at eligible institutions. Windows Pro Pack can be installed on a Windows 8.1 machine to add the functionality of Windows 8.1 Pro to the more basic edition. Windows 8.1 Pro supports homegroups, joining a domain, BitLocker, Client Hyper-V, Remote Desktop, and Group Policy. (You'll learn about these tools later in the text.)
- Windows 8.1 Enterprise allows for volume licensing in a large, corporate environment.
- Windows RT, a lighter edition, is available for tablets, netbooks, and other mobile devices.

Windows 7 editions include Windows 7 Starter, Windows 7 Home Basic, Windows 7 Home Premium, Windows 7 Professional, Windows 7 Enterprise, and Windows 7 Ultimate. Each edition comes at a different price with different features and capabilities.

Editions of Windows Vista are Windows Vista Starter, Windows Vista Home Basic, Windows Vista Home Premium, Windows Vista Business, Windows Vista Enterprise, and Windows Vista Ultimate.

> 🖉 **Notes**   An antitrust ruling (a ruling to break up monopolies) in Europe requires that Microsoft must offer editions of Windows that do not include multimedia utilities. Windows 8.1 and 7, therefore, come in N, K, and KN editions that do not include Windows Media Player and other media technologies or, in Windows 8.1, some media apps such as Sound Recorder and Skype. If you have an N or KN edition of Windows, you can, however, legally download the utilities from the Microsoft website.

OEM, FULL RETAIL, OR UPGRADE RETAIL LICENSE

When buying Windows, you can purchase a retail license or an Original Equipment Manufacturer (OEM) license. The OEM license costs less but can be installed only on a new computer. The boxed retail package contains the 32-bit DVD and 64-bit DVD (see Figure 2-1). You can also purchase and download Windows 8.1 from the Microsoft online store at *microsoftstore.com*. The retail license costs less if you purchase a license to upgrade from Windows 7 to Windows 8.1 using Microsoft's Windows 8.1 Upgrade Assistant, as explained below. You are required to purchase the Windows 8.1 full license for a new computer or any computer that has an OS other than Windows 8 or Windows 7 installed.

Figure 2-1 A Windows 8.1 package comes with two DVDs and one product key

> **Notes** The Windows 8.1 setup DVD is the same whether you're upgrading from Windows 7 or performing a clean installation. However, you cannot use an OEM disk for an upgrade installation.

32-BIT OR 64-BIT ARCHITECTURE

Recall that an operating system can process 32 bits or 64 bits at a time. A 64-bit installation of Windows generally performs better than a 32-bit installation if you have enough RAM. Table 2-1 shows how much RAM popular editions of Windows can support. Another advantage of 64-bit installations of Windows is they can support 64-bit applications, which run faster than 32-bit applications. Even though you can install 32-bit applications in a 64-bit OS, for best performance, always choose 64-bit applications. Keep in mind that 64-bit installations of Windows require 64-bit device drivers.

> **Notes** All processors (CPUs) used in personal computers today are hybrid processors and can handle a 32-bit or 64-bit OS. However, the Intel Itanium and Xeon processors used in high-end workstations and servers are true 64-bit processors and require a 64-bit OS.

Operating System	32-Bit Architecture	64-Bit Architecture
Windows 8.1	4 GB	128 GB
Windows 8.1 Pro Windows 8.1 Enterprise	4 GB	512 GB
Windows 7 Home Premium	4 GB	16 GB
Windows 7 Professional Windows 7 Enterprise Windows 7 Ultimate	4 GB	192 GB

Table 2-1 Maximum memory supported by Windows 8.1 and 7 editions and versions

> **Notes** How much memory or RAM you can install in a computer depends not only on the OS installed, but also on how much memory the motherboard can hold. To know how much RAM a motherboard can support, see the motherboard documentation.

VERIFY YOUR SYSTEM QUALIFIES FOR WINDOWS

A+
220-902
1.1, 1.2

The minimum hardware requirements for Windows 8/7/Vista are listed in Table 2-2. (These minimum requirements are also the Microsoft recommended requirements.) In addition to the requirements listed, Microsoft added to Windows 8 requirements three technologies used by the processor (NX, PAE, and SSE2). All processors built in the last 10 years use these technologies, so the move was intended to not allow Windows 8 to be installed on a system that was older than 10 years. Know, however, that Microsoft occasionally changes the minimum and recommended requirements for an OS.

Hardware	For 32-Bit Windows	For 64-Bit Windows
Processor	1 GHz or faster; for Windows 8, support for NX, PAE, and SSE2	
Memory (RAM)	1 GB	2 GB
Free hard drive space	16 GB	20 GB
Video device and driver	DirectX 9 device with WDDM 1.0 or higher driver	

Table 2-2   Minimum and recommended hardware requirements for Windows 8/7/Vista

> ✏ **Notes** The three processor technologies are NX (Never Execute or No Execute), which prevents malware from hiding in the data storage area of another program; PAE (Physical Address Extension), which was originally intended to allow 32-bit processors to use more than 4 GB of RAM but is no longer used for that purpose because it gave device drivers a big headache; and SSE2 (Streaming SIMD Extensions 2), which allows a processor to execute a single instruction multiple times.

WINDOWS 8 UPGRADE ASSISTANT

The simplest way to find out if a system can be upgraded to Windows 8.1 is to download, install, and run the Windows 8.1 Upgrade Assistant (called the Upgrade Advisor in Windows 7). You can find the software and instructions on how to use it at *windows.microsoft.com/en-US/windows-8/upgrade-from-windows-7-tutorial*. Microsoft also offers the Windows Compatibility Center at *microsoft.com/windows/compatibility* (see Figure 2-2). You can search under both software and hardware to find out if they are compatible with Windows 8.1. The site sometimes offers links to patches or fixes for a program or device so that it will work with Windows 8.1. Before you upgrade to Windows 8.1, research each item that's not compatible, install an update if available, or uninstall the software or device. You can deal with most problems after Windows 8.1 is installed unless it's a critical device such as your network adapter. (You don't want to install Windows 8.1 only to find out later you can't access the network or Internet.)

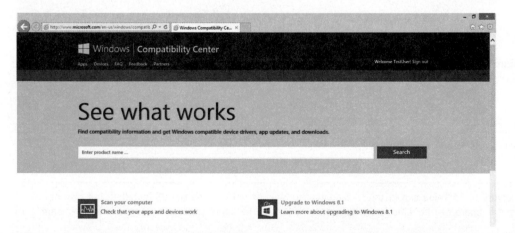

Figure 2-2   Use the Windows 8.1 Compatibility Center to find out if your hardware and software qualify for Windows 8.1

> ✏ **Notes** Websites change often. If you can't find the Upgrade Assistant at the link given, try this search string using *google.com*: **windows 8.1 upgrade assistant site: microsoft.com**.

To find out if a Vista system qualifies for an upgrade to Windows 7, download and run the Windows 7 Upgrade Advisor. To find it, type this search string at *google.com*: **windows 7 upgrade advisor site:microsoft.com** and click the top link in the search results.

MBR OR GPT PARTITIONING SYSTEM

You need to be aware of the partitioning method you will use on the hard drive. A hard drive is divided into one or more partitions. Windows can use one of two methods to partition a hard drive: The Master Boot Record (MBR) method is older, allows for four partitions, and is limited to 2-TB drives. The GUID Partition Table (GPT) method is newer, allows for any size hard drive, and, for Windows, can have up to 128 partitions on the drive. GPT is required for drives larger than 2 TB.

When an MBR or GPT partition is formatted with a file system and assigned a drive letter (such as drive C:), it is called a volume. A file system is the overall structure an OS uses to name, store, and organize files on a volume, and Windows is always installed on a volume that uses the NTFS file system. For most installations, you install Windows on the only hard drive in the computer and allocate all the space on the drive to one partition that Windows setup calls drive C:. Windows is installed in the C:\Windows folder.

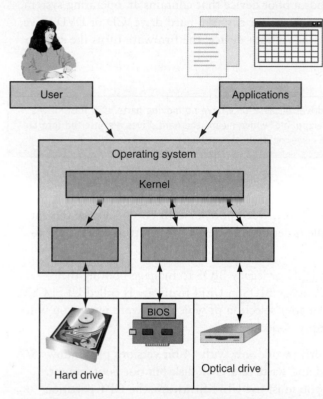

Figure 2-3 Windows relates to hardware by way of device drivers or system UEFI/BIOS

UEFI OR LEGACY BIOS FIRMWARE

To understand if your system qualifies for Windows 8/7, it helps to understand how Windows relates to hardware by using device drivers and system UEFI/BIOS, as shown in Figure 2-3. (In the figure, the kernel is that part of Windows responsible for relating to hardware.)

When a computer is first turned on, it uses some devices such as the keyboard, monitor, and hard drive before the OS starts up. The motherboard UEFI/BIOS is contained on a chip on the motherboard (see Figure 2-4) and manages these essential devices. This chip is called a firmware chip because it holds programs.

Figure 2-4 A chip on a motherboard contains UEFI or BIOS used to start the computer, hold motherboard settings, and run essential devices. The chip retains power from a nearby coin battery when the computer is turned off.

Older motherboards use firmware called BIOS (basic input/output system). A much-improved replacement for BIOS is UEFI (Unified Extensible Firmware Interface), which stores its setup information and some drivers on the motherboard and also on the hard drive. Most motherboards today support a combination of the two types of firmware, commonly called UEFI/BIOS. The motherboard UEFI/BIOS provides three main functions:

◢ The system UEFI/BIOS contains instructions for running essential hardware devices before an operating system is started. After the OS is started, it might continue to use system UEFI/BIOS or use device drivers to communicate with these devices.

◢ The startup UEFI/BIOS starts the computer and finds a boot device that contains an operating system. Boot devices that a system might support include an internal or external hard drive, CD or DVD drive, bootable USB flash drive, and the network. After it finds a boot device, the firmware turns the startup process over to the OS.

> **✎ Notes** Solid-state drives are faster than magnetic hard drives because they have no moving parts. USB flash drives are also solid-state devices. Some hard drives might be hot-swappable, which means the hard drives are inserted into an easily accessible hot-swap bay and can be exchanged without powering down the system.

◢ The setup UEFI/BIOS is used to change motherboard settings. You can use it to enable or disable a device on the motherboard (for example, the network port, video port, or USB ports), change the date and time that is later passed to the OS, and select the order of boot devices for startup UEFI/BIOS to search when looking for an operating system to load.

Most computers today give you the option of using UEFI or legacy BIOS to manage booting the computer and turning it over to the operating system. Legacy BIOS in UEFI firmware is called UEFI CSM (Compatibility Support Module) mode. You must make your selection of which firmware mode you will use *before* you install Windows. Here are points to help you decide:

◢ UEFI and the GPT partitioning system for the hard drive work only with 64-bit versions of Windows 8/7. However, a 32-bit version of Windows 8/7 can read and write to a GPT disk but not boot from it.

◢ If the computer has a hard drive larger than 2 TB, you must use UEFI firmware, the GPT partition system, and a 64-bit version of Windows.

◢ UEFI has a security system called Secure Boot, which helps to prevent malware from hijacking a system during or before the operating system load. UEFI and Windows work together to ensure that no unsecured device driver, application, or OS component is loaded. If you want to use Secure Boot, you must use UEFI, GPT, and a 64-bit edition of Windows.

◢ To install Windows on an MBR hard drive, you must run UEFI in CSM mode. To install Windows on a GPT drive, you must use UEFI and disable CSM mode.

APPLYING | CONCEPTS SELECT THE FIRMWARE MODE

**A+
220-902
1.2**

So how do you select your firmware mode before you start the Windows installation? Follow these steps:

1. To access UEFI/BIOS setup, press a key, such as **Del** or **F2**, early in the boot process before Windows starts to load. When the UEFI/BIOS setup screen appears, look for a screen to manage the boot. For example, the Boot screen for one motherboard's firmware is shown in Figure 2-5.

Source: American Megatrends, Inc.

Figure 2-5   The Boot screen for one UEFI/BIOS setup

2. To use legacy BIOS, which requires the MBR partitioning system:

    a. Click **CSM (Compatibility Support Module)** and make sure that CSM is enabled (see Figure 2-6).

Source: American Megatrends, Inc.

Figure 2-6   Enable or disable CSM mode

(continues)

b. On the Boot screen (Figure 2-5), click **Secure Boot**. In the Secure Boot menu, select **Other OS** for the OS Type (see Figure 2-7).

Source: American Megatrends, Inc.

Figure 2-7   Select Other OS to allow Windows to install on an MBR hard drive

To use UEFI firmware and the GPT partitioning system, use these same screens to disable **CSM** (see Figure 2-6) and set the OS Type to **Windows UEFI mode** (see Figure 2-7).

DEVICE DRIVERS

Device drivers are small programs stored on the hard drive that tell the computer how to communicate with a specific hardware device such as a printer, network card, or scanner. These drivers are installed on the hard drive when the OS is first installed, or when new hardware is added to the system. A device driver is written to work for a specific OS, such as Windows 8.1 or 7. In addition, a 32-bit OS requires 32-bit drivers, and a 64-bit OS requires 64-bit drivers.

Windows provides some device drivers, and the manufacturer of the hardware device provides others. When you purchase a printer, video card, digital camera, scanner, or other hardware device, a CD that contains the device drivers is usually bundled with the device along with a user manual (see Figure 2-8). You can also download the drivers for a device from the manufacturer's website.

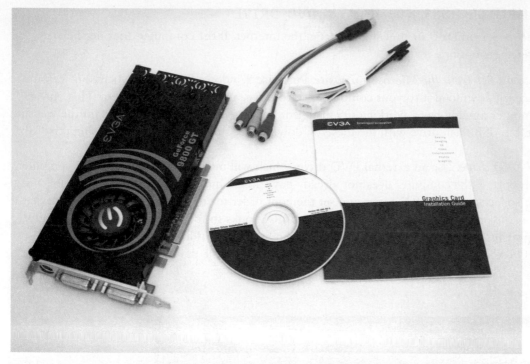

Figure 2-8 A device such as this video card comes packaged with its device drivers stored on a CD

Be sure you have the correct Windows device drivers for all your critical devices such as your network card or motherboard. To find the drivers, look on the CD that came bundled with the device or check the website of the device manufacturer. Remember that a 64-bit OS requires all 64-bit drivers.

If you are not sure if your devices will work with Windows 8/7, one solution is to set up a dual boot. A dual boot, also called a multiboot, allows you to install the new OS without disturbing the old one so you can boot to either OS. After the installation, you can test your software or hardware. If they work under the new OS, you can delete the old one. If they don't work, you can still boot to the old OS and use it. How to set up a dual boot is covered later in this chapter.

If you have applications written for Windows 7 or Vista that are not compatible with Windows 8, you can use compatibility mode to solve the problem. Compatibility mode is a group of settings that can be applied to older drivers or applications that might cause them to work in Windows 8. You learn more about compatibility mode later in this chapter.

Hands-On | Project 2-1 Prepare for an Upgrade

| A+ 220-902 1.1, 1.2 | On a computer with Windows 7 installed, access the Microsoft website *windows.microsoft.com/en-US/windows-8/upgrade-from-windows-7-tutorial* and locate, download, and run the Windows 8.1 Upgrade Assistant to find out if the computer is ready for a Windows 8.1 installation. Make a list of any hardware or software components found to be incompatible with Windows 8.1, and draw up a plan for getting the system ready for a Windows 8.1 upgrade. |

INSTALLATIONS WITH SPECIAL CONSIDERATIONS

| A+ 220-902 1.1, 1.2 | Depending on the circumstances and the available hardware, you might be faced with an installation on a computer that does not have a DVD drive, a computer that needs a factory recovery, or an installation in a virtual computer. All of these special considerations are discussed next. |

WHEN THE COMPUTER DOES NOT HAVE A DVD DRIVE

You can buy Windows 8.1 on DVD or download it from the Internet. If the computer does not have a DVD drive, consider these options:

◢ *Download Windows 8.1 from the Microsoft website.* Purchase Windows 8.1 on the Microsoft website (*microsoftstore.com*), download it to your computer's hard drive, and install it from there. This option assumes the computer already has a working OS installed. You can also follow directions on the website to create a bootable USB flash drive with the files you downloaded and install Windows using this USB flash drive.

◢ *Use an external DVD drive.* Use an external DVD drive, which will most likely connect to the computer by way of a USB port. If the computer does not already have an OS installed, you must boot from this USB port. To do so, access UEFI/BIOS setup and set the boot order for the USB as the first boot device. The boot order is the order of devices that startup UEFI/BIOS looks to for an OS. You can enter UEFI/BIOS setup by pressing a key at startup. Then locate the appropriate UEFI/BIOS setup screen. For example, the BIOS setup screen shown in Figure 2-9 shows a removable device as the first boot device. You can then boot from the external DVD drive and install Windows.

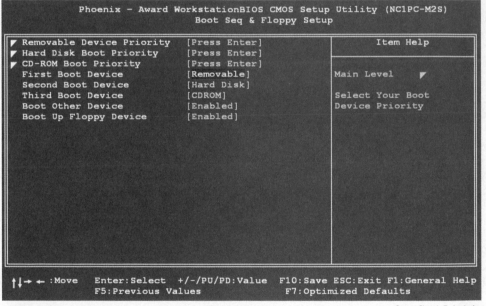

Source: Phoenix Technologies

Figure 2-9 Set the boot order in BIOS setup

◢ *Use a DVD drive on another computer on the network.* Share the DVD drive on another computer onto the network. Then go to the computer that is to receive the Windows installation and locate the DVD drive on the network. Double-click the setup.exe program to run the installation across the network. Alternately, you can copy the files on the DVD from the other computer to your hard drive. Again, this option assumes the computer already has a working OS installed. How to share folders and drives on a network is covered later in this text.

FACTORY RECOVERY PARTITION

If you have a laptop computer or a brand-name computer, such as a Dell, IBM, or Gateway, and you need to reinstall Windows, follow the recovery procedures given by the computer manufacturer. A hard drive is divided into one or more partitions, and the hard drive on a brand-name computer is likely to have a hidden recovery partition that contains a recovery utility and installation files.

To access the utilities on the hidden partition so that you can perform a repair installation, press a key during startup. The key to press is displayed on the screen early in the boot before the OS is loaded. If you don't see the message, search the website of the computer manufacturer to find the key combination. For one Dell laptop, you press Ctrl + F11 to start the recovery. One Gateway computer displays the message *Press F11 to start recovery.* When you press these keys, a menu displays, giving you the opportunity to reinstall Windows from setup files kept in the hidden partition.

Sometimes a manufacturer puts a utility in this hidden partition that can be used to create recovery discs (see Figure 2-10). However, the discs must have already been created if they are to be there to help you in the event the entire hard drive fails. You might also be able to purchase these CDs or DVDs on the computer manufacturer's website.

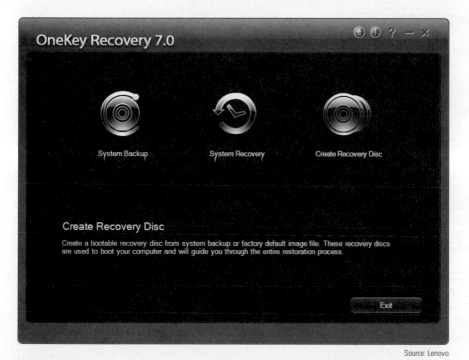

Figure 2-10 Use the recovery utility on this laptop to create DVDs that can be used to recover the system in the event the hard drive fails

> ✎ **Notes** In general, it's best not to upgrade an OS on a laptop unless you want to use some feature the new OS offers. For laptops, follow the general rule, "If it ain't broke, don't fix it." Many hardware components in a laptop are propri-etary, and the laptop manufacturer is the only source for these drivers. If you are considering upgrading a laptop to Windows 8.1, check the laptop manufacturer's website for advice and to download Windows 8.1 drivers, which are called third-party drivers because they are not included in UEFI/BIOS or Windows. It's very important you have available a Windows 8.1 driver for your network port without having to depend on the network or Internet to get one after Windows 8.1 is installed. Also know that many Windows 7 drivers work with Windows 8.1.

INSTALLATION IN A VIRTUAL COMPUTER

Another type of Windows installation is when you install Windows in a virtual computer. A virtual computer or virtual machine (VM) is software that simulates the hardware of a physical computer. Using this software, you can install and run multiple operating systems at the same time on a single computer, which is called the host machine. These multiple instances of operating systems can be used to train users, run legacy software, and support multiple operating systems. For example, help-desk technicians can run a virtual machine for each OS they support on a single computer and quickly and easily switch from one OS to another by clicking a window. Another reason to use a virtual machine is that you can capture screen shots of the boot process in a virtual machine, which is the way the screen shots during the boot were made for this text.

Software used to manage VMs installed on a workstation is called a hypervisor. Some popular hypervisors for Windows are Client Hyper-V and Virtual PC by Microsoft (*www.microsoft.com*), VirtualBox by Oracle (*www.virtualbox.org*), and VMware Player by VMware, Inc. (*www.vmware.com*). Client Hyper-V is embedded in Windows 8 Pro or Enterprise, but is not available for other Windows releases. Virtual PC is free for download in all other editions of Windows 7 or 8 except Windows 7 Starter. VirtualBox and VMware Player are freeware. Be aware that virtual machine programs require a lot of memory and might slow down your system. Figure 2-11 shows two virtual machines running under VirtualBox.

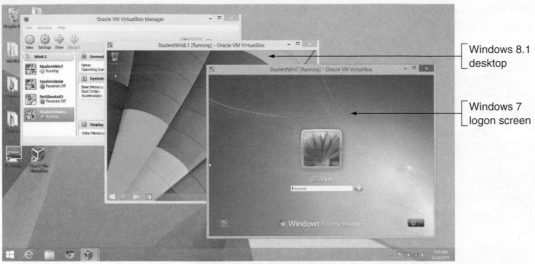

Windows 8.1 desktop

Windows 7 logon screen

Source: VirtualBox (Oracle)

Figure 2-11   Two virtual machines running under VirtualBox

> ✎ **Notes**   Windows XP Mode, which CompTIA calls virtual XP mode, is a Windows XP installation that runs under Virtual PC, and can be installed on a Windows 7 Professional, Enterprise, or Ultimate computer. When you install an OS in Virtual PC, normally you must have a valid product key for the installation, but an XP product key is not required for XP Mode. Windows XP Mode is not supported in Windows 8, although it is still possible to install Windows XP in a virtual machine in Windows 8.

If you are upgrading many computers to Windows 8.1 in a large enterprise, more automated methods are used for installations. Installation files are made available over the network or on bootable USB flash drives or DVDs. These automated methods are discussed later in this chapter.

Hands-On | Project 2-2   **Install and Run VirtualBox**

> ✎ **Notes**   If you don't want to use VirtualBox as your hypervisor, you can substitute another client hypervisor, such as VMware Player or Client Hyper-V. Note that Client Hyper-V does not play well on the same computer with other hypervisors, and can cause problems such as failed network connectivity. For that reason, don't enable Hyper-V on a Windows 8 computer that has another hypervisor installed.

On a Windows 8/7 computer, go to the Oracle VirtualBox website (*www.virtualbox.com*) and download and install VirtualBox on your computer. To set up a new virtual machine, open VirtualBox and click **New** at the top of the VirtualBox window. The *Create Virtual Machine* box shown in Figure 2-12 appears. Assign the VM a name and select **Windows 8.1 (32 bit)** from the Version drop-down menu. Click **Next**. Leave the default memory size selection of **1024 MB** and click **Next**. Be sure that **Create a virtual hard drive now** is checked and click **Create**.

Source: VirtualBox (Oracle)

Figure 2-12 Using VirtualBox to set up a new virtual machine

A wizard launches and steps you through the process of creating a new machine. During the process, you can select the virtual machine file type, the type of space allocation for the VM's hard drive, and the hard drive size. For the hard drive file type, make sure the default selection **VDI (VirtualBox Disk Image)** is checked (unless directed otherwise by your instructor), and click **Next**.

Be sure the default selection **Dynamically allocated** is checked so that space on the physical computer's hard drive is used only when it's needed by the VM. Click **Next**. Change the size of the virtual hard drive to **16 GB**, as shown at the bottom of Figure 2-13, and click **Create**. When you complete the wizard, the new virtual machine is listed in the VirtualBox window.

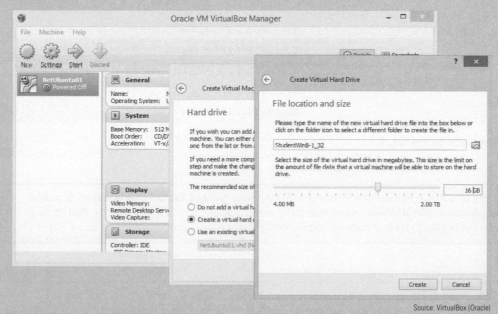

Source: VirtualBox (Oracle)

Figure 2-13 A 32-bit Windows installation requires at least 16 GB of hard drive space

In a project later in this chapter, you install Windows 8.1 in this VM.

CHOOSE THE TYPE OF INSTALLATION: IN-PLACE UPGRADE, CLEAN INSTALL, OR DUAL BOOT

A+
220-902
1.1, 1.2

If you are installing Windows on a new hard drive, you must perform a clean install. If an OS is already installed on the hard drive, you have three choices:

▲ *Clean install.* You can perform a clean install, overwriting the existing operating system and applications. In the Windows setup program, a clean install is called a custom installation. The main advantage of a clean install is that problems with the old OS are not carried forward and you get a fresh start. During the installation, you will have the option to reformat the hard drive, erasing everything on the drive. If you don't format the drive, the data will still be on the drive. The previous operating system settings and user profiles are collectively stored in the Windows.old folder that setup creates on the hard drive. After Windows is installed, you will need to install the applications. After you're sure the new installation is working as expected, you can delete the Windows.old folder to save space on the drive. Windows 8 automatically deletes most of the content of this folder 28 days after the installation.

▲ *In-place upgrade.* If the upgrade path allows it, you can perform an in-place upgrade installation. An in-place upgrade is a Windows installation that is launched from the Windows desktop and the installation carries forward user settings and installed applications from the old OS to the new one. A Windows OS is already *in place* before you begin the new installation. An in-place upgrade is faster than a clean install and is appropriate if the system is generally healthy and does not have problems. In order to perform an in-place upgrade, Microsoft requires that certain editions and versions of Windows be installed already. These qualifying OSs are called upgrade paths. Table 2-3 outlines the acceptable upgrade paths for Windows 8.1. There is no upgrade path from Windows Vista or XP to Windows 8.1. Even though you can purchase an upgrade license to install Windows 8.1 on these systems, you must perform a clean install.

From OS	To OS
Windows 7 Starter, Home Basic, Home Premium	Windows 8.1
Windows 7 Starter, Home Basic, Home Premium, Professional, Ultimate	Windows 8.1 Pro
Windows 7 Professional, Enterprise	Windows 8.1 Enterprise
Windows 8	Windows 8.1 or 8.1 Pro
Windows 8 Pro	Windows 8.1 Pro or 8.1 Enterprise
Windows 8.1	Windows 8.1 Pro
Windows 8.1 Pro	Windows 8.1 Enterprise

Table 2-3   In-place upgrade paths to Windows 8.1

> ✎ **Notes**   You can upgrade to a higher edition of Windows 8 or 8.1 by using the **Add features to Windows 8** or **Add features to Windows 8.1** option within Windows, which essentially means that you're purchasing the Pro Pack through Windows directly. The upgrade is easy to do and does not require going through the entire upgrade process.

> ⟨⟩ **OS Differences**   Because Windows 7 is quickly becoming outdated, most likely you won't be asked to upgrade a computer to Windows 7. However, if you need to see the upgrade paths to Windows 7, do a *google.com* web search on **windows 7 upgrade paths site:technet.microsoft.com**.

▲ *Multiboot.* You can install Windows in a second partition on the hard drive and create a dual-boot situation with the other OS, or even install three OSs, each in its own partition in a multiboot environment. Don't create a dual boot unless you need two operating systems, such as when you need to verify that applications and hardware work under Windows 8.1 before you delete the old OS. Windows 8/7/Vista all require that they be the only operating system installed on a partition. So to set up a dual boot, you'll need at least two partitions on the hard drive or a second hard drive.

In addition to the information given in Table 2-3, keep in mind these tips:

▲ A 64-bit version of Windows can only be upgraded to a 64-bit OS. A 32-bit OS can only be upgraded to a 32-bit OS.

▲ If you want to install a 64-bit version of Windows on a computer that already has a 32-bit OS installed, you must perform a clean install.

▲ You cannot upgrade from Windows XP or Vista to Windows 8, and you cannot upgrade from XP to Windows 7. You must perform a clean install.

UNDERSTAND THE CHOICES YOU'LL MAKE DURING THE INSTALLATION

While Windows is installing, you must choose which drive and partition to install Windows, the size of a new partition, and how Windows will connect to the network. Next you learn about what might affect your decisions regarding the size of the Windows partition and how Windows will connect to the network.

THE SIZE OF THE WINDOWS PARTITION

For a clean install or dual boot, you can decide to not use all the available space on the drive for the Windows partition. Here are reasons to not use all the available space:

▲ *You plan to install more than one OS on the hard drive, creating a dual-boot system.* For example, you might want to install Windows 7 on one partition and leave room for another partition where you intend to install Windows 8.1, so you can test software under both operating systems. (When setting up a dual boot, always install the older OS first.)

▲ *Some people prefer to use more than one partition or volume to organize data on their hard drives.* For example, you might want to install Windows and all your applications on one partition and your data on another. Having your data on a separate partition makes backing up easier. In another situation, you might want to set up a volume on the drive that is used exclusively to hold backups of data on another computer on the network. The size of the partition that will hold Windows 8/7 and its applications should be at least 16 GB for a 32-bit install and 20 GB for the 64-bit install, but a larger volume is nearly always preferred.

> ⚡ **Caution**   It's convenient to back up one volume to another volume on a different hard drive. However, don't back up one volume to another volume on the same hard drive, because when a hard drive fails, quite often all volumes on the drive are damaged and you will lose both your data and your backup.

Later in this text, you learn to use the Disk Management utility after Windows is installed to create partitions from unallocated space and to resize, delete, and split existing partitions.

NETWORK CONFIGURATION

Recall from the chapter, "Survey of Windows Features and Support Tools," that all editions of Windows 8/7/Vista can join a workgroup, Windows 8/7 can join a homegroup, and business editions of Windows 8/7 can join a homegroup or Windows domain. (Vista does not support homegroups.) To join a domain, you'll need the network ID and password assigned to you by the network administrator of the private network. To join a homegroup, you'll need the password to the homegroup, and to join a workgroup, you'll need the name of the workgroup. You can connect to a workgroup, homegroup, or domain during the installation, or you can wait and make the connection after the installation is complete.

You also need to know that the Windows installation process usually has no problems connecting to the network and the Internet without your help. However, you might need to know how the IP address is assigned. An IP address uniquely identifies a computer on the network. It might be assigned dynamically (IP address is assigned by a server each time the workstation connects to the network) or statically (IP address is permanently assigned to the workstation). If the network is using static IP addressing, you need the IP address for the workstation.

FINAL CHECKLIST BEFORE BEGINNING THE INSTALLATION

A+
220-902
1.1, 1.2

Before you begin the installation, complete the final checklist shown in Table 2-4 to verify that you are ready.

> **Notes** For new installations, look for the product key written on the cover of the Windows setup DVD, on a card inside the DVD case, or affixed to the back of the Windows documentation booklet, as shown in Figure 2-14. If you are reinstalling Windows on an existing system and you can't find the product key documentation, you can download and run freeware to tell you the key. For example, try Magical Jelly Bean freeware at *magicaljellybean.com/keyfinder*.

Questions to Answer	Further Information
Does the computer meet the minimum or recommended hardware requirement?	CPU: RAM: Hard drive partition size: Free space on the partition:
Do you have in hand the Windows device drivers for your hardware devices and application setup CDs?	List hardware and software that need to be upgraded:
Do you have the product key available?	Product key:
How will users be recognized on the network?	Homegroup password: Workgroup name: Domain name: Computer name: Network ID: Network password:
How will the computer be recognized on the network?	Static or dynamic IP addressing: IP address (for static addressing):
Will you do an upgrade or clean install?	Current operating system: Does the old OS qualify for an upgrade?
For a clean install, will you set up a dual boot?	List reasons for a dual boot: Size of the second partition: Free space on the second partition:
Have you backed up important data on your hard drive?	Location of backup:

Table 2-4 Checklist to complete before installing Windows

Product key for
OEM version

Product key for
retail version

Figure 2-14   The Windows product key found on the inside of a retail package or on the outside of an OEM package

Before getting into the step-by-step instructions of installing an OS, here are some general tips about installing Windows:

- Verify you have all application software CDs or DVDs available and all device drivers.
- Back up all important data on the drive. How to perform backups is covered in the chapter, "Maintaining Windows."
- For upgrade installations and clean installs in which you do not plan to reformat the hard drive, run antivirus/anti-malware software to make sure the drive is free from malware. If Windows will not start and you suspect malware might be a problem, plan to reformat the hard drive during the installation so you know the hard drive is clean of malware.
- If you want to begin the installation by booting from the Windows setup DVD or other media such as a USB device, use UEFI/BIOS setup to verify that the boot sequence is first the optical drive or USB device, and then the hard drive.
- In UEFI/BIOS setup, disable any virus protection setting that prevents the boot area of the hard drive from being altered.
- For a system that uses UEFI firmware, set the firmware to use UEFI mode (to use GPT and possibly Secure Boot) or UEFI CSM mode (to use MBR partitions on the hard drive). Know that Windows will install on a GPT drive only when UEFI CSM mode is disabled and will install on an MBR drive only when UEFI CSM mode is enabled.
- For a laptop computer, connect the AC adapter and use this power source for the complete OS installation, updates, and installation of hardware and applications. You don't want the battery to fail in the middle of the installation process.

✎ **Notes**   If your current installation of Windows is corrupted, you might be able to repair the installation rather than reinstalling Windows. The chapter, "Troubleshooting Windows Startup," covers what to do to fix a corrupted Windows installation.

INSTALLING WINDOWS 8.1 AND WINDOWS 7

 In this part of the chapter, you learn the steps to install Windows 8.1 and Windows 7 as an in-place upgrade, clean install, and dual boot, and how to handle the special situation of using a Windows upgrade product key to install Windows on a new hard drive. As you install and configure software, be sure to document what you did. This documentation will be helpful for future maintenance and troubleshooting. In a project at the end of this chapter, you will develop a documentation template.

Let's begin with how to perform an in-place upgrade of Windows 8.1.

STEPS TO PERFORM A WINDOWS 8.1 IN-PLACE UPGRADE

 The Windows 8.1 upgrade package comes with a 32-bit DVD and a 64-bit DVD. The product key is on a card found in a slip pocket inside the box. Here are the steps to perform an in-place upgrade from Windows 7 to Windows 8.1 when you're working with a Windows 8.1 setup DVD:

1. As with any upgrade installation, before you start the upgrade, do the following:

   a. Scan the system for malware using an updated version of anti-malware software. When you're done, be sure to close the anti-malware application so it's not running in the background.

   b. Uninstall any applications or device drivers you don't intend to use in the new installation.

   c. Make sure your backups of important data are up to date and then close any backup software running in the background.

2. Insert the Windows 8.1 setup DVD. If the setup program doesn't start automatically and the AutoPlay dialog box doesn't open, open Windows Explorer and double-click the **setup.exe** program in the root of the DVD. Respond to the UAC box. The setup program loads files, examines the system, and reports any problems it finds. If it finds the system meets minimum hardware requirements, setup asks permission to go online for updates (see Figure 2-15). Make your selection and click **Next**.

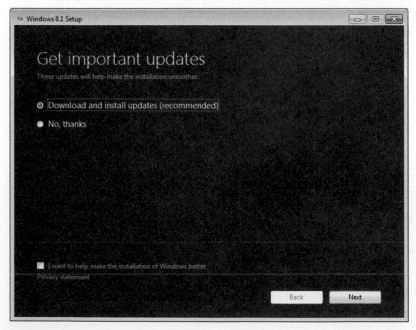

> **↻ OS Differences** The steps and screen shots for an in-place upgrade in this section are for Windows 8.1. The steps for Windows 8.0 work about the same way.

Figure 2-15   Decide how you will handle updates to the setup process

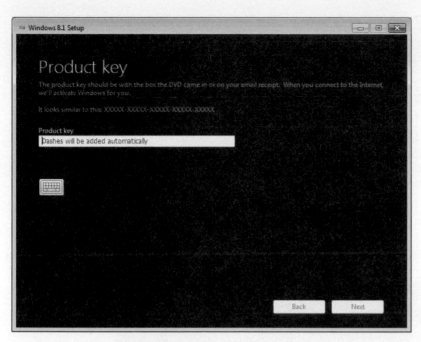

Figure 2-16 The product key is verified as a valid key before you can continue with the installation

3. The next window requests the product key (see Figure 2-16). Enter the product key and Windows verifies the key is a valid key. If the computer is connected to the Internet, setup will automatically activate Windows during the installation. Click **Next**.

4. The License terms window appears. Check **I accept the license terms** and click **Accept**.

5. On the Choose what to keep window (see Figure 2-17), decide what you want to do with Windows settings, personal files, and apps:

   ◢ The first two options perform upgrades to Windows 8.1.

   ◢ The Nothing option performs a clean install

of Windows 8.1. Everything on drive C: is deleted and the Windows.old folder is created, which holds files from the old installation. Other volumes on the hard drive are not disturbed.

For an upgrade installation, choose the first option and click **Next**. On the next screen, verify the choices listed and click **Install** to begin the installation.

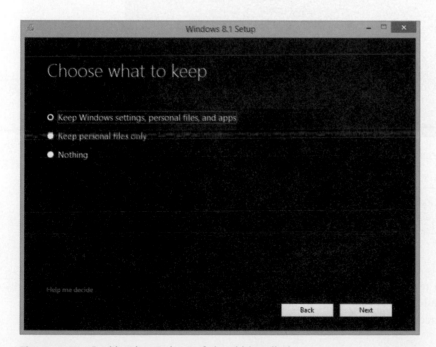

Figure 2-17 Decide what to keep of the old installation

> ✎ **Notes** When setup recognizes that it cannot perform an upgrade, but must perform a clean install, the first option on the window in Figure 2-17 is missing.

6. During the installation, setup might restart the system several times. Near the end of the installation, you are asked to select a screen color.

7. Next, the Settings screen appears (see Figure 2-18). To use the settings listed, click **Use express settings**. To customize the settings, click **Customize** and make your selections for these settings:

   ◢ Settings for sharing and connecting to devices

   ◢ Automatic Windows updates

   ◢ Privacy settings for apps and Internet Explorer

   ◢ Information sent to Microsoft

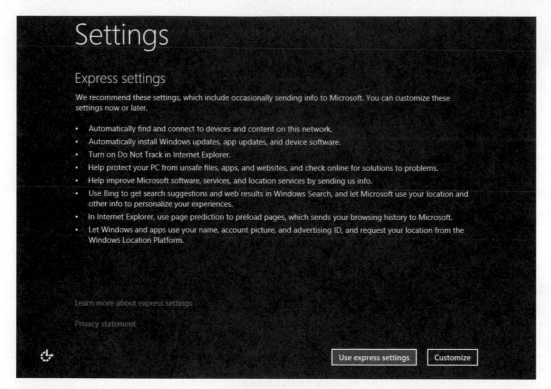

Figure 2-18 Decide which settings to accept

> ✎ **Notes** An in-place upgrade uses the existing selections for network connections and hard drive volumes; therefore, you're not asked to make these decisions during the upgrade process.

8. If the computer is connected to the Internet, on the next screen, you are given the opportunity to enter a Microsoft account that you can use to sign in to Windows (see Figure 2-19). Recall that a Microsoft account is associated with an email address registered at *live.com*. You also have the option to continue using a local account or domain account, although setup makes the option a little difficult to find.

Figure 2-19 Decide which account you will use to sign in to Windows 8.1

You have three options for setting up Windows 8.1 sign in:

◢ To use an existing Microsoft account, enter the email address and password and click **Next**.

◢ If you want to create a new Microsoft account, click **Create a new account**. On the next screen that appears (see Figure 2-20), enter the information for the new account and click **Next**. Notice on the screen you can get a new Microsoft email address (outlook.com, hotmail.com, or live.com address) or you can use an existing email address (one that is not managed by Microsoft).

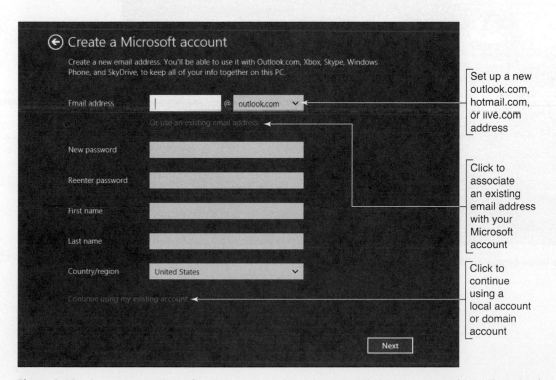

Figure 2-20 Create a new Microsoft account and use it to sign in to Windows 8.1 or continue using a local or domain account

◢ If you want to continue using a local account, on the screen shown in Figure 2-19, click **Create a new account**. On the next screen (see Figure 2-20), click **Continue using my existing account**. (You can switch to a Microsoft account later, after Windows 8.1 is installed.)

9. If you're signing in with a Microsoft account, follow directions on screen to set up how you want to secure your Microsoft account on this computer and set up your OneDrive.

10. Settings are applied and the Windows Start screen appears. You can now use the new installation of Windows 8.1.

> ✎ **Notes** If you have problems installing Windows, search the Microsoft website (*support.microsoft.com*) for solutions. Windows setup creates several log files during the installation that can help you solve a problem. Locations of Windows 8 setup log files are listed at this link: *technet.microsoft.com/en-us/library/hh824819.aspx*.
> For Windows 7, the list can be found in the Microsoft Knowledge Base Article 927521 at this link: *support.microsoft.com/kb/927521*.

> ✎ **Notes** When you first start using Windows 8.1 after an installation, it provides tips on screen to help you learn to use the OS (see Figure 2-21). The only way to get rid of a tip on screen is to follow its directions.

Figure 2-21 Tip boxes appear on Windows 8.1 screens to help you learn to use the OS

WINDOWS 8.1 UPGRADE FROM MICROSOFT WEBSITE

A+
220-902
1.2, 1.6

You just saw how to perform an upgrade using the Windows setup DVD. You can also download from the Microsoft website the files you need to perform the upgrade. To do that, Microsoft requires you first run the Upgrade Assistant. Here's how to get started:

1. After you have your Windows computer ready to upgrade, go to **windows.microsoft.com/en-gb/ windows-8/upgrade-assistant-download-online-faq**. Download and run the Windows 8.1 Upgrade Assistant. Make sure you have Windows 8.1 device drivers already downloaded for critical devices such as your network adapter.

2. If you're ready to proceed with the upgrade, click **Next** to continue.

3. The *Choose what to keep* window appears (refer back to Figure 2-17). Choose **Keep Windows settings, personal files, and apps,** and then click **Next**.

4. On the next screen, Microsoft recommends the right edition of Windows (see Figure 2-22). To buy the edition, click **Order**. On the next screen, click **Checkout**.

Source: Upgrade Assistant

Figure 2-22   Microsoft offers editions of Windows 8.1 for purchase

5. Follow directions on screen to enter your name, phone number, email address, and billing address, and pay for and start the download.

6. After the download completes, the Install Windows 8 screen appears. You can click *Install now* to continue with the installation. If you click *Install by creating media*, you are given the opportunity to create a bootable USB flash drive or DVD that contains the Windows setup files. Later, you can use the USB flash drive or DVD to perform the upgrade or a clean install of Windows 8.1. You're also given the opportunity to save the setup files to an ISO file. An ISO file, also called an ISO image or disc image, is an International Organization for Standardization image of an optical disc and includes the file system used. An ISO file has an .iso file extension. As you'll see later in the chapter, the ISO file is a handy tool when you want to install Windows in a virtual machine.

> ✎ **Notes** Best practice is to save the Windows setup files to a storage device or ISO image. You never know when you'll need the files to repair a corrupted Windows installation.

> ✎ **Notes** If you have an optical drive that can write to DVDs and you want to burn a DVD from an ISO file, insert a blank DVD in your optical drive and double-click the ISO file. Follow directions on screen and Windows does the rest.

WINDOWS 7 IN-PLACE UPGRADE

A+
220-902
1.2, 1.6,
4.1

When would you ever be called on to upgrade a Vista system to Windows 7? Suppose a Vista computer has several applications and device drivers installed that will not work in Windows 8.1, but will work in Windows 7. An in-place upgrade to Windows 7 will improve performance and security without having to deal with the hassle and expense of incompatible apps and drivers in Windows 8.1.

An in-place upgrade to Windows 7 is similar to that of Windows 8.1, with these exceptions:

◢ *Check for compatibility*. After inserting the Windows 7 DVD in the DVD drive, you then launch Windows 7 **setup.exe** just as you learned to do for Windows 8.1 setup. Respond to the Vista UAC box. If you have not yet performed the Windows 7 Upgrade Advisor process, do so by clicking **Check compatibility online** in the opening menu shown in Figure 2-23. To proceed with the installation, click **Install now**.

Figure 2-23 Opening menu when you launch Windows 7 setup from within Windows

> ↻ **OS Differences** A Vista installation works the same as a Windows 7 installation.

▲ *Product key.* Windows 8 setup asks for and requires you enter a product key early in the installation, but Windows 7 asks for the product key near the end of the installation (see Figure 2-24). You're not required to enter the product key in this window and you can uncheck **Automatically activate Windows when I'm online.** You can enter the product key and activate Windows after the installation is finished. You have 30 days before you must activate Windows 7.

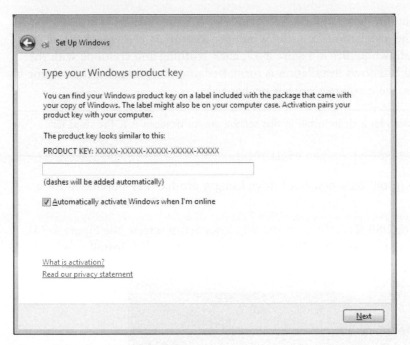

Figure 2-24 Enter the product key

▲ *Network location.* Windows 7 setup requires you select a network location (see Figure 2-25). Click the option that is appropriate to your network connection. You learned about these network locations in the chapter, "Survey of Windows Features and Support Tools." If you choose Home network, you are given the opportunity to create a homegroup or enter the homegroup password to join an existing homegroup. You can change these settings later using the Network and Sharing Center.

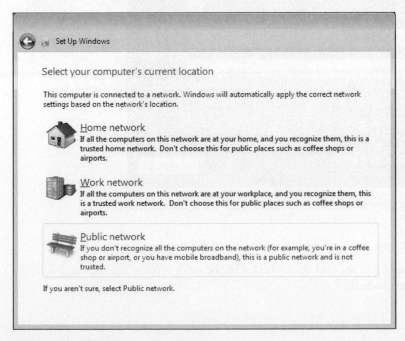

Figure 2-25 Select network settings

STEPS TO PERFORM A WINDOWS 8.1 CLEAN INSTALL

A+
220-902
1.2, 1.6

Recall that a clean install is the best option to use if the current installation is sluggish or giving problems, the currently installed OS does not allow for an in-place upgrade, or you're installing Windows 8.1 on a new desktop computer you're building.

If you have a Windows 7/Vista installation that qualifies for a Windows 8.1 upgrade and you need to do a clean install, begin by starting the installation from the Windows desktop as you would for an upgrade. When you get to the window shown earlier in Figure 2-17, click **Nothing** and continue with the installation. The volume holding the old Windows installation is formatted and everything on the volume is lost. If the hard drive has other volumes, these volumes are left unchanged.

> ○ **OS Differences** The steps and screen shots for a clean install in this section are for Windows 8.1. The steps for Windows 8.0 work about the same way.

Here are the steps to perform a clean install on a new hard drive using a product key purchased for a new installation of Windows 8.1:

1. Boot from the Windows setup DVD or USB flash drive. In the Windows Setup screen (see Figure 2-26), select the language and regional preferences and click **Next**. On the next screen, click **Install now**.

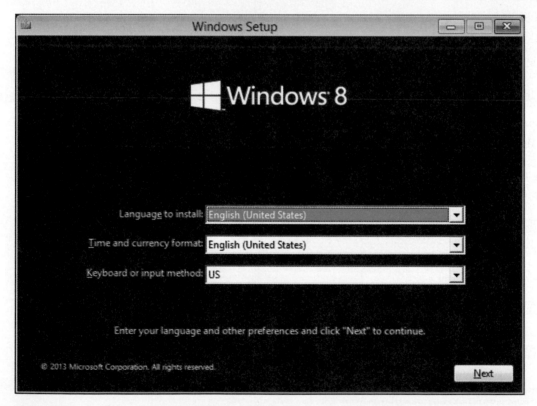

Figure 2-26   Decide on language and keyboard preferences

2. Enter your product key on the next screen. Setup verifies the key is a valid product key. Click **Next**.

3. Accept the license agreement on the next screen, and click **Next**. On the next screen (see Figure 2-27), click **Custom: Install Windows only (advanced)**.

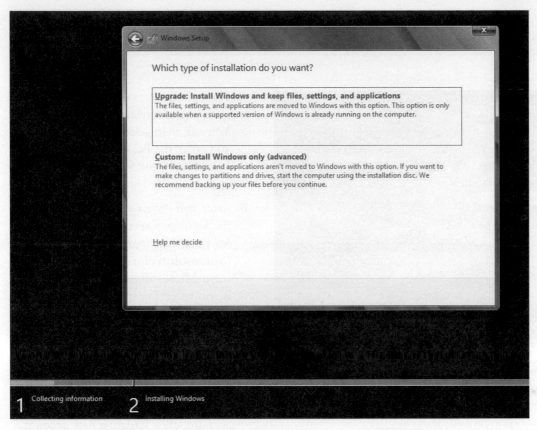

Figure 2-27 Decide between an upgrade and a clean install

4. The *Where do you want to install Windows?* screen appears. Select the drive and volume where you want to install Windows. Figure 2-28 shows the screen that appears for a new hard drive that has not been partitioned. By default, setup will use the entire unallocated space for the Windows volume. If you want to use only a portion of the space, click **New** and enter the size of the volume. (Setup will also create a small reserved partition that it later uses for system files and the startup process.) Click **Next** to continue.

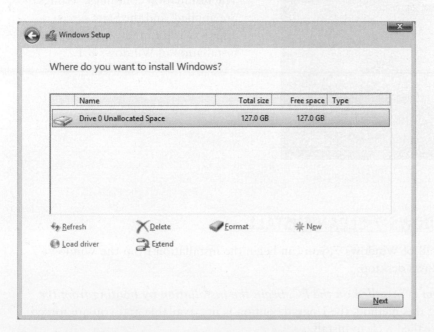

Figure 2-28 This hard drive has not yet been partitioned

> ✎ **Notes** If you don't see the *New* link on the *Where do you want to install Windows?* screen, click **Drive options (advanced)** to see this and other links you can use to manage the space on the hard drive.

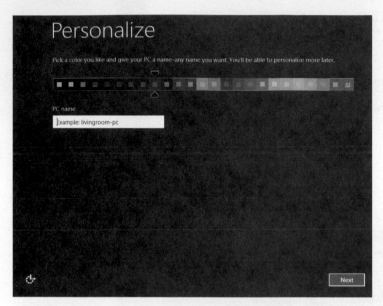

Figure 2-29 Decide on screen color, and enter a computer name

5. The installation begins, and the system might restart several times. You can then select a screen color and enter the PC name (see Figure 2-29). Next, the Settings screen appears (refer back to Figure 2-18).

6. After you have made your choices on the Settings screen, the *Sign in to your Microsoft account* screen appears (Microsoft *really* encourages you to use a Microsoft account). The screen is shown earlier in Figure 2-19. Just as with an in-place upgrade, you can sign in using an existing Microsoft account or create a new Microsoft account. In addition, you can create a new local account.

   If you want to create a new local account, click **Create a new account**. On the next screen, click **Sign in without a Microsoft account**. The screen shown in Figure 2-30 appears. Enter the local account name, password, and password hint, and then click **Finish**.

7. The installation continues, settings are applied, and the Start screen appears. You can now use the new installation of Windows 8.1.

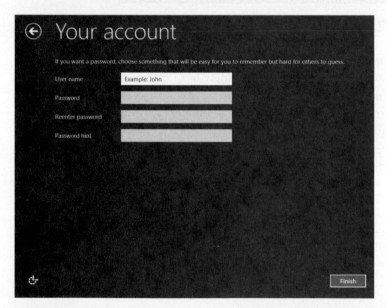

Figure 2-30 Set up a local account

STEPS TO PERFORM A WINDOWS 7 CLEAN INSTALL

> **A+**
> **220-902**
> **1.2, 1.6**

To perform a clean install of Windows 7, you can begin the installation from the Windows 7 DVD or from the Windows desktop:

▲ *If no operating system is installed on the PC, begin the installation by booting from the Windows 7 DVD.* Using this method, the Upgrade option is not available and you are forced to do a Custom installation, also called a clean install.

⊿ *If an operating system is already installed on the PC, you can begin the installation from the Windows desktop or by booting from the Windows 7 DVD.* Either way, you can perform a Custom installation. If you are using an upgrade license of Windows 7, setup will verify that a Windows OS is present, which qualifies you to use the upgrade license. This is the method to use when upgrading from Windows XP to Windows 7; you are required to perform a clean install even though setup verifies that Windows XP is present.

⊿ *If you are installing a 64-bit OS when a 32-bit OS is already installed or vice versa, you must begin the installation by booting from the DVD.* Setup still allows you to use the less-expensive upgrade license even though you are performing a clean install because it is able to verify a Windows installation is present.

Follow these steps to begin the installation by booting from the Windows 7 DVD:

1. Insert the Windows 7 DVD in the DVD drive and start the system, booting directly from the DVD. If you have trouble booting from the disk, go into UEFI/BIOS setup and verify that your first boot device is the optical drive. On the first screen (see Figure 2-31), select your language and regional preferences and click **Next**.

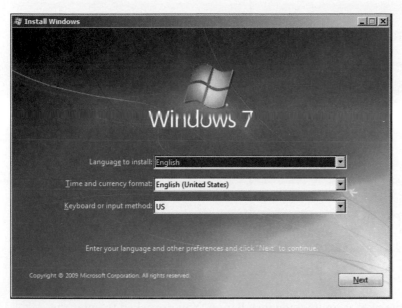

Figure 2-31   Select language, time, and keyboard options

2. The opening menu shown in Figure 2-32 appears. Click **Install now**.

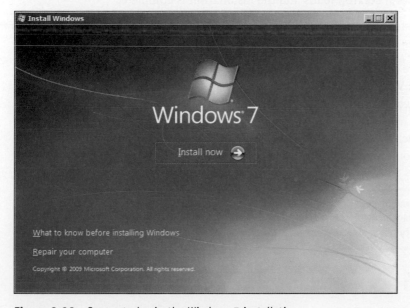

Figure 2-32   Screen to begin the Windows 7 installation

3. On the next screen, accept the license agreement. On the next screen, select the type of installation you want. Choose **Custom (advanced)**.

4. On the next screen, select an existing partition on the hard drive to hold the installation or select unallocated space for setup to use to create a partition.

5. The installation is now free to move forward. At the end of this process, the window in Figure 2-33 appears asking for a local account username and computer name. The next screen asks for a password for the local account.

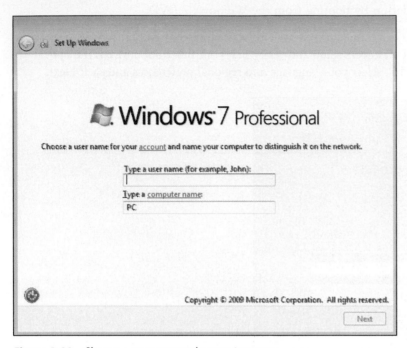

Figure 2-33   Choose a username and computer name

6. The installation now continues the same way as an upgrade installation. You are asked to enter the product key, Windows update settings, time and date settings, and network settings. Windows Update downloads and installs updates and you are asked to restart the system. After the restart, the logon screen appears. After you log in, the Windows 7 desktop loads and the installation is complete.

STEPS TO SET UP A WINDOWS MULTIBOOT

| A+ |
| 220-902 |
| 1.2, 1.6 |

You can install two or more operating systems on the same computer in a multiboot situation, for example, Windows 8.1, Windows 7, and Ubuntu Desktop. Each OS must have its own hard drive partition and each partition must have enough free space to hold the OS. Recall that Windows 8/7 needs *at least* 16 GB (32-bit) or 20 GB (64-bit) free space. Also know you cannot boot more than one OS at a time. To create a multiboot environment, always install Windows operating systems in order from older to newer.

> **Notes** If an OS is already installed, you might need to shrink a partition to make room for a second partition to hold the next OS. For Windows, use Disk Management to shrink a partition, create a new partition, or format a partition. Windows requires the NTFS file system. How to use Disk Management is covered in the chapter, "Maintaining Windows."

Here are the steps to set up a dual-boot system with two operating systems (using Windows 7 and 8.1 as examples):

1. Install Windows 7. If you plan to install Windows 8.1 on the same hard drive as Windows 7, leave some unallocated space for the Windows 8.1 partition. To do that, refer back to Figure 2-28. (This Windows setup screen works the same in Windows 7 as in Windows 8.1.) On this screen, click **New**. You can then specify how much of the total unallocated space you want to use for the Windows 7 installation.

2. To install Windows 8.1, first make sure you have (a) a second partition with enough free space to hold the Windows 8.1 installation, (b) enough unallocated space on the drive to create a new partition while installing Windows 8.1, or (c) a second hard drive to hold the Windows 8.1 installation.

3. Start the Windows 8.1 installation by booting from the Windows 8.1 setup DVD or USB flash drive. The Windows Setup screen shown earlier in Figure 2-26 appears. Follow steps given earlier in this chapter to perform a clean install.

4. When you're asked where to install Windows, select the partition or unallocated space to hold the installation. For example, select **Unallocated Space** to hold the Windows 8.1 installation, as shown in Figure 2-34. Don't select the partition where the older operating system is already installed; doing so causes setup to install Windows 8.1 in place of the older OS. Continue on to complete the clean install.

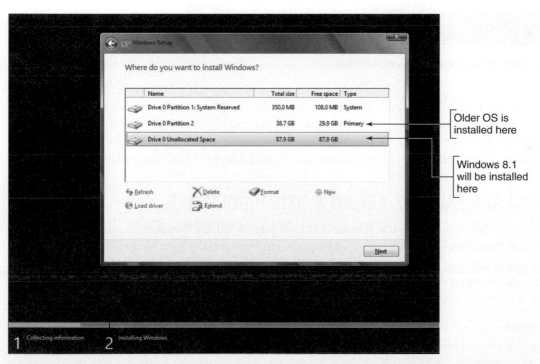

Figure 2-34   Select unallocated space or a partition other than the one used by the first OS installation

After the installation, when you boot with a dual boot, the boot loader menu automatically appears and asks you to select an operating system, as shown in Figure 2-35.

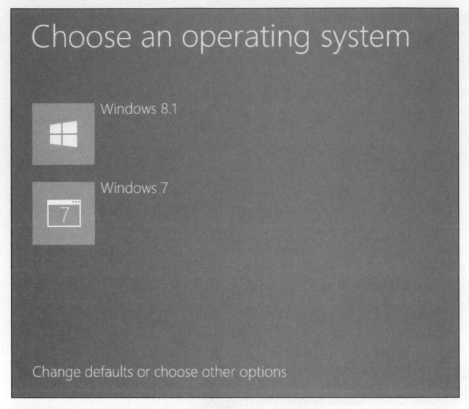

Figure 2-35   Boot loader menu in a dual-boot environment

When using a dual boot, you can execute an application while one OS is loaded even if the application is installed under the other OS if each OS is using the same architecture (32-bit or 64-bit). If the application is not listed on the Windows 8.1 Start screen or the Windows 7 Start menu, locate the program file in File Explorer (Windows 8.1) or Windows Explorer (Windows 7/Vista). Double-click the application to run it.

USING AN UPGRADE PRODUCT KEY ON A NEW HARD DRIVE

**A+
220-902
1.2, 1.6**

Suppose an upgrade license for Windows 8.1, Windows 8.0, or Windows 7 has been used to install Windows on a computer and later the hard drive fails. You replace the hard drive with a new one and now you need to reinstall Windows. You'll find lots of elegant and not so elegant shortcut solutions on the web, but here's the official Microsoft answer, using the example where a Windows 7 system was upgraded to Windows 8.0 and then updated to Windows 8.1:

1. Reinstall Windows 7. You don't need to enter the product key during the installation or activate Windows 7.

2. Reinstall Windows 8.0 using the upgrade product key and make sure Windows 8 is activated after the installation.

3. Download and install the free Windows 8.1 upgrade from the Windows Store.

In a situation where a Windows Vista system was upgraded to Windows 7, you can do the following so that you don't have to install Vista:

1. Install Windows 7 using your upgrade media. Don't enter the product key during the installation.

2. Reinstall Windows 7 as an upgrade. Windows setup should accept the upgrade product key during the installation and Windows should automatically activate.

APPLYING | CONCEPTS CONVERT AN MBR DRIVE TO GPT

Suppose you want to use a 64-bit version of Windows and UEFI firmware mode, thus requiring you to use the GPT partitioning system. However, your hard drive has already been partitioned with the MBR system. The error won't show up until you get to the step in the installation where you select the partition or unallocated space on the hard drive to hold the Windows installation (see Figure 2-36).

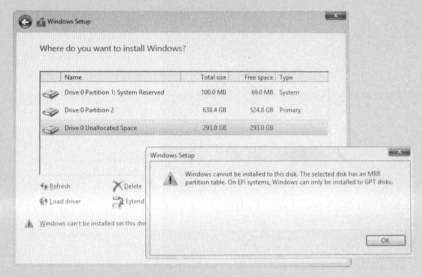

Figure 2-36 Error appears when Windows in UEFI mode requires the GPT partitioning system

Follow these steps to use the diskpart command to wipe the partition system off the hard drive. All data on the drive will be destroyed and then you can convert the drive to GPT:

1. Restart the computer from the Windows setup DVD and select your language and regional preferences. Click **Next**. On the next screen, select **Repair your computer** (see Figure 2-37).

Figure 2-37 Use the Windows setup DVD to repair your computer and launch a command prompt

(continues)

2. On the next screen, click **Troubleshoot**. On the Troubleshoot screen, click **Advanced options**. On the Advanced options screen, click **Command Prompt**. A command prompt window appears. Type **diskpart** and press **Enter**. The DISKPART> prompt appears, as shown in Figure 2-38.

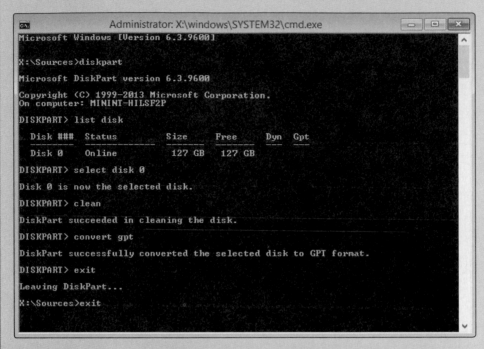

```
Administrator: X:\windows\SYSTEM32\cmd.exe

Microsoft Windows [Version 6.3.9600]

X:\Sources>diskpart

Microsoft DiskPart version 6.3.9600

Copyright (C) 1999-2013 Microsoft Corporation.
On computer: MININT-HILSF2P

DISKPART> list disk

  Disk ###  Status         Size     Free     Dyn  Gpt
  --------  -------------  -------  -------   ---  ---
  Disk 0    Online         127 GB   127 GB

DISKPART> select disk 0

Disk 0 is now the selected disk.

DISKPART> clean

DiskPart succeeded in cleaning the disk.

DISKPART> convert gpt

DiskPart successfully converted the selected disk to GPT format.

DISKPART> exit

Leaving DiskPart...

X:\Sources>exit
```

Figure 2-38   The command prompt window with diskpart running

3. At the DISKPART> prompt, use these commands to select the hard drive, clean it, and convert it to a GPT drive:

Command	Description
`list disk`	List the hard drives installed. If you have more than one hard drive, use the size of the drive to determine which one you want to clean. Most likely, you will have one hard drive identified as Disk 0.
`select disk 0`	Make Disk 0 the selected hard drive.
`clean`	Clean the partition table and all partitions from the drive.
`convert gpt`	Convert the partitioning system to GPT.
`exit`	Exit the diskpart utility.

4. Enter one more **exit** command to close the command prompt window. On the setup screen that appears, click **Turn off your PC**.

5. You can now restart the system and install Windows in UEFI mode, which uses the GPT partitioning system.

Hands-On | Project 2-3   Use the Internet for Problem Solving

Access the **support.microsoft.com** website for Windows 8.1 or Windows 7 support. Print one article from the Knowledge Base that addresses a problem when installing Windows 8.1 or Windows 7. In your own words, write a paragraph describing the problem and a paragraph explaining the solution. If you don't understand the problem or the solution from this article, do a search online for additional information so that you can give a well-rounded description of both the problem and the solution.

Hands-On | Project 2-4 Install Windows

Follow the instructions in the chapter to install Windows 8.1 or Windows 7 as either an upgrade or clean install. Write down each decision you had to make as you performed the installation. If you get any error messages during the installation, write them down and list the steps you took to recover from the error. How long did the installation take? If you have a hypervisor (virtual machine software) installed on your computer, you can do this project in a VM.

Hands-On | Project 2-5 Install Windows 8.1 in a VM

Earlier in the chapter, in Hands-On Project 2-2, you installed VirtualBox on your computer and created a VM. Use this VM to install a 32-bit version of Windows 8.1. You can use this VM installation of Windows 8.1 in projects later in the text.

To start this virtual machine and install an OS in it, first make sure you have the correct ISO file available to the host computer. Windows is best installed in a VM by using an ISO image.

Click on the VM you created earlier, then click **Start**. VirtualBox asks for the location of the startup disk (see Figure 2-39). Select the correct location then click **Start**. The VM boots up, finds the ISO file, and starts the OS installation, as shown in Figure 2-40.

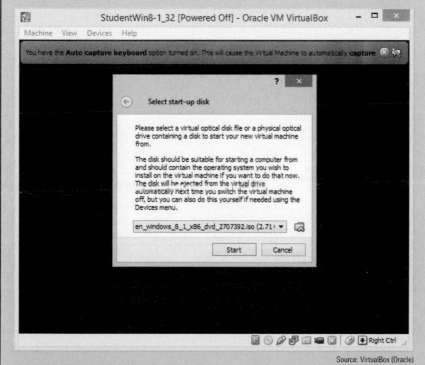

Source: VirtualBox (Oracle)

Figure 2-39 Locate the correct ISO file

(continues)

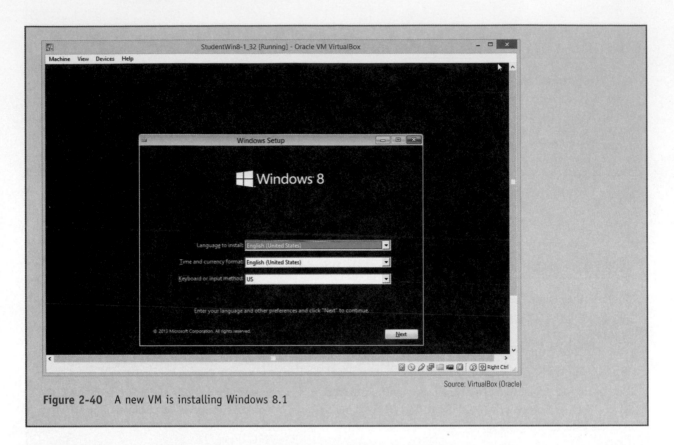

Figure 2-40   A new VM is installing Windows 8.1

WHAT TO DO AFTER A WINDOWS INSTALLATION

A+
220-902
1.1, 1.2,
1.4, 1.5,
4.1

After you have installed Windows, you need to do the following:

◢ Verify you have network access.
◢ Activate Windows.
◢ Install updates and service packs for Windows.
◢ Verify automatic updates are set as you want them.
◢ Install hardware.
◢ Install applications, including anti-malware software.
◢ Set up user accounts and transfer or restore from backup user data and preferences to the new system.
◢ Turn Windows features on or off.

> **⚡ Caution**   To protect your computer from malware, don't surf the web for drivers or applications until you have installed Windows updates and service packs and also installed and configured anti-malware software.

In addition, if you are installing Windows on a laptop, you will want to use Control Panel to configure power-management settings. If you are installing an OEM (Original Equipment Manufacturer) version of Windows 7, look for a sticker on the outside of the DVD case. This sticker contains the product key and is called the Certificate of Authenticity. Put the sticker on the bottom of a laptop or the side or rear of a desktop computer (see Figure 2-41). Windows 8 doesn't provide the sticker.

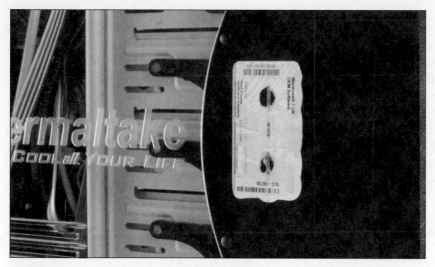

Figure 2-41 Paste the Windows 7 Certificate of Authenticity sticker on a new desktop

Now let's look at the details of the items in the preceding list.

VERIFY YOU HAVE NETWORK ACCESS

A+
220-902
1.2, 1.5

To make a wired connection to a network when using Windows, simply plug in the network cable and Windows does the rest. To create a wireless connection, follow the steps you learned in the chapter, "Survey of Windows Features and Support Tools."

To verify you have access to the local network and to the Internet, do the following:

1. Open File Explorer or Windows Explorer and verify you can see other computers on the network (see Figure 2-42). Try to drill down to see shared resources on these computers.

Figure 2-42 Use File Explorer to access resources on your network

2. To verify you have Internet access, open Internet Explorer and try to navigate to a couple of websites.

If a problem arises, consider that the problem might be that you need to install the drivers for the motherboard, including the drivers for the onboard network port. Also, the IP address, wireless network, or network security settings might be wrong. How to configure network settings and troubleshoot network connections are covered later in the chapter, "Connecting To and Setting Up a Network."

ACTIVATE WINDOWS

In order to make sure a valid Windows license has been purchased for each installation of Windows, Microsoft requires product activation. Windows 8.1 setup requires you enter a product key during the installation and, if the computer is connected to the Internet, Windows will automatically activate on the next restart after the installation completes. Recall from earlier in the chapter, you have more control over when to activate Windows 7. For Windows 7, you're not required to enter the product key during installation, and you can activate Windows 7 any time within the 30-day grace period.

To view the activation status, go to the System window. Figure 2-43 shows the window for one system that is not activated. To activate, make sure you're connected to the Internet and click **Activate Windows**. On the next screen, if necessary, you can enter a new product key and then activate Windows.

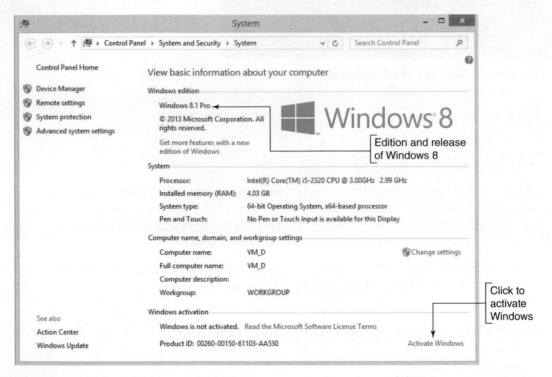

Figure 2-43 System window

 Notes If you change the product key after Windows is activated, you must activate Windows again because the activation is tied to the product key and the system hardware. If you replace the motherboard or replace the hard drive and memory at the same time, you must also reactivate Windows.

If you use the same product key to install Windows on a different computer, a dialog box appears telling you of the suspected violation of the license agreement. You can call a Microsoft operator and explain what caused the discrepancy. If your explanation is reasonable (for example, you uninstalled Windows from one computer and installed it on another), the operator can issue you a valid certificate. You can then type the certificate value into a dialog box to complete the boot process.

INSTALL WINDOWS UPDATES AND SERVICE PACKS

A+
220-902
1.1, 1.2,
1.5

The Microsoft website offers patches, fixes, and updates for known problems and has an extensive knowledge base documenting problems and their solutions. It's important to keep these updates current on your system to fix known problems and plug up security holes that might allow malware in. Be sure to install updates before you attempt to install software or hardware.

To view and manage Windows update settings, open the **System** window and click **Windows Update** in the left pane (refer back to Figure 2-43). In the Windows Update window (see Figure 2-44), you can view updates and install them. Before you move on, make sure all important updates are installed. To check for new updates, click **Check for updates** in the left pane. Windows selects the updates in the order the system can receive them, and will not necessarily list all the updates you need on the first pass. Keep installing important updates and checking for more updates until no more updates are available. You might need to restart the system after certain updates are installed.

Figure 2-44 View and manage Windows updates

If Windows 8.0 is installed, you can update it to Windows 8.1 for free. Open the Windows Store app on the Start screen, select the Windows 8.1 update, and follow directions on screen to download and install it.

> **⟲ OS Differences** Recall that Windows 7 releases major updates as a service pack. On a Windows 7 system, if you see a service pack listed in the updates, install all the updates listed above it. Then install the service pack as the only update to install. It takes about 30 minutes and a reboot to download and install a service pack. Only the latest service pack for an OS will install because the latest service pack includes all the content from previous service packs.

Hands-On | Project 2-6 Update Windows

On a Windows 8.1 system connected to the Internet, open the System window and click **Windows Update**. Windows Update searches the Microsoft website and recommends Windows updates. Print the webpage showing a list of recommended updates. For a lab computer, don't perform the updates unless you have your instructor's permission.

CONFIGURE AUTOMATIC UPDATES

Next, you need to make sure the update settings are as you want them. In the Windows Update window, click **Change settings**. In the Change settings window (see Figure 2-45), you can decide when and how updates are installed. The recommended setting is to allow Windows to automatically download and install updates daily. However, if you are not always connected to the Internet, your connection is very slow, or you want more control over which updates are installed, you might want to manage the updates differently. To change how and when updates are installed or to decide whether Windows can wake up your computer to perform updates, click **Updates will be automatically installed during the maintenance window**.

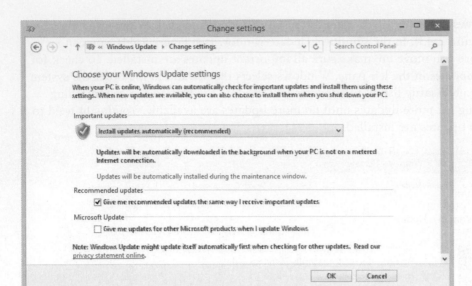

Figure 2-45   Manage how and when Windows is updated

UPDATE VIRUS AND SPYWARE DEFINITIONS

Windows 8 includes its own, preinstalled anti-malware software called Windows Defender. Although you might decide to install additional anti-malware software later, Windows Defender can provide adequate protection during the remainder of the setup process, and it's free. To verify Windows Defender settings, go to the Start screen and open Windows Defender. (On the Start screen, start typing **Defender**, then click **Windows Defender** in the search results.) The Windows Defender window appears on the desktop. Click the **Update** tab, then click **Update**.

After Defender has updated, click the **Settings** tab, and if necessary click **Real-time protection** in the menu on the left. Make sure the **Turn on real-time protection (recommended)** check box is checked. If not, check the box and click **Save changes**.

> **⟨⟩ OS Differences** Windows 7 comes with Windows Defender installed, but Defender only protects against spyware and not other types of malware. To install anti-malware software in Windows 7, you can go to the Microsoft website and download and install Microsoft Security Essentials The link is *windows.microsoft.com/en-us/windows/security-essentials-download*.

INSTALL HARDWARE

You're now ready to install the hardware devices that were not automatically installed during the Windows installation. As you install each device, reboot and verify the software or device is working before you move on to the next item. Most likely, you will need to do the following:

◢ *Install the drivers for the motherboard.* If you were not able to connect to the network earlier in the installation process, it might be because the drivers for the network port on the motherboard are not installed. Installing the motherboard drivers can solve the problem. These drivers might come on a CD bundled with the motherboard, or you can use another computer to download them from the motherboard manufacturer's website. To start the installation, double-click a setup program on the CD or a program that was previously downloaded from the web.

◢ *Even though Windows has embedded video drivers, install the drivers that came with the video card so that you can use all the features the card offers.* These drivers are on disc or downloaded from the video card manufacturer's website.

▲ *Install the printer*. For a network printer, run the setup program that came with the printer and this program will find and install the printer on the network. Alternately, open Control Panel in Classic view and open the Devices and Printers window. Then click **Add a printer** and follow the directions on screen. To install a local USB printer, all you have to do is plug in the USB printer, and Windows will install the printer automatically.

▲ *For other hardware devices, always read and follow the manufacturer's directions for the installation.* Sometimes you are directed to install the drivers before you connect the device, and sometimes you will first need to connect the device.

If a problem occurs while Windows is installing a device, it automatically launches the Action Center to help find a solution. For example, Figure 2-46 shows the error message window that appeared when a USB keyboard and USB printer were connected to a computer following a Windows 7 installation.

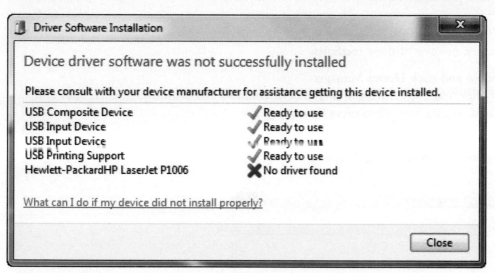

Figure 2-46   Windows 7 reports a problem with a driver for a USB printer

Immediately after this first window appeared, the window in Figure 2-47 appeared, which is provided by the Action Center. When the user clicked *Click to download and install the new driver from the Hewlett-Packard Company website*, the driver was immediately downloaded and installed with no errors.

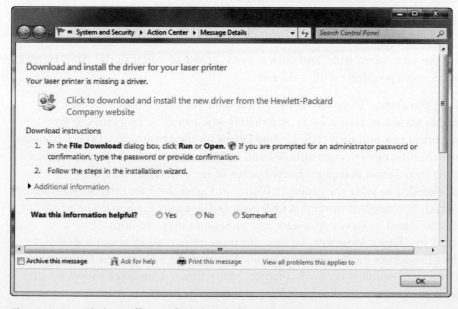

Figure 2-47   Windows offers to find the missing USB printer driver

You can also open the Action Center at any time to see a list of problems and solutions. If the problem is still not resolved after following the solutions offered by the Action Center, turn to Device Manager.

USE DEVICE MANAGER

Device Manager (its program file is named devmgmt.msc) is your primary Windows tool for managing hardware. It lists all installed hardware devices and the drivers they use. Using Device Manager, you can disable or enable a device, update its drivers, uninstall a device, and undo a driver update (called a driver rollback).

> ★ **A+ Exam Tip** The A+ 220-902 exam expects you to know in what scenarios it is appropriate to use Device Manager. You also need to know how to use the utility and how to evaluate its results.

To access Device Manager, use one of these methods:

◢ Open the System window and click **Device Manager**.
◢ For Windows 8, right-click **Start**, select **Run**, and type **devmgmt.msc**. For Windows 7, click **Start** and type **Devmgmt.msc** in the Search box. Then press **Enter**.
◢ For Windows 8, right-click **Start** and select **Device Manager**.

A Device Manager window is shown in Figure 2-48.

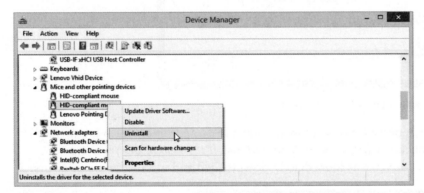

Figure 2-48   Use Device Manager to uninstall, disable, or enable a device

Click a white arrow to expand the view of an item, and click a black arrow to collapse the view. Here are ways to use Device Manager to solve problems with a device:

◢ *Try uninstalling and reinstalling the device.* To uninstall the device, right-click the device and click **Uninstall** on the shortcut menu, as shown in Figure 2-48. (Alternately, you can click **Properties** in the shortcut menu to open the Properties box and then click **Update Driver** on the Driver tab.) Then reboot the system. Windows will recognize that the device is not installed and will attempt to install the appropriate driver. Look for issues during the installation that point to the source of the problem. Sometimes reinstalling a device is all that is needed to solve the problem. Notice in Figure 2-48 that the device selected is an HID-compliant mouse, which is connected through a USB port. (HID stands for human interface device.) Sometimes USB devices are listed in Device Manager and sometimes they are not.
◢ *Look for error messages offered by Device Manager.* To find out more information about a device, right-click the device and select **Properties** on the shortcut menu. Figure 2-49 a shows the General tab of the Properties box for the onboard wireless network adapter. Many times, a message shows up in this box reporting the source of the problem and suggesting a solution.

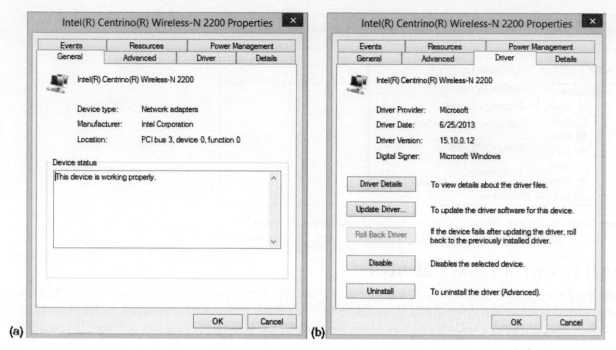

Figure 2-49   (a) Use the device Properties box to solve problems with device drivers, and (b) update device drivers.

▲ *Update the drivers.* Click the **Driver** tab (see Figure 2-49b) to update the drivers and roll back (undo) a driver update.

APPLYING | CONCEPTS   UPDATE DEVICE DRIVERS

Follow these steps to use Device Manager to update device drivers:

1. For best results, locate and download the latest driver files from the manufacturer's website to your hard drive. Be sure to use 64-bit drivers for a 64-bit OS and 32-bit drivers for a 32-bit OS. If possible, use Windows 8.1 drivers for Windows 8.1 and Windows 7 drivers for Windows 7.

2. Using Device Manager, right-click the device and select **Properties** from the shortcut menu. The Properties window for that device appears. Select the **Driver** tab and click **Update Driver**. The Update Driver Software box opens.

3. To search the Internet for drivers, click **Search automatically for updated driver software**. If you have already downloaded drivers to your PC, click **Browse my computer for driver software**, and point to the downloaded files. Note that Windows is looking for an .inf file to identify the drivers. Continue to follow the directions on screen to complete the installation.

✎ **Notes**   By default, Device Manager hides legacy devices that are not Plug and Play. To view installed legacy devices, click the **View** menu of Device Manager, and check **Show hidden devices** (see Figure 2-50).

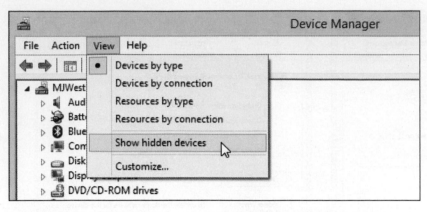

Figure 2-50   By default, Windows does not display legacy devices in Device Manager; you show these hidden devices by using the View menu

PROBLEMS WITH LEGACY DEVICES

Older hardware devices might present a problem. A Windows Vista driver is likely to work in the Windows 7 installation because Windows 7 and Vista are so closely related, but it might not work in Windows 8. If the driver does not load correctly or gives errors, first search the web for a Windows 8 driver. If you don't find one, try running the driver installation program in compatibility mode, which is explained next.

APPLYING | CONCEPTS   TROUBLESHOOT DEVICE DRIVERS

In the example that follows, the installation program for an older network printer worked under Windows 7 but did not load correctly on Windows 8.1. Follow these steps to use compatibility mode with the driver installation program:

1. Using File Explorer, locate the program file with an .exe file extension for the driver installation program. Right-click the program file and select **Troubleshoot compatibility** from the shortcut menu (see Figure 2-51). The Program Compatibility utility launches.

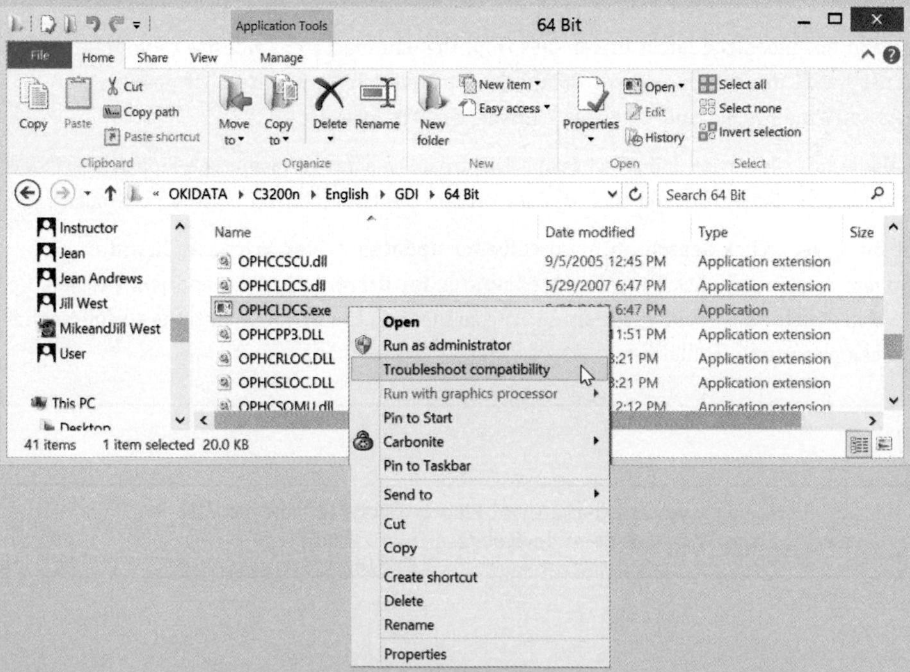

Figure 2-51   Run the Program Compatibility utility from the shortcut menu of the program that is giving a problem

2. On the first screen of the troubleshooter utility, select **Troubleshoot program** (see Figure 2-52).

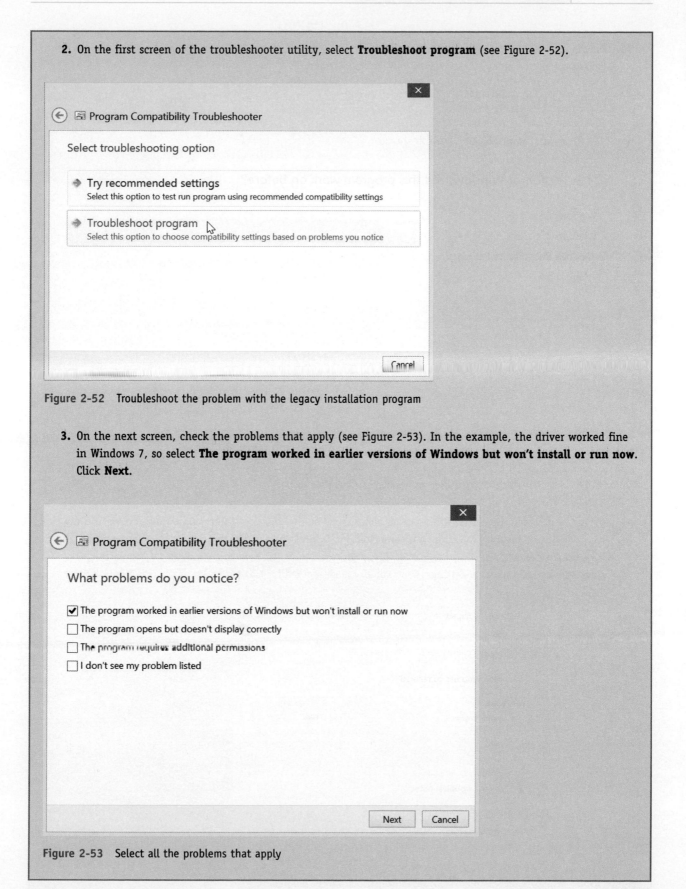

Figure 2-52 Troubleshoot the problem with the legacy installation program

3. On the next screen, check the problems that apply (see Figure 2-53). In the example, the driver worked fine in Windows 7, so select **The program worked in earlier versions of Windows but won't install or run now**. Click **Next**.

Figure 2-53 Select all the problems that apply

4. On the next screen, the troubleshooter asks for the OS with which the program worked (see Figure 2-54). For this example, you would select **Windows 7** and click **Next**.

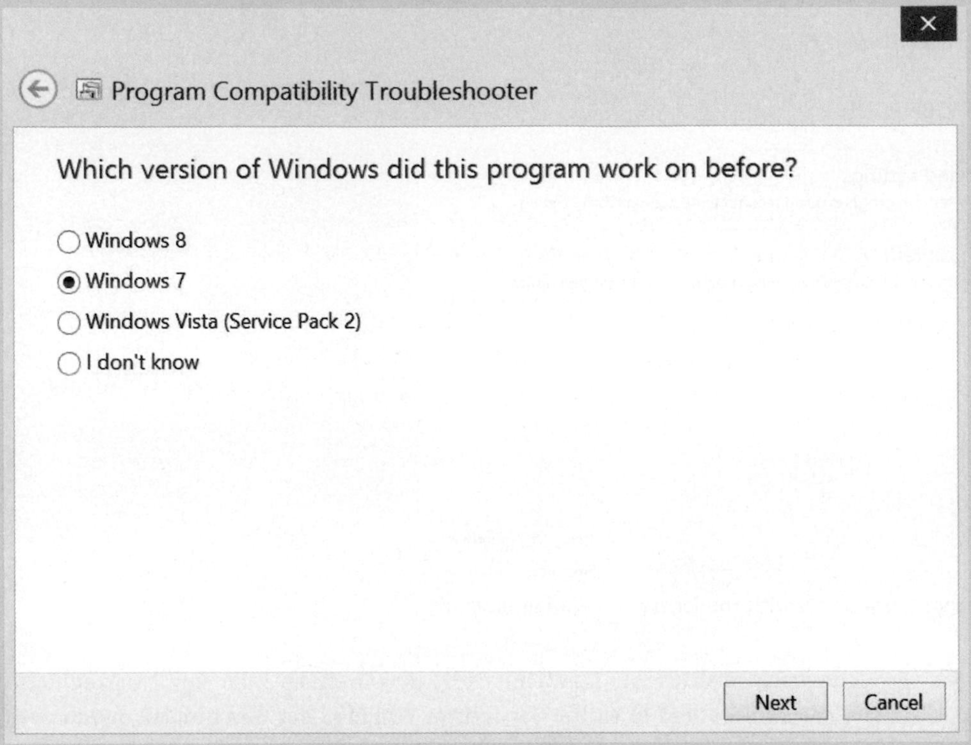

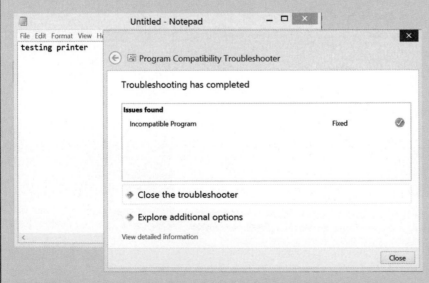

Program Compatibility Troubleshooter

Which version of Windows did this program work on before?

○ Windows 8
◉ Windows 7
○ Windows Vista (Service Pack 2)
○ I don't know

| Next | Cancel |

Figure 2-54   Select the operating system with which the program worked

5. On the next screen, click **Test the program** and respond to the UAC box. The program runs and successfully fixes the drivers for the printer. In this case, checking Devices and Printers in Control Panel shows no errors with the printer. Upon testing the printer, it can process a print job from this Windows 8.1 computer. Click **Next** and save the program settings. Compatibility mode worked for this particular driver (see Figure 2-55).

Untitled - Notepad
File Edit Format View H
testing printer

Program Compatibility Troubleshooter

Troubleshooting has completed

Issues found

Incompatible Program   Fixed   ✓

→ Close the troubleshooter

→ Explore additional options

View detailed information

| Close |

Figure 2-55   Windows successfully fixed the incompatible printer program

INSTALL APPLICATIONS

A+
220-902
1.2, 1.5

Applications can be installed in Windows 8/7 from CD or DVD, from a downloaded application file, directly from the web, or, for Windows 8, from the Windows Store.

To install applications from a disc, insert the setup CD or DVD, and follow the directions on screen to launch the installation routine. For software downloaded from the Internet, open File Explorer or Windows Explorer and double-click the program filename to begin the installation. When installing a program directly from the web, click the link on the website to install the software and follow directions on screen. To install apps in the Windows 8 interface, use the Store app on the Start screen. (Later in the text, you'll learn what to do when an installation fails.) After an application is installed, you might also need to install any updates available for the application on the manufacturer's website.

If you need to uninstall an application, open **Control Panel** and click **Programs and Features**. (For Windows 8, you can press **Win+X** and click **Programs and Features**.) The Programs and Features window appears, listing the programs installed on this computer where you can uninstall, change, or repair these programs. Select a program from the list. Based on the software, the buttons at the top of the list will change. For example, in Figure 2-56, the Camtasia Studio 8 software offers the option to Uninstall, Change, or Repair the software.

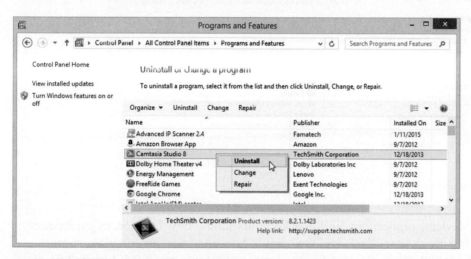

Figure 2-56 Select a program from the list to view your options to manage the software

Recall that you can also uninstall a Windows 8 app by using the Start screen or Apps screen. Right-click the app tile and then click **Uninstall** in the status bar that appears at the bottom of the screen.

SET UP USER ACCOUNTS AND TRANSFER USER DATA

A+
220-902
1.1, 1.2,
1.5

Remember that you can use the Windows 8 Settings charm or the Windows 7 User Accounts applet in Control Panel to create user accounts. In addition, you can use the Computer Management console in Windows 8/7 to create accounts. After you have created user accounts in a new installation of Windows, you might want to transfer user data and settings from another computer to this one.

For individuals or small organizations, use Windows Easy Transfer in Windows 8/7/Vista to copy user data and settings from one computer to another. The utility is easy to use and you can find directions in Windows Help and Support. For large corporations that use a Windows domain, a more advanced tool is required, the User State Migration Tool (USMT). This tool is discussed later in this chapter.

> ✎ **Notes** After moving user data and settings from one computer to another, the best practice is to leave the user data and settings on the original computer untouched for at least two months. This practice gives the user plenty of time to make sure everything has been moved over.

TURN WINDOWS FEATURES ON OR OFF

**A+
220-902
1.2, 1.5**

You can save on system resources by turning off Windows 8/7 features you will not use, and you might need to turn on some features that are, by default, turned off. To control Windows features, in the left pane of the Programs and Features window, click **Turn Windows features on or off** (refer to Figure 2-56). The Windows Features box opens (see Figure 2-57). Check or uncheck the features you want or don't want and then click **OK**. Sometimes a restart is necessary for the changes to take effect.

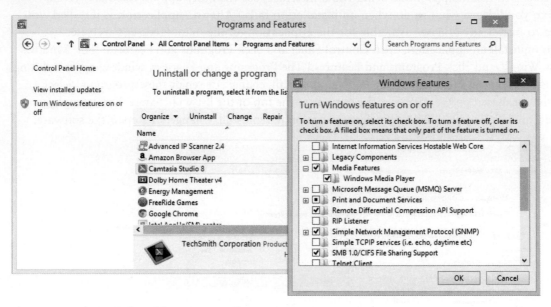

Figure 2-57   Turn Windows features on or off

The Windows installation, devices, applications, and user accounts should now be good to go. Restart the computer and make one last check that all is well. Now would be a good time to complete your documentation and make a backup of the entire Windows volume in the event of a hard drive failure or corrupted installation. How to make backups is covered in the chapter, "Maintaining Windows."

Hands-On | Project 2-7   Create a Documentation Form

Create a document that technicians can use when installing Windows and performing all the chores mentioned in the chapter that need doing before and after the installation. The document needs a checklist of what to do before the installation and a checklist of what to do after the installation. It also needs a place to record decisions made during the installation, the applications and hardware devices installed, user accounts created, and any other important information that might be useful for future maintenance or troubleshooting. Don't forget to include a way to identify the computer, the name of the technician doing the work, and when the work was done.

SPECIAL CONCERNS WHEN WORKING IN A LARGE ENTERPRISE

**A+
220-902
1.1, 1.2,
1.4**

Working as an IT support technician in a large corporate environment is different from working as an IT support technician for a small company or with individuals. In this part of the chapter, you learn how Windows is installed on computers in an enterprise and a little about providing ongoing technical support for Windows in these organizations.

DEPLOYMENT STRATEGIES FOR WINDOWS

A+
220-902
1.1, 1.2,
1.4

Earlier in the chapter, you learned how to install Windows using a setup DVD, USB flash drive, or files downloaded from the Microsoft website. You perform the installation while sitting at the computer, responding to each query made by the setup program. Then you must configure Windows and install device drivers and applications. If, however, you were responsible for installing Windows on several hundred computers in a large corporation, you might want a less time-consuming method to perform the installations. These methods are called deployment strategies. A deployment strategy is a procedure to install Windows, device drivers, and applications on a computer and can include the process to transfer user settings, application settings, and user data files from an old installation to the new installation.

Microsoft suggests four deployment strategies; the one chosen depends on the number of computers to be deployed and determines the amount of time you must sit in front of an individual computer as Windows is installed (this time is called the touch time). As an IT support technician in a large corporation, most likely you would not be involved in choosing or setting up the deployment strategy. But you need to be aware of the different strategies so that you have a general idea of what will be expected of you when you are asked to provide desk-side or help-desk support as Windows is being deployed in your organization.

The four deployment strategies are discussed next.

HIGH-TOUCH WITH RETAIL MEDIA (RECOMMENDED FOR FEWER THAN 100 COMPUTERS)

The high-touch with retail media strategy is the strategy used in the installations described earlier in the chapter. All the work is done by a technician sitting at the computer. To save time doing multiple installations, you can copy the Windows setup files to a file server on the network and share the folder. Then at each computer, you can execute the setup program on the server to perform a clean install or upgrade of the OS. A server used in this way is called a distribution server. Except for upgrade installations, applications must be manually installed after the OS is installed.

To transfer user settings, application settings, and user data files to a new installation (a process called migrating), you can use Windows Easy Transfer (a manual process that is easy to use) or the User State Migration Tool (more automated and more difficult to set up and use). Windows Easy Transfer is part of Windows 8/7/Vista. The User State Migration Tool (USMT) is a command-line tool that works only when the computer is a member of a Windows domain. USMT is included in the Windows Assessment and Deployment Kit (ADK) for Windows 8, and in the Windows Automated Installation Kit (AIK) for Windows 7. Both can be downloaded from the Microsoft website, and both contain a group of tools used to deploy Windows in a large organization.

HIGH-TOUCH WITH STANDARD IMAGE (RECOMMENDED FOR 100 TO 200 COMPUTERS)

To use the high-touch using a standard image strategy, a system administrator prepares an image called a standard image that includes the Windows OS, drivers, and applications that are standard to all the computers that might use the image. A standard image is hardware independent, meaning it can be installed on any computer. (In the chapter "Maintaining Windows," you learn to create other types of images that can only be used on the computer that created them.)

Drive-imaging software is used to copy the entire hard drive to another bootable media in the process called drive imaging. Tools included in the Windows ADK or AIK or third-party software can be used. Examples of third-party drive-imaging software are True Image by Acronis (*www.acronis.com*), Ghost by Symantec (*www.symantec.com*), and Todo Backup Free, a freeware version of the Todo Backup software by EaseUS (*www.easeus.com*). A standard image is usually stored on an 8-GB or larger bootable USB flash drive (UFD) or on a bootable DVD along with Windows setup files.

> **✎ Notes** To see a video introducing how to create a standard image, check out this video at the Microsoft Technet site: *technet.microsoft.com/en-us/windows/ee530017.aspx*.

Installing a standard image on another computer is called image deployment, which always results in a clean install rather than an upgrade. To begin, boot the computer from the bootable flash drive or DVD that contains the image. A menu appears to begin the Windows installation. When you finish this Windows installation, the standard image is installed. USMT can then be used to transfer user settings, user data files, and application settings to the new installation.

The high-touch using a standard image strategy takes longer to set up than the previous strategy because a system administrator must prepare the image and must set up USMT, but it takes less time to install on each computer and also assures the administrator that each computer has a standard set of drivers and applications that are configured correctly.

LITE-TOUCH, HIGH-VOLUME DEPLOYMENT (RECOMMENDED FOR 200 TO 500 COMPUTERS)

The lite-touch, high-volume deployment strategy uses a deployment server on the network to serve up the installation after a technician starts the process. The files in the installation include Windows, device drivers, and applications, and collectively are called the distribution share.

The technician starts the installation by booting the computer to Windows PE. Windows Preinstallation Environment (Windows PE) is a minimum operating system used to start the installation. It is included in the Windows ADK for Windows 8 or in the Windows AIK for Windows 7, and it can be installed on a USB flash drive, CD, or DVD to make the device bootable. The technician boots from the device, which might be configured to display a menu to choose from multiple distribution shares available on the deployment server.

The technician can also boot the computer directly to the network to receive Windows PE from the deployment server. For a legacy BIOS system, set the first item in the boot device priority to be Ethernet (see Figure 2-58). For a UEFI system, look for an advanced setup screen in UEFI setup to enable PXE Support. Then reboot the system. The computer boots to the Preboot eXecution Environment or Pre-Execution Environment (PXE) that is contained in the UEFI or BIOS code on the motherboard. PXE searches for a server on the network to provide a bootable operating system (Windows PE on the deployment server).

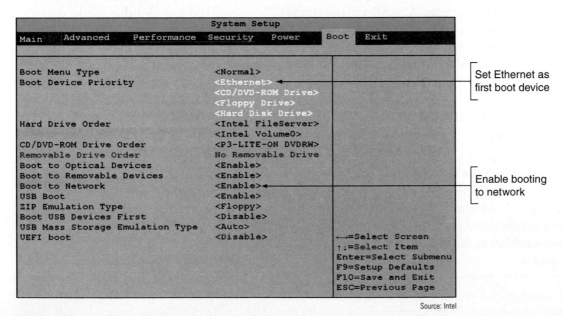

Figure 2-58   Configure BIOS setup to boot to the network

After the installation begins, the technician is not required to respond to prompts by the setup program, which is called an unattended installation. These responses, such as the administrator password or domain name, are stored in an answer file. The User State Migration Tool is then used to transfer user settings, user data files, and application settings to the new installation.

For high-touch strategies, a technician would normally sit at a computer and use the Windows 8 Upgrade Assistant or the Windows 7 Upgrade Advisor to determine if the system qualifies for the upgrade before performing the installation. Using lite-touch deployments, a more automated method of qualifying a computer is preferred. The Microsoft Assessment and Planning (MAP) Toolkit can be used by a system administrator from a network location to query hundreds of computers in a single scan. The software automatically examines hardware and applications on each computer to verify compatibility with Windows 7 or 8. The MAP software might also be used by the system administrator before deciding to deploy a new OS to determine what computer hardware upgrades or application software upgrades are required that must be included in the overall deployment budget.

ZERO-TOUCH, HIGH-VOLUME DEPLOYMENT (RECOMMENDED FOR MORE THAN 500 COMPUTERS)

The zero-touch, high-volume deployment strategy is the most difficult to set up and requires complex tools. The installation does not require a technician to start the process (called pull automation). Rather, the installation uses push automation, meaning that a server automatically pushes the installation to a computer when a user is not likely to be sitting at it. The entire remote network installation is automated and no user intervention is required. The process can turn on a computer that is turned off and even works when no OS is installed on the computer or the current OS is corrupted.

> 🖉 **Notes** IT support technicians find that large enterprises appreciate quick-and-easy solutions to desktop or laptop computer problems. Technicians quickly learn their marching orders are almost always "replace or reimage." Little time is given to trying to solve the underlying problem when hardware can quickly be replaced or a Windows installation can quickly be reimaged.

USING THE USMT SOFTWARE

A+
220-902
1.2, 1.4

Let's look briefly at what to expect when using the USMT software, which is included in the Windows 8 ADK software and the Windows 7 AIK software. To prepare to use USMT, a system administrator must first install the ADK or AIK software on his or her computer. In Microsoft documentation, this computer is called the technician computer. The source computer is the computer from which the user settings, application settings, and user data files are taken. The destination computer is the computer that is to receive this data. Sometimes the source computer and the destination computer are the same computer. An example is when you perform a clean installation of Windows 8/7 on a computer that has an earlier version of Windows installed and you want to transfer user files and settings from the older installation to the new installation.

> 🖉 **Notes** USMT uses hard-link migration of user files and settings when the source computer and the destination computer are the same computer. Hard-link migration does not actually copy files and settings, but leaves them on the hard drive without copying. This method makes USMT extremely fast when the hard drive is not formatted during the Windows installation.

The USMT software uses three commands:

- scanstate copies settings and files from the source computer to a safe location.
- loadstate applies these settings and files to the destination computer.
- usmtutils provides encryption options and hard-link management.

Here are the general steps to use USMT:

1. Download and install the ADK or AIK software on the technician computer.

2. Copy the USMT program files from the technician computer to the source computer.

3. Run the scanstate command on the source computer to copy user files and settings to a file server or other safe location.

4. Install Windows, device drivers, and applications on the destination computer.

5. Run the loadstate command to apply user files and settings from the file server to the destination computer.

> ★ **A+ Exam Tip**   The A+ 220-902 exam expects you to know about the User State Migration Tool (USMT).

The scanstate, loadstate, and usmtutils command lines can be lengthy and include references to .xml files in the command line along with other parameters. The details of these command lines are not covered in this text. Most likely, the commands are stored in batch files provided by the system administrator. A batch file has a .bat file extension and contains a list or batch of OS commands that are executed as a group. These batch files might be automatically executed as part of a zero-touch installation or manually executed in a lite-touch or high-touch installation. To manually execute a batch file, you type the name of the batch file at a command prompt.

> ✎ **Notes**   For detailed instructions on using USMT that a system administrator might use, go to *technet.microsoft.com* and search on *using USMT for IT professionals*.

>> CHAPTER SUMMARY

How to Plan a Windows Installation

- Editions of Windows 8 are Windows 8, Windows 8 Professional, Windows 8 Enterprise, and Windows RT. All editions come in 32- or 64-bit versions.

- The Windows 7 editions are Windows 7 Starter, Windows 7 Home Basic, Windows 7 Home Premium, Windows 7 Professional, Windows 7 Enterprise, and Windows 7 Ultimate.

- Windows can be purchased as the less-expensive OEM version or the more-expensive retail version. The OEM version can only be installed on a new computer.

- Each edition of Windows 8 and Windows 7 (except Windows 7 Starter) is available in either 32- or 64-bit versions. A 32-bit OS cannot address as much memory as a 64-bit OS. A 64-bit OS performs better and requires more memory than a 32-bit OS.

- Before purchasing Windows, make sure your system meets the minimum hardware requirements and all the hardware and applications will work under the OS. A 64-bit OS requires 64-bit drivers.

2

◢ A computer might have legacy BIOS installed on the motherboard or have the newer UEFI firmware installed. Most UEFI firmware offers the option to support legacy BIOS when in UEFI CSM mode.

◢ A hard drive contains one or more partitions or volumes and can use the MBR or GPT partitioning system. To use UEFI Secure Boot, the partitioning system must be GPT and the Windows installation must be 64 bit.

◢ Normally, Windows is installed on the C: volume in the C:\Windows folder. The volume in which Windows is installed must use the NTFS file system.

◢ Windows can be installed from the setup DVD, USB flash drive, files downloaded from the Internet, hidden partition on the hard drive (called a factory recovery partition), or in a virtual machine.

◢ Virtual machine software can provide multiple instances of operating systems for training users, running legacy software, and supporting multiple operating systems.

◢ Windows can be installed as an in-place upgrade, a clean installation, or in a multiboot environment with another OS.

Installing Windows 8.1 and Windows 7

◢ A technician needs to know how to perform an in-place upgrade, a clean install, or a multiboot with Windows.

◢ The steps for installing or upgrading Windows 8.0 are about the same as those for Windows 8.1.

◢ A clean install is the best option to use if the current installation is sluggish or giving problems, or if you're installing Windows on a new desktop computer that you're building.

◢ In a multiboot, each OS must be installed on its own partition. Make sure you have enough free space on a partition before installing Windows onto it, and make sure it doesn't currently hold an OS.

What to Do After a Windows Installation

◢ After a Windows installation, verify you have network access, activate Windows, install any Windows updates or Windows 7 service packs, verify automatic updates are configured correctly, install hardware and applications, create user accounts and transfer or restore from backup user data and preferences, and turn Windows features on or off.

Special Concerns When Working in a Large Enterprise

◢ Four deployment strategies for installing Windows in a large enterprise are high-touch with retail media, high-touch with a standard image, lite-touch with high volume, and zero-touch with high volume. Which strategy to use depends on the number of computers to deploy. Zero-touch deployments require the most time to set up, but do not require a technician to be at the computer when the installation happens.

>> KEY TERMS

For explanations of key terms, see the Glossary for this text.

answer file	compatibility mode	distribution server	hard-link migration
batch file	custom installation	distribution share	high-touch using a standard image
BIOS (basic input/output system)	deployment strategy	drive imaging	
	device driver	dual boot	high-touch with retail media
boot loader menu	Device Manager	file system	
Certificate of Authenticity	disc image	GUID Partition Table (GPT)	hot-swappable
clean install	diskpart		hypervisor

image deployment
in-place upgrade
ISO file
ISO image
lite-touch, high-volume deployment
loadstate
Master Boot Record (MBR)
Microsoft Assessment and Planning (MAP) Toolkit
multiboot
Original Equipment Manufacturer (OEM) license
Preboot eXecution Environment or Pre-Execution Environment (PXE)
product activation

Programs and Features
pull automation
push automation
recovery partition
remote network installation
repair installation
scanstate
Secure Boot
service pack
setup UEFI/BIOS
solid-state drive
standard image
startup UEFI/BIOS
system UEFI/BIOS
third-party driver
UEFI CSM (Compatibility Support Module) mode

unattended installation
Unified Extensible Firmware Interface (UEFI)
Upgrade Advisor
Upgrade Assistant
upgrade path
User State Migration Tool (USMT)
usmtutils
virtual machine (VM)
virtual XP mode
volume
Windows 7
Windows 8.1
Windows 8.1 Enterprise
Windows 8.1 Pro for Students

Windows 8.1 Professional (Windows 8.1 Pro)
Windows Assessment and Deployment Kit (ADK)
Windows Automated Installation Kit (AIK)
Windows Defender
Windows Easy Transfer
Windows Preinstallation Environment (Windows PE)
Windows Pro Pack
Windows RT
Windows Vista
Windows XP Mode
Windows.old folder
zero-touch, high-volume deployment

>> REVIEWING THE BASICS

1. How much free space on the hard drive is required to install a 64-bit version of Windows 8.1?

2. How do you start the process to reinstall an OS on a laptop computer using the backup files stored on a recovery partition?

3. What are three free applications mentioned in the chapter that can be used to create virtual machines?

4. When upgrading from Windows Vista to Windows 8.1, can you perform an in-place upgrade?

5. Which Windows architecture is required to enable the UEFI Secure Boot? Which partitioning system?

6. Which file system is used on the volume where Windows is installed?

7. When trying to install Windows in UEFI mode on a hard drive that is using the MBR partitioning system, which command can you use to get a special prompt in a command prompt window where you can then remove the partitioning system and convert the drive to GPT?

8. What is the minimum number of partitions that the MBR partitioning system can support?

9. Which partitioning method must you use for a 4-TB hard drive?

10. If you suspect a computer is infected with a virus, why is it not a good idea to perform an upgrade installation of Windows rather than a clean install?

11. After setting up a dual-boot installation with Windows 7 and Windows 8.1, how do you boot the system into Windows 7?

12. After a Windows installation, what is the easiest way to determine that you have Internet access?

13. What Windows 8 tool can you use to migrate user data and settings from a Windows 7 installation on one computer to the new Windows 8 installation on a different computer?

14. What is the primary Windows tool for managing hardware devices?

15. What window is used to uninstall a program in Windows 8? What Windows 8 screen is used to uninstall an app?

16. What three processor technologies are required to install Windows 8?

17. Why does Microsoft require these three processor technologies, even though they are currently available on all processors sold today?

18. How can you find out if a system qualifies for a Windows 8.1 upgrade?

19. Which window on the Windows 8 desktop can you use to find out if the Windows installation has been activated?

20. What is an advantage of using a dynamic hard drive in a VM?

21. Are you required to enter the product key during the Windows 7 installation?

22. Using an unattended installation of Windows, what is the name of the file that holds the responses a technician would normally give during the installation?

23. What are the three commands used by the User State Migration Tool?

24. To use the User State Migration Tool, how must a computer connect to the network?

25. Where is the PXE programming code stored that is used to boot a computer when it is searching for an OS on the network?

>> THINKING CRITICALLY

1. You are planning an upgrade from Windows 7 to Windows 8.1. Your system uses a network card that you don't find listed on the Microsoft Windows 8.1 list of compatible devices. What do you do next?

a. Abandon the upgrade and continue to use Windows 7.

b. Check the website of the network card manufacturer for a Windows 8.1 driver.

c. Buy a new network card.

d. Install a dual boot for Windows 7 and Windows 8.1 and only use the network when you have Windows 7 loaded.

2. You have just installed Windows 8.1 and now attempt to install your favorite game that worked fine under Windows 7. When you attempt the installation, you get an error. What is your best next step?

a. Purchase a new version of your game, one that is compatible with Windows 8.1.

b. Download any updates to Windows 8.1.

c. Reinstall Windows 7.

d. Install a VM running Windows 7.

3. You have 32-bit Windows 7 Home Premium installed on your computer, and you purchase the upgrade license of Windows 8.1 Professional. You want to install Windows 8.1 using the 64-bit architecture. Which way(s) can you install Windows 8.1?

a. You can perform an upgrade, but not a clean install.

b. You can perform an upgrade or a clean install.

c. You can perform a clean install, but not an upgrade.

d. In this situation, you cannot install Windows 8.1 using the upgrade license. You must go back and purchase the full license of Windows 8.1.

4. A laptop reports that it has made a wireless network connection, but it cannot access the network or the Internet. Arrange the following steps in the best order to troubleshoot the problem:

   a. Use Device Manager to uninstall the wireless adapter and install it again.

   b. Disable and enable the wireless network adapter.

   c. Disconnect the connection, and connect again to the wireless network.

   d. Use Device Manager to update the wireless adapter drivers.

>> REAL PROBLEMS, REAL SOLUTIONS

REAL PROBLEM 2-1 Recovering Data from a Corrupted Windows Installation

As an IT support technician for a small organization, it's your job to support the computers, the small network, and the users. One of your coworkers, Jason, comes to you in a panic. His Windows 8.1 system won't boot, and he has lots of important data files in several locations on the drive. He has no idea in which folder some of the files are located. Besides the application data he's currently working on, he's especially concerned about losing email addresses, email, and his Internet Explorer Favorites links.

After trying everything you know about recovering Windows 8.1, you conclude the OS is corrupted beyond repair. You decide there might be a way to remove the hard drive from Jason's computer and connect it to another computer so that you can recover the data. Search the Internet and find a device that you can use to connect Jason's hard drive to another computer using a USB port on that computer. The hard drive uses a SATA hard drive interface. Print the webpage showing the device and its price.

REAL PROBLEM 2-2 Troubleshooting an Upgrade

Your friend, Thomas, has upgraded his Windows 7 desktop to Windows 8.1. After the installation, he discovers his media card reader does not work. He calls you on the phone asking you what to do. Do the following to plan your troubleshooting approach:

1. List the questions you should ask Thomas to help diagnose the problem.

2. List the steps you would take if you were sitting at the computer solving the problem.

3. What do you think is the source of the problem? Explain your answer.

REAL PROBLEM 2-3 Creating Windows 8.1 Setup on a USB Flash Drive or DVD

Microsoft offers a solution to those who installed Windows 8.1 from the web but failed to save the Windows setup files to a DVD or USB flash drive and later need these files to reinstall Windows 8.1. Follow these steps to create Windows setup on a DVD or USB flash drive:

1. Go to the Microsoft webpage **windows.microsoft.com/en-us/windows-8/create-reset-refresh-media**. Download and run the Windows Installation Media Creation Tool. On the first window, select your language, edition of Windows 8.1, and architecture (see Figure 2-59).

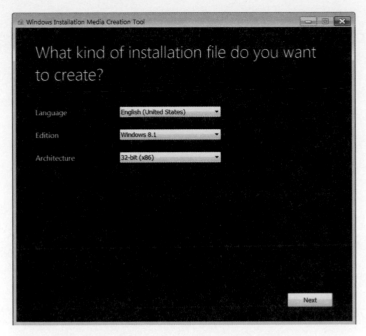

Figure 2-59 Select options to download Windows 8.1 setup files

2. On the next screen (see Figure 2-60), do one of the following:

▲ To create a bootable USB flash drive, select **USB flash drive**. When you click **Next**, the download begins and files are created on the drive.

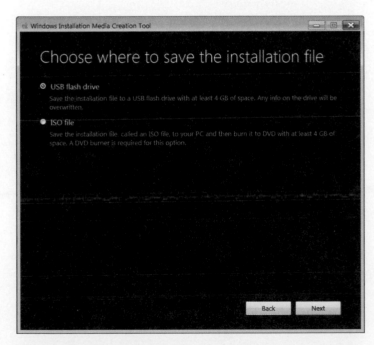

Figure 2-60 Select USB flash drive to hold Windows 8.1 setup files and folders

▲ If you want to burn a DVD, select **ISO file**. The file is created in the same folder where you saved the Windows Installation Media Creation Tool program that you downloaded in Step 1. (This ISO file is handy for installing Windows in a VM.) On the next screen, click **Open DVD burner** and follow directions on screen to burn the DVD.

Maintaining Windows

Earlier in the text, you learned how to install Windows. This
chapter takes you to the next step in learning how to support a
Windows operating system: maintaining the OS after it is installed.
Most Windows problems stem from poor maintenance. If you are an
IT support technician responsible for the ongoing support of several
computers, you can make your work easier and your users happier by
setting up and executing a good maintenance plan for each computer
you support. A well-maintained computer gives fewer problems and
performs better than one that is not maintained. In this chapter, you
learn how to schedule regular maintenance tasks, prepare for disaster
by setting up backup routines for user data and system files, use
commands to manage files and folders, and manage a hard drive.

This text covers Windows 8.1, 8.0, 7, and Vista. As you read,
you might consider following the steps in the chapter first using a
Windows 8.1 system, and then going through the chapter again using
a Windows 7 system.

SCHEDULE PREVENTIVE MAINTENANCE

 Regular preventive maintenance can keep a Windows computer performing well for years. At least once a month, you need to verify critical Windows settings and clean up the hard drive. These skills are covered in this part of the chapter. If you notice the system is slow as you do this maintenance, you need to dig deeper to optimize Windows. How to optimize Windows is covered later in the chapter "Optimizing Windows."

> **✎ Notes** When you're responsible for a computer, be sure to keep good records of all that you do to maintain, upgrade, or fix the computer. When performing preventive maintenance, take notes and include those in your documentation. The Computer Inventory and Maintenance document available at *cengagebrain.com* can help you organize your notes.

VERIFY CRITICAL WINDOWS SETTINGS

 Three Windows settings discussed here are critical for keeping the system protected from malware and hackers. Users sometimes change these settings without realizing their importance. Check the three settings and, if you find settings that are incorrect, take time to explain to the primary user of the computer how important these settings are. Here are the critical Windows settings you need to verify:

◢ **Windows updates.** Install any important Windows updates or Windows 7 service packs that are waiting to be installed and verify that Windows Update is configured to automatically allow updating. These updates may include updates to Windows, applications, device drivers, and firmware. You learned how to configure Windows Update in the chapter "Installing Windows."

◢ **Antivirus/anti-malware software.** To protect a system against malicious attack, you also need to verify that anti-malware software is configured to scan the system regularly and that it is up to date. If you discover it is not scanning regularly, take the time to do a thorough scan for viruses.

◢ **Network security setting.** To secure the computer against attack from the network, check that the network security type (public or private in Windows 8; public, work, or home in Windows 7) is set correctly for the optimum firewall settings. How to verify the network type was covered in the chapter "Survey of Windows Features and Support Tools." Further details of configuring network security are discussed in the chapter "Security Strategies."

> **✎ Notes** Don't forget that what you learn about maintaining Windows also applies to Windows in a VM. When maintaining a VM, make sure Windows in a VM is updated, anti-malware software is installed and running, and network settings are secure.

UPDATE DRIVERS AND FIRMWARE

 As part of routine maintenance, you normally would not update device drivers unless a device is having a problem or you want to use a new feature available with a driver update. In the chapter, "Installing Windows," you learned to use Device Manager to update drivers. A few devices have firmware on the device that can be updated, which is called flashing firmware. For example, after a RAID controller had its drivers updated by Device Manager, new tabs appeared on the controller's properties box that are put there by the drivers (see Figure 3-1). To flash the firmware on this controller card, you first download the flash image file from the device manufacturer's website. Then click **Browse** and locate the file. Next, click **Program Flash** to begin the firmware update.

Figure 3-1 Use the device's properties box to flash the firmware on some devices

PATCH MANAGEMENT

A+
220-902
1.7

When researching a problem, suppose you discover that Microsoft or a manufacturer's website offers a fix or patch for Windows, a device driver, or an application. To download and apply the right patch, you need to make sure you get a 32-bit patch for a 32-bit installation of Windows, a device driver, or an application. For a 64-bit installation of Windows, make sure you get a 64-bit device driver. An application installed in a 64-bit OS might be a 32-bit application or a 64-bit application.

The documentation on the Microsoft or other websites might be cryptic about the type of patch. Follow these guidelines when reading error messages or documentation:

◢ The term x86 refers to 32-bit CPUs or processors and to 32-bit operating systems. For example, suppose you need to download a patch from Microsoft to fix a Windows 8.1 problem you are having with USB devices. The article on the Microsoft website that applies to your problem says to download the patch if you are using a Windows 8.1, x86-based version. This means you can use this patch if you are using a 32-bit version of Windows 8.1.

◢ All CPUs installed in personal computers today are hybrid processors that can process either 32 bits or 64 bits. The term x86-64 refers to these processors, such as the Intel Core i5 or an AMD Phenom processor. (AMD64 refers specifically to these hybrid AMD processors.) The term x86-64 can also refer to a 64-bit OS. For example, a Windows message might say, "You are attempting to load an x86-64 operating system." Take that to mean you are attempting to load a 64-bit OS onto a computer that has a hybrid 32-bit/64-bit processor installed, such as the Phenom II X4 or Intel Core i5.

◢ The term IA64 refers specifically to 64-bit Intel processors such as the Xeon or Itanium used in servers or high-end workstations. For example, suppose you are selecting a utility to download from the Microsoft website. One choice for the utility specifies an IA64 platform. Only select this choice if you have installed an Itanium or Xeon processor. (By the way, a techie often uses the word *platform* to mean the processor and operating system on which other software is running. However, in this context, the operating system's platform is the processor.)

◢ The term x64 refers to 64-bit operating systems. For example, Microsoft offers two versions of Windows 8.1: the x86 version and the x64 version.

> ★ **A+ Exam Tip** The A+ 220-902 exam expects you to know the difference between Windows 32-bit and 64-bit versions. You are also expected to be familiar with the terms 32-bit, 64-bit, x86, and x64.

CLEAN UP THE HARD DRIVE

For best performance, Windows needs at least 15 percent free space on the hard drive that it uses for defragmenting the drive, for burning CDs and DVDs, and for a variety of other tasks, so it's important to delete unneeded files occasionally. In addition, you can improve drive performance and free up space by defragmenting magnetic hard drives, checking the drive for errors, compressing folders, and moving files and folders to other drives. All these tasks are discussed in the following subsections. We begin by learning where Windows puts important folders on the drive.

DIRECTORY STRUCTURES

Folder or directory locations you need to be aware of include those for user files, program files, and Windows data. In the folder locations given in this discussion, we assume Windows is installed on drive C:.

User Profile Namespace

When a user first signs in to Windows, a user profile is created, which is a collection of user data and settings, and consists of two general items:

◢ *A user folder together with its subfolders.* These items are created under the C:\Users folder, for example, C:\Users\Jean Andrews. This folder contains a group of subfolders collectively called the user profile namespace. (In general, a namespace is a container to hold data, for example, a folder.)

◢ *NTUSER.DAT.* NTUSER.DAT is a hidden file stored in the C:\Users*username* folder and contains user settings. Each time the user logs on, the contents of this file are copied to a location in the registry.

Program Files

Here is where Windows stores program files unless you select a different location when a program is installed:

◢ Program files are stored in C:\Program Files for 32-bit versions of Windows. Only 32-bit applications can be installed in a 32-bit installation of Windows.

◢ In 64-bit versions of Windows, 64-bit programs are stored in the C:\Program Files folder, and 32-bit programs are stored in the C:\Program Files (x86) folder. (For best performance, when you have the option, install 64-bit applications in a 64-bit installation of Windows.)

Here are folders that applications and some utilities use to launch programs at startup:

◢ A program file or shortcut to a program file stored in the C:\Users*username*\AppData\Roaming\ Microsoft\Windows\Start Menu\Programs\Startup folder launches at startup for an individual user.

◢ A program file or shortcut to a program file stored in the C:\ProgramData\Microsoft\Windows\Start Menu\Programs\Startup folder launches at startup for all users.

Folders for Windows Data

An operating system needs a place to keep hardware and software configuration information, user preferences, and application settings. This information is used when the OS is first loaded and when needed by hardware, applications, and users. Windows uses a database called the registry for most of this information. In addition, Windows keeps some data in text files called initialization files, which often have an .ini or .inf file extension.

Here are some important folder locations used for the registry and other Windows data:

▲ *Registry location.* The Windows registry is stored in the C:\Windows\System32\config folder.
▲ *Backup of the registry.* A backup of the registry is stored in the C:\Windows\System32\config\RegBack folder.
▲ *Fonts.* Fonts are stored in the C:\Windows\Fonts folder.
▲ *Temporary files.* These files, which are used by Windows when it is installing software and performing other maintenance tasks, are stored in the C:\Windows\Temp folder.
▲ *Offline files.* Offline files are stored in the client-side caching (CSC) folder, which is C:\Windows\CSC. This folder is created and managed by the Offline Files utility, which allows users to work with files in the folder when the computer is not connected to the corporate network. Later, when a connection happens, Windows syncs up the offline files and folders stored in the C:\Windows\CSC folder with those on the network.

> **✎ Notes** Most often, Windows is installed on drive C:, although in a dual-boot environment, one OS might be installed on C: and another on a different drive. For example, Windows 7 can be installed on C: and Windows 8 installed on E:. Also, drive C: for one OS in a dual-boot system is likely to have a different drive letter in the other OS.
>
> If the drive letter of the Windows volume is not known, it is written in Microsoft documentation as *%SystemDrive%*. For example, the location of the Program Files folder is written as *%SystemDrive%*\Program Files.

USE THE DISK CLEANUP UTILITY

Begin cleaning up the drive by finding out how much free space the drive has. Then use the Windows Disk Cleanup (cleanmgr.exe) utility to delete temporary files on the drive.

APPLYING | CONCEPTS USE DISK CLEANUP

A+
220-902
1.7

Follow these steps to find out how much free space is on the drive, and use Disk Cleanup:

1. Open Windows 8 File Explorer or Windows 7 Windows Explorer and right-click the volume on which Windows is installed, most likely drive C:. Select **Properties** from the shortcut menu. The drive Properties box appears, as shown on the left side of Figure 3-2. You can see the free space on this drive C: is 155 GB, which is about 37 percent of the volume.

(continues)

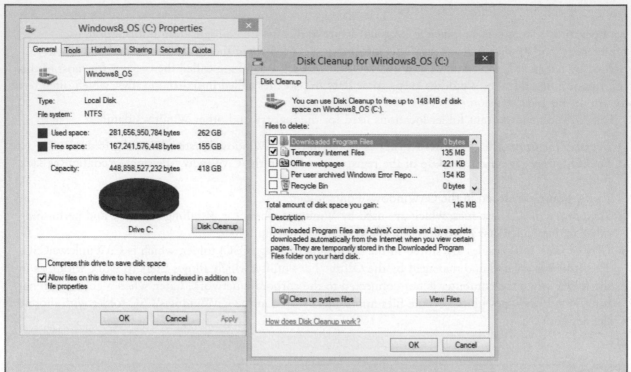

Figure 3-2   Use File Explorer to find out how much free space is on drive C:

2. On the General tab, click **Disk Cleanup**. (Alternatively, you can access the utility by executing the **cleanmgr.exe** program.) Disk Cleanup calculates how much space can be freed and then displays the Disk Cleanup box, shown on the right side of Figure 3-2. Select the files you want to delete.

3. Click **Clean up system files** to see temporary system files that you can also delete. The Disk Cleanup tab in Figure 3-3a shows the result for one computer. Notice in the figure the option to delete files from Previous Windows installation(s), which can free up additional hard drive space. This space is used by the Windows. old folder, which was created when Windows 8 was installed as an upgrade from Windows 7 and stored the old Windows, Program Files, and User folders in the Windows.old folder. If the user assures you that no information, data, or settings are needed from the old Windows installation, it's safe to delete these files to free up the space.

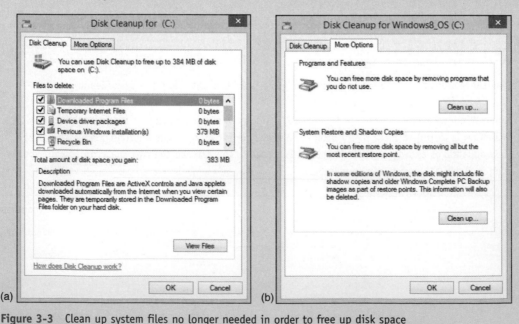

Figure 3-3   Clean up system files no longer needed in order to free up disk space

4. If you still need more free space, click the **More Options** tab (see Figure 3-3b) in the Disk Cleanup box. In the Programs and Features area, click **Clean up**. You are taken to the Programs and Features window where you can uninstall unneeded software to recover that space. Also on the More Options tab in the Disk Cleanup box, when you click **Clean up** under the System Restore and Shadow Copies area, Windows will delete all but the most recent restore points that are created by System Restore. (You will learn more about System Restore later in this chapter.)

DEFRAG THE HARD DRIVE

Two types of hard drives are magnetic hard disk drives (HDDs), which contain spinning platters, and solid-state drives (SSDs), which contain flash memory. For magnetic hard drives, Windows automatically defragments the drive once a week. To defragment is to rearrange fragments or parts of files on the drive so each file is stored on the drive in contiguous clusters.

In a file system, a cluster, also called a file allocation unit, is a group of whole sectors. The number of sectors in a cluster is fixed and is determined when the file system is first installed. A file is stored in whole clusters, and the unused space at the end of the last cluster, called slack, is wasted free space. As files are written and deleted from a drive, clusters are used, released, and used again. New files written on the drive can be put in available clusters spread over the drive. Over time, drive performance is affected when the moving read/write arm of a magnetic drive must move over many areas of the drive to collect all the fragments of a file. Defragmenting a drive rewrites files in contiguous clusters and improves drive performance.

Because a solid-state drive has no moving parts, defragmenting does not improve read/write time. In fact, defragmenting a solid-state drive can reduce the life of the drive and is not recommended. Windows disables defragmenting for solid-state drives.

> **Notes** To find out what type of hard drive is installed, use Device Manager or the System Information window (msinfo32.exe). For example, Figure 3-4 shows the Windows 8 System Information window drilled down to the Storage Disks area, and you can see the model information for two hard drives installed in the system. A quick search on the web shows the first hard drive is a magnetic HDD and the second hard drive is SSD.

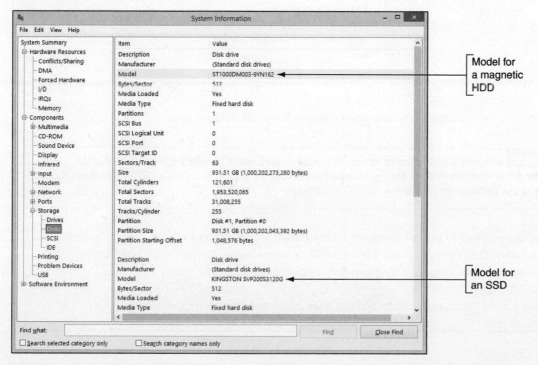

Figure 3-4 Use the System Information window to find the brand and model number for the hard drive

APPLYING | CONCEPTS   VERIFY SCHEDULED DRIVE MAINTENANCE

> **A+**
> **220-902**
> **1.7**

To verify that Windows 8/7/Vista is defragmenting a magnetic drive and not defragmenting a solid-state drive, do the following:

1. Use Explorer to open the Properties box for a drive and click the **Tools** tab (see the left side of Figure 3-5), and then click **Optimize** (or **Defragment now** in 7/Vista). In the Optimize Drives box (Disk Defragmenter in 7/Vista), as shown on the right side of Figure 3-5, verify the defrag settings. This system has two hard drives installed. Drive C: is an SSD and drive D: is a magnetic HDD. To have Windows tell you if a drive needs defragmenting, select a drive and click **Analyze** (**Analyze disk** in 7/Vista).

2. In Figure 3-5, you can see optimization is turned off. To turn it on for drive D:, select the drive and click **Turn on**. In the box that appears, which is showing in the bottom of the figure, check **Run on a schedule (recommended)** and select **Weekly** for the Frequency. Click **OK**.

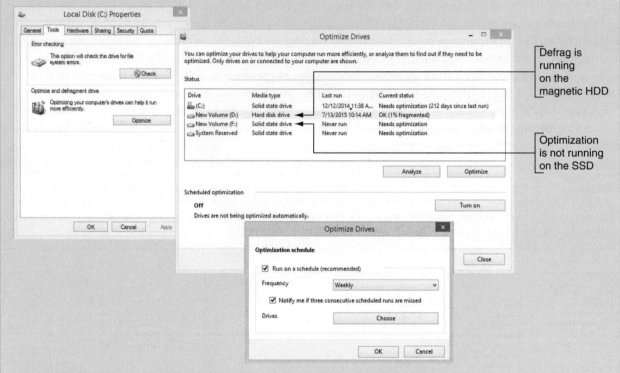

Figure 3-5   Windows is set to automatically defragment a magnetic hard drive once a week

---

◊ OS Differences   Windows 8 can optimize an SSD to release unused space to reduce the number of write operations to the drive. Windows 7/Vista does not support optimizing an SSD. To optimize an SSD in Windows 8, select the drive in the Optimize Drives window and click **Optimize.**

---

3. If the drive is more than 10 percent fragmented, click **Optimize** (**Defragment now** in 7/Vista) to defrag the drive immediately. The process can take a few minutes to several hours. If errors occur while the drive is defragmenting, check the hard drive for errors and try to defragment again.

You can also use the defrag command to defrag a drive from a command prompt window.

CHECK THE HARD DRIVE FOR ERRORS

Next, to make sure the drive is healthy, you need to search for and repair file system errors. The error-checking utility searches for bad sectors on a volume and recovers the data from them if possible. It then marks the sector as bad so that it will not be reused.

To use the error-checking utility in Explorer, right-click the drive, and select **Properties** from the shortcut menu. Click the **Tools** tab, and then click **Check** (**Check now** in 7/Vista). In the Error-checking dialog box, click **Scan drive**. (In 7/Vista, check **Automatically fix file system errors** and **Scan for and attempt recovery of bad sectors** in the Check Disk dialog box, and then click **Start**.) For the utility to correct errors on the drive, it needs exclusive use of all files on the drive. When Windows has exclusive use, the drive is called a locked drive. Therefore, a dialog box appears telling you about the problem and asking your permission to scan the drive the next time Windows starts. Reboot the system and let her rip.

You can also use the chkdsk command from the command prompt window to check a drive for errors.

FREE UP SPACE ON THE DRIVE

To free up some space on the hard drive, consider these tips:

▲ *Uninstall software you no longer use.* Doing so will free up some space on the hard drive, and, if the software loads a service or program during Windows startup, Windows startup might see performance improvement.

▲ *Move data off the drive.* Consider moving home videos, movies, photos, and other data to an external hard drive or burning them to DVDs or CDs, or transfer them to an online storage service such as Microsoft's OneDrive or Google's Drive.

▲ *Move programs off the drive.* If your Windows volume needs more free space, you can uninstall a program and reinstall it on a second hard drive installed in the system. An installation routine usually gives you the option to point to another location to install the program other than the default C:\Program Files or C:\Program Files (x86) folder.

▲ *Use drive or folder compression.* Windows offers drive and folder compression that can save on hard drive space. However, it is not recommended that you compress the volume on which Windows is stored. To compress a folder or file on an NTFS drive, open the file or folder **Properties** box, and click **Advanced** on the General tab. Then click **Compress contents to save disk space**, and click **OK**.

✎ **Notes** Windows installs on an NTFS volume, but if a second volume on the drive is formatted using the FAT32 file system, you can convert the volume to NTFS. For large drives, NTFS is more efficient and converting might improve performance. NTFS also offers better security and file and folder compression. For two Microsoft Knowledge Base articles about converting from FAT to NTFS, go to *support.microsoft.com* and search for articles 156560 and 314097. The first article discusses the amount of free space you'll need to make the conversion, and the second article tells you how to convert.

MOVE THE VIRTUAL MEMORY PAGING FILE

Windows uses a file, Pagefile.sys, in the same way it uses memory. This file is called virtual memory and is used to enhance the amount of RAM in a system. Normally, the file, pagefile.sys, is a hidden file stored in the root directory of drive C:. To save space on drive C:, you can move Pagefile.sys to another volume on the same hard drive or to a different hard drive, but don't move it to a different hard drive unless you know the other hard drive is at least as fast as this drive. If the drive is at least as fast as the drive on which Windows is installed, performance should improve. Also, make sure the new volume has plenty of free space to hold the file—at least three times the amount of installed RAM.

★ **A+ Exam Tip** The A+ 220-902 exam expects you to know how to configure virtual memory for optimal performance.

APPLYING | CONCEPTS   CHANGE THE LOCATION OF PAGEFILE.SYS

To change the location of Pagefile.sys in Windows 8/7/Vista, follow these steps:

1. Open the System window and click **Advanced system settings** in the left pane. The System Properties box appears with the Advanced tab selected (see Figure 3-6).

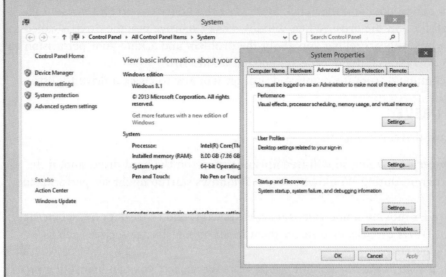

Figure 3-6   Manage virtual memory using the System Properties box

2. In the Performance section, click **Settings**. In the Performance Options box, select the **Advanced** tab and click **Change**. The Virtual Memory dialog box appears.

3. Uncheck **Automatically manage paging file size for all drives** (see Figure 3-7). Select the drive where you want to move the paging file. For best performance, allow Windows to manage the size of the paging file. If necessary, select **System managed size** and click **Set**.

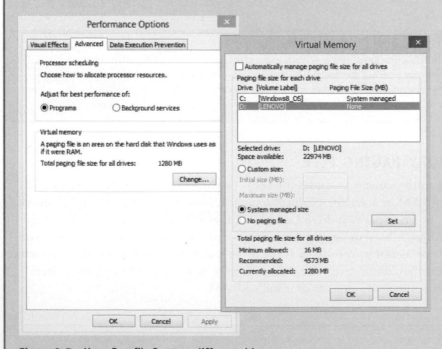

Figure 3-7   Move Pagefile.Sys to a different drive

3

4. Click **OK**. Windows informs you that you must restart the system for the change to take effect. Click **OK** to close the warning box.

5. Click **Apply** and close all boxes. Then restart the system.

If you still don't have enough free space on the Windows volume, consider adding a second hard drive to the system. In fact, if you install a second hard drive that is faster than the Windows hard drive, know that reinstalling Windows on the faster hard drive will improve performance. You can then use the slower and older hard drive for data.

 Notes If the Windows system is still slow and sluggish, know that later in the course you'll learn more about how to optimize Windows so it performs better.

Hands-On | Project 3-1 Perform Routine Maintenance

A+
220-902
1.7

Sign in to a Windows 8 or Windows 7 system using a Standard user account. Step through the process described in the chapter to do the following routine maintenance. As you work, note which chores you cannot perform unless you know the password to an administrator account. Do the following:

1. Verify critical Windows settings in Windows Update, anti-malware software, and the Network and Sharing Center.

2. Use the Disk Cleanup utility to clean up the hard drive.

3. Find out the brand and model of the hard drive that holds Windows. What is the brand and model? Is the drive a magnetic or solid-state drive? How do you know?

4. Check defrag settings and change them as necessary. Analyze the hard drive and determine if it needs defragmenting or optimizing. If so, optimize the drive.

5. Check the hard drive for errors.

6. Compress the My Documents folder.

Now let's look at how to perform on-demand backups and to schedule routine backups.

BACKUP PROCEDURES

A+
220-902
1.1, 1.4,
1.5, 1.7,
3.3

A backup is an extra copy of a data or software file that you can use if the original file becomes damaged or destroyed. Losing data due to system failure, a virus, file corruption, or some other problem really makes you appreciate the importance of having backups.

 Notes With data and software, here's a good rule of thumb: If you can't get along without it, back it up.

APPLYING | CONCEPTS BACKUPS PAY OFF

Dave was well on his way to building a successful career as an IT repair technician. His PC repair shop was doing well, and he was excited about his future. But one bad decision changed everything. He was called to repair a server at a small accounting firm. The call was on the weekend when he was normally off, so he was in a hurry to get the job done. He arrived at the accounting firm and saw that the problem was an easy one to fix, so he decided not to do a backup before working on the system. During his repairs, the hard drive crashed and all data on the drive was lost—four million dollars' worth! The firm sued, Dave's business license was stripped, and he was ordered to pay the money the company lost. A little extra time to back up the system would have saved his whole future. True story!

Because most of us routinely write data to the hard drive, in this section, we focus on backing up from the hard drive to another media. However, when you store important data on any media—such as a flash drive, external hard drive, or CD—always keep a copy of the data on another media. Never trust important data to only one media.

In this part of the chapter, you learn how to make a disaster recovery plan and then learn how to use Windows to back up user data, critical Windows system files, and entire volumes.

PLANNING FOR DISASTER RECOVERY

A+
220-902
1.1, 1.7

The time to prepare for disaster is before it occurs. If you have not prepared, the damage from a disaster will most likely be greater than if you had made and followed disaster recovery plans. Suppose the hard drive on your computer stopped working and you lost all its data. What would be the impact? Are you prepared for this to happen? Here are decisions you need to make for your backup and recovery plans:

▲ *Decide on the backup destination.* For example, options include online backup, network drive, CD, DVD, Blu-ray, SD card, USB flash drive, external hard drive, or other media. Here are points to keep in mind:

  ▲ For individuals or small organizations, an online backup service such as Carbonite (*carbonite.com*) or Mozy (*mozy.com*) is the easiest, most reliable, and most expensive solution. You pay a yearly subscription for the service, and they guarantee your backups, which are automatically done when your computer is connected to the Internet. If you decide to use one of these services, be sure to restore files from backup occasionally to make sure your backups are happening as you expect and that you can recover a lost file.

  ▲ Even though it's easy to do, don't make the mistake of backing up your data to another volume or folder on your same hard drive. When a hard drive crashes, most likely all volumes go down together and you will have lost your data and your backup. Back up to another media and, for extra safety, store it at an off-site location.

▲ *Decide on the backup software.* Windows offers a backup utility. However, you can purchase third-party backup software that might offer more features. An external hard drive often comes with backup software already installed on the drive. However, before you decide to use an all-in-one backup system, be certain you understand the risks of not keeping backups at an off-site location and keeping all your backups on a single media.

▲ *Decide how simple or complex your backup strategy needs to be.* A backup and recovery plan for individuals or small organizations might be very simple. But large organizations might require backups be documented each day, scheduled at certain times of the day or night, and recovery plans tested on a regular basis. Know the requirements of your organization when creating a backup and recovery plan. As a general rule of thumb, back up data for about every 4 to 6 hours of data entry. This might mean a backup needs to occur twice a day, daily, weekly, or monthly. Find out the data entry habits of workers before making your backup schedule and deciding on the folders or volumes to back up.

After you have a backup plan working, test the recovery plan. In addition, you need to occasionally retest the recovery plan to make sure all is still working as you expect. Do the following:

⬩ **Test the recovery process.** Erase a file on the hard drive, and use the recovery procedures to verify that you can re-create the file from the backup. This verifies that the backup medium works, that the recovery software is effective, and that you know how to use it. After you are convinced that the recovery works, document how to perform it.

⬩ **Keep backups in a safe place and routinely test them.** Don't leave a backup disk lying around for someone to steal. Backups of important and sensitive data should be kept under lock and key at an off-site location. In case of fire, keep enough backups off-site so that you can recover data even if the entire building is destroyed. Routinely verify that your backups are good by performing a test recovery of a backed-up file or folder. Backups are useless if the data on the backup is corrupted.

> ★ **A+ Exam Tip** The A+ 220-902 exam expects you to know how to create and use backups and best practices when scheduling backups.

Now let's see how to back up user data, important Windows system files, and the entire Windows volume. We begin with how to back up user data.

BACK UP USER DATA WITH WINDOWS 8 FILE HISTORY

A+
220-902
1.1, 1.4, 1.5,
1.7, 3.3

Windows 8 File History backs up user data stored in several locations, including Windows 8 libraries, user desktop, Internet Explorer favorites, contact folders, and offline OneDrive files (for Microsoft accounts). When the backup is enabled, it first makes a full backup to another media. By default, it scans for file and folder changes every hour and keeps as many generations of backups as it has free space on the storage device.

The File History utility is available as a window on the Windows desktop or an app in the Windows 8 interface. For most control over the utility, use the window on the desktop. Follow these steps:

1. First connect your backup device. Open Control Panel in Classic view, and then click **File History**. Figure 3-8 shows a File History window that recognizes a drive to hold the backups. The drive in the figure is an external hard drive with plenty of free space. To turn on File History, click **Turn on**.

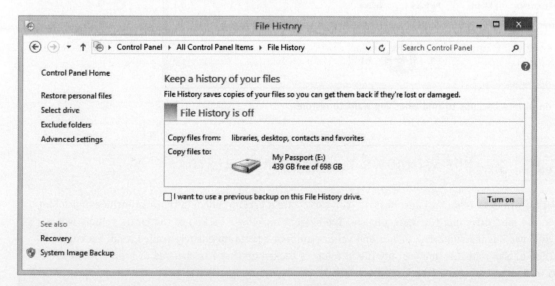

Figure 3-8 Turn on and off File History and control its settings

2. To manage these backups, click **Advanced settings**. On the Advanced Settings window, you can set
how often backups are made (every 10 minutes up to daily) and how long old backups should be kept
(forever, until space is needed, 1 month, 1 year, and so forth). You can also view a history of events and
clean up old backups to free up space.

> ✎ **Notes** To open File History in the Windows 8 interface, open the **Settings** charm and click **Change PC settings**. In
> the PC settings pane, click **Update and recovery** and then click **File History**.

USE FILE HISTORY TO RECOVER A CORRUPTED OR LOST FILE OR FOLDER

To recover items from File History backups, in the File History window, click **Restore personal files**. In the
window that appears (see Figure 3-9), use the left and right arrow keys on either side of the green button
at the bottom of the window to select a backup and drill down into a backup to find the file or folder you
need. Select an item to see a preview, and then click the green **Restore** button at the bottom of the window
to restore it. If you prefer to save the previous version in a different location so as not to lose the newest
version of that file, right-click the **Restore** button, and click **Restore to**. Navigate to the location where you
want to save the previous version, and then click **Select Folder**.

Figure 3-9   Drill down into backups to find what you want to restore

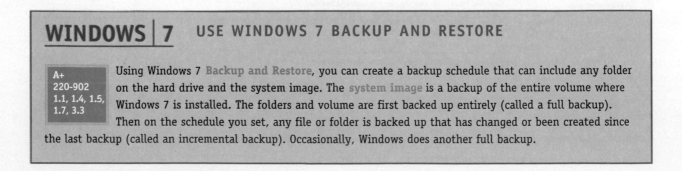

WINDOWS | 7   USE WINDOWS 7 BACKUP AND RESTORE

**A+
220-902
1.1, 1.4, 1.5,
1.7, 3.3**

Using Windows 7 Backup and Restore, you can create a backup schedule that can include any folder
on the hard drive and the system image. The system image is a backup of the entire volume where
Windows 7 is installed. The folders and volume are first backed up entirely (called a full backup).
Then on the schedule you set, any file or folder is backed up that has changed or been created since
the last backup (called an incremental backup). Occasionally, Windows does another full backup.

Follow these steps to learn how to set up a backup schedule using Windows 7 Backup and Restore:

1. Open Control Panel in Classic view, and click **Backup and Restore**. If no backup has ever been scheduled on the system, the window will look like the one shown in Figure 3-10. Click **Set up backup**.

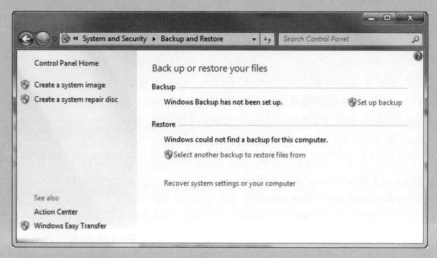

Figure 3-10 Use the Backup and Restore window in Windows 7 to create a system image

2. In the next dialog box (see Figure 3-11), select the media to hold the backup. In Figure 3-11, choices are volume E: (a second internal hard drive), the DVD drive, and OneTouch (an external hard drive). Make your selection and click **Next**.

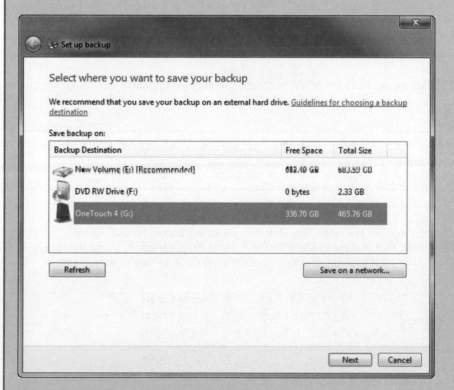

Figure 3-11 Select the destination media to hold the backup

(continues)

> ✎ **Notes** Windows 7 Professional, Ultimate, and Enterprise editions allow you to save the backup to a network location. To use a shared folder on the network for the backup destination, click **Save on a network** (see Figure 3-11). In the resulting box, click **Browse** and point to the folder. Also enter the user name and password on the remote computer that the backup utility will use to authenticate to that computer when it makes the backup. You cannot save to a network location when using Windows 7 Home editions. For these editions, the button *Save on a network* is missing in the window where you select the backup destination.

3. In the next box, you can allow Windows to decide what to back up or decide to choose for yourself. Select **Let me choose** so that you can select the folders to back up. Click **Next**.

4. In the next box, select the libraries and folders you want to back up. Click the white triangle beside Local Disk (C:) to drill down to any folder on the hard drive for backup. Check folders or libraries to back up. If the backup media can hold the system image, the option to include the image is selected by default. If you don't want to include the image, uncheck it. Click **Next** to continue. Here are folders that might contain important user data:

   ◢ Application data is usually found in C:\Users*username*\AppData.
   ◢ Internet Explorer favorites are in C:\Users*username*\Favorites.
   ◢ Better still, back up the entire user profile at C:\Users*username*.
   ◢ Even better, back up all user profiles at C:\Users.

5. In the next box, verify the correct folders and libraries are selected. To change the default schedule, click **Change schedule**. In the next box, you can choose to run the backup daily, weekly, or monthly and select the time of day. Make your selections, and click **OK**.

6. Review your backup settings, and click **Save settings and run backup**. The backup proceeds. A shadow copy is made of any open files so that files that are currently open are included in the backup.

> ★ **A+ Exam Tip** The A+ 220-902 exam expects you to know what a shadow copy is.

Later, you can return to the Backup and Restore window to change the backup settings or to turn off the backup.

> ✎ **Notes** One limitation of Windows Backup and Restore is that you can have only one scheduled backup routine.

> ✎ **Notes** After Windows does a full backup, it only backs up files that have changed since the last full backup. Occasionally, it does another full backup. Each full backup is called a backup period. It keeps as many backup periods as it has space on the backup media. As the media fills, it deletes the oldest backup periods. To see how space is used on your backup media, click **Manage space** in the Backup and Restore window. In the Manage Windows Backup disk space, you can click **View backups** to delete a backup period, but be sure to keep the most recent backup periods.

RECOVER BACKED-UP ITEMS

To recover backed-up items, open the Windows 7 Backup and Restore window and scroll down to the bottom of the window and click **Restore my files**. The Restore Files box appears (see Figure 3-12). Note that if the *Restore my files* button is missing from the Backup and Restore window, your backup media might not be available to Windows. You might need to plug in the media and then use Windows Explorer to verify you can access the backup folder on the media.

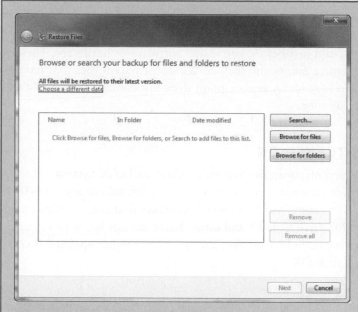

Figure 3-12   Locate the files and folders on the backup media to restore

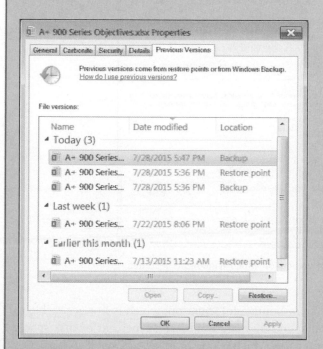

Figure 3-13   Restore a file or folder from a previous version

Use one of the three buttons on the window to locate the file or folder. *Search* allows you to search for a file or folder when you only know part of the file name or folder name. *Browse for files* allows you to drill down to the file to restore. *Browse for folders* allows you to search for the folder to restore. You can locate and select multiple files or folders to restore. Then follow the directions on screen to restore all the selected items.

To restore a folder or file to a previous version, follow these steps:

1. Use Windows Explorer to copy—not move—the corrupted folder or file to a new location. When you restore a file or folder to a previous version, the current file or folder can be overwritten by the previous version. By saving a copy of the current file or folder to a different location, you can revert to the copy if necessary.

2. Right-click the file or folder and select **Restore previous versions** from the shortcut menu. The Properties box for the file or folder appears with the Previous Versions tab selected. Windows displays a list of all previous versions of the file or folder it has kept (see Figure 3-13).

3. Select the version you want and click **Restore**. A message box asks if you are sure you want to continue. Click **Restore**, and then click **OK**.

4. Open the restored file or folder and verify it is the version you want. If you decide you need another version, delete the file or folder, and copy the file or folder you saved in Step 1 back into the original location. Then return to Step 2 and try again, this time selecting a different previous version.

BACK UP WINDOWS SYSTEM FILES

A+
220-902
1.1, 1.4, 1.5,
1.7, 3.3

The Windows System Protection utility automatically backs up system files and stores them on the hard drive at regular intervals and just before you install software or hardware. These snapshots of the system are called restore points and include Windows system files that have changed since the last restore point was made. A restore point does not contain all user data, and you can manually create a restore point at any time.

MAKE SURE SYSTEM PROTECTION IS TURNED ON

To make sure System Protection has not been turned off, open the System window, and click **System protection**. The System Protection tab of the System Properties box appears (see the left side of Figure 3-14). Make sure protection is turned on for the drive containing Windows, which indicates that restore points are created automatically. In Figure 3-14, protection for drive C: is on and other drives are not being protected. To make a change, click **Configure**. The System Protection box on the right side of the figure appears. If you make a change to this box, click **Apply**, and then click **OK**.

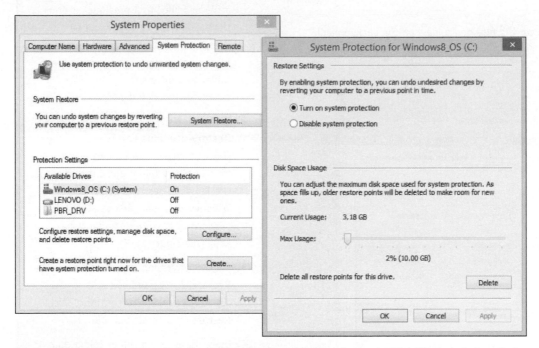

Figure 3-14   Make sure System Protection is turned on for the volume on which Windows is installed

Restore points are normally kept in the folder C:\System Volume Information, which is not accessible to the user. Restore points are taken at least every 24 hours, and they can use up to 15 percent of disk space. If disk space gets very low, restore points are no longer made, which is one more good reason to keep about 15 percent or more of the hard drive free.

MANUALLY CREATE A RESTORE POINT

To manually create a restore point, use the System Protection tab of the System Properties box, as shown on the left side of Figure 3-14. Click **Create**. In the System Protection box, enter a name for the restore point, such as "Before I tested software," and click **Create**. The restore point is created.

APPLY A RESTORE POINT

System Restore (rstrui.exe) restores the system to its condition at the time a restore point was made. If you restore the system to a previous restore point, user data on the hard drive will not be altered, but you can affect installed software and hardware, user settings, and OS configuration settings. When you use System Restore to roll back the system to a restore point, any changes made to these settings after the restore point was created are lost; therefore, always use the most recent restore point that can fix the problem so that you make the least intrusive changes to the system.

To return the system to a previous restore point and to practice opening a utility from the command prompt, do the following:

1. Click **Start**, type **rstrui.exe** in the Search box, and press **Enter**. The System Restore box opens. Click **Next**.

2. In the next box, the most recent restore points appear. For most situations, the most recent is the one to select so as to make the least possible changes to your system. Select a restore point (see Figure 3-15), and click **Next**.

3. Windows asks you to confirm your selection. Click **Finish** and respond to the warning box. The system restarts and the restore point is applied.

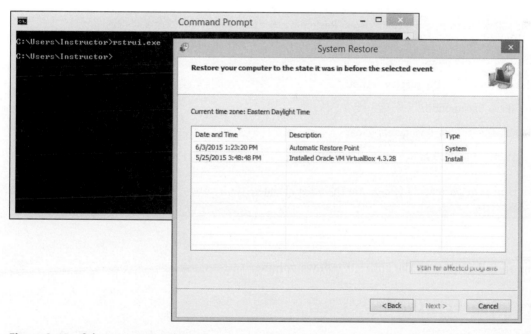

Figure 3-15 Select a restore point

POINTS TO REMEMBER ABOUT SYSTEM RESTORE

System Restore is a great tool to try to fix a device that is not working, restore Windows settings that are giving problems, or solve problems with applications. Although it's a great tool in some situations, it does have its limitations. Keep these points in mind:

▲ *Point 1:* System Restore won't help you if you don't have restore points to use. System Protection must be turned on so that restore points are automatically created.

▲ *Point 2:* Restore points replace certain keys in the registry but cannot completely rebuild a totally corrupted registry. Therefore, System Restore can recover from errors only if the registry is somewhat intact.

▲ *Point 3:* The restore process cannot remove a virus or worm infection. However, it might help you start a system that is infected with a virus that launches at startup. After Windows has started, you can then use anti-malware software to remove the infection.

▲ *Point 4:* System Restore might create a new problem. Often when using a restore point, anti-malware software gets all out of whack and sometimes even needs reinstalling. Therefore, use restore points sparingly.

▲ *Point 5:* System Restore might make many changes to a system. If you know which change caused a problem, try to undo that particular change first. The idea is to use the least invasive solution first. For example, if updating a driver has caused a problem, first try Driver Rollback to undo that change. Driver Rollback is performed using Device Manager.

▲ *Point 6:* Restore points are kept in a hidden folder on the hard drive. If that area of the drive is corrupted, the restore points are lost. Also, if a user turns System Protection off, all restore points are lost.

▲ *Point 7:* Viruses and other malware sometimes hide in restore points. To completely clean an infected system, you need to delete all restore points by turning System Protection off and back on.

▲ *Point 8:* If Windows will not start, you can launch System Restore using startup recovery tools, which are covered in the chapter, "Troubleshooting Windows Startup."

Hands-On | Project 3-2 Use System Restore

Do the following to find out how System Restore works and how it can affect a system:

1. Create a restore point.

2. Make a change to the display settings.

3. Change the desktop background.

4. Create a new text file in your Documents folder.

5. Restore the system using System Restore.

Is the text file still in your Documents folder? Are the other changes still in effect? Why or why not?

And now moving on to backing up the entire Windows volume.

WINDOWS 8 CUSTOM REFRESH IMAGE

A+
220-902
1.1, 1.4, 1.5,
1.7, 3.3

A custom refresh image is an image of the entire Windows volume, including the Windows installation, Windows 8 apps, desktop applications, and user settings and data. The best time to create the image is right after you've installed Windows, hardware, applications, and user accounts and customized Windows settings. The image is stored in a single file named CustomRefresh.wim in the folder you specify. The WIM file uses the Windows Imaging File (WIM) format, which is a compressed file that contains many related files.

Here are the steps to create a Windows 8 custom refresh image:

1. Open an elevated command prompt window. One way to do that is to press **Win+X** and click **Command Prompt (Admin)**. Respond to the UAC box. The Administrator: Command Prompt window opens.

2. Enter this command, substituting any drive and folder for that shown in the command line (see Figure 3-16):

```
recimg /createimage D:\MyImage
```

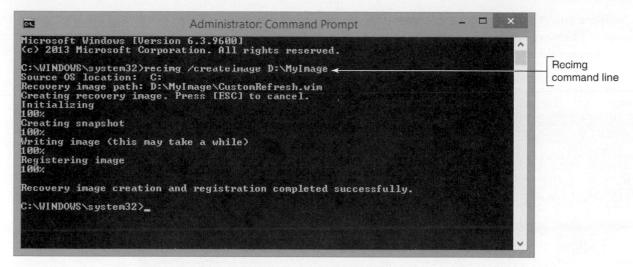

Figure 3-16 Use the recimg command to create a custom refresh image and register the image with the system

Creating the image takes some time and then the image and its location are registered as the active recovery image. The image is stored in a large file and you can view it using File Explorer (see Figure 3-17). You can create as many refresh images as you like, but only one is designated as the active recovery image, and it's the one that will be used when you refresh the Windows 8 installation. How to perform a Windows refresh is covered in the chapter, "Troubleshooting Windows Startup."

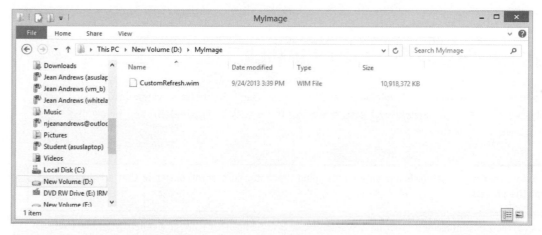

Figure 3-17 File Explorer shows the refresh image WIM file

The recimg command can also be used to manage refresh images. The parameters for the command are listed in Table 3-1.

Command	Description
recimg /createimage <path>	Creates the refresh image and registers its location as the active refresh image.
recimg /showcurrent	Displays the location of the active refresh image.
bcdedit /set {default} bootmenupolicy legacy	Deregisters the active recovery image. During the refresh process, Windows will not find an image and will revert to a hidden recovery partition on the hard drive or the Windows 8 setup files for the refresh.
recimg /setcurrent <path>	Registers a refresh image in the path given. The image at this location is now the active refresh image.

Table 3-1 The recimg command and parameters

Suppose you've created multiple refresh images and you want to select a particular image for a refresh. Figure 3-18 shows the commands you can use to change the active refresh image from the one stored in the D:\MyImage folder to one stored in the D:\MyImage2 folder.

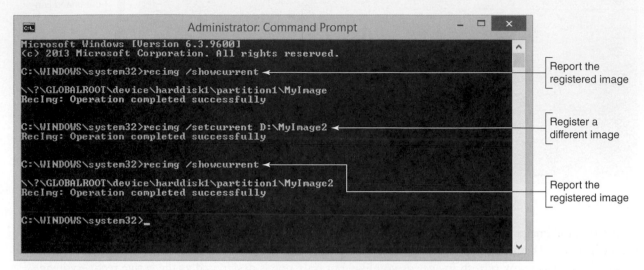

Figure 3-18 shows:

```
Administrator: Command Prompt                          –  □  ×

Microsoft Windows [Version 6.3.9600]
(c) 2013 Microsoft Corporation. All rights reserved.

C:\WINDOWS\system32>recimg /showcurrent          ◄── Report the
                                                      registered image
\\?\GLOBALROOT\device\harddisk1\partition1\MyImage
RecImg: Operation completed successfully

C:\WINDOWS\system32>recimg /setcurrent D:\MyImage2  ◄── Register a
RecImg: Operation completed successfully                different image

C:\WINDOWS\system32>recimg /showcurrent          ◄── Report the
                                                      registered image
\\?\GLOBALROOT\device\harddisk1\partition1\MyImage2
RecImg: Operation completed successfully

C:\WINDOWS\system32>_
```

Figure 3-18 Use the recimg command with parameters to manage refresh images

 Notes Because a refresh image must be named CustomRefresh.wim, you must store each image in a separate folder.

WINDOWS | 7   WINDOWS 7 SYSTEM IMAGE

A+
220-902
1.1, 1.4, 1.5,
1.7, 3.3

The backup of the Windows 7 volume is called a system image. To create a system image, click **Create a system image** in the Backup and Restore window (refer back to Figure 3-10) and follow directions on screen.

⚡ **Caution**   Before creating a system image on a laptop, plug the laptop into an AC outlet so that a failed battery will not interrupt the process.

Here are points to keep in mind when creating a system image and using it to recover a failed Windows volume:

▲ *A system image includes the entire drive C: or other drive on which Windows is installed.* When you restore a hard drive using the system image, everything on the volume is deleted and replaced with the system image.

▲ *A system image must always be created on an internal or external hard drive.* When scheduling the backup of your data folders, you can include the system image in the backup procedure. Even if the files and folders are being copied to a USB drive, CD, or DVD, the system image will always be copied to a hard drive.

▲ *Don't depend just on the system image as your backup.* You should also back up individual folders that contain user data. If individual data files or folders need to be recovered, you cannot rely on the system image because recovering data using the system image would totally replace the entire Windows volume with the system image.

▲ *You can create a system image any time after Windows is installed, and then you can use this image to recover from a failed hard drive.* Using the system image to recover a failed hard drive is called reimaging the drive. The details of how to reimage the drive are covered later in the chapter "Troubleshooting Windows Startup."

✎ **Notes** The system image you create can be installed only on the computer that was used to create it. A hardware-independent image is called a standard image and was discussed in the chapter "Installing Windows."

> 📝 **Notes** For backward compatibility, Windows 8 allows you to create a system image. To do so, click **System Image Backup** in the File History window. However, a custom refresh image is more flexible and easier to use than a system image.

> 🔄 **OS Differences** Windows Vista uses different backup methods than Windows 8 or 7 to back up user data, system files, and the Windows volume. The backup of the Vista volume is called the `Complete PC Backup`.

MANAGING FILES, FOLDERS, AND STORAGE DEVICES

A+
220-902
1.1, 1.2,
1.3, 1.4,
4.1

In this part of the chapter, you learn to manage files and folders on the hard drive and other storage devices using commands in a command prompt window and to manage hard drive partitions and volumes using the Disk Management utility. Let's begin the discussion with how partitions and file systems work in Windows.

HOW PARTITIONS AND FILE SYSTEMS WORK

A+
220-902
1.0

A hard drive is organized using sectors, blocks, partitions, volumes, and file systems. Let's see how it all works.

SECTORS AND BLOCKS

All data is stored on a magnetic hard drive in sectors, sometimes called records. Each sector on the drive is the same size, and for most hard drives, that size is 512 bytes. Sector markings used to organize the drive are done before it leaves the factory in a process called low-level formatting. The size of a sector and the total number of sectors on a drive determine the drive capacity. UEFI/BIOS and the OS can address groups of sectors on the drive in blocks, which is called Logical Block Addressing (LBA). SSD drives don't use sectors; space on an SSD drive is divided into blocks or LBAs that can be addressed by the UEFI/BIOS and OS. Today's drive capacities are measured in GB (gigabytes, roughly one million bytes) or TB (terabytes, roughly one trillion bytes).

> 📝 **Notes** For magnetic hard drives, each platter is divided into concentric circles called tracks, and each track is divided into sectors (see Figure 3-19). Magnetic drive sectors are usually 512 bytes, but blocks on SSDs can be larger: 4 KB or 16 KB.

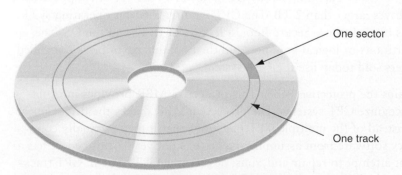

One sector

One track

Figure 3-19 A magnetic hard drive is divided into concentric circles called tracks, and tracks are divided into sectors

PARTITIONS

A drive is further divided into one or more partitions using one of two partitioning systems:

▲ *MBR partitions.* The Master Boot Record (MBR) partitioning system keeps a map of these partitions in a partition table stored in the very first sector on the hard drive called the MBR. The MBR system is required when a computer is using a 32-bit operating system, legacy BIOS, or UEFI in CSM mode. The MBR partition table can track up to four partitions on a drive. A drive can have one, two, or three primary partitions, also called volumes. The fourth partition is called an extended partition and can hold one or more volumes called logical drives, which are tracked in their own partition table separately from the primary partitions. Figure 3-20 shows how an MBR hard drive is divided into three primary partitions and one extended partition.

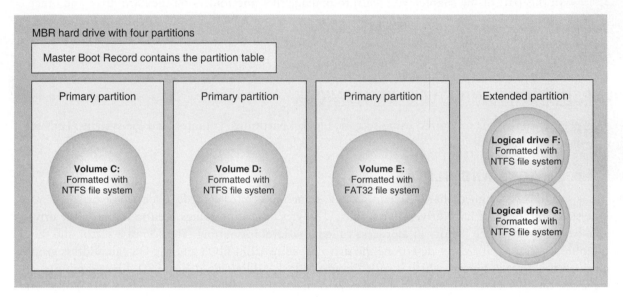

Figure 3-20   A hard drive with four partitions; the fourth partition is an extended partition

★ **A+ Exam Tip**   The A+ 220-902 exam expects you to know the difference between a primary and extended partition and between a volume and logical drive on an MBR hard drive.

▲ *GPT partitions.* The Globally Unique Identifier Partition Table (GUID or GPT) system can support up to 128 partitions and is required for drives larger than 2 TB. The GPT requires a 64-bit operating system and UEFI firmware enabled and is needed to use Secure Boot, a feature of UEFI and the OS. The GPT system does not use extended partitions or logical volumes, and the bootable partition is not called an active partition. Most new computers sold today use the GPT system.

The first sector in a GPT system contains the protective MBR. This protective MBR provides information to legacy software that doesn't recognize GPT systems. The protective MBR makes the drive appear to consist of a single MBR partition instead of the multiple GPT partitions that it might actually contain, but this is sufficient to keep legacy software from assuming the drive is not yet partitioned or has a corrupted MBR system, which it might attempt to repair and, thus, destroy the GPT system. GPT tracks all partitions in a single partition table, which it stores in the GPT header immediately following the protective MBR. GPT systems also back up the partition table at the end of the disk (see Figure 3-21). On Windows systems, there can be up to 128 partitions in between the two GPT headers.

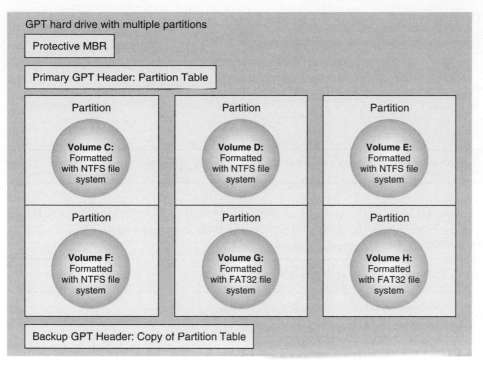

Figure 3-21 A hard drive using GPT

FILE SYSTEM

Before a partition or drive can be used, it must be assigned a drive letter such as C: or D: and formatted using a file system. Recall that the file system is the overall structure an OS uses to name, store, and organize files on a drive. Windows 8 and Windows 7 support three types of file systems for hard drives: NTFS, FAT32, and exFAT. NTFS is the most reliable and secure and is used for the volume on which Windows is installed. Installing a drive letter, file system, and root directory on a volume is called formatting the drive, also called high-level formatting, and can happen during the Windows installation.

> **✎ Notes** In most Microsoft documentation, a partition is called a partition until it is formatted with a file system, and then it is called a volume.

Here is a list of file systems supported by Windows that you can choose for volumes and drives that don't hold the Windows installation:

◢ *NTFS.* Choose the NTFS file system for hard drives because it uses smaller allocation units or cluster sizes than FAT32, which means it makes more efficient use of disk space when storing many small files. NTFS is more reliable; gives fewer errors; supports encryption, disk quotas (limiting the hard drive space available to a user), file and folder compression; and offers better security. As an example of the better security with NTFS, if you boot the system from another boot media such as a CD, you can access a volume using a FAT file system. If the volume uses NTFS, an administrator password is required to gain access.

◢ *ReFS.* The latest file system by Microsoft is the Resilient File System (ReFS), designed to improve on the NTFS file system by offering better fault tolerance (eliminating the need for repairs using chkdsk) and allowing for better compatibility with virtualization and data redundancy in a RAID system. ReFS is not widely used on personal computers, but it is expected to eventually replace NTFS. The 64-bit version of Windows 8.1 supports ReFS.

◢ *exFAT*. Choose the exFAT file system for large external storage devices that you want to use with other operating systems. For example, you can use a smart card formatted with exFAT in a Mac or Linux computer or in a digital camcorder, camera, or smart phone. exFAT uses the same structure as the older FAT32 file system, but with a 64-bit-wide file allocation table (FAT). exFAT does not use as much overhead as the NTFS file system and is designed to handle very large files, such as those used for multimedia storage.

◢ *FAT32*. Use FAT32 for small hard drives or USB flash drives because it does not have as much overhead as NTFS.

> ⭐ **A+ Exam Tip**   The A+ 220-902 exam expects you to know about the FAT32, exFAT, NTFS, and CDFS file systems.

◢ *CDFS and UDF*. CDFS (Compact Disk File System) is an older file system used by optical discs (CDs, DVDs, and BDs), and is being replaced by the newer UDF (Universal Disk Format) file system.

> ↻ **OS Differences**   For Windows Vista, the exFAT file system is available only if Service Pack 1 is installed.

HOW PARTITIONS ARE USED DURING THE BOOT

With MBR hard drives, one of the primary partitions is designated the active partition, which is the bootable partition that startup UEFI/BIOS turns to when searching for an operating system to start up. In GPT systems, this bootable partition is called the EFI System Partition (ESP), and UEFI turns to this partition to find and start the operating system. The OS program it looks for in this partition and starts is called the boot loader or boot manager.

In Windows, the MBR active partition or the ESP System Partition is called the system partition and, for Windows 8/7, the boot manager is named BootMgr (with no file extension). The boot manager turns to the volume that is designated the boot partition, where the Windows operating system is stored, and continues the process of starting Windows.

In Figure 3-22, you can see an example of an MBR hard drive in a two-drive system. In this computer, disk 0 is an SSD and disk 1 is a magnetic hard drive. The OS is stored on disk 0, which makes for a faster boot. On disk 0, the first partition is the System Reserved partition and is designated the active partition and the Windows system partition. The boot partition is drive C: where Windows is stored. Figure 3-23 shows a GPT system that contains a single hard drive. It contains a recovery partition, the EFI System Partition, and drive C:, which is designated the boot partition and holds the Windows 8 installation.

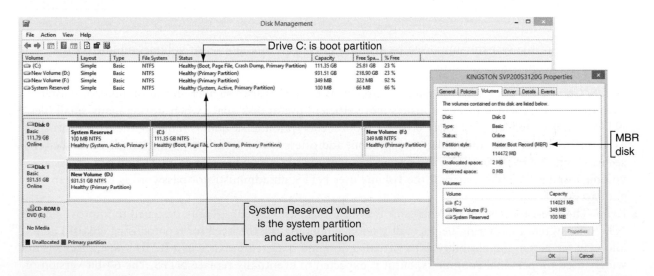

Figure 3-22   Two MBR disks with Windows 8 installed on disk 0

Notes In Figures 3-22 and 3-23, to view the Properties box for a hard drive, right-click the Disk box on the far-left side of the window and click **Properties** in the shortcut menu. Click the Volumes tab to see the type of disk, MBR or GPT.

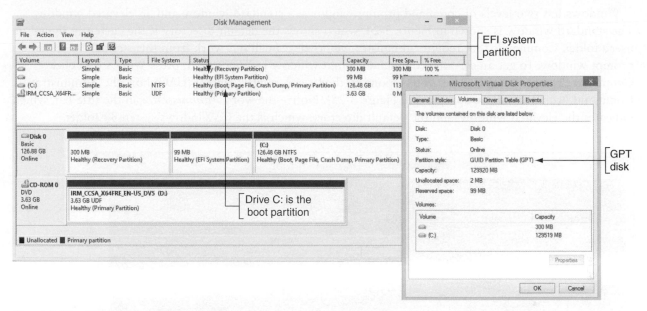

Figure 3-23 GPT disk with Windows 8 installed

Notes Don't be confused by the terminology here. It is really true that, according to Windows terminology, the Windows OS is on the boot partition, and the boot manager is on the system partition, although that might seem backward. The computer starts or boots from the system partition and loads the Windows operating system from the boot partition.

COMMANDS TO MANAGE FILES AND FOLDERS

A+
220-902
1.1, 1.2, 1.3,
1.4, 4.1

IT support technicians find it is much faster to manipulate files and folders using commands in a command prompt window than when using File Explorer (or Windows Explorer in Windows 7). In addition, in some troubleshooting situations, you have no other option but to use a command prompt window. For Windows 8, to open the command prompt window, press **Win+X** and click **Command Prompt**. The command prompt window is shown in Figure 3-24.

Figure 3-24 Use the exit command to close the command prompt window

Windows has two levels of command prompt windows: a standard window and an elevated window. The standard window is shown in Figure 3-24, which shows the default directory is the currently signed-in user's folder. Commands that require administrative privileges will not work from this standard command prompt window. To get an elevated command prompt window in Windows 8, press **Win+X** and click **Command Prompt** (**Admin**). After you respond to the User Account Control (UAC) box, the Administrator: Command Prompt window appears (see Figure 3-25). Notice the word *Administrator* in the title bar, which indicates the elevated window, and the default directory, which is the C:\Windows\system32 folder.

Figure 3-25   An elevated command prompt window has administrative privileges

Here are some tips for working in a command prompt window:

◢ Type **cls** and press **Enter** to clear the window.
◢ To retrieve the last command you entered, press the up arrow. To retrieve the last command line one character at a time, press the right arrow.
◢ To terminate a command before it is finished, press **Ctrl+C**, **Ctrl+Break**, or **Ctrl+Pause**.
◢ To close the window, type **exit** (see Figure 3-25) and press **Enter**.

If the command you are using applies to files or folders, the path to these files or folders is assumed to be the default drive and directory. The default drive and directory, also called the current drive and directory, shows in the command prompt. It is the drive and directory that the command will use if you don't give a drive and directory in the command line. For example, in Figure 3-24, the default drive is C: and the default path is C:\Users\Jill West. If you use a different path in the command line, the path you use overrides the default path. Also know that Windows makes no distinction between uppercase and lowercase in command lines (however, Linux does).

Now let's look at the file-naming conventions you will need to follow when creating files, wildcard characters you can use in command lines, and several commands useful for managing files and folders.

FILE-NAMING CONVENTIONS

When using the command prompt window to create a file, keep in mind that file name and file extension characters can be the letters *a* through *z*, the numbers *0* through *9*, and the following characters:

```
_ ^ $ ~ ! # % & - { } ( ) @ ' `
```

In a command prompt window, if a path or file name has spaces in it, it is sometimes necessary to enclose the path or file name in double quotation marks.

WILDCARD CHARACTERS IN COMMAND LINES

As you work at the command prompt, you can use wildcard characters in a file name to say that the command applies to a group of files or to abbreviate a file name if you do not know the entire name. The question mark (?) is a wildcard for one character, and the asterisk (*) is a wildcard for one or more characters. For example, if you want to find all files in a directory that start with *A* and have a three-letter file extension, you would use the following command:

```
dir a*.???
```

> **A+ Exam Tip** The A+ 220-902 exam expects you to know how to use the shutdown, md, rd, cd, del, format, copy, xcopy, robocopy, chkdsk, dir, exit, help, and expand commands, which are all covered in this section.

> **Notes** Many commands can use parameters in the command line to affect how the command will work. Parameters (also called options, arguments, or switches) often begin with a slash followed by a single character. In this chapter, you learn about the basic parameters used by a command for the most common tasks. For a full listing of the parameters available for a command, use the help command. Another way to learn about commands is to follow this link on the Microsoft website: *technet.microsoft.com/en-us/library/cc772390(WS.10).aspx*.

HELP OR <COMMAND NAME> /?

Use the help command to get help about any command. You can enter help followed by the command name or enter the command name followed by /?. Table 3-2 lists some sample applications of this command.

Command	Result
`help xcopy` `xcopy /?`	**Gets help about the xcopy command**
`help`	**Lists all commands**
`help xcopy | more`	**Lists information about the xcopy command one line at a time**

Table 3-2 Sample help commands

DIR [<FILENAME>] [/P] [/S] [/W]

Use the dir command to list files and directories. In Microsoft documentation about a command (also called the command syntax), the brackets [ ] in a command line indicate the parameter is optional. In addition, the parameter included in < >, such as <filename>, indicates that you can substitute any file name in the command. This file name can include a path or file extension. Table 3-3 lists some examples of the dir command.

Command	Result
dir /p	Lists one screen at a time
dir /w	Presents information using wide format, where details are omitted and files and folders are listed in columns on the screen
dir *.txt	Lists all files with a .txt file extension in the default path
dir d:\data*.txt	Lists all files with a .txt file extension in the D:\data folder
dir myfile.txt	Checks that a single file, such as myfile.txt, is present
dir /s	Includes subdirectory entries

Table 3-3   Sample dir commands

MD *[DRIVE:] PATH*

The md (make directory) command creates a subdirectory under a directory. Note that in the command lines in this section, the command prompt is not bolded, but the typed command is in bold. To create a directory named \game on drive C:, you can use this command:

C:\> **md C:\game**

The backslash indicates that the directory is under the root directory. If a path is not given, the default path is assumed. This command also creates the C:\game directory:

C:\> **md game**

To create a directory named chess under the \game directory, you can use this command:

C:\> **md C:\game\chess**

Figure 3-26 shows the result of the dir command on the directory game. Note the two initial entries in the directory table: . (dot) and .. (dot, dot). The md command creates these two entries when the OS initially sets up the directory. You cannot edit these entries with normal OS commands, and they must remain in the directory for the directory's lifetime. The . (dot) entry points to the subdirectory itself, and the .. (dot, dot) entry points to the parent directory, which, in this case, is the root directory.

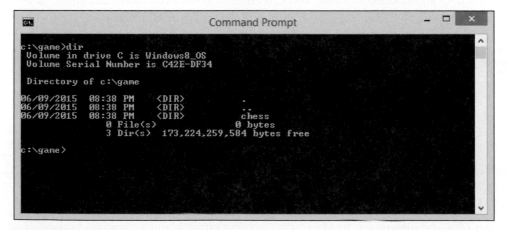

Figure 3-26   Results of the dir command on the game directory

CD [*DRIVE:*]*PATH OR CD..*

The cd (change directory) command changes the current default directory. You enter cd followed by the drive and the entire path that you want to be current, like so:

```
C:\> cd C:\game\chess
```

The command prompt now looks like this:

```
C:\game\chess>
```

To move from a child directory to its parent directory, use the .. (dot, dot) variation of the command:

```
C:\game\chess> cd..
```

The command prompt now looks like this:

```
C:\game>
```

Remember that .. (dot, dot) always means the parent directory. You can move from a parent directory to one of its child directories simply by stating the name of the child directory:

```
C:\game> cd chess
```

The command prompt now looks like this:

```
C:\game\chess>
```

Remember not to put a backslash in front of the child directory name; doing so tells the OS to go to a directory named chess that is directly under the root directory.

RD [*DRIVE:]PATH* [/S]

The rd (remove directory) command removes a directory. Unless you use the /s switch, three things must be true before you can use the rd command:

▲ The directory must contain no files.
▲ The directory must contain no subdirectories.
▲ The directory must not be the current directory.

A directory is ready for removal when only the . (dot) and .. (dot, dot) entries are present. For example, to remove the \game directory when it contains the chess directory, the chess directory must first be removed, like so:

```
C:\> rd C:\game\chess
```

Or, if the \game directory is the current directory, you can use this command:

```
C:\game> rd chess
```

After you remove the chess directory, you can remove the game directory. However, it's not good to attempt to saw off a branch while you're sitting on it; therefore, you must first leave the \game directory like so:

```
C:\game> cd..
```

```
C:\> cd \game
```

When you use the /s switch with the rd command, the entire directory tree is deleted, including all its subdirectories and files.

DEL OR ERASE *<FILENAME>*

The del or erase command erases files or groups of files. Note that in the command lines in this section, the command prompt is not bolded, but the typed command is in bold.

To erase the file named Myfile.txt, use the following command:

```
E:\> del myfile.txt
```

To erase all files in the current default directory, use the following command:

```
E:\Docs> del *.*
```

To erase all files in the E:\Docs directory, use the following command:

```
C:\> erase e:\docs\*.*
```

A few files don't have a file extension. To erase all files that are in the current directory and that have no file extensions, use the following command:

```
E:\Docs> del *.
```

REN *<FILENAME1>* *<FILENAME2>*

The ren (rename) command renames a file. *<filename1>* can include a path to the file, but *<filename2>* cannot. To rename Project.docx in the default directory to Project_Hold.docx:

```
E:\Docs> ren Project.docx Project_Hold.docx
```

To rename all .txt files to .doc files in the C:\Data folder:

```
ren C:\Data\*.txt *.doc
```

COPY *<SOURCE>* *[<DESTINATION>]* *[/V]* *[/Y]*

The copy command copies a single file or group of files. The original files are not altered. To copy a file from one drive to another, use a command similar to this one:

```
E:\> copy C:\Data\Myfile.txt E:\mydata\Newfile.txt
```

The drive, path, and file name of the source file immediately follow the copy command. The drive, path, and file name of the destination file follow the source file name. If you don't specify the file name of the destination file, the OS assigns the file's original name to this copy. If you omit the drive or path of the source or the destination, then the OS uses the current default drive and path.

To copy the file Myfile.txt from the root directory of drive C: to drive E:, use the following command:

```
C:\> copy myfile.txt E:
```

Because the command does not include a drive or path before the file name Myfile.txt, the OS assumes that the file is in the default drive and path. Also, because there is no destination file name specified, the file written to drive E: will be named Myfile.txt.

To copy all files in the C:\Docs directory to the USB flash drive designated drive E:, use the following command:

```
C:\> copy c:\docs\*.* E:
```

To make a backup file named System.bak of the System file in the \Windows\system32\config directory of the hard drive, use the following command:

```
C:\Windows\system32\config> copy system system.bak
```

If you use the copy command to duplicate multiple files, the files are assigned the names of the original files. When you duplicate multiple files, the destination portion of the command line cannot include a file name. Here are two switches or parameters that are useful with the copy command:

◢ */v.* When the /v switch is used, the size of each new file is compared with the size of the original file. This slows down the copying, but verifies that the copy is done without errors.

◢ */y.* When the /y switch is used, a confirmation message does not appear asking you to confirm before overwriting a file.

> ✎ **Notes** When trying to recover a corrupted file, you can sometimes use the copy command to copy the file to new media, such as from the hard drive to a USB drive. During the copying process, if the copy command reports a bad or missing sector, choose the option to ignore that sector. The copying process then continues to the next sector. The corrupted sector will be lost, but others can likely be recovered. The recover command can be used to accomplish the same thing.

RECOVER *<FILENAME>*

Use the recover command to attempt to recover a file when parts of the file are corrupted. The command is best used from the Windows Recovery Environment. To use it, you must specify the name of a single file in the command line, like so:

```
C:\Data> recover Myfile.txt
```

EXPAND [/D] *<SOURCE>* [*<DESTINATION>*]

The expand command extracts files from compressed distribution files, which are often used to distribute files for software installations. Table 3-4 lists examples of the command.

Command	Result
expand /d \installme	**Lists files contained in the \installme folder. Does not expand or extract the files.**
expand myprogram.cab	**Extracts the files in the myprogram.cab file. A .cab file is a cabinet file, which is a type of distribution file that contains compressed files.**
expand myprogram.cab -f:myfile.exe	**Extracts only the myfile.exe file from the myprogram.cab cabinet file.**

Table 3-4 Sample expand commands

XCOPY *<SOURCE>* [*<DESTINATION>*] [/S] [/C] [/Y] [/D:DATE]

The xcopy command is more powerful than the copy command. It follows the same general command-source-destination format as the copy command, but it offers several more options. Table 3-5 shows some of these options.

Command	Result
xcopy C:\docs*.* E: /s	**Use the /s switch to include subdirectories in the copy; this command copies all files in the directory C:\docs, as well as all subdirectories under \docs and their files, to drive E, unless the subdirectory is empty**
xcopy C:\docs*.* E: /e	**Same as /s but empty subdirectories are included in the copy**
xcopy C:\docs*.* E: /d:03-14-15	**The /d switch examines the date; this command copies all files from the directory C:\docs created or modified on or after March 14, 2015**
xcopy C:\docs*.* E: /y	**Use the /y switch to overwrite existing files without prompting**
xcopy C:\docs*.* E: /c	**Use the /c switch to keep copying even when an error occurs**

Table 3-5 Sample xcopy commands

ROBOCOPY *<SOURCE> <DESTINATION>* [/S] [/E] [/LOG:*FILENAME*] [/LOG+:*FILENAME*] [/MOVE] [/PURGE]

The robocopy (robust file copy) command is similar to the xcopy command. It offers more options than xcopy and is intended to replace xcopy. A few options for robocopy are listed in Table 3-6.

Command	Result
robocopy C:\docs*.* E: /s	The /s switch includes subdirectories in the copy but does not include empty directories
robocopy C:\docs*.* E: /e	The /e switch includes subdirectories, even the empty ones
robocopy C:\docs*.* E: /log:Mylog.txt	Records activity to a log file and overwrites the current log file
robocopy C:\docs*.* E: /log+:Mylog.txt	Appends a record of all activity to an existing log file
robocopy C:\docs*.* E: /move	Moves files and directories, deleting them from the source
robocopy C:\docs*.* E: /purge	Deletes files and directories at the destination that no longer exist at the source

Table 3-6   Sample robocopy commands

CHKDSK [*DRIVE*:] [/F] [/R]

The chkdsk (check disk) command fixes file system errors and recovers data from bad sectors. Earlier in the chapter, you learned to check for errors using the drive properties box, which does so by launching the chkdsk command. A file is stored on the hard drive as a group of clusters. The FAT32 and exFAT file systems use a FAT (file allocation table) to keep a record of each cluster that belongs to a file. The NTFS file system uses a database to hold similar information called the master file table (MFT). In Figure 3-27, you can see that each cell in the FAT represents one cluster and contains a pointer to the next cluster in a file.

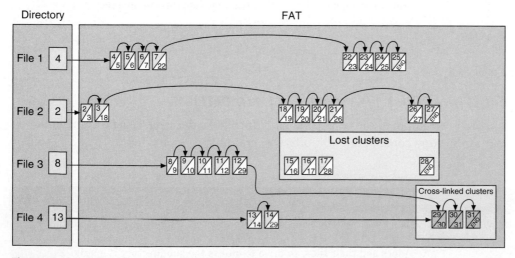

Figure 3-27   Lost and cross-linked clusters

Notes For an interesting discussion of how the FAT works, see the document FAT Details.pdf on the companion website for this text at *www.cengagebrain.com*. See the Preface for more information.

Used with the /f parameter, chkdsk searches for and fixes two types of file system errors made by the FAT or MFT:

▲ *Lost clusters (also called lost allocation units).* Lost clusters are clusters that are marked as used clusters in the FAT or MFT, but the cluster does not belong to any file. In effect, the data in these clusters is lost.
▲ *Cross-linked clusters.* Cross-linked clusters are clusters that are marked in the FAT or MFT as belonging to more than one file.

Used with the /r parameter, chkdsk checks for lost clusters and cross-linked clusters and also checks for bad sectors on the drive. The FAT and MFT keep a table of bad sectors that they normally do not use. However, over time, a sector might become unreliable. If chkdsk determines that a sector is unreliable, it attempts to recover the data from the sector and also marks the sector as bad so that the FAT or MFT will not use it again.

Used without any parameters, the chkdsk command only reports information about a drive and does not make any repairs.

In the following sample commands, the command prompt is not showing as the default drive and directory are not important. To check the hard drive for file system errors and repair them, use this command:

```
chkdsk C:/f
```

To redirect a report of the findings of the chkdsk command to a file that you can later print, use this command:

```
chkdsk C:>Myfile.txt
```

Use the /r parameter of the chkdsk command to fix file system errors and also examine each sector of the drive for bad sectors, like so:

```
chkdsk C:/r
```

If chkdsk finds data that it can recover, it asks you for permission to do so. If you give permission, it saves the recovered data in files that it stores in the root directory of the drive.

> **Notes** Use either the /f or /r parameter with chkdsk, but not both. Using both parameters is redundant. For the most thorough check of a drive, use /r.

The chkdsk command will not fix anything unless the drive is locked, which means the drive has no open files. If you attempt to use chkdsk with the /f or /r parameter when files are open, chkdsk tells you of the problem and asks permission to schedule the run the next time Windows is restarted. Know that the process will take plenty of time. Keep in mind that you must use an elevated command prompt window to run chkdsk.

> **Notes** The chkdsk command is also available from the Windows Recovery Environment.

DEFRAG [*DRIVE:*] [/C]

The defrag command examines a magnetic hard drive for fragmented files (files written to a disk in noncontiguous clusters) and rewrites these files to the drive in contiguous clusters. You use this command to optimize a magnetic hard drive's performance. Table 3-7 shows two examples of the command. It's not a good idea to defrag solid-state storage devices such as an SSD, flash drive, or smart card. Doing so can shorten the life of the drive.

Command	Result
defrag C:	**Defrag drive C:**
defrag /c	**Defrag all volumes on the computer, including drive C:**

Table 3-7   Sample defrag commands

The defrag command requires an elevated command prompt window in Windows. It is not available under the Windows Recovery Environment. Earlier in the chapter, you learned to defrag a drive using the Windows drive properties box.

FORMAT *<DRIVE:>* [/V:*LABEL*] [/Q] [FS:*<FILESYSTEM>*]

You can format a hard drive or other storage device using Disk Management. In addition, you can use the format command from a command prompt window and from the Windows Recovery Environment. This high-level format installs a file system on the device and *erases all data on the volume*. Table 3-8 lists various sample uses of the format command.

Command	Description
format D:	**Performs a full format of drive D: using the default file system for the volume type.**
format D: /q	**Performs a quick format of drive D: by re-creating an empty root directory. Use it to quickly format a previously formatted disk that is in good condition; /q does not read or write to any other part of the disk.**
format D: /fs:NTFS	**Formats drive D: using the NTFS file system.**
format D: /fs:FAT32	**Formats drive D: using the FAT32 file system.**
format D: /fs:EXFAT	**Formats drive D: using the extended FAT file system.**

Table 3-8   Sample format commands

SHUTDOWN [/M *COMPUTERNAME*] [/I] [/R] [/S] [/F] [/T *XX*]

Use the shutdown command to shut down the local computer or a remote computer. You must be signed in with an administrator account to use this command. By default, the command gives users a 30-second warning before shutdown. To shut down a remote computer on the network, you must have an administrator account on that computer and be signed on the local computer with that same account and password. Table 3-9 lists some shutdown commands.

Command	Description
shutdown /r	**Restart the local computer.**
shutdown /s /m \\bluelight	**Shut down the remote computer named \\bluelight.**
shutdown /s /m \\bluelight /t 60	**Shut down the \\bluelight computer after a 60-second delay.**
shutdown /i	**Displays the Remote Shutdown Dialog box so you can choose computers on the network to shut down.**
shutdown /s /full /t 0	**In Windows 8, immediately performs a full shutdown rather than hibernating the kernel, which is normally done to prepare for a Windows 8 QuickStart.**

Table 3-9   Sample shutdown commands

Hands-On | Project 3-3 Use a Batch File

A file with a .bat file extension is called a batch file. You can use a batch file to execute a group of commands, sometimes called a script, from a command prompt. Do the following to learn to use a batch file:

1. Using a command prompt window, copy the files in your Documents folder (My Documents in Windows 7) to a folder named \Save on a USB flash drive. Don't include subfolders in the copy.

2. Using Notepad, create a batch file named MyBatch.bat on the USB flash drive that contains the commands to do the following:

   a. Create the C:\Data folder and a subfolder named C:\Data\Documents.
   b. Copy all the files in your \Save folder to the C:\Data\Documents folder.
   c. List the contents of the C:\Data\Documents folder.

3. Using a command prompt window, execute the MyBatch.bat file and fix any problems you see. What happens when you execute the batch file and the C:\Data\Documents folder already exists?

WINDOWS POWERSHELL

Windows PowerShell is designed to replace the command prompt utility for providing a command-line interface. Like the command prompt utility, users enter commands to be executed. Unlike the command prompt, Windows PowerShell processes objects, called cmdlets (pronounced "command-lets"), that have been built with the .NET Framework programming tools instead of processing the text in a command line in order to perform tasks. This means that when entering a command into PowerShell, the utility is essentially running a prebuilt program, similar to the batch file you just created and ran in Hands-On Project 3-3. Windows PowerShell contains thousands of cmdlets so that users don't have to build their own. Technicians or programmers who program their own cmdlets can build customized objects using the pre-existing cmdlets as building blocks.

Let's see how a few cmdlets work in PowerShell. The get-help cmdlet gives help about a cmdlet and the get-process cmdlet lists all processes running on a computer. Do the following to practice using these and other cmdlets:

1. To open Windows 8 PowerShell, press **Win+X**, click **Run**, type **powershell** in the Run box, and press **Enter**.

> **OS Differences** In Windows 7, click **Start**, **All Programs**, **Accessories**, and **Windows PowerShell**. You might see other options in the Windows PowerShell folder, such as Windows PowerShell (x86), which is a 32-bit version of Windows PowerShell on 64-bit computers, or Windows PowerShell ISE, which is an administrator-level version of Windows PowerShell called the Integrated Scripting Environment (ISE). Click **Windows PowerShell** to open.

2. Enter the command **get-help get-process**, which requests information (get-help) on the get-process cmdlet.

3. View a more detailed description of the get-process cmdlet with the command **get-help get-process -detailed**.

4. Generate a list of all the processes running on your computer by entering the cmdlet **get-process**.

5. To list all cmdlets installed on a system, enter the cmdlet **get-command**.

6. As you can see, get cmdlets provide information on the item requested, but don't access the item itself. To start a program, use a start cmdlet instead. For example, to open Notepad, enter the cmdlet **start-process notepad.exe**.

USE DISK MANAGEMENT TO MANAGE HARD DRIVES

**A+
220-902
1.2, 1.4**

The primary tool for managing hard drives is Disk Management. In the "Installing Windows" chapter, you learned how to install Windows on a new hard drive. This installation process initializes, partitions, and formats the drive. After Windows is installed, you can use Disk Management to install and manage drives. In this part of the chapter, you learn to use Disk Management to manage partitions on a drive, prepare a new drive for first use, mount a drive, use Windows dynamic disks, and troubleshoot problems with the hard drive.

RESIZE, CREATE, AND DELETE PARTITIONS

Suppose you have installed Windows 8 on a hard drive and used all available space on the drive for the one partition. Now you want to split the partition into two partitions so you can install Windows 10 in a dual-boot installation with Windows 8. You can use Disk Management (diskmgmt.msc) to shrink the original partition, which frees up some space for the new Windows 10 partition. Follow these steps in Windows 8:

1. To open the Disk Management window, use one of these methods:

   ◢ Press **Win+X** and click **Disk Management**.

   ◢ Press **Win+X**, click **Run**, and enter **diskmgmt.msc** in the Run box.

> ◯ **OS Differences**   To open the Disk Management window in Windows 7, click **Start**, type **Disk Management** or **diskmgmt.msc** in the Search box, and press **Enter**.

2. The Disk Management window opens (see Figure 3-28). To shrink the existing partition, right-click in the partition space and select **Shrink Volume** from the shortcut menu (see Figure 3-28). The Shrink dialog box appears showing the amount of free space on the partition. Enter the amount in MB to shrink the partition, which cannot be more than the amount of free space so that no data on the partition will be lost. (For best performance, be sure to leave at least 15 percent free space on the disk.) Click **Shrink**. The disk now shows unallocated space.

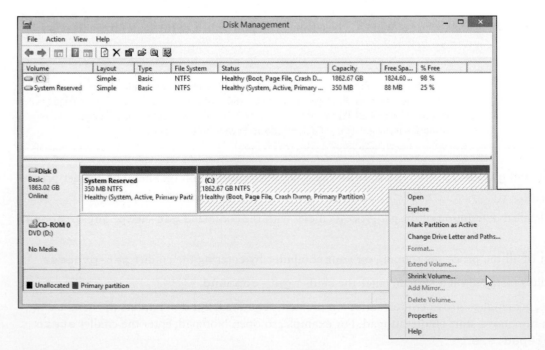

Figure 3-28   Shrink a volume to make room for a new partition

3. To create a new partition in the unallocated space, right-click in that space and select **New Simple Volume** from the shortcut menu (see Figure 3-29). The New Simple Volume Wizard opens.

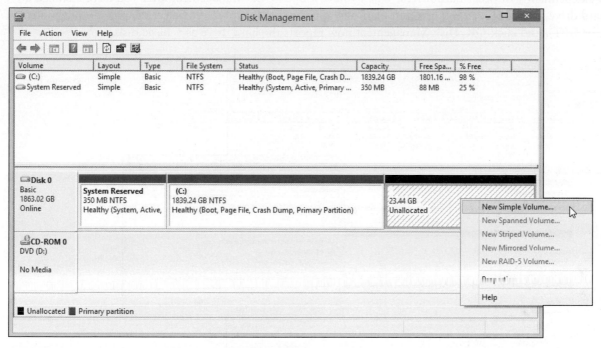

Figure 3-29 Use unallocated space to create a new partition

4. Follow the directions on screen to enter the size of the volume in MB and select a drive letter for the volume, a file system, and the size for each allocation unit (also called a cluster). It's best to leave the cluster size at the default value. You can also decide to do a quick format. The partition is then created and formatted with the file system you chose.

Notice in Figure 3-28 the options on the shortcut menu for this MBR system where you can make the partition the active partition (the one UEFI/BIOS looks to for an OS), change the drive letter for a volume, format the volume (erases all data on the volume), extend the volume (increase the size of the volume), and shrink or delete the volume. An option that is not available for the particular volume and situation is grayed.

> ★ **A+ Exam Tip** The A+ 220-902 exam expects you to know how to use Disk Management to extend and split partitions and configure a new hard drive in a system.

PREPARE A DRIVE FOR FIRST USE

When you install a new, second hard drive in a computer, use Disk Management to prepare the drive for use. This happens in a two-step process:

Step 1: Initialize the Disk

When the disk is initialized, Windows identifies the disk as a basic disk. A basic disk is a single hard drive that works independently of other hard drives. When you first open Disk Management after you have installed a new hard drive, the Initialize Disk box automatically appears (see Figure 3-30). Select the partitioning system (MBR or GPT), and click **OK**. Disk Management now reports the hard drive as a Basic disk.

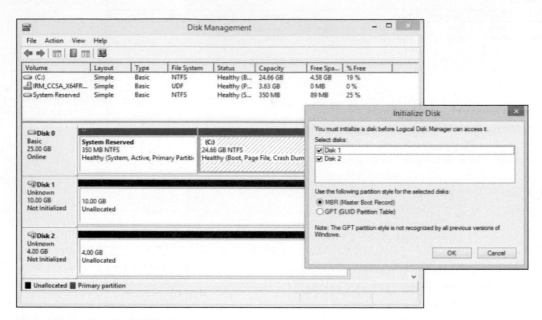

Figure 3-30   Use the Initialize Disk box to set up a partitioning system on new hard drives

> ✎ **Notes**   After installing a new hard drive, if you don't see the Initialize Disk box when you first open Disk Management, right-click in the Disk area and select **Initialize Disk** from the shortcut menu. The box will appear.

Step 2: Create a Volume and Format It with a File System

To create a new volume on a disk, right-click in the unallocated space, select **New Simple Volume** from the shortcut menu, and follow the directions on screen to select the size of the volume, assign a drive letter and name to the volume, and select the file system. When the process is finished, the drive is formatted and ready for use. When you open Explorer, you should see the new volume listed.

> ✎ **Notes**   You can use the diskpart command to convert an MBR disk to a GPT disk. However, all data on the disk is lost when you do the conversion. In the chapter "Troubleshooting Windows Startup," you learn more about diskpart and other commands used to manage a hard drive.

HOW TO MOUNT A DRIVE

A mounted drive is a volume that can be accessed by way of a folder on another volume so that the folder has more available space. A mounted drive is useful when a folder is on a volume that is too small to hold all the data you want in the folder. In Figure 3-31, the mounted drive gives the C:\Projects folder a capacity of 20 GB. The C:\Projects folder is called the mount point for the mounted drive.

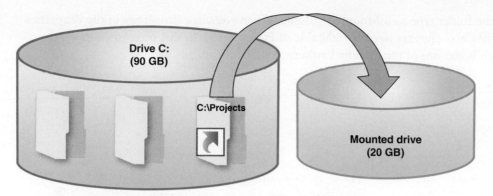

Figure 3-31   The C:\Projects folder is the mount point for the mounted drive

Follow these steps to mount a drive:

1. Make sure the volume that is to host the mounted drive uses the NTFS file system. The folder on this volume, called the mount point, must be empty. You can also create the folder during the mount process. In this example, we are mounting a drive to the C:\Projects folder.

2. Using Disk Management, right-click in the unallocated space of a disk. In our example, we're using Disk 1 (the second hard drive). Select **New Simple Volume** from the shortcut menu. The New Simple Volume Wizard launches. Using the wizard, specify the amount of unallocated space you want to devote to the volume. (In our example, we are using 20 GB, although the resulting size of the C:\Projects folder will only show about 19 GB because of overhead.)

3. As you follow the wizard, the box shown on the left side of Figure 3-32 appears. Select **Mount in the following empty NTFS folder,** and then click **Browse.** In the Browse for Drive Path box that appears (see the right side of Figure 3-32), you can drill down to an existing folder or click **New Folder** to create a new folder on drive C:.

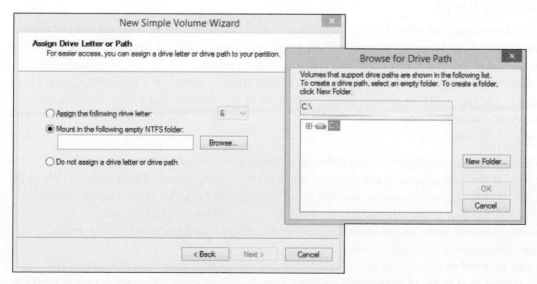

Figure 3-32   Select the folder that will be the mount point for the new volume

4. Complete the wizard by selecting a file system for the new volume and an Allocation unit size (the cluster size). The volume is created and formatted.

5. To verify the drive is mounted, open Explorer and then open the Properties box for the folder. In our example, the Properties box for the C:\Projects folder is shown in the middle of Figure 3-33. Notice the

Properties box reports the folder type as a Mounted Volume. When you click Properties in the Properties box, the volume Properties box appears (see the right side of Figure 3-33). In this box, you can see the size of the volume, which is the size of the mounted volume, less overhead.

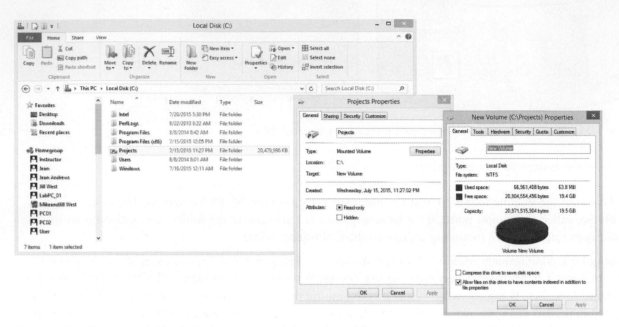

Figure 3-33   The mounted drive in Explorer appears as a very large folder

You can think of a mount point, such as C:\Projects, as a shortcut to a volume on a second hard drive. If you look closely at the left window in Figure 3-33, you can see the shortcut icon beside the Projects folder.

WINDOWS DYNAMIC DISKS

A basic disk works independently of other hard drives, but a dynamic disk can work with other hard drives to hold data. Volumes stored on dynamic disks are called dynamic volumes. Several dynamic disks can work together to collectively present a single dynamic volume to the system.

When dynamic disks work together, data to configure each hard drive is stored in a disk management database that resides in the last 1 MB of storage space on each hard drive. Note that Home editions of Windows do not support dynamic disks.

Here are three uses of dynamic disks:

▲ *For better reliability, you can configure a hard drive as a dynamic disk and allocate the space as a simple volume.* This is the best reason to use dynamic disks and is a recommended best practice. Because of the way a dynamic disk works, the simple volume is considered more reliable than when it is stored on a basic disk. A volume that is stored on only one hard drive is called a simple volume.

▲ *You can implement dynamic disks on multiple hard drives to extend a volume across these drives (called spanning).* This volume is called a spanned volume.

▲ *Dynamic disks can be used to piece data across multiple hard drives to improve performance.* The technology to configure two or more hard drives to work together as an array of drives is called RAID (redundant array of inexpensive disks or redundant array of independent disks). Joining hard drives together to improve performance is called striping or RAID 0. The volume is called a striped volume (see Figure 3-34). When RAID is implemented in this way using Disk Management, it is called software RAID. A more reliable way of configuring RAID is to use UEFI/BIOS setup on a motherboard that supports RAID, which is called hardware RAID.

One simple volume on a single disk

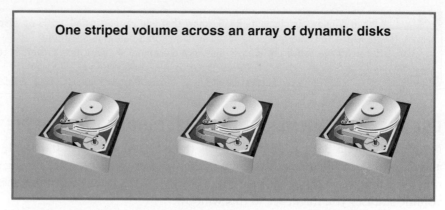

One striped volume across an array of dynamic disks

Figure 3-34 A simple volume is stored on a single disk, but a striped volume is stored on an array of dynamic disks

You can use Disk Management to convert two or more basic disks to dynamic disks. Then you can use unallocated space on these disks to create a simple, spanned, or striped volume. To convert a basic disk to dynamic, right-click the Disk area and select **Convert to Dynamic Disk** from the shortcut menu (see Figure 3-35), and then right-click free space on the disk and select **New Simple Volume**, **New Spanned Volume**, or **New Striped Volume** from the shortcut menu. If you were to use spanning or striping in Figure 3-35, you could make Disk 1 and Disk 2 dynamic disks that hold a single volume. The size of the volume would be the sum of the space on both hard drives.

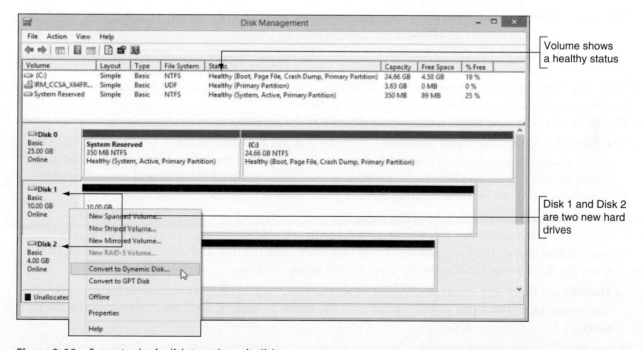

Figure 3-35 Convert a basic disk to a dynamic disk

Now for some serious cautions about software RAID where you use Windows for spanning and striping: Microsoft warns that when Windows is used for software RAID, the risk of catastrophic failure increases and can lead to data loss. Microsoft suggests you only use Windows spanning or striping when you have no other option. In other words, spanning and striping in Windows aren't very safe—to expand the size of a volume, use a mounted drive or use hardware RAID.

> ✎ **Notes** When Windows implements RAID, know that you cannot install an OS on a spanned or striped volume that uses software RAID. You can, however, install Windows on a hardware RAID drive.
>   Also, after you have converted a basic disk to a dynamic disk, you cannot revert it to a basic disk without losing all data on the drive.

USE DISK MANAGEMENT TO TROUBLESHOOT HARD DRIVE PROBLEMS

Notice in Figure 3-35 that this system has three hard drives, Disk 0, Disk 1, and Disk 2, and information about the disks and volumes is shown in the window. When you are having a problem with a hard drive, it helps to know what the information in the Disk Management window means. Here are the drive and volume statuses you might see in this window:

- *Healthy*. The healthy volume status shown in Figure 3-35 indicates that the volume is formatted with a file system and that the file system is working without errors.
- *Failed*. A failed volume status indicates a problem with the hard drive or that the file system has become corrupted. To try to fix the problem, make sure the hard drive data cable and power cable are secure. Data on a failed volume is likely to be lost. For dynamic disks, if the disk status is Offline, try bringing the disk back online (how to do that is coming up later in this list).
- *Online*. An online disk status indicates the disk has been sensed by Windows and can be accessed by either reading or writing to the disk.
- *Active*. One volume on an MBR system will be marked as Active. This is the volume that startup BIOS looks to for an OS boot manager to load.
- *EFI System Partition*. In GPT systems, one volume will be marked as the EFI System Partition. UEFI looks to this volume to find an OS boot manager to load an OS.
- *Unallocated*. Space on the disk is marked as unallocated if it has not yet been partitioned.
- *Formatting*. This volume status appears while a volume is being formatted.
- *Basic*. When a hard drive is first sensed by Windows, it is assigned the Basic disk status. A basic disk can be partitioned and formatted as a stand-alone hard drive.
- *Dynamic*. The following status indicators apply only to dynamic disks:
  - *Offline*. An offline disk status indicates a dynamic disk has become corrupted or is unavailable. The problem can be caused by a corrupted file system, loose drive cables, a failed hard drive, or another hardware problem. If you believe the problem is corrected, right-click the disk and select **Reactivate Disk** from the shortcut menu to bring the disk back online.
  - *Foreign drive*. If you move a hard drive that has been configured as a dynamic disk on another computer to this computer, this computer will report the disk as a foreign drive. To fix the problem, you need to import the foreign drive. To do that, right-click the disk and select **Import Foreign Disks** from the shortcut menu. You should then be able to see the volumes on the disk.
  - *Healthy (At Risk)*. The dynamic disk can be accessed, but I/O errors have occurred. Try returning the disk to online status. If the volume status does not return to healthy, back up all data and replace the drive.

If you are still having problems with a hard drive, volume, or mounted drive, check Event Viewer for events about the drive that might have been recorded there. These events might help you understand the nature of the problem and what to do about it. How to use Event Viewer is covered in the chapter, "Optimizing Windows."

Hands-On | Project 3-4   Use Disk Management on a Virtual Machine

A+
220-902
1.2, 1.4

To complete the Hands-On Projects in the chapter "Installing Windows," you used VirtualBox software to install Windows in a virtual machine. Use this VM to practice using Disk Management. Do the following:

1. Open Windows VirtualBox, but do not open the virtual machine.

2. With the virtual machine selected, click **Settings.** Use the Settings box to add a new hard drive to the VM, as shown in Figure 3-36: Click **Storage** in the left pane, click **Controller: SATA** in the center pane, and then click the **Add Hard Disk** icon. Click the **Create new disk** button.

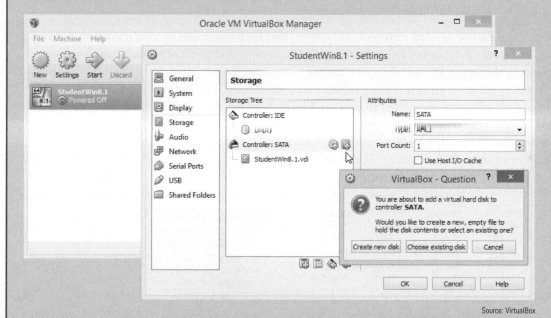

Source: VirtualBox

Figure 3-36   The Add Hard Disk icon is one option to the right of the SATA controller listing

3. In the Create Virtual Hard Drive dialog box, keep the default selection for **VDI (VirtualBox Disk Image)** unless directed otherwise by your instructor. Click **Next.** Keep the default **Dynamically allocated** option, and click **Next.** Keep the default drive name and location, change the size to **4 GB**, and then click **Create.** Click **OK.**

4. Start up the VM, sign in to Windows, and open Disk Management.

5. Use Disk Management to initialize the new disk and partition it. Create two partitions on the disk, one formatted using the NTFS file system and one using the FAT32 file system.

6. View the new volumes using File Explorer.

7. Create and save a snip of your screen showing the virtual machine with the new volumes created. Email the snip to your instructor.

WINDOWS STORAGE SPACES

A+
220-902
1.4

Storage Spaces is new with Windows 8 and is a potential replacement for traditional Windows software RAID. With Storage Spaces, you can create a storage pool using any number of internal or external backup drives that use interfaces such as SATA (Serial ATA), SAS (Serial Attached SCSI), or even USB. Then you create one or more virtual drives, called spaces, from this pool, which appear as normal drives in File Explorer. Drives used for Storage Spaces can be formatted with the NTFS or ReFS file system.

Storage Spaces is designed for resiliency, which resists data loss in the event of drive failure. The following storage options offer varying degrees of resiliency in Storage Spaces:

▲ *Simple*. A simple storage space combines multiple physical drives into a single logical drive with no built-in data backup. This option offers no resiliency.

▲ *Two-way mirroring*. A logical drive can be mirrored, which means the data is duplicated across multiple physical drives used to create the space.

▲ *Three-way mirroring*. In three-way mirroring, data is stored in triplicate to provide additional resiliency against data loss, although this feature requires that at least five physical drives be used to create the storage pool.

▲ *Parity*. To provide even greater resiliency, parity spaces maintain multiple copies of data (depending upon the configuration) plus parity checking, which is a way to check backed-up data for any loss and re-create compromised data through parity calculations.

A single storage pool can be divided into multiple spaces, and each space can be configured with different resiliency settings. As pool capacity is depleted, more drives can be added to increase the available space without reconfiguring the space. In fact, the space can be configured as if it has more virtual storage than the physical drives actually offer by using a feature called thin provisioning. For example, in Figure 3-37, you can see the total of storage spaces presented to users is 12 TB; however, the physical hard drive capacities add up to only 8 TB. As the space actually used approaches 8 TB, the administrator is prompted to add more physical storage to the pool, which can eventually meet the 12-TB maximum capacity.

To set up a system to use Storage Spaces, do the following:

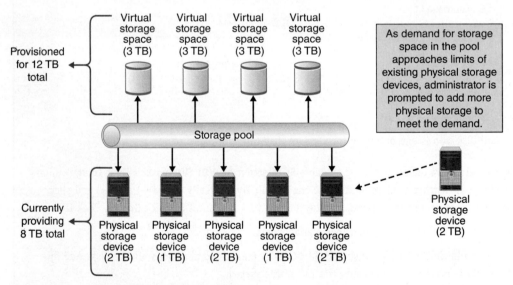

Figure 3-37 Thin provisioning allows for additional physical devices as needed without reconfiguring space available to users

1. Attach any drives to the computer that you intend to use for your storage pool. These can include SATA, SAS, or certain USB devices, and they do not have to match in capacity. All data on the storage drives will be lost during formatting, so be sure to back up anything important.

2. Open Control Panel and click **Storage Spaces**. Click **Create a new pool and storage space**. Respond to the UAC dialog box.

3. Any drives that are compatible with Storage Spaces will be listed. Select the drives to format. All data on the selected drives will be lost.

4. In the Create a storage space window (see Figure 3-38), assign a name and drive letter for the storage space, and select a file system. File system options include NTFS and ReFS.

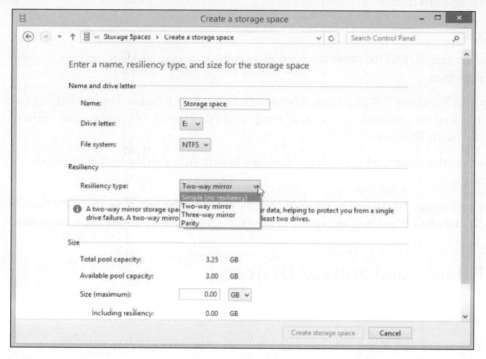

Figure 3-38 Select a resiliency type for a new storage space

5. Select a resiliency type. Options include simple (no resiliency), two-way mirror, three-way mirror, and parity. Then, if you plan to use thin provisioning, adjust the maximum size of the storage pool. Sizes can be set in GB or TB. Click **Create storage space**. The storage space is created and formatted.

6. After the storage space is created, you can return to the Storage Spaces window to change the name, drive letter, and size of an existing storage space.

>> CHAPTER SUMMARY

Schedule Preventive Maintenance

◢ Regular preventive maintenance includes verifying Windows settings, cleaning up the hard drive, defragmenting the hard drive, checking the drive for errors, uninstalling unwanted software, and doing whatever else is necessary to free up enough space on the hard drive for Windows to perform well.

◢ Windows stores user profiles in the C:\Users folder.

◢ For best performance, allow at least 15 percent of free space on the Windows volume. The easiest way to clean up temporary files is to use the Disk Cleanup utility in the drive properties box.

◢ You can defrag a magnetic hard drive by using the drive properties box or the defrag command. By default, Windows automatically defrags magnetic hard drives weekly.

◢ Use the chkdsk utility to check the drive for errors and recover data. The utility can be accessed from a command prompt or the drive properties box.

◢ Windows supports compressed (zipped) folders and NTFS folder and file compression. You can also compress an NTFS volume.

▲ Virtual memory uses hard drive space as memory to increase the total amount of memory available. Virtual memory is stored in a paging file named pagefile.sys. To save space on drive C:, you can move the file to another volume or hard drive.

Backup Procedures

▲ You need a plan for disaster recovery in the event the hard drive fails. This plan needs to include routine backups of data and system files.

▲ Windows 8 File History and Windows 7 Backup and Restore can be used to schedule routine backups of user data files. Backup and Restore can back up a system image and File History offers the same option for backward compatibility with Windows 7.

▲ System Protection creates restore points, which include Windows system files that have changed since the last restore point was made.

▲ A Windows 8 custom refresh image backs up the entire Windows volume. The best time to create the image is right after you've installed Windows, hardware, applications, and user accounts and customized Windows settings.

Managing Files, Folders, and Storage Devices

▲ A hard drive is divided into sectors (for magnetic hard drives only), blocks, and partitions. Each partition is formatted with a file system.

▲ The MBR partitioning system requires legacy BIOS and can support only three primary partitions and one extended partition.

▲ The GPT partitioning system requires UEFI and a 64-bit OS. It can support up to 128 partitions, Secure Boot, and hard drives larger than 2 TB.

▲ Commands useful to manage files, folders, and storage media include help, dir, del, ren, copy, recover, expand, xcopy, robocopy, md, cd, rd, chkdsk, defrag, and format.

▲ Use Disk Management to manage hard drives and partitions. Use it to create, delete, and resize partitions, mount a drive, manage dynamic disks, and solve problems with hard drives.

▲ Windows 8 Storage Spaces is expected to replace the Windows solution for software RAID and can support thin provisioning, which allows for physical hard drives to be added to the storage pool as need demands.

>> KEY TERMS

For explanations of key terms, see the Glossary for this text.

active partition	custom refresh image	expand	high-level formatting
active recovery image	defrag	extended partition	initialization files
Backup and Restore	defragment	FAT (file allocation table)	logical drive
basic disk	del		low-level formatting
boot partition	dir	file allocation unit	Master Boot Record (MBR)
BootMgr	Disk Cleanup	File History	
cd (change directory)	dynamic disk	formatting	master file table (MFT)
CDFS (Compact Disk File System)	dynamic volume	fragmented file	md (make directory)
	EFI System Partition (ESP)	Globally Unique Identifier Partition Table (GUID or GPT)	mount point
chkdsk (check disk)			mounted drive
cluster	elevated command prompt window	hardware RAID	Offline Files
Complete PC Backup		help	pagefile.sys
copy	erase		partition table

primary partition
quick format
RAID (redundant array
   of inexpensive disks
   or redundant array of
   independent disks)
RAID 0
rd (remove directory)
recover
registry

ren (rename)
resiliency
Resilient File System
   (ReFS)
restore point
robocopy (robust file copy)
sector
shadow copy
shutdown
simple volume

slack
software RAID
Storage Spaces
striping
system image
system partition
System Protection
System Restore
thin provisioning
track

UDF (Universal Disk
   Format)
user profile
user profile namespace
virtual memory
wildcard
Windows PowerShell
xcopy

>> REVIEWING THE BASICS

1. What are the three Windows settings critical to securing a computer that need to be verified as part of regular maintenance?

2. What folder holds the Windows registry? What folder holds a backup of the registry?

3. What folder holds 32-bit programs installed in a 64-bit installation of Windows?

4. What file in the user account folder stores user settings?

5. What is the purpose of the C:\Windows\CSC folder?

6. What is the purpose of the Windows.old folder?

7. How can you manually delete the Windows.old folder?

8. By default, how often does Windows automatically defrag a magnetic hard drive?

9. On what type of hard drive does Windows disable defragmenting?

10. What are two reasons to uninstall software you no longer use?

11. What is the file name and default path of the Windows paging file used for virtual memory?

12. What type of storage media must be used to create a Windows system image?

13. What Windows 8 utility is used to back up user data? What Windows 7 utility is used to back up user data?

14. Why is it important to not store a backup of drive C: on another partition on the same hard drive?

15. What is the *%SystemRoot%* folder as used in Microsoft documentation?

16. What Windows utility creates restore points?

17. How can you delete all restore points?

18. In what folder are restore points kept?

19. Which dialog box can you use to manually create a restore point?

20. To use the GPT partitioning system on a hard drive, what firmware is required? What operating system architecture?

21. In a command line, what is the purpose of the ? in a file name?

22. What is the purpose of the |more parameter at the end of a command line?

23. What is the command to list all files and subdirectories in a directory?

24. What type of command prompt window is needed to run the chkdsk command?

25. When you want to use chkdsk to fix file system errors and the drive is not locked, when does Windows schedule the chkdsk command to run?

3

26. What command is intended to replace xcopy?

27. Which Windows utility can you use to split a partition into two partitions?

28. Which is more stable, RAID implemented by Windows or RAID implemented by hardware?

29. When you move a dynamic disk to a new computer, what status will Disk Management first assign the drive?

30. What is the feature of Windows 8 Storage Spaces that allows an administrator to add physical hard drives to the storage pool as available space fills up?

>> THINKING CRITICALLY

1. Write and test commands to do the following. (Answers can vary.)

   a. Create a folder named C:\data

   b. Create a folder named C:\data\test1 and a folder named C:\data\test2

   c. Copy Notepad.exe to the test1 folder

   d. Move Notepad.exe from the test1 folder to the test2 folder

   e. Make C:\ the default folder

   f. Without changing the default folder, list all files in the test2 folder

   g. Delete the test2 folder

   h. Delete the C:\data folder

2. You are trying to clean up a slow Windows 8 system that was recently installed in place of the old Windows 7 installation, and you discover that the 75-GB hard drive has only 5 GB of free space. The entire hard drive is taken up by drive C:. What is the best way to free up some space?

   a. Compress the entire hard drive.

   b. Move the /Program Files folder to an external hard drive.

   c. Delete the Windows.old folder.

   d. Reduce the size of the paging file.

3. Which is the best first step to protect important data on your hard drive?

   a. Use dynamic disks to set up a striped volume so that the data has redundancy.

   b. Back up the data to another media.

   c. Compress the folder that holds the data.

   d. Put password protection on the data folder.

4. The A+ exams expect you to be able to launch many Windows utilities by using the program file name of the utility. What is the program file name for each of the following utilities? (*Hint*: You might need to look online for some of these.)

   a. Command prompt

   b. System Information

   c. System Restore

   d. Device Manager

   e. Disk Cleanup

   f. Disk Management

>> REAL PROBLEMS, REAL SOLUTIONS

REAL PROBLEM 3-1 Researching the WinSxS Folder

While cleaning up a hard drive, you begin to look for folders that are excessively large and discover the C:\Windows\WinSxS folder is more than 7 GB. That's almost half the size of the entire C:\Windows folder on this drive. Use the web to research the purpose of the WinSxS folder. What goes in this folder and how does it get there? How can the size of the folder be reduced without causing major trouble with the OS? Write a brief one-page paper about this folder and cite at least three articles you find on the web about it.

REAL PROBLEM 3-2 Cleaning Up a Sluggish Windows System

Do you have a Windows system that is slow and needs optimizing? If not, talk with family and friends and try to find a slow system that can use your help. Using all the tools and techniques presented in this chapter, clean up this sluggish Windows system. Take detailed notes as you go, listing what you checked before you started to solve the problems, describing what you did to solve the problems, and describing the results of your efforts. What questions did you have along the way? Bring these questions to class for discussion.

REAL PROBLEM 3-3 Creating a Virtual Hard Drive

You can use the Disk Management tool or the diskpart command to create a Virtual Hard Drive (VHD) on a physical computer. The VHD is a file that takes up some free space on the physical hard drive, but to Windows it appears as a second hard drive. You can store data in folders and files on the VHD and even install Windows in the VHD. Follow these steps to create a VHD:

1. In Disk Management, click **Action** in the menu bar and click **Create VHD**. Follow directions on screen to create the VHD, specifying its location on the hard drive and its size. You can make the size dynamically expanding. The VHD is listed as a Disk in the Disk Management window.

2. Right-click the new disk and click **Initialize Disk**. Use the GPT partitioning system for the disk.

3. To format the disk, right-click the unallocated space on the disk and click **New Simple Volume**. The VHD is now ready for use and appears in File Explorer or Windows Explorer as a new volume.

Discuss in your class and research online how a VHD might be useful. What are two uses of a VHD, in which a VHD offers advantages over using a physical hard drive?

Optimizing Windows

In the chapter, "Maintaining Windows," you learned about the tools and strategies to maintain Windows and about the importance of keeping good backups. This chapter takes you one step further as an IT support technician so that you can get the best performance out of Windows. We begin the chapter learning about the Windows tools you'll need to optimize Windows. Then we turn our attention to the steps you can follow to cause a sluggish Windows system to perform at its best and how to manually remove software that does not uninstall using normal methods. As you read the chapter, you might consider following along using a Windows 8 or Windows 7 system.

> **Notes** Windows installed in a virtual machine is an excellent environment to use when practicing the skills in this chapter.

WINDOWS UTILITIES AND TOOLS TO SUPPORT THE OS

A+
220-902
1.1, 1.4,
1.5, 4.1

Knowledge is power when it comes to supporting Windows. In this part of the chapter, you learn more about how Windows works and to use some Windows tools to poke around under the hood to see what is really happening that is slowing Windows down or giving other problems.

WHAT ARE THE SHELL AND THE KERNEL?

A+
220-902
4.1

It might sound like we're talking about a grain of wheat, but Windows has a shell and a kernel and you need to understand what they are and how they work so you can solve problems with each. A shell is the portion of an OS that relates to the user and to applications. The kernel is responsible for interacting with hardware. Figure 4-1 shows how the shell and kernel relate to users, applications, and hardware. In addition, the figure shows a third component of an OS, the configuration data. For Windows, this data is primarily contained in the registry.

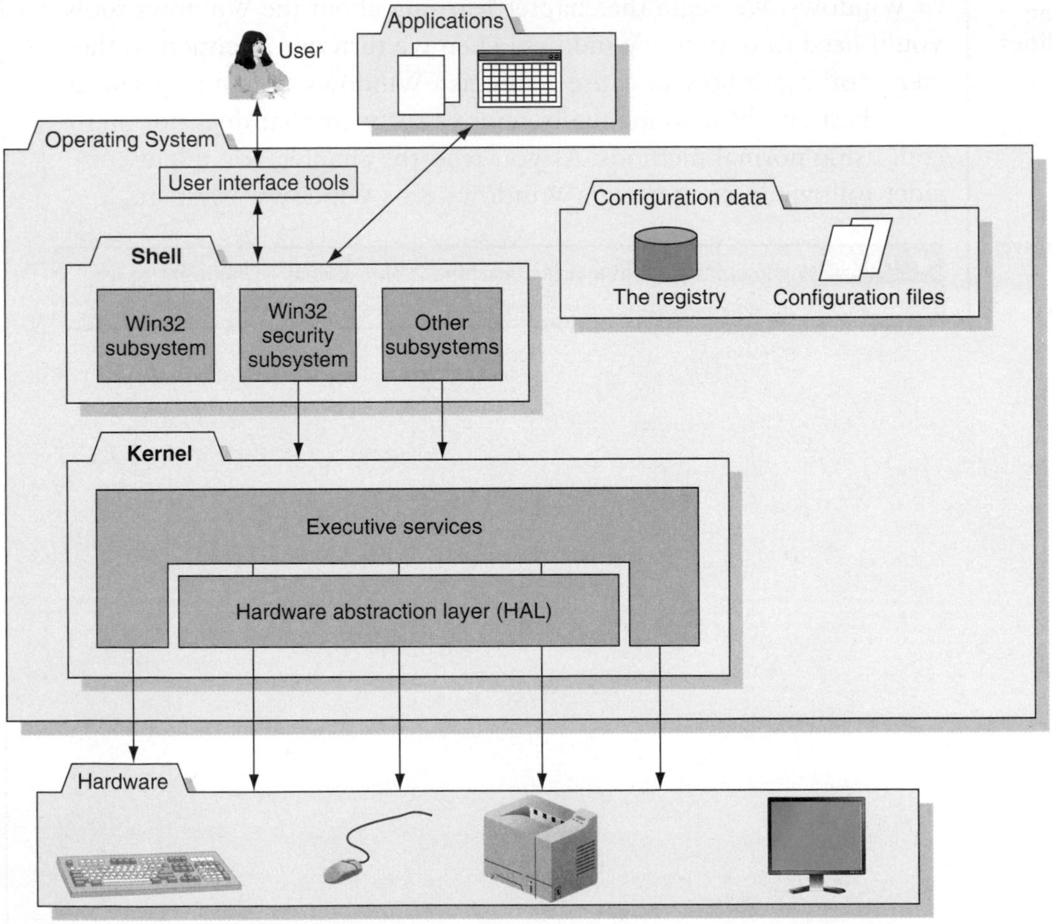

Figure 4-1 Inside an operating system, different components perform various functions

THE WINDOWS SHELL

The shell provides tools such as File Explorer or the Windows desktop as a way for the user to do such things as select music to burn to a CD or launch an application. For applications, the shell provides commands and procedures that applications can call on to do such things as print a document, read from a storage device, or display a photograph on screen.

The shell is made up of several subsystems that all operate in user mode, which means these subsystems have only limited access to system information and can access hardware only through other OS services. One of these subsystems, the Win32 security subsystem, provides sign-in to the system and other security functions, including privileges for file access. All applications relate to Windows by way of the Win32 subsystem.

THE WINDOWS KERNEL

The kernel, or core, of the OS is responsible for interacting with hardware. Because the kernel operates in kernel mode, it has more power to communicate with hardware devices than the shell has. Applications operating under the OS cannot get to hardware devices without the shell passing those requests to the kernel. This separation of tasks provides for a more stable system and helps to prevent a wayward application from destabilizing the system.

The kernel has two main components: (1) the HAL (hardware abstraction layer), which is the layer closest to the hardware, and (2) the executive services interface, which is a group of services that operate in kernel mode between the user mode subsystems and the HAL. Executive services contained in the ntoskrnl.exe program file manage memory, I/O devices, file systems, some security, and other key components directly or by way of device drivers.

When Windows is first installed, it builds the HAL based on the type of CPU installed. The HAL cannot be moved from one computer to another, which is one reason you cannot copy a Windows installation from one computer to another.

HOW WINDOWS MANAGES APPLICATIONS

A+
220-902
1.4

When an application is first installed, its program files are normally stored on the hard drive. When the application is launched, the program is copied from the hard drive into memory and there it is called a process. A process is a program that is running under the authority of the shell, together with the system resources assigned to it. System resources might include other programs it has started and memory addresses to hold its data. When the process makes a request for resources, this request is made to the Win32 subsystem and is called a thread. A thread is a single task, such as the task of printing a file that the process requests from the kernel. Figure 4-2 shows two threads in action, which is possible because the process and Windows support multithreading. Sometimes a process is called an instance, such as when you say to a user, "Open two instances of Internet Explorer." Technically, you are saying to open two Internet Explorer processes.

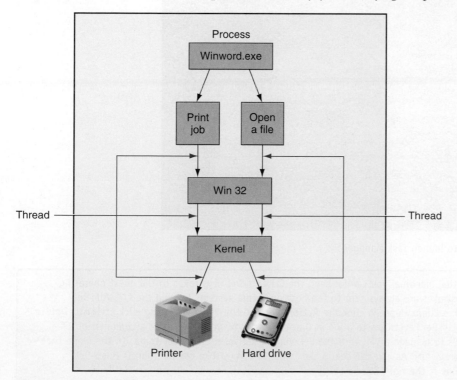

Figure 4-2 A process with more than one thread is called multithreading

> ⭐ **A+ Exam Tip**   The A+ 220-902 exam expects you to know how to use Task Manager, System Configuration, Services console, Computer Management console, MMC, Event Viewer, Task Scheduler, Registry Editor, Performance Monitor, and Print Management. All these tools are covered in this part of the chapter.

Now that you are familiar with the concepts of how Windows works, let's see how to use some tools that can help us manage Windows components and processes.

TASK MANAGER

Task Manager (taskmgr.exe) lets you view the applications and processes running on your computer as well as information about process and memory performance, network activity, and user activity. Several ways to access Task Manager are:

◢ Press **Ctrl+Alt+Del**. Depending on your system, the security screen (see Figure 4-3) or Task Manager appears. If the security screen appears, click **Task Manager**. This method works well when the system has a problem and is frozen.

◢ Right-click a blank area in the taskbar on the desktop, and select **Task Manager** in Windows 8 or **Start Task Manager** in Windows 7 from the shortcut menu.

◢ Press **Ctrl+Shift+Esc**.

◢ For Windows 8, press **Win+X** and click **Task Manager** in the Quick Launch menu. For Windows 7, click **Start**, enter **taskmgr.exe** in the Search box, and press **Enter**.

Figure 4-3   Use the security screen to launch Task Manager

> ✏ **Notes**   When working with a virtual machine, you cannot send the Ctrl+Alt+Del keystrokes to the guest operating system in the VM because these keystrokes are always sent to the host operating system. To send the Ctrl+Alt+Del keystrokes to a VM in Windows 8.1 Pro Client Hyper-V, click the **Action** menu in the VM window and click **Ctrl+Alt+Delete** (see Figure 4-4a). To send the Ctrl+Alt+Del keystrokes to a VM in Oracle VirtualBox, you must press a combination of keystrokes. To find out the keystrokes to manage a VM, with the VM window active, press **Host+Home**. In the menu that appears, point to **Machine** (see Figure 4-4b). As you can see in the figure, the keystroke combination is Host+Del. (By default, the Host key in VirtualBox is the right Ctrl key.)

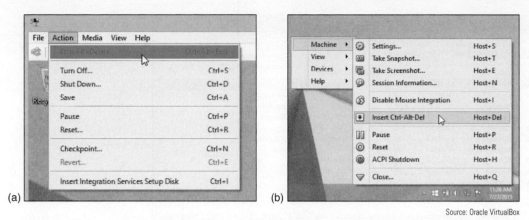

Figure 4-4   Send the Ctrl+Alt+Del keystrokes to a VM managed by (a) Windows 8.1 Pro Client Hyper-V or (b) Oracle VirtualBox

The Windows 8 Task Manager window is shown in Figure 4-5. If you see very limited information in the window, click **More details** to see the details shown in the figure.

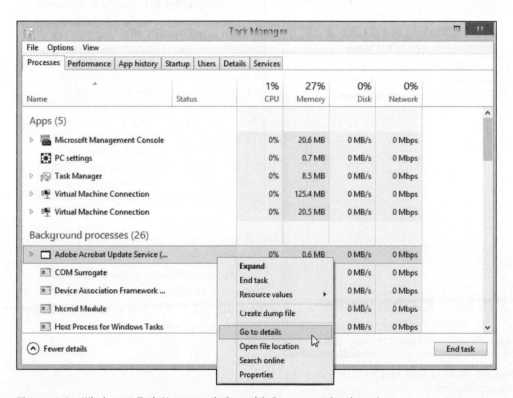

Figure 4-5   Windows 8 Task Manager window with Processes tab selected

Let's take a look at the Task Manager tabs.

PROCESSES TAB AND DETAILS TAB

The Processes tab shows running processes organized by Apps, Background processes, and Windows processes. Right-click a process, and click **Go to details** (see Figure 4-5) to jump to the Details tab where you see the name of the program file and other details about the running program. On the Details tab (see Figure 4-6), if a process is hung, it is reported as Not Responding. To end the task, select it and click **End task**. The application will attempt a normal shutdown; if data has not been saved, you are given the opportunity to save it.

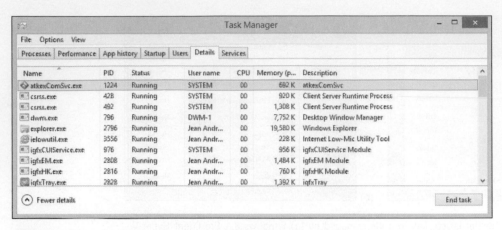

Figure 4-6 Use the Details tab to end a task that is not responding

Figure 4-7 The Applications tab in Windows 7 Task Manager shows the status of active applications

Notes If your desktop locks up, you can use Task Manager to refresh it. To do so, press **Ctrl+Alt+Del** and open **Task Manager**. Click the **Processes** tab. In the Windows processes group, select **Windows Explorer** and click **Restart**. (Yes, Windows 8 Task Manager really does call Explorer "Windows Explorer.")

In Windows 7, on the Processes tab, select and end the **explorer.exe** process. Then click **File** in the menu bar and click **New Task (Run)**. Enter **Explorer.exe** in the Create New Task box, and click **OK**. Your desktop will be refreshed and any running programs will still be open.

If you want to end the process and all related processes, on the Details tab, right-click the process and select **End Process Tree** from the shortcut menu. Be careful to not end critical Windows processes; ending these might crash your system.

OS Differences The Windows 7/Vista Task Manager window has six tabs: Applications, Processes, Services, Performance, Networking, and Users. The Applications tab of Task Manager (see Figure 4-7) is used to view a list of running processes. You can end a process that is not responding on this tab or end it on the Processes tab.

A+ Exam Tip The A+ 220-902 exam expects you to understand the purposes of each tab in Task Manager for Windows 8 and Windows 7.

PERFORMANCE TAB

The Performance tab of Task Manager (see Figure 4-8) allows you to monitor performance of key devices in the system and network connections. For example, Figure 4-8 shows Memory selected where you can monitor how much RAM is currently used. When you select CPU, the Performance tab reports whether Hardware-assisted Virtualization is enabled.

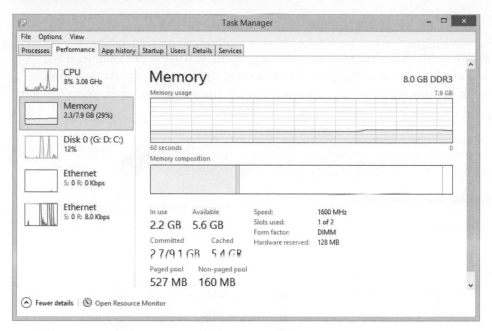

Figure 4-8   Use the Performance tab to view system resource usage

Click **Open Resource Monitor** on this tab to open the Resource Monitor, which monitors the CPU, hard drive, network, and memory in real time (see Figure 4-9). If you suspect CPU, memory, disk, or network resources are being used excessively by a process, you can use Resource Monitor to identify the process. Check for such a process if you suspect malware might be at work in a denial-of-service (DoS) attack.

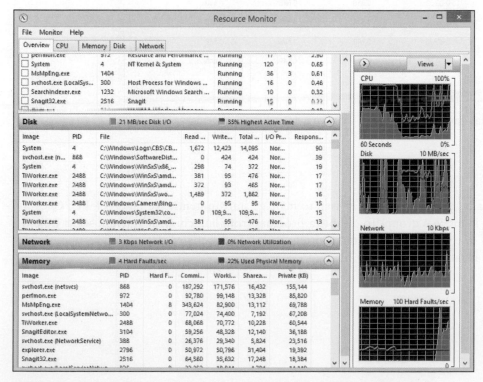

Figure 4-9   Resource Monitor monitors devices and the network in real time

> **⟳ OS Differences** In Windows 7/Vista, the Performance tab of Task Manager monitors performance of the CPU and memory and also gives you access to the Resource Monitor. To monitor the performance of network connections, see the Networking tab of Task Manager. Alternately, you can use the Windows 7 Resource Monitor to monitor the performance of the CPU, memory, hard drive, and network connections.

APP HISTORY TAB

The App history tab (see Figure 4-10) shows the resources that a program is using. For example, it's useful when deciding if a live tile for an app on the Start screen is using up too many system resources as it provides live information on the tile. If you want to disable a live tile from updating itself, go to the **Start** screen, right-click the tile, and click **Turn live tile off** in the shortcut menu.

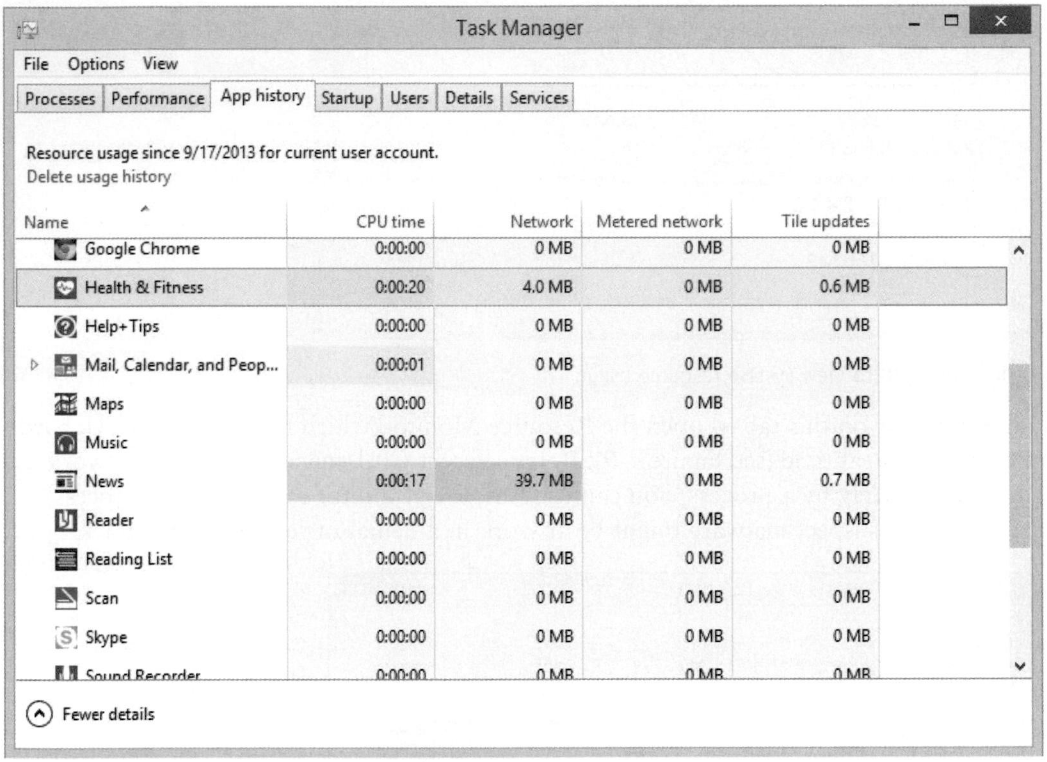

Name	CPU time	Network	Metered network	Tile updates
Google Chrome	0:00:00	0 MB	0 MB	0 MB
Health & Fitness	0:00:20	4.0 MB	0 MB	0.6 MB
Help+Tips	0:00:00	0 MB	0 MB	0 MB
Mail, Calendar, and Peop...	0:00:01	0 MB	0 MB	0 MB
Maps	0:00:00	0 MB	0 MB	0 MB
Music	0:00:00	0 MB	0 MB	0 MB
News	0:00:17	39.7 MB	0 MB	0.7 MB
Reader	0:00:00	0 MB	0 MB	0 MB
Reading List	0:00:00	0 MB	0 MB	0 MB
Scan	0:00:00	0 MB	0 MB	0 MB
Skype	0:00:00	0 MB	0 MB	0 MB
Sound Recorder	0:00:00	0 MB	0 MB	0 MB

Figure 4-10   The App history tab can help you decide if a background program is hogging system resources

STARTUP TAB

The Startup tab of Task Manager in Windows 8 is used to manage startup items (see Figure 4-11). Click a white arrow to expand the items in a group. To disable a program from launching at startup, select it, and click **Disable** at the bottom of the window or in the shortcut menu. To see the program file location, right-click it, and click **Open file location**, as shown in the figure.

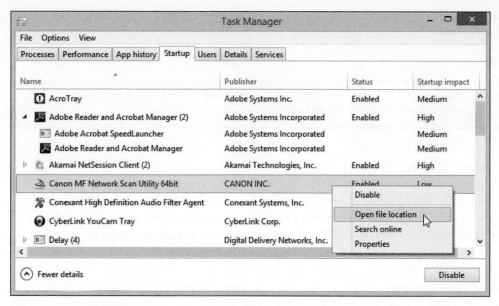

Figure 4-11   Startup processes are managed on the Startup tab of Task Manager

USERS TAB

The Users tab (see Figure 4-12) lists currently signed-in users and gives performance information that can help you identify processes started by a signed-in user that might be affecting overall system performance. Notice that the statuses of some programs on this tab are listed as Suspended. In Windows 8, if certain apps remain idle for a short time, they're suspended so they don't require the attention of the CPU. When the app is used again, it automatically comes out of suspension, and the CPU once again begins servicing it.

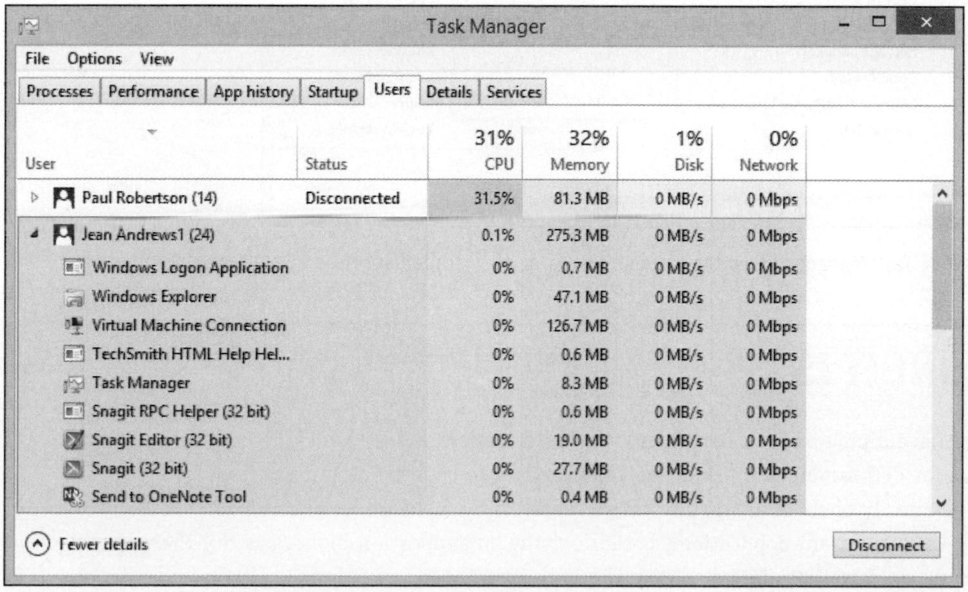

Figure 4-12   The Users tab shows system resources used by each signed-in user

To disconnect a remote user from the system, select the user and click **Disconnect** at the bottom of the screen. To sign out a user who signed in at the workstation, select the user and click **Sign out** at the bottom of the screen.

> ✎ **Notes** On the Users tab of Task Manager, you might need to click the white arrow beside a user account name to expand the view so you can see processes running under the user account.

SERVICES TAB

The Services tab (see Figure 4-13) lists the services currently installed along with the status of each service. Recall that a service is a program that runs in the background and is called on by other programs to perform a background task. Running services are sometimes listed in the notification area of the taskbar. A problem with a service can sometimes be resolved by stopping and restarting the service. For example, stopping and restarting the Spooler service might solve a problem with print jobs not moving on to the printer. To stop or restart, right-click the service and use the shortcut menu, as shown in Figure 4-13. The Services console can also be used to manage services, and you can open the console by clicking **Open Services** at the bottom of the window. How to use this console is discussed later in the chapter.

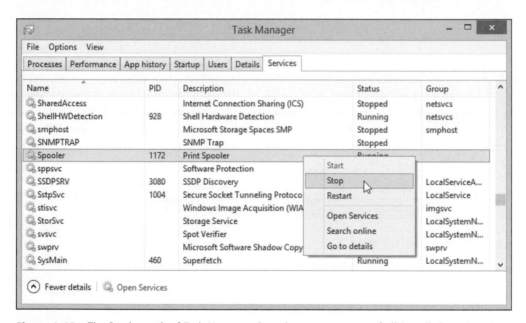

Figure 4-13   The Services tab of Task Manager gives the current status of all installed services

APPLYING | CONCEPTS   ADJUST THE PRIORITY LEVEL OF AN APPLICATION

**A+
220-902
1.4**

Each application running on your computer is assigned a priority level, which determines its position in the queue for CPU resources. You can use Task Manager to change the priority level for an application that is already open. If an application performs slowly, increase its priority. You should only do this with very important applications, because giving an application higher priority than certain background system processes can sometimes interfere with the operating system.

To use Task Manager to change the priority level of an open application, do the following:

1. In Task Manager, on the Processes tab, right-click the application and click **Go to details**.

2. On the Details tab, right-click the selected program and point to **Set priority**. Set the new priority to **Above normal** (see Figure 4-14). If that doesn't give satisfactory performance, then try **High**.

Remember that any changes you make to an application's priority level affect only the current session.

Figure 4-14 Change the priority level of a running application

⟨⟩ OS Differences For Windows 7/Vista, to set the priority for a process, begin with the **Applications** tab. Right-click the application and select **Go To Process**. On the Processes tab, right-click the selected process and point to **Set Priority**. You can then set the new priority.

ADMINISTRATIVE TOOLS

A+
220-902
1.4
Windows offers a group of Administrative Tools in Control Panel that are used by technicians and developers to support Windows. To see the list of tools, open Control Panel in Classic view and then click **Administrative Tools**. Figure 4-15 shows the Administrative Tools window for Windows 8 Pro. The Home editions of Windows don't include the Local Security Policy (controls many security settings on the local computer) or Print Management (manages print servers on a network).

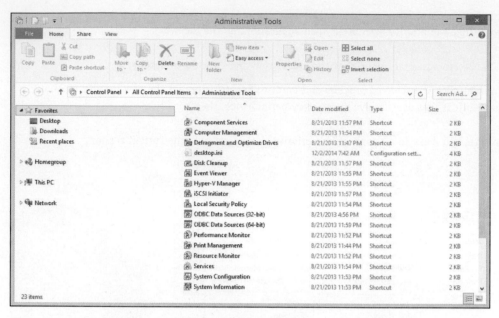

Figure 4-15   Administrative tools available in Windows 8 Pro

Several Administrative tools are covered next, including System Configuration, Services console, Computer Management, Microsoft Management Console (MMC), Event Viewer, Print Management, Task Scheduler, and Performance Monitor. Later in the text, you learn to use more Administrative tools.

SYSTEM CONFIGURATION

A+
220-902
1.4

You can use the System Configuration (msconfig.exe) utility, which is commonly pronounced "*M-S-config*," to temporarily disable programs from launching at startup in order to troubleshoot a startup problem. To open the System Configuration box, enter **msconfig.exe** in the Windows 8 Run box or in the Windows 7 Search box. The Windows 8 System Configuration box is shown in Figure 4-16 with the General tab selected.

Notes   To open the Windows 8 Run box, press **Win+X** and click **Run** in the Quick Launch menu. To open the Windows 7 Search box, click **Start**.

Caution   Don't depend on System Configuration to be a permanent fix to disable a startup program or service. Once you've decided you want to make the change permanent, use other methods to permanently remove that process from Windows startup. For example, you might uninstall a program, remove it from a startup folder, or use the Services console to disable a service.

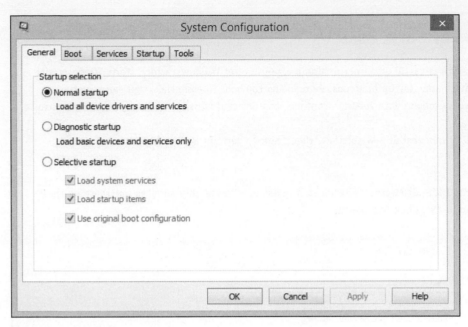

Figure 4-16 Use the General tab to control how Windows starts

Use the Boot tab (see Figure 4-17) to see information about the boot and control some boot settings. For example, in Figure 4-17, you can see this computer is set for a dual boot and, using this box, you can delete one of the choices for a dual boot from the boot loader menu. Also notice on the Boot tab the Boot options to apply when starting Windows. You learn more about these options in the chapter, "Troubleshooting Windows Startup."

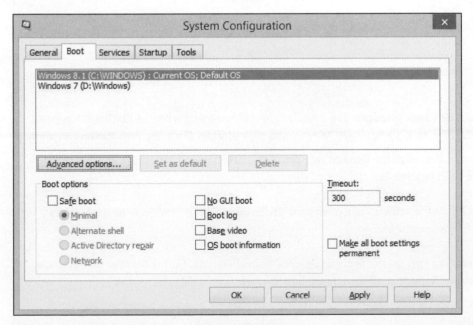

Figure 4-17 Use the Boot tab to control boot settings

APPLYING | CONCEPTS   PERFORM A CLEAN BOOT

A+
220-902
1.4

System Configuration is useful when performing a clean boot of Windows, which starts Windows with a basic set of drivers and startup programs. By reducing the boot to essentials, you can sometimes identify and solve a problem with software conflicts, bad device drivers, or startup processes that cause slow performance.

Suppose, for example, you cannot install new software. Here's how to perform a clean boot to verify other software is not in conflict:

1. On the Services tab, check **Hide all Microsoft services**. The list now shows only services put there by third-party software (see Figure 4-18). Click **Disable all**.

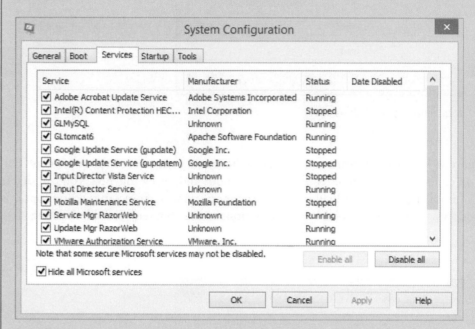

Figure 4-18   Use the Services tab of System Configuration to view and control services launched at startup

2. On the Startup tab, click **Open Task Manager**. The Task Manager window opens with the Startup tab selected (refer back to Figure 4-11). For each startup item, select it and click **Disable**. Close the Task Manager window.

3. In the System Configuration box, click the **General** tab. Notice that Selective startup is now selected. Click **Apply**. Close the System Configuration box and restart Windows.

Now you can try again to install the software in a clean boot environment. If the problem is resolved, here's how to return to a normal Windows startup:

1. Open the System Configuration box. On the General tab, click **Normal startup**. On the Services tab, uncheck **Hide all Microsoft services**. Verify that all services are now checked.

2. On the Startup tab, click **Open Task Manager**. In the Task Manager window, select each startup item and enable it. Close all windows.

The Tools tab in the System Configuration box gives you quick access to other Windows tools you might need during a troubleshooting session (see Figure 4-19).

Figure 4-19 The Tools tab makes it easy to find troubleshooting tools

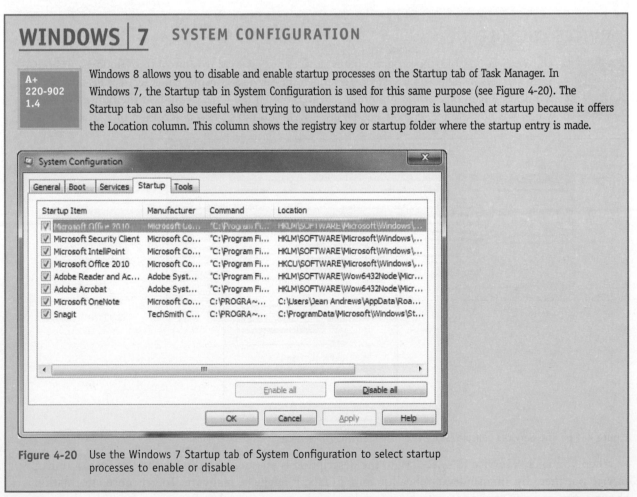

WINDOWS | 7   SYSTEM CONFIGURATION

A+
220-902
1.4

Windows 8 allows you to disable and enable startup processes on the Startup tab of Task Manager. In Windows 7, the Startup tab in System Configuration is used for this same purpose (see Figure 4-20). The Startup tab can also be useful when trying to understand how a program is launched at startup because it offers the Location column. This column shows the registry key or startup folder where the startup entry is made.

Figure 4-20   Use the Windows 7 Startup tab of System Configuration to select startup processes to enable or disable

(continues)

Here's how to use Windows 7 System Configuration to perform a clean boot:

1. Click **Start**, type **msconfig.exe** in the Search box, and then press **Enter**.

2. In the System Configuration box on the Services tab, check **Hide all Microsoft services** and click **Disable all**.

3. On the Startup tab (see Figure 4-20), click **Disable all**. Close System Configuration and restart the system.

🖉 **Notes** System Configuration reports only what it is programmed to look for when listing startup programs and services. It looks only in certain registry keys and startup folders, and sometimes does not report a startup process. Therefore, don't consider its list of startup processes to be complete.

◇ **OS Differences** Windows Vista uses the System Configuration utility to control startup programs just as does Windows 7. In addition, Vista offers Software Explorer, a user-friendly tool to control startup programs.

Hands-On | Project 4-1 Research Running Processes

Boot to the Windows desktop and then use Task Manager to get a list of all the running processes on your machine. Use the Windows Snipping Tool to save and print the Task Manager screens showing the list of processes. Next, perform a clean boot. Which processes that were loaded normally are not loaded when the system is running after a clean boot?

SERVICES CONSOLE

A+
220-902
1.4

The Services console (the program file is services.msc) is used to control the Windows and third-party services installed on a system. To launch the Services console, enter **services.msc** in the Windows 8 Run box or the Windows 7 Search box. If the Extended tab at the bottom of the window is not selected, click it (see Figure 4-21). This tab gives a description of a selected service.

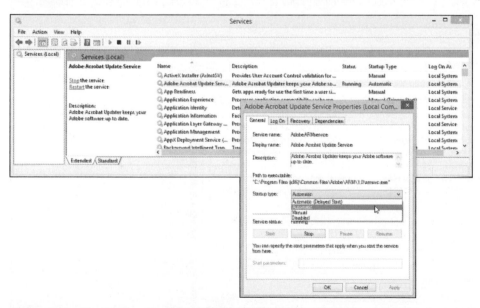

Figure 4-21 The Services console is used to manage Windows services

When you click a service to select it and the description is missing, most likely the service is a third-party service put there by an installed application and, in fact, it might be malware. To get more information about a service or to stop or start a service, right-click its name and select **Properties** from the shortcut menu. In the Properties box (see Figure 4-21), the startup types for a service are:

▲ *Automatic (Delayed Start).* Starts shortly after startup, after the user signs in, so as not to slow down the startup process

▲ *Automatic.* Starts when Windows loads

▲ *Manual.* Starts as needed

▲ *Disabled.* Cannot be started

> ✎ **Notes** If you suspect a Windows system service is causing a problem, you can use System Configuration to disable the service. If this works, then try replacing the service file with a fresh copy from the Windows setup DVD.

COMPUTER MANAGEMENT

Computer Management (compmgmt.msc) contains several tools that can be used to manage the local computer or other computers on the network. The window is called a console because it consolidates several Windows Administrative tools. To use most of these tools, you must be signed in as an administrator, although you can view certain settings in Computer Management if you are signed in with lesser privileges.

As with most Windows tools, there are several ways to access Computer Management:

▲ Enter **compmgmt.msc** in the Windows 8 Run box or the Windows 7 Search box.

▲ For Windows 8, press **Win+X** and click **Computer Management** in the Quick Launch menu. For Windows 7, click **Start**, right-click **Computer**, and select **Manage** from the shortcut menu.

▲ In Control Panel, look in the **Administrative Tools** group.

The Computer Management window is shown in Figure 4-22. Using this window, you can access Task Scheduler, Event Viewer, Shared Folders, Local Users and Groups, Performance Monitor, Device Manager, Disk Management, and the Services console. Several tools available from the Computer Management window are covered in this chapter.

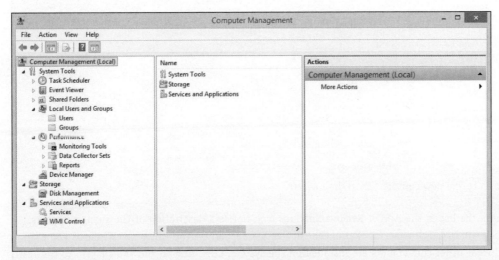

Figure 4-22 Windows Computer Management combines several Administrative tools into a single, easy-to-access window

MICROSOFT MANAGEMENT CONSOLE (MMC)

Microsoft Management Console (MMC; the program file is mmc.exe) is a Windows utility that can be used to build your own customized console windows. In a console, these individual tools are called snap-ins. A console is saved in a file with an .msc file extension, and a snap-in in a console can itself be a console. To use all the functions of MMC, you must be signed in with administrator privileges.

Notes A program that can work as a snap-in under the MMC has an .msc file extension.

APPLYING | CONCEPTS   CREATE A CONSOLE

**A+
220-902
1.4**

If you find yourself often using a few Windows tools, consider putting them in a console stored on your desktop. Follow these steps to create a console:

1. Enter **mmc.exe** in the Windows 8 Run box or the Windows 7 Search box. Respond to the UAC box. An empty console window appears, as shown in Figure 4-23.

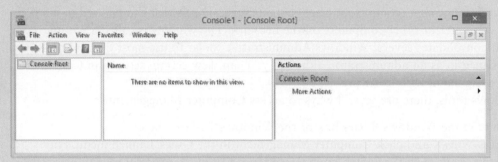

Figure 4-23   An empty console

2. Click **File** in the menu bar and then click **Add/Remove Snap-in**. The Add or Remove Snap-ins box opens, as shown on the left side of Figure 4-24.

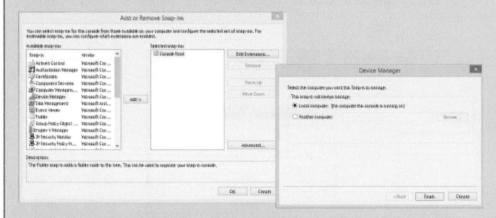

Figure 4-24   Add a snap-in to the new console

3. Select a snap-in from the list in the Add or Remove Snap-ins box. Notice a description of the snap-in appears at the bottom of the window. The snap-ins that appear in this list depend on the edition of Windows you have installed and what other components are installed on the system. Click **Add** to add the snap-in to the console.

4. If parameters for the snap-in need defining, a dialog box opens that allows you to set up these parameters. The dialog box offers different selections, depending on the snap-in being added. For example, when Device Manager is selected, a dialog box appears, asking you to select the computer that Device Manager will monitor (see the right side of Figure 4-24). Select **Local computer (the computer this console is running on)** and click **Finish**. The snap-in now appears in the list of snap-ins for this console.

5. Repeat Steps 3 and 4 to add all the snap-ins that you want to the console. When you finish, click **OK** in the Add or Remove Snap-ins box.

6. To save the console, click **File** in the menu bar and then click **Save As**. The Save As dialog box opens. A good place to save a console is the Windows desktop. Then close all windows.

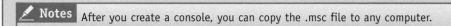

✎ **Notes**   After you create a console, you can copy the .msc file to any computer.

Hands-On | Project 4-2   Use the Microsoft Management Console

A+
220-902
1.4

Using the Microsoft Management Console in Windows 8 or Windows 7, create a customized console. Put two snap-ins in the console: Device Manager and Event Viewer. Store your console on the Windows desktop. Copy the console to another computer and install it on the Windows desktop.

EVENT VIEWER

A+
220-902
1.1, 1.4,
4.1

Just about anything that happens in Windows is logged by Windows, and these logs can be viewed using Event Viewer (eventvwr.msc). You can find events such as a hardware or network failure, OS error messages, a device or service that has failed to start, or General Protection Faults, which can cause Windows to lock up or hang.

Event Viewer is a Computer Management console snap-in, and you can open it by using the Computer Management window, by entering **Event Viewer** or **Eventvwr.msc** in the Windows 8 Run box or the Windows 7 Search box, or by using the Administrative Tools group in Control Panel. The Event Viewer window is shown in Figure 4-25.

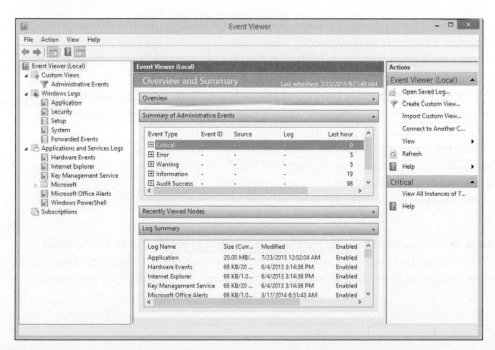

Figure 4-25   Use Event Viewer to see logs about hardware, Windows, security, and applications events

The different views of logs are listed in the left pane, and you can drill down into subcategories of these logs. First select a log in the left pane. To sort a list of events, click a column heading in the middle pane. Click an event in the middle pane to see details about the event. For example, in Figure 4-26, the Administrative Events log shows Windows had a problem loading a device driver.

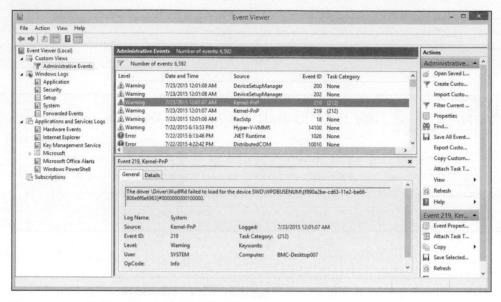

Figure 4-26   Click an event to see details about the event

The types of events are Critical, Error, Warning, Information, and Audit Success. Error events are the most important and indicate something went wrong with the system, such as a scheduled backup failed to work. Warning events indicate failure might occur in the future, and Critical events indicate a problem occurred with a critical Windows process.

Here are the views of logs that are the most useful:

▲ **Administrative Events log.** This log is a filtered log that shows only Critical, Error, and Warning events intended for the administrator. This log is in the Custom Views category and is selected in Figure 4-26.

▲ **Application log.** In the Windows Logs group, look in the Application log for events recorded by an application. This log might help you identify why an application is causing problems.

▲ **Security log.** Events in the Security log are called audits and include successful and unsuccessful sign-ins to a user account and attempts from another computer on the network to access shared resources on this computer.

▲ **Setup log.** Look in the Setup log for events recorded when applications are installed.

▲ **System log.** Look in the System log to find events triggered by Windows components, such as a device driver failing to load or a problem with hardware.

▲ **Forwarded Events log.** This log receives events that were recorded on other computers and sent to this computer.

When you first encounter a Windows, hardware, application, or security problem, get in the habit of checking Event Viewer as one of your first steps toward investigating the problem. To save time, first check the Administrative Events log because it filters out all events except Critical, Error, and Warning events.

CREATE CUSTOM LOG FILES

You can filter events and create a log of only your filtered events. Then you can save this custom view to an .evtx file, which you can use to document a problem or email to someone who is helping you troubleshoot a problem. To create a custom view, right-click any log in the left pane and select **Create Custom View** from the shortcut menu. The Create Custom View box appears (see Figure 4-27), which offers many ways to filter events.

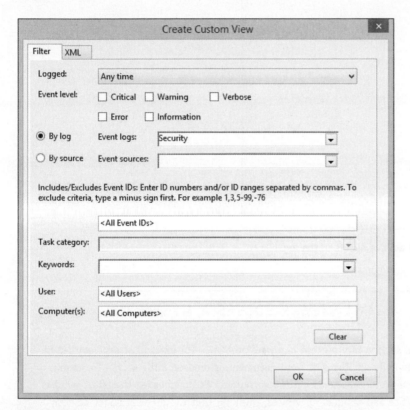

Figure 4-27   Criteria to filter events in Event Viewer for a custom view

After you select the filters, click **OK**. In the next box, name your custom view and click **OK**. Your custom view is now listed in the left pane. To save the view to an .evtx file, right-click it and click **Save All Events in Custom View As**. In the Save As box that appears, name the file and browse to where you want to save it. Then click **Save**. A good place to save an event log file is the desktop. Later, to view the log file, double-click the file name and it will open in Event Viewer.

LIMIT SIZE OF LOGS

To control the size of a log in Event Viewer, you can clear it. Right-click a log and click **Clear Log** in the shortcut menu. Before clearing the log, Event Viewer gives you a chance to save it. Be default, Event Viewer sets a maximum size for each log and overwrites older events with newer ones when the maximum size is reached. To change this setting so that you can control the maximum size of a log file and to cause the events to be archived before they are overwritten, right-click a log and select **Properties** from the log's shortcut menu. The properties box for the Application log is shown in Figure 4-28.

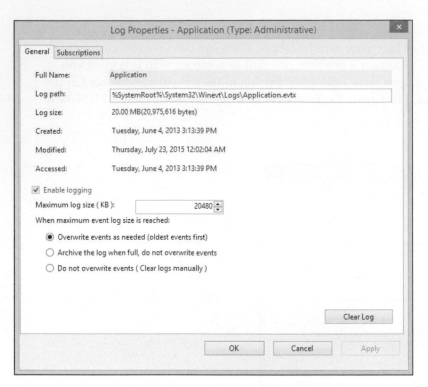

Figure 4-28   Control the size of a log file and archive events in the log

APPLYING | CONCEPTS   EVENT VIEWER SOLVES A MYSTERY

A+
220-902
1.1, 1.4,
4.1

Event Viewer can be useful in solving intermittent hardware problems. For example, I once worked in an office where several people updated Microsoft Word documents stored on a file server. For weeks, people complained about these Word documents getting corrupted. We downloaded the latest patches for Windows and Microsoft Office and scanned for viruses, thinking that the problem might be with Windows or the application. Then we suspected a corrupted template file for building the Word documents. But nothing we did solved our problem of corrupted Word documents. Then one day someone thought to check Event Viewer on the file server. Event Viewer had faithfully been recording errors when writing to the hard drive. What we had suspected to be a software problem was, in fact, a failing hard drive, which was full of bad sectors. We replaced the drive and the problem went away. That day I learned the value of checking Event Viewer very early in the troubleshooting process.

Hands-On | Project 4-3   Use Event Viewer

A+
220-902
1.1, 1.4,
4.1

Event Viewer can be intimidating to use but is really nothing more than a bunch of logs to search and manipulate. If you have Microsoft Office installed, open a Word document, make some changes in it, and close it without saving your changes. Now look in **Applications and Services Logs** and **Microsoft Office Alerts**. What event is recorded about your actions?

PRINT MANAGEMENT

A+
220-902
1.4

Windows professional and business editions offer the Print Management (printmanagement .msc) utility in the Administrative Tools group of Control Panel. (Home editions don't provide the Print Management tool.) You can use it to monitor and manage printer queues for all printers on the network. In Print Management, each computer on the network that shares a printer with other computers on the network is considered a print server.

4

APPLYING | CONCEPTS   LEARN TO USE PRINT MANAGEMENT

A+
220-902
1.4

Follow these steps to learn to use Print Management:

1. Open **Control Panel** in Classic view, click **Administrative Tools**, and double-click **Print Management**. The Print Management window appears.

2. In the Print Servers group, drill down to your local computer and click **Printers**. The list of printers installed on your computer appears, as shown in Figure 4-29.

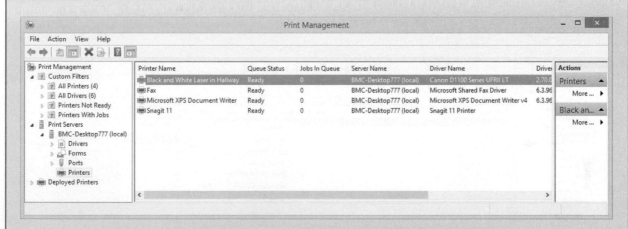

Figure 4-29   Use Print Management to monitor and manage printers on the network

3. To add other print servers to the list, right-click **Print Servers** in the left pane and click **Add/Remove Servers**. In the Add/Remove Servers box (see the left side of Figure 4-30), click **Browse**. Locate the computer (see the right side of Figure 4-30) and click **Select Server**. The computer is now listed under Add servers in the Add/Remove Servers box. Click **Add to List**. The computer is listed in the Print servers area. Click **OK** to close the Add/Remove Servers box.

(continues)

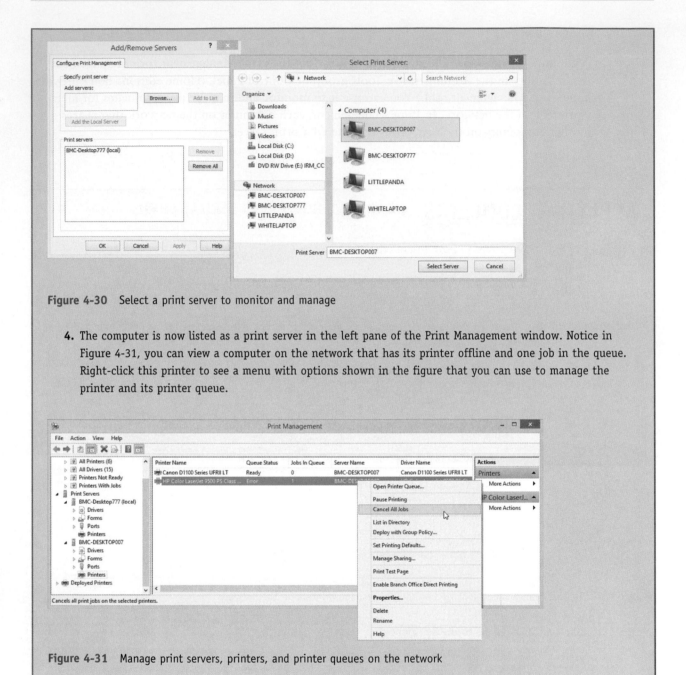

Figure 4-30   Select a print server to monitor and manage

4. The computer is now listed as a print server in the left pane of the Print Management window. Notice in Figure 4-31, you can view a computer on the network that has its printer offline and one job in the queue. Right-click this printer to see a menu with options shown in the figure that you can use to manage the printer and its printer queue.

Figure 4-31   Manage print servers, printers, and printer queues on the network

TASK SCHEDULER

**A+
220-902
1.4**

Windows Task Scheduler (taskschd.msc) is also among the Administrative Tools in Control Panel and is a Computer Management console that can be set to launch a task or program at a future time, including at startup. When applications install, they might schedule tasks to check for and download their program updates. Task Scheduler stores tasks in a file stored in the C:\ Windows\System32\Tasks folder. For example, in Figure 4-32, File Explorer shows 10 scheduled tasks in the folder and other tasks are stored in two subfolders.

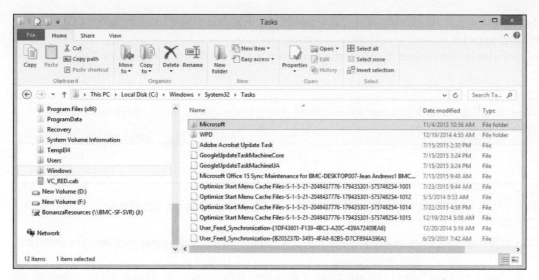

Figure 4-32   The Tasks folder contains tasks managed by Task Scheduler

To open Task Scheduler, enter **taskschd.msc** in the Windows 8 Run box or the Windows 7 Search box. Alternately, from Control Panel, double-click **Task Scheduler** in the Administrative Tools group. The Task Scheduler window is shown in Figure 4-33.

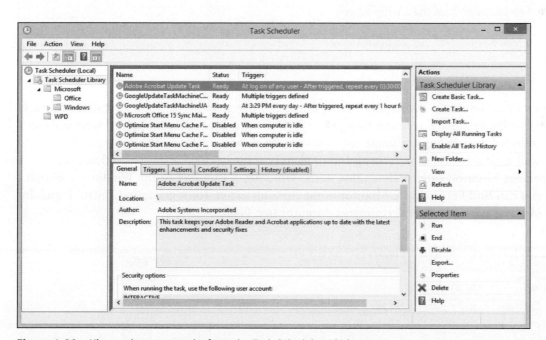

Figure 4-33   View and manage tasks from the Task Scheduler window

Here is what you need to know to use the Task Scheduler window:

◢ In the left pane, drill down into groups and subgroups. Notice in the left pane of Figure 4-33, the groups and subgroups match up with the folder structure in the Tasks folder of File Explorer, shown in Figure 4-32. Tasks in a group are listed in the middle pane.

◢ To see details about a task, including what triggers it, what actions it performs, the conditions and settings related to the task, and the history of past actions, select the task and then click the tabs in the lower-middle pane. For example, in the list of tasks shown in Figure 4-33, you can see that the Adobe Acrobat Update Task is scheduled to run when any user signs in.

◢ To add a new task, first select the group for the new task. In the Actions pane on the right, click **Create Basic Task**. A wizard appears to step you through creating the task.

◢ To delete, disable, or run a task, select it and in the Actions pane, click Delete, Disable, or Run.

> ✎ **Notes** Tasks can be hidden in the Task Scheduler window. To be certain you're viewing all scheduled tasks, unhide them. In the menu bar, click **View** and make sure **Show Hidden Tasks** is checked.

Hands-On | Project 4-4 Practice Launching Programs at Startup

A+ 220-902 1.4

Do the following to practice launching programs at startup, listing the steps you took for each activity:

1. Configure Scheduled Tasks to launch Notepad each time the computer starts and any user signs in. List the steps you took.

2. Put a shortcut in a startup folder so that any user launches a command prompt window at startup. See the appendix, "Entry Points for Windows Startup Programs," for a list of startup folders.

3. Restart the system and verify that both programs are launched. Did you receive any errors?

4. Remove the two programs from the startup process.

PERFORMANCE MONITOR

A+ 220-902 1.4, 4.1

Performance Monitor is a Microsoft Management Console snap-in (perfmon.msc) that can track activity by hardware and software to measure performance. It can monitor in real time and can save collected data in logs for future use. Software developers might use this tool to evaluate how well their software is performing and to identify software and hardware bottlenecks.

To open Performance Monitor, enter **perfmon.msc** in the Windows 8 Run box or the Windows 7 Search box. Alternately, you can find Performance Monitor in the Administrative Tools group in Control Panel. In the Performance Monitor window, click Performance Monitor (see Figure 4-34).

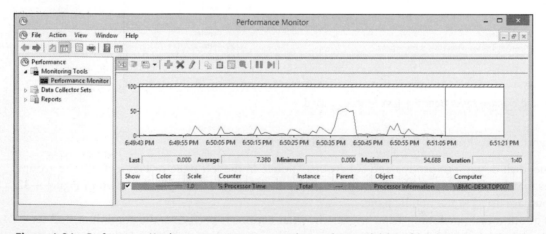

Figure 4-34 Performance Monitor uses counters to monitor various activities of hardware and software

Performance Monitor offers hundreds of counters used to examine many aspects of the system related to performance. The Windows default setting is to show the %Processor Time counter the first time you open the window (see Figure 4-34). This counter appears as a red line in the graph and tracks activity of the processor.

To keep from unnecessarily using system resources, only use the counters you really need. For example, suppose you want to track hard drive activity. You first remove the %Processor Time counter. To delete a counter, select the counter from the list so that it is highlighted and click the red **X** above the graph.

Next add two counters: the % Disk Time counter and Avg. Disk Queue Length counter in the PhysicalDisk group. The % Disk Time counter tracks the percentage of time the hard drive is in use, and the Avg. Disk Queue Length counter tracks the average number of processes waiting to use the hard drive. To add a counter, click the green **plus sign** above the graph. Then, in the Add Counters box, select a counter and click **Add**. Figure 4-35 shows the Add Counters box with two counters added. After all your counters are added, click **OK**.

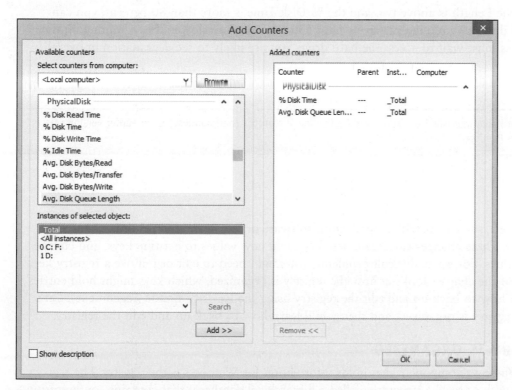

Figure 4-35   Add counters to set up what Performance Monitor tracks

Allow Performance Monitor to keep running while the system is in use, and then check the counters. The results for one system are shown in Figure 4-36. Select each counter and note the average, minimum, and maximum values for the counter.

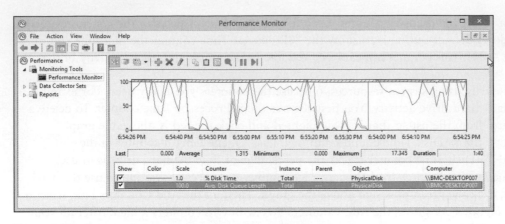

Figure 4-36 Two counters can measure hard drive performance

If the Avg. Disk Queue Length is above two and the % Disk Time is more than 80 percent, you can conclude that the hard drive is working excessively hard and processes are slowed down waiting on the drive. Anytime a process must wait to access the hard drive, you are likely to see degradation in overall system performance.

> **⟳ OS Differences** The Windows Vista Reliability and Performance Monitor (perfmon.msc) is an earlier version of Windows 8/7 Performance Monitor.

REGISTRY EDITOR

A+
220-902
1.4, 4.1

Many actions, such as installing application software or hardware, can result in changes to the registry. These changes can create new keys, add new values to existing keys, and change existing values. For a few difficult problems, you might need to edit or remove a registry key. This part of the chapter looks at how the registry is organized, which keys might hold entries causing problems, and how to back up and edit the registry using the Registry Editor (regedit.exe). Let's first look at how the registry is organized, and then you'll learn how to back up and edit the registry.

HOW THE REGISTRY IS ORGANIZED

The most important Windows component that holds information for Windows is the registry. The registry is a database designed with a treelike structure (called a hierarchical database) that contains configuration information for Windows, users, software applications, and installed hardware devices. During startup, Windows builds the registry in memory and keeps it there until Windows shuts down. During startup, after the registry is built, Windows reads from it to obtain information to complete the startup process. After Windows is loaded, it continually reads from many of the subkeys in the registry.

Windows builds the registry from the current hardware configuration and from information it takes from these files:

◢ Five files stored in the C:\Windows\System32\config folder; these files are called hives, and they are named the SAM (Security Accounts Manager), SECURITY, SOFTWARE, SYSTEM, and DEFAULT hives. (Each hive is backed up with a log file and a backup file, which are also stored in the C:\Windows\System32\config folder.)

◢ C:\Users*username*\Ntuser.dat file, which holds the preferences and settings of the currently signed-in user.

After the registry is built in memory, it is organized into five high-level keys (see Figure 4-37). Each key can have subkeys, and subkeys can have more subkeys and can be assigned one or more values. The way data is organized in the hive files is different from the way it is organized in registry keys. Figure 4-38 shows the relationship between registry keys and hives. For example, in the figure, notice that the HKEY_CLASSES_ROOT key contains data that comes from the SOFTWARE and DEFAULT hive, and some of this data is also stored in the larger HKEY_LOCAL_MACHINE key.

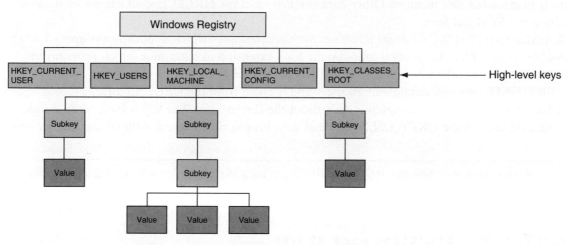

Figure 4-37   The Windows registry is logically organized in five keys with subkeys

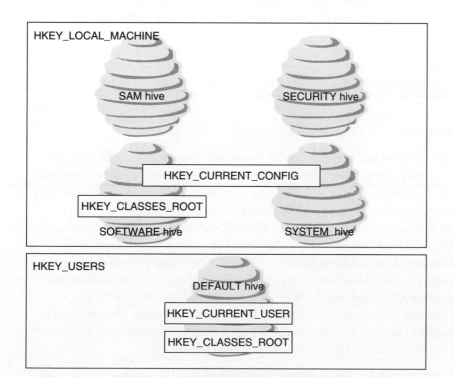

Figure 4-38   The relationship between registry keys and hives

Here are the five keys, including where they get their data and their purposes:

▲ HKEY_LOCAL_MACHINE (HKLM) is the most important key and contains hardware, software, and security data. The data is taken from four hives: the SAM hive, the SECURITY hive, the SOFTWARE hive, and the SYSTEM hive. In addition, the HARDWARE subkey of HKLM is built when the registry is first loaded, based on data collected about the current hardware configuration.

▲ HKEY_CURRENT_CONFIG (HKCC) contains information that identifies each hardware device installed on the computer. Some of the data is gathered from the current hardware configuration when the registry is first loaded into memory. Other data is taken from the HKLM key, which got its data primarily from the SYSTEM hive.

▲ HKEY_CLASSES_ROOT (HKCR) stores information that determines which application is opened when the user double-clicks a file. This process relies on the file's extension to determine which program to load. Data for this key is gathered from the HKLM key and the HKCU key.

▲ HKEY_USERS (HKU) contains data about all users and is taken from the DEFAULT hive.

▲ HKEY_CURRENT_USER (HKCU) contains data about the current user. The key is built when a user signs in using data kept in the HKEY_USERS key and data kept in the Ntuser.dat file of the current user.

> **✎ Notes** Device Manager reads data from the HKLM\HARDWARE key to build the information it displays about hardware configurations. You can consider Device Manager to be an easy-to-view presentation of this HARDWARE key data.

BEFORE YOU EDIT THE REGISTRY, BACK IT UP!

When you need to edit the registry, if possible, make the change from the Windows tool that is responsible for the key—for example, by using the Programs and Features applet in Control Panel. If that doesn't work and you must edit the registry, always back up the registry before attempting to edit it. Changes made to the registry are implemented immediately.

> **⚡ Caution** There is no undo feature in the Registry Editor, and no opportunity to change your mind once the edit is made.

Here are the ways to back up the registry:

▲ *Use System Protection to create a restore point.* A restore point keeps information about the registry. You can restore the system to a restore point to undo registry changes, as long as the registry is basically intact and not too corrupted. Also know that, if System Protection is turned on, Windows automatically makes a daily backup of the registry hive files to the C:\Windows\System32\Config\RegBack folder.

▲ *Back up a single registry key just before you edit the key.* This method, called exporting a key, should always be used before you edit the registry. How to export a key is coming up in this chapter.

▲ *Make an extra copy of the C:\Windows\System32\config folder.* This is what I call the old-fashioned shotgun approach to backing up the registry. This backup will help if the registry gets totally trashed. You can boot from the Windows setup DVD and use the Windows Recovery Environment to get a command prompt window that you can use to restore the folder from your extra copy. This method is drastic and not recommended except in severe cases. But, still, just to be on the safe side, you can make an extra copy of this folder just before you start any serious digging into the registry.

In some situations, such as when you're going to make some drastic changes to the registry, you'll want to play it safe and use more than one backup method. Extra registry backups are always a good thing! Now let's look at how to back up an individual key in the registry, and then you'll learn how to edit the registry.

Backing Up and Restoring Individual Keys in the Registry

A less time-consuming method of backing up the registry is to back up a particular key that you plan to edit. However, know that if the registry gets corrupted, having a backup of only a particular key most likely will not help you much when trying a recovery. Also, although you could use this technique to back up the entire registry or an entire tree within the registry, it is not recommended.

To back up a key along with its subkeys in the registry, follow these steps:

1. Open the Registry Editor. To do that, enter **regedit** in the Windows 8 Run box or the Windows 7 Search box and respond to the UAC box. Figure 4-39 shows the Registry Editor with the five main keys and several subkeys listed. Click the triangles on the left to see subkeys. When you select a subkey, such as KeyboardClass in the figure, the names of the values in that subkey are displayed in the right pane along with the data assigned to each value.

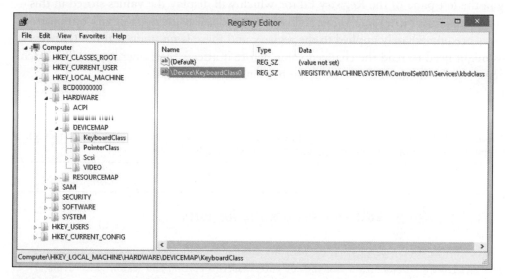

Figure 4-39 The Registry Editor showing the five main keys, subkeys, values, and data

> **Notes** The full path to a selected key displays in the status bar at the bottom of the editor window. If the status bar is missing, click **View** in the menu bar and make sure **Status Bar** is checked.

2. Suppose we want to back up the registry key that contains a list of installed software, which is HKLM\ SOFTWARE\Microsoft\Windows\CurrentVersion\Uninstall. (HKLM stands for HKEY_LOCAL_MACHINE.) First click the appropriate triangles to navigate to the key. Next, right-click the key and select **Export** from the shortcut menu, as shown in Figure 4-40. The Export Registry File dialog box appears.

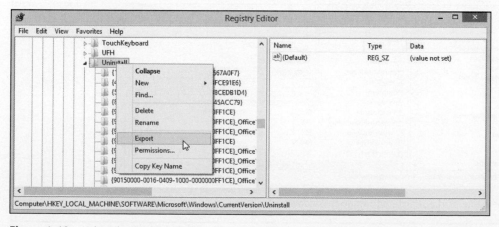

Figure 4-40 Using the Registry Editor, you can back up a key and its subkeys with the Export command

3. Select the location to save the export file and name the file. A convenient place to store an export file while you edit the registry is the desktop. Click **Save** when done. The file saved will have a .reg file extension.

4. You can now edit the key. Later, if you need to undo your changes, exit the Registry Editor and double-click the saved export file. The key and its subkeys saved in the export file will be restored. After you're done with an export file, delete it so that no one accidentally double-clicks it and reverts the registry to an earlier setting.

Editing the Registry

Before you edit the registry, you should use one or more of the four backup methods just discussed so that you can restore it if something goes wrong. To edit the registry, open the **Registry Editor (regedit.exe)**, and locate and select the key in the left pane of the Registry Editor, which will display the values stored in this key in the right pane. To edit, rename, or delete a value, right-click it and select the appropriate option from the shortcut menu. Changes are immediately applied to the registry and there is no undo feature. (However, Windows or applications might need to read the changed value before it affects their operations.) To search the registry for keys, values, and data, click **Edit** in the menu bar and then click **Find**.

> ⚡ **Caution**   Changes made to the registry take effect immediately. Therefore, take extra care when editing the registry. If you make a mistake and don't know how to correct a problem you create, then double-click the exported key to recover. When you double-click an exported key, the registry is updated with the values stored in this key.

Hands-On | Project 4-5   Edit and Restore the Registry

A+
220-902
1.4, 4.1

When you install Windows on a new computer, Windows setup gives you opportunity to enter the registered owner and registered organization of the computer. Practice editing and restoring the registry by doing the following to change the registered owner name:

1. In the Windows 8 Run box or the Windows 7 Search box, enter **winver.exe**, which displays the About Windows box. Who is the registered owner and registered organization of your computer?

2. Using the Registry Editor, export the registry key HKEY_LOCAL_MACHINE\SOFTWARE\Microsoft\Windows NT\ CurrentVersion to an export file stored on the desktop.

3. With the HKEY_LOCAL_MACHINE\SOFTWARE\Microsoft\Windows NT\CurrentVersion key selected in the left pane, double-click **RegisteredOwner** value in the right pane. The Edit String box appears (see Figure 4-41). Change the Value data, which is highlighted in the box and click **OK**. Close the Registry Editor window.

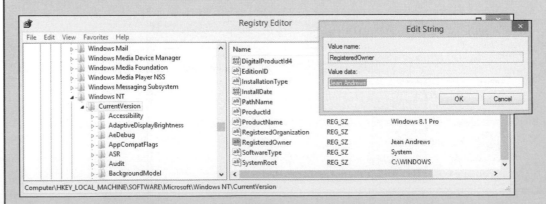

Figure 4-41   Change the name of the registered owner of Windows

4. Use the **winver** command again to display the About Windows box. Did the new name show as the registered owner? Close the box.

5. To restore the Value data to its original name, double-click the exported key on your desktop. Once again, use the **winver** command to display the About Windows box and verify the original name is restored. Close the box.

6. Delete the exported registry key stored on the desktop.

From these directions, you can see that changes made to the registry take effect immediately. Therefore, take extra care when editing the registry. If you make a mistake and don't know how to correct a problem you create, then you can restore the key that you exported by exiting the Registry Editor and double-clicking the exported key.

DISPLAY SETTINGS AND GRAPHICS SOFTWARE

**A+
220-902
1.1, 1.5,
4.1**

Use the Display applet in Control Panel to manage display settings. In Control Panel, open the Display applet and the Display window shown in Figure 4-42 appears.

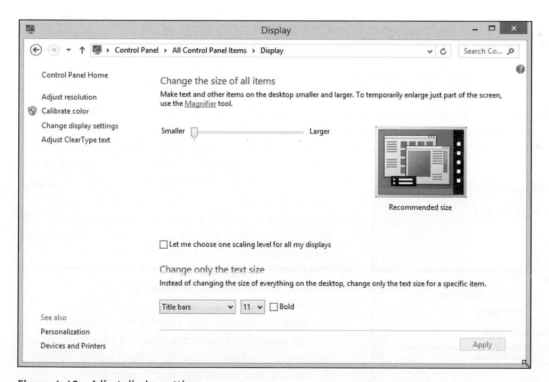

Figure 4-42 Adjust display settings

Here are a few basic display settings:

◢ To adjust color depth, click **Calibrate color** on the Display window and follow directions on screen.
◢ To adjust resolution (the number of horizontal and vertical pixels used to build one screen), click Adjust resolution. On the Screen Resolution window (see the right side of Figure 4-43), select the highest or recommended resolution. The recommended resolution is usually the native resolution, which is the optimal resolution the monitor was designed to support.

◢ The refresh rate is the number of times the monitor refreshes the screen in one second. To set the rate, click **Advanced settings** on the Screen Resolution window. The video adapter properties box appears. Click the **Monitor** tab and select the highest value available under Screen refresh rate (see Figure 4-43).

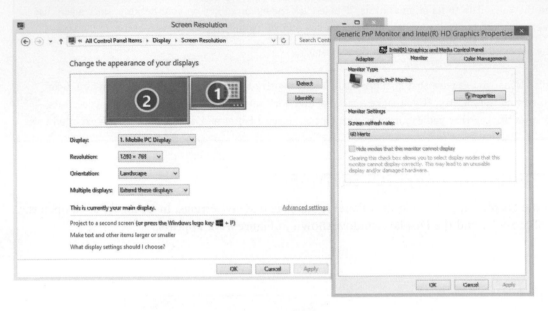

Figure 4-43 Adjust refresh rate on the monitor properties box

◢ For a dual-monitor setup, use the Screen Resolution window to configure multiple displays. For a multiple monitor orientation problem, drag the two monitor boxes on the Screen Resolution window so that the boxes represent the relative positions of each monitor. (For example, in Figure 4-43, the right monitor is represented by box 1 and the left monitor is represented by box 2.) You can also adjust the boxes so they are horizontal or vertical relative to each other. If you stack the boxes vertically, the pointer moves vertically from monitor to monitor. For either a horizontal or vertical multiple monitor misalignment problem, align the two boxes evenly and not staggered so that the pointer moves straight across or straight up or down to the second monitor without staggering. For best results, use the same screen resolution for both monitors.

◢ Windows 8 offers a multimonitor taskbar, which is the option to extend the desktop taskbar across both monitors. (Windows 7/Vista does not have this option.) To make the adjustment, right-click the taskbar and click **Properties**. You can manage the taskbar for multiple displays on the Taskbar tab of the taskbar properties box (see Figure 4-44).

Figure 4-44 Use the taskbar properties box to manage the taskbar on multiple displays

Recall from the chapter, "Installing Windows," that Windows requires the video adapter and drivers support DirectX 9. DirectX is a Microsoft software development tool that software developers can use to write multimedia applications, such as games, video-editing software, and computer-aided design software. The video firmware on the video card or motherboard chipset can interpret DirectX commands to build 3D.

If an application, such as a game or desktop publishing app that relies heavily on graphics is not performing well or giving errors, the problem might be the version of DirectX the system is using. You can use the dxdiag.exe command to display information about hardware and diagnose problems with DirectX. To use the command, enter **dxdiag.exe** in the Windows 8 Run box or the Windows 7 Search box. The first time you use the command, a message box appears asking if you want to check if your drivers are digitally signed. Then the opening window shown in Figure 4-45 appears. Look for the version of DirectX installed (version 11 in the figure).

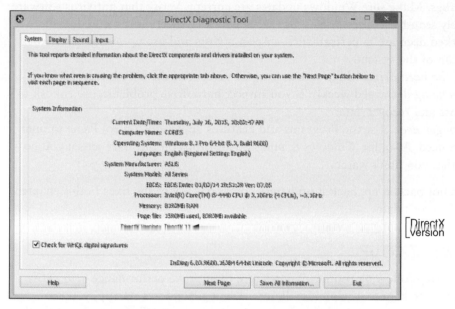

Figure 4-45 The DirectX Diagnostic tool reports information about DirectX components

To find out the latest version of DirectX published by Microsoft, go to *www.microsoft.com* and search on "DirectX End-User Runtime Web Installer." You can use a link on the page to download and install a new version of DirectX.

Now let's turn our attention to the step-by-step procedures using the tools you just learned about to improve Windows performance.

IMPROVING WINDOWS PERFORMANCE

**A+
220-902
1.1, 4.1**

In this part of the chapter, you learn to search for problems affecting performance and to clean up the Windows startup process. These step-by-step procedures go beyond the routine maintenance tasks you learned about in the chapter, "Maintaining Windows." We're assuming Windows starts with no errors. If you are having trouble loading Windows, it's best to address the error first rather than to use the tools described here to improve performance. How to handle errors that keep Windows from starting is covered in the chapter, "Troubleshooting Windows Startup."

★ **A+ Exam Tip** The A+ 220-902 exam expects you to know how to troubleshoot and solve problems with slow system performance.

Now let's look at five steps you can take to improve Windows performance.

STEP 1: PERFORM ROUTINE MAINTENANCE

It might seem pretty mundane, but the first things you need to do to improve performance of a sluggish Windows system are the routine maintenance tasks that you learned in the chapter, "Maintaining Windows." These tasks are summarized here:

◢ *Verify critical Windows settings.* Make sure Windows updates are current. Verify that antivirus software is updated and set to routinely scan for viruses. Make sure the network connection is secured. If the system is experiencing a marked decrease in performance, suspect a virus and use up-to-date antivirus software to perform a full scan of the system.

◢ *Clean up, defrag, and check the hard drive.* Make sure at least 15 percent of drive C: is free. Make sure a magnetic hard drive is being defragged weekly. If you suspect hard drive problems, use chkdsk to check the hard drive for errors and recover data.

◢ *Uninstall software you no longer need.* Use the Programs and Features applet in Control Panel to uninstall programs you no longer need. Also, for Windows 8, uninstall any apps on the Start screen you no longer use and turn off live tiles you don't watch.

As always, if valuable data is not backed up, back it up before you apply any of the fixes in this chapter. You don't want to risk losing the user's data.

STEP 2: CLEAN WINDOWS STARTUP

The most important step following routine maintenance to improve performance is to verify that startup programs are kept to a minimum. Before cleaning Windows startup, you can perform a clean boot to set a benchmark for the time it takes to start Windows when only the bare minimum of programs are launched.

OBSERVE PERFORMANCE IN A CLEAN BOOT

To find out if programs and services are slowing down Windows startup, perform a clean boot, which was described earlier in the chapter, and watch to see if performance improves. Do the following:

1. Use a stopwatch or a watch with a second hand to time a normal startup from the moment you press the power button until the wait icon on the Windows desktop disappears.

2. Time the boot again, this time using a clean boot.

If the difference is significant, follow the steps in this part of the chapter to reduce Windows startup to essentials. If the performance problem still exists after a clean boot, you can assume that the problem is with hardware or Windows settings and you can proceed to *Step 3: Check If the Hardware Can Support the OS.*

INVESTIGATE AND ELIMINATE STARTUP PROGRAMS

To speed up startup, search for unnecessary startup programs you can eliminate. Tools that can help are System Configuration (msconfig.exe), startup folders, and Task Manager. Follow these steps to investigate startup:

1. Open the **Startup** tab in Windows 8 Task Manager or the **Startup** tab in Windows 7 System Configuration. In the list of startup items, look for a specific startup program you don't want. If you're not sure of the purpose of a program, for Windows 8, right-click the program and click **Search online** in the shortcut menu. (For Windows 7, scroll to the right in the Command column to see the location and name of the startup program file and use that information for a web search.) Then search the web for information on this program. Be careful to use only reliable sites for credible information.

4

> ⚡ **Caution** A word of caution is important here: Many websites will tell you a legitimate process is malicious so that you will download and use their software to get rid of the process. However, their software is likely to be adware or spyware that you don't want. Make sure you can trust a site before you download from it or take its advice.

2. If you want to find out if disabling a startup entry gives problems or improves performance, temporarily disable it using Windows 8 Task Manager or Windows 7 System Configuration. To permanently disable a startup item, it's best to uninstall the software or remove the entry from a startup folder. See the appendix, "Entry Points for Windows Startup Processes," for a list of startup folders.

> ✏ **Notes** The startup folder for all users is hidden by default. In the chapter, "Survey of Windows Features and Support Tools," you learned how to unhide folders that are hidden.

3. As you research startup processes, Task Manager can tell you what processes are currently running. Open Task Manager and select the **Processes**. If you see a process and want to know its program file location, in Windows 8, right-click the process and click **Open file location**. File Explorer opens at the program file's location.

> ◇ **OS Differences** For Windows 7, to find out the file location, click **View** and click **Select Columns**. In the Select Process Page Columns, check **Image Path Name** and click **OK**. The Image Path Name column is added to the Processes tab.

For extremely slow systems that need a more drastic fix, set Windows for a clean boot. Then restart the system and see what problems you get into with a program disabled that you really need. Then enable just the ones you decide you need.

Regardless of the method you use, be sure to restart the system after each change and note what happens. Do you get an error message? Does a device or application not work? If so, you have probably disabled a service or program you need.

Has performance improved? If performance does not improve by disabling services or startup programs, go back and enable them again. If no non-Microsoft service or startup program caused the problem, then you can assume the problem is caused by a Microsoft service or startup program. Start disabling them one at a time.

> ⚡ **Caution** You might be tempted to disable all Microsoft services. If you do so, you are disabling Networking, Event Logging, Error Reporting, Windows Firewall, Windows Installer, Windows Backup, Print Spooler, Windows Update, System Protection, and other important services. These services should be disabled only when testing for performance problems and then immediately enabled when the test is finished. Also, know that if you disable the Volume Shadow Copy service, all restore points kept on the system will be lost. If you intend to use System Restore to fix a problem with the system, don't disable this service. If you are not sure what a service does, read its description in the Services console before you change its status.

Remember that you don't want to permanently leave System Configuration or Task Manager in control of startup. After you have used these two tools to identify the problem, use other tools to permanently remove a service or program from startup that is causing a problem. Use the Services console to disable a service, use the Programs and Features window to uninstall software, and remove program files from startup folders. After the problem is fixed, return System Configuration and/or Task Manager to a normal startup.

Don't forget to restart the computer after making a change to verify that all is well.

CHECK FOR UNWANTED SCHEDULED TASKS

When applications install, they often schedule tasks to check for and download their program updates, and malware sometimes hides as a scheduled task. Scheduled tasks might be unnecessary and can slow a system down. The best way to uninstall a scheduled task is to uninstall the software that is responsible for the task. Open the Task Scheduler window and search through tasks looking for those you think are unnecessary or causing trouble. Research the software the task works with and then you might decide to uninstall the software or disable the task.

Don't forget to restart the system to make sure all is well before you move on.

MONITOR THE STARTUP PROCESS

Now that you have the startup process clean, you will want to keep it that way. You can use several third-party tools to monitor any changes to startup. A good one is WinPatrol by Ruiware (*www.winpatrol.com*). Download and install the free version of the program to run in the background to monitor all sorts of things, including changes to the registry, startup processes, Internet Explorer settings, and system files. In Figure 4-46, you can see how WinPatrol gave an alert when it detected malware about to register itself as a service to launch at startup. WinPatrol displays a little black Scotty dog in the notification area of the taskbar to indicate it's running in the background and guarding your system. Also, many antivirus programs monitor the startup process and inform you when changes are made.

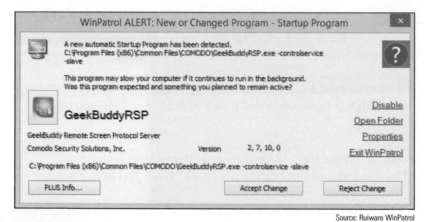

Source: Ruiware WinPatrol

Figure 4-46 WinPatrol by Ruiware alerts you when a program is making a system change

---

Hands-On | Project 4-6 Monitor Startup Items with WinPatrol

1. Using Task Manager and/or System Configuration, disable all the non-Windows startup items and services. Restart your computer.

2. Download and install WinPatrol from *www.winpatrol.com*.

3. Using Task Manager and/or System Configuration, enable all of the disabled startup items and services and restart the computer.

4. Are the startup programs and services able to start? What messages are displayed on the screen?

STEP 3: CHECK IF THE HARDWARE CAN SUPPORT THE OS

The system might be slow because the OS does not have the hardware resources it needs. Use System Information (msinfo32.exe) to find the model and speed of the installed processor and hard drive and the amount of memory installed. Compare all these values with the minimum and recommended requirements for Windows listed in the chapter, "Installing Windows."

If you suspect that the processor, hard drive, or memory is a bottleneck, use Performance Monitor to get more information. If the bottleneck appears to be graphics, the problem might be solved by updating the graphics drivers or video adapter.

If you find that the system is slow because of a hardware component, discuss the situation with the user. You might be able to upgrade the hardware or install another OS that is compatible with the hardware that is present. Upgrading from Windows 7 to Windows 8.1 can often improve performance in a computer that has slow hardware components. Better still, perform a clean installation of Windows 8.1 so that you get a fresh start with installed applications, plug-ins, and background services that might be slowing down the system.

STEP 4: CHECK FOR A HISTORY OF PROBLEMS

**A+
220-902
4.1**

If you have the opportunity to interview the user, try to identify when the slow performance problem began. You can then use the Action Center and Reliability Monitor to find out what changes were made to the system around that time and what other problems occurred. Open Control Panel in Classic view and then open **Action Center**. In the Action Center, expand the **Maintenance** group and click **View reliability history**. The Reliability Monitor opens (see Figure 4-47).

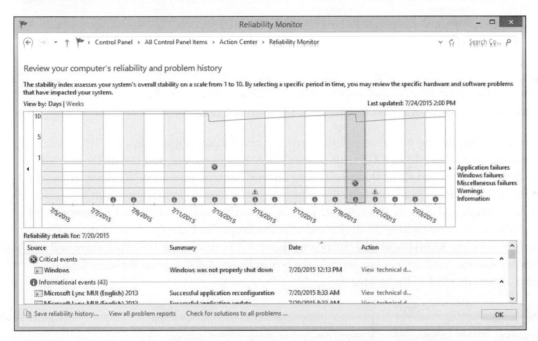

Figure 4-47   Use the Reliability Monitor to search for when a problem began and what else happened about that time

Click a date to see a list of activities on that day. If you don't know when the problem started, skim through the line graph at the top of the Reliability Monitor window and look for drops in the graph. Also look for critical events indicated by a red X (refer to Figure 4-47).

STEP 5: CONSIDER USING READYBOOST

**A+
220-902
1.1, 4.1**

Windows ReadyBoost uses a flash drive or secure digital (SD) memory card to boost hard drive performance. The faster flash memory is used as a buffer to speed up hard drive access time. You see the greatest performance increase using ReadyBoost when you have a slow magnetic hard drive (running at less than 7200 RPM). To find out what speed your hard drive is using, use System Information (msinfo32.exe) and drill down into the Components, Storage group, and select Disks (see Figure 4-48). The model of the hard drive appears in the right pane. Use Google to search on this brand and model; a quick search shows this drive runs at 5400 RPM. It's, therefore, a good candidate to benefit from ReadyBoost.

★ **A+ Exam Tip** The A+ 220-902 exam expects you to know how to use ReadyBoost to improve performance.

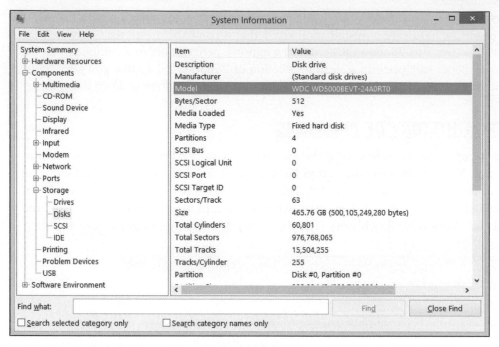

Figure 4-48   Use the System Information window to find out the brand and model of your hard drive

When you first connect a flash device, Windows will automatically test it to see if it qualifies for ReadyBoost. To qualify, it must have a capacity of 256 MB to 4 GB with at least 256 MB of free space, and run at about 2 MB/sec of throughput. If the device qualifies and ReadyBoost will speed up hard drive performance, Windows displays a dialog box that can be used to activate ReadyBoost. Follow directions on screen to decide how much of the device memory to allot for ReadyBoost and activate ReadyBoost. You can manually have Windows test a memory card or flash drive for ReadyBoost by right-clicking the device and selecting **Properties** from the shortcut menu. On the device properties box, click the **ReadyBoost** tab. The box in Figure 4-49a reports the USB flash drive will not improve performance because the hard drive is fast enough; the box in Figure 4-49b reports the same USB flash drive will help another system that has a slower hard drive.

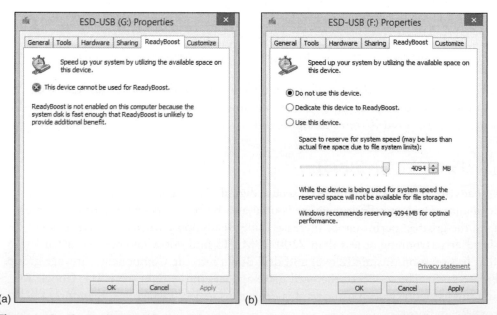

Figure 4-49   The ReadyBoost tab gives information about a device and system qualifying for ReadyBoost

The best flash devices to use for ReadyBoost are the ones that can take advantage of the faster ports. For example, a SuperSpeed USB (USB 3.0) device and port is about 10 times faster than a Hi-Speed USB (USB 2.0) device and port. Incidentally, when you remove the device, no data is lost because the device only holds a copy of the data.

WINDOWS | 7   DISABLE THE AERO INTERFACE

> **A+**
> **220-902**
> **1.1, 4.1**

The Windows 7/Vista Aero interface might be slowing down the system because it uses memory and computing power. Try disabling it. If performance improves, you can conclude that the hardware is not able to support the Aero interface. At that point, you might want to upgrade memory, upgrade the video card, or leave the Aero interface disabled.

To disable the Aero interface using Windows 7, do the following:

1. Right-click the desktop and select **Personalize** from the shortcut menu. The Personalization window opens (see Figure 4-50).

2. Scroll down to and click **Windows 7 Basic** and close the window.

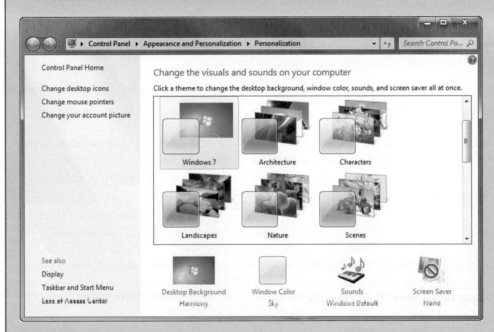

Figure 4-50 Disable the Windows 7 Aero interface to conserve system resources

> **✪ OS Differences** Recall that the Vista sidebar appears on the Windows desktop to hold apps called gadgets. The sidebar uses system resources and disabling it can improve performance. To do that, right-click the sidebar and select **Properties** from the shortcut menu. In the Sidebar Properties box, uncheck **Start Sidebar when Windows starts** and click **OK**.

MANUALLY REMOVING SOFTWARE

> **A+**
> **220-902**
> **1.1, 1.4,**
> **4.1**

In this part of the chapter, we focus on getting rid of programs that refuse to uninstall or give errors when uninstalling. In these cases, you can manually uninstall a program. Doing so often causes problems later, so use the methods discussed in this section only as a last resort after normal uninstall methods have failed.

This part of the chapter discusses the following steps to manually remove software:

1. First try to locate and use an uninstall routine provided by the software. If this works, you are done and can skip the next steps.

2. Delete the program folders and files that hold the software.

3. Delete the registry entries used by the software.

4. Remove the entries in the Start menu and delete any shortcuts on the desktop.

5. Remove any entries that launch processes at startup.

> ✎ **Notes** Before uninstalling software, make sure it's not running in the background. For example, antivirus software cannot be uninstalled if it's still running. You can use Task Manager to end all processes related to the software, and you can use the Services console to stop services related to the software. Then remove the software.

Now let's step through the process of manually removing software.

STEP 1: FIRST TRY THE UNINSTALL ROUTINE

Most programs written for Windows have an uninstall routine that can be accessed from the Programs and Features window and Windows 8 apps can be uninstalled on the Start screen. First, try one of these methods before moving on to Step 2.

STEP 2: DELETE PROGRAM FILES

If the uninstall routine is missing or does not work, the next step is to delete the program folders and files that contain the software. In our example, we'll delete the RegServe software without using its uninstall routine. (RegServe is utility software that can clean the registry of unused keys.)

Look for the program folder in one of these folders:

◢ C:\Program Files
◢ C:\Program Files (x86)

In Figure 4-51, you can see the RegServe folder under the C:\Program Files (x86) folder. Keep in mind, however, the program files might be in another location that was set by the user when the software was installed. Delete the **RegServe** folder and all its contents.

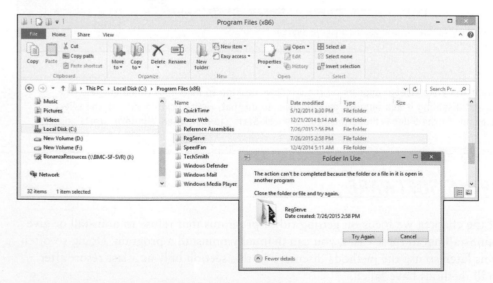

Figure 4-51 Program files are usually found in the Program Files or Program Files (x86) folder

As you do, you might see the Folder In Use box shown on the right side of Figure 4-51 saying the program is in use. In this situation, do the following:

1. Look for the program file reported on the Processes tab of Task Manager. If you see it listed, end the process. For Windows 8, be sure to look in the Windows Explorer group (see Figure 4-52). For Windows 7, the Command Line column can help you find the right program.

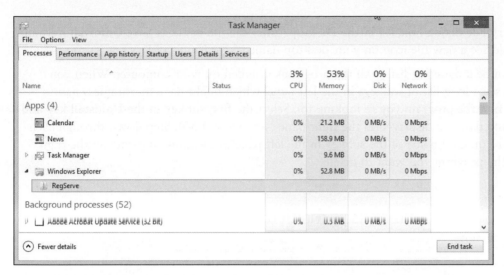

Figure 4-52 Task Manager shows a service is running and needs to be stopped before the program files can be deleted

2. If you don't find the program on the Processes tab, check the **Services** tab. If you find it there, select it and stop the service.

3. After the program or service is stopped, try to delete the program folder again. If you still cannot delete the folder, look for other running programs or services associated with the software. Look for a program or service that has a program file location in the RegServe folder or its subfolders.

STEP 3: DELETE REGISTRY ENTRIES

Editing the registry can be dangerous, so do this with caution and be sure to back up first! Do the following to delete registry entries that cause a program to be listed as installed software in the Programs and Features window of Control Panel:

1. To be on the safe side, back up the entire registry using one or more of the methods discussed earlier in the chapter.

2. Open the Registry Editor by using the **regedit** command in the Search box.

3. Locate a key that contains the entries that make up the list of installed software. Use this criteria to decide which key to locate:

◢ For a 32-bit program installed in a 32-bit OS or for a 64-bit program installed in a 64-bit OS, locate this key:
HKEY_LOCAL_MACHINE\Software\Microsoft\Windows\CurrentVersion\Uninstall

◢ For a 32-bit program installed in a 64-bit OS, locate this key:
HKEY_LOCAL_MACHINE\SOFTWARE\Wow6432Node\Microsoft\Windows\CurrentVersion\Uninstall

> ✎ **Notes** Recall that 32-bit programs normally install in the \Program Files (x86) folder on a 64-bit system. These 32-bit programs normally use the Wow6432Node subkey in the registry of a 64-bit OS.

4. Back up the Uninstall key to the Windows desktop so that you can backtrack, if necessary. To do that, right-click the **Uninstall** key and select **Export** from the shortcut menu (see Figure 4-40 earlier in the chapter).

5. In the Export Registry File dialog box, select the **Desktop**. Enter the file name as **Save Uninstall Key**, and click **Save**. You should see a new file icon on your desktop named Save Uninstall Key.reg.

6. The Uninstall key can be a daunting list of all the programs installed on your computer. When you expand the key, you see a long list of subkeys in the left pane, which might have meaningless names that won't help you find the program you're looking for. Select the first subkey in the Uninstall key and watch as its values and data are displayed in the right pane (see Figure 4-53). Step down through each key, watching for a meaningful name of the subkey in the left pane or meaningful details in the right pane until you find the program you want to delete.

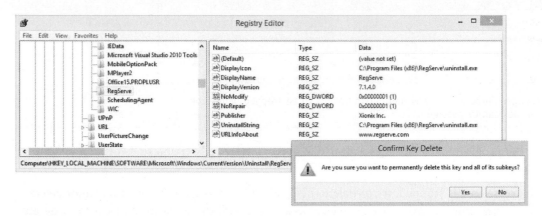

Figure 4-53 Select a subkey under the Uninstall key to display its values and data in the right pane

7. To delete the key, right-click the key and select **Delete** from the shortcut menu. Confirm the deletion, as shown in Figure 4-53. Be sure to search through all the keys in this list because the software might have more than one key. Delete them all and exit the Registry Editor.

8. Open the Programs and Features window and verify that the list of installed software is correct and the software you are uninstalling is no longer listed.

9. If the list of installed software is not correct, to restore the Uninstall registry key, double-click the **Save Uninstall Key.reg** icon on your desktop.

10. As a last step when editing the registry, clean up after yourself by deleting the Save Uninstall Key.reg file on your desktop. Right-click the icon and select **Delete** from the shortcut menu.

STEP 4: REMOVE PROGRAM SHORTCUTS

A+
220-902
1.1, 4.1

For Windows 8, go to the Start screen and type the name of the program. The Problem with Shortcut box appears (see Figure 4-54). Click **Yes** and the program will no longer be listed on the Start screen or Apps screen. For Windows 7, to remove the program from the All Programs menu, right-click it and select **Delete** from the shortcut menu. If the program has shortcuts on the desktop, delete these.

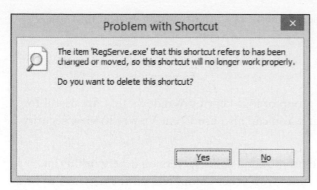

Figure 4-54 Delete the program shortcut from the
Windows 8 Start screen or Apps screen

STEP 5: REMOVE STARTUP PROCESSES

A+
220-902
1.1, 4.1

Restart the system and watch for any startup errors about a missing program file. The
software might have stored startup entries in the registry, in startup folders, or as a service that
is no longer present and causing an error. If you see an error, use System Configuration or Task
Manager to find out how the program is set to start. This entry point is called an orphaned
entry. You'll then need to delete this startup entry by editing the registry, deleting a shortcut in a startup
folder, or disabling a service using the Services console.

It's unlikely you will be able to completely remove all keys in the registry that the software put there. A
registry cleaner can help you find these orphaned keys, but if no errors appear at startup, you can just leave
these keys untouched. Also, an installation might put program files in the C:\Program Files\Common Files
or the C:\Program Files (x86)\Common Files folder. Most likely you can just leave these untouched as well.
Address all error messages you encounter and stop there.

>> CHAPTER SUMMARY

Windows Utilities and Tools to Support the OS

◢ The Windows OS is made up of two main components, the shell and the kernel. The shell provides an
interface for users and applications. The kernel is responsible for interacting with hardware.

◢ A process is a program running under the shell, together with all the resources assigned to it. A thread is
a single task that a process requests from the kernel.

◢ Task Manager (taskmgr.exe) lets you view services and other running programs, CPU and memory
performance, network activity, and user activity. It is useful to stop a process that is hung.

◢ Tools listed in the Administrative Tools group of Control Panel are used by technicians and developers
to support Windows and applications.

◢ System Configuration (msconfig.exe) can be used to temporarily disable startup processes to test for
performance improvement and find a startup program causing a problem.

◢ System Configuration and Task Manager can be used to perform a clean boot, which reduces the boot
to essentials.

◢ The Services console (services.msc) is used to manage Windows and application services. When and if a
service starts can be controlled from this console.

◢ The Computer Management console (compmgmt.msc) contains a group of Windows Administrative tools useful for managing a system.

◢ The Microsoft Management Console (MMC) can be used to build your own custom consoles from available snap-ins.

◢ The Event Viewer (eventvwr.msc) console displays a group of logs kept by Windows that are useful for troubleshooting problems with software and hardware. You can also use Event Viewer to view security audits made by Windows.

◢ The Print Management utility can be used to manage printers and print servers on a network. Print Management considers any computer that shares a printer with other computers on the network to be a print server.

◢ Task Scheduler (taskschd.msc) schedules and runs tasks, which are stored in C:\Windows\System32\ Tasks folder.

◢ Performance Monitor (perfmon.msc) uses counters to track activity by hardware and software to evaluate performance.

◢ The Registry Editor (regedit.exe) is used to edit the registry in real time. There is no way to use the Registry Editor to undo changes you make to the registry. Therefore, you should always make a backup before editing it.

◢ The Display applet in Control Panel can be used to change the screen resolution and refresh rate and adjust color depth. The taskbar properties box can be used to extend the Windows 8 taskbar across both monitors in a dual-monitor setup.

◢ The dxdiag command can be used to verify the version of DirectX.

Improving Windows Performance

◢ The five high-level steps to improve Windows performance are (1) routine maintenance, (2) clean Windows startup, (3) check if hardware can support the OS, (4) check for a history of problems to find the source of a problem, and (5) consider using ReadyBoost to improve a slow hard drive's performance. For Windows 7/Vista, disable the Aero interface.

Manually Removing Software

◢ To manually delete software, delete the program files, registry keys, shortcuts to the program on the Start screen, Apps screen, or Windows 7 All Programs menu, and items in startup folders.

>> KEY TERMS

For explanations of key terms, see the Glossary for this text.

Administrative Tools	HKEY_CURRENT_ CONFIG (HKCC)	multiple monitor misalignment	Reliability and Performance Monitor
clean boot	HKEY_CURRENT_USER (HKCU)	multiple monitor orientation	Reliability Monitor
Computer Management console	HKEY_LOCAL_ MACHINE (HKLM)	native resolution	resolution
DirectX	HKEY_USERS (HKU)	Performance Monitor	Services console
dxdiag.exe	kernel	Print Management	shell
Event Viewer	kernel mode	process	snap-in
executive services	Microsoft Management Console (MMC)	ReadyBoost	System Configuration
HAL (hardware abstraction layer)	multimonitor taskbar	refresh rate	Task Manager
HKEY_CLASSES_ROOT (HKCR)		registry	Task Scheduler
		Registry Editor	thread
			user mode

>> REVIEWING THE BASICS

1. If a program is hung and not responding, how can you stop it?

2. If a necessary program is using too much of system resources and bogging down other applications, what can you do to fix the problem?

3. How can you view a list of users currently signed in to the computer?

4. What is the program file name and extension of System Configuration?

5. If a nonessential service is slowing down startup, how can you permanently disable it?

6. What should be the startup type of a service that should not load at startup but might be used later after startup? What tool can you use to set the startup type of a service?

7. List three snap-ins that can be found in the Computer Management console that are used to manage hardware and track problems with hardware.

8. What is the file extension of a console that is managed by Microsoft Management Console?

9. What is the program file name and extensions of the Microsoft Management Console?

10. Which log in Event Viewer would you use to find out about attempted sign-ins to a computer?

11. Which log in Event Viewer would you use if you suspect a problem with the hard drive?

12. Which log in Event Viewer lists only Critical, Error, and Warning events?

13. Which Administrative tool can you use to clear the print queue of another computer on the network that has a shared printer?

14. Does Windows 8 allow you to extend the desktop taskbar across both monitors in a dual-monitor setup? Windows 7?

15. What is the path to the Ntuser.dat file?

16. How is the Ntuser.dat file used?

17. What command do you use to find out what version of DirectX your video card is using?

18. Which Windows tool can you use to find out if the hard drive is slowing down Windows performance?

19. Which registry key contains information that Device Manager uses to display information about hardware?

20. If performance improves when Windows is loaded in a clean boot, what can you conclude?

21. If performance does not improve when Windows is loaded in a clean boot, what can you conclude?

22. When using System Configuration to stop startup services including Microsoft services, which service should you not stop so that restore points will not be lost?

23. In what folder does Task Scheduler keep scheduled task?

24. What is the purpose of the Wow6432Node subkey in the Windows registry?

25. What is the name of the window used to uninstall software?

>> THINKING CRITICALLY

1. You need to install a customized console on 10 computers. What is the best way to do that?

   a. When installing the console on the first computer, write down each step to make it easier to do the same chore on the other nine.

   b. Create the console on one computer and copy the .mmc file to the other nine.

   c. Create the console on one computer and copy the .msc file to the other nine.

2. What is the name of the program that you can enter in the Windows 8 Run box to execute Event Viewer? What is the process that is running when Event Viewer is displayed on the screen? Why do you think the running process is different from the program name?

3. When cleaning up the startup process, which of these should you do first?

   a. Use the Registry Editor to look for keys that hold startup processes.

   b. Run System Configuration to see what processes are started.

   c. After you have launched several applications, use Task Manager to view a list of running tasks.

   d. Run the Defrag utility to optimize the hard drive.

4. Using the Internet, investigate each of the following startup processes. Identify the process and write a one-sentence description:

   a. Acrotray.exe

   b. Ieuser.exe

5. Using Task Manager, you discover an unwanted program that is launched at startup. Of the items listed below, which ones might lead you to the permanent solution to the problem? Which ones would not be an appropriate solution to the problem? Explain why they are not appropriate.

   a. Look at the registry key that launched the program to help determine where in Windows the program was initiated.

   b. Use Task Manager to disable the program.

   c. Search Task Scheduler for the source of the program being launched.

   d. Use System Configuration to disable the program.

   e. Search the startup folders for the source of the program.

6. List the program file name and path for the following utilities. (*Hint:* You can use Explorer or a Windows search to locate files.)

   a. Task Manager

   b. System Configuration

   c. Services Console

   d. Microsoft Management Console

   e. Registry Editor

>> REAL PROBLEMS, REAL SOLUTIONS

REAL PROBLEM 4-1 Using RegServe

RegServe by Xionix can be downloaded free from the *regserve.com* website. Download, install, and run the software. How many orphaned registry keys did it find on your computer? Which software installed on your computer is responsible for these orphaned keys? Do you think your system would benefit from allowing RegServe to clean your registry? If you decide to use RegServe to clean the registry, be sure to create a restore point first so you can undo the changes to your registry, if necessary.

REAL PROBLEM 4-2 Cleaning Up Startup

Using a computer that has a problem with a sluggish startup, apply the tools and procedures you learned in this chapter to clean up the startup process. Take detailed notes of each step you take and its results. (If you are having a problem finding a computer with a sluggish startup, consider offering your help to a friend, a family member, or a nonprofit organization.)

REAL PROBLEM 4-3 Manually Removing Software

To practice your skills of manually removing software, install WinPatrol from *www.winpatrol.com*. (If you did Project 4-6, the software is already installed.) Then, following the directions in the chapter, manually remove the software, listing the steps you used. (Do not use the uninstall routine provided by WinPatrol.) After you have manually removed the software, reboot the system. Did you get any error messages?

## CHAPTER 5

Supporting Customers and Troubleshooting Windows

After completing this chapter, you will be able to:

- Support customers in the nontechnical ways that they want and expect, beyond your technical skills
- Apply general strategies and steps to troubleshoot and solve any computer problem
- Troubleshoot application problems using appropriate Windows tools

When a computer gives you problems, a good plan for solving that problem can help you to not feel so helpless. This chapter is designed to give you just that—a plan with all the necessary details and tools so that you can determine just what has gone wrong and what to do about it.

Equally important when troubleshooting computers is handling customer concerns. Knowing how to effectively work with people in a technical world is one of the most sought-after skills in today's service-oriented work environments. Just before writing this chapter, an employer told me, "It's not hard to find technically proficient people these days. But it's next to impossible to find people who know how to get along with others and can be counted on when managers are not looking over their shoulders." I could sense his frustration, but I also felt encouraged to know that good social skills and good work ethics can take you far in today's world. My advice to you is to take this chapter seriously. It's important to be technically proficient, but the skills learned in this chapter just might be the ones that make you stand out above the crowd to land that new job or promotion.

In this chapter, we begin with interpersonal skills (people skills, sometimes called soft skills) needed by an IT support technician. Then we move on to how to troubleshoot any computer problem, and drill down into the specifics of troubleshooting applications.

> ✎ **Notes** This chapter focuses on problems that occur after the Windows desktop has loaded. You'll learn how to solve software problems when Windows refuses to start in the chapter, "Troubleshooting Windows Startup." For solving hardware problems, consult the companion volume to this text, *A+ Guide to Hardware, 9th edition.*

WHAT CUSTOMERS WANT: BEYOND TECHNICAL KNOW-HOW

A+
220-902
5.4

Probably the most significant indication that an IT technician is doing a good job is that customers are consistently satisfied. In your career as an IT support technician, commit to providing excellent service and to treating customers as you would want to be treated in a similar situation. One of the most important ways to achieve customer satisfaction is to do your best by being prepared, both technically and personally. Being prepared includes knowing what customers want, what they don't like, and what they expect from an IT technician.

> ✎ **Notes** People respond in kind to the position of facial muscles presented to them. Try smiling when you first greet someone and watch to see what happens.

BECOMING A COMPETENT AND HELPFUL SUPPORT TECHNICIAN

A+
220-902
5.4

The following traits distinguish a competent and helpful technician from a technician who is incompetent or unhelpful in the eyes of the customer:

▲ *Trait 1. Be dependable and reliable.* Customers appreciate and respect those who do as they say. If you promise to be back at 10:00 the next morning, be back at 10:00 the next morning. If you cannot keep your appointment, never ignore your promise. Call, apologize, let the customer know what happened, and reschedule your appointment. Also, do your best to return phone calls the same day and email within two days.

> ✎ **Notes** Quote from R.C., an employer: "When I choose a person to work for me, in a lot of cases, I choose based on his or her past dependability or attendance. I am less concerned about a person's ability because I can train anyone to do a specific job. I cannot, however, train anyone to do anything if he or she is not present for me to train. Being dependable and reliable has a profound impact on customer relationships as well."

▲ *Trait 2. Keep a positive and helpful attitude.* This helps establish good customer relationships. You communicate your attitude in your tone of voice, the words you choose, how you use eye contact, your facial expressions, how you dress, and in many other subjective and subtle ways. Generally, your attitudes toward your customers stem from how you see people, how you see yourself, and how you see your job. Your attitude is a heart issue, not a head issue. To improve your attitude, you must do it from your heart. That's pretty subjective and cannot be defined with a set of rules, but it always begins with a decision to change. As you work with customers or users, make it a habit to not talk down to or patronize them. Don't make the customers or users feel inferior. People appreciate it when they feel your respect for them, even when they have made a mistake or are not knowledgeable. If a problem is simple to solve, don't make the other person feel he or she has wasted your time. Your customer or user should always be made to feel that the problem is important to you.

APPLYING | CONCEPTS   CUSTOMER SERVICE

A+
220-902
5.4

Josie walked into a computer parts store and wandered over to the cleaning supplies looking for Ace monitor wipes. She saw another brand of wipes, but not the ones she wanted. Looking around for help, she noticed Mary stocking software on the shelves in the next aisle. She walked over to Mary and asked her if she could help her find Ace monitor wipes. Mary put down her box, walked over to the cleaning supply aisle without speaking, picked up a can of wipes and handed them to Josie, still without speaking a word. Josie explained she was looking for Ace wipes. Mary yells over three aisles to a coworker in the back room, "Hey,

Billy! This lady says she wants Ace monitor wipes. We got any?" Billy comes from the back room and says, "No, we only carry those," pointing to the wipes in Mary's hand, and returns to the back room. Mary turns to Josie and says, "We only carry these," and puts the wipes back on the shelf. She turns to walk back to her aisle when Josie says to Mary, "Well, those Ace wipes are great wipes. You might want to consider carrying them." Mary says, "I'm only responsible for software." Josie leaves the store.

Discuss this situation in a small group of students and answer the following questions:

1. If you were Josie, how would you feel about the service in this store?

2. What would you have expected to happen that did not happen?

3. If you were Mary, how could you have provided better service?

4. If you were Billy, is there anything more you could have done to help?

5. If you were the store manager, what principles of good customer service would you want Billy and Mary to know that would have helped them in this situation?

◢ *Trait 3. Listen without interrupting your customer.* When you're working with or talking to a customer, focus on him or her. Don't assume you know what your customer is about to say. Let her say it, listen carefully, and don't interrupt. Make it your job to satisfy this person, not just your organization, your boss, your bank account, or the customer's boss.

© iStockphoto.com/Sportstock

Figure 5-1 Learn to listen before you decide what a user needs or wants

◢ *Trait 4. Use proper and polite language.* Speak politely and use language that won't confuse your customer. Avoid using slang or jargon (technical language that only technical people can understand). Avoid acronyms (initial letters that stand for words). For example, don't say to a nontechnical customer, "I need to ditch your KVM switch," when you could explain yourself better by saying to the customer, "I need to replace that little switch box on your desk that controls your keyboard, monitor, and mouse."

◢ *Trait 5. Show sensitivity to cultural differences.* Cultural differences happen because we are from different countries and societies or because of physical disabilities. Culture can cause us to differ in how we define or judge good service. For example, culture can affect our degree of tolerance for uncertainty. Some cultures are willing to embrace uncertainty, and others strive to avoid it. Those who tend to avoid uncertainty can easily get upset when the unexpected happens. For these people, you need to make special efforts to communicate early and often when things are not going as expected. For the physically disabled, especially the hearing- or sight-impaired, communication can be more difficult. It's your responsibility in these situations to do whatever is necessary to find a way to communicate. And it's especially important to have an attitude that expresses honor and patience, which you will unconsciously express in your tone of voice, your choice of words, and your actions.

▲ *Trait 6. Take ownership of the problem.* Taking ownership of the customer's problem means to accept the customer's problem as your own problem. Doing that builds trust and loyalty because the customer knows you can be counted on. Taking ownership of a problem also increases your value in the eyes of your coworkers and boss. People who don't take ownership of the problem at hand are likely to be viewed as lazy, uncommitted, and uncaring. One way to take ownership of a problem is to not engage your boss in unproductive discussions about a situation that he expects you to handle on your own.

APPLYING | CONCEPTS   SELF-CONTROL

**A+
220-902
5.4**

Jack had had a bad day on the phones at the networking help desk in Atlanta. An electrical outage coupled with a generator failure had caused servers in San Francisco to be down most of the day. The entire help-desk team had been fielding calls all day explaining to customers why they did not have service and about expected recovery times. The servers were finally online, but it was taking hours to get everything reset and functioning. No one had taken a break all afternoon, but the call queue was still running about 20 minutes behind. Todd, the boss, had asked the team to work late until the queue was empty. It was Jack's son's birthday and his family was expecting Jack home on time. Jack moaned as he realized he might be late for Tyler's party. Everyone pushed hard to empty the queue. As Jack watched the last call leave the queue, he logged off, stood up, and reached for his coat.

And then the call came. Jack was tempted to ignore it, but decided it had to be answered. It was Lacy. Lacy was the executive assistant to the CEO (chief executive officer over the entire company) and when Lacy calls, all priorities yield to Lacy, and Lacy knows it. The CEO was having problems printing to the laser printer in his office. Would Jack please walk down to his office and fix the problem? Jack asks Lacy to check the simple things like, "Is the printer turned on? Is it plugged in?" Lacy gets huffy and says, "Of course, I've checked that. Now come right now. I need to go." Jack walks down to the CEO's office, takes one look at the printer, and turns it on.

He turns to Lacy and says, "I suppose the on/off button was just too technical for you." Lacy glares at him in disbelief. Jack says, "I'll be leaving now." As he walks out, he begins to form a plan as to how he'll defend himself to his boss in the morning, knowing the inevitable call to Todd's office will come.

In a group of two or four students, role-play Jack and Todd and discuss these questions:

1. Todd is informed the next morning of Jack's behavior. Todd calls Jack into his office. He likes Jack and wants him to be successful in the company. Jack is resistant and feels justified in what he did. As Todd, what do you think is important that Jack understand? How can you explain this to Jack so he can accept it? What would you advise Jack to do? In role-play, one student plays the role of Jack, and another the role of Todd.

2. Switch roles or switch team members and replay the roles.

3. What are three principles of relating to people that would be helpful for Jack to keep in mind?

▲ *Trait 7. Portray credibility.* Convey confidence to your customers. Don't allow yourself to appear confused, afraid, or befuddled. Troubleshoot the problem in a systematic way that portrays confidence and credibility. Get the job done, and do it with excellence. Credible technicians also know when the job is beyond their expertise and when to ask for help.

▲ *Trait 8. Work with integrity and honesty.* Don't try to hide your mistakes from your customer or your boss. Everyone makes mistakes, but don't compound them by a lack of integrity. Accept responsibility and do what you can to correct the error.

▲ *Trait 9. Know the law with respect to your work.* For instance, observe the laws concerning the use of software. Don't use or install pirated software.

▲ *Trait 10. Look and behave professionally.* A professional at work knows to not allow his emotions to interfere with business relationships. If a customer is angry, allow the customer to vent, keeping your own professional distance. (You do, however, have the right to expect a customer not to talk to you in an abusive way.) Dress appropriately for the environment. Take a shower each day, and brush your teeth after each meal. Use mouthwash. Iron your shirt. If you're not in good health, try as best you can to take care of the problem. Your appearance matters. And finally—don't use rough language. It is *never* appropriate.

> ✎ **Notes** Your customers might never remember what you said or what you did, but they will always remember how you made them feel.

Hands-On | Project 5-1 Evaluate Your Own Interpersonal Skills with Customers and Coworkers

Assume that you are working as an IT support technician for a corporation. Your job requires you to give desk-side support to users, answer the phone at the help desk, and make an occasional on-site call at corporate branches. Answer the following questions:

1. In the role of desk-side support to users, what do you think is your strongest social skill that would help you succeed in this role?

2. What is likely to be your greatest interpersonal weakness that might present a challenge to you in this role?

3. What is one change you might consider making that will help you to improve on this weakness?

4. In the role of phone support at the help desk, what part of that job would you enjoy the most? What part would give you the greatest challenge?

5. When making on-site calls to corporate branches, what part of this job would you enjoy the most? What interpersonal skills, if any, would you need to develop so that you could do your best in this role?

Hands-On | Project 5-2 The Johari Window Online Game

The Johari (pronounced "Joe-Harry" after the two men who created it) window reveals an interesting view of how we relate to others. Sometimes when we evaluate our own interpersonal skills, we overlook our greatest assets that others can see. This project is designed to help others reveal to you those assets. The house in Figure 5-2 represents who we are. Room 1 is what we know about ourselves that we allow others to see. Room 2 is what others see about us that we don't see ourselves (our blind spots). Room 3 is what we see about ourselves that we hide from others. And Room 4 contains traits in us that we don't know about and neither do others see—traits yet to be discovered.

As we move Bar A to the right, we are making a conscious decision to reveal more about ourselves to others, which is a technique successful salespeople often use to immediately connect with their customers. The theory is that if you move Bar A to the right, not only are you choosing to reveal what you normally would hide, but you are also moving the bar so that more of Room 4 can be seen in Room 2. This means that others can see more about you that you don't see. When we allow others to tell us something about ourselves, we are moving Bar B away from us, which, in effect,

(continues)

5

allows us to see more of who we really are. Therefore, to learn more about yourself, you can do two things: Reveal more of yourself to others and allow others to tell you more about yourself. Try playing the Interactive Johari Window game by Kevan Davis. You can find it at *www.kevan.org*.

Then answer the following questions:

1. What five or six descriptive words did you use to describe yourself at the beginning of the game?

2. What words did others use to describe you?

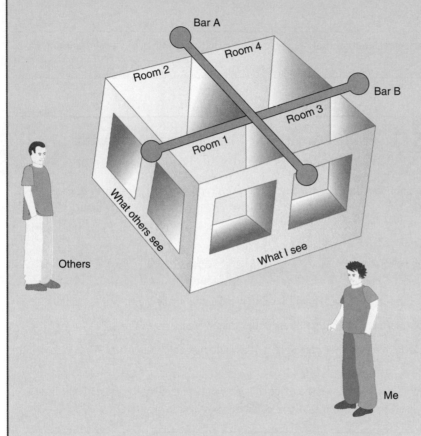

Figure 5-2 Johari Window demonstrates the complexity of how we see ourselves and how others see us

3. How has input from your friends adjusted how you see yourself?

4. How might this adjustment affect the way you will relate to customers and coworkers on the job?

5. If you were to play the Interactive Johari Window game a second time, would you still use the same five or six descriptive words you used the first time? If your answer is no, what new words would you use?

PLANNING FOR GOOD SERVICE

A+
220-902
5.4

Your customers can be "internal" (you both work for the same company, in which case you might consider the customer your colleague) or "external" (your customers come to you or your company for service). Customers can be highly technical or technically naive, represent a large company or simply own a home computer, be prompt or slow at paying their bills, want only the best (and be willing to pay for it) or be searching for bargain service, be friendly and easy to work with or demanding and condescending. In each situation, the key to success is always the same: Don't allow circumstances or personalities to affect your commitment to excellence and to treat the customer as you would want to be treated.

> ★ **A+ Exam Tip** The A+ 220-902 exam expects you to know that when servicing a customer, you should be on time, avoid distractions, set and meet expectations and timelines, communicate the status of the solution with the customer, and deal appropriately with customers' confidential materials.

Most good service for customers of IT support begins with entries in call tracking software, so let's begin there.

CALL TRACKING SOFTWARE

Your organization is likely to use call tracking software to track support calls and give technicians a place to keep their call notes. Figure 5-3 shows a window in *everything HelpDesk* software, which is a popular call tracking application.

Source: everything HelpDesk

Figure 5-3 Call tracking software allows you to create, edit, and close tickets used by technicians

When someone initiates a call for help, whoever receives the call starts the process by creating a ticket, which is a record of the request and what is happening to resolve it. The call tracking software might track: (1) the date, time, and length of help-desk or on-site calls, (2) causes of and solutions to problems already addressed, (3) who is currently assigned to the ticket and who has already worked on it, (4) who did what and when, and (5) how each call was officially resolved. The ticket is entered into the call tracking system and stays open until the issue is resolved. Support staff assigned to the ticket document their progress under this ticket in the call tracking system. As an open ticket ages, more attention and resources are assigned to it, and the ticket might be escalated (passed on to someone more experienced or who has more resources available) until the problem is finally resolved and the ticket closed. Help-desk personnel and managers acknowledge and sometimes even celebrate those who consistently close the most tickets!

As you support customers and solve computer problems, it's very important to include detailed information in your call notes so that you have this information as you problem solve or later, when faced with a similar problem. Sometimes another person must pick up your open ticket and should not have to waste time finding out information you already knew. Also, tracking-system notes are sometimes audited.

INITIAL CONTACT WITH A CUSTOMER

Your initial contact with a customer might be when the customer comes to you, such as in a retail setting, when you go to the customer's site, when the customer calls you on the phone, when the customer reaches you by chat or email, or when you are assigned a ticket already entered in a call tracking system. In each situation, always follow the specific guidelines of your employer. Let's look at some general guidelines for handling first contact with customers.

When you answer the phone, identify yourself and your organization. (Follow the guidelines of your employer on what to say.) Follow company policies to obtain specific information you should take when answering an initial call, such as name (get the right spelling), phone number, and business name. For example, your company might require that you obtain a licensing or warranty number to determine whether the customer is entitled to receive your support. After you have obtained all the information you need in order to know that you are authorized to help the customer, open up the conversation for the caller to describe the problem.

Prepare for on-site visits by reviewing information given to you by whoever took the call. Know the problem you are going to address; the urgency of the situation; and what computer, software, and hardware need servicing. Arrive with a complete set of equipment appropriate to the visit, which might include a toolkit, flashlight, multimeter, ESD strap and mat, and bootable media.

© iStockphoto.com/killerb10

Figure 5-4 If a customer permits it, begin each new relationship with a handshake

When you arrive at the customer's site, greet the customer in a friendly manner and shake his or her hand. Use Mr. or Ms. and last names or Sir or Ma'am rather than first names when addressing the customer, unless you are certain the customer expects you to use a first name. If the site is a residence, know that you should never stay at a site when only a minor is present. If a minor child answers the door, ask to speak with an adult and don't allow the adult to leave the house with only you and the child present.

After initial greetings, the first thing you should do is listen and ask questions. As you listen, it's fine to take notes, but don't start the visit by filling out your paperwork. Save the paperwork for later, or have the essentials already filled out before you reach the site.

INTERVIEW THE CUSTOMER

Troubleshooting begins by interviewing the user. As you ask the user questions, take notes and keep asking questions until you thoroughly understand the problem. Have the customer reproduce the problem, and carefully note each step taken and its results. This process gives you clues about the problem and about the customer's technical proficiency, which helps you know how to communicate with the customer.

> ★ **A+ Exam Tip** The A+ 220-902 exam expects you to be able to clarify customer statements by asking open-ended questions to narrow the scope of the problem and by restating the issue or question.

Use diplomacy and good manners when you work with a user to solve a problem. For example, if you suspect that the user dropped the computer, don't ask, "Did you drop the laptop?" Put the question in a less accusatory manner: "Could the laptop have been dropped?"

SET AND MEET CUSTOMER EXPECTATIONS

A professional technician knows that it is her responsibility to set and meet expectations with a customer. It's important to create an expectation of certainty with customers so that they are not left hanging and don't know what will happen next.

Part of setting expectations is to establish a timeline with your customer for the completion of a project. If you cannot solve the problem immediately, explain to the customer what needs to happen and the timeline that he should expect for a solution. Then keep the customer informed about the progress of the solution. For example, you can say to a customer, "I need to return to the office and research the cost of parts that need replacing. I'll call you tomorrow before 10:00 a.m. with an estimate." If later you find out you need more time, call the customer before 10:00 a.m., explain your problem, and give him a new time to expect your call. This kind of service is very much appreciated by customers and, if you are consistent, you will quickly gain their confidence.

Another way to set expectations is to give the customer an opportunity to make decisions about repairs to the customer's equipment. When explaining to the customer what needs to be done to fix a problem, offer repair or replacement options if they apply. Don't make decisions for your customer. Explain the problem and what you must do to fix it, giving as many details as the customer wants. When a customer must make a choice, state the options in a way that does not unfairly favor the solution that makes the most money for you as the technician or for your company. For example, if you must replace a motherboard (a costly repair in parts and labor), explain to the customer the total cost of repairs and then help him decide if it is to his advantage to purchase a new system or repair this one.

© iStockphoto.com/Dean Mitchell

Figure 5-5 Advise and then allow a customer to make repair or purchasing decisions

WORKING WITH A CUSTOMER ON SITE

As you work with a customer on site, avoid distractions as you work. Don't accept personal calls or texts on your cell phone, and definitely don't check social media sites when you're on the job. Most organizations require that you answer calls from work, but keep the calls to a minimum. Be aware that the customer might be listening, so be careful to not discuss problems with coworkers, the boss, or other situations that might put the company, its employees, or products in a bad light with the customer. If you absolutely must excuse yourself from the on-site visit for personal reasons, explain to the customer the situation and return as soon as possible.

When working at a user's desk, follow these general guidelines:

1. As you work, be as unobtrusive as possible. Consider yourself a guest in the customer's office or residence. Don't make a big mess. Keep your tools and papers out of the customer's way. Don't pile your belongings and tools on top of the user's papers, books, and so forth.

2. Protect the customer's confidential and private materials. For example, if you are working on the printer and discover a budget report in the out tray, quickly turn it over so you can't read it, and hand it to the customer. If you notice a financial spreadsheet is displayed on the customer's computer screen, step away and ask the user if she wants to first close the spreadsheet before you work with the computer. If sensitive documents are lying on the customer's desk, you might let him know and ask if he would like to put them out of your view or in a safe place.

3. Don't take over the mouse or keyboard from the user without permission.

4. Ask permission again before you use the printer or other equipment.

5. Don't use the phone without permission.

6. Accept personal inconvenience to accommodate the user's urgent business needs. For example, if the user gets an important call while you are working, don't allow your work to interfere. You might need to stop work and perhaps leave the room.

7. Also, if the user is present, ask permission before you make a software or hardware change, even if the user has just given you permission to interact with the computer.

8. Don't disclose information about a customer on social media sites, and don't use those public outlets to complain about difficulties with a customer.

In some IT support situations, it is appropriate to consider yourself a support to the user as well as to the computer. Your goals can include educating the user, as well as repairing the computer. If you want users to learn something from a problem they caused, explain how to fix the problem and walk them through the process if necessary. Don't fix the problem yourself unless they ask you to. It takes a little longer to train the user, but it is more productive in the end because the user learns more and is less likely to repeat the mistake.

© iStockphoto.com/Sportstock

Figure 5-6   Teaching a user how to fix her problem can prevent it from reoccurring

WORKING WITH A CUSTOMER ON THE PHONE

Phone support requires more interaction with customers than any other type of IT support. To understand the problem and also give clear instructions, you must be able to visualize what the customer sees at his or her computer. Patience is required if the customer must be told each key to press or command button to click. Help-desk support requires excellent communication skills, good phone manners, and lots of patience. As your help-desk skills improve, you will learn to think through the process as though you were sitting in front of the computer yourself. Drawing diagrams and taking notes as you talk can be very helpful. In some cases, help-desk support personnel might have software that enables the remote control of customers' computers. Examples of this type of software are GoToAssist by Citrix at *www.netviewer* *.com* and LogMeIn Rescue by LogMeIn at *secure.logmeinrescue.com*. Always communicate clearly with customers when using this type of software, so that they understand what type of access they are allowing you to have on their computers.

If your call is accidentally disconnected, call back immediately. Don't eat or drink while on the phone. If you must put callers on hold, tell them how long it will be before you get back to them. Speak clearly and don't talk too fast. Don't complain about your job, your boss or coworkers, your company, or other companies or products to your customers. A little small talk is okay and is sometimes beneficial in easing a tense situation, but keep it upbeat and positive.

DEALING WITH DIFFICULT CUSTOMERS

Most customers are polite and appreciate your help. And, if you make it a habit to treat others as you want to be treated, you'll find that most of your customers will tend to treat you well, too. However, occasionally you'll have to deal with a difficult customer. In this part of the chapter, you learn how to work with customers who are not knowledgeable, who are overly confident, and who complain.

When the Customer Is Not Knowledgeable

When on site, you can put a computer in good repair without depending on a customer to help you. But when you are trying to solve a problem over the phone, with a customer as your only eyes, ears, and hands, a computer-illiterate user can present a challenge. Here are some tips for handling this situation:

◢ *Tip 1.* Be specific with your instructions. For example, instead of saying, "Open File Explorer," say, "Using your mouse, right-click the Start button, and click File Explorer from the menu."

© iStockphoto.com/mediaphotos

Figure 5-7 Learn to be patient and friendly when helping users

◢ *Tip 2.* Don't ask the customer to do something that might destroy settings or files without first having the customer back them up carefully. If you think the customer can't handle your request, ask for some on-site help.

◢ *Tip 3.* Frequently ask the customer what is displayed on the screen to help you track the keystrokes and action.

◢ *Tip 4.* Follow along at your own computer. It's easier to direct the customer, keystroke by keystroke, if you are doing the same things.

◢ *Tip 5.* Give the customer plenty of opportunity to ask questions.

◢ *Tip 6.* Genuinely compliment the customer whenever you can to help the customer gain confidence.

◢ *Tip 7.* If you determine that the customer cannot help you solve the problem without a lot of coaching, you might need to tactfully request that the caller have someone with more experience call you. The customer will most likely breathe a sigh of relief and have someone take over the problem.

> ✎ **Notes** When solving computer problems in an organization other than your own, check with technical support within that organization instead of working only with the user. The user might not be aware of policies that have been set on his computer to prevent changes to the OS, hardware, or applications.

When the Customer Is Overly Confident

Sometimes customers might want to give advice, take charge of a call, withhold information they think you don't need to know, or execute commands at the computer without letting you know, so you don't have enough information to follow along. A situation like this must be handled with tact and respect for the customer. Here are a few tips:

◢ *Tip 1.* When you can, compliment the customer's knowledge, experience, or insight.

◢ *Tip 2.* Slow the conversation down. You can say, "Please slow down. You're moving too fast for me to follow. Help me catch up."

◢ *Tip 3.* Don't back off from using problem-solving skills. You must still have the customer check the simple things, but direct the conversation with tact. For example, you can say, "I know you've probably already gone over these simple things, but could we just do them again together?"

◢ *Tip 4.* Be careful not to accuse the customer of making a mistake.

◢ *Tip 5.* Even though the customer might be using technical jargon, keep to your policy of not using jargon back to the customer unless you're convinced he truly understands you.

> ★ **A+ Exam Tip** The A+ 220-902 exam expects you to know that it is important to not minimize a customer's problem and to not be judgmental toward a customer.

When the Customer Complains

When you are on site or on the phone, a customer might complain to you about your organization, products, or service or the service and product of another company. Consider the complaint to be helpful feedback that can lead to a better product or service and better customer relationships. Here are a few suggestions that can help you handle complaints and defuse customer anger:

◢ *Suggestion 1.* Be an active listener, and let customers know they are not being ignored. Look for the underlying problem. Don't take the complaint or the anger personally.

◢ *Suggestion 2.* Give the customer a little time to vent, and apologize when you can. Then start the conversation from the beginning, asking questions, taking notes, and solving problems. Unless you must have the information for problem solving, don't spend a lot of time finding out exactly whom the customer dealt with and what happened to upset the customer.

◢ *Suggestion 3.* Don't be defensive. It's better to leave the customer with the impression that you and your company are listening and willing to admit mistakes. No matter how much anger is expressed, resist the temptation to argue or become defensive.

▲ *Suggestion 4.* Know how your employer wants you to handle a situation where you are verbally abused. If this type of language is happening, you might say something like this in a very calm tone of voice: "I'm sorry, but my employer does not require me to accept this kind of talk."

▲ *Suggestion 5.* If the customer is complaining about a product or service that is not from your company, don't start off by saying, "That's not our problem." Instead, listen to the customer complain. Don't appear as though you don't care.

▲ *Suggestion 6.* If the complaint is against you or your product, identify the underlying problem if you can. Ask questions and take notes. Then pass these notes on to people in your organization who need to know.

▲ *Suggestion 7.* Sometimes simply making progress or reducing the problem to a manageable state reduces the customer's anxiety. As you are talking to a customer, summarize what you have both agreed on or observed so far in the conversation.

▲ *Suggestion 8.* Point out ways that *you* think communication could be improved. For example, you might say, "I'm sorry, but I'm having trouble understanding what you want. Could you please slow down, and let's take this one step at a time."

© iStockphoto.com/Kameleon007

Figure 5-8 When a customer is upset, try to find a place of agreement

---

APPLYING | CONCEPTS   CULTURE OF HONOR

**A+
220-902
5.4**

Andy was one of the most intelligent and knowledgeable support technicians in his group working for CloudPool, Inc. He was about to be promoted to software engineer and today was his last day on the help desk. Sarah, a potential customer with little computer experience, calls asking for help accessing the company website. Andy says, "The URL is www dot cloud pool dot com." Sarah responds, "What's a URL?" Andy's patience grows thin. He's thinking to himself, "Oh, help! Just two more hours and I'm off these darn phones." He answers Sarah in a tone of voice that says, hey, I really think you're an idiot! He says to her, "You know, lady! That address box at the top of your browser. Now enter www dot cloud pool dot com!" Sarah gets all flustered and intimidated and doesn't know what to say next. She really wants to know what a browser is, but instead she says, "Wait. I'll just ask someone in the office to help me," and hangs up the phone.

Discuss the situation with others in a small group and answer these questions:

1. If you were Andy's manager and overheard this call, how would you handle the situation?

2. What principles of working with customers does Andy need to keep in mind?

Two students sit back-to-back, one playing the role of Andy and the other playing the role of Sarah. Play out the entire conversation. Others in the group can offer suggestions and constructive criticism.

THE CUSTOMER DECIDES WHEN THE WORK IS DONE

When you think you've solved the problem, allow the customer to decide when the service is finished to his or her satisfaction. For remote support, generally, the customer ends the call or chat session, not the technician. If you end the call too soon and the problem is not completely resolved, the customer can be frustrated, especially if it is difficult to contact you again.

For on-site work, after you have solved the problem, complete these tasks before you close the call:

1. If you changed anything on the computer after you booted it, reboot one more time to make sure you have not caused a problem with the boot.

2. Allow the customer enough time to be fully satisfied that all is working. Does the printer work? Print a test page. Does the network connection work? Can the customer sign in to the network and access data on it?

3. If you backed up data before working on the problem and then restored the data from backups, ask the user to verify that the data is fully restored.

4. Review the service call with the customer. Summarize the instructions and explanations you have given during the call. This is an appropriate time to fill out your paperwork and explain to the customer what you have written. Then ask if she has any questions.

5. Explain preventive maintenance to the customer (such as deleting temporary files from the hard drive or cleaning the mouse). Most customers don't have preventive maintenance contracts for their computers and appreciate the time you take to show them how they can take better care of their equipment. One technician keeps a pack of monitor wipes in his toolkit and ends each call by cleaning the customer's monitor screen.

To demonstrate a sincere concern for your customer's business and that you have owned their problem, it's extremely important to follow up later with the customer and ask if he is still satisfied with your work and if he has any more questions. For example, you can say to the customer, "I'll call you on Monday to make sure everything is working and you're still satisfied with the work." And then on Monday make that call. As you do, you're building customer loyalty.

> ★ **A+ Exam Tip** The A+ 220-902 exam expects you to know to follow up with the customer at a later date to verify his or her satisfaction.

SOMETIMES YOU MUST ESCALATE A PROBLEM

You are not going to solve every computer problem you encounter. Knowing how to escalate properly so the problem is assigned to those higher in the support chain is one of the first things you should learn on a new job. Know your company's policy for escalation. What documents or entries in the call-tracking software do you use? Who do you contact? How do you pass the problem on (email, phone call, or an online entry in a database)? Do you remain the responsible "support" party, or does the person now addressing the problem become the new contact? Are you expected to keep in touch with the customer and the problem, or are you totally out of the picture?

When you escalate, let the customer know. Tell the customer you are passing the problem on to someone who is more experienced or has access to more extensive resources. If you check back with the customer only to find out that the other support person has not called or followed through to the customer's satisfaction, don't lay blame or point fingers. Just do whatever you can to help within your company guidelines. Your call to the customer will go a long way toward helping the situation.

WORKING WITH COWORKERS

Learn to be a professional when working with coworkers. A professional at work is someone who puts business matters above personal matters. In big bold letters, I can say **the key to being professional is to learn to not be personally offended when someone lets you down or does not please you.** Remember, most people do the best they can considering the business and personal constraints they're up against. Getting offended leads to becoming bitter about others and about your job. Learn to keep negative opinions to yourself, and to expect the best of others. When a coworker starts to gossip, try to politely change the subject.

Know your limitations and be willing to admit when you can't do something. For example, Larry's boss stops by his desk and asks him to accept one more project. Larry already is working many hours overtime just to keep up. He needs to politely say to his boss, "I can accept this new project only if you relieve me of some of these tasks."

© iStockphoto.com/Chris Schmidt

Figure 5-9 Coworkers who act professionally are fun to work with

---

APPLYING | CONCEPTS ACTIVE LEARNING

A+ 220-902 5.4

Ray was new at the corporate help desk that supported hospitals across the nation. He had only had a couple of weeks of training before he was turned loose on the phones. He was a little nervous the first day he took calls without a mentor sitting beside him. His first call came from Fernanda, a radiology technician who was trying to sign in to the network to start the day. When Fernanda entered her network ID and passcode, an error message appeared saying her user account was not valid. She told Ray she had tried it several times on two different computers. Ray checked his database and found her account, which appeared to be in good order. He asked her to try it again. She did and got the same results. In his two weeks of training, this problem had never occurred. He told her, "I'm sorry, I don't know how to solve this problem." She said, "Okay, well, thank you

(continues)

anyway," and hung up. She immediately called the help-desk number back and the call was answered by Jackie, who sits across the room from Ray. Fernanda said, "The other guy couldn't fix my problem. Can you help me?"

"What other guy?" Jackie asks. "I think his name was Ray." "Oh, him! He's new and he doesn't know much, and besides that he should have asked for help. Tell me the problem." Jackie resets the account and the problem is solved.

In a group of three or more students, discuss and answer the following questions:

1. What mistake did Ray make? What should he have done or said?

2. What mistake did Jackie make? What should she have done or said?

3. What three principles of relating to customers and coworkers would be helpful for Ray and Jackie to keep in mind?

Hands-On | Project 5-3   Handle Conflict at Work

Jenny works with a team of seven other professionals. Linda, a team member, is a very close personal friend of the boss. With the boss's approval, Linda took a sudden and unexpected two-week vacation to go on a cruise during the team's most difficult month of the year. One team member, Jason, had to work 16 days nonstop, without a day off during Linda's vacation. Other team members soon began complaining and resenting Linda for the unbearable workload her vacation caused them. A few weeks back from vacation, Linda began to notice that she was being excluded from informal luncheons and after-work gatherings. She confided in Jenny that she could not understand why everyone seemed to be mad at her. Jenny, not wanting to cause trouble, said nothing to Linda. In a group of four or five classmates, discuss the answers to the following questions:

1. If you were Jenny, what would you do?

2. What would you do if you were Linda?

3. What would you do if you were Jason?

4. What would you do if you were another team member?

5. If you were the boss and got wind of the resentment against Linda, what would you do?

Hands-On | Project 5-4   Learn to Be a Good Communicator

Working with a partner, discuss ways to respond to the following statements made by a customer. Then decide on your best response.

1. My computer is all dark.

2. I got so mad at my laptop, I threw it on the floor. Now it won't start. I think it's still under warranty.

3. My dog chewed the mouse cord and now nothing works.

4. I heard you tell that other customer that your product stinks. I came here to buy one. Now what am I to do?

5. I don't see the "any" key. Where is it?

Hands-On | Project 5-5 Learn to Interact with the User

Rob, an IT service technician, has been called on site to repair a desktop computer. He has not spoken directly with the user, Lisa, but he knows the floor of the building where she works and can look for her name on her cubicle. The following is a description of his actions. Create a table with two columns. List in one column the mistakes he makes in the following description, and in the next column describe the correct actions he should have taken.

Rob's company promised that a service technician would come sometime during the next business day after the call was received. Rob was given the name and address of the user and the problem, which was stated as "PC will not boot." Rob arrived the following day at about 10:00 a.m. He found Lisa's cubicle, but she was not present. Because Lisa was not present, Rob decided not to disturb the papers all over her desk, so he laid his notebooks and tools on top of her work.

Rob tried to boot the computer, and it gave errors indicating a corrupted file system on the hard drive. He successfully booted from a DVD and was able to access a directory list of drive C:. The list was corrupted and jumbled and he realized most of the files were corrupted. Next, Rob used a recovery utility to try to recover the files and directories but was unable to do so. He began to suspect that a virus had caused the problem, so he ran a virus scan program that did not find the suspected virus.

He made a call to his technical support to ask for suggestions. Technical support suggested he try erasing everything on the hard drive to remove any possible viruses and then reinstall Windows. Rob cleaned everything off the hard drive and was on the phone with technical support, in the process of reloading Windows from the company's file server, when Lisa arrived.

Lisa took one look at her computer and gasped. She caught her breath and asked where her data was. Rob replied, "A virus destroyed your hard drive. I had to reformat."

Lisa tried to explain the importance of the destroyed data. Rob replied, "Guess you'll learn to make backups now." Lisa left to find her manager.

Hands-On | Project 5-6 Learn from the Best

Relate a firsthand experience when a technician, coworker, help-desk personnel, or salesperson followed best practices while helping a customer or coworker. What is a principle this person applied that could help you when working with your own customers or coworkers?

Now let's turn our attention to general strategies and tips that can help you troubleshoot any computer problem.

STRATEGIES TO TROUBLESHOOT ANY COMPUTER PROBLEM

A+ 220-902 5.5 When a computer doesn't work and you're responsible for fixing it, you should generally approach the problem first as an investigator and discoverer, always being careful not to compound the problem through your own actions. If the problem seems difficult, see it as an opportunity to learn something new. Ask questions until you understand the source of the problem. Once you understand it, you're almost done because most likely the solution will be evident. If you take the attitude that you can understand the problem and solve it, no matter how deeply you have to dig, you probably *will* solve it.

One systematic method to solve a problem used by most expert troubleshooters is the six steps diagrammed in Figure 5-10, which can apply to both software and hardware problems.

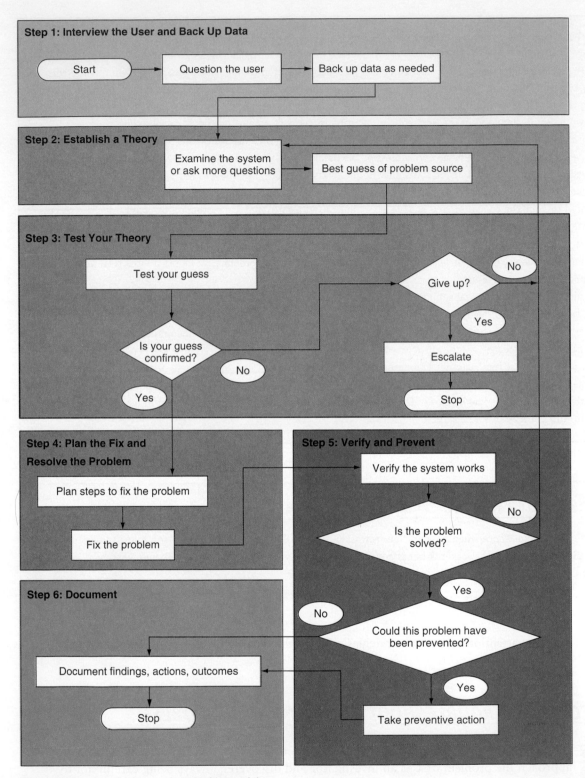

Figure 5-10 General approach to problem solving

Here are the steps:

1. Interview the user and back up data before you make any changes to the system.

2. Examine the system, analyze the problem, and make an initial determination of what is the source of the problem.

3. Test your theory. If the theory is not confirmed, form another theory or escalate the problem to someone higher in your organization with more experience or resources.

4. After you know the source of the problem, plan what to do to fix the problem and then fix it.

5. Verify the problem is fixed and that the system works. Take any preventive measures to make sure the problem doesn't happen again.

6. Document activities, outcomes, and what you learned.

Now let's examine the process step-by-step. As you learn about these six steps, you'll also learn about 13 rules useful when troubleshooting. Here's the first rule.

Rule 1: Approach the Problem Systematically

When trying to solve the problem, start at the beginning and walk through the situation in a thorough, careful way. This one rule is invaluable. Remember it and apply it every time. If you don't find the explanation to the problem after one systematic walkthrough, then repeat the entire process. Check and double-check to find the step you overlooked the first time. Most problems with computers are simple, such as a loose cable or incorrect Windows setting. Computers are logical through and through. Whatever the problem is, it's also very logical. Also, if you are faced with more than one problem on the same computer, work on only one problem at a time. Trying to solve multiple problems at the same time can get too confusing.

STEP 1: INTERVIEW THE USER AND BACK UP DATA

A+
220-902
5.5

Every troubleshooting situation begins with interviewing the user if he or she is available. If you have the opportunity to speak with the user, ask questions to help you identify the problem, how to reproduce it, and possible sources of the problem. Also ask about any data on the hard drive that is not backed up.

⭐ **A+ Exam Tip** The A+ 220-902 exam expects you to know how to interact with a user and know what questions to ask, given a troubleshooting scenario.

Here are some questions that can help you learn as much as you can about the problem and its root cause:

1. Please describe the problem. What error messages, unusual displays, or failures did you see? (Possible answer: I see this blue screen with a funny-looking message on it that makes no sense to me.)

2. When did the problem start? (Possible answer: When I first booted after loading this neat little screen saver I downloaded from the web.)

3. What was the situation when the problem occurred? (Possible answers: I was trying to start up my laptop. I was opening a document in Microsoft Word. I was using the web to research a project.)

4. What programs or software were you using? (Possible answer: I was using Internet Explorer.)

5. What changes have recently been made to the system? For example, did you recently install new software or move your computer system? (Possible answer: Well, yes. Yesterday I moved the computer case across the room.)

6. Has there been a recent thunderstorm or electrical problem? (Possible answer: Yes, last night. Then when I tried to turn on my computer this morning, nothing happened.)

7. Have you made any hardware, software, or configuration changes? (Possible answer: No, but I think my sister might have.)

8. Has someone else used your computer recently? (Possible answer: Sure, my son uses it all the time.)

9. Is there some valuable data on your system that is not backed up that I should know about before I start working on the problem? (Possible answer: Yes! Yes! My term paper! It's not backed up! You gotta save that!)

10. Can you show me how to reproduce the problem? (Possible answers: Yes, let me show you what to do.)

Based on the answers you receive, ask more penetrating questions until you feel the user has given you all the information he or she knows that can help you solve the problem. As you talk with the user, keep in mind rules 2, 3, and 4.

Rule 2: Establish Your Priorities
This rule can help make for a satisfied customer. Decide what your first priority is. For example, it might be to recover lost data or to get the computer back up and running as soon as possible. When practical, ask the user or customer for help deciding on priorities.

Rule 3: Beware of User Error
Remember that many problems stem from user error. If you suspect this is the case, ask the user to show you the problem and carefully watch what the user is doing.

Rule 4: Keep Your Cool and Don't Rush
In some situations, you might be tempted to act too quickly and to be drawn into the user's sense of emergency. But keep your cool and don't rush. For example, when a computer stops working, if unsaved data is still in memory or if data on the hard drive has not been backed up, look and think carefully before you leap! A wrong move can be costly. The best advice is not to hurry. Carefully plan your moves. Research the problem using documentation or the web if you're not sure what to do, and don't hesitate to ask for help. Don't simply try something, hoping it will work, unless you've run out of more intelligent alternatives!

After you have talked with the user, be sure to back up any important data that is not currently backed up before you begin work on the computer. If the computer is working well enough to boot to the Windows desktop, you can use File Explorer or Windows Explorer to copy data to a flash drive, another computer on the network, or other storage media.

⭐ **A+ Exam Tip**   The A+ 220-902 exam expects you to know the importance of making backups before you make changes to a system.

If the computer is not healthy enough to use Explorer, don't do anything to jeopardize the data. If you must take a risk with the data, let it be the user's decision to do so, not yours. Try to boot the system. If the system will not boot to the Windows desktop, know that you can remove the hard drive from the system and use a converter to connect the drive to a USB port on another computer. You can then copy the data to the other computer. Next, return the hard drive to the original computer so you can begin troubleshooting the problem.

If possible, have the user verify that all important data is safely backed up before you continue to the next troubleshooting step. If you're new to troubleshooting and don't want the user looking over your shoulder while you work, you might want to let him or her know you'd prefer to work alone. You can say something like, "Okay, I think I have everything I need to get started. I'll let you know if I have another question."

STEP 2: EXAMINE THE SYSTEM AND MAKE YOUR BEST GUESS

A+ 220-902 5.5

You're now ready to start solving the problem. Rules 5 and 6 can help.

5

Rule 5: Make No Assumptions

This rule is the hardest to follow because there is a tendency to trust anything in writing and assume that people are telling you exactly what happened. But documentation is sometimes wrong, and people don't always describe events as they occurred, so do your own investigating. For example, if the user tells you that the system boots up with no error messages but that the software still doesn't work, boot for yourself. You never know what the user might have overlooked.

Rule 6: Try the Simple Things First

Most problems are so simple and obvious that we overlook them because we expect the problem to be difficult. Don't let the complexity of computers fool you. Most problems are easy to fix. Really, they are! To save time, check the simple things first, such as whether a power switch is not turned on or a cable is loose. Generally, it's easy to check for a hardware problem before you check for a software problem. For example, if a USB drive is not working, verify the drive works on another computer before verifying the drivers are installed correctly.

Follow this process to form your best guess (best theory) and test it:

1. *Reproduce the problem and observe for yourself what the user has described.* For example, if the user tells you the system is totally dead, find out for yourself. Plug in the power and turn on the system. Listen for fans and look for lights and error messages. Suppose the user tells you that Internet Explorer will not open. Try opening it yourself to see what error messages might appear. As you investigate the system, refrain from making changes until you've come up with your theory as to what the source of the problem is. Can you duplicate the problem? Intermittent problems are generally more difficult to solve than problems that occur consistently.

2. *Decide if the problem is hardware or software related.* Sometimes you might not be sure, but make your best guess. For example, if the system fails before Windows starts to load, chances are the problem is a hardware problem. If the user tells you the system has not worked since the lightning storm the night before, chances are the problem is electrical. If the problem is that Explorer will not open even though the Windows desktop loads, you can assume the problem is software related. In another example, suppose a user complains that his Word documents are getting corrupted. Possible sources of the problem might be that the user does not know how to save documents properly, the application or the OS might be corrupted, the computer might have a virus, or the hard drive might be intermittently failing. Investigate for yourself, and then decide if the problem is caused by software, hardware, or the user.

3. *Make your best guess as to the source of the problem, and don't forget to question the obvious.* Here are some practical examples of questioning the obvious and checking the simple things first:

   ◢ The video doesn't work. Your best guess is the monitor cables are loose or the monitor is not turned on.

   ◢ Excel worksheets are getting corrupted. Your best guess is the user is not saving the workbook files correctly.

   ◢ The DVD drive is not reading a DVD. Your best guess is the DVD is scratched.

◢ The system refuses to boot and gives the error that the hard drive is not found. Your best guess is internal cables to the drive are loose.

Rule 7: Become a Researcher

Following this rule is the most fun. When a computer problem arises that you can't easily solve, be as tenacious as a bulldog. Search the web, ask questions, read more, make some phone calls, and ask more questions. Take advantage of every available resource, including online help, documentation, technical support, and books such as this one. Learn to perform advanced searches using a good search engine on the web, such as *www.google.com*. What you learn will be yours to take to the next problem. This is the real joy of computer troubleshooting. If you're good at it, you're always learning something new.

If you're having a problem deciding what might be the source of the problem, keep in mind Rule 7 and try searching these resources for ideas and tips:

◢ The specific application, operating system, or hardware you support must be available to you to test, observe, and study and to use to re-create a customer's problem whenever possible.

◢ In a corporate setting, hardware and software products generally have technical documentation available. If you don't find it on hand, know that you are likely to find user manuals and technical support manuals as .pdf files that can be downloaded from the product manufacturers' websites. These sites might offer troubleshooting and support pages, help forums, chat sessions, email support, and links to submit a troubleshooting ticket to the manufacturer (see Figure 5-11). For Windows problems, the best websites to search are *technet.microsoft.com* or *support.microsoft.com*.

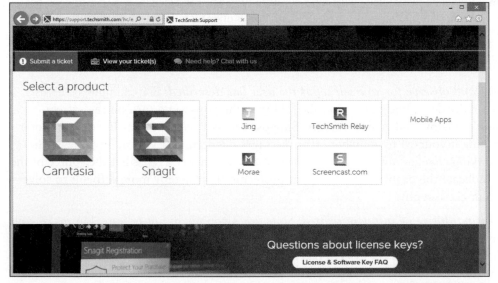

Source: Techsmith Corporation

Figure 5-11   Search manufacturer websites for help with a hardware or software product

◢ Use a search engine to search the web for help. In your search string, include an error message, symptom, hardware device, or description of the problem. The chances are always good that someone has had exactly the same problem, presented the problem online, and someone else has presented a step-by-step solution. All you have to do is find it! As you practice this type of web research, you'll get better and better at knowing how to form a search string and which websites are trustworthy and present the best information. If your first five minutes of searching doesn't turn up a solution, please don't give up! It might take patience and searching for 20 minutes or more to find the solution you need. As you search, most likely you'll learn more and more about the problem, and you'll slowly zero in on a solution.

◢ Some companies offer an expert system for troubleshooting. An expert system is software that is designed and written to help solve problems. It uses databases of known facts and rules to simulate human experts' reasoning and decision making. Expert systems for IT technicians work by posing questions about a problem to be answered by the technician or the customer. The response to each question triggers another question from the software until the expert system arrives at a possible solution or solutions. Many expert systems are "intelligent," meaning the system will record your input and use it in subsequent sessions to select more questions to ask and approaches to try. Therefore, future troubleshooting sessions on this same type of problem tend to zero in more quickly toward a solution.

> ✎ **Notes** To limit your search to a particular site when using *www.google.com*, use the *site:* parameter in the Search box. For example, to search only the Microsoft site for information about the defrag command, enter this search string: **defrag site:*microsoft.com***

STEP 3: TEST YOUR THEORY

**A+
220-902
5.5**

For simple problems, you can zip right through Steps 3, 4, and 5 in Figure 5-10. Here are two examples where Steps 3, 4, and 5 go very fast:

◢ The video does not work and you suspect loose cables or the monitor is not turned on. You check the video cable connection (Step 3) and discover it's loose. As you connect it (Step 4), the video display works. Problem solved. You now can take the time to screw the video cable to the connection (Step 5) so that the problem won't happen again.

◢ Excel worksheets are getting corrupted. As you watch the user save a file, you discover he is saving files in an incorrect format that other software in the office cannot read (Step 3). You step the user through saving the file correctly and then verify that others can open the file (Step 4). You explain to the user which format to use (Step 5). The problem is then solved, and it's not likely to happen again.

Here are two examples of Step 3 that include testing a guess that is not correct:

◢ The optical drive won't read a DVD and you suspect the DVD is scratched. When you check the disc, it looks fine. Your next guess is the optical drive is not recognized by Windows. You check Device Manager, and it reports errors with the drive. Your next guess is that drivers are corrupted.

◢ The system refuses to boot and gives the error message that the hard drive is not found. Internal cable connections are solid. Your next guess is the drive is not getting power.

Here are two examples of Step 3 where your guess is correct, and then you move on toward Step 4 to plan a solution:

◢ Word files are getting corrupted. After eliminating several simple causes, you guess that the hard drive is going bad. You check Event Viewer and discover Windows has recorded write errors to the drive multiple times (Step 3). Your theory is confirmed that the drive is bad and needs replacing (Step 4).

◢ The video display does not work. You check cables and power and verify monitor settings controlled by buttons on the front of the monitor are all okay, but still no video. You guess the video cable might be bad and exchange it with one you know is good, but still no video. Therefore, you guess that the monitor is bad. You move the monitor to a working computer and it still does not work. You try a good monitor on the first computer, and it works fine. Your guess that the monitor is bad has been confirmed (Step 3). Next, you plan how to purchase a new monitor (Step 4).

As you test your guesses, keep in mind rules 8 through 11.

5

Rule 8: Divide and Conquer
This rule is the most powerful. Isolate the problem. In the overall system, remove one hardware or software component after another until the problem is isolated to a small part of the whole system. As you divide a large problem into smaller components, you can analyze each component separately. You can use one or more of the following to help you divide and conquer:

- In Windows, perform a clean boot to eliminate all nonessential startup programs and services as a possible source of the problem.
- Boot from a bootable DVD or flash drive to eliminate the Windows installation and the hard drive as the problem.

Rule 9: Write Things Down
Keep good notes as you're working. They'll help you think more clearly. Draw diagrams. Make lists. Clearly and precisely write down what you're learning. If you need to leave the problem and return to it later, it's difficult to remember what you have observed and already tried. When the problem gets cold like this, your notes will be invaluable.

Rule 10: Don't Assume the Worst
When it's an emergency and your only copy of data is on a hard drive that is not working, don't assume that the data is lost. Much can be done to recover data. If you want to recover lost data on a hard drive, don't write anything to the drive; you might write on top of lost data, eliminating all chances of recovery.

Rule 11: Reboot and Start Over
This is an important rule. Fresh starts are good, and they uncover events or steps that might have been overlooked. Take a break! Get away from the problem. Begin again.

By the time you have finished Step 3, the problem might already be solved or you will know the source of the problem and will be ready to plan a solution.

STEP 4: PLAN YOUR SOLUTION AND THEN FIX THE PROBLEM

 Some solutions, such as replacing a hard drive or a motherboard, are expensive and time consuming. You need to carefully consider what you will do and the order in which you will do it. When planning and implementing your solution, keep rules 12 and 13 in mind.

A+
220-902
5.5

Rule 12: Use the Least Invasive Solution First
As you solve computer problems, always keep in mind that you don't want to make things worse, so you should use the least invasive solution. Keep in mind that you want to fix the problem in such a way that the system is returned to normal working condition with the least amount of effort and least changes to the system. For example, don't format the hard drive until you've first tried to fix the problem without having to erase everything on the drive. In another example, don't reinstall Microsoft Office until you have tried applying patches to the existing installation.

Rule 13: Know Your Starting Point
Find out what works and doesn't work before you take anything apart or try some possible fix. Suppose you decide to install a new anti-malware program. After the installation, you discover Microsoft Office gives errors and you cannot print to the network printer. You don't know if the anti-malware program is causing problems or the problems existed before you began work. As much as possible, find out what works or what doesn't work before you attempt a fix.

Do the following to plan your solution and fix the problem:

1. Consider different solutions and select the least invasive one.

2. Before applying your solution, as best you can, determine what works and doesn't work about the system so you know your starting point.

3. Fix the problem. This might be as simple as plugging up a new monitor. Or it might be as difficult as reinstalling Windows and applications software and restoring data from backups.

STEP 5: VERIFY THE FIX AND TAKE PREVENTIVE ACTION

**A+
220-902
5.5**

After you have fixed the problem, reboot the system and verify all is well. Can you reach the Internet, use the printer, or use Microsoft Office? If possible, have the user check everything and verify that the job is done satisfactorily. If either of you finds a problem, return to Step 2 in the troubleshooting process to examine the system and form a new theory as to the cause of the problem.

After you and the user have verified all is working, ask yourself the question, "Could this problem have been prevented?" If so, go the extra mile to instruct the user, set Windows to automatically install updates, or do whatever else is appropriate to prevent future problems.

STEP 6: DOCUMENT WHAT HAPPENED

**A+
220-902
5.5**

Good documentation helps you take what you learned into the next troubleshooting situation, train others, develop effective preventive maintenance plans, and satisfy any audits or customer or employer queries about your work. Most companies use call tracking software for this purpose. Be sure to include initial symptoms, the source of the problem, and what you did to fix it. Make the notes detailed enough so that you can use them later when solving similar problems.

For on-site support, a customer expects documentation about your services. Include in the documentation sufficient details broken down by cost of individual parts, hours worked, and cost per hour. Give the documentation to the customer at the end of the service and keep a copy for yourself. For phone support, the documentation stays in-house.

APPLYING | CONCEPTS   TAKE GOOD NOTES

**A+
220-902
5.5**

Daniel had not been a good note taker in school, and this lack of skill was affecting his work. His manager, Jonathan, had been watching Daniel's notes in the ticketing system at the help desk he worked on and was not happy with what he saw. Jonathan had pointed out to Daniel more than once that his cryptic notes with sketchy information would one day cause major problems. On Monday morning, calls were hammering the help desk because a server had gone down over the weekend and many internal customers were not able to get to their data. Daniel escalated one call from a customer named Matt to a tier-two help desk. Later that day, Sandra, a tier-two technician, received the escalated ticket, and to her dismay the phone number of the customer was missing. She called Daniel. "How am I to call this customer? You only have his first name, and these notes about the problem don't even make sense!" Daniel apologized to Sandra, but the damage was done.

Two days later, an angry Matt calls the manager of the help desk to complain that his problem is still not solved. Jonathan listens to Matt vent and apologizes for the problem his help desk has caused. It's a little embarrassing to Jonathan to have to ask Matt for his call-back information and to repeat the details of the problem. He gives the information to Sandra and the problem gets a quick resolution.

Discuss this situation in a small group and answer the following questions:

1. If you were Daniel, what could you do to improve note taking in the ticketing system?

2. After Sandra called, do you think Daniel should have told Jonathan about the problem? Why or why not?

3. If you were Jonathan, how would you handle the situation with Daniel?

Two students play the role of Daniel and Jonathan when Jonathan calls Daniel into his office to discuss the call he just received from Matt. The other students in the group can watch and make suggestions as to how to improve the conversation.

Hands-On | Project 5-7 Document an Intermittent Problem

Intermittent problems can make troubleshooting challenging. The trick in diagnosing problems that come and go is to look for patterns or clues as to when the problems occur. If you or the user can't reproduce the problem at will, ask the user to keep a log of when the problems occur and exactly what messages appear. Tell the user that intermittent problems are the hardest to solve and might take some time, but you won't give up. Show the user how to take a screen shot of the error messages when they appear. It might also be appropriate to ask him to email the screen shot to you. Do the following:

1. Use the Windows 8/7 Snipping Tool to take a snip of your Windows desktop showing the Task Manager window open. If you need help using the Snipping Tool, see Windows Help and Support.

2. Save the snip and email it to your instructor.

Hands-On | Project 5-8 Research IT Support Sites

The web is an excellent resource to use when problem solving, and it's helpful to know which websites are trustworthy and useful. Access each of the websites listed in Table 5-1, and print one webpage from each site that shows information that might be useful for a support technician. If the site offers a free email newsletter, consider subscribing to it. Answer the following questions about these sites:

1. Which site can help you find out what type of RAM you can use on your computer?

2. Which site explains Moore's Law? What is Moore's Law?

3. Which site offers a free download for data recovery software?

4. Which site gives a review about registry cleaning software?

5. Which two sites allow you to post a question about computer repair to a forum?

6. Which site offers a tutorial to learn C programming?

7. Which site offers free antivirus software published by the site owners?

Organization	Website
CNET, Inc.	cnet.com
Experts Exchange (subscription site)	experts-exchange.com
F-Secure Corp	f-secure.com
How Stuff Works	howstuffworks.com
How-To Geek	howtogeek.com
iFixit	ifixit.com
Kingston Technology (information about memory)	kingston.com
Microsoft Technical Resources	support.microsoft.com technet.microsoft.com
PC World	pcworld.com
TechRepublic	techrepublic.com
Tom's Hardware Guide	tomshardware.com

Table 5-1 Technical information websites

With tons of information in hand about serving customers and solving problems, let's dig into some actual troubleshooting.

TROUBLESHOOTING APPLICATIONS

A+
220-902
1.3, 1.4,
3.3, 4.1

A problem with an application might be caused by the application, the hardware, the operating system, the data, other applications in conflict with this one, or the user. We begin this part of the chapter by looking at some general steps to help you solve a problem with an application. We then look at some Windows tools to help you solve application problems, and some specific error messages and what to do about them.

> 🖊 **Notes** As you are troubleshooting a problem and make a change to the system, be sure to restart Windows and check to see if the problem is resolved before you move on to the next fix.

GENERAL STEPS FOR SOLVING APPLICATION ERRORS

A+
220-902
4.1

This section covers a variety of steps you can take to try to solve a problem with an application. As you work your way through these steps, keep in mind where each step fits in the overall strategy given earlier in the chapter for solving any computer problem.

STEP 1: INTERVIEW THE USER AND BACK UP DATA

Worth saying again: Start with interviewing the user:

1. *Interview the user and back up data.* Find out as much information as you can from the user about the problem, when it started, and what happened to the system around the time the problem started. Also ask if valuable data is on the system. If so, back it up.

2. *Ask the user to reproduce the problem while you watch.* Many problems with applications are caused by user error. Watch carefully as the user shows you the problem. If you see him making a mistake, be tactful as you explain the problem and its solution.

3. *Try a reboot.* Reboots solve a lot of application problems and one might be a shortcut to your solution. If that doesn't work, no harm is done and you're ready to begin investigating the system.

STEP 2: ERROR MESSAGES, THE WEB, COWORKERS, AND LOGS MIGHT HELP

Windows might display an error message and offer a solution. Logs kept by Windows can offer clues. Here are a few examples of how to get help from Windows, the web, and coworkers:

◢ *View error messages in the Action Center.* The Action Center tracks problems with applications, hardware, and Windows (see Figure 5-12). In the Action Center, click **View archived messages** to see a history of past problems and double-click a problem to read the details about it.

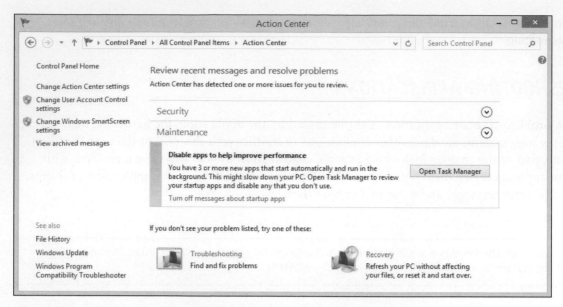

Figure 5-12   Windows 8 suggests disabling some startup applications to increase the system's performance

▲ *Use Event Viewer and Reliability Monitor to look for clues.* The Event Viewer logs might give clues about applications and the system. Hard drive errors often appear as application errors. Use Reliability Monitor to look for errors with other applications or with key hardware components such as the hard drive. You learned to use both tools in the chapter, "Optimizing Windows."

▲ *Find and ask for help.* You might find more information about a problem by searching the website of the application manufacturer for support and help. Also, search the web on the error message, application, or description of the problem. Look for forums where others have posted the same problem with the same app. Someone else has likely posted a solution. However, be careful and don't take the advice unless you trust the website. After you've made a reasonable effort to find help on your own, ask for help from coworkers who are more experienced.

> ✎ **Notes** Working while a customer looks over your shoulder can be awkward. A customer needs her IT support technician to appear confident and in charge. To maintain your customer's confidence in your technical abilities, you might want to find privacy when searching the web or talking with coworkers.

STEP 3: CONSIDER THE DATA OR THE APPLICATION IS CORRUPTED

Now that you've interviewed the user, backed up important data, examined the system, and investigated the problem, it's time to come up with a theory as to the cause of the problem. Consider and do these things:

▲ *Consider data corruption.* For applications that use data files such as Microsoft Office, it might appear that the application has a problem when the problem is really a corrupted data file. Try creating an entirely new data file. If that works, then suspect that previous errors might be caused by corrupted data. You might be able to recover part of a corrupted file by changing its file extension to .txt and importing it into the application as a text file.

▲ *Check application settings for errors.* Maybe a user has made one too many changes to the application settings, which can cause a problem with missing toolbars and other functions. Write down each setting the user has changed and then restore all settings back to their default values. If the problem is solved, restore each setting to the way the user had it until you find the one causing the problem. The process will take some time, but users can get upset if you change their application settings without justification.

▲ *Repair the application.* The application setup might have the option to repair the installation. Look for it in the Programs and Features window, on the setup disc for the application, or on the manufacturer's website.

▲ *Uninstall and reinstall the application.* Do so with caution because you might lose any customized settings, macros, or scripts. Also know this still might not solve a problem with a corrupted application because registry entries might not be properly reset during the uninstall process.

STEP 4: CONSIDER OUTSIDE INTERFERENCE

The problem might be caused by a virus, Windows, other applications, or hardware. Check these things:

▲ *A virus might be causing the problem.* Scan for viruses and check Task Manager to make sure some strange process is not interfering with your applications.

▲ *The computer might be low on system resources or another application might be interfering.* Close all other applications.

▲ *Maybe a service failed to start.* Research the application documentation and find out if the app relies on a service to work. Use the Services console to make sure the service has started. If the service has failed to start, make sure it has an Automatic or Manual setting.

▲ *The problem might be bad memory.* Following the directions given later in this chapter, use the Memory Diagnostics tool (mdsched.exe) to test memory. If it finds errors, replace the memory modules.

▲ *The problem might be a corrupted hard drive.* To eliminate the hard drive as the source of an application error, use the chkdsk command with the /r parameter to check the drive and recover data in bad sectors.

▲ *A background program or other software might be conflicting with the application.* To eliminate compatibility issues with other software, run the application after a clean boot. You learned to perform a clean boot in the chapter, "Optimizing Windows." Recall a clean boot eliminates third-party software from starting during the boot. If a clean boot allows the application to run without errors, you need to methodically disable each third-party program one-by-one until you discover the one in conflict.

STEP 5: CONSIDER WINDOWS MIGHT BE THE PROBLEM

A problem with an application can sometimes be solved by updating or restoring Windows system files. Do the following:

▲ *Download Windows updates.* Make sure all critical and important Windows updates are installed. Microsoft Office updates are included in Windows updates.

▲ *Use System File Checker.* For essential hardware devices, use the System File Checker (SFC), which is covered later in this section, to verify and replace system files. Use the command **sfc /scannow**.

▲ *Boot Windows in Safe Mode.* Safe Mode loads Windows with a minimum configuration and can create a stable environment when Windows gets corrupted. It goes beyond a clean boot in that it eliminates third-party software from launching at the boot and also reduces Windows startup processes to only those essential to launch Windows. There are several ways to start Safe Mode, which you learn about in the chapter, "Troubleshooting Windows Startup." One way is to use System Configuration. Enter **msconfig.exe** in the Windows 8 Run box or the Windows 7 Search box to open the System Configuration window and click the **Boot** tab. Check **Safe boot** (see Figure 5-13). If the application needs the Internet to work, select **Network**. Click **OK** and restart the system.

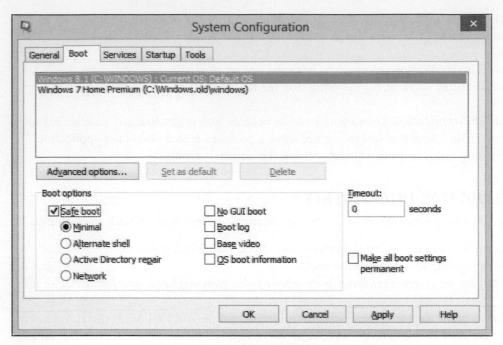

Figure 5-13 Restart Windows in a Safe boot with minimal Windows configuration

If the application works in Safe Mode, you can assume the problem is not with the application but with the operating system, device drivers, or other software that loads at startup. To return the system to a normal startup, open System Configuration again and click **Normal startup** on the General tab.

◢ *Use System Restore.* If you can identify the approximate date the error started and that date is in the recent past, use System Restore (rstrui.exe). Select a restore point just before the problem started. Reverting to a restore point can solve problems with registry entries the application uses that have become corrupted. However, System Restore can cause problems of its own, so use it with caution.

★ **A+ Exam Tip** The 220-902 exam expects you to know when and how to use System Restore to solve a Windows, hardware, or application problem.

★ **A+ Exam Tip** If an often-used Windows utility can be launched from a command prompt, the A+ 220-902 exam expects you to know the program name of that utility.

⚡ **Caution** When researching a problem, suppose you discover that Microsoft or a manufacturer's website offers a fix or patch you can download and apply. To get the right patch, recall you need to make sure you get a 32-bit patch for a 32-bit installation of Windows, a device driver, or an application. For a 64-bit installation of Windows, make sure you get a 64-bit device driver. An application installed in a 64-bit OS might be a 32-bit application or a 64-bit application.

Now let's learn to use the Memory Diagnostics and System File Checker tools, which can be useful when troubleshooting application problems.

MEMORY DIAGNOSTICS

Errors with memory are often difficult to diagnose because they can appear intermittently and might be mistaken as application errors, user errors, or other hardware component errors. Sometimes these errors cause the system to hang, a BSOD (blue screen of death) error might occur, or the system continues to function with applications giving errors or data getting corrupted. You can quickly identify a problem with memory or eliminate memory as the source of a problem by using the Windows Memory Diagnostics (mdsched.exe) tool. It works before Windows is loaded to test memory for errors, and can be used on computers that don't have Windows installed. Use one of these two methods to start the utility:

▲ **Method 1.** In a command prompt window on the Windows desktop, enter **mdsched.exe** and press **Enter**. A dialog box appears (see Figure 5-14) asking if you want to run the test now or on the next restart.

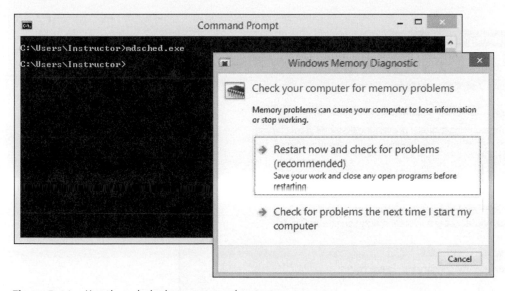

Figure 5-14 Use the mdsched.exe command to test memory

▲ **Method 2.** If you cannot boot from the hard drive, boot the computer from the Windows setup DVD or some other recovery media such as a Windows 8 recovery drive or a Windows 7 repair disc. (You learn more about these options in the chapter, "Troubleshooting Windows Startup.") On the opening screen, select your language. On the next screen (see Figure 5-15), click **Repair your computer**.

Figure 5-15 Opening menu when you boot from the Windows 8 setup DVD

On the next screen, do one of the following:

◢ For Windows 8, click **Troubleshoot** and then **Advanced options**. On the Advanced options screen, click **Command Prompt**. A command prompt window appears. At the command prompt, enter **mdsched.exe** and press **Enter**.

◢ For Windows 7, select the Windows installation to repair. On the System Recovery Options screen (see Figure 5-16), click **Windows Memory Diagnostic** and follow the directions on screen.

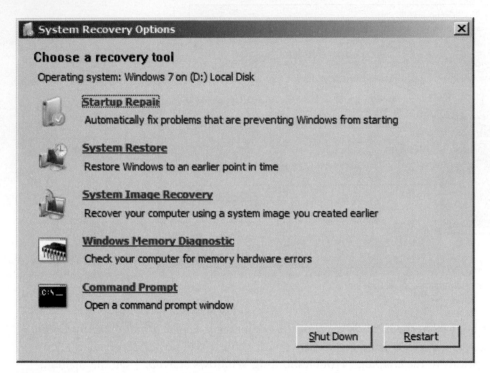

Figure 5-16   Test memory using the Windows 7 System Recovery Options menu

If the tool reports memory errors, replace all memory modules installed on the motherboard.

SYSTEM FILE CHECKER

A+
220-902
1.3, 4.1

A Windows application or hardware problem might be caused by a corrupted Windows system file. That's where System File Checker might help. System File Checker (SFC) protects system files and keeps a cache of current system files in case it needs to refresh a damaged file. To use the utility to scan all system files and verify them, first close all applications and then enter the command **sfc /scannow** in an elevated command prompt window (see Figure 5-17). If corrupted system files are found, you might need to provide the Windows setup DVD to restore the files. If you have problems running the SFC utility, boot the computer into Safe Mode and run the sfc /scannow command again in Safe Mode. If you still have problems, know that you will learn more about repairing system files in the chapter, "Troubleshooting Windows Startup."

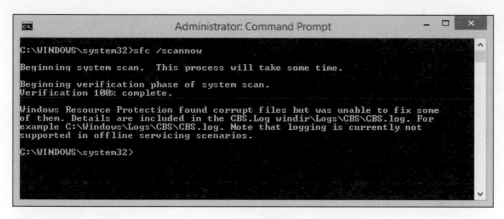

Figure 5-17 Use System File Checker to verify Windows system files

> **Notes** Recall from the chapter, "Maintaining Windows," that you can get an elevated command prompt window in Windows 8 by right-clicking **Start** and clicking **Command Prompt (Admin)**. In Windows 7, click **Start**, **All Programs**, and **Accessories**. Then right-click **Command Prompt** and select **Run as administrator** from the shortcut menu.

RESPONDING TO SPECIFIC ERROR MESSAGES

A+
220-902
1.3, 1.4,
3.3, 4.1

In this part of the chapter, we look at some specific error messages that relate to problems with applications.

WHEN AN APPLICATION HANGS

If an application is locked up and not responding, use Task Manager to end it. If Task Manager can't end a process, use the tasklist and taskkill commands. The tasklist command returns the process identifier (PID), which is a number that identifies each running process. The taskkill command uses the process ID to kill the process. Using Notepad as a sample application, do the following:

1. Open a command prompt window and start Notepad with the command **notepad.exe**. Be sure the Notepad window and the command prompt window are positioned so both are visible on your screen. Use the **tasklist | more** command to get a list of processes currently running (press the Spacebar to scroll to the next page). Note the PID of the Notepad process, for example, 7132.

2. Enter the command **taskkill /f /pid:7132**, using the PID you noted in Step 1. The /f parameter forcefully kills the process. Be careful using this command; it is so powerful that you can end critical system processes that will cause the system to shut down.

WHEN A FILE FAILS TO OPEN

Windows depends on the file extension to associate a data file with an application used to open it, which it calls the file association. An application associated with a file extension is called its default program. When you double-click a data file and Windows examines the file extension and doesn't know which application to call on to open the file, it displays an error message. The solution to this problem is to change the file association for the data file's file extension.

APPLYING | CONCEPTS   SOLVE FILE ASSOCIATION PROBLEMS

In our example, the Transact.dbf file shown in Figure 5-18a is a legacy database file created by dBASE, and the error box in Figure 5-18a appeared when the user double-clicked the file.

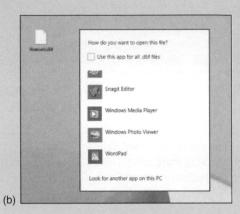

(a)   (b)

Figure 5-18   Windows does not know which application to use to open the data file

Follow these steps to instruct Windows 8 to use Microsoft Excel to open files with a .dbf file extension:

1. Click **More options** (see Figure 5-18a). At the bottom of the box (see Figure 5-18b), click **Look for another app on this PC**. (For Windows 7, click **Select a program from a list of installed programs**.)

2. The *Open with* window appears. Locate the program file for Microsoft Excel, as shown in Figure 5-19 and click **Open**. (If you don't know an application's program file and location, launch the application and then open Task Manager. On the Processes tab of Task Manager, right-click the application and click **Open file location**. File Explorer or Windows Explorer opens and highlights the program file. You can see the path to the program file at the top of the Explorer window.)

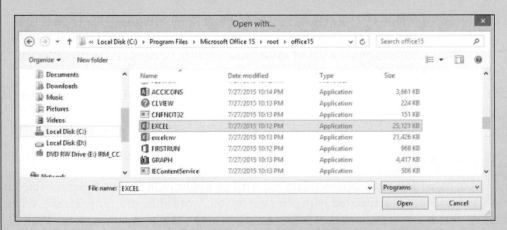

Figure 5-19   Locate and select the EXCEL.exe application program file

3. When you double-click the **Transact.dbf** file, the file opens in an Excel window. Also the icon used for the file on the desktop is now the Excel icon.

If you need to change the program associated with a file extension, use the Default Programs applet in Control Panel. For example, suppose you tried to associate the Transact.dbf file with Microsoft Access and when you opened the file, Access gave an error. Follow these steps to change the file association to Excel:

1. Open Control Panel in Classic view and click **Default Programs**. The Default Programs window opens. Click **Associate a file type or protocol with a program**. The list of current associations appears in the Set Associations window.

2. Select the file extension you want to change (see Figure 5-20) and click **Change program**. A dialog box appears asking how you want to open the file (as shown in the middle of Figure 5-20).

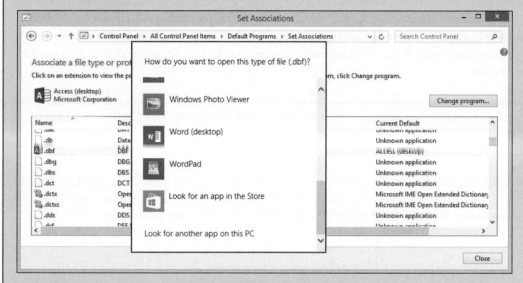

Figure 5-20   Select the default program to associate with a file extension

3. The box displays installed programs that can handle the selected file extension. If you don't see the program you want, click **More options** and scroll to the bottom of the list. Then click **Look for another app on this PC** (in Windows 7, click **Browse**) to find it in the Program Files or Program Files (x86) folder on your hard drive. Otherwise, make your selection (and in Windows 7, click **OK**). Then close all windows.

WHEN A SERVICE FAILS TO START

A message about a service failing to start can be caused by a corrupted or missing service program, or the service might not be configured to launch at startup. Recall from the "Optimizing Windows" chapter that you can use the Services console (services.msc) to enable, disable, start, or stop a service. A service can be disabled at startup using the System Configuration tool (msconfig.exe), and Task Manager (taskmgr.exe) can give you a list of all running services.

If you get an error message that a service has failed to start, check the Services console to make sure the service is set to start automatically. Make sure the Startup type is set to Automatic or Automatic (Delayed Start). Use the service's Properties box in the console to find the path and file name to the executable program. Then use Explorer to make sure the program file is not missing. You might need to reinstall the service or the application that uses the service.

WHEN A DLL IS MISSING OR A COMPONENT IS NOT REGISTERED

Most applications have a main program file that uses a collection of many small programs called components or objects that serve the main program. The main program for an application has an .exe file extension and relies on several component services that often have a .dll file extension. (DLL stands for

Dynamic Link Library.) Problems with applications can be caused by a missing DLL program or a broken association between the main program and a component.

If you get an error message about a missing DLL, the easiest way to solve this problem might be to reinstall the application. However, if that is not advisable, you can identify the path and name of the missing DLL file and recover it from backup or from the application installation files.

On the other hand, the file might be present and undamaged, but the application cannot find it because the relationship between the two is broken. Relationships between a main program and its components are normally established by entries in the registry when the application is installed. The process is called registering a component. In addition, the Component Services (also called COM+) tool, which is a Microsoft Management Console snap-in, can be used to register components. The tool is often used by application developers and system administrators when developing and deploying an application. For example, a system administrator might use COM+ when installing an application on servers or client computers where an application on one computer calls an application on another computer on the network. COM+ is more automated than the older and more manual Regsvr32 utility that is also used to register component services.

> ★ **A+ Exam Tip** The A+ 220-902 exam expects you to know how to handle missing DLL errors and to know when it's appropriate to use the Component Services and Regsvr32.

The regsvr32.exe program requires an elevated command prompt. Note in Figure 5-21, the first regsvr32 command uses the /u parameter to unregister a component. The second regsvr32 command registers the component again. Also notice that you need to include the path to the DLL file in the command line.

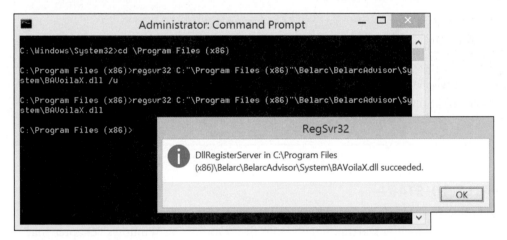

Figure 5-21 Use the regsvr32 command to register or unregister an application component

As an IT support technician, you might be asked by a system administrator or software provider to use the COM+ or Regsvr32 tool to help solve a problem with an application giving errors. Suppose you get this error when installing an application:

Error 1928 "Error registering COM+ application."

When you contact the help desk of the application provider, you might be instructed to use the COM+ tool to solve the problem. To open the tool, open Control Panel and click **Administrative Tools**, then double-click **Component Services**. The Component Services window is shown in Figure 5-22. To learn how to use the tool, click **Help** in the menu bar.

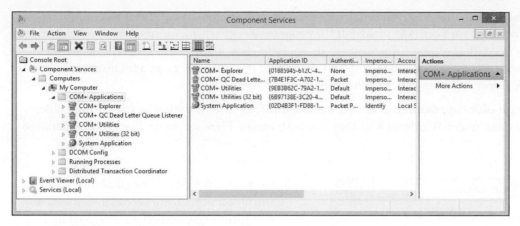

Figure 5-22 Use the Component Services window to register components used by an application

WHEN THE APPLICATION HAS NEVER WORKED

If the application has never worked, follow these steps:

1. *Update Windows and search the web.* Installing all important and critical Windows updates can sometimes solve a problem with an application that won't install. Also check the website of the software manufacturer and the Microsoft support site (*support.microsoft.com*) for solutions. Search on the application name or the error message you get when you try to run it.

2. *Run the installation program or application as an administrator.* The program might require that the user have privileges not assigned to the current user account. Try running the application with administrator privileges, which Windows calls a secondary logon. If the installation has failed, use Explorer to locate the installation executable file. Right-click it and select **Run as administrator** from the shortcut menu (see Figure 5-23).

> **✎ Notes** To run a program using a user account other than administrator, hold down the Shift key and right-click the program file. Then select **Run as different user** from the shortcut menu. You must then enter the user name and password of another user account in the Windows Security box.

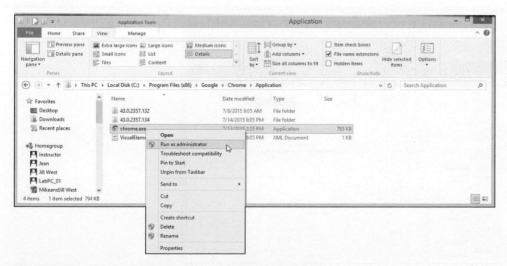

Figure 5-23 Execute a program using administrative privileges

If the application has failed after it is installed, locate the installed program. Look for it in a subfolder of the Program Files or Program Files (x86) folder. If the program works when you run it with administrative privileges, you can make that setting permanent. To do so, right-click it and select **Properties** from the shortcut menu. Then click the **Compatibility** tab and check **Run this program as an administrator** (see Figure 5-24). Click **Apply** and then close the Properties box.

3. *Consider whether an older application is having compatibility problems with Windows.* Some older applications cannot run under Windows 8 or they run with errors. Here are some steps you can take to fix the problem:

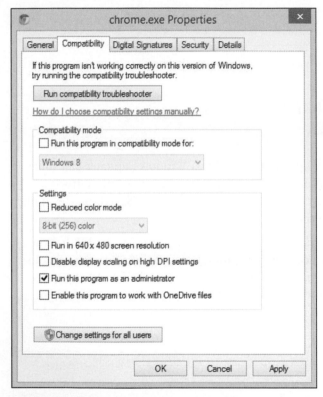

Figure 5-24   Permanently change the privilege level of an application

a. Go to the Windows Compatibility Center site at *www.microsoft.com/en-us/windows/compatibility/CompatCenter/Home* and search for the application. The site reports problems and solutions for known legacy software. For example, search on the application **WinPatrol**, then under the *Compatible with* menu, click **Windows 8.1**. You find that Microsoft recommends Version 25 or 28 for Windows 8.1 (see Figure 5-25). Use the 32-bit or 64-bit type appropriate for your system. If the version and type you are using are not compatible, try to replace or upgrade the software.

b. Try running the application in compatibility mode. To do that, on the Compatibility tab of the program file Properties box shown earlier in Figure 5-24, check **Run this program in compatibility mode for:**. Then, from the drop-down menu, select the operating system that the application was written to run under. Click **Apply** and close the Properties box.

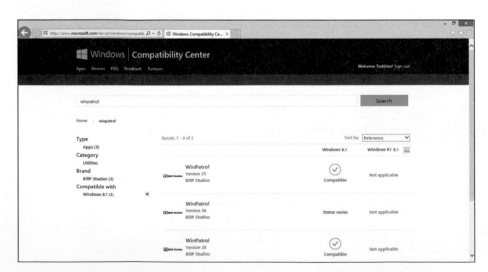

Figure 5-25   Microsoft tracks software and hardware compatible with Windows 8.1

> **OS Differences** For Windows 7 Professional, Ultimate, or Enterprise editions, try running the program in Windows XP Mode. Recall from the chapter, "Installing Windows," that Windows XP Mode can be used to install XP in a virtual machine under Windows 7. Applications installed in XP Mode work in the XP environment. Only use this option as a last resort because XP Mode takes up a lot of system resources.

4. *Verify that the application is digitally signed.* Although applications that are not digitally signed can still run on Windows, a digital signature does verify that the application is not a rogue application and that it is certified as Windows-compatible by Microsoft. To view the digital signature, select the **Digital Signatures** tab of the program file's Properties box. Select a signer in the list and click **Details** (see Figure 5-26). If the Digital Signatures tab is missing, the program is not digitally signed.

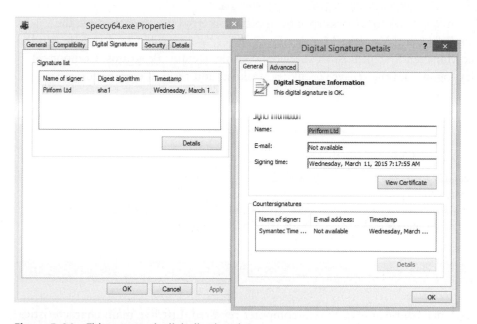

Figure 5-26   This program is digitally signed

>> CHAPTER SUMMARY

What Customers Want: Beyond Technical Know-How

▲ Customers want more than just technical know-how. They want a positive and helpful attitude, respect, good communication, sensitivity to their needs, ownership of their problem, dependability, credibility, integrity, honesty, and professionalism.

▲ Customers expect their first contact with you to be professional and friendly, and they want you to put listening to their problem or request as your first priority.

▲ Know how to ask penetrating questions when interviewing a customer about a problem or request.

▲ Set and meet customer expectations by using good communication about what you are doing or intending to do and allowing the customer to make decisions where appropriate.

▲ Deal confidently and gracefully with customers who are difficult, including those who are not knowledgeable, are overly confident, or complain.

▲ When you first start a new job, find out how to escalate a problem you cannot solve.

Strategies to Troubleshoot Any Computer Problem

▲ The six steps in the troubleshooting process are (1) interview the user and back up data, (2) examine the system and form a theory of probable cause (your best guess), (3) test your theory, (4) plan a solution and implement it, (5) verify that everything works and take appropriate preventive measures, and (6) document what you did and the final outcome.

Troubleshooting Applications

▲ A problem with an application might be caused by the application, the hardware, the operating system, the data, other applications in conflict with this one, or the user.

▲ Windows error messages and logs can help you examine a system looking for the source of an application problem.

▲ Tools and features available in Windows to address specific application error messages include the Action Center, Event Viewer, Reliability Monitor, Memory Diagnostics, System File Checker, Safe Mode, System Configuration, Task Manager, System Restore, Services console, Default Programs, Component Services (COM+), secondary logon, and the regsvr32, chkdsk, tasklist, and taskkill commands.

>> KEY TERMS

For explanations of key terms, see the Glossary for this text.

call tracking software	escalate	Regsvr32	taskkill
Component Services (COM+)	expert system	Safe Mode	tasklist
	file association	secondary logon	technical documentation
default program	Memory Diagnostics	System File Checker (SFC)	ticket

>> REVIEWING THE BASICS

1. Assume that you are a customer who wants to have a computer repaired. List five main characteristics that you would want to see in your computer repair person.

2. What is one thing you should do when you receive a phone call requesting on-site support, before you make an appointment?

3. You make an appointment to do an on-site repair, but you are detained and find out that you will be late. What is the best thing to do?

4. When making an on-site service call, what should you do before making any changes to software or before taking the case cover off a computer?

5. What should you do after finishing your computer repair?

6. What is a good strategy to follow if a conflict arises between you and your customer?

7. You have exhausted your knowledge of a problem and it still is not solved. Before you escalate it, what else can you do?

8. If you need to make a phone call while on a customer's site and your cell phone is not working, what do you do?

9. What is one thing you can do to help a caller who needs phone support and is not a competent computer user?

10. Describe what you should do when a customer complains to you about a product or service that your company provides.

11. What are the six steps that you can use to solve any computer problem?

12. How many bits does an x86-based operating system process at one time?

13. What is the command to use the Memory Diagnostics tool?

14. What is the command to use the System File Checker to immediately verify system files?

15. What GUI tool can you use to stop a program that is hung?

16. What command-line tool can you use to stop a program that is hung?

17. How can you eliminate the possibility that an application error is caused by another application or service running in the background?

18. How does Windows know which application to use to open a file when you double-click the file in File Explorer or Windows Explorer?

19. Which two tools might a software developer or system administrator use to register a component of an application in the Windows registry?

20. If an application works when the system is loaded in Safe Mode, but does not work when Windows is loaded normally, what can you assume?

>> THINKING CRITICALLY

1. You own a small computer repair company and a customer comes to you with a laptop that will not boot. After investigating, you discover the hard drive has crashed. What should you do first?

   a. Install a hard drive the same size and speed as the original.

   b. Ask the customer's advice about the size drive to install, but select a drive the same speed as the original drive.

   c. Ask the customer's advice about the size and speed of the new drive to install.

   d. If the customer looks like he can afford it, install the largest and fastest drive the system can support.

2. You have repaired a broken LCD panel in a laptop computer. However, when you disassembled the laptop, you bent the hinge on the laptop lid so that it now does not latch solidly. When the customer receives the laptop, he notices the bent hinge and begins shouting at you. What do you do first? Second?

   a. Explain to the customer you are sorry but you did the best you could.

   b. Listen carefully to the customer and don't get defensive.

   c. Apologize and offer to replace the bent hinge.

   d. Tell the customer he is not allowed to speak to you like that.

3. As a help-desk technician, list four good detective questions to ask if a user calls to say, "My computer won't boot."

4. A user tells you that Microsoft Word gives errors when saving a file. What should you do first?

   a. Install Windows updates, which also include patches for Microsoft Word.

   b. Ask the user when the problem first started.

   c. Ask the user to save the error message as a screen shot the next time the error occurs and email it to you.

   d. Use Task Manager to end the Microsoft Word program.

>> REAL PROBLEMS, REAL SOLUTIONS

REAL PROBLEM 5-1 Summarizing Windows Troubleshooting Tools

When you're stuck on a problem, it's helpful to have a quick-and-easy reference of the tools available to you in Windows. In this project, you create a table to gather all of this information into one place. In the "Troubleshooting Windows Startup" chapter, you will add more tools to this table.

1. Using your choice of word-processing software (such as Microsoft Word) or spreadsheet software (such as Microsoft Excel), create a table with the following headings: **Tool**, **Steps to access**, and **Description**.

2. Under the *Tool* heading, list all of the Windows tools covered in this chapter and in earlier chapters, such as Event Viewer, Task Manager, Action Center, and Memory Diagnostics.

3. Complete the remainder of the table with the steps needed to access each tool and a brief, one- or two-sentence description of each. For Computer Management, for example, you might say, "Access from the Control Panel, or enter compmgmt.msc at a command prompt." Be sure to include the program name of the utility if it can be launched from the command prompt. The description for Disk Management might say, "Use it to view and modify partitions on hard drives and to format drives." Be sure to note whether a tool is available only for certain releases of Windows, such as "New with Windows 8."

Keep this table handy, as it can be very useful when troubleshooting problems in Windows.

REAL PROBLEM 5-2 Writing Your Own Scenario for Developing Interpersonal Social Skills

In the chapter, you read several scenarios where technical support people failed to serve their customers well or failed to relate professionally with coworkers. Recall a similar situation where you observed poor service from a technician or salesperson. Write the scenario using fictitious names. Then write three questions to help other students think through what went wrong, what should have happened, and some principles of relating to customers or coworkers that could have helped if they had been applied. Present your scenario in class or with a student group for discussion.

REAL PROBLEM 5-3 Installing and Using Help-Desk Software

Go to *www.spiceworks.com* and watch a few of the videos about Spiceworks Help Desk Software. Then download, install, and run the software. Practice using the software to add help-desk workers, open a ticket, assign a worker to a ticket, and resolve and close the ticket.

Consider setting up an IT help desk where your classmates can provide end-user support to other students and instructors at your school as they have problems with their personal computers. One computer in the class would be designated the help-desk computer that holds the Spiceworks Help Desk Software for the entire class. Classmates are entered in Spiceworks as help-desk workers and are assigned tickets as users request help. Spiceworks can be set up to receive requests for help through an email account, and you can advertise the email address as a way to offer support for students and instructors on campus. What other ways can you use to advertise your help desk and provide a way for your customers to contact the help desk? Some IT support classes have run extremely successful help desks and have received small donations for services.

Troubleshooting Windows Startup

Y ou've already learned how to deal with Windows and application problems that occur after Windows has started. In this chapter, you take your troubleshooting skills one step further by learning to deal with startup problems caused by Windows. When Windows fails to start, it can be stressful if important data has not been backed up or the user has pressing work to do with the computer. What helps more than anything else is to have a good understanding of Windows startup and a good plan for approaching startup problems.

We begin the chapter with a discussion of what happens when you first turn on a computer and Windows starts. The more you understand about startup, the better your chances of fixing startup problems. Then you learn about Windows tools specifically designed to handle startup problems. Finally, you learn about strategies for solving startup problems.

UNDERSTANDING THE BOOT PROCESS

Knowledge is power. The better you understand what happens when you first turn on a computer until Windows is loaded and the Windows Start screen or desktop appears, the more likely you will be able to solve a problem when Windows cannot start. Let's begin by noting the differences between a hard boot and a soft boot.

> ✏ **Notes** Most techies use the terms *boot* and *startup* interchangeably. However, in general, the term *boot* refers to the hardware phase of starting up a computer. Microsoft consistently uses the term *startup* to refer to how its operating systems are booted, well, started, I mean.

DIFFERENT WAYS TO BOOT

The term booting comes from the phrase "lifting yourself up by your bootstraps" and refers to the computer bringing itself up to a working state without the user having to do anything but press the on button. Two fundamental ways to boot a computer are:

- ◢ A hard boot, or cold boot, involves turning on the power with the on/off switch.
- ◢ A soft boot, or warm boot, involves using the operating system to reboot. In Windows, a soft boot is called a restart.

A hard boot takes more time than a soft boot because in a soft boot, the initial steps performed by UEFI/BIOS in a hard boot don't happen. To save time in most circumstances, you should use a soft boot (Windows restart). A hard boot initializes the processor and clears memory. So if a restart doesn't work or you want to make certain you get a fresh start, use a Windows shutdown followed by a hard boot.

WINDOWS SHUTDOWN AND RESTART

Windows shutdown orderly closes all open applications, user sessions, services, devices, and system processes and then powers down the computer. The Windows 8 Fast Startup feature speeds up startup by performing a partial hibernation at shutdown. At shutdown, Windows saves the drivers and kernel state in the Windows hibernate file, hiberfil.sys, and then reads from this file on the next cold boot. The feature is enabled by default and can be disabled in the Power Options applet in Control Panel. A shutdown from the Start screen (see Figure 6-1a) uses Fast Startup hibernation when the feature is enabled. Even when Fast Startup is enabled, a shutdown from the desktop always performs a full shutdown (see Figure 6-1b).

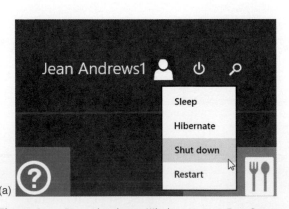
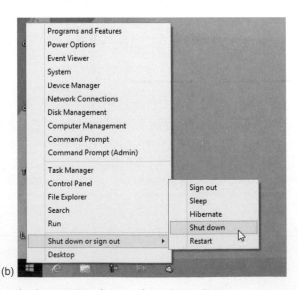

Figure 6-1   For a shutdown, Windows 8 uses Fast Startup on the Start screen, but not from the desktop

A restart in Windows 8 does not use Fast Startup hibernation, which means the kernel and drivers are completely reloaded at startup as is done with a full shutdown.

> **⟲ OS Differences** Windows 7 doesn't have the Fast Startup feature. A Windows 7 shutdown always performs a full shutdown and a Windows 7 restart always reloads the kernel and drivers.

POWER BUTTONS AND SWITCHES ON A COMPUTER CASE

If Windows is hung and you can't use the OS to perform a restart or shutdown, look for power or reset buttons on the front or rear of the case. For example, one computer has three power switches: a power button and a reset button on the front of the case and a power switch on the rear of the case (see Figure 6-2).

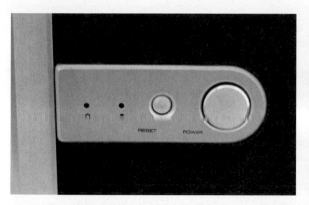 

Figure 6-2 This computer case has two power buttons on the front and one power switch on the rear of the case

They work like this:

▲ The power button in front can be configured as a "soft" power button, causing a Windows restart.

▲ The reset button initializes the CPU so that it restarts at the beginning of the UEFI/BIOS startup program. The computer behaves as though the power were turned off and back on and then goes through the entire boot process.

▲ The switch on the rear of the case simply turns off the power abruptly and is a "hard" power button. If you use this switch, wait 30 seconds before you press the power button on the front of the case to boot the system. This method gives you the greatest assurance that memory will clear. However, if Windows is abruptly stopped, it might give an error message when you reboot.

How the front two buttons work can be controlled in UEFI/BIOS setup. Know, however, that different cases offer different options.

STARTUP UEFI/BIOS CONTROLS THE BEGINNING OF THE BOOT

The startup UEFI/BIOS is programming contained on the firmware chip on the motherboard that is responsible for getting a system up and going and finding an OS to load. Recall that UEFI is a mini-operating system that is gradually replacing the legacy BIOS standards. UEFI improves on processes for booting, securing the boot, loading device drivers and applications before the OS loads, and handing over the boot to the OS.

If Secure Boot in UEFI is enabled, UEFI systems run security checks to protect against malware designed to attack during the boot. UEFI stores device drivers and information about Secure Boot on a nonvolatile RAM (NVRAM) chip and in a hidden partition on the hard drive called the EFI System Partition (ESP). Recall UEFI/BIOS searches for and then turns to a boot device to find an operating system to launch. During startup, you can change the boot device priority order used for this search by accessing UEFI/BIOS setup.

Next let's see what happens during the boot, from the time power is turned on until Windows is started. In these steps, we assume the OS is loaded from the hard drive.

STEPS TO BOOT THE COMPUTER AND START WINDOWS

A+
220-902
4.1

Before we get into the steps, check out Table 6-1. It lists the components and files stored on the hard drive that are necessary to start Windows. The table can serve as a guide as you study the steps.

Component or File	Path*	Description
BIOS systems using MBR partitioning		
MBR	First sector of the hard drive is called the Master Boot Record (MBR)	BIOS looks to the partition table in the MBR to locate the active partition.
System partition	Also called the active partition or System Reserved partition	The system partition holds the Boot Manager, Boot Configuration Data (BCD) store, and other files and folders needed to begin Windows startup. For Windows, these files are stored in the root and \Boot directory of the hidden system partition.
Boot Manager	In the root of the system partition	Windows Boot Manager, bootmgr (with no file extension), accesses the BCD store and locates the Windows Boot Loader.
BCD store	\Boot directory on the system partition	The Boot Configuration Data (BCD) store is a database file named BCD (no file extension) and is organized the same as a registry hive. It contains boot settings that control the Boot Manager and can be viewed and edited with the bcdedit command.
UEFI systems using GPT partitioning		
GPT partition table	At the beginning of the hard drive and a backup copy at the end of the drive	UEFI looks to the GPT partition table to locate the EFI System Partition.
System partition	EFI System Partition (ESP) is normally 100 MB to 200 MB in size.	The system partition holds the Windows Boot Manager, BCD, and other supporting files. For Windows, the Boot Manager is bootmgfw.efi and is stored in \EFI\Microsoft\Boot. A backup copy of bootmgfw.efi is at \EFI\Boot\bootx64.efi.
Boot Manager	For Windows, \EFI\Microsoft\ Boot on the ESP	Bootmgfw.efi loads EFI applications based on variables stored in NVRAM and reads the BCD store to find out other boot parameters (such as a dual boot).
BCD store	\EFI\Microsoft\Boot on the ESP	BCD store entries point the Windows Boot Manager to the location of the Windows Boot Loader program.
All Windows BIOS and UEFI systems		
Windows Boot Loader	C:\Windows\System32*	Windows Boot Manager turns control over to the Windows Boot Loader, which loads and starts essential Windows processes. Two versions of the program file are: winload.exe (BIOS) winload.efi (UEFI)
Resume from hibernation	C:\Windows\System32	This Windows Boot Loader is used when Windows resumes from hibernation: winresume.exe (BIOS) winresume.efi (UEFI)

Table 6-1   Software components and files needed to start Windows (continues)

Component or File	Path*	Description
Ntoskrnl.exe	C:\Windows\System32	Windows kernel
Hal.dll	C:\Windows\System32	Dynamic link library handles low-level hardware details
Smss.exe	C:\Windows\System32	Sessions Manager program responsible for starting user sessions
Csrss.exe	C:\Windows\System32	Win32 subsystem manages graphical components and threads
Winlogon.exe	C:\Windows\System32	Logon process
Services.exe	C:\Windows\System32	Service Control Manager starts and stops services
Lsass.exe	C:\Windows\System32	Authenticates users
System registry hive	C:\Windows\System32\Config	Holds data for the HKEY_LOCAL_MACHINE key of the registry
Device drivers	C:\Windows\System32\Drivers	Drivers for required hardware

* It is assumed that Windows is installed in C:\Windows.

Table 6-1 Software components and files needed to start Windows (continued)

A successful boot depends on essential hardware devices, UEFI/BIOS, and the operating system all performing without errors. Let's look at the steps to start a Windows computer. Several of these steps are diagrammed in Figures 6-3 and 6-4 to help you visually understand how the steps work.

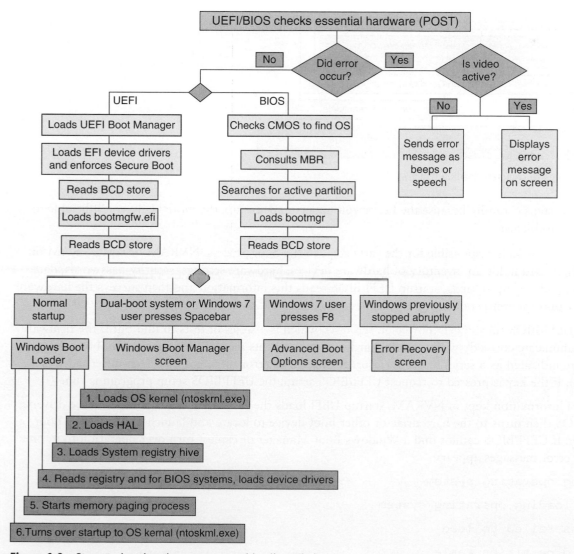

Figure 6-3 Steps to booting the computer and loading Windows

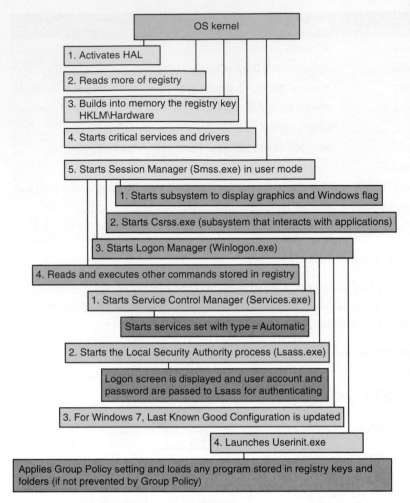

Figure 6-4   Steps to complete loading Windows

Study these steps carefully because the better you understand startup, the more likely you'll be able to solve startup problems:

1. Startup UEFI/BIOS is responsible for the early steps in the boot process. NVRAM or CMOS RAM on the motherboard holds an inventory of hardware devices, hardware settings, security passwords, date and time, and startup settings. Startup UEFI/BIOS reads this information and then surveys the hardware devices it finds present, comparing it with the list kept in its RAM.

2. Startup UEFI/BIOS runs POST (power-on self test), which is a series of tests to find out if the firmware can communicate correctly with essential hardware components required for a successful boot. Any errors are indicated as a series of beeps, recorded speech, or error messages on screen (after video is checked). If the key is pressed to request UEFI/BIOS setup, the UEFI/BIOS setup program is run.

3. Based on information kept in NVRAM, startup UEFI loads the UEFI boot manager and device drivers. UEFI/BIOS then turns to the hard drive or other boot device to locate and launch the Windows Boot Manager. If UEFI/BIOS cannot find a Windows Boot Manager or cannot turn over operation to it, one of these error messages appears:

```
Missing operating system

Error loading operating system

Windows failed to load

Invalid partition table
```

4. The Windows Boot Manager does the following:

   a. It reads the settings in the BCD.

   b. The next step, one of three, depends on entries in the BCD and these other factors:

      ▲ *Option 1.* For normal startups that are not dual booting, no menu appears and Boot Manager finds and launches the Windows Boot Loader program.

      ▲ *Option 2.* If the computer is set up for a dual-boot environment, Boot Manager displays the *Choose an operating system* screen, as shown in Figure 6-5.

      ▲ *Option 3.* If Windows was previously stopped abruptly or another error occurs, the Windows 8 Startup Menu appears (see Figure 6-6) to give you the option to troubleshoot the problem.

6

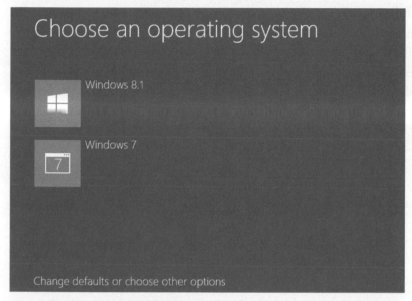

Figure 6-5   In a dual-boot setup, Windows Boot Manager provides a choice of operating systems

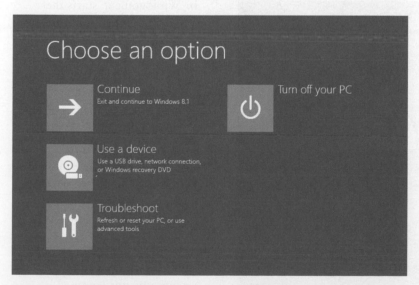

Figure 6-6   Windows 8 Startup Menu offers the opportunity to troubleshoot a problem with startup

5. Windows Boot Loader (winload.exe or winload.efi) is responsible for loading Windows components. It does the following:

   a. For normal startups, Boot Loader loads into memory the OS kernel, Ntoskrnl.exe, but does not yet start it. Boot Loader also loads into memory the Hardware Abstraction Layer (Hal.dll), which will later be used by the kernel.

   b. Boot Loader loads into memory the system registry hive (C:\Windows\System32\Config\System).

   c. Boot Loader then reads the registry key just created, HKEY_LOCAL_ MACHINE\SYSTEM\Services, looking for and loading into memory device drivers that must be launched at startup. The drivers are not yet started.

   d. Boot Loader starts up the memory paging process and then turns over startup to the OS kernel (Ntoskrnl.exe).

6. The kernel (Ntoskrnl.exe) does the following:

   a. It activates the HAL, reads more information from the registry, and builds into memory the registry key HKEY_LOCAL_ MACHINE\HARDWARE, using information that has been collected about the hardware.

   b. The kernel then starts critical services and drivers that are configured to be started by the kernel during the boot. Drivers interact directly with hardware and run in kernel mode, while services interact with drivers. Most services and drivers are stored in C:\Windows\System32 or C:\Windows\System32\Drivers and have an .exe, .dll, or .sys file extension.

   c. After the kernel starts all services and drivers configured to load during the boot, it starts the Session Manager (Smss.exe), which runs in user mode.

7. The Session Manager (Smss.exe) loads the graphical interface and starts the client/server run-time subsystem (csrss.exe), which also runs in user mode. Csrss.exe is the Win32 subsystem component that interacts with applications.

8. Smss.exe starts the Logon Manager (winlogon.exe) and reads and executes other commands stored in the registry, such as a command to replace system files placed there by Windows Update.

9. Winlogon.exe does the following:

   a. It starts the Service Control Manager (services.exe). Services.exe starts all services listed with the startup type of Automatic in the Services console.

   b. Winlogon.exe starts the Local Security Authority process (lsass.exe). The sign-in screen appears (see Figure 6-7), and the user account and password are passed to the lsass.exe process for authenticating.

   c. Winlogon.exe launches userinit.exe. For Windows 8, the Start screen or desktop (explorer.exe) is launched. For Windows 7, the desktop is launched.

10. Userinit.exe applies Group Policy settings and any programs not trumped by Group Policy that are stored

Figure 6-7   Windows 8 sign-in screen

in startup folders and startup registry keys. See the appendix, "Entry Points for Windows Startup Processes," for a list of these folders and registry keys.

The Windows startup is officially completed when the Windows Start screen or desktop appears and the pinwheel wait icon disappears.

WINDOWS | 7 STARTUP

| A+ 220-902 4.1 |

Windows 8 and Windows 7 generally use the same startup processes, which are outlined in earlier in Figures 6-3 and 6-4. However, here are a few key differences:

◢ If Windows 7 was previously stopped abruptly or another error occurs, the Windows 7 Error Recovery screen (see Figure 6-8) appears.

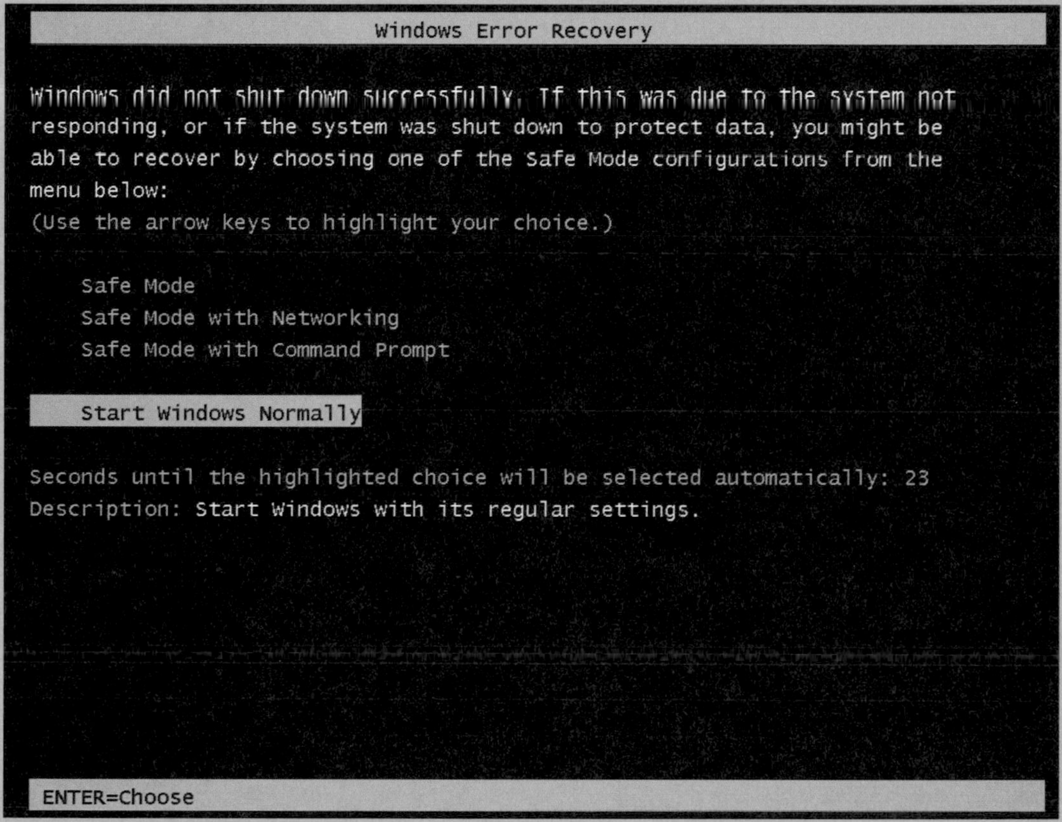

```
                           Windows Error Recovery

Windows did not shut down successfully. If this was due to the system not
responding, or if the system was shut down to protect data, you might be
able to recover by choosing one of the Safe Mode configurations from the
menu below:
(Use the arrow keys to highlight your choice.)


    Safe Mode
    Safe Mode with Networking
    Safe Mode with Command Prompt

    Start Windows Normally

Seconds until the highlighted choice will be selected automatically: 23
Description: Start Windows with its regular settings.




ENTER=Choose
```

Figure 6-8 This window appears if Windows 7 has been abruptly stopped

◢ If the user presses the Spacebar near the beginning of Windows startup, the Windows 7 Boot Manager screen appears, which allows you to run Windows Memory Diagnostics.

◢ If the user presses F8 at startup, the Windows 7 Advanced Boot Options screen appears (see Figure 6-9).

(continues)

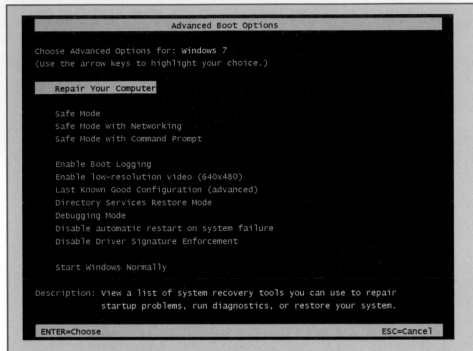

Figure 6-9   Press F8 during the boot to launch the Windows 7 Advanced Boot Options menu

Hands-On | Project 6-1   Examine the System Partition Contents

A+
220-902
4.1

Normally, you cannot see the contents of the system partition. However, if you first assign the partition a drive letter, you can view its contents. First, open the **Folder Options** applet in Control Panel and verify that system files and all file extensions are not hidden and can be viewed. Then open **Disk Management** and find out if the hard drive on which Windows is installed is using the MBR or GPT partitioning system.

Do the following if the hard drive is using the MBR system:

1. In **Disk Management**, right-click the **System Reserved** partition and click **Change Drive Letter and Paths**. Click **Add** and follow directions on screen to assign the partition a drive letter.

2. Open File Explorer or Windows Explorer and drill down into the new volume (see Figure 6-10). You should find bootmgr in the root and BCD in the \Boot folder on the volume.

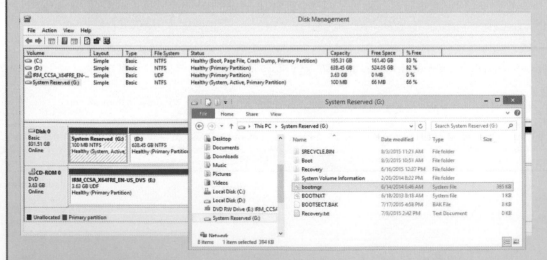

Figure 6-10   Assign a drive letter to the System Reserved partition so that you can view its contents

Do the following if the hard drive is using the GPT system:

1. Open an elevated command prompt window. Then enter the following commands:

`diskpart`	**Open the diskpart command prompt**
`list disk`	**List installed hard drives**
`select disk 0`	**Select the hard drive on which Windows is installed**
`list partition`	**List the partitions on the selected drive**
`select partition 2`	**Select the system partition (it's about 100 MB in size)**
`assign letter=z`	**Assign drive letter z to the partition**
`exit`	**Exit the diskpart utility**

2. At the command prompt, use the dir and cd commands to examine the folders and files on drive z:. Are you able to locate the BCD and bootmgfw.efi files?

When you are finished, remove the drive letter from the system partition so that users won't accidentally change its contents.

With this basic knowledge of the boot in hand, let's turn our attention to the Windows tools that can help you solve problems when Windows refuses to load.

TOOLS FOR TROUBLESHOOTING WINDOWS STARTUP PROBLEMS

A+
220-902
1.2, 1.3,
1.7, 4.1

When troubleshooting startup, it helps to have a road map, which is the purpose of the diagram in Figure 6-11. It can help you organize in your mind the various ways to boot the system and the menus and procedures available to you depending on how you boot the system.

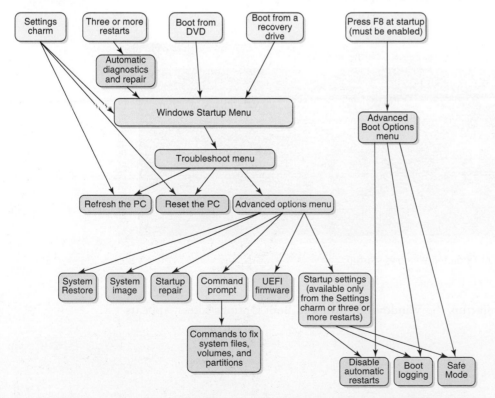

Figure 6-11 Methods to boot the system, menus that appear, and tools available on menus used to troubleshoot startup problems

As you learn to use each tool, keep in mind that you want to use the tool that makes as few changes to the system as possible to fix the problem. In this part of the chapter, the tools are divided into three groups: the least invasive and easy solutions, tools that can affect Windows system files and user settings, and tools to rebuild the Windows installation, even to the point of reinstalling Windows. Before we dig into these tools, let's look at what you can do before a problem occurs in order to make troubleshooting easier and more effective.

WHAT TO DO BEFORE A PROBLEM OCCURS

A+
220-902
4.1

Good preparation will make troubleshooting startup problems much simpler and more successful. When you are responsible for a computer and while the computer is still healthy, be sure to complete the following tasks:

▲ *Keep good backups.* The chapter "Maintaining Windows" covers methods to back up data, applications, and user settings.

▲ *Create a Windows 8 custom refresh image.* Windows 8 offers the option of creating a custom refresh image of the Windows 8 volume. As you learned in the chapter "Maintaining Windows," this image should be created right after you've installed Windows, hardware, applications, and user accounts, and customized Windows settings. You can store the image on the hard drive so it's easy for an end user to get to it when needed or copy it to a network drive, external drive, or some other safe location.

▲ *Configure Windows 8 to use the F8 key at startup.* The F8 key gives you access to the Advanced Boot Options menu in Windows, which you'll learn about later in this chapter. Windows 8 has the feature disabled by default, and Windows 7 has it enabled. In Windows 8, to enable the F8 key at startup, you'll need an elevated command prompt window. Press **Win+X**, click **Command Prompt (Admin)**, and respond to the UAC box. In the command prompt window, enter this command (see Figure 6-12):

```
bcdedit /set {default} bootmenupolicy legacy
```

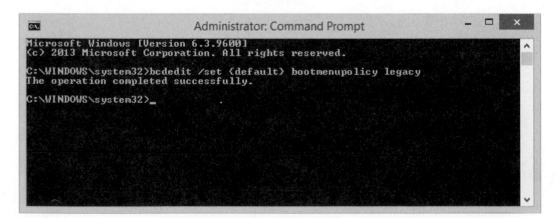

Figure 6-12   Enable the use of F8 during Windows startup

When you press **F8** at startup, the Windows 8 Advanced Boot Options screen appears (see Figure 6-13).

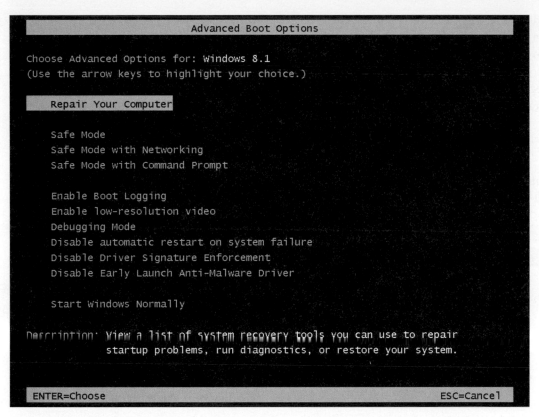

```
                        Advanced Boot Options

Choose Advanced Options for: Windows 8.1
(Use the arrow keys to highlight your choice.)

    Repair Your Computer

    Safe Mode
    Safe Mode with Networking
    Safe Mode with Command Prompt

    Enable Boot Logging
    Enable low-resolution video
    Debugging Mode
    Disable automatic restart on system failure
    Disable Driver Signature Enforcement
    Disable Early Launch Anti-Malware Driver

    Start Windows Normally

Description: View a list of system recovery tools you can use to repair
            startup problems, run diagnostics, or restore your system.


ENTER=Choose                                          ESC=Cancel
```

Figure 6-13   Use the Advanced Boot Options menu to troubleshoot difficult startup problems

Later, if you want to disable the use of F8 at startup, open an elevated command prompt window and enter this command:

```
bcdedit /set {default} bootmenupolicy standard
```

> ⚡ **Caution**   As you learn to troubleshoot Windows 8 startup, don't depend on the F8 key to work during the boot because you never know when you'll work on a computer that has it disabled.

▲ *Create a recovery drive.* Although it's possible to use recovery media created on a different computer than the one you are troubleshooting, the process is simplified if you already have these tools on hand. Let's learn how to do that now.

CREATE A RECOVERY DRIVE

If the computer won't start up, you'll need a bootable device with Windows repair tools on it to start the system and fix problems. Windows 8 provides two recovery device options, depending on the drive hardware available. Here are options for that device:

▲ If the computer has an optical drive, you can boot from the Windows setup DVD and use Windows RE to fix problems, which is discussed later in this section.

▲ You can use a tool new to Windows 8, called a recovery drive. A recovery drive is a bootable USB flash drive. Many mobile computers don't have an optical drive, which can make a recovery drive an essential troubleshooting tool.

> 🖉 **Notes**   A recovery drive is bit-specific: Use a 32-bit recovery drive to repair a 32-bit Windows installation and a 64-bit recovery drive to repair a 64-bit installation.

The key to optimal success with a recovery drive is to create it *before* it's needed. You can use a recovery drive on a broken computer that was created on a different computer. However, if a computer has an OEM recovery partition put there by the manufacturer of a laptop, all-in-one, or other brand-name computer, you have the option to copy this partition to the recovery drive in order to retain OEM resources. If the drive is to hold the OEM recovery partition, it should be about 16 GB. Otherwise, an 8-GB flash drive is large enough.

Here are the steps to create the recovery drive:

1. Plug in a USB flash drive. Know that the entire drive will be formatted and everything on the drive will be lost.

2. Open the **Control Panel** in Classic view and click **Recovery**. In the Recovery window that appears (see Figure 6-14), click **Create a recovery drive**. Respond to the UAC box.

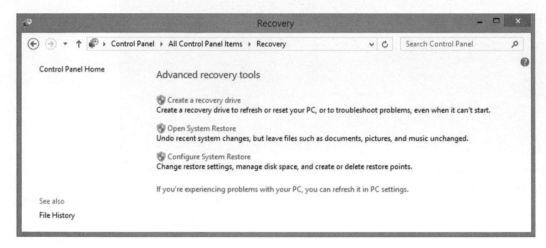

Figure 6-14   The Recovery window in Control Panel is used to create a recovery drive

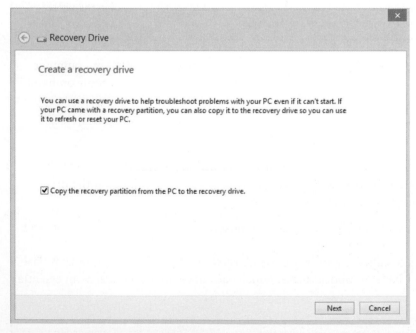

Figure 6-15   If the computer has a recovery partition, you have the option to copy it to the recovery drive

3. The Recovery Drive dialog box appears (see Figure 6-15). If the computer doesn't have an OEM recovery partition, the check box on this dialog box is gray and not available. If the computer has an OEM recovery partition, the check box is available and you can check it to copy the recovery partition to the recovery drive. Click **Next** to continue.

4. A list of installed drives appears (see Figure 6-16). Be careful to select the USB flash drive because everything on the drive will be lost. Click **Next**. A message on the next screen warns you that everything on the drive will be deleted. Click **Create**. The drive is created, which takes some time. Then click **Finish**.

Figure 6-16   Select the USB flash drive that will become the recovery drive

Be sure to label the flash drive well and put it in a safe place. For example, you can put it in an envelope and label it "Recovery drive for John Hawkins 64-bit Windows 8 Sony laptop" and store it in the computer's documentation file.

> ✎ **Notes** If you copied the OEM recovery partition to the USB flash drive and are short on hard drive space on the computer, you can use Disk Management to delete the recovery partition to free up some space and then expand the Windows volume.

6

WINDOWS | 7   CREATE A SYSTEM REPAIR DISC

A+
220-902
4.1

In Windows 7, you can create a Windows 7 system repair disc, which you can use to launch Windows RE. To create a Windows 7 system repair disc, click **Create a system repair disc** in the Windows 7 Backup and Restore window (see Figure 6-17). A 32-bit Windows 7 installation will create a 32-bit version of the repair disc, and a 64-bit Windows 7 installation will create a 64-bit version of the repair disc. A repair disc created on one computer can be used on a different computer even if they are using different editions of Windows 7, but be sure to use a 32-bit disc for a 32-bit installation and a 64-bit disc for a 64-bit Windows installation.

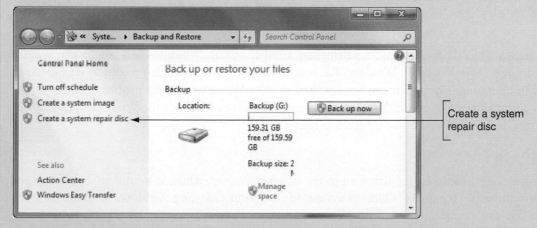

Figure 6-17   Use Windows 7 Backup and Restore to create a system repair disc to use instead of the Windows setup DVD

> ✎ **Notes** To launch Windows RE from a Windows setup DVD or Windows 7 repair disc, be sure to use a 64-bit DVD for a 64-bit installation of Windows and a 32-bit DVD for a 32-bit installation of Windows. To boot from a DVD, you might have to change the boot sequence in UEFI/BIOS setup to put the optical drive first above the hard drive.

TOOLS FOR LEAST INVASIVE SOLUTIONS

Looking back at the diagram in Figure 6-11, tools to repair Windows are shown in purple boxes. In this part of the chapter, we discuss several tools that are easy to use and don't make major changes to Windows system files or user settings, including the Windows 8 self-healing feature and several options on the Windows advanced startup screens.

USE WINDOWS 8'S SELF-HEALING FEATURE

If you restart the computer at least three times within a few minutes, Windows 8 automatically launches diagnostics (see Figure 6-18) and takes you through steps to attempt to repair the system. Sometimes a few restarts is all you need to do.

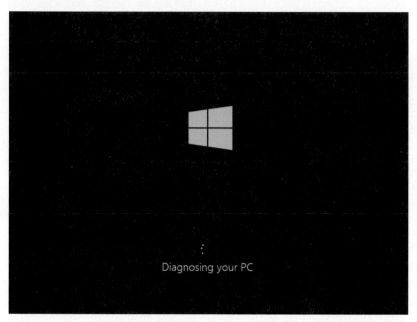

Figure 6-18   Windows automatically launches diagnostic procedures after the third restart within a few minutes

If the system hangs while diagnosing and repairing, try another restart. Windows will launch the Windows Recovery Environment (Windows RE). Windows RE is normally stored on a hidden partition on the hard drive and is a lean operating system that can be launched to solve Windows startup problems and provides a graphical and command-line interface. You can also launch Windows RE from the Windows setup DVD or a recovery drive. In Windows RE, first try startup repair.

STARTUP REPAIR

When addressing startup problems, the first tool to try is startup repair, which is a built-in diagnostic and repair tool in Windows 8/7. It can fix Windows system files without changing Windows settings, user data, or applications. You can't cause additional problems with the tool and it's easy to use. Figure 6-11 shows that startup repair can be launched from the Windows 8 Settings charm, by three or more restarts, or by booting from the Windows setup DVD or a recovery drive.

Follow these steps to use startup repair from the Settings charm:

1. On the Windows 8 charms bar, click **Settings**. In the Settings pane, click **Change PC settings**. In the left pane of the PC settings window, click **Update and recovery**. In the Update and recovery pane, click **Recovery** and click **Restart now** (see Figure 6-19).

6

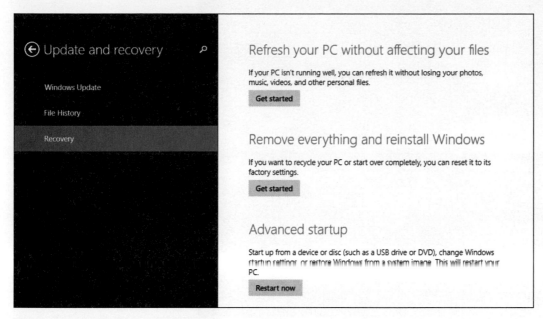

Figure 6-19 Refresh or reset a computer or restart the computer in advanced startup mode

2. Windows restarts and launches Windows RE. The first screen provided by Windows RE is called the Windows Startup Menu and is shown in Figure 6-20. When you click **Troubleshoot**, the Troubleshoot screen in Figure 6-21 appears. Using this screen, notice you can refresh or reset the computer, which are more invasive solutions than startup repair. Click **Advanced options**.

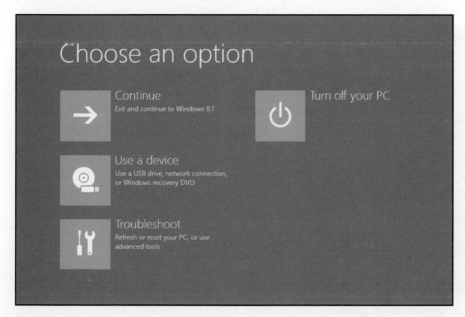

Figure 6-20 Windows Startup Menu indicates Windows RE is launched

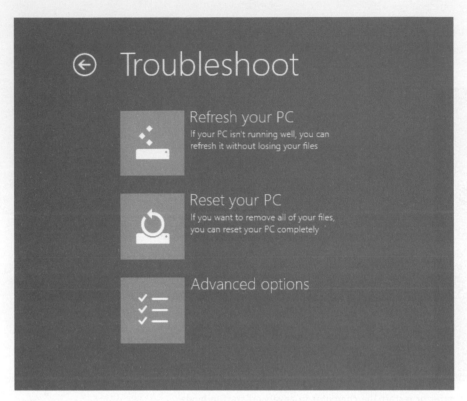

Figure 6-21   Windows RE offers refresh and reset options to solve a computer problem

3. From the Advanced options screen (see Figure 6-22), you can perform a System Restore (apply a restore point), use a system image to recover the Windows volume (for backward compatibility with the Windows 7 system image), perform a startup repair, get to a command prompt, and change startup settings. Click **Startup Repair**. Windows RE examines the system, fixes problems, reports what it did, and might offer suggestions for further fixes. A log file of the process can be found at C:\Windows\System32\ LogFiles\SRT\SRTTrail.txt.

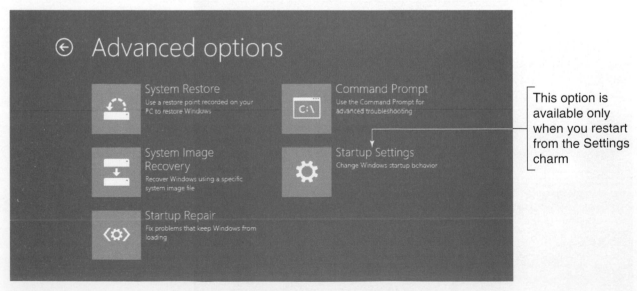

Figure 6-22   More advanced tools for solving startup problems

---

✎ Notes Depending on the situation, you might see a sixth option on the Advanced options screen, which is UEFI Firmware Settings. Use this option to change settings in a computer's UEFI firmware.

6

WINDOWS | 7 STARTUP REPAIR

A+
220-902
4.1

Windows RE in Windows 7 offers many of the same startup troubleshooting tools as does Windows 8. In Windows 7, to perform a startup repair, press **F8** at startup to launch the Advanced Boot Options screen. Click **Repair Your Computer**, which launches Windows RE. On the next screen, enter an administrator user account and password. Then the System Recovery Options box appears (see Figure 6-23). Click **Startup Repair** and follow directions on screen.

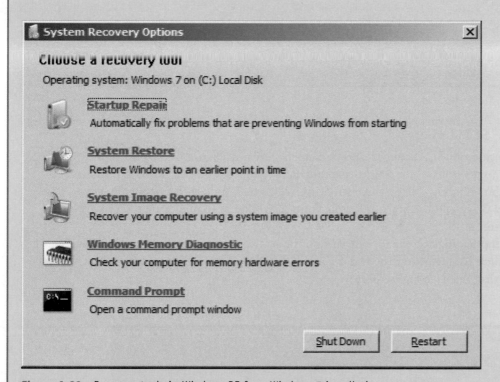

Figure 6-23 Recovery tools in Windows RE for a Windows 7 installation

If Windows is totally trashed, pressing F8 at startup won't work. In this situation, boot the computer from the Windows 7 setup DVD. On the Install Windows screen (see Figure 6-24), click **Repair your computer**. Windows RE launches. On the following screens, select your language and enter an administrator user account and password. The System Recovery Options window appears where you can select **Startup Repair**.

(continues)

Figure 6-24   Launch Windows RE after booting from the Windows 7 setup DVD

CHANGE STARTUP SETTINGS

The Startup Settings option on the Advanced options screen shown in Figure 6-22 is available only when Windows RE is launched from the hard drive rather than another media. If you have launched Windows RE from within Windows or by three successive restarts, Windows RE will have been launched from the hard drive and the Startup Settings option will be available to help solve problems with critical Windows settings.

When you click **Startup Settings** on the Advanced options screen, the Startup Settings screen shown in Figure 6-25 appears. Click **Restart**. After the restart, another Startup Settings screen appears, which has more options than the first one (see Figure 6-26).

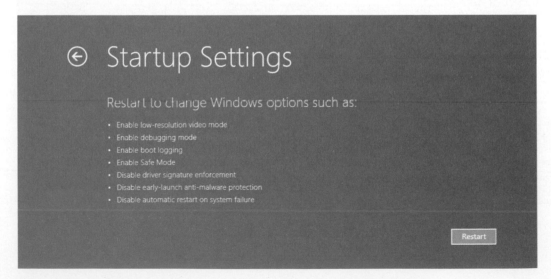

Figure 6-25   Restart the computer to get to more advanced troubleshooting tools

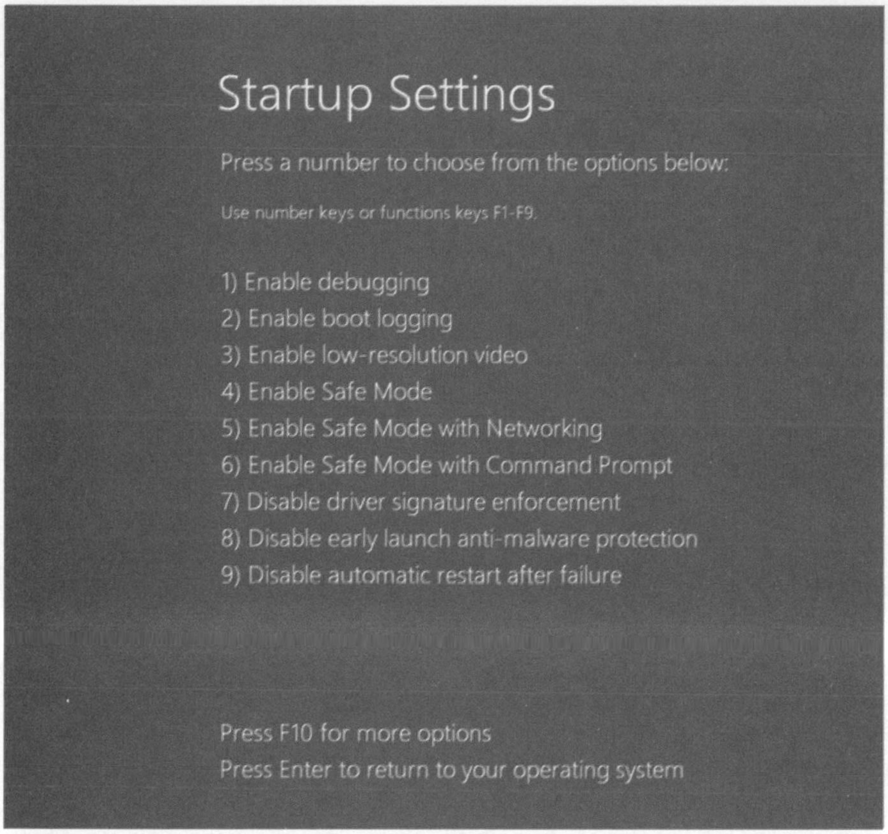

Startup Settings

Press a number to choose from the options below:

Use number keys or functions keys F1-F9.

1) Enable debugging
2) Enable boot logging
3) Enable low-resolution video
4) Enable Safe Mode
5) Enable Safe Mode with Networking
6) Enable Safe Mode with Command Prompt
7) Disable driver signature enforcement
8) Disable early launch anti-malware protection
9) Disable automatic restart after failure

Press F10 for more options
Press Enter to return to your operating system

Figure 6-26 Press a function key or number to restart the system in a given mode

Press numbers or function keys F1 through F9 to launch the tools on this screen. Windows 7 offers similar tools on its Advanced Boot Options screen (refer back to Figure 6-9). Here's a quick rundown of what the Windows 8/7 tools do.

Press 1 or F1: Enable Debugging

This tool moves system boot logs from the failing computer to another computer for evaluation. The computers must be connected by way of a serial port.

Press 2 or F2: Enable Boot Logging

Windows loads normally and all files used during the load process are recorded in a log file, C:\Windows\ Ntbtlog.txt (see Figure 6-27). Use this option to see what did and did not load during the boot. For instance, if you have a problem getting a device to work, check Ntbtlog.txt to see what driver files loaded. Boot logging is much more effective if you have a copy of Ntbtlog.txt that was made when everything worked as it should. Then you can compare the good load with the bad load, looking for differences.

Notes The Ntbtlog.txt file is also generated when you boot into Safe Mode.

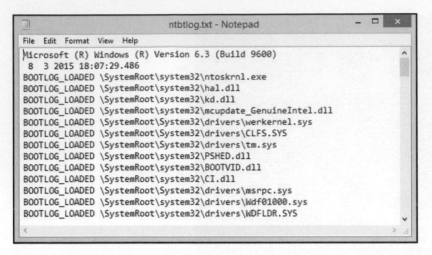

Figure 6-27 Sample Ntbtlog.txt file

Notes If Windows hangs during the boot, try booting using the option Enable Boot Logging. Then look at the last entry in the Ntbtlog.txt file. This entry might be the name of a device driver causing the system to hang.

Press 3 or F3: Enable Low-Resolution Video (640 × 480)

Use this option when the video settings don't allow you to see the screen well enough to fix a bad setting (for example, black fonts on a black background). Booting in this mode gives you a very plain, standard VGA video. You can then go to the Display settings, correct the problem, and reboot normally. You can also use this option if your video drivers are corrupted and you need to update, roll back, or reinstall the video drivers.

Press 4 or F4: Enable Safe Mode

After you sign in to Windows, the Safe Mode desktop appears (see Figure 6-28). Launching Safe Mode and then restarting the system can sometimes solve a startup problem. However, you can also go to the Start screen in Safe Mode to launch anti-malware software to scan the system for malware. You can open Event Viewer to find events helpful in troubleshooting the system, run the System File Checker command (**sfc /scannow**) to restore system files, use Device Manager to roll back a driver, use Memory Diagnostics to verify memory, use the **chkdsk /r** command to check for file system errors, configure Windows for a clean boot on the next restart, and perform other troubleshooting tasks.

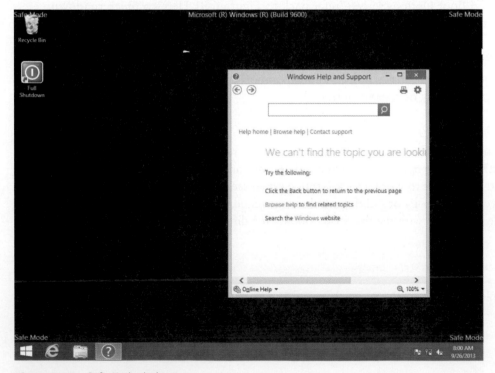

Figure 6-28 Safe Mode desktop

6

★ **A+ Exam Tip** The A+ 220-902 exam expects you to know how to use Safe Mode and chkdsk to help resolve a Windows startup problem.

Press 5 or F5: Enable Safe Mode with Networking

Use this option when you need access to the network to solve the problem. For example, you might need to download updates to your anti-malware software. Also use this mode when the Windows installation files are available on the network, rather than the Windows setup DVD, and you need to access those files.

Press 6 or F6: Enable Safe Mode with Command Prompt

If Safe Mode can't start, try Safe Mode with Command Prompt, which doesn't attempt to load the graphical interface. At the command prompt, use the **sfc /scannow** command to verify system files (see Figure 6-29). If the problem is still not solved, you can use this command to launch System Restore: **C:\Windows\ system32\rstrui.exe.** Then follow the directions on screen to select a restore point (see Figure 6-30).

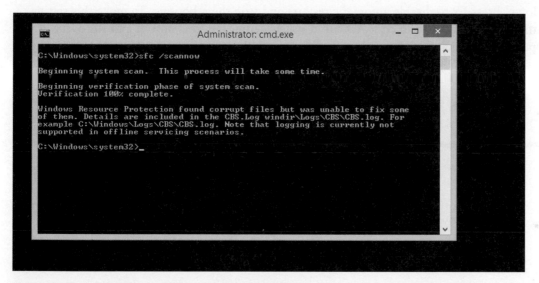

Figure 6-29 SFC finds and repairs corrupted system files

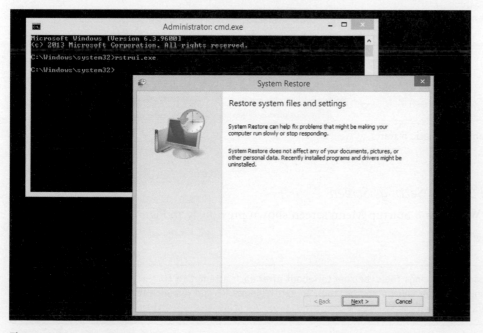

Figure 6-30 Use System Restore after booting to Safe Mode with Command Prompt

Press 7 or F7: Disable Driver Signature Enforcement

All 64-bit editions of Windows require that kernel-mode drivers be digitally signed. Disabling driver signature enforcement is used by developers who are testing kernel-mode device drivers that are not yet digitally signed. Don't use this option for troubleshooting Windows startup because doing so might allow malware drivers to load.

Press 8 or F8: Disable Early Launch Anti-Malware Driver

Windows 8 allows anti-malware software to launch a driver before any third-party drivers are launched so it can scan these drivers for malware. Unless you're sure a driver is the problem, don't disable this security feature. (Windows 7 doesn't offer this option on its Advanced Boot Options screen.)

Press 9 or F9: Disable Automatic Restart on System Failure

By default, Windows automatically restarts immediately after a blue screen of death (BSOD) stop error, which is described in more detail later in this chapter. The error can cause the system to continually reboot rather than shut down. Press **F9** to disable automatic restarts and stop the rebooting. To make this setting permanent, open the **System** window and click **Advanced system settings**. In the Startup and Recovery group of the System Properties box, click **Settings**, and on the Startup and Recovery box, uncheck **Automatically restart** (see Figure 6-31). Click **OK** twice and close the System window.

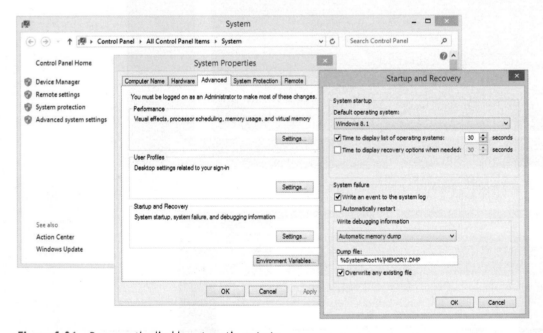

Figure 6-31   Permanently disable automatic restarts

Press F10: Return to the Startup Settings Screen

Press F10 to return to the Windows 8 Startup Menu screen shown previously in Figure 6-20.

> ✎ **Notes**   As you use these startup settings tools, be sure to reboot after each attempt to fix the problem to make sure the problem has not been resolved before you try another tool. To exit Windows RE and relaunch Windows, press **Enter** on the Startup Settings screen.

WINDOWS | 7 LAST KNOWN GOOD CONFIGURATION

A+ 220-902 4.1

One option available in the Advanced Boot Options menu for Windows 7 (refer back to Figure 6-9) that is no longer available for Windows 8 is the Last Known Good Configuration, which has been replaced by System Restore and a computer refresh for Windows 8. For Windows 7, registry settings collectively called the Last Known Good Configuration are saved in the registry each time the user successfully logs on to the system. If your problem is caused by a bad hardware or software installation and you get an error message the first time you restart the system after the installation, using the Last Known Good can, in effect, undo your installation and solve your problem.

Remember, the Last Known Good registry settings are saved each time a user logs on to Windows 7. Therefore, it's important to try the Last Known Good early in the troubleshooting session before a good one is overwritten with a bad Last Known Good. (However, know that if you sign in to Safe Mode, the Last Known Good is not saved.)

6

Hands-On | Project 6-2 Use Boot Logs and System Information to Research Startup

A+ 220-902 4.1

Boot logs can be used to generate a list of drivers that were loaded during a normal startup and during the Safe Mode startup. Do the following to use boot logs to research startup:

1. Boot to the normal Windows desktop with boot logging enabled. Save the boot log just created to a different name or location so it will not be overwritten on the next boot.

2. Reboot the system in Safe Mode, which also creates a boot log. Compare the two logs, identifying differences in drivers loaded during the two boots. To compare the files, you can print both files and lay them side by side for comparison. An easier method is to compare the files using the Compare tool in Microsoft Word.

3. Use the System Information utility or other methods to identify the hardware devices loaded during normal startup but not loaded in Safe Mode. Which devices on your system did not load in Safe Mode?

As you identify the drivers not loaded during Safe Mode, these registry keys might help with your research:

◢ Lists drivers and services loaded during Safe Mode: HKLM\System\CurrentControlSet\Control\SafeBoot\Minimal

◢ Lists drivers and services loaded during Safe Mode with Networking: HKLM\System\CurrentControlSet\Control\SafeBoot\Network

Hands-On | Project 6-3 Take Ownership and Replace a Windows System File

A+ 220-902 4.1

The System File Checker (SFC) tool can be used to find and replace corrupted Windows system files. The tool keeps a log of its actions (refer back to Figure 6-29), and, if it cannot replace a corrupted file, you can find that information in the log file. Then you can manually replace the file. To do so, you can use the takeown command to take ownership of a system file and the icacls command to get full access to the file. The Microsoft Knowledge Base Article 929833 at *support.microsoft.com* explains how to use these two commands.

(continues)

Do the following to practice manually replacing a system file:

1. Boot the computer into Safe Mode with Command Prompt.

2. Take ownership and gain full access to the C:\Windows\System32\jscript.dll file. What commands did you use?

3. Rename the jscript.dll file to jscript.dll.hold. Run the **sfc /scannow** command. Did SFC restore the jscript.dll file? What is the path and file name of the log file listing repairs?

4. SFC restores a file using files stored on the Windows setup DVD or other folders on the hard drive. If SFC cannot restore a file, you might find a fresh copy in the C:\Windows\winsxs folder or its subfolders. Search these folders. Did you find a version of jscript.dll that is the same file size as the one in C:\Windows\System32? Other than the C:\Windows\winsxs folder, where else can you find a known good copy of a corrupted system file?

✎ **Notes** To use a command prompt window to search for a file in a folder and its subfolders, use the **dir /s** command.

TOOLS THAT CAN AFFECT WINDOWS SYSTEM FILES AND SETTINGS

A+
220-902
4.1

Tools that affect Windows system files, Windows settings, user settings, and applications include System Restore and several commands that you can execute from a command prompt in Windows RE. These tools are discussed next.

SYSTEM RESTORE

Windows gives you several opportunities during the startup troubleshooting process to use System Restore to restore the system to an earlier point in time when a restore point was made. You can select System Restore from the Windows 8 Advanced options screen (refer back to Figure 6-22) or the Windows 7 Advanced Boot Options screen (refer back to Figure 6-9). You can also perform System Restore in Safe Mode or from a command prompt.

System Restore can cause problems of its own because Windows updates and updates to anti-malware software can be lost and hardware devices and applications might need to be reinstalled. System Restore won't help if the file system is corrupted or the registry is trashed. In these situations, the command prompt might help.

THE COMMAND PROMPT WINDOW IN WINDOWS RE

A+
220-902
1.3, 4.1

Use the command prompt window in Windows RE when the graphical interface is missing or corrupted or you want to use a specific command to fix a problem when Windows refuses to start. Using this command prompt, you have administrator privileges and full read and write access to all files on all drives. Many commands you learned about in the chapter, "Maintaining Windows," can be used at this command prompt. To access the Windows RE command prompt, follow these steps:

1. Depending on the health of your Windows system, do one of the following:

   ◢ If you can start Windows, launch Windows RE from the Settings charm as you learned to do earlier in the chapter. The system restarts and the Windows Startup Menu (refer back to Figure 6-6) appears.

   ◢ If you cannot launch Windows, boot from the Windows setup DVD or a recovery drive. (You might need to first change the boot device priority order in UEFI/BIOS to boot first from the optical drive or USB device.) On the Windows Setup screen (see Figure 6-32), click **Repair your computer**. On the next screen, choose your keyboard. The Windows Startup Menu appears.

Figure 6-32 Use the Windows setup DVD to launch Windows RE

2. On the Windows Startup Menu, click **Troubleshoot**. On the Troubleshoot screen (refer back to Figure 6-21), click **Command Prompt** (refer back to Figure 6-22).

3. If Windows RE is able to read registry entries on the hard drive, it will ask you to sign in using an administrator account.

Next are some examples of how to use the Windows RE command prompt to repair a system.

MANAGE DATA FILES AND SYSTEM FILES

Use the **sfc /scannow** command to restore critical Windows system files. Use the cd, copy, rename, and delete commands to manage data and system files. For example, if key registry files are corrupted or deleted, the system will not start. You can restore registry files using those saved in the C:\Windows\System32\Config\RegBack folder. This RegBack folder contains partial backups of the registry files put there after a successful boot. Use the commands in Table 6-2 to restore the registry files. In the table, we assume Windows is installed on drive C:. However, know that Windows RE is likely to assign a different drive letter to the Windows volume.

Command Line	Description
1. `c:`	Makes drive C: the current drive. The default directory is root.
2. `dir`	Examines the contents of drive C:. If this is not your Windows volume, try a different drive letter.
3. `cd \windows\system32\config`	Makes the Windows registry folder the current folder.
4. `ren default default.save` 5. `ren sam sam.save` 6. `ren security security.save` 7. `ren software software.save` 8. `ren system system.save`	Renames the five registry files.
9. `cd regback`	Makes the registry backup folder the current folder.

Table 6-2 Steps to restore the registry files (continues)

Command Line	Description
10. `copy system` `c:\windows\system32\config`	For hardware problems, first try copying just the System hive from the backup folder to the registry folder and then reboot.
11. `copy software` `c:\windows\system32\config`	For software problems, first try copying just the Software hive to the registry folder, and then reboot.

12. `copy system`
    `c:\windows\system32\config`
13. `copy software`
    `c:\windows\system32\config`
14. `copy default`
    `c:\windows\system32\config`
15. `copy sam`
    `c:\windows\system32\config`
16. `copy security`
    `c:\windows\system32\config`
	If the problem is still not solved, try copying all five hives to the registry folder and reboot.

Table 6-2   Steps to restore the registry files (continued)

After you try each fix, reboot the system to see if the problem is solved before you do the next fix.

REPAIR AND MANAGE A HARD DRIVE

A corrupted file system or partition can cause a failure to boot. Use the chkdsk /r command to repair the file system. Use the format command to reformat the volume (all files will be lost). Use the diskpart command to manage hard drives, partitions, and volumes. When you enter diskpart at a command prompt, the DISKPART> prompt appears where you can enter diskpart commands. Some important diskpart commands are listed in Table 6-3; you have already learned to use several. Diskpart can also be used in a normal command prompt window.

Diskpart Command	Description
`list disk`	Lists installed hard disk drives.
`select disk`	Selects a hard disk or other storage device. For example: `select disk 0`
`list partition`	Lists partitions on selected disk.
`select partition`	Selects a partition on the selected disk. For example: `select partition 1`
`clean`	Removes any partition or volume information from the selected disk. Can be useful to remove dynamic disk information or a corrupted partition table or if you just want a fresh start when partitioning a hard disk. All data and partition information on the disk are deleted.
`convert gpt`	Converts an empty disk from MBR to GPT.
`create partition primary`	Creates a primary partition on the currently selected hard disk.
`assign`	Assigns a drive letter to a partition. For example: `assign letter=z`
`remove`	Removes a drive letter from a volume. For example: `remove letter=z`

`format`	Formats the currently selected partition. For example:
	`format fs=ntfs quick`
	`format fs=fat32`

`active`	Makes the selected partition the active partition.

Table 6-3   Important diskpart commands used at the DISKPART> prompt (continues)

Diskpart Command	Description
inactive	Makes the selected partition inactive.
detail	Shows details about the selected disk, partition, or volume: detail disk detail partition detail volume
exit	Exits the diskpart utility.

Table 6-3   Important diskpart commands used at the DISKPART> prompt (continued)

> ✎ **Notes** For a complete list of diskpart commands, go to the Microsoft support site (*technet.microsoft.com*) and search on "DiskPart Command-Line Options".

ENABLE NETWORKING

Networking is not normally available from the Windows RE command prompt. Use the **wpeinit** command to enable networking. The wpeinit command initializes Windows PE. Recall from the chapter, "Installing Windows," that Windows PE is the preinstallation-environment operating system that is launched prior to installing Windows in a clean install and includes networking components.

USE BOOTREC AND BCDEDIT TO REPAIR THE FILE SYSTEM AND KEY BOOT FILES

A failure to boot can be caused by a corrupted BCD. Use the bootrec command to repair the BCD and boot sectors. Use the bcdedit command to manually edit the BCD. (Be sure to make a copy of the BCD before you edit it.) Use the bootsect command to repair a dual-boot system. To get helpful information about these commands, enter the command followed by /?, such as **bcdedit /?**. Some examples of the bootrec and bcdedit commands are listed in Table 6-4.

Command Line	Description
bootrec /scanOS	Scans the hard drive for Windows installations not stored in the BCD
bootrec /rebuildBCD	Scans for Windows installations and rebuilds the BCD
bootrec /fixboot	Repairs the boot sector of the system partition
bootrec /fixmbr	Repairs the MBR
bcdedit /enum	Displays the contents of the BCD

Table 6-4   Bootrec and bcdedit commands to repair system files and the file system

Although a startup repair should solve the problem when you get an error message at startup that "Bootmgr is missing," rebuilding the BCD store should also be able to resolve the same problem on a BIOS and MBR system.

> ★ **A+ Exam Tip** The A+ 220-901 and 220-902 exams expect you to know how to use the bootrec and diskpart commands.

Hands-On | Project 6-4 View the BCD Store

A+
220-902
4.1

On two or more computers, open an elevated command prompt window and use the bcdedit /enum command to view the BCD store. One BCD store is shown in Figure 6-33.

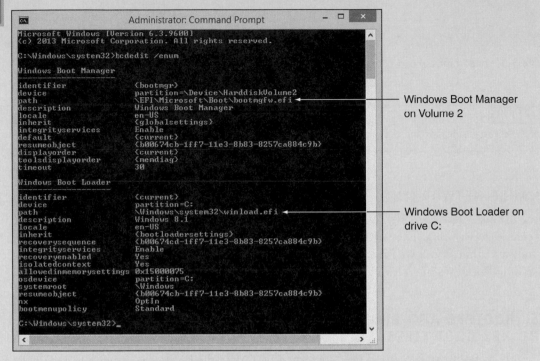

Figure 6-33   A BCD store on a computer that uses the GPT partitioning system

Answer the following questions:

1. Can you view the BCD store and determine if the system is using the MBR or GPT partitioning system? Why or why not?

2. Explain how you can look at the BCD store and tell if the system is a single boot or multiboot system.

TOOLS FOR REINSTALLING WINDOWS

A+
220-902
1.2, 1.7,
4.1

All of the startup troubleshooting tools so far in this chapter are designed to repair a Windows installation. However, sometimes Windows is beyond repair and you need to reinstall it. The following startup troubleshooting tools affect the entire Windows installation on a computer rather than a few files or settings. Let's discuss your options for a reinstall, including an OEM recovery partition, Windows 8 refresh and reset, and Windows 8/7 system image.

OEM RECOVERY PARTITION

Laptops, all-in-one computers, and brand-name desktops come with the OS preinstalled at the factory. This OEM (original equipment manufacturer) build of the OS is likely to be customized, and, for laptops, the drivers might be specific to proprietary devices installed in the laptop.

The laptop or brand-name computer is likely to have a recovery partition on the hard drive that contains a copy of the OS build, device drivers, diagnostics programs, and preinstalled applications needed to restore the system to its factory state. This partition might or might not be hidden. For example, Figure 6-34 shows the Disk Management information for a hard drive on one laptop that has a 14.75-GB recovery partition.

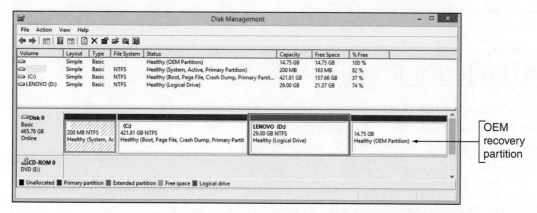

Figure 6-34   This laptop hard drive has a 14.75-GB recovery partition that can be used to recover the system

To know how to access the recovery tools stored on a recovery partition, see the manufacturer's website or look for a message at the beginning of the boot, such as "Press ESC for diagnostics" or "Press F12 to recover the system." For one Sony laptop, you press the red **Assist** button during the boot (see Figure 6-35). When you press the key or button, a menu appears giving you options to diagnose the problem, to repair the current OS installation, or to completely rebuild the entire hard drive to its factory state.

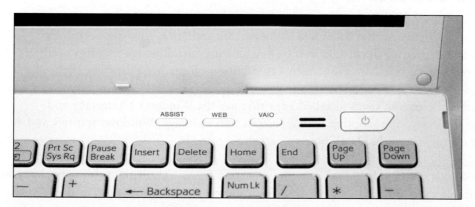

Figure 6-35   For this laptop, press the Assist button during the boot to launch programs on the recovery partition

Recall that an OEM recovery partition can be saved when you create a recovery drive for Windows 8. Unless the recovery partition has been saved, it won't be any help at all if the hard drive is broken or corrupted. In this situation, you're dependent on other recovery media. Older laptops came bundled with the full recovery on CDs. For today's laptops, you might have the option to use a working computer to download the recovery media from the manufacturer's website and use it to create a bootable USB flash drive or DVD. You can then use the media to install Windows to its factory state on a new hard drive installed in the laptop.

> **Notes**   When you first become responsible for a laptop, make a Windows 8 recovery drive to a USB flash drive that includes the OEM recovery partition in case you must replace the laptop's hard drive. Know that, if the laptop is more than three years old, the manufacturer might no longer provide the recovery media.

> ⚡ **Caution** Upgrading Windows on a laptop is not a good idea unless you have a good reason to do so. If you do decide to upgrade, upgrade the OS using an OS build purchased from the laptop manufacturer, which should include the OS and device drivers specific to your laptop. If you decide to upgrade the OS using an off-the-shelf version of Windows, be careful to determine that all components in the system are compatible with the upgrade.

Hands-On | Project 6-5 Research Laptop Online Resources

Suppose the hard drive in a laptop has failed and you must replace the hard drive with a new one and install Windows on the new drive. What online resources can help you? Do the following to find a service manual and recovery files for a laptop that you have access to, such as one you or a friend owns:

1. What are the brand, model, and serial number of the laptop?

2. What is the website of the laptop manufacturer? Print a webpage on that site that shows you what recovery files are available for download to install Windows on a new hard drive for this laptop.

3. If the website provides a service manual, download the manual and print the pages that show how to replace the hard drive.

4. Based on what you have learned about online support for this laptop, what backups or recovery media do you think need to be created now before a hard drive crash occurs.

REFRESH A WINDOWS 8 COMPUTER

In the chapter, "Maintaining Windows," you learned to create a Windows 8 custom refresh image of the Windows volume. To solve a problem with a corrupted Windows 8 installation, you can perform a Windows 8 refresh. The refresh can recover the installation from a custom refresh image that has been designated as the active recovery image, a hidden OEM recovery partition on the hard drive, or the Windows 8 setup DVD.

When you refresh a computer, the refresh saves installed apps that use the Windows 8 interface and current user settings and data. Unless you're working with a custom refresh image, Windows settings and desktop applications are lost during a refresh. Here's how to perform a refresh:

1. Because the system will restart a couple of times during the refresh, remove any discs in the optical drive and unplug any bootable external hard drive or USB flash drives. For a laptop, plug in the AC adapter so you don't lose battery power during the refresh. If the computer doesn't have a recovery partition and you haven't made a custom refresh image, insert the Windows setup DVD in the optical drive, which the refresh will use to perform a partial in-place upgrade of Windows 8.

2. Do one of the following, depending on the health of the Windows installation:

   ◢ If you can launch Windows, on the charms bar, click **Settings**, click **Change PC settings**, click **Update and recovery**, and click **Recovery**. Click **Get started** under *Refresh your PC without affecting your files* (refer back to Figure 6-19). A warning message appears (see Figure 6-36). Click **Next**. Click **Refresh**.

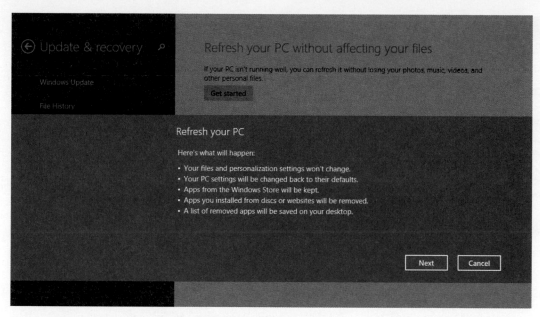

Figure 6-36 Windows lists what to expect from a refresh

◢ If you cannot launch Windows, boot from the Windows setup DVD or a recovery drive. When booting from the Windows setup DVD, the Windows Setup screen appears, as shown earlier in Figure 6-32. Click **Repair your computer**. (When booting from a recovery drive, the Setup screen doesn't show.) On the next screen, choose your keyboard. The Windows Startup Menu appears (refer back to Figure 6-20). Click **Troubleshoot**. On the Troubleshoot screen (refer back to Figure 6-21), click **Refresh your PC**.

3. Windows verifies there's enough free space on the hard drive to perform the refresh. A lot of space (as much as half the space on the Windows volume) is needed because Windows will store the old Windows installation in a Windows.old folder and will also need space to back up apps and data. If there's not enough space, an error occurs, and you'll need to delete files or folders or move them to a different location to free up enough space and start the refresh again.

4. Another warning message appears. Click **Refresh** to continue. Next, user settings and data and Windows 8 apps are backed up, and Windows searches for media or an image to use to reinstall Windows. It uses this order for the search:

   a. *It checks for a custom refresh image.* If a custom refresh image was previously made and registered with the system, this image is used to refresh the system. (If desktop applications were included in the image, they are included in the refresh. Any desktop applications that were installed after the refresh image was created are lost and must be manually reinstalled.)

   b. *If no custom refresh image is found, it checks for an OEM recovery partition.* If it finds an OEM recovery partition, the image on the partition is used to refresh the computer to its factory state.

   c. *If no image or recovery partition is found, it requests the Windows setup DVD if it's not already available.* The refresh process will use the Windows setup DVD to perform a partial in-place upgrade of Windows 8.

5. The system restarts and the refresh begins. Progress is reported on screen as a percentage of completion. The Windows volume is formatted, and Windows is reinstalled from an image or from the Windows setup files. User settings, data, and Windows 8 apps are restored from backup, and the system restarts.

6. The names of desktop applications lost during the refresh are stored in a file on the Windows desktop named Removed Apps.html (see Figure 6-37). Open the file to see the list of applications. You'll need to reinstall these applications.

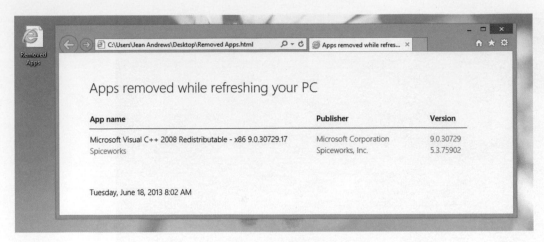

Figure 6-37 View a list of desktop applications lost during the refresh

7. The refresh created a Windows.old folder containing the old Windows installation. After you're sure you don't need anything in it, you can delete the folder to free up the disk space.

RESET A WINDOWS 8 COMPUTER

You might want to reset a computer when you're about to give it away or recycle it or totally want to start over. The Windows volume is formatted and Windows is reinstalled. If an OEM recovery partition is present, the system is reset to its factory state. If there's no recovery partition, the process requests the Windows setup DVD, which it uses to reinstall Windows. All user data and settings and installed apps are lost. You can use the recovery methods provided by the manufacturer (for example, press F12 or F10 at startup) or you can use Windows 8 to reset the system.

Here are the Windows 8 steps to reset a computer:

1. If a recovery partition is present, it will be used for the reset. If there's no recovery partition, insert the Windows setup DVD in the optical drive, which the reset process uses to perform a clean install of Windows.

2. Do one of the following:

   ◢ If you can launch Windows, go to the **Update and recovery** screen and click **Get started** under *Remove everything and reinstall Windows* (refer back to Figure 6-19). A warning message appears. Click **Next**.

   ◢ If you cannot launch Windows, boot from the Windows setup DVD or a recovery drive and make your way to the Troubleshoot screen shown earlier in Figure 6-21. Click **Reset your PC**.

3. If the system contains more than one volume or hard drive, Windows asks if you want to format all drives or just the Windows volume. Click a box to make your selection.

4. On the next screen (see Figure 6-38), you're asked to decide between a quick format and a thorough format. A thorough format makes it less likely someone can recover data on the drive. Make your selection by clicking a box.

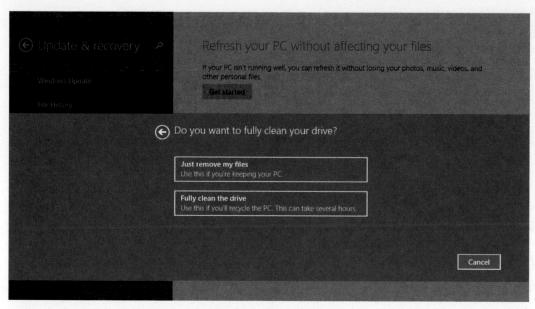

Figure 6-38 Decide the type of format the reset will use

5. On the next screen, another warning appears. Click **Reset** to start the process. The system restarts and resetting begins. After another restart, you can step through the process of preparing Windows for first use.

WINDOWS | 7   SYSTEM IMAGE

> **A+**
> **220-902**
> **4.1**

Recall from the chapter, "Maintaining Windows," a Windows 7 system image is a backup of the entire Windows volume and Windows 8 allows you to create a system image for backward compatibility with Windows 7. For Windows 8, always use a custom refresh image over a system image because it's more flexible and easier to use than a system image.

In Windows 7, to recover the system using a system image, launch Windows 7 from the Windows setup DVD or a recovery drive. When booting from a Windows setup DVD, on the Install Windows screen (refer back to Figure 6-24), click **Repair your computer**. Windows RE launches. On the following screens, select your language and enter an administrator user account and password.

The System Recovery Options box appears, listing a menu of Windows RE recovery tools (refer back to Figure 6-23). Click **System Image Recovery** and follow directions on screen to point to the location of the system image. Everything on the Windows volume is erased and replaced with the system image.

INSTALL WINDOWS OVER THE NETWORK

Recall from the chapter "Installing Windows" that in an enterprise environment you can install Windows from a deployment image on the network. You must boot the computer to the network where it finds and loads Windows PE on the deployment server. For a legacy BIOS system, go into BIOS setup and set the first boot device to be Ethernet. For a UEFI system, look for an advanced setup screen in UEFI setup to enable PXE Support. The computer then boots to the Preboot eXecution Environment (PXE) and PXE then searches for a server on the network to provide Windows PE and the deployment image.

★ **A+ Exam Tip** The A+ 220-902 exam expects you to know how to use a preinstallation environment and a recovery image to help resolve a Windows startup problem.

Hands-On | Project 6-6 Practice Using System Recovery Options

Using Windows 8 or 7, launch Windows RE and do the following:

1. Execute the startup repair process. What were the results?

2. Launch System Restore. What is the most recent restore point? (Do not apply the restore point.)

3. Using the command prompt window, open the Registry Editor. What command did you use? Close the editor.

4. Using the command prompt window, copy a file from your Documents folder to a flash drive. Were you able to copy the file successfully? If not, what error message(s) did you receive?

TROUBLESHOOTING WINDOWS STARTUP

And now the fun begins! With your understanding of the boot process and Windows tools for troubleshooting startup in hand, let's work through a bunch of errors and problems that can affect Windows startup and see what can be done about them. When troubleshooting a startup problem, follow procedures to interview the user, back up important data or verify you have current backups, research and identify any error messages, and determine what has just changed that might be the source of the problem.

When you know the source of the problem, decide which tool will be the least invasive to use, yet still will fix the problem. If that doesn't work, move on to the next tool. Remember that tools are described earlier in the chapter from least to most invasive. Here's a recap of some of the more important tools discussed earlier:

- Multiple restarts of Windows 8
- Startup repair
- Boot logging to help you better understand the problem
- From a command prompt, chkdsk and SFC
- Memory Diagnostics
- Safe Mode and then a clean boot
- Use anti-malware software to scan for malware
- System Restore
- System Configuration and Task Manager to reduce startup programs and services
- Refresh the computer
- Reset the computer

IMPORTANT DATA ON THE HARD DRIVE

Troubleshooting a computer problem should always start with the most important question: Is there important data on the hard drive not backed up? Even if data is lost or corrupted, you might be able to recover it using Windows tools, third-party file recovery software, or commercial data recovery services. One good product is GetDataBack by Runtime Software (*www.runtime.org*), which can recover data and program files even when Windows cannot recognize the drive.

For less than $30, you can purchase a SATA-to-USB converter kit (see Figure 6-39) that includes a data cable and power adapter. You can use one of these kits to temporarily connect a desktop or laptop hard drive to a USB port on a working computer. Set the drive beside your computer and plug one end of the data cable into the drive and the other into the USB port. The AC adapter supplies power to the drive. While power is getting to the drive, be careful to not touch the circuit board on the drive.

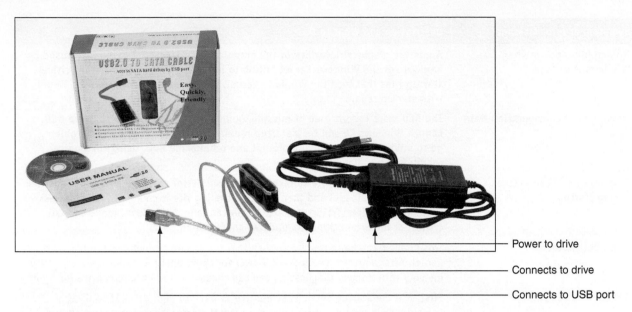

Figure 6-39 Use a SATA-to-USB converter to recover data from a drive using a SATA connector

Using File Explorer or Windows Explorer, you can browse the drive and copy data to other media. After you have saved the data, you can use diagnostic software from the hard drive manufacturer to examine the drive and possibly repair it or return the drive to its own computer and start troubleshooting there.

ERROR MESSAGES AND PROBLEMS

A+
220-902
4.1

Table 6-5 summarizes some symptoms and error messages caused by hardware, device drivers, or Windows that prevent Windows from booting. Hardware errors can present as errors messages on a black screen or a Windows blue screen of death (BSOD) stop error. A stop error can be caused by a corrupted registry, a system file that is missing or damaged, a device driver that is missing or damaged, bad memory, or a corrupted or failing hard drive. Also, sometimes Windows hangs with the pinwheel spinning, continuously restarts, or does an abrupt and improper shutdown.

Symptom or Error Message	Description and What to Do
A disk read error occurred Nonsystem disk or disk error Invalid boot disk Hard drive not found Disk boot failure No boot device found	Startup UEFI/BIOS cannot communicate with the hard drive. Check UEFI/BIOS setup for the boot sequence and try to boot from another device. This is likely a hardware problem. For Windows 8, try going into UEFI/BIOS setup and disabling any quick boot features. This causes UEFI/BIOS to do a more thorough job of POST and reports more information on the screen as it performs POST. The drive might be failing. To recover data from the drive, move it to another computer and install it as a second hard drive.
Invalid partition table Invalid drive specification Error loading operating system Missing operating system Drive not recognized	MBR sector is damaged or the active partition is corrupt or missing. Use the repair commands from the Windows RE command prompt window.
Operating system not found Missing operating system Missing bootmgr	Windows system files are missing or corrupted. Boot to Windows RE and use tools there. First try startup repair. Use chkdsk to fix hard drive errors. Use System File Checker (SFC) to restore Windows system files. Try System Restore.
Automatically boots into Safe Mode	This action can occur when Windows recognizes a problem with the registry or other startup files. Attempt to use System Restore to apply a restore point. For Windows 7, use the Last Known Good Configuration on the Advanced Boot Options menu.

Table 6-5 Error messages and what to do about them (continues)

Symptom or Error Message	Description and What to Do
No graphics appear when Windows is started	A missing graphical interface or the graphical interface fails to load is caused by hardware or the Windows kernel failing to load. To solve problems with critical startup files that load the Windows kernel, use the tools in Windows RE. Begin with startup repair.
Missing Boot Configuration Data	The BCD store is corrupted or missing. Sometimes a virus can corrupt the BCD. Launch Windows RE and try a startup repair. If this doesn't solve the problem, go to a Windows RE command prompt and rebuild the BCD, using the bootrec / rebuildBCD command.
Stop error, or BSOD occurs during startup	Use the Microsoft website to research the exact error message and error code. Use the startup repair tool and then examine the log file it creates at C:\Windows\ System32\LogFiles\Srt\Srttrail.txt. If you can launch Windows, make sure all critical or important Windows updates are installed.
Improper shutdown	This problem can be caused by overheating, a hardware problem, or the Windows kernel. After a restart, check Event Viewer for clues, apply Windows updates, verify memory with Memory Diagnostics, and use chkdsk to check the hard drive for errors.
Spontaneous shutdowns and restarts	First, use the Startup Settings screen (refer back to Figure 6-26) to disable the automatic restarts so that you can view the error messages on screen and troubleshoot the underlying problem. Research the error messages on screen as you would a BSOD error. Use the startup repair tool and then examine the log file it creates at C:\Windows\System32\LogFiles\Srt\Srttrail.txt.
Device fails to start or is not detected	Address this issue first as a hardware problem. Check the device's cable connections. Try the device in a working computer. Check Device Manager for errors reported. Use Device Manager to uninstall the device and restart Windows. Search the device manufacturer's website for troubleshooting procedures and to download diagnostic software for the device. Restart the system and enable boot logging. Check the Ntbtlog.txt file to see if the correct driver files loaded.
Errors after the user has signed in to Windows	For application errors, use System Configuration (msconfig.exe) and Task Manager to perform a clean boot. If the error goes away, research each non-Microsoft program or service to find the problem. Try to repair the application. If the error persists, uninstall and reinstall the application. For Windows errors, boot into Safe Mode and run System File Checker, System Restore, chkdsk /r, and Memory Diagnostics. Install all critical and important Windows updates. Check the Ntbtlog.txt log file for clues. Compare it with one made during a normal boot with Enable Boot Logging selected.

Table 6-5   Error messages and what to do about them (continued)

★ **A+ Exam Tip**   The A+ 220-902 exam expects you to know how to use System Information (msconfig.exe) to help you resolve a Windows startup problem.

★ **A+ Exam Tip**   The A+ 220-902 exam expects you to know about the Windows XP Ntldr boot loader program, a repair disk, and the Recovery Console. When starting Windows XP, a "missing Ntldr" error message can be resolved by booting the system from a Windows XP repair disk. After booting from the floppy disk, you can launch the Windows XP Recovery Console and use commands in this console to copy the Ntldr program file on the floppy disk to the hard drive.

Next, we give a few more details about several of the errors listed in Table 6-5.

BSOD OR STOP ERRORS

A BSOD, or stop error, happens when processes running in kernel mode encounter a problem and Windows must stop the system. In such situations, a blue screen appears with a cryptic error message such as the one in Figure 6-40. Look on the blue screen for the stop error at the top and the specific number of the error near the bottom of the screen, as labeled in Figure 6-40.

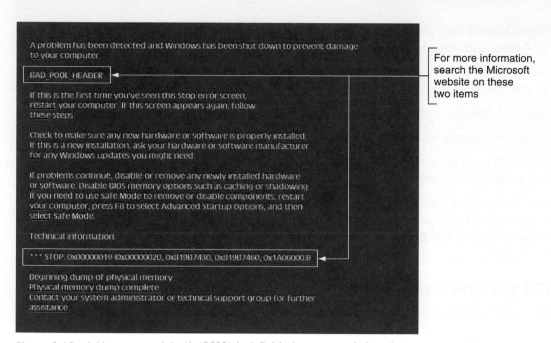

For more information, search the Microsoft website on these two items

Figure 6-40 A blue screen of death (BSOD) is definitively not a good sign; time to start troubleshooting

Stop errors can occur during or after startup. Here's what to do when you get a stop error:

1. As for the tools useful in solving stop errors, put the web at the top of your list! (But don't forget that some sites are unreliable and others mean you harm.) Search the Microsoft website on the two items labeled in Figure 6-40.

2. If the blue screen names the device driver or service that caused the problem, use File Explorer or Windows Explorer on a working computer to locate the program file. Driver files are stored in the C:\Windows\System32\drivers folder. Right-click the file and select **Properties** from the shortcut menu. The Details tab of the Properties box tells you the purpose of the file (see Figure 6-41). You can then reinstall the device or program that caused the problem.

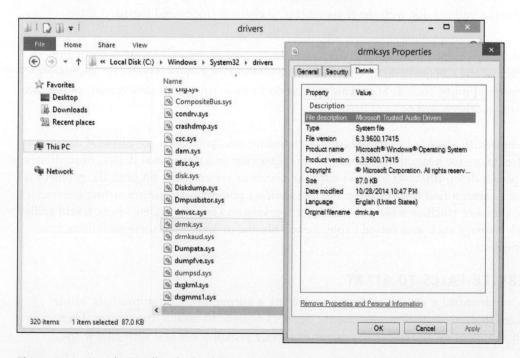

Figure 6-41 Use the Details tab of a driver's Properties box to identify the purpose of the driver

3. Reboot the system. Immediately after a reboot following a stop error, Windows displays an error message box or bubble with useful information. Follow the links in the box.

4. Check Event Viewer, which might provide events it has logged. Recall that critical errors and warnings are recorded in the Administrative Events log.

5. Also check Archived Messages in the Action Center for clues.

6. Use Windows Updates to apply all important and critical updates.

7. Undo any recent changes to the system. If you are not sure which changes to undo, consider using System Restore to restore the system to the point in time before the problem started.

8. Use the Memory Diagnostics tool to check memory and use chkdsk with the /r parameter to check the hard drive for errors. If the problem is still not resolved, you might need to repair Windows system files by using System File Checker, Safe Mode, or other Windows startup repair tools discussed in this chapter.

DEALING WITH IMPROPER SHUTDOWNS

Improper shutdowns and a system lockup that cause a computer to freeze and require that it be restarted are most likely caused by hardware. Hardware that can cause these errors include memory, the motherboard, CPU, video card, or the system overheating. I/O devices such as the keyboard, mouse, or monitor or application errors don't usually cause these types of catastrophic problems.

> ★ **A+ Exam Tip** The 220-902 exam expects you to know how to solve problems when the system shuts down improperly.

When these types of errors occur, try and check these things:

1. Check Event Viewer to see if it has reported a hardware failure.

2. Apply any important or critical Windows updates.

3. Use Memory Diagnostics and chkdsk with the /r parameter to check memory and the hard drive for errors.

4. If you suspect overheating is a problem, immediately after the lockup, go into UEFI/BIOS setup and check the temperature of the CPU, which, for most CPUs, should not exceed 38 degrees C. Alternately, you can install a freeware utility, such as SpeedFan by Alfredo Comparetti (*www.almico.com*) to monitor the temperature of the motherboard or hard drive.

When solving problems with any kind of hardware, it's important that you check for physical damage to the device. If you feel excessive heat coming from the computer case or a peripheral device, immediately unplug the device or power down the system. Don't turn the device or system back on until the problem is solved; you don't want to start a fire! Other symptoms that indicate potential danger are strong electrical odors, unusual noises, no noise (such as when the fan is not working to keep the system cool), liquid spills on a device, and visible damage such as a frayed cable, melted plastic, or smoke. In these situations, turn off the equipment immediately.

A DEVICE OR SERVICE FAILS TO START

After you believe you've identified a service or device preventing a normal boot, boot into Safe Mode and use Device Manager to disable the device or use the Services console to disable the service. Then reboot, and, if the problem goes away, replace the driver or service program file and then enable the driver or service.

If you cannot boot into Safe Mode, open the command prompt window in Windows RE. Then back up the registry and open the Registry Editor using the regedit command. Drill down to the service or device key. The key that loads services and drivers can be found in this location:

HKEY__LOCAL__MACHINE\System\CurrentControlSet\Services

Disable the service or driver by changing the Start value to 0x4. Close the Registry Editor and reboot. If the problem goes away, use the copy command to replace the service or driver program file, and restart the service or driver.

Hands-On | Project 6-7 Rebuild Pagefile.sys

**A+
220-902
4.1**

If a stop error indicates that Pagefile.sys is corrupted, you can rebuild the file. Search the *support. microsoft.com* website for the steps to rebuild Pagefile.sys and then practice these steps by rebuilding Pagefile.sys. List the steps you took to rebuild the file.

Hands-On | Project 6-8 Use Windows RE to Solve a Startup Problem

**A+
220-902
4.1**

On a system that uses the MBR partitioning method for the hard drive, use File Explorer or Windows Explorer to rename the bootmgr file in the root directory of the hidden System Reserved partition. Reboot the system. What error message do you see? Now use Windows RE to restore the bootmgr file. List the steps taken to complete the repair.

>> CHAPTER SUMMARY

Understanding the Boot Process

◢ When you first turn on a system, startup UEFI/BIOS on the motherboard takes control to examine hardware components and find an operating system to load.

◢ UEFI stores information, drivers, and applications used for the startup in NVRAM and the EFI System Partition (ESP).

◢ Windows startup is managed by the Windows Boot Manager. For a BIOS system, the program is bootmgr. For a UEFI system, the program is bootmgfw.efi. The Windows Boot Loader is winload.exe or winload.efi. The Boot Configuration Data (BCD) store contains Windows startup settings.

Tools for Troubleshooting Windows Startup Problems

◢ Before a problem occurs, make sure you have good backups of user data and a Windows 8 custom refresh image or a Windows 7 system image. You might also want to create a Windows 8 recovery drive and configure Windows 8 to use F8 at startup, which launches the Advanced Boot Options screen.

◢ The Windows Recovery Environment (Windows RE) can be started from within Windows, from the Windows setup DVD, or from a recovery drive. For Windows 7, press F8 at startup to launch Windows RE.

◢ Tools for startup troubleshooting include startup repair, Memory Diagnostics, System Restore, Safe Mode, enabling boot logging, refresh, reset, and applying a Windows 7 system image.

◢ Commands that might be useful when repairing Windows include bootrec, bcdedit, diskpart, chkdsk, and sfc.

Troubleshooting Windows Startup

◢ If a hard drive contains valuable data but will not boot, you might be able to recover the data by installing the drive in another system as the second, nonbooting hard drive in the system.

◢ Use the web to research stop errors on the error title and error number listed on the blue screen.

◢ Improper shutdowns are most likely hardware related. Event Viewer might record failures. Use Memory Diagnostics and chkdsk to check memory and the hard drive. Consider overheating and monitor the system temperature.

◢ When a device or service causes the system to hang during a normal boot, boot into Safe Mode and disable the device or service. Then you can replace the drivers or service program file.

>> KEY TERMS

For explanations of key terms, see the Glossary for this text.

bcdedit	chkdsk /r	Last Known Good	soft boot
blue screen of death	cold boot	Configuration	startup repair
(BSOD)	diskpart	nonvolatile RAM	system repair disc
Boot Configuration Data	EFI System Partition	(NVRAM)	warm boot
(BCD) store	(ESP)	POST (power-on self test)	Windows Boot Loader
booting	Fast Startup	recovery drive	Windows Recovery
bootrec	format	refresh	Environment
bootsect	hard boot	reset	(Windows RE)

>> REVIEWING THE BASICS

1. What test does startup UEFI/BIOS perform when you first turn on a computer to verify it can communicate with essential hardware devices?

2. Where is the MBR partition table on a hard drive found?

3. Is the bootmgr file stored in the boot partition or the system partition?

4. What is the name of the Boot Manager program in a UEFI system? On which partition is the program stored?

5. What is the name of the Windows boot loader program for a BIOS system? For a UEFI system?

6. What is the name of the Windows kernel program?

7. What is the name of the program that manages Windows logon?

8. Which registry hive is loaded first during Windows startup?

9. Where does Windows store device driver files?

10. Stop errors happen when which type of processes encounter an error?

11. What is the command to use the System File Checker to immediately verify system files?

12. In Windows 7, which key do you press to launch the Advanced Boot Options window during Windows startup?

13. A stop error halts the system while it is booting, and the booting starts over in an endless loop of restarts. How can you solve this problem using the Windows 8 Startup Settings screen?

14. When is the Windows startup process completed?

15. What command in Windows RE can you use to rebuild the BCD file?

16. What command in Windows RE gives you opportunity to manage partitions and volumes installed on the system?

17. Which log in Event Viewer only tracks errors and warnings?

18. If you are having a problem with a driver, which of the following is the least invasive solution: update the driver or use System Restore?

19. What is the name of the log file and its location that is created when you enabled boot logging on the Windows 8 Startup Setting menu or the Windows 7 Advanced Boot Options menu?

20. What information is contained in the C:\Windows\System32\LogFiles\SRT\SRTTrail.txt file?

>> THINKING CRITICALLY

1. When the Windows registry is corrupted and you cannot boot from the hard drive, what tool or method is the best option to fix the problem?

   a. Boot into Safe Mode and use System Restore to repair the registry.

   b. Use the Last Known Good Configuration on the Advanced Boot Options menu.

   c. Use commands from the Windows Recovery Environment to recover the registry from backup.

   d. Refresh Windows using a custom refresh image.

2. Your Windows system boots to a blue screen stop error and no Start screen or desktop. What do you do first?

   a. Reinstall Windows.

   b. Use the web to research the stop error messages and numbers.

   c. Attempt to boot into Windows RE using the Windows setup DVD or a recovery drive.

   d. Verify the system is getting power.

3. You have important data on your hard drive that is not backed up and your Windows installation is so corrupted you know that you must refresh the entire installation. What do you do first?

   a. Use System Restore.

   b. Make every attempt to recover the data.

   c. Perform an in-place upgrade of Windows.

   d. Reformat the hard drive and reinstall Windows.

4. Your computer displays the error message "A disk read error occurred." You try to boot from the Windows setup DVD and you get the same error. What is most likely the problem?

   a. The Windows setup DVD is scratched or damaged in some way.

   b. The hard drive is so damaged the system cannot read from the DVD.

   c. Both the optical drive and the hard drive have failed.

   d. Boot device order is set to boot from the hard drive before the optical drive.

5. When a driver is giving problems in Windows 8, which tool offers the least intrusive solution?

   a. Device Manager

   b. Windows 8 reset

   c. System Restore

   d. Windows 8 refresh

6. An error message is displayed during Windows startup about a service that has failed to start and then the system locks up. You try to boot into Safe Mode, but get the same error message. What do you try next?

   a. Use the command prompt to edit the registry.

   b. Boot to Windows RE and enable boot logging.

   c. Perform an in-place upgrade of Windows 7.

   d. Boot to Windows RE and perform a startup repair.

>> REAL PROBLEMS, REAL SOLUTIONS

REAL PROBLEM 6-1 Summarizing Windows Troubleshooting Tools

In the chapter "Supporting Customers and Troubleshooting Windows," you started building a reference table of tools available in Windows for troubleshooting. In this project, you will expand your table to include new tools covered in this chapter.

1. Return to your tools reference table from the chapter, "Supporting Customers and Troubleshooting Windows." Under the *Tool* heading, add to your list all of the Windows tools covered in this chapter, such as Safe Mode and startup repair.

2. Complete the remainder of the table with the steps needed to access each tool and a brief, one- or two-sentence description of each. Be sure to include the program name of the utility if it can be launched from the command prompt. Also be sure to note whether a tool is available only for certain releases of Windows, such as "New with Windows 8."

REAL PROBLEM 6-2 Sabotaging a Windows System

In a lab environment, follow these steps to find out if you can corrupt a Windows system so that it will not boot, and then repair the system. (This problem can be done using a Windows installation in a virtual machine.) Don't forget about the takeown and icacls commands discussed in this chapter.

1. Rename or move one of the program files listed in Table 6-1. Which program file did you select? In what folder did you find it?

2. Restart your system. Did an error occur? Check in Explorer. Is the file restored? What Windows feature repaired the problem?

3. Try other methods of sabotaging the Windows system, but carefully record exactly what you did to sabotage the boot. Can you make the boot fail?

4. Now recover the Windows system. List the steps you took to get the system back to good working order.

REAL PROBLEM 6-3 Creating a Stop Error

This project is more difficult than it might first appear. Using a VM with Windows 8 installed, create a BSOD or stop error. Take a screen shot of the BSOD. List the steps you took to make Windows 8 crash.

REAL PROBLEM 6-4 Recovering Data from a Hard Drive

To practice recovering data from a hard drive that won't boot, create a folder on a VM with Windows 8 installed. Put data files in the folder. What is the name of your folder? Move the hard drive to another working VM and install it as a second hard drive in the system. Copy the data folder to the primary hard drive in this second VM. Now return the hard drive to the original VM and verify the VM starts with no errors. List the steps you used in this project.

6

Connecting To and Setting Up a Network

After completing this chapter, you will be able to:

• Explain the TCP/IP protocols and standards Windows uses for networking

• Connect a computer to a wired or wireless network

• Configure and secure a multifunction router on a local network

In this chapter, you learn how Windows uses TCP/IP protocols and standards to create and manage network connections, including how computers are identified and addressed on a network. You also learn to connect a computer to a network and how to set up and secure a small wired or wireless network.

This chapter prepares you to assume total responsibility for supporting both wired and wireless networks in a small-office/home-office (SOHO) environment. So let's get started by looking at how TCP/IP works in the world of Windows networking.

⭐ **A+ Exam Tip**   Much of the content in this chapter applies to both the A+ 220-901 exam and the A+ 220-902 exam. This text includes icons for the A+ 220-902 (software) exam only. For markup of content relating to the A+ 220-901 (hardware) exam, see the companion volume to this text, *A+ Guide to Hardware, 9th ed.*

UNDERSTANDING TCP/IP AND WINDOWS NETWORKING

When two computers communicate using a local network or the Internet, communication happens at three levels (hardware, operating system, and application). The first step in communication is one computer must find the other computer. The second step is both computers must agree on the methods and rules for communication (called protocols). Then one computer takes on the role of making requests from the other computer. A computer making a request from another is called the client and the one answering the request is called the server. Most communication between computers on a network or the Internet uses this client/server model. For example, in Figure 7-1, someone uses a web browser on a client to request a webpage from a web server. To handle this request, the client computer must first find the web server, the protocols for communication are established, and then the request is made and answered. Hardware, the OS, and the applications on both computers are all involved in this process.

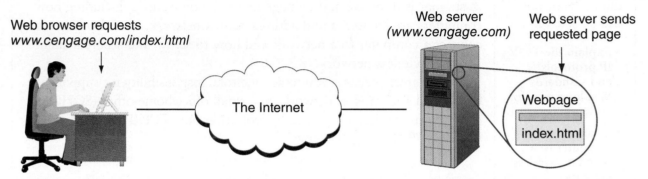

Figure 7-1   A web browser (client software) requests a webpage from a web server (server software); the web server returns the requested data to the client

Let's first look at the layers of communication that involve hardware, the OS, and applications and then see how computers are addressed and found on a network or the Internet. Then we'll see how a client/server request is made by the client and answered by the server.

LAYERS OF NETWORK COMMUNICATION

When your computer at home is connected to your Internet service provider (ISP) off somewhere in the distance, your computer and a computer on the Internet must be able to communicate. When two devices communicate, they must use the same protocols so that the communication makes sense. For almost all networks today, including the Internet, the group or suite of protocols used is called TCP/IP (Transmission Control Protocol/Internet Protocol).

Communication between two computers happens in layers. In Figure 7-2, you can see how communication starts with an application (browser) passing a request to the OS, which passes the request to the network card and then on to the network. When the request reaches the network card on the server, the network card passes it on to the OS and then the OS passes it on to the application (the web server).

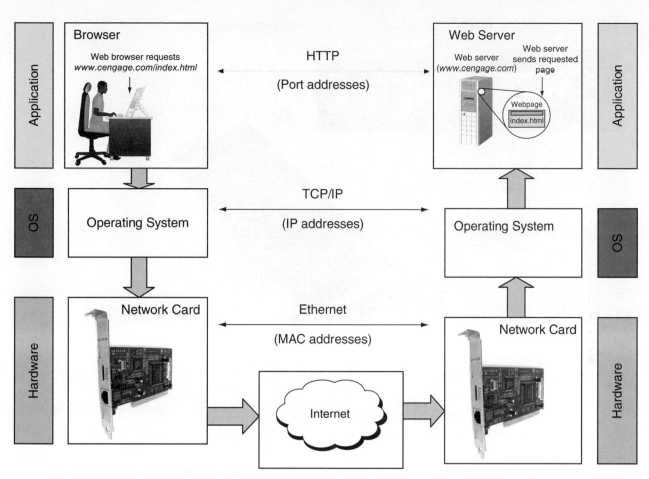

Figure 7-2 Network communication happens in layers

Listed next is a description of each level of communication:

◢ *Level 1: Hardware level.* At the root level of communication is hardware. The hardware or physical connection might be wireless or might use network cables, phone lines (for DSL or dial-up), or TV cable lines (for a cable modem). For local wired or wireless networks, a network adapter (also called a network card, a network interface card, or a NIC) inside your computer is part of this physical network. Every network adapter (including a network card, network port on a motherboard, onboard wireless, or wireless NIC) has a 48-bit (6-byte) number hard-coded on the card by its manufacturer that is unique for that device (see Figure 7-3). The number is written in hexadecimal, and is called the MAC (Media Access Control) address, hardware address, physical address, adapter address, or Ethernet address. Part of the MAC address identifies the manufacturer that is responsible for making sure that no two network adapters have the same MAC address. MAC addresses are used to locate a computer on a local area network (LAN). A local area network (LAN) is a network bound by routers or other gateway devices. A router is a device that manages traffic between two or more networks and can help find the best path for traffic to get from one network to another. A gateway is any device or computer that network traffic can use to leave one network and go to a different network.

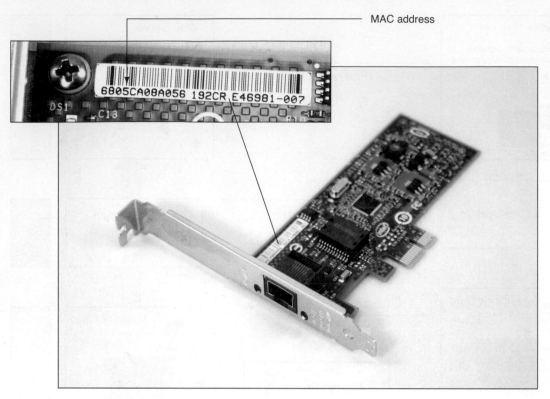

MAC address

Figure 7-3 This Gigabit Ethernet adapter by Intel uses a PCIe x1 slot

▲ *Level 2: Operating system level.* Operating systems use IP addresses to find other computers on a network. An IP address is a 32-bit or 128-bit string that is assigned to a network connection when the connection is first made. Whereas a MAC address is only used to find a computer on a local network, an IP address can be used to find a computer anywhere on the Internet (see Figure 7-4) or on an intranet. An intranet is any private network that uses TCP/IP protocols. A large enterprise might support an intranet that is made up of several local networks. A local network can further be divided into smaller networks and each of these smaller networks is called a subnetwork or subnet. IP addresses are used to find computers on subnets, an intranet, or the Internet.

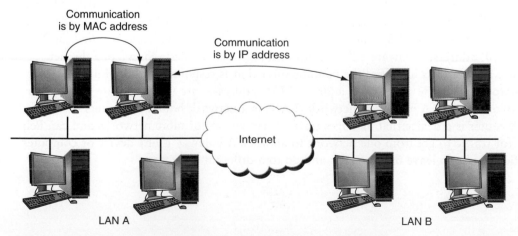

Communication
is by MAC address

Communication
is by IP address

Internet

LAN A   LAN B

Figure 7-4 Computers on the same LAN use MAC addresses to communicate, but computers on different LANs use IP addresses to communicate over the Internet

▲ *Level 3: Application level.* Most applications used on the Internet or a local network are client/server applications. Client applications, such as Internet Explorer, Google Chrome, or Outlook, communicate with server applications such as a web server or email server. Each client and server application installed on a computer listens at a predetermined address that uniquely identifies the application on the computer. This address is a number and is called a port number, port, or port address. For example, you can address a web server by entering into a browser address box an IP address followed by a colon and then 80, which is the port number for a web server application. Suppose a computer with an IP address of 136.60.30.5 is running both an email server, which listens at port 25, and a web server application listening at port 80. If a client computer sends a request to 136.60.30.5:25, the email server that is listening at that port responds. On the other hand, if a request is sent to 136.60.30.5:80, the web server listening at port 80 responds (see Figure 7-5).

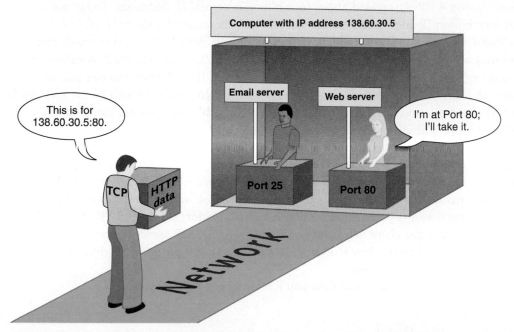

Figure 7-5   Each server running on a computer is addressed by a unique port number

Figure 7-6 shows how communication moves from a browser to the OS to the hardware on one computer and on to the hardware, OS, and web server on a remote computer. As you connect a computer to a network, keep in mind that the connection must work at all three levels. And when things don't work right, it helps to understand that you must solve the problem at one or more levels. In other words, the problem might be with the physical equipment, with the OS, or with the application.

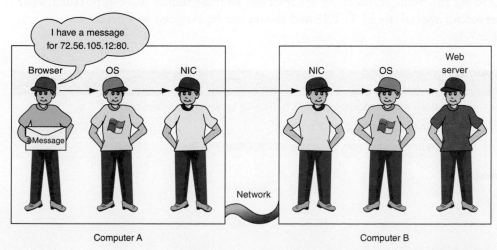

Figure 7-6   How a message gets from a browser to a web server using three levels of communication

Before a message is transmitted on a network, if it is too long, it's broken up into segments. Also, header and trailer information are added, including the IP addresses of the source computer and destination computer, the application's port number, and the protocols for communication the message uses on the network. When this information is added, the message is called a segment, datagram, packet, or frame depending on what information has been added to the header and trailer and which layer of communication added the information.

HOW IP ADDRESSES GET ASSIGNED

An IP address has 32 bits or 128 bits. When the Internet and TCP/IP were first invented, it seemed that 32 bits were more than enough to satisfy any needs we might have for IP addresses because this standard, called Internet Protocol version 4 (IPv4), created about four billion potential IP addresses. Today we need many more than four billion IP addresses over the world. Partly because of a shortage of 32-bit IP addresses, Internet Protocol version 6 (IPv6), which uses an IP address with 128 bits, was developed. Currently, the Internet uses a mix of 32-bit and 128-bit IP addresses. The Internet Assigned Numbers Authority (IANA at *iana.org*) is responsible for keeping track of assigned IP addresses and has already released all its available 32-bit IP addresses. IP addresses leased from IANA today are all 128-bit addresses.

A MAC address is embedded on a network adapter at the factory, but IP addresses are assigned manually or by software. Recall that an IP address can be a dynamic IP address (IP address is assigned by a server each time the computer or device connects to the network) or a static IP address (IP address is permanently assigned to the computer or device).

For dynamic IP addresses, a DHCP (Dynamic Host Configuration Protocol) server gives an IP address to a computer when it first attempts to initiate a connection to the network and requests an IP address. A computer or other device (such as a network printer) that requests an address from a DHCP server is called a DHCP client. It is said that the client is leasing an IP address. A DHCP server that serves up IPv6 addresses is often called a DHCPv6 server. How to configure a Windows computer to use dynamic or static IP addressing is covered later in the chapter.

Next, let's see how IPv4 addresses are used, and then you'll learn about IPv6 addresses.

HOW IPv4 ADDRESSES ARE USED

A 32-bit IP address is organized into four groups of 8 bits each, which are presented as four decimal numbers separated by periods, such as 72.56.105.12. The largest possible 8-bit number is 11111111, which is equal to 255 in decimal, so the largest possible IP address in decimal is 255.255.255.255, which in binary is 11111111.11111111.11111111.11111111. Each of the four numbers separated by periods is called an octet (for 8 bits) and can be any number from 0 to 255, making a total of about 4.3 billion IP addresses (256 × 256 × 256 × 256). Some IP addresses are reserved, so these numbers are approximations. IP addresses that are reserved for special use by TCP/IP and should not be assigned to a device on a network are listed in Table 7-1.

IP Address	How It Is Used
255.255.255.255	Used for broadcast messages by TCP/IP background processes
0.0.0.0	Currently unassigned IP address
127.0.0.1	Indicates your own computer and is called the loopback address

Table 7-1 Reserved IP addresses

The first part of an IP address identifies the network, and the last part identifies the host. When messages are routed over the Internet, the network portion of the IP address is used to locate the right local network. After the message arrives at the local network, the host portion of the IP address is used to identify the one computer on the network that is to receive the message. How does a computer or other network device know what part of an IP address identifies the network and what part identifies the host? It relies on a subnet mask for this information.

SUBNET MASKS

The subnet mask identifies which part of an IP address is the network portion and which part is the host portion. A computer or other device can use its subnet mask to know if an IP address of another computer is on its network or another network (see Figure 7-7).

Figure 7-7 A host (router, in this case) can always determine if an IP address is on its network

A subnet mask has 32 bits and is a string of 1s followed by a string of 0s, for example, 11111111.1111 1111.11110000.00000000. The 1s in a subnet mask say, "On our network, this part of an IP address is the network part," and the group of 0s says, "On our network, this part of an IP address is the host part." On Windows screens, a subnet mask is displayed in decimal, for example the subnet mask of 11111111.11111 111.00000000.00000000 is 255.255.0.0 in decimal.

Suppose the IP address of a computer on Network A is 201.18.20.160 and the subnet mask is 11111111 .11111111.00000000.00000000. The subnet mask tells Windows that the first 16 bits or two octets of the IP address is the network ID. Therefore, when Windows is deciding how to communicate with a computer that has an IP address of 201.18.20.208, it knows the computer is on its own network, but a computer with an IP address of 201.19.23.160 is on another network.

Let's look at one more example. Suppose the IP address of a computer is 19.200.60.6 and its subnet mask is 255.255.240.0. Is a computer with the IP address 19.200.51.100 on its network? Here's the logic to find out:

Question	Answer
1. What is my IP address in binary?	19.200.60.6 in binary is: 00010011.11001000.00111100.00000110.
2. What is the other IP address in binary?	19.200.51.100 in binary is: 00010011.11001000.00110011.01100100.
3. Based on my subnet mask, how many bits in my IP address identify my network?	255.255.240.0 in binary is: 11111111.11111111.11110000.00000000. 20 bits identify the network.
4. Do the first 20 bits in my IP address match the first 20 bits in the other IP address?	Compare the 20 red bits in the two IP addresses: 00010011.11001000.00111100.00000110 00010011.11001000.00110011.01100100 Yes, they match.
5. Is the other IP address on my network?	Yes.

Sometimes an IP address and subnet mask are written using a shorthand notation like 15.50.212.59/20, where the /20 means that the first 20 bits in the IP address identify the network. This notation is sometimes called slash notation or CIDR notation (pronounced "*cider notation*"), named after the CIDR (Classless Interdomain Routing) standards that were written in 1993 about subnetting.

Hands-On | Project 7-1 Practice Using Subnet Masks

To practice your skills using subnet masks, fill in Table 7-2. First, convert decimal values to binary and then record your decisions in the last column.

Local IP Address	Subnet Mask	Other IP Address	On the Same Network? (Yes or No)
15.50.212.59 Binary: _____	255.255.240.0 Binary: _____	15.50.235.80 Binary: _____	
192.168.24.1 Binary: _____	255.255.248.0 Binary: _____	192.168.31.198 Binary: _____	
192.168.0.1 Binary: _____	255.255.255.192 Binary: _____	192.168.0.63 Binary: _____	
192.168.0.10 Binary: _____	255.255.255.128 Binary: _____	192.168.0.120 Binary: _____	

Table 7-2 Practice using subnet masks

That brings us to a fun way of explaining subnet masks. Suppose all the tall sticks shown in Figure 7-8 belong to the same large network that has been subnetted. The short stick represents the subnet mask for all subnets. How many subnets are in the network? Which sticks belong in the same subnet as Stick 5? As Stick 6?

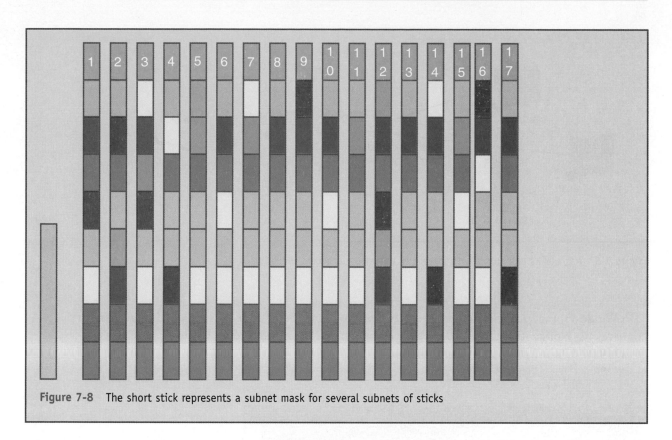

Figure 7-8   The short stick represents a subnet mask for several subnets of sticks

PUBLIC, PRIVATE, AND AUTOMATIC PRIVATE IP ADDRESSES

IP addresses available to the Internet are called public IP addresses. To conserve the number of public IP addresses, some blocks of IP addresses have been designated as private IP addresses that are not allowed on the Internet. Private IP addresses are used within a company's private network, and computers on this network can communicate with one another using these private IP addresses.

IEEE recommends that the following IP addresses be used for private networks:

◢ 10.0.0.0 through 10.255.255.255
◢ 172.16.0.0 through 172.31.255.255
◢ 192.168.0.0 through 192.168.255.255

If a computer first connects to the network that is using dynamic IP addressing and is unable to lease an IP address from the DHCP server, it generates its own Automatic Private IP Address (APIPA) in the address range 169.254.*x.y.*

> ✎ **Notes** IEEE, a nonprofit organization, is responsible for many Internet standards. Standards are proposed to the networking community in the form of an RFC (Request for Comment). RFC 1918 outlines recommendations for private IP addresses. To view an RFC, visit the website *www.rfc-editor.org.*

NAT (Network Address Translation) is a technique designed to conserve the number of public IP addresses needed by a network. A router or other gateway device stands between a private network and the Internet and substitutes the private IP addresses used by computers on the private network with its own public IP address when these computers need access to the Internet. See Figure 7-9. Besides conserving public IP addresses, another advantage of NAT is security; the gateway hides the entire private network behind this one address.

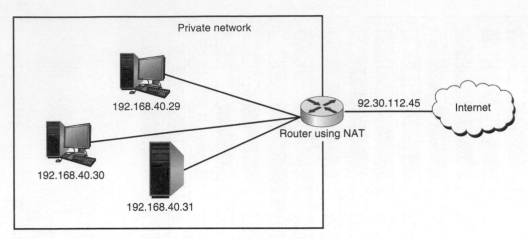

Figure 7-9   NAT allows computers with private IP addresses to access the Internet

In Windows, the ipconfig command can be used to show the IP addresses assigned to all network connections. Notice in Figure 7-10 that the computer has been assigned a private IPv4 address of 192.168.31.198 for the wireless connection.

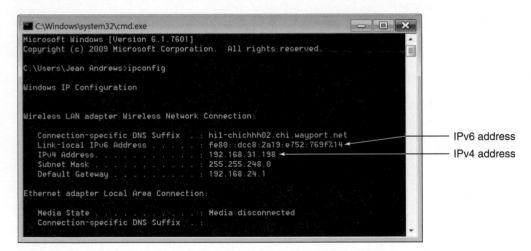

Figure 7-10   The wireless network connection has been assigned a private IPv4 address

HOW IPv6 ADDRESSES ARE USED

Using the IPv6 standards, more has changed than just the number of bits in an IP address. To improve routing capabilities and speed of communication, IPv6 changed the way IP addresses are used to find computers on the Internet. Let's begin our discussion of IPv6 by looking at how IPv6 addresses are written and displayed:

◢ An IPv6 address has 128 bits that are written as eight blocks of hexadecimal numbers separated by colons, like this: 2001:0000:0B80:0000:0000:00D3:9C5A:00CC.
◢ Each block is 16 bits. For example, the first block in the address above is 2001 in hex, which can be written as 0010 0000 0000 0001 in binary.
◢ Leading zeros in a four-character hex block can be eliminated. For example, the IP address above can be written as 2001:0000:B80:0000:0000:D3:9C5A:CC.

◢ If blocks contain all zeros, they can be written as double colons (::). The IP address above can be written two ways:

    ◢ 2001::B80:0000:0000:D3:9C5A:CC

    ◢ 2001:0000:B80::D3:9C5A:CC

To avoid confusion, only one set of double colons is used in an IP address. In this example, the preferred method is the second one: 2001:0000:B80::D3:9C5A:CC because the address is written with the fewest zeros.

The way computers communicate using IPv6 has changed the terminology used to describe TCP/IP communication. Here are a few terms used in the IPv6 standards:

◢ A link, sometimes called the local link, or local network, is a local area network (LAN) or wide area network (WAN) bounded by routers.

◢ A node is any device that connects to the network, such as a computer, printer, or router. An interface is a node's attachment to a link. The attachment can be a logical attachment, such as when a virtual machine connects to the network, or a physical attachment, such as when a network adapter connects to the wired network.

◢ The last 64 bits or 4 blocks of an IP address identify the interface and are called the interface ID or interface identifier. These 64 bits uniquely identify an interface on the local network.

◢ Neighbors are nodes on the same local network.

So far, very few networks solely use IPv6. Most networks, including the Internet, rely on IPv4 protocols. On IPv4 networks, tunnels are used to allow IPv6 messages to travel on the network. A tunnel works by encapsulating an IPv6 message inside an IPv4 message. Two common tunneling protocols are ISATAP (pronounced "eye-sa-tap" and stands for Intra-Site Automatic Tunnel Addressing Protocol) and Teredo (pronounced "ter-EE-do"), which is named after the Teredo worm that bores holes in wood. Teredo IPv6 addresses begin with 2001.

IPv6 supports these three types of IP addresses:

◢ A unicast address is used to send messages to a single node on a network. Three types of unicast addresses are link-local addresses, unique local addresses, and global addresses.

◢ A multicast address is used to deliver messages to all nodes in a targeted, multicast group, such as when video is streaming from a server to multiple nodes on a network.

◢ An anycast address is used by routers and can identify multiple destinations and a message is delivered only to the closest destination.

Recall that with IPv4 broadcasting, messages are sent to every node on a local network. However, IPv6 doesn't use broadcasting, which reduces network traffic. The concepts of broadcasting, multicasting, anycasting, and unicasting are illustrated in Figure 7-11.

Table 7-3 lists the currently used address prefixes for these types of IP addresses. In the future, we can expect more prefixes to be assigned as they are needed.

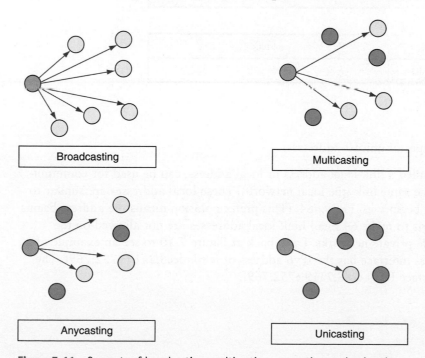

Figure 7-11 Concepts of broadcasting, multicasting, anycasting, and unicasting

IP Address Type	Address Prefix
Link-local address	FE80::/64 (First 64 bits are always 1111 1110 1000 0000…)
Unique local address	FC00::/7 (First 7 bits are always 1111 1100)
Global address	2000::/3 (First 3 bits are always 001)
Multicast	FF00::/8 (First 8 bits are always 1111 1111)
Unassigned address	0::0 (All zeroes)
Loopback address	0::1, also written as ::1 (127 zeroes followed by 1)

Table 7-3   Address prefixes for types of IPv6 addresses

Three types of unicast addresses are link-local, unique link-local, and global addresses, which are graphically shown in Figure 7-12.

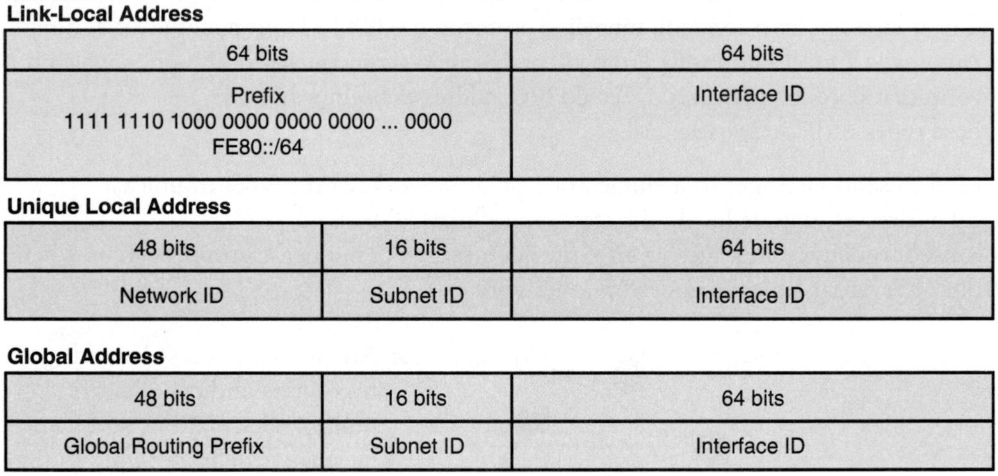

Link-Local Address

64 bits	64 bits
Prefix 1111 1110 1000 0000 0000 0000 … 0000 FE80::/64	Interface ID

Unique Local Address

48 bits	16 bits	64 bits
Network ID	Subnet ID	Interface ID

Global Address

48 bits	16 bits	64 bits
Global Routing Prefix	Subnet ID	Interface ID

Figure 7-12   Three types of IPv6 addresses

Here is a description of the three types of unicast addresses:

▲ A link-local unicast address, also called a link-local address or local address, can be used for communicating with neighboring nodes in the same link (the local network). These local addresses are similar to IPv4 private IP addresses and most begin with FE80::/64. (This prefix notation means the address begins with FE80 followed by enough zeros to make 64 bits.) Link-local addresses are not allowed on the Internet or allowed to travel outside private networks. Look back at Figure 7-10 to see an example of a link-local address where the wireless interface has the IPv6 address of fe80::dcc8:2a19:e752:769f. The first 64 bits are fe80:: and the interface ID is dcc8:2a19:e752:769f.

◢ A unique local address is a private address that can travel across subnets within the private network. These addresses are used by network administrators when subnetting a large network.

◢ A global unicast address, also called a global address, can be routed on the Internet. These addresses are similar to IPv4 public IP addresses. The first 48 bits of the address is the Global Routing Prefix. When an ISP assigns a global address to a customer, it's these 48 bits that it assigns. An organization that leases one Global Routing Prefix from its ISP can use it to generate many IPv6 global addresses.

SUBNETS

IPv6 uses subnetting but doesn't need a subnet mask because the subnet ID that identifies a subnet is part of the IPv6 address. The subnet ID is the 16 bits following the first 48 bits of the address. When a large IPv6 network is subnetted, a DHCPv6 server assigns a node in a subnet a global address or unique local address that contains the correct subnet ID for the node's subnet.

> **✎ Notes** An excellent resource for learning more about IPv6 and how it works is the e-book, *TCP/IP Fundamentals for Microsoft Windows*. To download the free PDF, search for it at *www.microsoft.com/download*.

7

VIEW IP ADDRESS SETTINGS

In summary, let's use the ipconfig command to take a look at the IPv4 and IPv6 addresses assigned to all network connections on a computer (see Figure 7-13).

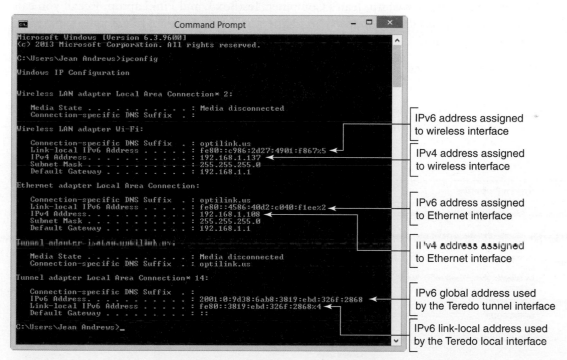

Figure 7-13 The ipconfig command showing IPv4 and IPv6 addresses assigned to this computer

Notice in the figure the four IP addresses that have been assigned to the physical connections:

◢ Windows has assigned the wireless connection two IP addresses, one IPv4 address and one IPv6 address.
◢ The Ethernet LAN connection has also been assigned an IPv4 address and an IPv6 address.

The IPv6 addresses are followed by a % sign and a number; for example, %5 follows the first IP address. This number is called the zone ID or scope ID and is used to identify the interface in a list of interfaces for this computer.

IPv6 addressing is designed so that a computer can self-configure its own link-local IP address, which is similar to how IPv4 uses an Automatic Private IP Address (APIPA). Here's what happens when a computer using IPv6 first makes a network connection:

1. The computer creates its IPv6 address by using the FE80::/64 prefix and uses its MAC address to generate an interface ID for the last 64 bits.

2. It then performs a duplicate address detection process to make sure its IP address is unique on the network.

3. Next, it asks if a DHCPv6 server is present on the network to provide configuration information. If a server responds with DHCP information, the computer uses whatever information this might be, such as the IP addresses of DNS servers or its own IP address. Because a computer can generate its own link-local IP address, a DHCPv6 server usually serves up only global or unique local addresses.

CHARACTER-BASED NAMES IDENTIFY COMPUTERS AND NETWORKS

Remembering an IP address is not always easy, so character-based names are used to substitute for IP addresses. Here are the possibilities:

◢ A host name, also called a computer name, is the name of a computer and can be used in place of its IP address. The name can have up to 63 characters, including letters, numbers, and special characters. Examples of computer names are www, ftp, Jean's Computer, TestBox3, and PinkLaptop. Recall you can assign a computer name while installing Windows. In addition, you can change the computer name at any time using the System window:

1. For Windows 8, press **Win+X** and click **System**. For Windows 7, open Control Panel in Classic view and click **System**. In the System window, click **Advanced system settings**.

2. In the System Properties box, on the Computer Name tab (see Figure 7-14), click **Change**. You will need to restart your computer for the change to take effect.

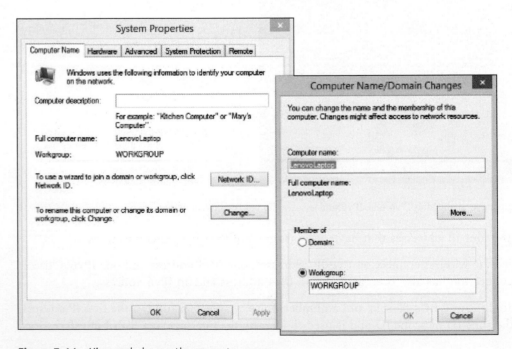

Figure 7-14   View and change the computer name

⬛ Recall that a workgroup is a group of computers on a peer-to-peer network that are sharing resources. The workgroup name assigned to this group is only recognized within the local network.

⬛ A domain name identifies a network. Examples of domain names are the names that appear before the period in *microsoft.com*, *course.com*, and *mycompany.com*. The letters after the period are called the top-level domain and tell you something about the domain. Examples are .com (commercial), .org (nonprofit), .gov (government), and .info (general use).

⬛ A fully qualified domain name (FQDN) identifies a computer and the network to which it belongs. An example of an FQDN is *www.cengage.com*. The host name is *www* (a web server), *cengage* is the domain name, and *com* is the top-level domain name of the Cengage network. Another FQDN is *joesmith.mycompany.com*.

On the Internet, a fully qualified domain name must be associated with an IP address before this computer can be found. This process of associating a character-based name with an IP address is called name resolution. The DNS (Domain Name System or Domain Name Service) protocol is used by a DNS server to find an IP address for a computer when the fully qualified domain name is known. On home or small company networks, the ISP is responsible for providing access to one or more DNS servers as part of the service it provides for Internet access. Larger corporations have their own DNS servers to perform name resolution for the enterprise network. When an individual or organization, which has its own DNS servers, leases a public IP address and domain name and sets up a website, it is responsible for entering the name resolution information into its primary DNS server. This server can present the information to other DNS servers on the web and is called the authoritative name server for the website.

7

⭐ **A+ Exam Tip** The A+ 220-902 exam expects you to be able to configure DNS on a client computer.

✏️ **Notes** When you enter a fully qualified domain name such as *www.cengage.com* in a browser address bar, that name is translated into an IP address followed by a port number. It's interesting to know that you can skip the translation step and enter the IP address and port number in the address box. See Figure 7-15.

Figure 7-15 A website can be accessed by its IP address and port number: http://69.32.208.74:80

When Windows is trying to resolve a computer name to an IP address, it first looks in the DNS cache it holds in memory. If the computer name is not found in the cache, Windows then turns to a DNS server if it has the IP address of the server. When Windows queries the DNS server for a name resolution, it is called the DNS client.

Hands-On | Project 7-2 View and Clear the DNS Cache

Open a command prompt window and use the **ipconfig /displaydns** command to view the DNS cache on your computer. Then use the **ipconfig /flushdns** command to clear the DNS cache.

TCP/IP PROTOCOL LAYERS

Recall that a protocol is an agreed-to set of rules for communication between two parties. Operating systems and client/server applications on the Internet all use protocols that are supported by TCP/IP. The left side of Figure 7-16 shows these different layers of protocols and how they relate to one another. As you read this section, this figure can serve as your road map to the different protocols.

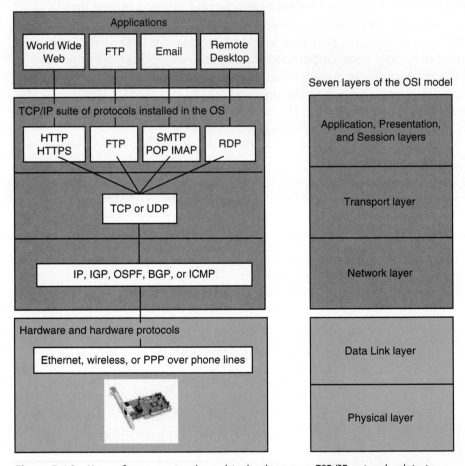

Figure 7-16   How software, protocols, and technology on a TCP/IP network relate to each other

> ✎ **Notes**   When studying networking theory, the OSI model is used, which divides network communication into seven layers. In the OSI model, protocols used by hardware are divided into two layers (Data Link and Physical layers), and TCP/IP protocols used by the OS are divided into five layers (Network, Transport, Session, Presentation, and Application layers). These seven layers are shown on the right side of Figure 7-16.

In the following sections, the more significant applications and operating system protocols are introduced. However, you should know that the TCP/IP protocol suite includes more protocols than just those mentioned in this chapter; only some of them are shown in Figure 7-16.

TCP/IP PROTOCOLS USED BY THE OS

Looking back at Figure 7-16, you can see three layers of protocols between the applications and the hardware protocols. These three layers make up the heart of TCP/IP communication. In the figure, TCP or UDP manages communication with the applications protocols above them as well as the protocols shown underneath TCP and UDP, which control communication on the network.

TCP Guarantees Delivery

Remember that all communication on a network happens by way of messages delivered from one location on the network to another. In TCP/IP, the protocol that guarantees message delivery is TCP (Transmission Control Protocol). TCP makes a connection, sends the data, checks whether the data is received, and resends it if it is not. TCP is, therefore, called a connection-oriented protocol. TCP is used by applications such as web browsers and email. Guaranteed delivery takes longer and is used when it is important to know that the data reached its destination.

For TCP to guarantee delivery, it uses protocols at the IP layer to establish a session between client and server to verify that communication has taken place. When a TCP message reaches its destination, an acknowledgment is sent back to the source (see Figure 7-17). If the source TCP does not receive the acknowledgment, it resends the data or passes an error message back to the higher-level application protocol.

UDP Provides Fast Transmissions

On the other hand, UDP (User Datagram Protocol) does not guarantee delivery by first connecting and checking whether data is received; thus, UDP is called a connectionless protocol or best-effort protocol. UDP is used for broadcasting, such as streaming video or sound over the web, where guaranteed delivery is not as important as fast transmission. UDP is also used to monitor network traffic.

Figure 7-17 TCP guarantees delivery by requesting an acknowledgment

TCP/IP PROTOCOLS USED BY APPLICATIONS

Some common applications that use the Internet are web browsers, email, chat, FTP, Telnet, Remote Desktop, and Remote Assistance. Here is a bit of information about several of the protocols used by these and other applications:

◢ **HTTP.** HTTP (Hypertext Transfer Protocol) is the protocol used for the World Wide Web and used by web browsers and web servers to communicate. You can see when a browser is using this protocol by looking for http at the beginning of a URL in the address bar of a browser, such as *http://www.microsoft.com.*

◢ **HTTPS.** HTTPS (HTTP secure) refers to the HTTP protocol working with a security protocol such as Secure Sockets Layer (SSL) or Transport Layer Security (TLS), which is better than SSL, to create a secured socket. A socket is a connection between a browser and web server. HTTPS is used by web browsers and servers to secure the socket by encrypting the data before it is sent and then decrypting it before the data is processed. To know a secured protocol is being used, look for https in the URL, as in *https://www.wellsfargo.com.*

▲ **SMTP.** SMTP (Simple Mail Transfer Protocol) is used to send an email message to its destination (see Figure 7-18). The email server that takes care of sending email messages (using the SMTP protocol) is often referred to as the SMTP server.

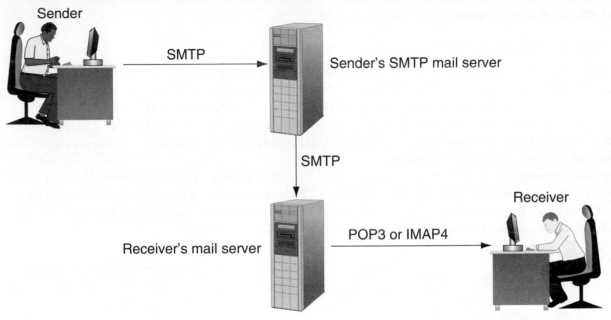

Figure 7-18   The SMTP protocol is used to send email to a recipient's mail server, and the POP3 or IMAP4 protocol is used by the client to receive email

▲ **POP and IMAP.** After an email message arrives at the destination email server, it remains there until the recipient requests delivery. The recipient's email server uses one of two protocols to deliver the message: POP3 (Post Office Protocol, version 3) or IMAP4 (Internet Message Access Protocol, version 4). Using POP3, email is downloaded to the client computer and, unless the default setting is changed, the email is then deleted from the email server. Using IMAP, the client application manages the email stored on the server.

▲ **Telnet.** The Telnet protocol is used by Telnet client/server applications to allow an administrator or other user to control a computer remotely. Telnet is not considered secure because transmissions in Telnet are not encrypted.

▲ **LDAP.** Lightweight Directory Access Protocol (LDAP) is used by various client applications when the application needs to query a database. For example, an email client on a corporate network might query a database that contains the email addresses for all employees or an application might query a database of printers looking for a printer on the corporate network or Internet. Data sent and received using the LDAP protocol is not encrypted; therefore, an encryption layer is sometimes added to LDAP transmissions.

▲ **SMB.** Server Message Block (SMB) is a file access protocol originally developed by IBM and used by Windows to share files and printers on a network. The current release of the SMB protocol is CIFS, also called SMB2.

▲ **AFP.** AFP (Apple Filing Protocol) is a file access protocol used by early editions of the Mac operating system by Apple and is one protocol in the suite of Apple networking protocols called AppleTalk. (TCP/IP has replaced AppleTalk for most networking protocols in the Mac OS.) Current Mac OS releases use SMB2 for file access, and support AFP for backward compatibility with earlier versions of the Mac OS.

▲ **CIFS.** CIFS (Common Internet File System), also called SMB2, is a file access protocol and the cross-platform version of SMB used between Windows, Linux, Mac OS, and other operating systems.

▲ **FTP.** FTP (File Transfer Protocol) is used to transfer files between two computers. Web browsers can use the protocol. Also, third-party FTP client software, such as CuteFTP by GlobalSCAPE (*www.cuteftp.com*) and others, offers more features for file transfer than does a browser. By default, FTP transmissions are not secure. Secure FTP (SFTP) uses SSH encryption.

▲ **SSH.** The Secure Shell (SSH) protocol encrypts transmission so they cannot be intercepted by a hacker. SSH is used in various situations for encryption, such as SFTP. SSH is commonly used in Linux to pass sign-in information to a remote computer and control that computer over a network. Because it's secure, SSH is preferred over Telnet on Linux systems.

▲ **SNMP.** Simple Network Management Protocol (SNMP) is used to monitor network traffic. It is used by the Microsoft SNMP Agent application that monitors traffic on a network and helps balance that traffic.

▲ **RDP.** Remote Desktop Protocol (RDP) is used by the Windows Remote Desktop and Remote Assistance utilities to connect to and control a remote computer.

7

APPLYING | CONCEPTS   INTERNET EXPLORER AND FTP

To use FTP in Internet Explorer, enter the address of an FTP site in the address box, for example, *ftp.cengage.com*. A logon dialog box appears where you can enter a user name and password (see Figure 7-19). When you click **Log on**, you can see folders on the FTP site and the FTP protocol displays in the address bar, as in *ftp://ftp.cengage.com*. It's easier to use File Explorer or Windows Explorer to transfer files rather than Internet Explorer.

Figure 7-19   Log on to an FTP site

After you have located the FTP site, to use Explorer for file transfers, press **Alt**, which causes the menu bar to appear. In the menu bar, click **View, Open FTP site in File Explorer** (see Figure 7-20). Explorer opens, showing files and folders on the FTP site. You can copy and paste files and folders from your computer to the site.

(continues)

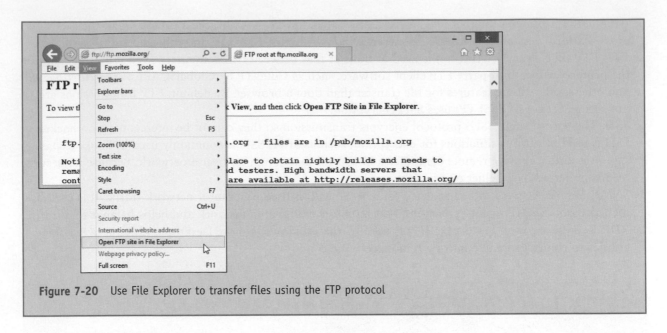

Figure 7-20 Use File Explorer to transfer files using the FTP protocol

Recall that client/server applications use ports to address each other. Table 7-4 lists the port assignments for common applications.

Port	Protocol and App	Description
20	FTP client	The FTP client receives data on port 20 from the FTP server.
21	FTP server	The FTP server listens on port 21 for commands from an FTP client.
22	SSH server	A server using the SSH protocol listens at port 22.
23	Telnet server	A Telnet server listens at port 23.
25	SMTP email server	An email server listens at port 25 to receive email from a client computer.
53	DNS server	A DNS server listens at port 53.
80	Web server using HTTP	A web server listens at port 80 when receiving HTTP requests.
110	POP3 email client	An email client using POP3 receives email at port 110.
143	IMAP email client	An email client using IMAP receives email at port 143.
443	Web server using HTTPS	A web server listens at port 443 when receiving HTTPS transmissions.
3389	RDP apps, including Remote Desktop and Remote Assistance	Remote Desktop and Remote Assistance listen at port 3389.
137, 138, and 139	SMB over NetBIOS	NetBIOS is a legacy suite of protocols used by Windows before TCP/IP. To support legacy NetBIOS applications on a TCP/IP network, TCP offers NetBIOS over TCP/IP. Earlier versions of SMB required NetBIOS over TCP/IP be enabled. Ports used on these networks are: ▲ SMB over UDP uses ports 137 and 138. ▲ SMB over TCP uses ports 137 and 139. Current versions of SMB don't require NetBIOS over TCP.

Table 7-4 Common TCP/IP port assignments for client/server applications (continues)

Port	Protocol and App	Description
445	SMB direct over TCP/IP	Current releases of SMB and SMB2 use port 445 for both TCP and UDP traffic.
427	SLP and AFP	Service Location Protocol (SLP) uses port 427 to find printers and file sharing devices on a network. AFP relies on SLP and port 427 to find resources on a local network.
548	AFP	AFP over TCP/IP is used for file sharing and file services.

Table 7-4   Common TCP/IP port assignments for client/server applications (continued)

Now that you have an understanding of TCP/IP and Windows networking, let's apply that knowledge to making network connections.

CONNECTING A COMPUTER TO A NETWORK

Connecting a computer to a network is quick and easy in most situations. In the chapter, "Survey of Windows Features and Support Tools," you learned to connect to a wired and wireless network. We begin with a summary of that information and then you learn to connect to a WWAN (cellular network), how to make a dial-up connection, and how to connect to a VPN.

> ★ **A+ Exam Tip** The A+ 220-902 exam expects you to know how to connect to a wired, wireless, cellular, dial-up, or VPN network.

CONNECT TO AN ETHERNET WIRED OR WIRELESS WI-FI LOCAL NETWORK

A+
220-902
1.5, 1.6

To connect a computer to a network using an Ethernet wired or Wi-Fi wireless connection, follow these steps:

1. In general, before you connect to any network, the network adapter and its drivers must be installed and Device Manager should report no errors.

2. Do one of the following to connect to the network:

   ◢ For a wired network, plug in the network cable to the Ethernet port. The port is also called an RJ-45 port (RJ stands for registered jack) and looks like a large phone jack. Indicator lights near the network port should light up to indicate connectivity and activity. For Ethernet, Windows should automatically configure the connection.

   ◢ For a wireless network, in Windows 8, you can use the charms bar or the Network icon in the taskbar on the Windows 8/7 desktop. On the desktop, click the Network icon in the taskbar and select a wireless network. Click **Connect**. If the network is secured, you must enter the security key to the wireless network to connect.

3. Open your browser and make sure you can access the web. For wireless connections, some hotspots provide a home page where you must enter a code or agree to the terms of use before you can use the network. On a private network, open File Explorer or Windows Explorer and drill down into the Network group to verify network resources are available (see Figure 7-21).

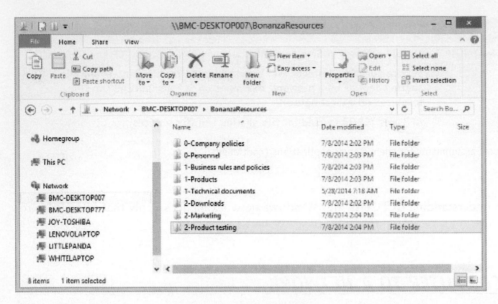

Figure 7-21   File Explorer shows resources on the network

For wireless connections, you can view the status of the connection, including the security key used to make the connection. Do the following:

1. For Windows 8/7, open **Control Panel** in Classic view and open the **Network and Sharing Center**. Alternately, you can right-click the Network icon in the desktop taskbar and click **Open Network and Sharing Center**. The Network and Sharing Center is shown in Figure 7-22. Click **Change adapter settings**. The Network Connections window appears (see Figure 7-23).

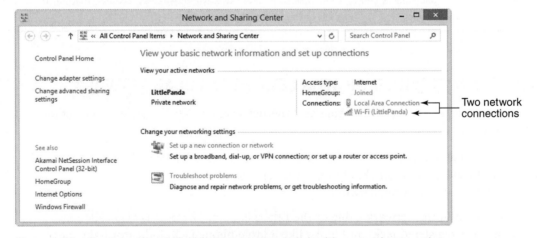

Figure 7-22   The Network and Sharing Center reports two healthy network connections

Figure 7-23   The Network Connections window can be used to repair broken connections

Notes For Windows 8, a shortcut to open the Network Connections window is to press **Win+X** and click **Network Connections**.

2. In the Network Connections window, right-click the **Wi-Fi** connection and click **Status**. In the Wi-Fi Status box (see Figure 7-24), click **Wireless Properties**. On the Wireless Properties box, select the **Security** tab. To view the security key, check **Show characters**. You can also see the security and encryption types that Windows automatically sensed and applied when it made the connection.

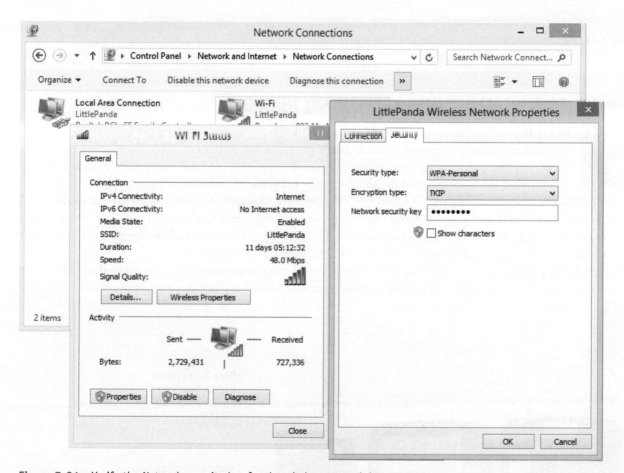

Figure 7-24 Verify the Network security key for the wireless network is correct

If you have a problem making a network connection, you can reset the connection. Open the Network Connections window and right-click the network connection. Select **Disable** from the shortcut menu as shown in Figure 7-25. Right-click the connection again and select **Enable**. The connection is reset. Try again to browse the web or access resources on the network. If you still don't have local or Internet access, consider that the problem might be with the network or its connection to the ISP.

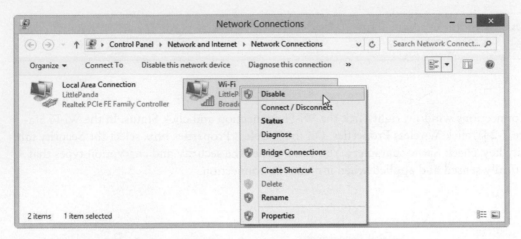

Figure 7-25   To repair a connection, disable and then enable the connection

CONNECT TO A WIRELESS WAN (CELLULAR) NETWORK

A+
220-902
1.6

To connect a computer using mobile broadband to a wireless wide area network (WWAN), also called a cellular network, such as those provided by Verizon or AT&T, you need the hardware and software to connect and, for some networks, a SIM card. A cellular network can support both voice and data and currently uses one of two technologies: GSM (Global System for Mobile Communications) or CDMA (Code Division Multiple Access). Most carriers in the United States use CDMA, but GSM is more popular globally. Long Term Evolution (LTE) and Voice over LTE (VoLTE) provide data and voice transmissions and are expected to ultimately replace both GSM and CDMA. Many carriers use a combination of GSM and LTE or CDMA and LTE.

Those cellular devices that use GSM or LTE require a SIM (Subscriber Identification Module) card be installed in the device, which contains the information that identifies your device to the carrier (see Figure 7-26).

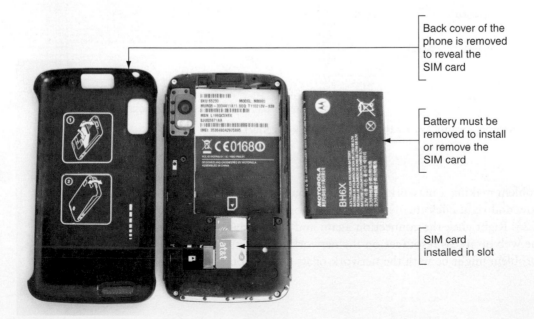

Back cover of the phone is removed to reveal the SIM card

Battery must be removed to install or remove the SIM card

SIM card installed in slot

Figure 7-26   A SIM card contains proof that your device can use a cellular network

Here are your options for software and hardware devices that can connect to a cellular network:

▲ *Use an embedded mobile broadband modem.* A laptop or other mobile device might have an embedded broadband modem. In this situation, you still need to subscribe to a carrier.

▲ *Tether your cell phone to your computer.* You can tether your cell phone to your computer. The cell phone connects to the cellular network and provides communication to your computer. The phone and computer can connect by way of a USB cable (see Figure 7-27), a proprietary cable provided by your cell phone manufacturer, or a Bluetooth or Wi-Fi wireless connection. Your contract with the carrier must allow tethering.

Figure 7-27   Tether your cell phone to your laptop using a USB cable

▲ *Use a USB broadband modem.* For any computer, you can use a USB broadband modem (sometimes called an air card), such as the one shown in Figure 7-28. The device requires a contract with a cellular carrier.

When you purchase any of these devices from a carrier or manufacturer, most likely detailed instructions are included for connecting to the cellular network. Follow those instructions rather than the generic ones presented here. Generally, here's how you can connect to a cellular network:

▲ *Use an embedded broadband modem.* For laptops or other mobile devices that have an embedded modem, if a SIM card is required, insert the card in the device. For some laptops, the card slot might be in the battery bay, and you must remove the battery to find the slot. Then use

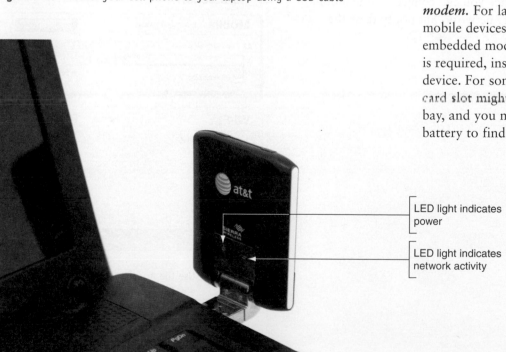

LED light indicates power

LED light indicates network activity

Figure 7-28   A USB broadband modem by Sierra Wireless

a program installed on the device to connect to the cellular network. In addition, the mobile operator might provide software for you to use.

▲ ***Tether your cell phone.*** To tether your cell phone to your computer, your carrier is likely to provide you software to make the connection. If software is provided, install the software first and then tether your cell phone to your computer. Use the software to make the connection.

▲ ***Use a USB broadband modem.*** When using a USB broadband modem, if needed, insert the SIM card in the modem (see Figure 7-29). When you insert the modem into a USB port, Windows finds the device, and the software stored on the device automatically installs and runs. A window then appears provided by the software that allows you to connect to the cellular network.

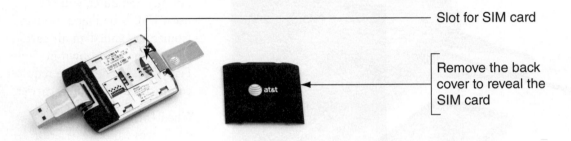

Slot for SIM card

Remove the back cover to reveal the SIM card

Figure 7-29   A SIM card with subscription information on it might be required to use a cellular network

The software might prompt you to go to the website of your carrier and activate the phone number used by the modem. Figure 7-30 shows the software provided by one modem. Notice you can connect to the mobile network or the Wi-Fi network, but not both at the same time.

Source: AT&T Communications Manager

Figure 7-30   Use the management software to connect and disconnect from the Mobile (cellular) or Wi-Fi network

CREATE A DIAL-UP CONNECTION

A+
220-902
1.6

You never know when you might be called on to support an older dial-up connection. Here are the bare-bones steps you need to set up and support this type of connection:

1. Install an internal or external dial-up modem. Make sure Device Manager recognizes the card without errors.

2. Plug the phone line into the modem port on your computer and into the wall jack.

3. Open the **Network and Sharing Center** window. In the Network and Sharing Center window (refer back to Figure 7-22), click **Set up a new connection or network**. In the dialog box that appears (see Figure 7-31), select **Connect to the Internet - Set up a broadband or dial-up connection to the Internet** and click **Next**.

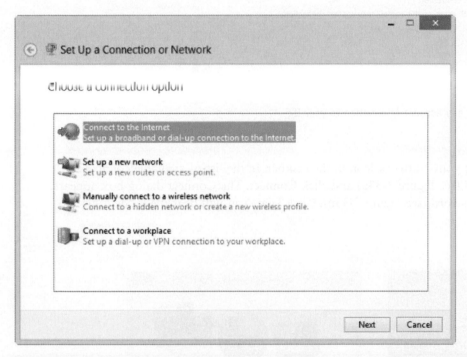

Figure 7-31 Create a dial-up connection to an ISP

4. In the next box, click **Dial-up**. In the next box (see Figure 7-32), enter the phone number to your ISP, your ISP user name and password, and the name you decide to give the dial-up connection, such as the name and city of your ISP. Then click **Create**.

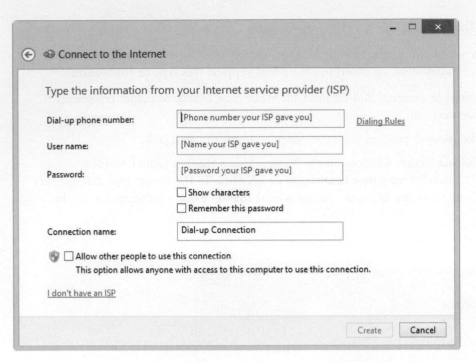

Figure 7-32 Enter phone number and account information to your ISP

To use the connection, click your Network icon in the taskbar. In the list of available connections, select your dial-up connection (see Figure 7-33a) and click **Connect**. The Connect dialog box appears, where you can enter your password (see Figure 7-33b). Click **Dial**. You will hear the modem dial up the ISP and make the connection.

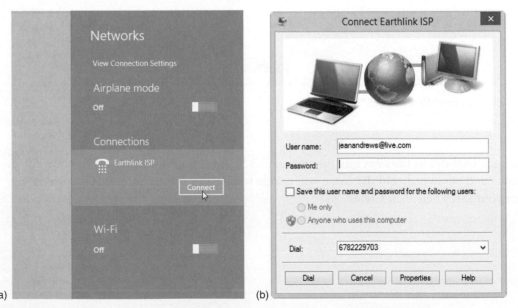

(a)   (b)

Figure 7-33 (a) Select your dial-up connection, and (b) enter the password to your ISP

If the dial-up connection won't work, here are some things you can try:

▲ Is the phone line working? Plug in a regular phone and check for a dial tone. Is the phone cord securely connected to the computer and the wall jack?

▲ Does the modem work? Check Device Manager for reported errors about the modem. Does the modem work when making a call to another phone number (not your ISP)?

▲ Check the Dial-up Connection Properties box for errors. To do so, click **Change adapter settings** in the Network and Sharing Center, and then right-click the dial-up connection and select **Properties** from the shortcut menu. Is the phone number correct? Does the number need to include a 9 to get an outside line? Has a 1 been added in front of the number by mistake? If you need to add a 9, you can put a comma in the field like this "9,4045661200", which causes a slight pause after the 9 is dialed.

▲ Try dialing the number manually from a phone. Do you hear beeps on the other end? Try another phone number.

▲ When you try to connect, do you hear the number being dialed? If so, the problem is most likely with the phone number, the phone line, or the user name and password.

▲ Try removing and reinstalling the dial-up connection.

CREATE A VPN CONNECTION

A+
220-902
1.6

A virtual private network (VPN) is often used by employees when they telecommute to connect to the corporate network by way of the Internet. A VPN protects data by encrypting it from the time it leaves the remote computer until it reaches a server on the corporate network. The encryption technique is called a tunnel or tunneling (see Figure 7-34).

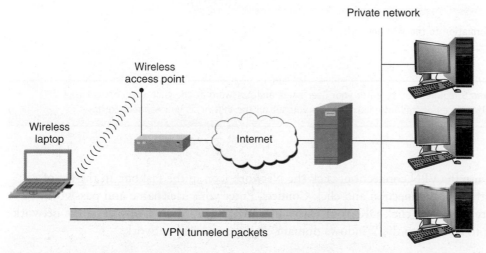

Figure 7-34   With a VPN, tunneling is used to send encrypted data over wired and wireless networks and the Internet

A VPN can be managed by operating systems, routers, or third-party software such as OpenVPN (*openvpn.net*). A VPN connection is a virtual connection, which means you are really setting up the tunnel over an existing connection to the Internet. When creating a VPN connection on a personal computer, always follow directions given by the network administrator who set up the VPN. The company website might provide VPN client software to download and install on your computer.

Here are the general steps to use Windows to connect to a VPN:

1. In the Network and Sharing Center (refer back to Figure 7-22), click **Set up a new connection or network**. Then select **Connect to a workplace - Set up a dial-up or VPN connection to your workplace** (refer back to Figure 7-31) and click **Next**.

2. In the Connect to a Workplace box, click **Use my Internet connection (VPN)**. In the next box, enter the IP
address or domain name of the network (see Figure 7-35). Your network administrator can provide this
information. Name the VPN connection and click **Create**.

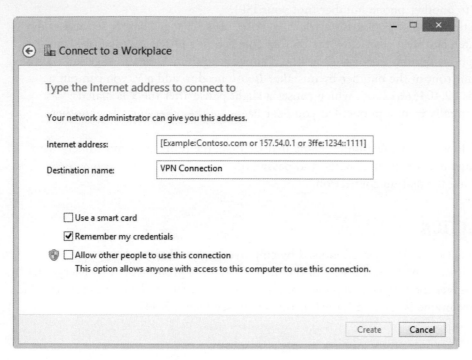

Figure 7-35 Enter logon information to the VPN network

> **◇ OS Differences** Windows 8 requires you to enter your user name and password at the time you connect to a VPN.
> Windows 7 gives you the option to enter this information when you set up the VPN or as you connect to it.

Whenever you want to use the VPN connection, click the Network icon in the taskbar. In the list of
available networks, click the **VPN connection** and click **Connect**. Enter your user name and password
(for Windows 8, see Figure 7-36) and click **OK**. Your user name and password are likely to be the network
ID and password you use to connect to the Windows domain on the corporate network.

Figure 7-36 Enter your user name and password to connect to your VPN

After the connection is made, you can use your browser to access the corporate secured intranet websites or other resources. The resources you can access depend on the permissions assigned the user account.

Problems connecting to a VPN can be caused by the wrong authentication protocols used when passing the user name and password to the VPN. To configure these settings, in the Network and Sharing Center, click **Change adapter settings**. In the Network Connections window, right-click **VPN Connection** and click **Properties**. In the Properties box, select the **Security** tab (see Figure 7-37). Here you can select the authentication protocols given to you by the network administrator.

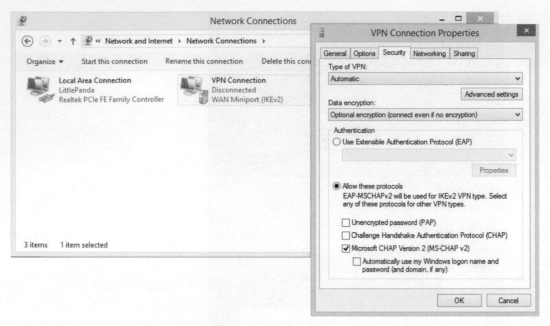

Figure 7-37 Select the VPN's authentication protocol

Now let's turn our attention to how to configure TCP/IP settings for a network connection, including dynamic, static, and alternate address configurations.

DYNAMIC AND STATIC IP CONFIGURATIONS

By default, Windows assumes dynamic IP addressing and automatically configures the network connection. However, some networks use static IP addresses.

To configure dynamic and static IP addresses, follow these steps:

1. Open the **Network Connections** window. Right-click the network connection and click **Properties**. In the Properties box, click the **Networking** tab, which is the middle box shown in Figure 7-38 for the Local Area Connection (Ethernet). Select **Internet Protocol Version 4 (TCP/IPv4)** and click **Properties**. The TCP/IPv4 Properties box appears (see the right side of Figure 7-38).

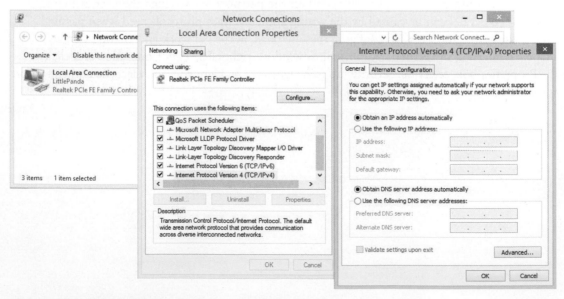

Figure 7-38 Configure TCP/IPv4 for static or dynamic addressing

2. By default, dynamic IP addressing is used, which selects *Obtain an IP address automatically* and *Obtain DNS server address automatically*. To change the settings to static IP addressing, select **Use the following IP address**. Then enter the IP address, subnet mask, and default gateway. (A default gateway is the gateway a computer uses to access another network if it does not have a better option.)

3. If you have been given the IP addresses of DNS servers, select **Use the following DNS server addresses** and enter up to two IP addresses. If you have other DNS IP addresses, click **Advanced** and enter them on the **DNS** tab of the Advanced TCP/IP Settings box.

> **Notes** Notice in Figure 7-38 that you can select Internet Protocol Version 6 (TCP/IPv6) and click Properties to change IPv6 properties, including static and dynamic address configuration.
> You can also uncheck Internet Protocol Version 6 (TCP/IPv6) to disable it. For most situations, you need to leave it enabled. A bug in Windows 7 might prevent you from joining a homegroup if IPv6 is disabled.

ALTERNATE IP ADDRESS CONFIGURATION

A+
220-902
1.6

Suppose an employee with a laptop often travels, and her work network uses static IP addressing, and, as you know, most public networks use dynamic IP addressing. How do you configure her computer's TCP/IP settings? For travel, you would configure the computer to use dynamic IP addressing for public networks. However, when the computer attempts to connect to the corporate network, the computer won't be able to find a DHCP server to get an IP address, subnet mask, default gateway, and DNS server addresses, and it will default to an Automatic Private IP Address (APIPA) and won't have the information it needs to connect to the network or Internet. The solution is to create an alternate configuration that the computer will use if it cannot find a DHCP server.

To create an alternate configuration, on the TCP/IPv4 Properties box shown in Figure 7-38, click the **Alternate Configuration** tab. By default, the alternate configuration is Automatic private IP address. See Figure 7-39. Select **User configured**. Then enter a static IP address, subnet mask, default gateway, and DNS server addresses for the alternate configuration to be used on the company network. Click **OK** and close all boxes.

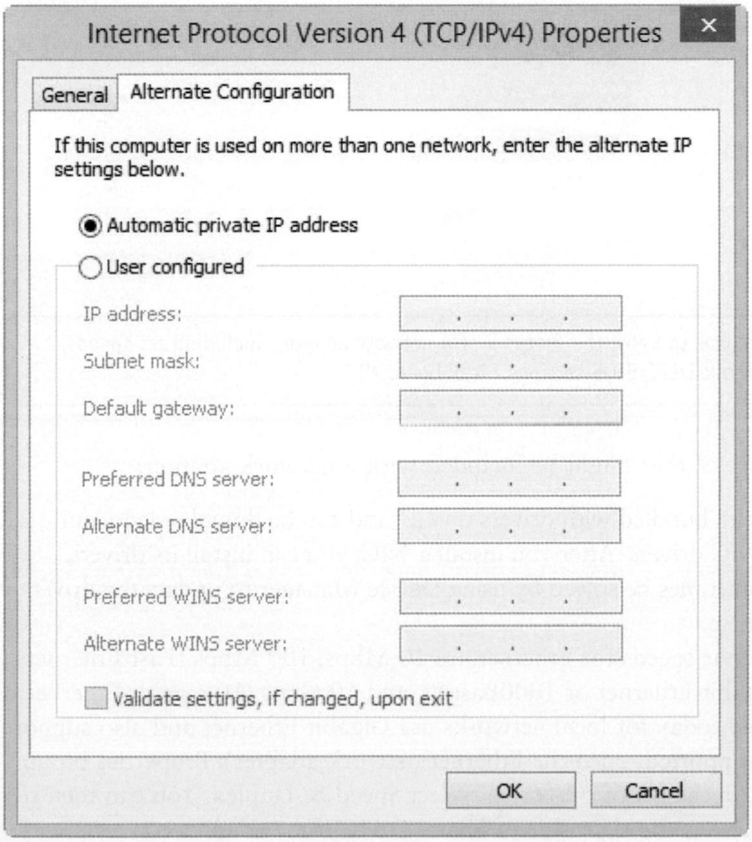

Figure 7-39 Create an alternate static IP address configuration

> ★ A+ Exam Tip   The A+ 220-902 exam expects you to know how to configure an alternate IP address, including setting the static IP address, subnet mask, DNS addresses, and gateway address.

MANAGE NETWORK ADAPTERS

A+
220-902
1.6

A computer makes a direct connection to a local wired network by way of a network adapter, which might be a network port embedded on the motherboard or a network interface card (NIC) designed for installation in an expansion slot on the motherboard (refer back to Figure 7-3). In addition, the adapter might also be an external device plugged into a USB port (see Figure 7-40). The wired network adapter provides a network port. A network adapter is often called a NIC, even when it's not really a card but a USB device or a network port embedded on the motherboard, which can be called an onboard NIC.

Figure 7-40   USB device provides an Ethernet port

> ★ A+ Exam Tip   The A+ 220-902 exam expects you to know the features of a network adapter, including its speeds, half duplex, full duplex, Wake-on-LAN, QoS, and about UEFI/BIOS settings for onboard NICs.

Here are the features you need to be aware of that might be included with a network adapter:

▲ *The drivers a NIC uses.* A NIC usually comes bundled with drivers on CD and can be downloaded from the web. Windows has several embedded NIC drivers. After you install a NIC, you can install its drivers. Problems with the network adapter can sometimes be solved by using Device Manager to update the drivers or uninstall the drivers and then reinstall them.

▲ *Ethernet speeds.* For wired networks, the four speeds for Ethernet are 10 Mbps, 100 Mbps (Fast Ethernet; technical name is 100BaseT), 1 Gbps (Gigabit Ethernet or 1000BaseT), and 10 Gbps (10-gigabit Ethernet or 10GBaseT). Most network adapters sold today for local networks use Gigabit Ethernet and also support the two slower speeds. To see the speeds supported, open the Ethernet network adapter's Properties box in Device Manager. Select the Advanced tab. In the list of properties, select Speed & Duplex. You can then see available speeds in the Value dropdown list (see the right side of Figure 7-41). If the adapter connects with slower network devices on the network, the adapter works at the slower speed. Notice in the dropdown list choices for half duplex or full duplex. Full duplex sends and receives transmissions at the same time. Half duplex works in only one direction at a time. Select Auto Negotiation for Windows to use the best possible speed and duplex.

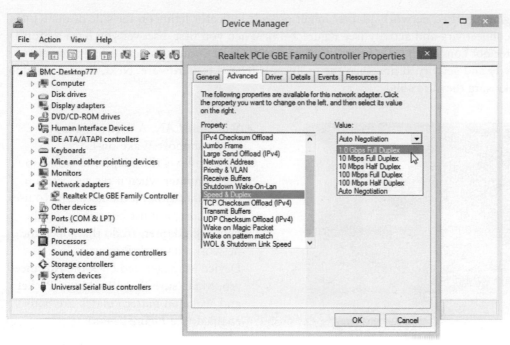

Figure 7-41 Set the speed and duplex for the network adapter

> **Notes** The speed of a network depends on the speed of each device on the network and how well a router manages that traffic. Routers, switches, and network adapters currently run at three speeds: Gigabit Ethernet (1000 Mbps or 1 Gbps), Fast Ethernet (100 Mbps), or Ethernet (10 Mbps). If you want your entire network to run at the fastest speed, make sure all your devices are rated for Gigabit Ethernet.

▲ *MAC address.* Every network adapter (wired or wireless) has a 48-bit (6-byte) identification number, called the MAC address or physical address, hard-coded on the card by its manufacturer that is unique for that adapter, and this number is used to identify the adapter on the network. An example of a MAC address is 00-0C-6E-4E-AB-A5. Most likely, the MAC address is printed on the device. You can also have Windows tell you the MAC address by entering the **ipconfig /all** command in a command prompt window (see Figure 7-42).

Figure 7-42 Use the ipconfig /all command to show the MAC address of a network adapter

▲ *Status indicator lights.* A wired network adapter might provide indicator lights on the side of the RJ-45 port that indicate connectivity and activity (see Figure 7-43). When you first discover you have a problem with a computer not connecting to a network, be sure to check the status indicator lights to verify you have connectivity and activity. If not, then the problem is related to hardware. Next, check the cable connections to make sure they are solid.

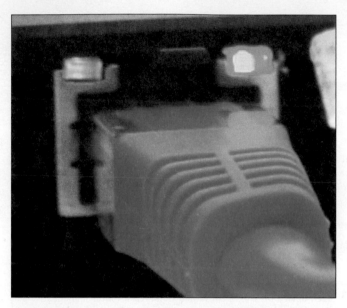

Figure 7-43   Status indicator lights for the onboard network port

▲ *Wake-on-LAN.* A network adapter might support Wake-on-LAN, which allows the adapter to wake up the computer when it receives certain communication on the network. To use the feature, it must be enabled on the network adapter. To do that, open the network adapter's Properties box in Device Manager and click the **Advanced** tab. Make sure **Wake on Magic Packet** and **Wake on pattern match** are both enabled (see Figure 7-44a).

> ✎ **Notes** Some network adapters provide a Power Management tab in the Properties box. To use the Power Management tab to enable Wake-on-LAN, check **Allow this device to wake the computer** (see Figure 7-44b).

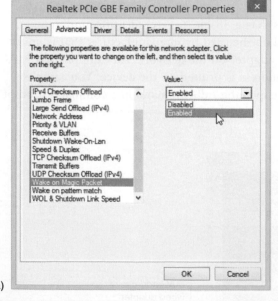

(a)

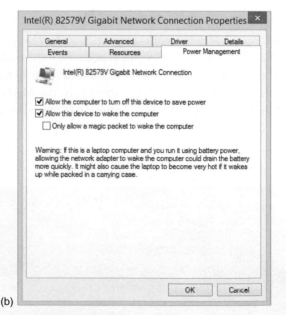

(b)

Figure 7-44   Enable Wake-on-LAN (a) using the Advanced tab, or (b) using the Power Management tab of the network adapter Properties box

For an onboard NIC, you must also enable Wake-on-LAN in UEFI/BIOS setup. Reboot the computer and enter UEFI/BIOS setup and look for the option on a power-management screen in UEFI/BIOS setup. Figure 7-45 shows the BIOS screen for one onboard NIC. It is not recommended that you enable Wake-on-LAN for a wireless network adapter.

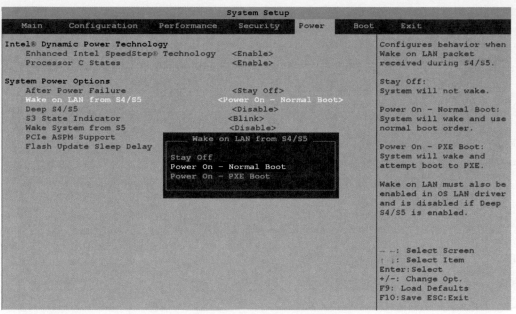

Source: Intel

Figure 7-45 Use the Power screen in the BIOS setup to enable Wake on LAN

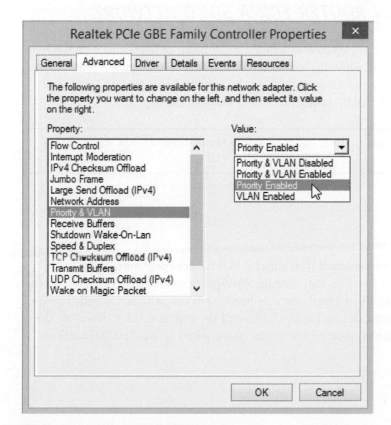

Figure 7-46 Select Priority Enabled to allow the network adapter to support QoS on the network

▲ *Quality of Service (QoS).* Another feature of a network adapter is the ability to control which applications have priority on the network. The feature must be enabled and configured on the router and also enabled on the network adapters and configured in Windows for every computer on the network using the high-priority applications. To enable Quality of Service (QoS) for a NIC, open the network adapter Properties box in Device Manager. On the Advanced tab, make sure **Priority Enabled** is selected, as shown in Figure 7-46. (If the option is not listed, the adapter does not support QoS.) Later in this chapter, you learn how to configure a router to use QoS. To configure an application to use QoS, you can use Group Policy in professional and business editions of Windows. How to use Group Policy is covered in the chapter, "Windows Resources on a Network."

7

Hands-On | Project 7-3   Investigate TCP/IP Settings

**A+
220-902
1.6**

Using a computer connected to a network, answer these questions:

1. What is the hardware device used to make this connection (network card, onboard port, wireless)? List the device's name as Windows sees it in the Device Manager window.

2. What is the MAC address of the wired or wireless network adapter? What command or window did you use to get your answer?

3. For a wireless connection, is the network secured? If so, what is the security type? What is the encryption type?

4. What is the IPv4 address of the network connection?

5. Are your TCP/IP version 4 settings using static or dynamic IP addressing?

6. What is the IPv6 address of your network connection?

7. Disable and enable your network connection. Now what is your IPv4 address?

SETTING UP A MULTIFUNCTION ROUTER FOR A SOHO NETWORK

**A+
220-902
3.2, 3.7**

An IT support technician is likely to be called on to set up a small office or home office (SOHO) network. As part of setting up a small network, you need to know how to configure a multipurpose router to stand between the network and the Internet. You also need to know how to set up and secure a wireless access point. Most SOHO routers are also a wireless access point.

> ★ **A+ Exam Tip**   The A+ 220-902 exam expects you to be able to install, configure, and secure a SOHO wired and wireless router.

FUNCTIONS OF A SOHO ROUTER

Routers can range from small ones designed to manage a SOHO network connecting to an ISP (costing around $75 to $200) to those that manage multiple networks and extensive traffic (costing several thousand dollars). On a small office or home network, a router stands between the ISP network and the local network (see Figure 7-47), and the router is the gateway to the Internet. Note in the figure that computers can connect to the router using wired or wireless connections.

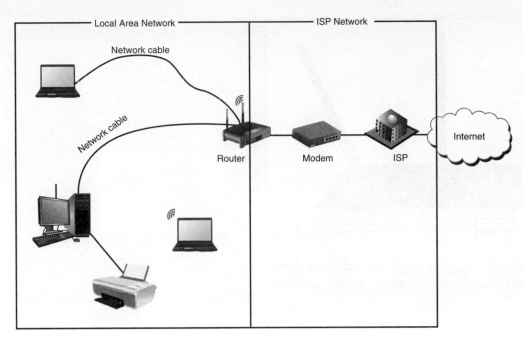

Figure 7-47 A router stands between a local network and the ISP network and manages traffic between them

A typical SOHO router is usually several devices in one:

◢ *Function 1:* As a router, it stands between two networks, the ISP network and the local network, and routes traffic between the two networks.

◢ *Function 2:* As a switch, it manages several network ports that can be connected to wired computers or to a switch that provides more ports for more computers.

◢ *Function 3:* As a DHCP server, it can provide IP addresses to networked computers.

◢ *Function 4:* As a wireless access point (WAP), it enables a wireless computer to connect to the network. This wireless connection can be secured using wireless security features.

◢ *Function 5:* As a firewall, it blocks unwanted traffic initiated from the Internet and can restrict Internet access for local computers behind the firewall. Restrictions on local computers can apply to days of the week, time of day, keywords used, or certain websites. It can limit network and Internet access to only specified computers, based on their MAC addresses. It also provides Network Address Translation (NAT) so that computers on the LAN can use private or link-local IP addresses.

◢ *Function 6:* As an FTP server, you can connect an external hard drive to the router, and the FTP firmware on the router can be used to share files with network users.

An example of a multifunction router is the Nighthawk AC1900 by NETGEAR shown in Figures 7-48 and 7-49. It has one Internet port for the broadband modem (cable modem or DSL modem) and four ports for computers on the network. The USB port can be used to plug in a USB external hard drive for use by any computer on the network. The router is also a wireless access point having multiple antennas to increase speed and range.

Source: Amazon.com

Figure 7-48 NETGEAR Nighthawk AC1900 Dual band Wi-Fi Gigabit router

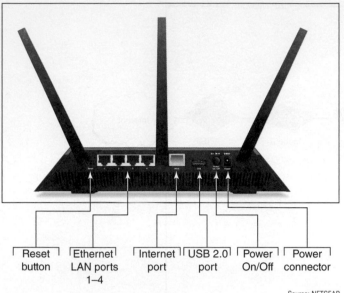

Reset | Ethernet | Internet | USB 2.0 | Power | Power
button | LAN ports | port | port | On/Off | connector
| 1–4 | | | |

Source: NETGEAR

Figure 7-49 Connections and ports on the back of the NETGEAR router

INSTALL AND CONFIGURE A ROUTER ON THE LOCAL NETWORK

A+
220-902
3.2, 3.7

When deciding where to physically place a router, consider the physical security of the router and, as a wireless access point, make sure the router is centrally located to create the best Wi-Fi hotspot for users. For physical security, don't place the router in a public location in a small business, such as the lobby. For best security, place the router behind a locked door accessible only to authorized personnel in a location with access to network cabling. The indoor range for a Wi-Fi hotspot is up to 70 meters; the range is affected by many factors, including interference from walls, furniture, electrical equipment, and other nearby hotspots. For the best Wi-Fi strength, position your router or a stand-alone wireless access point in the center of where you want your hotspot and know that a higher position (near the ceiling) works better than a lower position (on the floor).

> **📝 Notes** Some wireless access points are plenum rated, meaning that, according to fire codes, they can be installed in the plenum area between floors in a building or above a suspended ceiling. For these types of installation, network technicians are careful to follow local fire codes and must take into account how the device might affect airflow in the plenum.

For routers that have external antennas, raise the antennas to vertical positions. Plug in the router and connect network cables to the local network. Connect the network cable from the ISP modem or other device to the uplink port on the router.

To configure a router for the first time or change its configuration, always follow the directions of the manufacturer rather than the general directions given here. You can use any computer on the network that uses a wired connection (it doesn't matter which one) to configure the firmware on the router. You'll need the IP address of the router and the default user name and password to the router setup. To find this information, look in the router documentation or search online for your model and brand of router.

Here are the general steps for one router, the Nighthawk AC1900 by NETGEAR, although the setup screens for your router may be different:

1. Open your browser and enter the IP address of the router in the address box. In our example, the address is 192.168.1.1. The Windows Security box appears (see Figure 7-50). For our router, the default user name and password is **admin**, although yours might be different.

Figure 7-50 Enter the user name and password to the router firmware utility

2. The main setup page of the router firmware appears in your browser window. Figure 7-51 shows the main page for a router that has already been configured. Notice the BASIC tab is selected. Most of the settings you'll need are on the ADVANCED tab. Begin by poking around to see what's available and to find the setting you need. If you make changes, be sure to save your changes. When finished, click **Logout** and close the browser window.

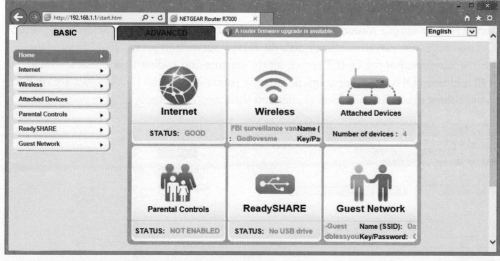

Source: NETGEAR

Figure 7-51 Main screen for router firmware setup

Following are some changes that you might need to make to the router's configuration. The first setting should always be done.

CHANGE THE ROUTER PASSWORD

It's extremely important to protect access to your network and prevent others from hijacking your router. If you have not already done so, change the default password to your router firmware. For our router, click the **ADVANCED** tab, click **Administration**, and click **Set Password** (see Figure 7-52). Change the password and click **Apply**. If the firmware offers the option, disable the ability to configure the router from over the wireless network. Know that this password to configure the router firmware is different from the password needed to access the router's wireless network.

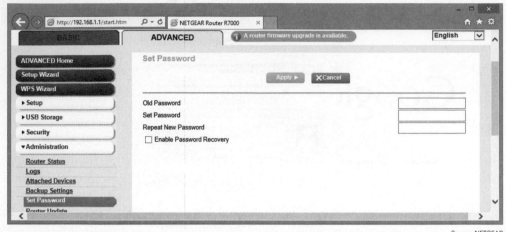

Source: NETGEAR

Figure 7-52   Change the router firmware password

⚡ **Caution**   Changing the router password is especially important if the router is a wireless router. Unless you have disabled or secured the wireless access point, anyone outside your building can use your wireless network. If they guess the default password to the router, they can change the password to hijack your router. Also, your wireless network can be used for criminal activity. When you first install a router, before you do anything else, change your router password and disable the wireless network until you have time to set up and test the wireless security. And, to give even more security, change the default user name to another user name if the router utility allows that option.

CONFIGURE THE DHCP SERVER

To configure the DHCP server for our sample router, click the **ADVANCED** tab and then **LAN Setup** in the Setup group (see Figure 7-53). On this page, you can enable or disable the DHCP server and set the IP address of the router and subnet mask for the network. For the DHCP server, set the starting and ending IP addresses, which determines the number of IP addresses DHCP can serve up. Be sure the router and all the IP addresses are on the same subnet, according to the subnet mask. After making changes on this page, click **Apply** to save your changes.

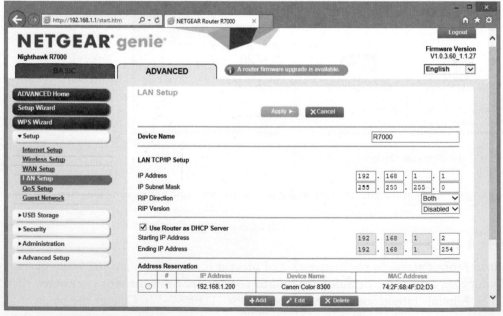

Source: NETGEAR

Figure 7-53   Configure the DHCP server in the router firmware

ASSIGN STATIC IP ADDRESSES

A computer or network printer might require a static IP address, which is called address reservation. For example, when a computer is running a web server on the local network, it needs a static IP address so that other computers on the network that need access to this intranet website can find the web server. A network printer also needs a static IP address so computers will always be able to find the printer. Do the following:

1. To identify the computer or printer, you'll need its MAC address. When the client is connected to the network, on the ADVANCED tab, click **Attached Devices** in the Administration group (see Figure 7-54). Copy the MAC address (select it and press **CTRL+C**) or write it down.

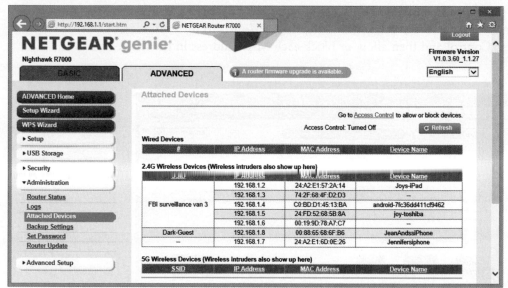

Source: NETGEAR

Figure 7-54 View the MAC addresses of devices connected to the network

2. To assign a static IP address to the client, on the LAN Setup page shown in Figure 7-53, click **Add** under **Address Reservation**. In the IP address field, enter the IP address to assign to the computer or printer. Be sure to use an IP address in the LAN's subnet, such as 192.168.1.200 in our example. Select the MAC address from the list of attached devices or copy or type the MAC address in the field. Click **Apply** to save your changes. In Figure 7-55, a Canon network printer is set to receive the IP address 192.168.1.200 each time it connects to the network.

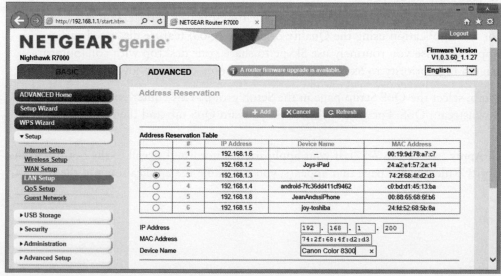

Source: NETGEAR

Figure 7-55 Use address reservation to assign a static IP address to a computer or other device

> ✎ **Notes** If you are running a web server on the Internet, you will need a public IP address for your router and a static private IP address for the web server. For this situation, you can lease a public IP address from your ISP at an additional cost. You will also need to enable port forwarding to the server, which is discussed later in this chapter.

MAC ADDRESS FILTERING

MAC address filtering allows you to control access to your network to only certain computers or devices. If a MAC address is not entered in a table of MAC addresses, the computer is not allowed to connect to the network. For our sample router, the MAC address table can be viewed and edited on the ADVANCED tab on the Access Control page in the Security group (see Figure 7-56). To turn on Access Control, check the box **Turn on Access Control** and then allow or block each MAC address in the table.

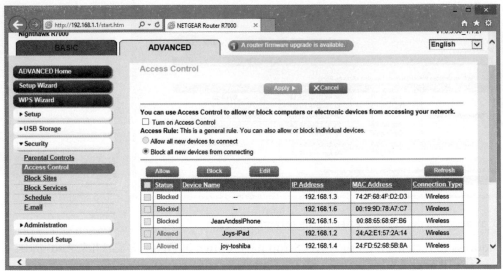

Source: NETGEAR

Figure 7-56   Use MAC address filtering to allow and block devices on the network

IMPROVE QoS FOR AN APPLICATION

As you use your network and notice that one application is not getting the best service, you can improve network performance for this application using the Quality of Service (QoS) feature discussed earlier in this chapter. For example, suppose you routinely use Skype to share your desktop with collaborators over the Internet. To assign a high priority to Skype for our sample router, do the following:

1. On the ADVANCED tab, select the **QoS Setup** page in the Setup group. This router configures both upstream QoS and downstream QoS. For Skype, click the **Upstream QoS** tab and then click **Setup QoS rule.**

2. Select **Skype** and click **Apply** (see Figure 7-57). If your application is not listed, scroll to the bottom of the list and click **Add Priority Rule.** On the page that appears, you can name the application and the port(s) it uses.

Source: NETGEAR

Figure 7-57   Apply a QoS rule to the selected app

UNIVERSAL PLUG AND PLAY

Universal Plug and Play (UPnP) helps computers on the local network automatically discover and communicate with services provided by other computers on the local network. Enable UPnP if computers on the network use applications, such as messaging, gaming, or Windows Remote Assistance, which run on other local computers and there is a problem establishing communication. Basically, a computer can use the router to advertise its service and automatically communicate with other computers on the network. UPnP is considered a security risk because shields between computers are dropped, which hackers might exploit. Therefore, use UPnP with caution.

For our sample router, UPnP is enabled on the UPnP page in the Advanced Setup group on the ADVANCED tab (see Figure 7-58). Any computers and their ports that are currently using UPnP are listed.

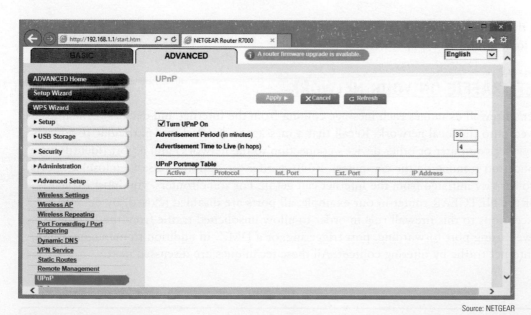

Source: NETGEAR

Figure 7-58   Turn on UPnP

UPDATE ROUTER FIRMWARE

As part of maintaining a router, know the router manufacturers often release updates to the router firmware. The router setup utility can be used to download and apply these updates. For our sample router, when you click **A router firmware update is available** on any of the setup screens (for example, see Figure 7-58), the Firmware Upgrade Assistant page appears (see Figure 7-59). Use this page to perform the upgrade.

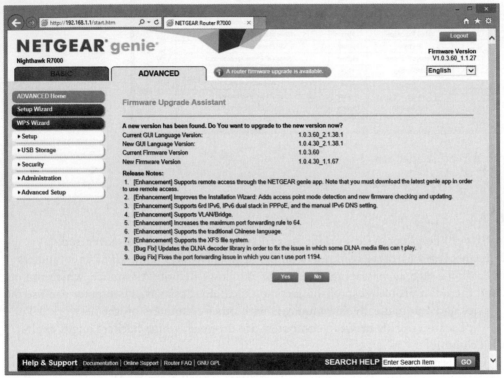

Source: NETGEAR

Figure 7-59   Update router firmware

Now let's look at the concepts and steps to allow certain activity initiated from the Internet past your firewall. Then we'll look at how to set up a wireless network.

LIMIT INTERNET TRAFFIC ON YOUR NETWORK

A+
220-902
3.2, 3.7 A router's firewall examines each message coming from the Internet and decides if the message is allowed onto the local network. Recall that a message is directed to a particular IP address (identifying a computer or other device's connection to the network) and a port (identifying the application running on the computer). Routers offer the option to disable (close) all ports, which means that no activity initiated from the Internet can get in. For some routers, you must explicitly disable all ports. For the NETGEAR router in our example, all ports are disabled (closed) by default. You must specify exceptions to this firewall rule in order to allow unsolicited traffic from the Internet. Exceptions are allowed using port forwarding, port triggering, or a DMZ. In addition to managing ports, you can also limit Internet traffic by filtering content. All these techniques are discussed next.

> ⭐ **A+ Exam Tip**   The A+ 220-902 exam expects you to know how to implement port forwarding, port triggering, and a DMZ.

PORT FORWARDING

Suppose you're hosting an Internet game or website or want to use Remote Desktop to access your home computer from the Internet. In these situations, you need to enable (open) certain ports to certain computers so that activity initiated from the Internet can get past your firewall. This technique, called port forwarding or port mapping, means that when the firewall receives a request for communication from the Internet to the specific computer and port, the request will be allowed and forwarded to that computer on the network. The computer is defined to the router by its static IP address. For example, in Figure 7-60a, port 80 is open and requests to port 80 are forwarded to the web server that is listening at that port. This one computer on the network is the only one allowed to receive requests at port 80.

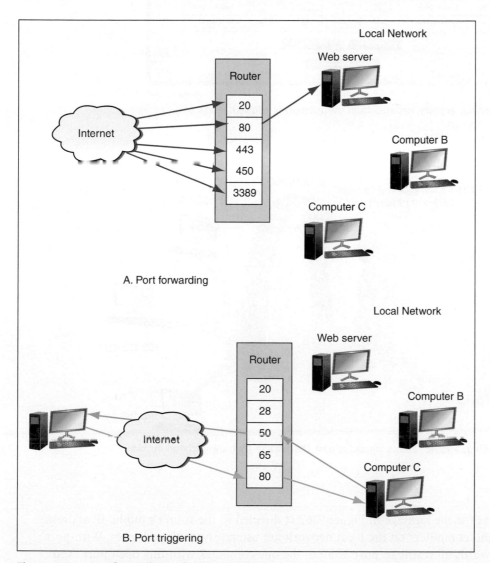

Figure 7-60   Port forwarding and port triggering

To configure port forwarding for our sample router, on the ADVANCED tab, click **Port Forwarding/ Port Triggering** in the Advanced Setup group (see Figure 7-61) and verify **Port Forwarding** is selected. Select the **Service Name** and enter the static IP address of the computer providing the service in the Server IP Address field and click **Add**. Notice in the figure that the Remote Desktop application outside the network can use port forwarding to communicate with the computer whose IP address is 192.168.1.90 using port 3389. The situation is illustrated in Figure 7-62. This computer is set to support the Remote Desktop server application. You will learn to use Remote Desktop in the chapter, "Windows Resources on a Network."

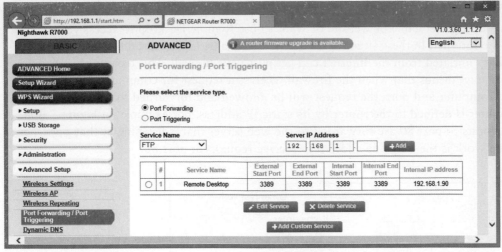

Source: NETGEAR

Figure 7-61 Using port forwarding, activity initiated from the Internet is allowed access to a computer on the network

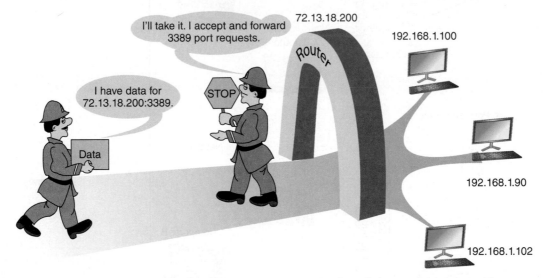

Figure 7-62 With port forwarding, a router allows messages past the firewall that are initiated outside the network

Also notice the IP address for the message in Figure 7-62 is directed to the router's public IP address. The router is using NAT and computers on the local network are using private IP addresses. With port forwarding, the router forwards all traffic to port 3389 to the one computer with this open port even though traffic is directed to the router's public IP address. For this reason, port forwarding is sometimes called Destination Network Address Translation (DNAT).

> **✎ Notes** By the way, if you want to use a domain name rather than an IP address to access a computer on your network from the Internet, you'll need to purchase the domain name and register it in the Internet name space to associate it with your static IP address assigned by your ISP. Several websites on the Internet let you do both; one site is by Network Solutions at *networksolutions.com*.

PORT TRIGGERING

Port triggering opens a port when a computer on the network initiates communication through another port, and is often used with Internet gaming. For example, in Figure 7-60b, Computer C sends a message to port 50 to a computer on the Internet. The router is configured to open port 80 for communication from this remote computer. Port 80 is closed until this trigger occurs. Port triggering does not require a static IP address for the computer inside the network, and any computer can initiate port triggering. The router will leave port 80 open for a time. If no more data is received from port 50, then it closes port 80.

To configure port triggering on our sample router, select **Port Triggering** on the page shown in Figure 7-61. Click **Add Service**. In the Port Triggering page that appears (see Figure 7-63), type a descriptive name for the service. For Service User, selecting **Any** allows any computer to use the service or you can enter a specific IP address of a remote computer. Select the Service Type (TCP, UDP, or both) and enter the triggering port (the outbound traffic port that will open the inbound ports). Under Inbound Connection, select the Connection Type (TCP, UDP, or both) and the range of ports that will be open for inbound traffic. This information about types of service and ports should be available from the documentation for the application you are using.

7

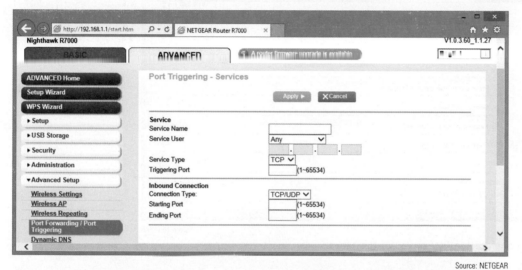

Source: NETGEAR

Figure 7-63   For port triggering, identify the service, the triggering port, and the ports to open

Here are some tips to keep in mind when using port forwarding or port triggering.

- You must lease a static IP address for your router from your ISP so that people on the Internet can find you. Most ISPs will provide you a static IP address for an additional monthly fee.
- For port forwarding to work, the computer on your network must have a static IP address so that the router knows where to send the communication.
- If the computer using port triggering stops sending data, the router might close the triggered port before communication is complete. Also, if two computers on the network attempt to trigger the same port, the router will not allow data to pass to either computer.
- Using port forwarding, your computer and network are more vulnerable because you are allowing external users directly into your private network. For better security, turn on port forwarding only when you know it's being used.

DMZ

A DMZ (demilitarized zone) in networking is a computer or network that is not protected by a firewall or has limited protection. You can drop all your shields protecting a computer by putting it in a DMZ and the firewall no longer protects it. If you are having problems getting port forwarding or port triggering to work, putting a computer in a DMZ can free it to receive any communication from the Internet. All unsolicited traffic from the Internet that the router would normally drop is forwarded to the computer designated as the DMZ server.

> ⚡ **Caution**   If a DMZ computer is compromised, it can be used to attack other computers on the network. Use it only as a last resort when you cannot get port forwarding or port triggering to work. It goes without saying to not leave the DMZ enabled unless you are using it.

To set up a DMZ server for our sample router, on the ADVANCED tab, select **WAN Setup** in the Setup group (see Figure 7-64). Check **Default DMZ Server** and enter the static IP address of the computer.

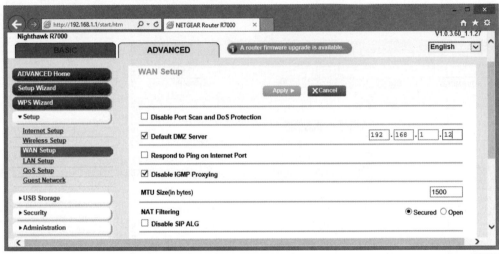

Source: NETGEAR

Figure 7-64   Set up an unprotected DMZ server for the network

CONTENT FILTERING AND PARENTAL CONTROLS

Routers normally provide a way for employers or parents to limit the content that computers on the local network can access on the Internet. Filtering can apply to specific computers, users, websites, categories of websites, keywords, services, time of day, and day of week. Filters can apply to black lists (lists what cannot be accessed) or white lists (lists what can be accessed).

For our sample router, content filtering and parental controls are managed in the Security group on the ADVANCED tab. Here are the options:

▲ The Parental Controls page provides access to the Live Parental Controls application and website at *www.netgear.com/lpc* where parents can manage content allowed from the Internet and monitor websites and content accessed.

▲ The Block Sites page (see Figure 7-65) allows you to enter keywords or websites to block. Notice you can also specify a trusted IP address of a computer on the network that is allowed access to this content.

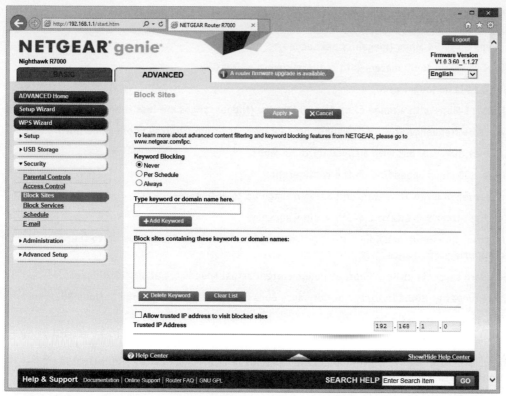

Source: NETGEAR

Figure 7-65 Block sites by keyword or domain names

◢ The Block Services page can block services on the Internet. For example, you can block Internet gaming services or email services or allow the service based on a schedule. You will need to know the ports these services use. You can also specify the IP addresses of computers to which the block applies.

◢ The Schedule page allows you to specify the schedule of time and day a blocked service can be used.

◢ The E-mail page gives you the option for the router to email to you a log of router activities.

Now let's turn our attention to configuring a wireless access point provided by a router.

SET UP A WIRELESS NETWORK

A+
220-902
3.2, 3.7

A wireless network is created by a wireless access point (WAP). The standards for a local wireless network are called Wi-Fi (Wireless Fidelity), and their technical name is IEEE 802.11. The IEEE 802.11 standards, collectively known as the 802.11 a/b/g/n/ac standards, have evolved over the years and are summarized in Table 7-5.

Wi-Fi Standard	Speeds, Distances, and Frequencies
IEEE 802.11a	◢ Speeds up to 54 Mbps (megabits per second). ◢ Short range up to 50 meters with radio frequency of 5.0 GHz. ◢ 802.11a is no longer used.
IEEE 802.11b	◢ Up to 11 Mbps with a range of up to 100 meters. (Indoor ranges are less than outdoor ranges.) ◢ The radio frequency of 2.4 GHz experiences interference from cordless phones and microwaves.
IEEE 802.11g	◢ Same as 802.11b, but with a speed up to 54 Mbps.
IEEE 802.11n	◢ Up to 600 Mbps depending on the configuration. ◢ Indoor range up to 70 meters and outdoor range up to 250 meters. ◢ Can use either 5.0-GHz or 2.4-GHz radio frequency. ◢ Uses multiple input/multiple output (MIMO), which means a WAP can have up to four antennas to improve performance.
IEEE 802.11ac	◢ Standard supports up to 7 Gbps, although current actual speeds are about 1300 Mbps. ◢ Same ranges as 802.11n except performance does not weaken at long range as does 802.11n. ◢ Uses the 5.0-GHz radio frequency. ◢ Supports up to eight antennas. ◢ Supports beamforming, which detects the locations of connected devices and increases signal strength in that direction.

Table 7-5   Older and current Wi-Fi standards

Wireless computers and other devices on the wireless LAN (WLAN) must support the latest wireless standard for it to be used. If not, the connection uses the latest standard both the WAP and client support. Figure 7-66 shows a wireless adapter that has two antennas and supports the 802.11n standard. Most new adapters, wireless computers, and mobile devices support 802.11ac and are backward compatible with older standards.

Figure 7-66   Wireless network adapter with two antennas supports 802.11b/g/n Wi-Fi standards

Now let's look at the various features and settings of a wireless access point and how to configure them.

✎ Notes When configuring your wireless access point, it's important you are connected to the router by way of a wired connection. If you change a wireless setting and you are connected wirelessly, your wireless connection will immediately be dropped and you cannot continue configuring the router until you connect again.

SECURITY KEY

The most common and effective method of securing a wireless network is to require a security key before a client can connect to the network. By default, a network that uses a security key encrypts data on the network. Use the router firmware to set the security key. For best security, enter a security key that is different from the password you use to the router utility.

✎ Notes To make the strongest passphrase or security key, use a random group of numbers, uppercase and lowercase letters, and, if allowed, at least one symbol. Also use at least eight characters in the passphrase.

7

For our sample router, the security key can be set on the ADVANCED tab, Wireless Setup page in the Setup group (see Figure 7-67) and is called the Password or Network Key. Click **Apply** to save your changes.

Source: NETGEAR

Figure 7-67 Configure the router's wireless access point

SET ENCRYPTION

When you set a security key, routers by default encrypt wireless transmissions, and you can change the encryption protocols used or disable encryption. (Encrypting transmissions slows down the network; disabling encryption can improve performance and might be appropriate when you are not concerned about transmissions being hacked.) The three main protocols for encryption for 802.11 wireless networks are:

▲ **WEP.** WEP (Wired Equivalent Privacy) is no longer considered secure because the key used for encryption is static (it doesn't change).
▲ **WPA.** WPA (Wi-Fi Protected Access), also called TKIP (Temporal Key Integrity Protocol) encryption, is stronger than WEP and was designed to replace it. With WPA encryption, encryption keys are constantly changing.
▲ **WPA2.** WPA2 (Wi-Fi Protected Access 2), also called the 802.11i standard, is the latest and best wireless encryption standard. It is based on the AES (Advanced Encryption Standard), which improved on the way TKIP generated encryption keys. All wireless devices sold today support the WPA2 standard.

To configure encryption for our sample router, first, notice in Figure 7-67 that this router supports two wireless frequencies: 2.4 GHz used by 802.11 b/g/n standards and 5 GHz used by 802.11 a/n/ac. The security key applies to either band, but each band can have its own encryption type. For the best security, set both bands to **WPA-PSK [TKIP] + WPA2-PSK [AES]** encryption. This setting means a wireless connection will use WPA2 encryption unless an older device does not support it, in which case the connection reverts to WPA encryption. Click **Apply** to save your changes.

CHANGE THE DEFAULT SSID AND DISABLE SSID BROADCASTING

The Service Set Identifier (SSID) is the name of a wireless network. When you look at Figure 7-67, you can see that each frequency band has its own SSID and you can change that name. Each band is its own wireless network, which the access point (router) connects to the local wired network. When you give each band its own SSID and connect a wireless computer to your network, you can select the band by selecting the appropriate SSID. If your computer supports 802.11ac, you would want to select the SSID for the 5-GHz band in order to get the faster speeds of the 802.11ac standard. If you selected the SSID for the 2.4-GHz band, the connection would revert to the slower 802.11n standard.

> ✎ **Notes** Notice in Figure 7-67 the option to select the mode a wireless network will use, which determines the speed of the wireless network. Recall the 802.11ac standard currently supports the speed of 1300 Mbps. If you select a slower mode for the 5-GHz band, such as 600 Mbps, in effect you are preventing the 802.11ac standard from being used on the network and connections will revert to the 802.11n standard that uses the 600-Mbps speed. For best results, use the fastest mode the band supports.

Also notice in Figure 7-67 the option to Enable SSID Broadcast. When you disable SSID broadcasting, the wireless network will appear as Unnamed or Unknown Network. When a client selects this network, you are given the opportunity to enter the SSID. If you don't enter the name correctly, you will not be able to connect. This security method is not considered strong security because software can be used to discover an SSID that is not broadcasted.

SELECT CHANNELS FOR THE WLAN

A channel is a specific radio frequency within a broader frequency. For example, two channels in the 5-GHz band are 5.180-GHz and 5.200-GHz channels. In the United States, eleven channels are available for wireless communication in the 5-GHz or 2.4-GHz bands. In North America, the 5-GHz band uses channels 36, 40, 44, and 48, and the 2.4-GHz band uses channels 1 through 14 (preferred nonoverlapping channels are 1, 6, and 11). For most networks, you can allow auto channel selection so that any channel in the frequency range (5-GHz or 2.4-GHz) will work. The device scans for the least-busy channel. However, if you are trying to solve a problem with interference from a nearby wireless network, you can set each network to a different channel and make the channels far apart to reduce interference. For example, for the 2.4-GHz band, set the network on one WAP to channel 1 and set the other WAP's network to channel 11.

RADIO POWER LEVELS

Some high-end access points allow you to adjust the radio power levels the wireless network can use. To reduce interference, limit the range of the network, or to save on electricity, reduce the power level.

WI-FI PROTECTED SETUP (WPS)

You also need to know about Wi-Fi Protected Setup (WPS), which is designed to make it easier for users to connect their computers to a wireless network when a hard-to-remember SSID and security key are used. WPS generates the SSID and security key using a random string of hard-to-guess letters and numbers. The SSID is not broadcasted, so both the SSID and security key must be entered to connect. Rather than having to enter these difficult strings, a user presses a button on a wireless computer or on the router or enters an eight-digit PIN assigned to the router (see Figure 7-68). All computers on the wireless network must support WPS for it to be used, and you must enable WPS on the router, as shown in the figure.

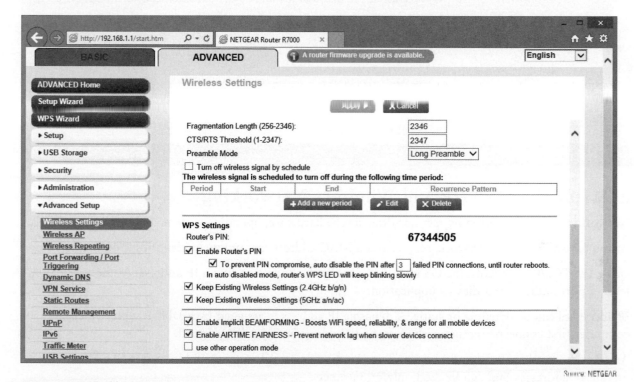

Figure 7-68 Enable WPS and decide how the router's PIN is used

WPS might be a security risk if it's not managed well. To improve WPS security, turn on auto disable so that WPS will disable after a few failed PIN entries. If routers don't have the auto disable feature, don't use WPS because an eight-digit PIN is easy to hack with repeated attempts. In addition, if the router has a WPS button to push, don't use WPS unless the router is in a secured physical location. For improved security, turn on WPS only when you are working with a user to connect to the wireless network and then turn it off.

★ **A+ Exam Tip** The A+ 220-902 exam expects you to know about installing and configuring a wireless network, including setting encryption, changing the default SSID and password, disabling SSID broadcasting, antenna and access point placements, radio power levels, and WPS.

Hands-On | Project 7-4 Research a Wireless LAN

A+
220-902
3.2, 3.7

Suppose you have a DSL connection to the Internet in your home and you want to connect two laptops and a desktop computer in a wireless network to the Internet. You need to purchase a multifunction wireless router like the one you learned to configure in this chapter. You also need a wireless adapter for the desktop computer. (The two laptops have built-in wireless networking.) Use the web to research the equipment needed to create the wireless LAN and answer the following:

1. Save or print two webpages showing two different multifunctional wireless routers. What are the brand, model, and price of each router?

2. Save or print two webpages showing two different wireless adapters a desktop computer can use to connect to the wireless network. Include one external device that uses a USB port and one internal device. What are the brand, model, and price of each device?

3. Which router and wireless adapter would you select for your home network? What is the total cost of both devices?

>> CHAPTER SUMMARY

Understanding TCP/IP and Windows Networking

▲ Networking communication happens at three levels: hardware, operating system, and application levels.

▲ At the hardware level, a network adapter has a MAC address that uniquely identifies it on the network.

▲ Using the TCP/IP protocols, the OS identifies a network connection by an IP address. At the application level, a port address identifies an application.

▲ IP addresses can be dynamic or static. A dynamic IP address is assigned by a DHCP server when the computer first connects to a network. A static IP address is manually assigned.

▲ An IP address using IPv4 has 32 bits, and an IP address using IPv6 has 128 bits. Some IP addresses are private IP addresses that can be used only on intranets.

▲ Using IPv4, a subnet mask determines the number of left most bits in an IP address that identify the local network. The remaining right most bits identify the host.

▲ Using IPv6, three types of IP addresses are a unicast address (used by a single node on a network), multicast address (used for one-to-many transmissions), and anycast address (used by routers).

▲ Types of unicast addresses are a global address (used on the Internet), a link-local address (used on a private network), and a unique local address (used on subnets in a large enterprise).

▲ A computer can be assigned a computer name (also called a host name), and a network can be assigned a domain name. A fully qualified domain name (FQDN) includes the computer name and the domain name. An FQDN can be used to find a computer on the Internet if this name is associated with an IP address kept by DNS servers.

▲ TCP/IP uses protocols at the application level (such as FTP, HTTP, and Telnet) and at the operating system level (such as TCP and UDP).

Connecting a Computer to a Network

◢ An IT support person needs to know how to configure TCP/IP settings and make a wired or wireless connection to an existing network.

◢ To connect to a wireless WAN or cellular network, you need a mobile broadband modem and a subscription to the cellular network. For some carriers, a SIM card is also required.

◢ A dial-up connection uses a telephone modem to make a connection to an ISP.

Setting Up a Multifunction Router for a SOHO Network

◢ A multifunction router for a small office/home office network might serve several functions, including a router, a switch, a DHCP server, a wireless access point, a firewall using NAT, and an FTP server.

◢ It's extremely important to change the password to configure your router as soon as you install it, especially if the router is also a wireless access point.

◢ To allow certain network traffic initiated on the Internet past your firewall, you can use port forwarding, port triggering, and a DMZ.

◢ To secure a wireless access point, you can require a security key, disable SSID broadcasting, and enable encryption (WPA2, WPA, or WEP). As with wired networks, you can also enable MAC address filtering.

7

>> KEY TERMS

For explanations of key terms, see the Glossary for this text.

802.11 a/b/g/n/ac
adapter address
address reservation
AES (Advanced
    Encryption Standard)
AFP (Apple Filing
    Protocol)
anycast address
AppleTalk
Automatic Private IP
    Address (APIPA)
beamforming
best-effort protocol
CDMA (Code Division
    Multiple Access)
channel
CIDR notation
CIFS (Common Internet
    File System)
client/server
computer name
connectionless protocol
connection-oriented
    protocol
default gateway
Destination Network
    Address Translation
    (DNAT)
DHCP (Dynamic Host
    Configuration Protocol)

DHCP client
DHCPv6 server
DMZ (demilitarized zone)
DNS (Domain Name
    System or Domain
    Name Service)
DNS client
DNS server
domain name
dynamic IP address
firewall
FTP (File Transfer Protocol)
FTP server
full duplex
fully qualified domain
    name (FQDN)
gateway
global address
global unicast address
GSM (Global
    System for Mobile
    Communications)
half duplex
hardware address
host name
HTTP (Hypertext Transfer
    Protocol)
HTTPS (HTTP secure)
IEEE 802.11ac

IEEE 802.11n
IMAP4 (Internet
    Message Access Protocol,
    version 4)
interface
interface ID
Internet Protocol
    version 4 (IPv4)
Internet Protocol
    version 6 (IPv6)
intranet
IP address
ipconfig
ISATAP
Lightweight Directory
    Access Protocol (LDAP)
link (local link)
link-local address
link-local unicast address
local area network (LAN)
Long Term Evolution (LTE)
loopback address
MAC (Media Access
    Control) address
MAC address filtering
multicast address
multiple input/multiple
    output (MIMO)
name resolution

NAT (Network Address
    Translation)
neighbors
NetBIOS
NetBIOS over TCP/IP
network adapter
network interface
    card (NIC)
node
octet
onboard NIC
OSI model
physical address
POP3 (Post Office
    Protocol, version 3)
port
port address
port forwarding
port mapping
port number
port triggering
private IP address
protocol
public IP address
Quality of Service (QoS)
Remote Desktop
    Protocol (RDP)
RJ-45
router

Secure FTP (SFTP)
Secure Shell (SSH)
Server Message
 Block (SMB)
Service Set Identifier
 (SSID)
SIM (Subscriber
 Identification
 Module) card
Simple Network
 Management
 Protocol (SNMP)
SMB2
SMTP (Simple Mail
 Transfer Protocol)

socket
static IP address
subnet
subnet ID
subnet mask
switch
TCP (Transmission
 Control Protocol)
TCP/IP (Transmission
 Control Protocol/Internet
 Protocol)
Telnet
Teredo
TKIP (Temporal Key
 Integrity Protocol)

UDP (User Datagram
 Protocol)
unicast address
unique local address
Universal Plug and
 Play (UPnP)
virtual private
 network (VPN)
Voice over LTE (VoLTE)
Wake-on-LAN
WEP (Wired Equivalent
 Privacy)
Wi-Fi (Wireless Fidelity)
Wi-Fi Protected
 Setup (WPS)

wireless access point (WAP)
wireless LAN (WLAN)
wireless wide area
 network (WWAN)
WPA (Wi-Fi Protected
 Access)
WPA2 (Wi-Fi Protected
 Access 2)

>> REVIEWING THE BASICS

1. How many bits are in a MAC address?

2. How many bits are in an IPv4 address? In an IPv6 address?

3. How does a client application identify a server application on another computer on the network?

4. What are IP addresses called that begin with 10, 172.16, or 192.168?

5. Describe the difference between public and private IPv4 addresses. If a network is using private IP addresses, how can the computers on that network access the Internet?

6. Why is it unlikely that you will find the IP address 192.168.250.10 on the Internet?

7. If no DHCP server is available when a computer configured for dynamic IP addressing connects to the network, what type of IPv4 address is assigned to the computer?

8. If a computer is found to have an IP address of 169.254.1.1, what can you assume about how it received that IP address?

9. What are the last 64 bits of an IPv6 address called? How are these bits used?

10. Name two tunneling protocols that are used for IPv6 packets to travel over an IPv4 network.

11. How is an IPv6 address used that begins with 2000::? That begins with FE80::?

12. How many bits are in the Subnet ID block? What are the values of these bits for a link-local IP address?

13. Which type of IPv6 address is used to create multiple subnets within a large organization?

14. What type of server serves up IP addresses to computers on a network?

15. Which TCP/IP protocol that manages packet delivery guarantees that delivery? Which protocol does not guarantee delivery, but is faster?

16. At what port does an SMTP email server listen to receive email from a client computer?

17. Which protocol(s) does a web server use when transmissions are encrypted for security?

18. What type of server resolves fully qualified domain names to IP addresses?

19. Which email protocol allows a client application to manage email stored on an email server?

20. What technology is used to present a public IP address to computers outside the LAN to handle requests to use the Internet from computers inside the LAN?

21. Which protocol is used when an application queries a database on a corporate network such as a database of printers?

22. What type of encryption protocol does Secure FTP (SFTP) use to secure FTP transmissions?

23. What two Windows applications use the RDP protocol and port 3389?

24. Which two versions of the 802.11 technologies can use multiple antennas at both the access point and the network adapter?

25. Which wireless encryption standard is stronger, WEP or WPA?

26. When securing a Wi-Fi wireless network, which is considered better security: to filter MAC addresses, use encryption, or not broadcast the SSID?

27. Would you expect WPS to be used when a wireless network is using strong security, weak security, or no security (as in a public hotspot)?

>> THINKING CRITICALLY

1. You have just installed a network adapter and have booted up the system, installing the drivers. You open File Explorer on a remote computer and don't see the computer on which you just installed the NIC. What is the first thing you check?

   a. Has TCP/IPv6 been enabled?

   b. Is the computer using dynamic or static IP addressing?

   c. Are the lights on the adapter functioning correctly?

   d. Has the computer been assigned a computer name?

2. Your boss asks you to transmit a small file that includes sensitive personnel data to a server on the network. The server is running a Telnet server and an FTP server. Why is it not a good idea to use Telnet to reach the remote computer?

   a. Telnet transmissions are not encrypted.

   b. Telnet is not reliable and the file might arrive corrupted.

   c. FTP is faster than Telnet.

   d. FTP running on the same computer as Telnet causes Telnet to not work.

3. You have just installed a SOHO router in a customer's home and the owner has called you saying his son is complaining that Internet gaming is too slow. His son is using a wireless connection to the network. Which possibilities should you consider in order to speed up the son's gaming experience? Select all that apply.

   a. Verify the wireless connection is using the fastest wireless standard the router supports.

   b. Disable encryption on the wireless network to speed up transmissions.

   c. Suggest the son use a wired Gigabit Ethernet connection to the network.

   d. Enable QoS for the gaming applications on the router and on the son's computer.

>> REAL PROBLEMS, REAL SOLUTIONS

REAL PROBLEM 7-1 Setting Up a Small Network

The simplest possible wired network is two computers connected together using a crossover cable. In a crossover cable, the send and receive wires are crossed so that one computer can send and the other computer receive on the same wire. At first glance, a crossover cable looks just like a regular network cable (also called a patch cable) except for the labeling (see Figure 7-69).

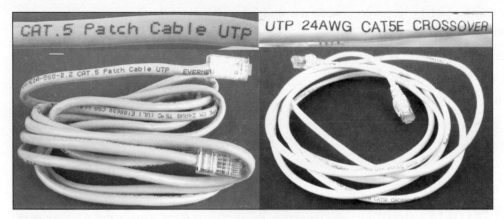

Figure 7-69   A patch cable and crossover cable look the same but are labeled differently

Do the following to set up and test the network:

1. Connect two computers using a crossover cable. Using the Network and Sharing Center, verify your network is up. What is the IPv4 address of Computer A? Of Computer B?

2. Join the two computers to the same homegroup. Then use File Explorer or Windows Explorer to view the files on the other computer shared with the homegroup.

3. Convert the TCP/IP configuration to static IP addressing. Assign a private IP address to each computer. Make sure the two computers are in the same subnet. What is the subnet mask? What is the IP address of Computer A? Of Computer B?

4. Verify you can still see files shared with the homegroup on each computer.

5. Assign a new IP address to each computer so they are not in the same subnet. What are the two IP addresses? Can you still see files shared with the homegroup on each computer?

6. Return the computers to the same subnet and verify each computer can find the other and its shared resources.

REAL PROBLEM 7-2 Using the Hosts File

The hosts file in the C:\Windows\System32\drivers\etc folder has no file extension and contains computer names and their associated IP addresses on the local network. An IT support technician can manually edit the hosts file when the association is needed for address resolution on the local network and a DNS server is not available on the local network.

> ✎ **Notes** For an entry in the hosts file to work, the remote computer must always use the same IP address. One way to accomplish this is to assign a static IP address to the computer. Alternately, if your DHCP server supports this feature, you can configure it to assign the same IP address to this computer each time it connects to the network.

Using your small network you set up in Real Problem 7-1, do the following to use the hosts file:

1. The ping command sends a request to a remote computer and the computer responds to verify communication. On Computer A, open a command prompt window and ping Computer B using its IP address. For example, if the IP address is 192.168.10.10, use this command: ping 192.168.10.10.

2. Try to ping Computer B, this time using its computer name. Did the ping work?

3. Use Notepad to edit the hosts file on Computer A and add the entry that associates the IP address of Computer B with its computer name.

4. Try to ping Computer B, this time using its computer name rather than IP address. Did the ping work?

CHAPTER
8

Supporting Mobile Operating Systems

After completing this chapter, you will be able to:

- Identify and use significant features of Android, iOS, and Windows mobile operating systems

- Configure, synchronize, and troubleshoot mobile devices that use iOS

- Configure, synchronize, and troubleshoot mobile devices that use Android

- Configure, synchronize, and troubleshoot Windows mobile devices

Previous chapters have focused on supporting personal computers. This chapter deviates from this topic as we discuss operating systems on mobile devices such as smart phones and tablets. As mobile devices become more common, many people use them to surf the web, access email, and manage apps and data. As an IT support technician, you need to know about the operating systems used with mobile devices and how to help a user configure and troubleshoot these devices.

Because many employees expect to be able to use their mobile devices to access, synchronize, and edit data on the corporate network, data, settings, and apps stored on mobile devices need to be secured and synchronized to other storage locations. In this chapter, you learn how you can synchronize content on mobile devices to a personal computer or to storage in the cloud (on the Internet). Finally, in this chapter, you learn about tools and resources available for troubleshooting mobile operating systems.

OPERATING SYSTEMS USED ON MOBILE DEVICES

**A+
220-902
2.5**

The operating system for a mobile device is installed at the factory. Here are the three most popular ones in the United States:

◢ Android OS by Google (*android.com*) is based on Linux and is used on various smart phones and tablets. Currently, Android is the most popular OS for smart phones. Nearly 80 percent of the smart phones sold today use Android. Combining both smart phones and tablets, Android holds about 50 percent of the market.

◢ iOS by Apple (*apple.com*) is based on Mac OS X and is currently used on the iPhone, iPad, and iPod touch by Apple. Almost 20 percent of smart phones sold today are made by Apple and use iOS. About 40 percent of smart phones and tablets combined use iOS.

◢ Windows Phone (WP) by Microsoft (*microsoft.com*) is based on Windows and is used on various smart phones (not on tablets). Less than 3 percent of smart phones sold today use Windows Phone. (Windows tablets use the 32-bit version of the same Windows operating system used on desktop and laptop systems.)

The remaining market share for smart phones and tablets in the United States is shared by these mobile OSs:

◢ Java Micro Edition (ME) by Oracle (*oracle.com*) provides a basic platform for everything from smart phones to TV set-top boxes to printers. Most of these devices have limited computing power, and Java ME enables Java applications to run on these devices.

◢ The Symbian OS from the Symbian Foundation (*symbian.org*) is popular outside the United States and is used on devices made by multiple manufacturers, including Nokia, Samsung, Sony, and others.

◢ BlackBerry OS by BlackBerry Limited (*blackberry.com*) is a proprietary OS used on devices built by BlackBerry.

◢ Kindle Fire by Amazon (*amazon.com*) runs the Fire OS, which is based on Android and is deeply customized to meet the needs of Amazon's e-reader audience.

This chapter focuses on the Android, iOS, and Windows Phone operating systems used on smart phones and/or tablets.

> ★ **A+ Exam Tip**   The A+ 220-902 exam expects you to know how to support the Android, iOS, and Windows Phone operating systems used with mobile devices.

ANDROID BY THE OPEN HANDSET ALLIANCE AND GOOGLE

**A+
220-902
2.5**

The Android operating system is based on the Linux OS and uses a Linux kernel. Linux and Android are open source, which means the source code for the operating system is available for free and anyone can modify and redistribute the source code. Open source software is typically developed as a community effort by many contributors. Android was originally developed by the Open Handset Alliance (*www.openhandsetalliance.com*), which is made up of many technology and mobile phone companies and led by Google, Inc.

In 2005, Google acquired this source code. Google does not own Android, but it has assumed a leadership role in development, quality control, and distributions of the Android OS and Android apps. Ongoing development of the Android OS code by Google and other contributors is released to the public as open source code.

GETTING TO KNOW AN ANDROID DEVICE

Releases of Android are named after desserts and include Froyo (frozen yogurt; version 2.2.x), Gingerbread (version 2.3.x), Honeycomb (version 3.x), Ice Cream Sandwich (version 4.0.x), Jelly Bean (version 4.1-4.3.x), KitKat (version 4.4+), and Lollipop (version 5.0-5.1.1). (Future releases of Android will follow in alphabetic order: M, N, O, and P.) At the time of this writing, most new phones and tablets ship with KitKat or Lollipop installed.

> ✏ **Notes** Google has announced that Marshmallow is the next release of Android and will be released by the time this text is in print.

Android's launcher, or graphical user interface (GUI), starts with multiple home screens and supports windows, panes, and 3D graphics. The Android OS can use an embedded browser, manage a database using SQLite, and connect to Wi-Fi, Bluetooth, and cellular networks. Most current Android mobile devices have no physical buttons on the front of the device. However, the user can configure up to five custom software buttons, called Home touch buttons, on the Action bar at the bottom of the screen, with the three default buttons typically being back, home, and overview (see Figure 8-1).

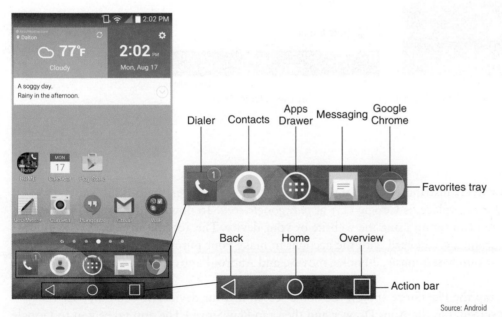

Figure 8-1 This LG smart phone has the Android Lollipop OS installed

On Android phones, up to seven apps or groups of apps can be pinned to the Favorites tray just above the Action bar. The pinned apps shown in Figure 8-1 are the Dialer (for making phone calls), Contacts, the Apps Drawer (lists and manages all your apps), Android's native Messaging app, and Google Chrome (web browser). Apps in the Favorites tray stay put as you move from home screen to home screen by swiping left or right. All but the Apps Drawer can be replaced by third-party apps.

Notifications provide alerts and related information about apps and social media. Notifications are accessed by swiping down from the top of the screen, as shown in Figure 8-2a. The Notifications shade provides access to the Quick Settings menu, such as Wi-Fi, Bluetooth, Volume, and Brightness. Tap the **Settings** (cog) icon in the upper-right corner to open the Settings app (see Figure 8-2b), or tap the back button in the Action bar to return to the home screen.

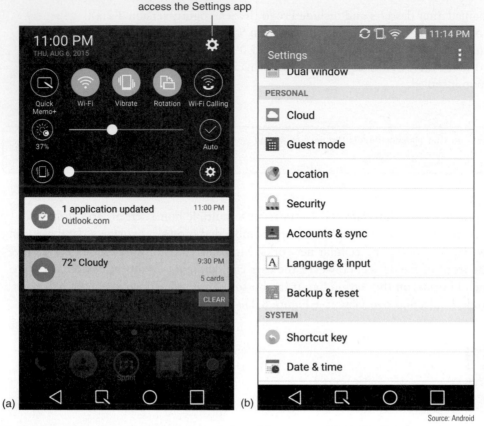

Figure 8-2   (a) The Notifications shade includes quick access to (b) the Settings app

ANDROID APPS

Android apps are sold or freely distributed from any source or vendor. However, the official source for apps, called the Android marketplace, is Google Play at *play.google.com*. To download content, you need a Google account, which you can set up using the website or your device. The account is associated with any valid email address. Associate a credit card with the account to make your purchases at Google Play. Then you can download free or purchased music, e-books, movies, and Android apps from Google Play to your mobile device.

To download an app, tap the **Play Store** app on the home screen of your device. (If you don't see the app icon on your home screen, tap the **Apps Drawer** and then tap **Play Store**.) The app takes you to Google Play, where you can search for apps, games, movies, music, e-books, and magazines (see Figure 8-3a). In addition, you can get apps and data from other sources, such as the Amazon Appstore for Android at *amazon.com* or directly from a developer. You can also use the Play Store app to manage updates to installed apps, as shown in Figure 8-3b.

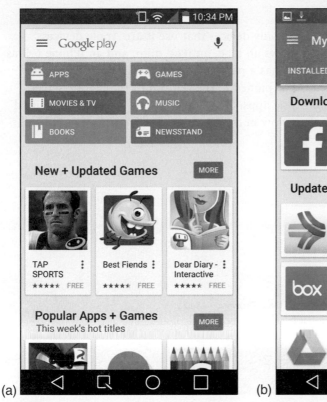
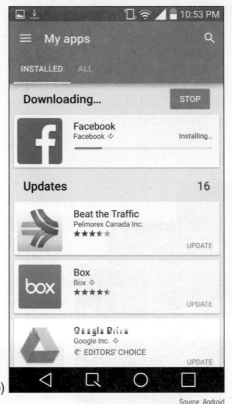

Source: Android

Figure 8-3   Use the Play Store app to (a) search Google Play for apps, music, e-books, movies, and more that you can download, as well as (b) updates to apps you already have

Google maintains the Android website at *android.com* where an app developer can download Android Studio, which includes Android SDK tools and an Android emulator, from *developer.android.com*. An SDK (Software Development Kit) is a group of tools that developers use to write apps. Android Studio is free and is released as open source. Most Android apps are written using the Java programming language. All the parts of an app are published as a package of files wrapped into one file with an .apk file extension using the APK (Android Application Package) package file format.

Now let's see how Apple's iOS differs from Android.

iOS BY APPLE

A+
220-902
2.5

Apple, Inc. (*www.apple.com*) owns, manufactures, and sells the Apple iPhone (a smart phone), iPad (a handheld tablet), and iPod touch (a multimedia recorder and player *and* a game player). These devices all use the iOS operating system, also developed and owned by Apple. iOS is based on Mac OS X, the operating system used by Apple desktop and laptop computers. There have been eight major releases of the iOS with a ninth released in beta at the time of this writing; the latest full version is iOS version 8.

GETTING TO KNOW AN iOS DEVICE

Because Apple is the sole owner and distributor of iOS, the only devices that use it are Apple devices (currently the iPhone, iPad, and iPod touch). Figure 8-4 shows an iPad, an iPad mini, and an iPhone 6 Plus (the iPhone 6 Plus is larger than the iPhone 6). Each device has a physical Wake/sleep button at the top of the device and a Home button on the bottom front. Apps pinned to the bottom of the iPhone screen in Figure 8-4 are the Phone, Mail, Safari browser, and Music apps. (The Music app is also called the iPod app.) Apps pinned to the bottom of the iPad screens that show in the figure are the Safari browser, Mail, and Videos apps.

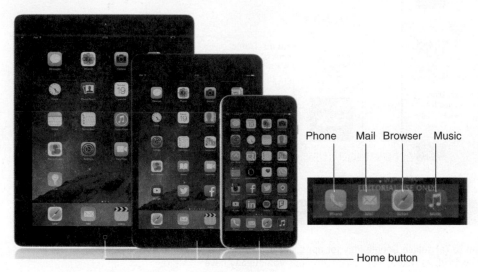

© iStockphoto.com/Hocus-focus

Figure 8-4   An iPad, an iPad mini, and an iPhone 6 Plus iPhone by Apple have iOS version 5.1 installed

Also, because Apple is the sole developer and manufacturer, it can maintain strict standards on its products, which means iOS is extremely stable and bug free. Apple's iOS is also a very easy and intuitive operating system to use. As with Mac OS X, iOS makes heavy use of icons.

Knowing a few simple navigation tips on an iOS device can help you get around a little more easily:

◢ Swipe down from the top of the screen to see the Notifications screen. Slide a notification, such as an iMessage, up to remove it and slide it down to access options for responding to it, such as replying to an iMessage. The types of notifications shown and other notification settings can be customized in the Settings app. For example, on an iPhone you can turn on or off government alerts such as AMBER alerts and other emergency notifications.

⟨⟩ OS Differences You can adjust settings for emergency notifications in Android, too, but the steps to accomplish this task vary by device. Many Android devices offer these options in the Settings menu of the default Messaging app. Look for an option such as Emergency alerts. On other devices, on the Settings app tap **More**, then tap **Cell broadcasts**.

◢ To delete or move an app icon on the screen, press and hold the icon until all icons start to jiggle. As the icons jiggle, to delete an icon, press the X beside it. To move an icon, press and drag it to a new location. You can add new home screens by dragging an app icon off the screen to the right. To stop the jiggling, tap the Home button.

◢ Double-click the Home button to show the app switcher. Tap an app to switch to that screen, or swipe an app to the top of the screen to close it. Closing apps you're not using can save battery life.

◢ Press and hold the Home button to open Siri, iOS's virtual assistant service. A virtual assistant service or app, also called a personal assistant, responds to a user's voice commands with a personable, conversational interaction to perform tasks and retrieve information. iOS's Siri, as shown in Figure 8-5a, was the first of these virtual assistant services (Siri is more of a service than an app because of how deeply embedded it is within iOS), and has been around long enough to have become quite sophisticated. Siri uses information within the device to provide a customized experience.

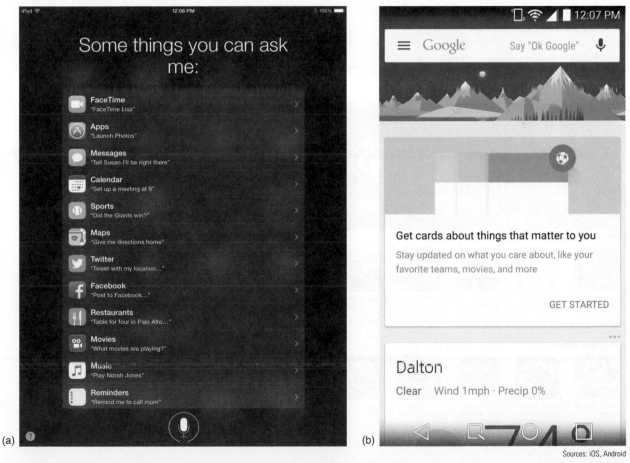

(a) (b)

Sources: iOS, Android

Figure 8-5   (a) Siri settings are changed in the Settings app; (b) Google Now gives helpful information on cards

◯ **OS Differences** Android offers Google Now virtual assistant (see Figure 8-5b), which can be accessed through a web interface in addition to the installed app on the mobile device, and uses search histories and information collected during setup or later to customize a user's experience. Windows Phone 8.1 has a virtual assistant called Cortana that also customizes the user's experience.

iOS APPS

You can get Android apps from many sources, but the only place to go for an iOS app is Apple. Apple is the sole distributer of iOS apps at its App Store. Other developers can write apps for the iPhone, iPad, or iPod, but these apps must be sent to Apple for their close scrutiny. If they pass muster, they are distributed by Apple on its website. One requirement is that an app be written in the Objective-C, C, or C++ programming language. Apple offers app development tools, including the iOS SDK (Software Development Kit) at *developer.apple.com*.

When you first purchase an iPad or an iPod touch, you activate it by signing into the device with an Apple ID, or user account, using a valid email address and password, and associate this account with a credit card number. You can then go to the Settings app to download the latest updates to the iOS. Here are options for obtaining apps and other content:

◢ Use the App Store app on your mobile device (see Figure 8-6 for an iPad example) to search, purchase, and download (or download for free) apps, games, e-books, periodical content such as newspapers and magazines, and iTunes U content. (iTunes U contains lectures and even complete courses from many schools, colleges, and universities.)

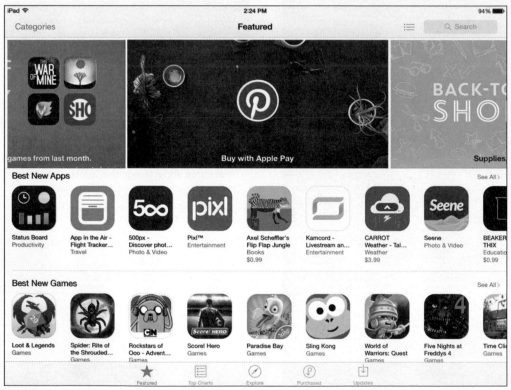

Source: Apple iOS

Figure 8-6   Use the App Store app to download content from the iTunes Store

◢ Use the iTunes Store app to search, purchase, and download (or download for free) content, including music, movies, TV shows, podcasts, and iTunes U content. Download and install the iTunes software on a Mac or Windows personal computer. Then connect your mobile device to the computer by way of a USB port. iTunes can then sync the device to iOS updates downloaded from *iTunes.com* and to content on your computer, which can be a helpful troubleshooting option, as you'll see later. You can also purchase content that is downloaded to your device by way of iTunes on your computer. Figure 8-7 shows the iTunes window when an iPhone is connected to the computer. How to use iTunes to sync data and apps on your device is covered later in the chapter.

Figure 8-7   iTunes window shows summary information for an attached iPhone

Recall that apps can be downloaded to an iOS device only from Apple. People have discovered that it is possible to break through this restriction in a process called jailbreaking. Jailbreaking gives you root or administrative privileges to the operating system and the entire file system (all files and folders) and complete access to all commands and features. Jailbreaking was once illegal, but in 2010, the U.S. Copyright Office and the Library of Congress made a copyright ruling that a user has the right to download and use software that will jailbreak his or her iPhone. Note, however, that this ruling applies only to iPhones (and other smart phones), not iPads (or other tablets), due to some ambiguity in the definition of the word *tablet*. Also, jailbreaking voids any manufacturer warranty on the device, violates the End User License Agreement (EULA) with Apple, and might violate BYOD (Bring Your Own Device) policies in an enterprise environment. This jailingbreaking ruling applies only in the United States; other countries have addressed this issue differently.

Android and iOS hold the lion's share of the mobile operating system market. However, Microsoft offers some valid competition with its latest Windows mobile OS developments.

WINDOWS PHONE BY MICROSOFT

A+
220-902
2.5

The Windows Phone operating system by Microsoft is more or less a simplified version of the Windows operating system designed for desktop computers, laptops, and tablets. Windows Phone and Windows version numbers correspond: Windows Phone 8.1 corresponds to Windows 8.1. One of the biggest differences between Windows and Windows Phone is that Windows Phone does not have a desktop screen. Everything is accessed initially from the Start screen. As of the writing of this text, Microsoft has released its preview version of Windows 10 Mobile.

> ⭐ **A+ Exam Tip**   The A+ 220-902 exam expects you to be able to use and support Windows 8.1/8/7 and Windows Phone 8.1. It does not cover Windows 10 or Windows 10 Mobile.

GETTING TO KNOW A WINDOWS PHONE MOBILE DEVICE

Most Windows phones have three buttons below the screen (see Figure 8-8). These buttons might be physical buttons or software buttons. The Start button accesses the Start screen; the Back button goes back one screen, and the Search button opens a Bing or Cortana Search box. Also, if you press and hold the Back button, it displays recent apps. For most phones, these buttons aren't true software buttons, but they're also not true physical buttons, because they might not work when the OS is malfunctioning.

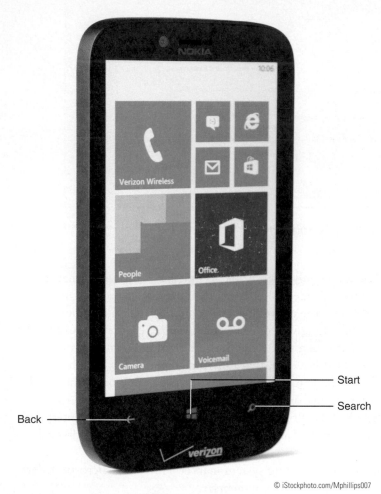

© iStockphoto.com/Mphillips007

Figure 8-8   Press and hold the Start button to activate Cortana, the Windows virtual assistant

Windows phones rely primarily on the Start screen for accessing apps. Just as with Windows 8, a tile icon on the Start screen represents an app. Here are some tips for getting around Windows Phone:

▲ Tap a tile on the Start screen to open its app. Scroll up or down to see more tiles. Press and hold to resize or reposition tiles. On many smart phones, pressing and holding a link functions like right-clicking with a mouse on a Windows desktop computer.

◢ Swipe down from the very top of the screen to see notifications in the Action Center (Figure 8-9a), similar to both Android and iOS. Like Android, there is also a Settings icon here to open the Settings app (Figure 8-9b). Settings can also be accessed via the Settings tile.

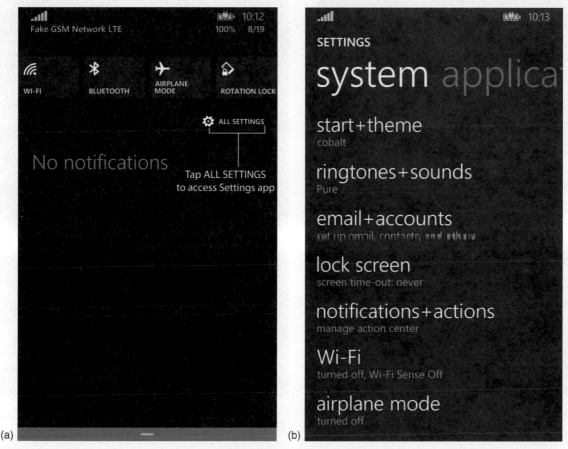

(a) (b)

Figure 8-9   (a) Notifications appear in the Action Center; (b) the Settings app provides an extensive toolkit for customizing a Windows smart phone

◢ Swipe from the right to see the apps list (similar to clicking the down arrow on a Windows Start screen). Press and hold an app on the list to pin the app to the Start screen (see Figure 8-10a). On the Start screen, press and hold the app tile and then you can change its size and other characteristics. Tap the Store tile on the Start screen to find more apps (Figure 8-10b).

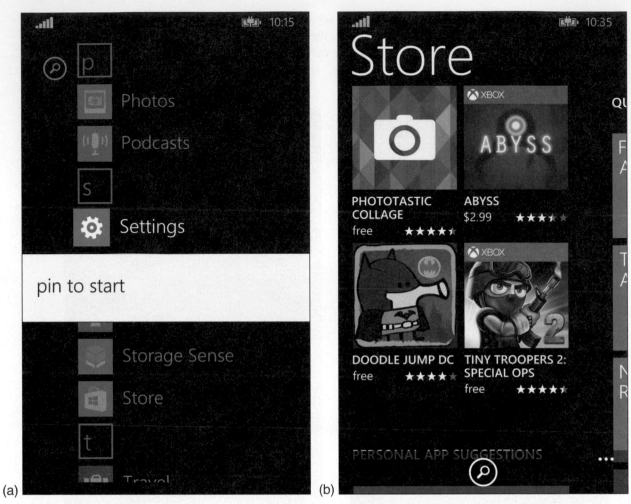

(a)   (b)

Figure 8-10   (a) To pin an app to the Start screen, press and hold the app's icon and then tap **pin to start**; (b) get more apps from the Store

◢ While a menu is displayed in the Settings app, you can sometimes swipe from the right to see a submenu. Windows Phone is rich with settings options, making it easier to integrate Windows phones in an enterprise environment.

WINDOWS PHONE APPS

The availability of apps for Windows mobile devices is much more limited than what can be found for Android or iOS. Windows apps are obtained through the Microsoft Store (*microsoftstore.com*). The number of apps for Windows smart phones should increase soon, as Microsoft has announced that Windows 10 Mobile will be more compatible with both Android and iOS apps. This means app developers will more easily be able to adapt their existing apps for posting in the Microsoft Store. Additionally, like Android apps, Windows Phone apps can be obtained from third-party websites.

COMPARING OPEN SOURCE AND CLOSED SOURCE OPERATING SYSTEMS

Open source operating systems (such as Android) and closed source, also called vendor-specific or commercial license, operating systems (such as iOS) have their advantages and disadvantages. Here are some key points to consider about releasing or not releasing source code:

◢ Apple carefully guards its iOS source code and internal functions of the OS. Third-party developers of apps have access only to APIs, which are calls to the OS. An app must be tested and approved by Apple before it can be sold in its online App Store. These policies assure users that apps are high quality. It also assures developers they have a central point of contact for users to buy their apps.

◢ The Android source code and the development and sale of apps are not closely guarded. Apps can be purchased or downloaded from Google Play, but they can also be obtained from other sources such as *Amazon.com* or directly from a developer. This freedom comes with a cost because users are not always assured of high-quality, bug-free apps, and developers are not always assured of a convenient market for their apps.

◢ Because any smart phone or tablet manufacturer can modify the Android source code, many variations of Android exist. These variations can make it difficult for developers to write apps that port to any Android platform. It can also make it difficult for users to learn to use new Android devices because of these inconsistencies.

★ **A+ Exam Tip** The A+ 220-902 exam expects you to understand the advantages and disadvantages of open source and closed source operating systems on mobile devices.

CONFIGURE, SYNC, AND TROUBLESHOOT iOS DEVICES

In this part of the chapter, you learn to configure network connections, and to update, secure, and back up data, content, and settings on an iOS device. Later in the chapter, you learn similar skills using Android and Windows devices. We begin with iOS because it's so easy to use and understand.

This chapter is intended to show you how to support a device that you might not own or normally use. Technicians are often expected to do such things! If you don't have an iPhone or iPad to use as you read through these sections, you can still follow along, paying careful attention to the screen shots taken on each device. Learning to use an iOS device is fun, and supporting one is equally easy.

Most of the settings you need to know to support an iOS device are contained in the Settings app, which you can find on the home screen (see Figure 8-11a). Basically, you can tap the Settings app and search through its menus and submenus until you find what you need. So let's get started.

(a) Tap Settings to access
the Settings app

Source: iOS

Figure 8-11   (a) Tap the Settings app to configure iOS and apps; (b) in the Settings app, Airplane Mode turns off all three antennas that connect the iPhone or iPad to networks

CONFIGURE iOS NETWORK CONNECTIONS

A+
220-902
2.5, 2.6,
2.7

An iOS mobile device can contain up to four antennas (Wi-Fi, GPS, Bluetooth, and cellular). The device uses a Wi-Fi, Bluetooth, or cellular antenna to connect to each type of network, and settings on the device allow you to enable or disable each antenna. Let's look at each type of connection.

> 🖉 **Notes** You can disable the three antennas in a mobile device that can transmit signals by enabling Airplane mode so that the device can neither transmit nor receive signals. To use Airplane mode, tap the **Settings** app and turn **Airplane Mode** on or off (see Figure 8-11b). It's not necessary to disable the GPS antenna because it only receives and never transmits.

> ★ **A+ Exam Tip** The A+ 220-902 exam expects you to know how to configure Wi-Fi, cellular data, Bluetooth, and VPN connections using the iOS, Android, and Windows mobile operating systems.

CELLULAR CONNECTION

A cellular network provided by a carrier (for example, AT&T or Verizon) is used for voice, text, and data communication. A cellular network uses GSM or CDMA for voice and another layer of technology for data transmissions. Options are 2G, EDGE (an earlier version of 3G), 3G, 4G, and 4G LTE. GSM and LTE require a SIM card installed in the device, and CDMA does not use a SIM card. (Although a CDMA and LTE carrier does require the SIM card for the LTE technology to work.) To make a cellular data connection, you must have a subscription with your carrier that includes a cellular data plan and then connect your device.

Here is information that might be used when a connection is first made to the network:

▲ The IMEI (International Mobile Equipment Identity) is a unique number that identifies each mobile phone or tablet device worldwide. It's usually reported within the *About* menu in the OS, and it might also be printed on a sticker on the device, such as behind the battery.

▲ The IMSI (International Mobile Subscriber Identity) is a unique number that identifies a cellular subscription for a device or subscriber, along with its home country and mobile network. This number is stored on the SIM card for networks that use SIM cards. For networks that don't use SIM cards, the number is kept in a database maintained by the carrier and is associated with the IMEI.

▲ The ICCID (Integrated Circuit Card ID) identifies the SIM card if the card is used. To know if a device is using a SIM card, look in the Settings app on the *About* menu in the General group. An ICCID entry indicates a SIM card is present.

When a carrier uses a SIM card, you can move the card from one device to another and the new device can connect to the carrier's network. When a carrier does not use a SIM card, you must contact the carrier and request permission to switch devices. If the carrier accepts the new device, the new IMEI will be entered in the carrier's database.

To connect an iOS device to a cellular data network, tap **Settings, Cellular Data,** then **Set Up Cellular Data.** Select a carrier (see Figure 8-12a) and follow the on screen instructions. Also you can enable or disable Data Roaming and Cellular Data. Using data roaming might mean additional charges if you are in a different country, and disabling cellular data might save on carrier charges in certain situations.

★ **A+ Exam Tip** The A+ 220-902 exam expects you to know how to identify and distinguish between the IMEI and the IMSI.

✎ **Notes** The advantage of disabling cellular data and using Wi-Fi for data transmissions is that data transmissions over Wi-Fi are not charged against your cellular data subscription plan. Also, Wi-Fi is generally faster than most cellular connections.

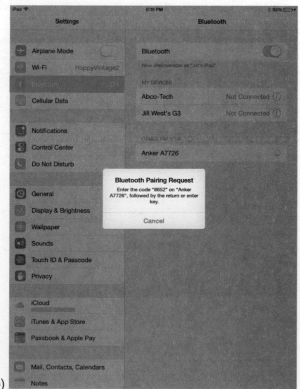

Source: iOS

Figure 8-12 (a) Connect to a cellular data network; (b) a PIN code is required to pair these two Bluetooth devices

CDMA carriers are likely to require that a cellular device have a Removable User Identity Module (R-UIM), which is a small card similar to a SIM card. The card contains a database file called the PRL (Preferred Roaming List), which lists the preferred service providers or radio frequencies your carrier wants the device to use. You can reset or update the list in the Settings app. For example, for an iPad, tap **Settings**, **General**, then scroll down and tap **Reset**. Tap **Subscriber Services**, then tap **Reprovision Account** and tap **OK**. Tap **OK** again when the update is complete.

> **OS Differences** Android devices on CDMA networks also require updated PRLs. To see the current PRL version, open the **Settings** app, scroll down and tap **About phone** or **About tablet**, then tap **Status**. To update the PRL, go back to the Settings app, then tap **System updates**. Tap **Update PRL**, and tap **OK** when the update is complete.

BLUETOOTH CONNECTION

To configure an iOS Bluetooth connection, first turn on the other Bluetooth device you want to connect to. Then on your mobile device, tap **Settings** and turn on Bluetooth. The device searches for other Bluetooth devices. If it discovers a Bluetooth device, tap it to connect. The two Bluetooth devices now begin the pairing process. The devices might require a Bluetooth PIN code to complete the Bluetooth connection. For example, in Figure 8-12b, an iPad and Bluetooth keyboard are pairing. To complete the connection, enter the four-digit PIN on the keyboard. To test the connection, enter text on the keyboard and make sure the text appears on the iPad screen in the active app.

If you have a problem connecting to a Bluetooth device, try turning that device off and back on. The device might also offer a pairing button or combination of buttons to enable pairing. When you press this button, a pairing light blinks, indicating the device is ready to receive a Bluetooth connection.

WI-FI CONNECTION

To configure an iOS Wi-Fi connection, tap **Settings, Wi-Fi**. On the Wi-Fi screen (Figure 8-13a), you can view available Wi-Fi hotspots, see which Wi-Fi network you are connected to, turn Wi-Fi off and on, and decide whether the device needs to ask before joining a Wi-Fi network. A Wi-Fi hotspot is an area where access to Wi-Fi Internet connectivity is made available, such as at a coffee shop, retail store, or airport.

Source: iOS

Figure 8-13   (a) Turn on Wi-Fi and choose a Wi-Fi network; (b) configure Wi-Fi connection settings

When the device is within range of a Wi-Fi network, it displays the list of networks. Select one to connect. If the Wi-Fi network is secured, enter the security key to complete the connection. To change a network's settings, tap the name of the network (see Figure 8-13b).

VPN CONNECTION

Like desktop computers, a mobile device can be configured to communicate information securely over a virtual private network (VPN) connection. To create a VPN connection in iOS, tap **Settings**, **General**, then scroll down and tap **VPN**. Tap **Add VPN Configuration**. Follow directions to complete the connection, which will require you know the type of encryption protocol used (L2TP, PPTP, or IPsec), the IP address or domain name of the VPN server, and the user name and password to the corporate network.

CONFIGURE iOS EMAIL

A+
220-902
2.6, 2.7

Using a personal computer or mobile device, email can be managed in one of two ways:

▲ *Use a browser.* Using a browser, go to the website of your email provider and manage your email on the website. In this situation, your email is never downloaded to your computer or mobile device, and your messages remain on the email server until you delete them.

▲ *Use an email client.* An email client, such as Microsoft Outlook, can be installed on your personal computer, and/or you can use an email app on your mobile device. The client or app can either download email messages to your device (using the POP3 protocol) or can manage email on the server (using the IMAP protocol). When the client or app downloads the email, you can configure the server to continue to store the email on the server for later use or delete the email from the server. The built-in Mail app for managing email is available on iPhones and iPads.

Here is the information you'll need to configure the Mail app on an iOS device:

▲ *Your email address and password.* If your email account is with iCloud, Microsoft Exchange, Google, Yahoo!, AOL, or Outlook, your email address and password are all you need because the iOS can automatically set up these accounts.

▲ *The names of your incoming and outgoing email servers.* To find this information, check the support page of your email provider's website. For example, the server you use for incoming mail might be *pop.mycompany.com*, and the server you use for outgoing mail might be *smtp.mycompany.com*. The two servers might have the same name.

▲ *The type of protocol your incoming server uses.* The incoming server will use POP3 or IMAP. Using IMAP, you are managing your email on the server. For example, you can move a message from one folder to another and that change happens on the remote server. Using POP3, the messages are downloaded to your device where you manage them locally. Using POP3, the Mail app leaves the messages on the server (does not delete them), but you can change this setting if you want.

▲ *Security used.* Most likely, if email is encrypted during transmission using the SSL protocol, the configuration will happen automatically without your involvement. However, if you have problems, you need to be aware of these possible settings:

　▲ An IMAP server uses port 143 unless it is secured and using SSL. IMAP over SSL (IMAPS) uses port 993.

　▲ A POP3 server uses port 110 unless it is secured and using SSL. POP3 over SSL uses port 995.

　▲ Outgoing email is normally sent using the protocol SMTP. A more secure alternative called S/MIME (Secure/Multipurpose Internet Mail Extensions) is now available, however. S/MIME encrypts the email message and includes a digital signature, which validates the identity of the sender of the email message. This feature is enabled after the email account is set up on the device. The activation process is automated for accounts through Microsoft Exchange, and can be set up manually for other types of accounts. Look for this option on the Advanced settings screen, which you'll soon see how to access.

APPLYING | CONCEPTS   CONFIGURE iOS EMAIL

A+
220-902
2.6, 2.7

Follow these steps to configure the email client on an iOS device:

1. Tap **Settings** and then tap **Mail, Contacts, Calendars**. On the Mail, Contacts, Calendars screen, you
can add a new email account and decide how email is handled. To add a new email account, tap
Add Account. On the next screen, select the type of account (see Figure 8-14a) and enter your email address
and password. If your email account type is not in the list, tap **Other** at the bottom of the list.

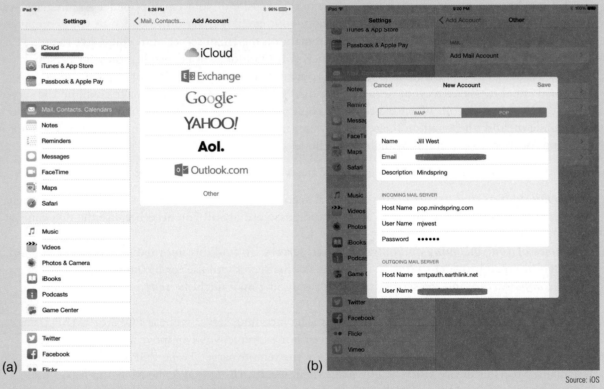

Source: iOS

Figure 8-14   (a) iOS can automatically set up several types of email accounts; (b) an email account is set up to use
IMAP or POP3 for incoming mail

2. On the Other screen, tap **Add Mail Account**. On the New Account screen, enter your name, email address, password, and description (optional). Tap **Next**.

3. The device might be able to successfully establish your email account based on this information alone. When
prompted, select the account elements you want to sync to this device, such as Mail, Notes, and Calendar.
However, sometimes the Mail app chooses the wrong default settings (such as assuming POP3 when you want
IMAP). To force the Mail app to allow manual selection of these settings, first enter a bogus email address or
password. The account connection will fail, and the screen in Figure 8-14b will appear. Tap IMAP or POP and
enter the correct settings. This includes the Host Name, User Name, and Password for both the incoming and
outgoing mail servers. Then tap **Save**.

4. The Mail app assumes it is using SSL (to secure email in transit using encryption) and attempts to make the connection. If it cannot, it asks if you want it to try to make the connection without using SSL. Click **OK** to make that attempt.

5. To use the account, tap the **Mail** app on your home screen.

If you later need to verify the email account settings or delete the account, follow these steps:

1. Tap **Settings**, and then tap **Mail, Contacts, Calendars**. In the list of Accounts, tap the account. On the account screen, you can enable and disable the account and change the account settings.

2. To delete the account, tap **Delete Account** at the bottom of the screen (see Figure 8-15a).

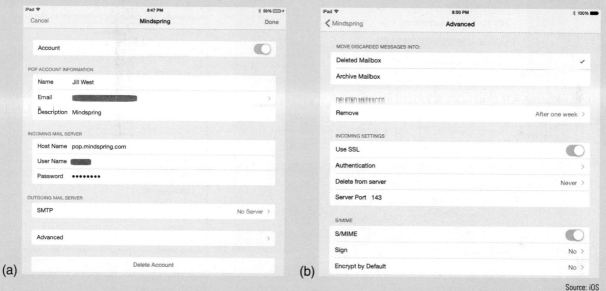

(a)   (b)

Source: iOS

Figure 8-15   (a) Delete an email account or use Advanced settings; (b) decide how messages are handled on the server after you receive them

3. To see advanced settings, tap **Advanced**. On the Advanced screen (see Figure 8-15b), tap **Delete from server** to decide how to handle mail you have downloaded using the POP3 protocol. Choices are *Never*, *Seven Days*, or *When removed from Inbox*.

4. Notice on the Advanced screen that you can enable and disable SSL. The server port that the app addresses might also need to be changed. You can also enable S/MIME to encrypt outgoing email messages. When this feature is enabled, you'll see a blue lock icon when creating new email messages, which you can click to activate S/MIME for that message.

> ✏️ **Notes**   For IMAP accounts, tapping the account on the **Mail, Contacts, Calendars** screen shows a list of IMAP accounts, options for syncing Mail and Notes, and the option to delete the account. Tap the account again for configuration options, as shown in Figure 8-16a. Tap **Advanced** to see additional options, as shown in Figure 8-16b.

(continues)

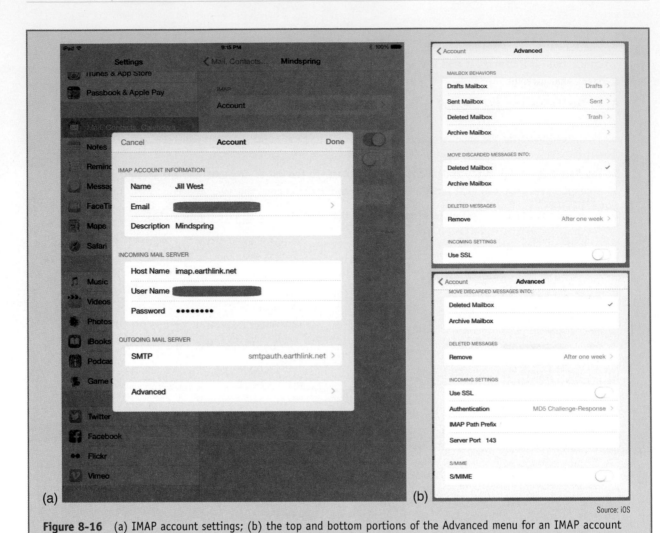

Figure 8-16   (a) IMAP account settings; (b) the top and bottom portions of the Advanced menu for an IMAP account

You need to know about an exception in how email is managed when using a Gmail account. Gmail is an email service provided by Google at *mail.google.com*. Normally, when you use the Mail app, you can delete a message by selecting it and tapping **Delete** (see Figure 8-17a). However, using Gmail, by default, you archive a message rather than delete it (see Figure 8-17b).

Using most email services, a message arrives in your Inbox, which is a folder on the email server. You organize these messages by moving them to other folders or deleting them. Deleted messages are placed in the Trash folder and permanently deleted after a period of time. Using Gmail, a message remains in the Inbox, and you organize these messages by assigning each message one or more labels. When you archive a message, you move the message from the Inbox to the All Mail folder out of sight but still accessible. Therefore, when using the Mail app on an Apple device with a Gmail account, the Delete button is replaced with the Archive button.

To change the Gmail account so that you can delete messages, go to the home screen and tap **Settings** and then tap **Mail, Contacts, Calendars**. Tap the Gmail account and go into **Advanced** settings. On the Advanced screen (refer to Figure 8-16b) under *Move discarded messages into*, tap to select **Deleted Mailbox**. Return to the Account screen and tap **Done**. The Mail app will now have a Delete button for Gmail, as shown in Figure 8-17a.

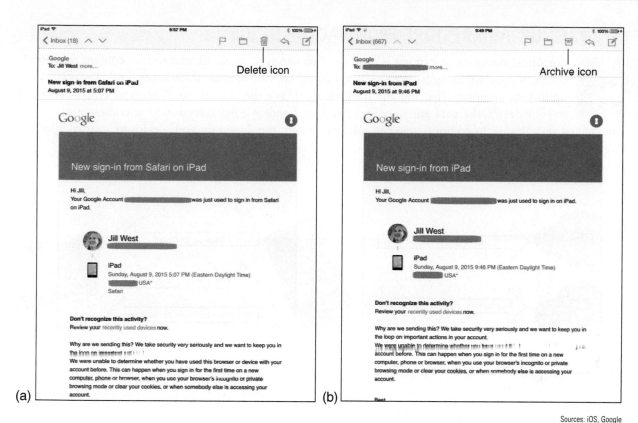

Sources: iOS, Google

Figure 8-17 Two methods for dealing with messages you no longer need: a) Using most email clients, delete a message, or b) using Gmail, archive a message

Microsoft Exchange is a server application that is popular with large corporations for handling employee email, contacts, and calendars. When you set up a Microsoft Exchange email account, the Mail app automatically enables ActiveSync, which causes all email, contacts, and calendar updates made on the Exchange server or on your mobile device to stay in sync. Any changes at either location are automatically and immediately transmitted to the other. You can change the ActiveSync settings by doing the following:

1. On the home screen, tap **Settings,** and tap **Mail, Contacts, Calendars.**

2. Select your Exchange email account. On the account screen, you can turn on or off the Mail, Contacts, Calendars, Reminders, and Notes settings. You can set the number of days, weeks, or months of email you want to stay in sync. You can also set up automatic out-of-office replies, and decide whether you want folders in addition to the Inbox folder to be pushed to you from the Exchange server.

★ **A+ Exam Tip** The A+ 220-902 exam expects you to know about special considerations when configuring Gmail and Exchange email accounts.

SYNC, BACK UP, AND RESTORE FROM BACKUP IN iOS

> **A+**
> **220-902**
> **2.6, 2.7**

For Apple devices, you can use iCloud or iTunes to sync, back up, and restore content on your device. iCloud backs up to storage on the Apple website at *www.icloud.com*, and iTunes backs up to your computer. Syncing and backing up are not the same thing. When you sync a computer to your device, the data and apps you purchased and/or downloaded to your computer are transferred to your device. In addition, you can transfer content purchased on your device to your computer. Figure 8-18 helps sort out all these options.

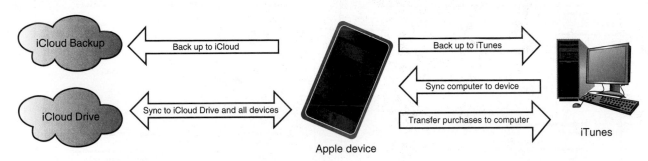

Figure 8-18   Options for backing up and syncing an Apple device

The advantages of backing up to iCloud are your devices automatically back up to iCloud whenever your device is connected to Wi-Fi and Apple is responsible for protecting your backups. The advantages of backing up to iTunes are you have more control over your backups and the cost for storage is less; however, you are responsible for maintaining your backups on your computer. Next, let's see how to sync and back up your content using iCloud and iTunes.

USE iCLOUD DRIVE TO SYNC CONTENT

Your Apple ID gives you a free iCloud account at *icloud.com* that can hold your iCloud Backup, iCloud Drive, iCloud Photo Library, iCloud Mail (using your *@icloud.com* email addresss), and data from apps that can interface with iCloud. The first 5 GB of storage is free. Music, apps, books, TV shows, and My Photo Stream you purchase from the Apple Store don't count against your 5 GB of storage.

You can sync files stored on iCloud Drive with any Apple mobile device or personal computer, and, when the iCloud Drive software is installed, you can sync content with a Windows computer. When you turn on iCloud Drive on an Apple device, content stored on your iCloud Drive is automatically synced with your device. To turn on iCloud Drive, open the **Settings** app, tap **iCloud**, and verify **iCloud Drive** is turned on. Now, any app on your device that can interact with iCloud Drive can use content at iCloud Drive.

APPLYING | CONCEPTS   USE AN APP TO EXPORT A DOCUMENT TO iCLOUD DRIVE

A+
220-902
2.6, 2.7

The Documents Free app on an iPad can interface with iCloud Drive. Follow these steps to create a document in the app and save it to iCloud Drive:

1. To use the app to create a new document file, open the app, tap **iCloud** in the left pane to select the location where the file will be saved, then tap the "**+**" sign at the bottom of the screen. Select the type of document to create, as shown in Figure 8-19a.

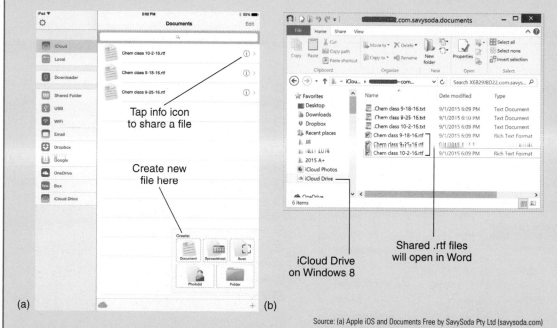

(a)   (b)

Source: (a) Apple iOS and Documents Free by SavySoda Pty Ltd (savysoda.com)

Figure 8-19   (a) Access iCloud Drive through compatible apps on your device; (b) iCloud Drive files are automatically synced to all devices where it is installed, including Windows computers

2. After you're finished creating the document, to save it, tap **File** in the upper-left corner of the app and tap **Save** (to use the app's default name for the file) or **Save As** (to rename the file). To return to your Documents list, tap **File** and tap **Don't Save**. The file is now available inside the app's own folder in iCloud Drive at *icloud.com* and also on any device or computer that syncs with your iCloud Drive account.

In Windows 8 on a personal computer, iCloud Drive is listed under Favorites in File Explorer, and there you can find the document file uploaded from your iPad, as shown in Figure 8-19b. (The app saves two copies of each file, one is an .rtf, or rich text format, file associated by default with Word, and one is a .txt, or text, file associated by default with WordPad.)

3. To download a document from iCloud Drive to the Documents Free app, on the Documents list screen, tap the **menu icon** in the upper-left corner. In the menu list that appears on the left side of the screen (see Figure 8-19a), tap **iCloud Drive**. You can then drill down into folders on your iCloud Drive and tap a file you want to download. The file can then be viewed and edited in the app.

✎ **Notes** Using any computer, open a browser and go to *icloud.com*. When you sign in with your Apple ID account, you can upload or download any file stored on your iCloud Drive to your computer.

USE iCLOUD BACKUP TO BACK UP CONTENT

To use iCloud Backup to back up your content to the cloud, follow these steps:

1. iCloud Backup requires iOS 5 or higher. To verify your Apple device is updated to iOS 5 or higher, tap **Settings, General, About** (see Figure 8-20a for an iPad screen).

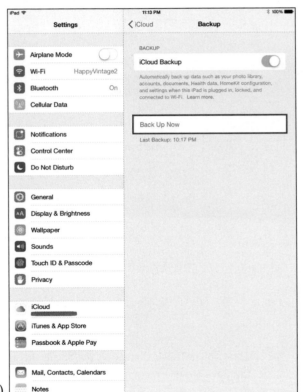

Figure 8-20   (a) Verify your iOS is using version 5 or higher; (b) perform an iCloud backup at any time by tapping Back Up Now

Source: iOS

2. To turn on iCloud Backup, tap **Settings**, then **iCloud**. Tap **Backup** and make sure iCloud Backup is turned on (see Figure 8-20b).

3. Select the items you want to back up (see Figure 8-21a), such as Mail, Contacts, Calendars, Reminders, Safari bookmarks, and so forth. Note that iCloud does not back up content already stored in the cloud, including apps, movies, podcasts, audio books, or data stored on your iCloud Drive. It also does not back up content you did not obtain from the iTunes Store, such as imported MP3s, videos, or CDs. To monitor your storage, tap **Storage**. The Storage pane is shown in Figure 8-21b.

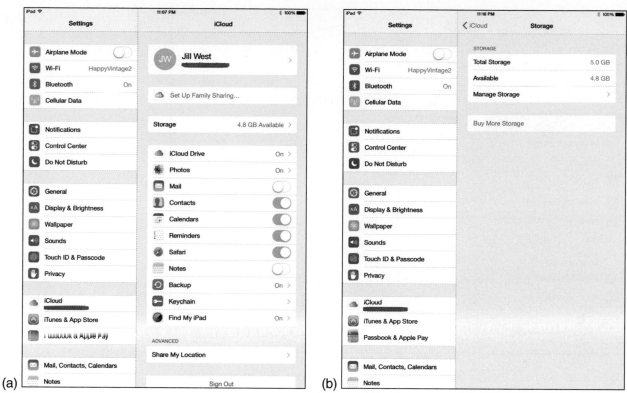

Figure 8-21   (a) Decide what type of content to back up to iCloud; (b) view available storage on iCloud

4. iCloud Backup normally backs up whenever your device is connected to Wi-Fi. To back up manually to iCloud at any time, on the Backup screen shown in Figure 8-20b, you can tap **Back Up Now**.

> ✏️ **Notes**   To have your device report its location to iCloud, turn on **Find My iPad** or **Find My iPhone** (see Figure 8-21a). Later, if you lose your device, sign in to iCloud and this location data can be used to find your device on a map.

If you need to restore your data from iCloud Backup to your current device or to a new Apple device, here are your options:

◢ When you are setting up a new iOS device, the Setup process provides a screen asking if you want to restore from backup. Tap **Restore from iCloud Backup**. If you don't restore from backup during setup, the only way you can do it later is to erase everything on the new device and set up the device again.

◢ If you lose the content and settings on a device, to restore from backup, tap **Settings**, then **General**. Scroll to the bottom and tap **Reset**, then tap **Erase All Content and Settings** (refer to Figure 8-22). You will be given the opportunity to select a backup from iCloud through the Setup Assistant.

8

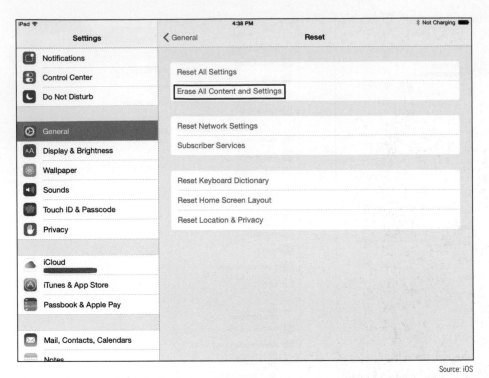

Source: iOS

Figure 8-22 Restoring a device from an iCloud backup can make setup easy when configuring a replacement device, such as when replacing a lost or stolen iPhone

Apps, music, and e-books you have previously downloaded from the iTunes Store can be downloaded again to this and other devices tied to your Apple ID. To automatically sync this content, tap **Settings** on the home screen and tap **iTunes & App Store**. On the iTunes & App Store screen (see Figure 8-23 for an iPad), turn on and configure Automatic Downloads for each type of content. Here you can also decide whether to use cellular data for automatic downloads.

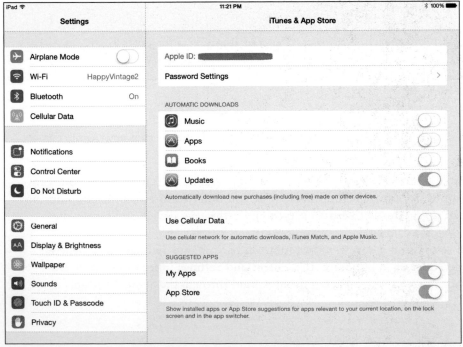

Source: iOS

Figure 8-23 Decide how to handle Automatic Downloads

USE iTUNES TO BACK UP AND SYNC CONTENT

After you have installed iTunes software on your computer, you can use it to back up and sync content, transfer purchased content from your device to your computer, and update iOS on your device. Follow these steps:

1. Make sure your computer qualifies for iTunes. For a Windows computer, iTunes can install under Windows 8/7 and needs 400 MB of free hard drive space. Install a 64-bit version of iTunes on a 64-bit OS and a 32-bit version of iTunes on a 32-bit OS.

2. Go to **apple.com/itunes/download** and download and install the software. After the software is installed, restart your computer.

3. Connect your device to your computer by way of a USB port. iTunes automatically launches and displays the window shown in Figure 8-24.

Source: iTunes

Figure 8-24 Opening window when you first connect a new device to iTunes

To see your options for backups, syncing, and transferring, in the iTunes window, click **File** and click **Devices**. Notice the four options shown in Figure 8-25 are Sync (transfers apps and data from the computer to the device), Transfer Purchases (transfers apps and data purchased on the device to the computer), Back Up (backs up content from the device to the computer), and Restore from Backup (restores backups to the device). To back up the device to the computer, click **Back Up.**

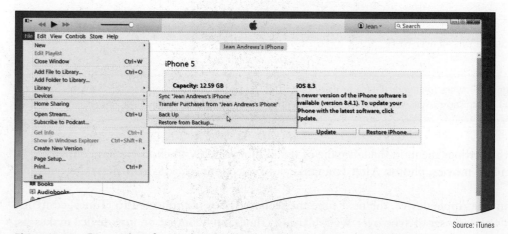

Source: iTunes

Figure 8-25 Four options for syncing, backing up, and restoring an Apple device

You can also perform a backup by clicking **Back Up Now** on the Summary screen in the Backups group (refer back to Figure 8-7).

When you back up content with iTunes, the backup is stored on your computer at this location when using Windows 8/7:

C:\Users*username*\AppData\Roaming\Apple Computer\MobileSync\Backup\

> ✏️ **Notes** For best protection, be sure you make routine backups of the user profile folder on your computer. The user profile folder contains user settings and data, and part of this data is your iOS device backups.

iTunes automatically syncs the contacts, app data and app settings, documents, calendar, call history, photos and videos taken by the device, Wi-Fi and email passwords, Microsoft Exchange information, bookmarks, text messages and pictures, and voice messages.

To verify and customize exactly what iTunes is syncing, do the following:

1. With your device connected to your computer, select your device in the upper-left corner of the iTunes window. The Summary page was shown in Figure 8-7.

2. Scroll down to see the lower part of the Summary page, where you can choose how to sync, including allowing to sync when the iPad is in the same Wi-Fi network as the computer, as shown in Figure 8-26. You can also control what to sync.

Source: iTunes

Figure 8-26   iOS devices can be synced over Wi-Fi

> ✏️ **Notes** You can manage Wi-Fi syncs from your iPhone or iPad. To do this, go to the Settings app and tap **General**. Scroll down and tap **iTunes Wi-Fi Sync**. Recent syncs are shown on the screen, and a new sync can be initiated here as well.

3. Select options from the Settings menu in the left pane of the iTunes window to choose what content to sync, such as apps, music, movies, photos. After you make your selections, click **Sync** to start the sync.

If you have more than one Apple device, the next time the second device is connected to iTunes, content is synced to it (unless it's already set to sync over Wi-Fi). Using iTunes, any content on any device makes its way to the other devices and to your computer for backup.

RESTORE FROM AN iTUNES BACKUP

To restore from backup, connect the device to iTunes, select the device to show the Summary page, and in the Backups section, click **Restore Backup** in the shortcut menu (refer back to Figure 8-7). Also, when you are setting up a new device and you first connect it to iTunes on your computer, it will ask if you want to restore from backup or set up the device as a new device. You can also see in Figure 8-7 where you can update an iOS device through iTunes. From iOS version 5 and later, this is not necessary, as the device can receive updates automatically through a cellular or Wi-Fi connection.

> ✎ **Notes** To check for and install updates on the device itself, open the **Settings** app, then tap **General** in the left pane. On the right side, tap **Software Update**. Any available updates will be reported here and can be installed.

USE AIRDROP AND HANDOFF TO SYNC CONTENT

Beginning with iOS 7, iPhones and iPads can easily transfer files, such as photos, videos, and documents, between devices that belong to you or to someone else using a feature called AirDrop. Embedded in iOS, AirDrop uses Bluetooth to detect nearby compatible devices, then creates a peer-to-peer network using a Wi-Fi signal between the devices. The connections are protected by a firewall at each device, and transmissions are encrypted. AirDrop can be enabled for contacts only, or it can detect any compatible devices nearby regardless of who owns them, or it can be disabled completely. AirDrop settings are accessed through the Control Center, as shown in Figure 8-27a. To open the Control Center, swipe up from the bottom of the screen. To share files from within an app, open the app and tap **Share**. For example, Figure 8-27b shows the Maps app and the option to share the map location by AirDrop to a nearby MacBook.

8

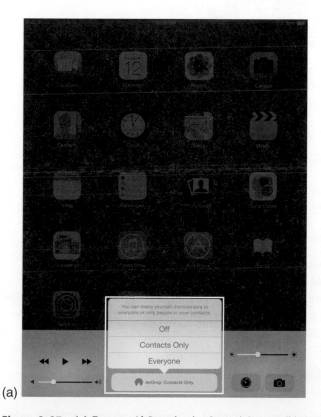

(a)

(b)

Source: iOS

Figure 8-27 (a) Turn on AirDrop in the Control Center; (b) many iOS apps, such as this Maps app, include the AirDrop sharing feature

Another synchronization tool designed to connect devices that all use the same Apple ID is Handoff. Handoff lets you start a task on one device, such as an iPad, then pick up that task on another device, such as a Mac desktop or laptop. To use Handoff, make sure that both devices are signed into iCloud with the same Apple ID, and that both devices have Bluetooth activated. To turn on Handoff on the iOS device, tap **Settings, General, Handoff & Suggested Apps,** and turn on **Handoff** (see Figure 8-28a). Now you're ready to use Handoff. For example, open a supported app on the iOS device, such as Safari, and then look for that app's icon on a Mac laptop. On the Mac computer, you'll see a small mobile device icon appended to the app's icon, as shown in Figure 8-28b. Click to open the app, and the app will pick up where you left off with the other device.

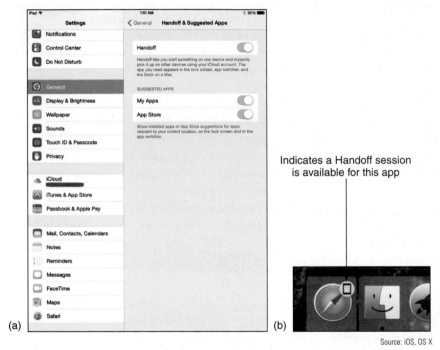

Figure 8-28   (a) Turn on Handoff, and then (b) Handoff can transfer your current work in an app to a different device, such as a Mac laptop

TROUBLESHOOT iOS DEVICES

When learning to troubleshoot any OS or device, remember the web is a great source of information. Depend on the *support.apple.com* website to give you troubleshooting tips and procedures for its iOS and mobile devices. Let's first look at some troubleshooting tools and then some common problems and their solutions.

TOOLS FOR TROUBLESHOOTING THE iOS

For iPhones or iPads, you can sometimes solve a problem by restarting, resetting, updating, or restoring the device. Try the first step that follows and if that does not solve the problem, move on to the next step. The steps are ordered so as to solve the problem while making the least changes to the system (least intrusive solution). With each step, first make sure the device is plugged in or already has sufficient charge to complete the step. After you try one step, check to see if the problem is solved before you move on to the next step. Here are the tools in the order you should use them:

1. **Close running apps.** Press the Wake/sleep button twice and swipe each app up to close it. Reopen an app that you want to use. Too many open apps can shorten battery life.

2. **Uninstall and reinstall an app.** If an app is giving problems, uninstall it. (Press the app icon until it jiggles and then press the X beside the app icon.) Use the iTunes Store to download and reinstall the app.

3. **Restart the device.** To restart the device (perform a soft reset), press and hold the Wake/sleep button until the red slider bar appears and then drag the slider. Then press and hold the Wake/sleep button until the Apple logo appears. A soft reset puts the device in hibernation and does not clear memory.

> **↻ OS Differences** Each mobile OS defines a soft reset and hard reset differently. For iOS, a soft reset puts the device in hibernation and then restarts the device, and a hard reset is a hard boot, which involves a full shutdown of the device. For Android devices, a soft reset is a hard boot, and a hard reset, also called a factory reset, erases all data and restores the device to factory default state.

4. **Reset the device.** To reset the device (called a forced restart or hard reset), press and hold the Wake/sleep button and the Home button at the same time for at least 10 seconds until the Apple logo appears. A hard reset is like a full shutdown in Windows and performs a full clean boot.

5. **Update iOS.** To update iOS with the latest patches, first back up content and settings if possible. Then tap **Settings** and **Software Update**.

6. **Update from Recovery mode using iTunes.** This process attempts to update iOS without losing data or settings. Follow these steps:

   a. Make sure the latest version of iTunes is installed on your computer (you can also use someone else's computer and iTunes installation so long as iTunes is up to date).

   b. Connect the device to the computer and force it to restart by pressing and holding the Wake/sleep and Home buttons at the same time. Keep holding both buttons until the Recovery mode screen appears.

   c. Tap **Update** to reinstall iOS without erasing personal data.

   d. Don't unplug or interrupt the device during the update. If the device exits Recovery mode before the update is complete, force a restart again, and tap Update again.

7. **Reset all settings.** If you have not already done so, back up the data and settings. Then to erase settings, tap **Settings**, **General** and **Reset**. On the Reset screen (refer back to Figure 8-22), tap **Reset All Settings**.

8. **Erase all data and settings.** First, make every attempt to back up data and settings. Then to erase all data and settings, tap **Settings**, **General** and **Reset**. On the Reset screen (see Figure 8-22), tap **Erase All Content and Settings**.

9. **Restore the device.** This process reinstalls iOS and you will lose all your data on the device. The device is restored to its factory default condition, but you can then apply a backup if you have one. Before you perform a restore, try to back up all your data and settings. Then follow these steps:

   a. Make sure the latest version of iTunes is installed on your computer (you can also use someone else's computer and iTunes installation so long as iTunes is up to date). Also, if possible, make sure *Find My iPhone* or *Find My iPad* is turned off in the iCloud settings menu on the device.

   b. Connect the device to your computer and select it in iTunes. Click the **Summary** panel and click **Restore**. Click **Restore** again to confirm that you know all data and content will be deleted.

   c. Don't unplug or interrupt the device during the restore. iOS is reinstalled and all data and settings are lost.

   d. Next, restore your data and settings from backup. How to do that was covered earlier in the chapter.

10. **Restore the device from Recovery mode using iTunes.** This process might work to restore the device to its factory state when the restore process fails or when you cannot start the restore process, such as when the device restarts repeatedly, gets stuck during the startup process, or is frozen and not responding at all. The process does a firmware upgrade. All content and data are lost and the OS is refreshed. Follow these steps:

    a. Turn off the device and leave it off for a few minutes. If you have trouble turning off the device, press and hold the Wake/sleep button and the Home button at the same time.

    b. While holding down the Home button, connect the device to your computer. If you see the device charging, wait a few minutes while it charges. Do not release the Home button while it is charging. When you see the Connect to iTunes screen, release the Home button.

    c. iTunes should recognize the device and display a message saying the device is in Recovery mode and ask if you want to restore the device. Tap Restore and follow the directions on screen to restore the device to factory state.

    d. Restore data and settings using the most recent backup.

    If the device is still not working properly, search for more troubleshooting tips on the Apple website at *support.apple.com*, review the list of common problems below, or take the device to an Apple store for repair.

COMMON PROBLEMS AND SOLUTIONS

Some common problems with iOS devices can be addressed by checking specific settings or identifying particular malfunctions. If the suggestions listed here don't work, then move on to perform a soft reset, hard reset, and more invasive tools discussed earlier. Here are some problems and their solutions:

▲ *Touch screen not responsive.* Recall that Apple devices use a capacitive touch screen that does not get out of alignment unless there is a hardware problem. Here are some tips to try when a touch screen is giving you problems:

    ▲ Clean the screen with a soft, damp cloth.

    ▲ Don't use the touch screen when your hands are wet or you are wearing gloves.

    ▲ Remove any plastic sheet or film protecting the touch screen.

▲ *Dim display.* When the display is dim, open the Control Center and adjust the screen brightness. To open the Control Center, swipe up from the bottom of the screen.

▲ *Weak cellular signal.* If you have a weak cellular signal or just want to save your cellular minutes, you can use Wi-Fi to connect to the Internet for VoIP voice communication. In the United States, Sprint and T-Mobile offer a feature called Wi-Fi calling, which uses VoIP over a Wi-Fi connection to the Internet. To enable Wi-Fi calling on an iPhone that uses one of these two carriers, tap **Settings** and **Phone**, then turn on **Wi-Fi Calling**. You can also install an app, such as Skype or LINE, on your iPhone and use it to make VoIP phone calls on a Wi-Fi network, regardless of the carrier you are using.

> ⚡ **Caution**   When using Wi-Fi calling on your iPhone, confirm your Emergency Address from the link on the Wi-Fi Calling screen so that 911 services can respond to an emergency call from your phone if needed. Federal law requires that your carrier have a validated home address on file before activating Wi-Fi calling on your account. Your actual location can be updated on your phone each time you switch to a different wireless network.

▲ *No sound or distorted sound from speakers.* First, make sure the volume is turned up by pressing the device's physical **Up** volume button, or by checking Control Center, which you can access by swiping up from the bottom of the screen. Also, the problem could be that the sound output for the device is being misdirected. Check to see if Bluetooth is on, and if so, turn it off in order to make sure the device is not inadvertently connected to a Bluetooth headset or car stereo system. Also check Accessibility settings by tapping **Settings, General, Accessibility**. Some of the Accessibility audio settings can interfere with normal operation of the device's built-in speaker system. On iPhones, check that **Phone Noise Cancellation** is disabled.

▲ *Screen won't rotate.* A gyroscope is a device that contains a disc that is free to move and respond to gravity as the device is moved. An accelerometer is a type of gyroscope used in mobile devices to sense the physical position of the device, which helps the OS know when to adjust the screen orientation from portrait to landscape. In iPhones and iPads, the accelerometer also enables features such as shake, where the user literally shakes the device to perform actions such as undoing the deletion of an email. If the screen won't rotate between portrait and landscape orientations, check to ensure the orientation isn't locked. Swipe up from the bottom of the screen to reveal the Control Center. The Orientation Lock icon is a padlock symbol with an arrow circling around it. Tap it to turn it on and off.

◢ *Bluetooth connectivity issues.* Sometimes an iOS update will cause issues with Wi-Fi network connectivity or Bluetooth pairings. For Bluetooth issues, first delete all known devices by tapping **Settings, Bluetooth,** then tap the info icon for each device and tap **Forget This Device.** Then, in the left panel, tap **General,** and scroll down and tap **Reset.** Tap **Reset Network Settings** and tap **Reset** on the warning box. This restores network settings to factory defaults, then you can attempt to re-pair a Bluetooth device with the iPad or iPhone.

◢ *Wi-Fi connectivity issues.* Lack of wireless connectivity or intermittent connectivity is often caused by problems with the signal that is being broadcast from the router or access point. First make sure the access point and router are working correctly, that the Wi-Fi network you want to connect to is visible to the device (not hidden), and that you're using the correct security key. For Wi-Fi issues on the device side, first start with Wi-Fi settings (in the Settings app, tap **Wi-Fi**) for the network you're trying to connect to. Tap the info icon, and try renewing the IP address (tap **Renew Lease** then tap **Renew**). If that doesn't work, tap **Forget This Network,** then retry connecting to the network. Finally, try resetting the network settings, as described above for Bluetooth connectivity issues.

◢ *Overheating.* For a true overheating problem, where the device is too hot to touch safely, power off and replace the device. However, all devices can get fairly warm if the display is left on for too long, if the surrounding environment is particularly hot, if the device is sitting on a soft surface, if the battery is going bad, or if the device remains plugged in to a power source for a long period of time. Don't use a mobile device in direct sunlight for long periods of time, try to turn off the display when you're not using it, and close apps that you're not using. This will also help conserve battery power.

> ✎ **Notes** If you know where the battery is located inside a mobile device, check for heat originating from that area of the device. If so, replacing the battery might be your solution. For most mobile devices, you can find tear-down instructions, videos, tools, and replacement parts for purchase at *ifixit.com.* Be aware you might void the warranty when you open the case.

◢ *Location services not working in apps.* A mobile device provides location-specific information by using Bluetooth and GPS information as well as crowd-sourced Wi-Fi and cellular databases built from anonymous, encrypted geo-tagged locations of Wi-Fi hotspots and cell towers. A GPS (Global Positioning System) receiver determines its position by using the GPS satellite data or data from the position of nearby cellular towers. Geotracking, which is the identification of a device's location in order to track the device's movements, relies heavily on location information. Many apps can only access this information if Location Services is enabled on the device (emergency calls can use location information even if Locations Services is not enabled). For example, Siri checks the device's current location before recommending Italian restaurants in the area.

If an app is having trouble accessing location-specific information, check the Location Services settings by tapping **Settings, Privacy,** and then **Location Services,** which shows the screen in Figure 8-29. Tap **Share My Location** to determine whether apps like Messages and Find My Friends can share your location information with contacts. On the Location Services screen, tap the **About Location Services & Privacy** link to read more information about how your privacy is affected by sharing your location information.

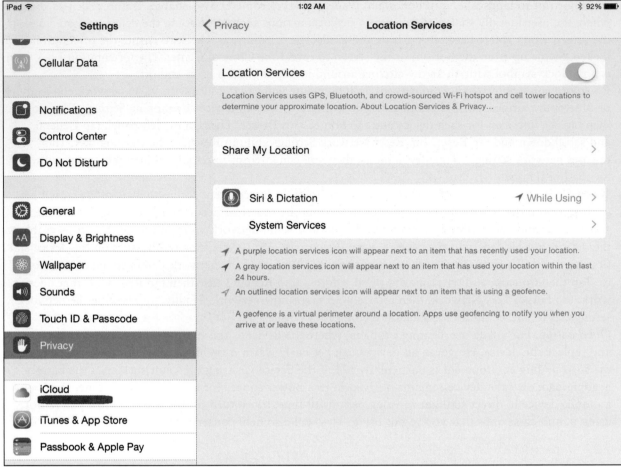

Source: iOS

Figure 8-29   The Location Services screen shows which apps have recently used your device's location information

▲ *System lockout.* If your iOS device is locked because of too many failed attempts at entering your passcode to sign in to the device, you can wait until the timer counts down on the screen and then attempt to enter the passcode again. If you have forgotten the passcode, Apple advises your only solution is to reset the device, which erases all data and settings, and then you can restore the device from backup. You have a few options for resetting the device:

    ▲ If you set up Find My iPhone or Find My iPad, you can go to *icloud.com/find*, sign in with your Apple ID, select your device, and then erase it. The erase process resets the device to its factory state.

    ▲ If you have previously synced the device with iTunes, connect the device to iTunes and allow it to sync. After the sync is completed, use iTunes to restore your device. When you reach the setup screen, tap **Restore from iTunes backup.**

    ▲ If you have not set up Find My iPhone or Find My iPad and you've never synced with iTunes, install iTunes on your computer and connect your device. Then force restart the device: Press and hold the Wake/sleep button and Home button at the same time until you see the Apple logo appear and then the recovery mode screen appear. Tap **Restore.** iTunes will reset the device to factory state.

8

Hands-On | Project 8-1   Research iOS Browser Apps

A+
220-902
2.5

A smart phone or tablet comes with a built-in browser, but you can replace it with a third-party browser. Research browser apps and answer the following questions:

1. List three browser apps that are popular with Apple devices using iOS. List one feature for each app that makes it stand out.

2. The iPhone and iPad don't use Adobe Flash, and many websites depend on Flash. What workaround app can be used with iOS so that the iPhone and iPad can view content on these websites?

CONFIGURE, SYNC, AND TROUBLESHOOT ANDROID DEVICES

A+
220-902
2.5, 2.6,
2.7, 4.3

Because the Android operating system is open source, manufacturers can customize the OS and how it works in many variations. Therefore, it is not always possible to give specific step-by-step directions similar to those given for iOS. In this part of the chapter, you learn about general procedures you can follow to support an Android device. We also give a few examples for specific Android devices so that you can see how the step-by-step directions might work on an Android device.

Most of the settings you need to support an Android device are found in the Settings app; however, settings options might not be in the Settings app and some settings options might rely on third-party apps.

On the other hand, Android is usually fun to use and support because it offers so much flexibility and the potential to customize. Once you get comfortable with Android, you can do amazing things with it. Technicians who love to tinker with devices tend to gravitate to Android, and those who just want a quick and easy tool to use without a hassle choose iOS.

When you are assigned responsibility for supporting an Android device, begin with the user guide for the device, which you can download from the device manufacturer's website. The user guide is likely to tell you the detailed steps of how to connect to a network, configure email, update the OS, sync and back up settings and data, secure the device, and what to do when things go wrong.

> ✎ **Notes** Most of us rarely follow step-by-step directions when learning to use a new device until when "all else fails, read the directions." This part of the chapter can give you an idea of what to look for on an Android device, and you can likely figure out the specific steps for yourself.

Now let's look at what to expect when supporting an Android device.

CONFIGURE ANDROID NETWORK CONNECTIONS

A+
220-902
2.5, 2.6,
2.7, 4.3

To configure settings on an Android device, use the Settings app, which can be found in the Apps Drawer or on the Notifications shade, as shown earlier in Figure 8-2. Figure 8-30 shows the Settings screen in list view on the left and in tab view on the right. Switch from list view to tab view by tapping the ellipsis icon in the upper-right corner, then tap **Switch to tab view** and tap **OK**.

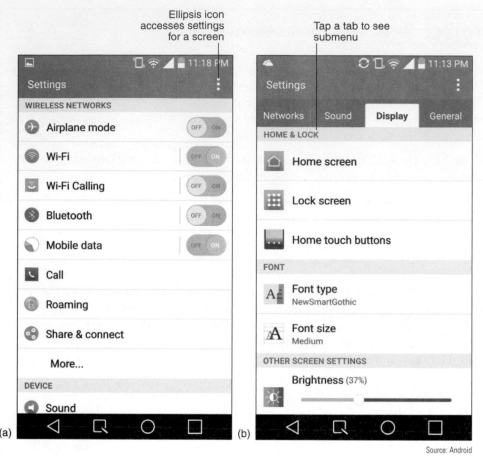

Figure 8-30   The Settings menu can be organized (a) by one long list or (b) by tabs and submenus

Network connections are configured using the Settings screen. Available settings can include:

▲ *Turn Airplane mode on or off.* Airplane mode disables all wireless network antennas and can help conserve data usage or battery power when your battery is low.

▲ *Turn Wi-Fi on or off and configure Wi-Fi access points.* Tap **Wi-Fi**. On the Wi-Fi settings screen, as shown in Figure 8-31a, you can add a Wi-Fi connection, manage existing networks, access the Advanced Wi-Fi settings screen (see Figure 8-31b), or explore the tutorial. When you first attempt to connect to a secured Wi-Fi network, you need its security key.

> ✎ **Notes** Searching for a Wi-Fi network can drain battery power. To make a battery charge last longer, disable Wi-Fi when you're not using it.

▲ *Turn Wi-Fi calling on or off.* Wi-Fi calling, available through certain carriers, allows you to make phone calls over a Wi-Fi network rather than needing a cellular network. Turn on Wi-Fi calling, then input 911 information, as shown in Figure 8-32a. You can also enable address notification (Figure 8-32b) so that you're prompted to update your location each time you connect with a new Wi-Fi network. These addresses are saved so the information won't have to be reentered the next time you visit that location.

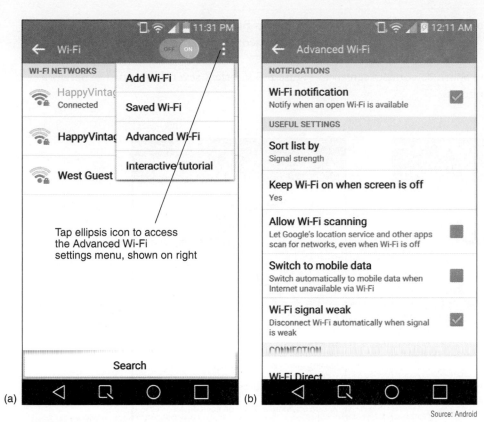

Figure 8-31   Configure Wi-Fi settings

Source: Android

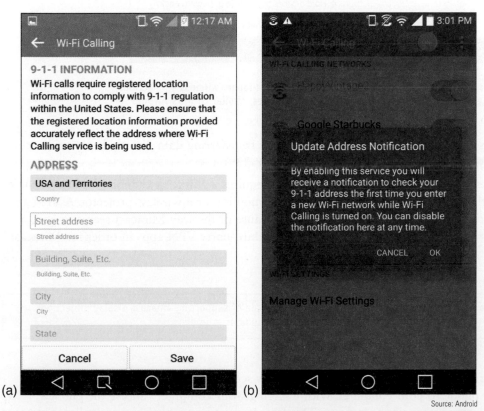

Figure 8-32   (a) 911 address information is required in order to use Wi-Fi calling service; (b) your phone can remind you to update your current location information when joining a new wireless network

Source: Android

▲ *Turn Bluetooth on or off.* To configure Bluetooth settings, tap **Bluetooth** (refer back to Figure 8-30a). On the Bluetooth settings screen, you can make the device discoverable so it can pair with other Bluetooth devices.

▲ *Share and connect.* The Share & connect screen in Figure 8-33a offers several options for network connections to share content:

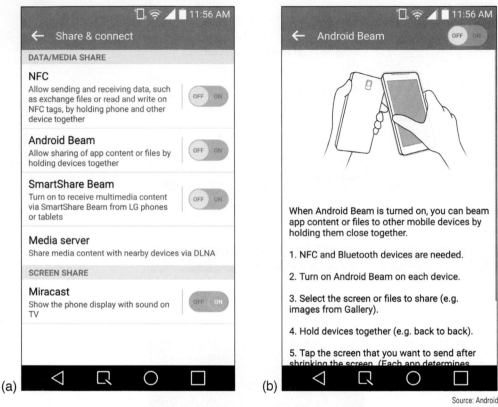

Source: Android

Figure 8-33   (a) This version of Android provides several options for short-range, wireless connections; (b) Android Beam uses both NFC and Bluetooth technologies, similar to iOS's AirDrop

▲ NFC and Bluetooth technologies both provide options for transferring data directly between devices that are held in close proximity to each other (see Figure 8-33b).

▲ Miracast is a wireless display-mirroring technology that requires a Miracast-capable screen or dongle in order to mirror the phone's display to a TV, a wireless monitor, or a wireless projector. A VPN app on the device sometimes disables the Miracast feature because of the way Miracast seems to pose a threat to VPN security. It might be necessary to uninstall third-party VPN apps in order for Miracast to work properly.

> **⟨⟩ OS Differences** Windows 8.1 and Windows Phone 8.1 are also capable of supporting Miracast display projections. If it's not working in Windows, be sure to check for driver and firmware updates.

▲ *Set up tethering.* Figure 8-34 shows the Wireless & networks screen on an Android phone, which you can use to tether your phone to your computer. With tethering, your computer can use the phone's cellular network connection to access the Internet. This feature must be enabled on your cellular plan

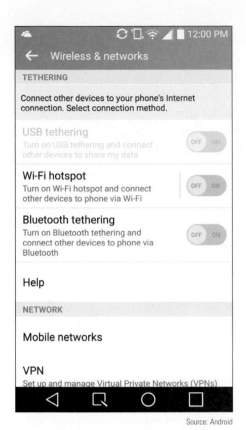

Source: Android

Figure 8-34 The Wireless & network settings
screen on an Android phone

in order to use it; some carriers include the tethering feature as a standard service in their plans, whereas others charge extra. To set up tethering, tap one of the tethering options. (A tablet that does not have cellular capability will not have tethering options.)

◢ *Set up a VPN.* To set up a VPN in Android, tap **VPN** on the Wireless & network settings screen (see Figure 8-34). Figure 8-35a shows the configuration options, including the Type (which refers to the VPN protocol used, such as PPTP, L2TP/IPsec, and IPsec Xauth), Server address, and any encryption options. The advanced options shown in Figure 8-35b allow configuration of the DNS search domain, DNS server (Google's public DNS server is at IP address 8.8.8.8), and any forwarding routes. In addition to the built-in Android VPN client just shown, some Android devices also provide proprietary VPN configuration options.

8

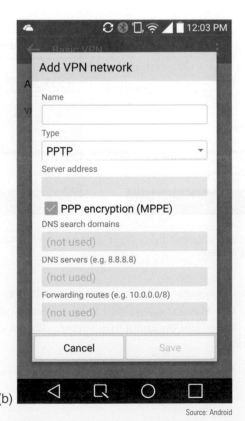

Source: Android

Figure 8-35 (a) Basic configuration for a VPN connection and (b) advanced VPN configuration options

CONFIGURE ANDROID EMAIL

A+
220-902
2.6, 2.7

Because Google owns Gmail, Google makes it very easy to configure a Gmail account on an Android device. To set up a Gmail account, tap the **Gmail** app on the home screen and enter your Gmail account and password. (If you don't see the app on your home screen, tap the Apps Drawer, and then tap Gmail.) You can change settings for this account later by going to the Settings app, tapping **Accounts & sync,** and selecting your **Google** account.

Here are the steps to set up email accounts other than Gmail or any other type of account such as Skype, YouTube, Photobucket, Dropbox, or Facebook accounts:

1. Tap **Settings, Accounts & sync, Add account.** On the Add account screen (see Figure 8-36a), Android can automatically configure several types of accounts. For an email account, tap **Email.** On the next screen, you might be given options for different email account types, such as Yahoo!. If none of these is correct, tap **Other.** Next, enter your email account and password and tap **Next** (see Figure 8-36b). The account is automatically set up.

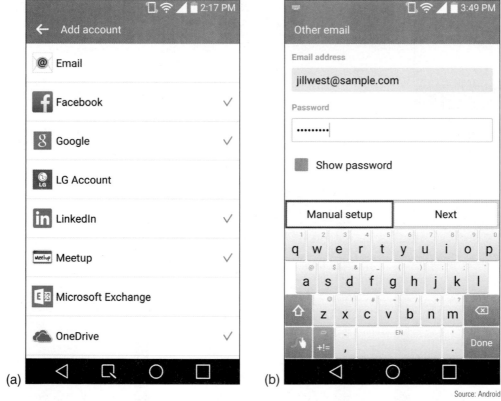

Source: Android

Figure 8-36 (a) Android can automatically configure several types of accounts, but (b) manual setup is available if needed

2. If you get errors using automatic configuration, try again with a manual setup. Enter the email address and password and tap **Manual setup** (see Figure 8-36b). You can then select the type of account (POP3 or IMAP4), enter incoming and outgoing mail server addresses, POP3 or IMAP4 protocols, port numbers, and email encryption.

SYNC, UPDATE, BACK UP, AND RESTORE FROM BACKUP WITH ANDROID

A+
220-902
2.5, 2.6,
2.7

Syncing, backing up, and restoring from backup with Android is much simpler now than it has been in the past. Additionally, Android offers more methods and options for these chores, and third-party apps can often be used. In this part of the chapter, you learn to sync with online accounts, sync all your apps to an app store, and back up any content to your personal computer.

SYNC USING ONLINE ACCOUNTS

Each Google product automatically syncs across devices when you're signed in to your account on that device. For example, the Gmail app on your phone will show the same information and configuration settings as the Gmail interface in your Chrome browser on your computer. Google Drive makes documents available to all of your Google-connected devices, and Google Calendar syncs appointments and reminders across devices. All data is web-based, so everything is accessible through a web browser (Google products work best in Chrome, of course). You can also sync contacts, calendars, photos, newsfeeds, messages, games, and other data with social media accounts such as Facebook, Twitter, Dropbox, LinkedIn, and others. If you notice an account is not syncing correctly, re-sync information for the account through the same *Accounts & sync* menu used to create the account. On the **Settings** app, tap **Accounts & sync**. Select an existing account to turn on sync, force a re-sync, or adjust other account settings.

USE THIRD-PARTY SYNCING APPS

For other content, such as pictures, music, and videos, third-party apps might better suit your needs. Some Android devices come preinstalled with sync apps. Some apps like OneDrive will sync entire folders in the background with no user intervention required, while others like Dropbox only sync files placed in the app's own folder. Some apps sync between a mobile device and computer, while others maintain those files in the cloud and the service is linked to the user's account.

SYNC APPS WITH YOUR APP SOURCE

Google Play maintains records of all apps for a particular Google account. A Google account is associated with an email address (Gmail or some other email address). To tie a Google account to your device, tap **Settings**, **Accounts & sync**, **Add account**, **Google Accounts**, and follow the directions on screen. The process allows you to create a Google account if you don't already have one.

You can sometimes solve a problem with an app by uninstalling it and then installing it again. To uninstall an app, open the Settings app and tap **Apps**. Press and hold the app you want to uninstall and then tap **Uninstall**.

To update an app or restore an app you uninstalled, follow these steps:

1. On the home screen, tap **Play Store**. The Google Play screen appears (see Figure 8-37a for an Android phone). Apps are tied to the Google account you used when you downloaded the app. Tap the menu icon, then tap **My apps** (see Figure 8-37b) to manage settings for your existing apps, including updates.

Menu icon

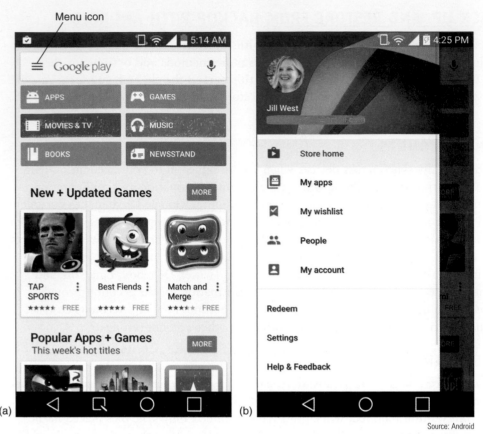

Source: Android

Figure 8-37   (a) Search for new apps in the Play Store and (b) manage your existing apps

2. On the My apps screen, the INSTALLED tab shows a list of apps already installed on the device. To update an app, tap **Update**, then tap **UPDATE** again on the app's screen and accept any access permission changes. To reinstall an app that has been uninstalled, tap **ALL** at the top of the screen. In the list of apps that you have previously downloaded or purchased from the Play Store, select the app and tap **INSTALL**. The app installs again. Notice on these screens that you're given information on permissions assigned to each app, including how it can use storage, the network, GPS locator service, and other hardware controls.

You can control how an app is updated. To do so, return to the Google Play screen and tap the menu icon (refer back to Figure 8-37a). Then tap **Settings**. On the Settings screen, tap **Auto-update apps** and choose to not auto-update apps, which gives you manual control over updates, or **Auto-update apps over Wi-Fi only** to conserve battery charge and use of the cellular data network.

In addition to the Play Store, you can purchase apps from other sites like *Amazon.com*. When you purchase an app from a source other than the Play Store, make sure the site provides the opportunity to restore the app if that becomes necessary.

UPDATE THE ANDROID OS

Updates to the Android OS are automatically pushed to the device from the manufacturer. Because each manufacturer maintains its own versions of Android, these updates might not come at the same time Google announces a major update. When the device receives notice of an update, it might display a message asking permission to install the update. With some devices, you can also manually check for updates at any time, although not all devices provide the option to perform a manual update of the Android OS. To see if manual updates can be performed on your device, go to the **Settings** app and tap

About. On the About screen, tap **System updates** or **Software update** or a similar item. The device turns to the manufacturer's website for information and reports updates available.

Before installing an OS update, you might want to read on the website the release instructions about the update, called Product Release Instructions (PRI), such as new features or patches the update provides and how long the update will take. Later, if a device is giving problems after an OS update or after the device has been rooted, which is similar to the concept of jailbreaking an iOS phone, check the PRI for information that might help you understand the nature of the problem.

BACK UP AND RESTORE ANDROID

Syncing your emails, contacts, calendar, photos, and other data through online accounts serves as a useful backup for that data should something happen to your phone. On the other hand, your app data, Wi-Fi passwords, and other settings can be backed up directly through the Android OS. To do this, go to the **Settings** app, then tap **Backup & reset.** Make sure that **Back up my data** is checked and change the backup account if needed. Your backup data is stored on Google's servers and is connected with your Google account. You can access much of this information directly through your account on the Google website, including recent browser searches, contacts, calendars, location history, alarms, and network connection settings like Wi-Fi passwords. On your mobile device, you can also choose to restore backed-up settings and data to an app that you reinstall after removing it.

You can back up the layout of your home screen and the wallpaper as well. In the **Settings** app, tap **Home screen.** Tap **Home backup & restore,** then **Backup.** Tap **Yes** to save the current home screen settings as a new backup file. To restore these settings later, return to the Home screen menu, tap **Home backup & restore,** and this time tap **Restore.** Tap **Yes** to confirm the restore request.

Hands-On | Project 8-2 Research Apps for Mobile Payment Services

A+
220-902
2.5

iPhone and Android phones both offer some kind of mobile payment service, which allows you to use your smart phone to pay for merchandise or services at a retail checkout counter. iPhone has Apple Pay. Android can use the Google Wallet app and Android Pay will soon be embedded in the newest Android phones. Microsoft has announced that Windows 10 phones will also have a similar service.

Mobile payment services use NFC (near field communication) technology, a short-range, low-power wireless technology, to exchange financial information between your phone and the reader at the checkout counter. You might want to pay with a credit card stored on your phone or get discounts with a store rewards account reported by your phone as you check out. But how secure is your sensitive financial information?

Research the following topics, then answer the following questions:

1. Research how mobile payment systems use NFC technology. How does NFC work? How can you activate NFC on an Android phone? An iPhone? A Windows phone?

2. Find and read some articles online or watch videos that describe the details of storing financial information for mobile payment systems, accessing the information when needed, and transmitting the information securely. What security measures are in place? Where is the data actually stored? What information is actually transmitted at the point of transaction?

3. List three third-party mobile payment apps available either in Apple's App Store, in Android's Play Store, or in Microsoft's Store. On which mobile OS versions will the apps work? What are advantages and disadvantages of each app? How much do the apps cost? What security measures do the apps use?

4. If you were to purchase one of these apps, which one would it be? Why?

TROUBLESHOOT ANDROID DEVICES

A+
220-902
2.5, 2.6,
4.3

Follow these general tips to solve problems with Android devices. For more specific instructions, search the website of the device manufacturer:

1. *Force reboot or soft reset.* You can forcefully reboot the device, which, for Android devices is called a soft reset, by pressing and holding the power button. Power cycling a smart phone every few days is a good idea anyway to keep the phone functioning at peak efficiency. If this doesn't work, you can open the back cover of the device, remove the battery, and then reinstall the battery. Not all Android devices allow removal of the battery. In those cases, some devices offer a simulated battery pull. Research online to find out if this is an option.

2. *Uninstall and reinstall an app.* If you suspect an app is giving a problem, uninstall it and use the app store to reinstall it. How to do this was covered earlier in the chapter.

3. *Update Android.* Try installing Android updates, if available.

4. *Use Safe Mode.* Similar to Windows computers, Android offers a Safe Mode for troubleshooting OS and device issues. Be aware, however, that booting to Safe Mode might result in loss of some settings such as synchronization accounts. The combination of buttons to access Safe Mode varies by device, so consult the manufacturer's website for specific instructions. For one LG smart phone, to access Safe Mode you hold down the power button until the power menu appears. Tap and hold the **Power Off** option until the pop-up shown in Figure 8-38a appears. Tap **OK**, and the phone restarts into Safe Mode, as shown in Figure 8-38b. Notice the *Safe mode* flag at the bottom of the screen, and the default appearance of the home screen. In Safe Mode, only apps native to the Android installation can run, and troubleshooting tools can be accessed through the Settings app to back up data, test configuration issues, or reset the device. To exit Safe Mode, on the Notifications shade, tap the shield icon to restart the device and restore third-party apps.

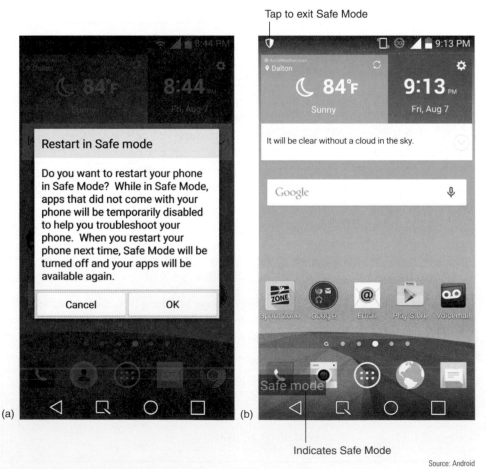

Tap to exit Safe Mode

Indicates Safe Mode

Source: Android

Figure 8-38   (a) Restart in Safe Mode, and (b) in Safe Mode, third-party apps don't load and default configuration settings are used

5. *Update firmware.* Updating the device's firmware can solve problems with network connections and other issues where the Android OS must interact with hardware. A firmware update, also called a baseband update, is distributed by the manufacturer of the device. Usually the firmware update is pushed out from the carrier along with an OS update, but not always. To determine the current baseband version of an Android device, on the **Settings** app, tap **About**, then **Software info**. You can take a screen shot to save the baseband version information before checking for an update. To update the firmware, on the **Settings** app, tap **System updates**, then **Update Firmware** (this menu might vary slightly between manufacturers). When the update is complete or it's reported that no update is available, tap **OK**.

6. *Use Recovery mode.* Take the device into Recovery mode, which is somewhat similar in concept to UEFI/BIOS setup in Windows. To do so, look for instructions on the manufacturer's website. Most likely, you need to hold down a combination of buttons. Once there, Android presents a menu where you can reboot the system, restore the system to factory state, and possibly other options. Try the reboot before you try the factory state, because this last option causes all your apps and data to be lost.

7. *Factory reset or hard reset.* As a last resort, you can perform a factory reset, which, for Android devices is also called a hard reset. The reset erases all data and settings and resets the device to its original factory default state. To do this, from the **Settings** app, tap **Backup & reset**, then tap **Factory data reset**.

Several issues commonly faced with Android devices can be addressed with a little understanding of what has gone wrong behind the scenes. Here's a description of how to handle some common problems:

▲ *Dropped calls.* Sometimes updating the device's firmware can solve problems with dropped calls because the update might apply to the radio firmware, which manages the cellular, Wi-Fi, and Bluetooth radios.

▲ *Wireless connectivity problems.* Intermittent connectivity problems might be caused by a weak Wi-Fi signal. By default, Android stops attempting to reconnect to a weak Wi-Fi signal in order to conserve battery power, but you can change this setting. On the Wi-Fi screen, tap the menu icon and then tap **Advanced Wi-Fi**. Uncheck **Wi-Fi signal weak** (see Figure 8-39a) so that the device will attempt to

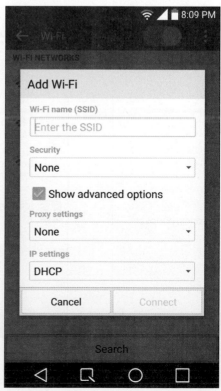

(a)   (b)

Source: Android

Figure 8-39 (a) Uncheck this setting to cause Wi-Fi to work even with a weak signal, and (b) connect to a hidden wireless network that is not broadcasting its SSID

maintain a connection even with a weak signal. Also check to make sure *Keep Wi-Fi on when screen is off* is set to **Yes** so the device won't have to reconnect to Wi-Fi every time the screen is turned back on. Some wireless networks are hidden and must be added manually. On the **Settings** app, tap **Wi-Fi**. Tap the menu icon in the upper-right corner of the screen (the three-dot ellipsis icon, as shown earlier in Figure 8-31a), then tap **Add Wi-Fi**. On the screen shown in Figure 8-39b, enter the SSID and security key for the hidden wireless network.

▲ ***Bluetooth not connecting.*** Make sure that Bluetooth is turned on by tapping the Bluetooth icon on the Notifications shade or on the Settings app. Also check Bluetooth settings. To do this, on the **Settings** app, tap **Bluetooth**, then tap the menu icon in the upper-right corner. From this menu, you can edit the phone's name, and most importantly, you can adjust the visibility time. Tap **Visibility timeout** and increase the visibility time so that the device you're attempting to pair with will have more time to identify the Android device for pairing.

▲ ***Apps not loading.*** You might find that there is insufficient space available on the device, especially if one app is taking up all of its allocated space, or memory is not available for the app you want to load. Uninstalling unused apps and deleting files no longer needed might solve the storage problem. You can download an app from the Play Store that can help clean up storage space, and other apps that report on how apps are using memory. You can also install a file manager app, such as ES File Explorer, to navigate through the directory and delete files or folders one at a time.

To view used and available storage space, go to the **Settings** app and tap **Storage**. You can see in Figure 8-40a where nearly 17 GB is still available on this device, apps are taking up almost 6 GB of the used space, and multimedia files (pictures, videos, and audio files) are taking up less than 100 MB total. From the **Settings** app, tap **Smart cleaning** for suggestions on files to delete and clear up space (see Figure 8-40b).

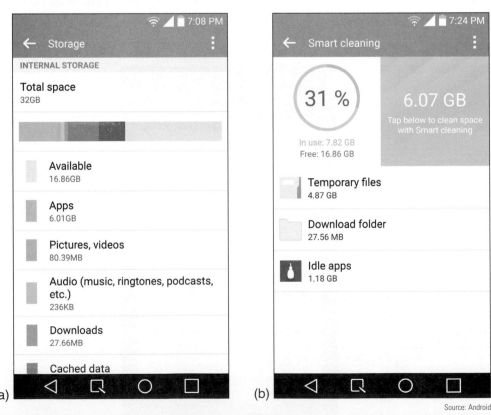

Source: Android

Figure 8-40 (a) Android reports how storage is used and (b) makes suggestions to free some storage space

▲ *Slow performance.* Having too many apps open at once will slow down overall performance (see Figure-8-41a). Tap the overview button on the Action bar, and swipe off to the side as many apps as possible to close them. You can also force stop an app. To see all installed apps, go to the **Settings** app and tap **Apps**. Swipe to the left to see the *Running* tab, which shows all running apps (see Figure 8-41b). Tap an app to force stop the app.

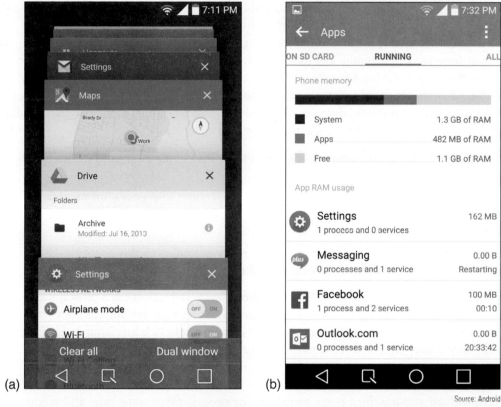

(a)   (b)

Source: Android

Figure 8-41   (a) View open apps and close the ones you're not using to conserve memory; (b) tap an app in the running apps list to force stop the app

▲ *Short battery life.* Too many apps running in the background will drain the battery quickly, as will Wi-Fi, Bluetooth, or other wireless technologies. Disable wireless connections and close apps when you're not using them to save battery juice. Many Android devices have replaceable batteries, so if a battery is performing poorly, consider replacing it.

▲ *Dim display.* Swipe down from the top of any screen to open the Notifications shade, then slide the Brightness slider to the right to brighten the screen. Make sure the **Auto** option is not selected so that you have more control over the screen's brightness level. This is especially helpful when trying to view the screen in bright daylight, but increasing the brightness level will also drain the battery more quickly.

▲ *Inaccurate touch screen response.* A cover on the screen can result in inaccurate touch screen responses. Also, accessibility settings can alter a touch screen's performance. Check accessibility settings in the Settings app. Scroll down and tap **Accessibility**. Touch feedback time is a particular suspect, as is Touch control areas and Auto-rotate screen. You can also perform a motion sensor calibration. In the Settings app, tap **Gestures**, then tap **Motion sensor calibration**. Tap **Calibrate sensor** and follow on screen instructions.

▲ *Overheating.* Running several apps or keeping a smart phone's screen on for more than just a few minutes can heat up the device. Try turning the screen off for a while, and close unneeded apps. If this doesn't work, there might be something wrong with the device's battery, which would need to be checked by a technician at a service center.

▲ *Unable to decrypt email.* Email encryption is done using a public key and private key. You distribute your public key to those who want to send you encrypted email and you keep the private key on your device. If your device is unable to decrypt email, most likely you'll need to generate a new public key and private key and distribute your new public key to those who send you encrypted email. Search the website of the email app that you are using for encryption to find instructions for setting up new public and private keys and for other tips on troubleshooting decrypting problems.

▲ *System lockout.* If a device is locked because of too many failed attempts to sign in (such as when a child has attempted to unlock your device), you can do the following:

1. Wait until the timer on the device counts down and gives you another opportunity to sign in. Enter your passcode or screen swipe.

2. If the passcode or screen swipe doesn't work, enter your Google account and password associated with your device. After you have entered the account and password, you must reset your passcode or screen swipe pattern.

3. If you still can't unlock the device, know that Google offers many solutions to this problem. Go to *accounts.google.com* and search for additional methods and tools to unlock your device.

If you find you are unable to do all you want to do with your Android device (such as install a powerful app or download the latest Android release before your device manufacturer makes it available), you can root your device. Rooting, similar to jailbreaking an iOS device, is the process of obtaining root or administrator privileges to an Android device, which then gives you complete access to the entire file system (all folders and files) and all commands and features. As with jailbreaking an iOS device, it's legal in the United States to root only smart phones, not tablets.

To root a device, you download and use third-party software. The process takes some time and might even involve restoring the device to its factory state. The process of rooting might corrupt the OS, and after the device is rooted, installed apps that require root access can corrupt the OS. For some manufacturers, rooting will void your warranty, and some carriers refuse to provide technical support for a rooted device. In addition, BYOD (Bring Your Own Device) policies in enterprise environments might not allow rooting. Avoid rooting if you can; if you decide to root a device, do so with caution!

CONFIGURE, SYNC, AND TROUBLESHOOT WINDOWS MOBILE DEVICES

Windows Phone tiles and menus are remarkably different from Android and iOS icon-based launchers. But the settings, options, and troubleshooting tools will feel familiar to you because they closely resemble those of Windows 8. Here's a quick overview of settings and troubleshooting tools on a Windows Phone device.

CONFIGURE WINDOWS PHONE NETWORK CONNECTIONS

**A+
220-902
2.5, 2.6,
2.7**

The Action Center, by default, provides direct links to Wi-Fi and Bluetooth connection apps, as well as the Airplane mode app. You can access the Action Center by swiping down from the top of the Start screen. Note that buttons in the Action Center are links to their respective apps, not toggle switches. Tapping Wi-Fi, for example, opens the Wi-Fi app, as shown in Figure 8-42a. The list of shortcuts in the Action Center can be customized by tapping **notifications+actions** in the Settings app, as shown in Figure 8-42b. Also use the Settings app to access cellular+SIM, NFC, Internet sharing (which is the same as tethering), and VPN connections.

(a)   (b)

Figure 8-42   (a) Use the Wi-Fi app to toggle Wi-Fi off and on; (b) several different apps can be added to the Action Center

CONFIGURE WINDOWS PHONE EMAIL, SYNC, AND BACKUP

**A+
220-902
2.5, 2.6,
2.7**

Windows Phone automatically syncs contacts, calendars, and email with an online email account such as a Microsoft account, and, similar to Windows on a desktop computer, documents can be automatically synced through OneDrive. The first Microsoft account used to set up the phone determines the apps and other benefits that will be available to that device, and is the account that will be associated with the device's backup data. Other Microsoft accounts such as Outlook.com or Live.com can be added later, but photos in those accounts will not be synced with the phone, and certain Xbox features will not be available through those accounts.

To add a Microsoft account to a Windows Phone, open the **Settings** app, then tap **email+accounts**. Tap **add an account**, then **Microsoft account**. An information screen, as shown in Figure 8-43a, describes the importance of this first Microsoft account configured on the device. Tap **sign in**.

8

(a)   (b)

Figure 8-43   (a) The first Microsoft account configured on a Windows phone will hold the phone's backups; (b) Windows Phone automatically backs up photos, text messages, phone settings, and app data

Enter your email address and password, then tap **next**. If you use two-factor authentication, you'll be required to verify your identity using the second form of authentication, such as a code sent by text message. After authentication is complete, you're asked if you want to back up content online from the phone (see Figure 8-43b). Tap **yes** to back up photos, text messages, phone settings, and app data. These options can be changed later in the backup app in Settings (see Figure 8-44a).

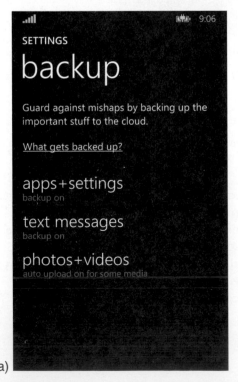

(a)   (b)

Figure 8-44   (a) Tap each item to change its settings; (b) turn backup on to perform a manual backup

✎ **Notes** Windows Phone performs automatic backups only when the device is connected to a Wi-Fi network and plugged in to a power source. To perform a manual backup, go to the **Settings** app, tap **backup**, then **apps+settings**. As shown in Figure 8-44b, tap the toggle switch to turn on **Settings backup** if it's not already on, then tap **back up now**.

The email tile on the Start screen gives direct access to this primary email account; Figure 8-45a shows an email notification on the Outlook tile. Other types of email accounts, as shown in Figure 8-45b, can also be configured automatically (meaning you won't have to provide server information or port numbers).

Figure 8-45 (a) The Outlook tile shows one new email; (b) Exchange, Yahoo!, Google, and iCloud email accounts can all be configured automatically

Microsoft account settings, such as theme and password, can be synced across devices using the **sync my settings** app in Settings. Location data can be synced through the **location** app. See Figure 8-46 to take a look at both of these menus.

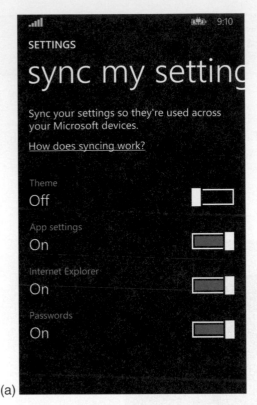

(a)   (b)

Figure 8-46   (a) Sync your Microsoft account settings or (b) your location across devices

UPDATE AND RESTORE WINDOWS PHONE FROM BACKUP

| A+ |
| 220-902 |
| 2.5, 2.7 |

Check for Windows Phone updates by opening the **Settings** app, then tap **phone update**. If no updates are currently pending, tap **check for updates**. On the phone update screen, you can also set the phone to automatically download updates.

Microsoft occasionally issues a critical update for Windows Phone, which generates an update notification; the update should be installed right away. Prompts remind users to install the update if the phone is not configured to install updates automatically. Even when configured for manual updates, Windows Phone will automatically install a required update in three days if the user does not manually install the update sooner.

Restoring a Windows phone from backup, or installing a backup on a new device, requires that you use the same Microsoft account that was used to create the backup. First connect the phone to a Wi-Fi network so you don't risk incurring charges for cellular data. When you first sign in with your Microsoft account, you're given the opportunity to restore from backup. Select the correct backup, then tap **next**. Complete the two-factor authentication process if required, then tap **next**. After the restore process is complete, tap **next**. You can enter passwords for accounts that were restored to the phone, or you can tap **skip** to wait until later. Tap **done** to complete the process.

TROUBLESHOOT WINDOWS MOBILE DEVICES

| A+ |
| 220-902 |
| 2.5, 4.3 |

The following lists options for troubleshooting Windows mobile devices. Before you start troubleshooting, back up your phone's data, and then attempt the following options, which are listed in order from least invasive to most invasive:

1. *Power down and power up.* As with troubleshooting other mobile devices, begin with restarting the phone. Press and hold the **power** button for about three seconds until **slide down to power off** appears

on the screen. Swipe down, wait several seconds, and then press the **power** button again to turn the phone back on.

2. *Force a restart.* You can force the phone to restart by pressing and holding the **volume down** button and the **power** button together for 10–15 seconds until the phone restarts. This option is not available on all Windows Phone devices. Check the manufacturer's documentation for specific directions for these devices.

3. *Remove the battery.* If the battery can be removed, pull it out then put it back in. Press the **power** button to turn the phone back on. If removing power causes issues with signing in to your Microsoft account, go to **Settings** and tap **Date+time** to reset the time.

4. *Update Windows Phone.* Go to **Settings** and tap **update**. Check for updates and install any updates that are available.

5. *Reset.* Reset the phone to factory defaults. This wipes all user data and settings off the phone, so make sure you back up your data and settings first, if possible. On the **Settings** app, tap **about**, then tap **reset your phone**. A warning screen indicates that user content is about to be removed from the device. Tap **yes** to continue, and then tap **yes** on the second warning screen as well. Wait until the reset process is complete.

6. *Force reset.* Some Windows phones offer the ability to force a reset using the phone's physical buttons. This is helpful if the phone is completely unresponsive and you can't get to the Settings app. Check the manufacturer's documentation for specific steps. For some phones, the following procedure forces a reset: Press and hold the **volume down** and **power** buttons until the phone vibrates. Immediately release the volume down and power buttons, then press and hold the **volume down** button again until a large exclamation mark appears on the screen. Finally, press these four buttons in this order: **volume up, volume down, power, volume down**. The phone resets.

7. *Software Recovery Tool.* Some Windows phones can be reset and recovered using the Software Recovery Tool on your computer. Check the manufacturer's documentation for specific information on a particular model. The Software Recovery Tool erases all user content and settings on the phone. If you have a backup of this content, you can restore from backup after the reset. Complete the following steps to use your Windows computer to reset your Windows phone:

a. First make sure the phone is fully charged.

b. On a Windows 8/7 computer, download the Software Recovery Tool (search for article FA142987 on *microsoft.com*) that is designed for your device and install it.

c. Open the application. Then connect the phone to the computer via a USB cable. Once the phone is detected, follow the on screen instructions.

Hands-On | Project 8-3 Select a Mobile Device

A+
220-902
2.5

Shop for a new smart phone or tablet that uses iOS, Android, or Windows Phone. Be sure to read some reviews about a device you are considering. Select two devices that you might consider buying and answer the following questions:

1. What is the device brand, model, and price?

2. What is the OS and version? Amount of storage space? Screen size? Types of network connections? Battery life? Camera pixels?

3. What do you like about each device? Which would you choose and why?

>> CHAPTER SUMMARY

Operating Systems Used on Mobile Devices

◢ The most popular operating systems used on mobile devices include Android by Google, iOS by Apple, and Windows and Windows Phone by Microsoft.

◢ Android is an open source OS, and anyone can develop and sell Android apps or variations in the Android OS. Google is the major distributor of Android and Android apps from its Google Play website.

◢ The iOS by Apple is used only on Apple devices, including the iPhone, iPad, and iPod touch. Apps for the iOS are distributed solely by Apple.

◢ Windows Phone by Microsoft works on smart phones and tracks version numbers alongside Windows for desktops, laptops, and tablets.

Configure, Sync, and Troubleshoot iOS Devices

◢ A cellular network provided by a carrier is used by cell phones for voice communication and text messaging. A smart phone or tablet might also contain the technology to connect to a cellular network for data transmission.

◢ iCloud Backup can be used to back up your device's content to the cloud and iCloud Drive can sync content to all of your iOS devices associated with an Apple ID.

◢ iTunes installed on a personal computer can be used to back up iOS content, sync content from the computer to the device, update iOS, and restore iOS from backup or to its factory state.

◢ To troubleshoot an iOS device, you can restart, reset, update, erase, restore, and recover iOS on the device.

Configure, Sync, and Troubleshoot Android Devices

◢ The Settings app on an Android device can be used to manage network connections, email, online accounts, updates to Android, and security.

◢ Each Google product, such as Gmail, Calendars, and Hangouts, syncs across devices when you're signed in to your account on that device. All data is web-based, so everything is also accessible through a web browser.

◢ Tools and techniques used to solve problems with Android devices include a forced reboot, uninstall and reinstall apps, update the Android OS, use Safe Mode, update firmware, use Recovery mode, and perform a factory reset.

Configure, Sync, and Troubleshoot Windows Mobile Devices

◢ The buttons in the Windows Phone Action Center provide direct links to their respective apps, not toggle switches for features.

◢ The first Microsoft account used to set up a phone determines the apps and other benefits that will be available to that device, and is the account that will be associated with the device's backup data.

◢ Even when configured for manual updates, Windows Phone will automatically install a required update in three days if the user does not manually install the update sooner.

◢ Some Windows phones offer the ability to force a reset using the phone's physical buttons. This is helpful if the phone is completely unresponsive and the Settings app is inaccessible.

>> *KEY TERMS*

For explanations of key terms, see the Glossary for this text.

accelerometer
Action bar
AirDrop
Airplane mode
Android
APK (Android Application Package)
App Store
Apple ID
Apps Drawer
Bluetooth PIN code
closed source
emergency notifications
factory default
Favorites tray
force stop

geotracking
Gmail
Google account
Google Play
GPS (Global Positioning System)
gyroscope
Handoff
hard reset
hotspot
iCloud Backup
iCloud Drive
IMEI (International Mobile Equipment Identity)
IMSI (International Mobile Subscriber Identity)

iOS
iPad
iPhone
iPod touch
iTunes Store
iTunes U
jailbreaking
launcher
location data
Microsoft Exchange
Microsoft Store
Miracast
mobile payment service
notifications
open source
pairing

PRL (Preferred Roaming List)
Product Release Instructions (PRI)
rooting
screen orientation
SDK (Software Development Kit)
S/MIME (Secure/ Multipurpose Internet Mail Extensions)
soft reset
tethering
virtual assistant
Wi-Fi calling
Windows Phone (WP)

8

>> *REVIEWING THE BASICS*

1. List four types of antennas a smart phone might contain. Which three antennas are disabled in Airplane mode?

2. What company provides and oversees the Android Play Store? What is the website of this store?

3. List three Apple devices that use iOS.

4. Who is the sole distributor of apps for iOS?

5. What is one disadvantage to users when using an open source operating system on a mobile device?

6. Which programming language is used to write most Android apps? Apple requires that iOS apps be written in one of which three programming languages?

7. How can you configure a mobile device so it cannot connect to any network?

8. Which type of network connection requires that two devices pair before the connection is completed?

9. Which email protocol downloads email to be managed on the client machine? Which email protocol manages email on the server?

10. Which database needs to be updated so a smart phone knows which cell towers to connect with inside and outside the carrier's network?

11. Which email protocol uses port 110? 143? 993? 995?

12. Which security protocol is used to encrypt email?

13. Which protocol is a more secure alternative to using SMTP for outgoing email?

14. Which email server uses ActiveSync to sync all emails, contacts, and calendar updates on the server and client machines, including mobile devices?

15. Which procedure is the least intrusive solution to a problem with iOS, to reset an iOS device or to restore an iOS device?

16. What is the location of an iOS backup stored on a local Windows computer via iTunes?

17. What technology is available on both Windows Phone and Android to mirror the phone's display through a wireless connection with a TV?

18. What is the difference between tethering and hotspots?

19. What Google product provides free storage for photos, documents, and other content?

20. What type of item does an IMEI identify?

>> THINKING CRITICALLY

1. Suppose you find an app that cost you $4.99 is missing from your Android. What is the best way to restore the missing app?

    a. Go to backup storage and perform a restore to recover the lost app.

    b. Purchase the app again.

    c. Go to the Play Store where you bought the app and install it again.

    d. Go to the Settings app and perform an application restore.

2. Suppose you and your friend want to exchange lecture notes taken during class. She has an iPhone and you have an iPad. What is the easiest way to do the exchange?

    a. Cope the files to an SD card and move the SD card to each device.

    b. Drop the files in OneDrive and share notebooks with each other.

    c. Send a text to each other with the files attached.

    d. Transfer the files through an AirDrop connection.

3. You have set up your Android phone using one Google account and your Android tablet using a second Google account. Now you would like to download the apps you purchased on your phone to your tablet. What is the best way to do this?

    a. Set up the Google account on your tablet that you used to buy apps on your phone and then download the apps.

    b. Buy the apps a second time from your tablet.

    c. Back up the apps on your phone to your SD card and then move the SD card to your tablet and transfer the apps.

    d. Call Google support and ask them to merge the two Google accounts into one.

>> REAL PROBLEMS, REAL SOLUTIONS

REAL PROBLEM 8-1 Using the Microsoft Windows Phone Emulator

Microsoft offers a Windows Phone emulator embedded in its Visual Studio software, which can be used by developers of mobile apps for Windows Phone. You will need a Microsoft account to do this project. Follow these general directions to download, install, and run the emulator:

1. On a Windows 8.1 computer, go into UEFI/BIOS setup and verify that hardware-assisted virtualization is turned on. This UEFI/BIOS feature supports VMs running on the system and is required for the Windows emulator to work. You learned to use UEFI/BIOS setup earlier in the text.

2. Go to **visualstudio.com** and click the link **Download Community 2015** to download Visual Studio Community 2015. The downloaded file is vs_community.exe. Double-click the file to install the software. Under *Choose the type of installation*, select **Custom**. On the next screen, check **Windows 8.1 and Windows Phone 8.0/8.1 Tools** and continue with the installation, which can take some time.

3. After installation is complete, open **Visual Studio 2015** and create a new project. You will be asked to sign in to your Microsoft account and the account will be given a free developer license.

4. For the project template, in the left pane, click **Visual C#**, click **Windows**, click **Windows 8,** and click **Windows Phone**. In the middle pane, click **Blank App (Windows Phone)**. Click **OK** and the project is created.

5. To select the emulator for your project, click **Device** and select any of the emulator devices, as shown in Figure 8-47.

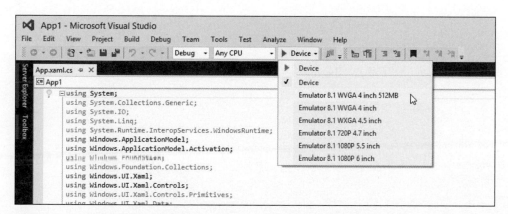

Figure 8-47 Select the emulator to use with your Visual Studio project

6. To start the emulator, click the **Emulator** button that replaces the Device button. The emulator tool opens (see Figure 8-48). Click the **Start** button at the bottom of the emulator to show the Start screen in the emulator. Explore the menus in the Windows Phone emulator.

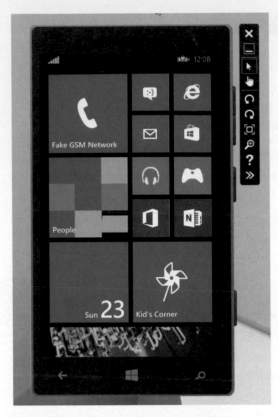

Figure 8-48   Windows Phone 8.1 emulator

7. Take a screen shot of your emulator and email it to your instructor.

REAL PROBLEM 8-2 Using the Android SDK to Run an Android Emulator

This Real Problem is a challenging project and you might want to work with a partner so that you will have someone with whom to discuss solutions and share the work. Go to *Youtube.com* and watch some videos on downloading and installing the Android SDK and using it to install a virtual Android device using the Android Emulator. Then do the work to use the Android SDK and the Android Emulator to emulate an Android device. To prove you have accomplished this feat, take a screen shot of your virtual Android device running on your computer and email it to your instructor. Write a one-page report of your experience and include in it five or six tips that you think would help a student through this project.

Windows Resources on a Network

After completing this chapter, you will be able to:

- Support some client/server applications

- Share and secure files and folders on a network

- Support cloud computing services on a network

I n the chapter, "Connecting To and Setting Up a Network," you learned how to create and manage a network connection. This chapter focuses on using a network for client/server applications, for sharing files and folders with network users, and for providing cloud computing services.

Security is always a huge concern when dealing with networks. In this chapter, you learn how to share resources on the network and still protect these resources from those who should not have access. In the chapter, "Security Strategies," we take security to a higher level and discuss many tools and techniques you can use to protect a computer or a SOHO network.

SUPPORTING CLIENT/SERVER APPLICATIONS

Resources available on a network might include network services, such as email or file storage, or applications hosted by a server and used by a client. Client/server applications you will likely be expected to support include Internet Explorer, Remote Desktop, and other remote applications. You also need to know how to use Group Policy to configure Quality of Service (QoS) for client/server applications and how to link a data source through a network to database applications. All of these skills are covered in this part of the chapter.

NETWORK SERVERS

A+
220-902
2.4

Recall from the chapter, "Connecting To and Setting Up a Network," that a client computer contacts a server in order to request information or perform a task, such as when a web browser connects with a web server and requests a webpage. Many other types of server resources exist on a typical network. Some of these servers are standalone devices, but often multiple network services are provided by a single server computer, or servers might be embedded in other devices. For example, servers are sometimes embedded in router firmware (such as a SOHO router providing FTP services) or in an operating system (such as web server capabilities embedded in Windows Server 2012). Each time any of these components is updated, any legacy technology present on the network must be taken into consideration, which can result in a complex web of network server resources. Here's a brief list of several popular client/server resources used on networks and the Internet:

▲ *Mail server.* Email is a client/server application that involves two mail servers. Recall that SMTP is used to send email messages, and either POP3 or IMAP4 is used to deliver an email message to a client. An example of a popular email server application is Microsoft Exchange Server. Outlook, an application in the Microsoft Office suite of applications, is a popular email client application.

▲ *File server.* A file server stores files and makes them available to other computers. A network administrator can make sure this data is backed up regularly and kept secure.

▲ *Print server.* A print server manages network printers and makes them available to computers throughout the network. Expensive network printers can handle high-capacity print jobs from many sources, eliminating the need for a desktop printer at each workstation. If a network printer fails, a technician can sometimes diagnose and solve the problem from her workstation.

▲ *DHCP server.* Recall from the chapter, "Connecting To and Setting Up a Network," that a DHCP server leases an IP address to a computer when it first attempts to initiate a connection to the network and requests an IP address. The DHCP server is configured to pull from a range of IP addresses, which is called the DHCP scope.

▲ *DNS server.* DNS servers, as you learned in the chapter, "Connecting To and Setting Up a Network," store domain names and their associated IP addresses for computers on the Internet or a large enterprise network. DNS servers are responsible for name resolution, which happens when a client computer sends an FQDN (fully qualified domain name) to a DNS server and requests the IP address associated with this character-based name.

> ✎ **Notes** A telltale sign that the network's DNS server is malfunctioning is when you can reach a website by its IP address, but not by its FQDN (fully qualified domain name).

▲ *Proxy server.* A proxy server is a computer that intercepts requests that a client, such as a browser, makes of another server, such as a web server. The proxy server substitutes its own IP address for the request using NAT protocols. An example of using a proxy server is when an ISP caches webpages to speed up requests for the same pages. After it caches a page, if another browser requests the same content, the proxy server can provide the content that it has cached. In addition, a proxy server sometimes acts as a gateway to the Internet, a firewall to protect the network, a filter for email, and to restrict Internet access by employees in order to force those employees to follow company policies.

◢ *Authentication server.* An authentication server authenticates users or computers to the network so that they can access network resources. Active Directory, which is a directory service included in Windows Server, is often used for this purpose on a Windows domain. The authentication server stores user or device credentials, such as user names and passwords, validates an authentication request, and determines the permissions assigned to each user, device, or group.

◢ *Web server.* A web server serves up webpages to clients. Many corporations have their own web servers, which are available privately on the corporate network. Other web servers are public, accessible from anywhere on the Internet. The most popular web server application is Apache (see *apache.org*), which primarily runs on UNIX or Linux systems and can also run on Windows. The second most popular web server is Internet Information Services (IIS), which is embedded in the Windows Server operating system.

INTERNET EXPLORER

A+
220-902
1.5, 1.6

By far, the most popular client/server applications on the Internet are a browser and web server. The latest release of Internet Explorer (IE) is version 11, although Windows 10 features a new browser called Microsoft Edge to replace Internet Explorer going forward. Windows 8.1 comes with IE version 11 installed, and earlier versions of Windows can upgrade to IE version 11 using Windows Update. To upgrade, open Windows Update and find and install the Internet Explorer 11 update. You can also go to the *microsoft.com* website and follow links to download and install IE11.

Here are some tips about using IE11:

◢ *Menu bar.* Internet Explorer has a menu bar, which you can see by pressing the **Alt** key. The menu appears for a long enough time for you to make one selection from the menu. If you want the menu bar to be permanently visible, right-click a blank area in the title bar and check **Menu bar** in the shortcut menu (see Figure 9-1). Notice in Figure 9-1, you can also add the command bar to the IE window.

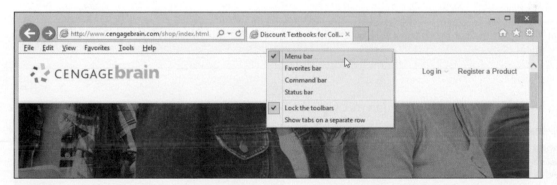

Figure 9-1 Access the shortcut menu from the title bar to control the Internet Explorer window

◢ *HTTP Secure.* Some web servers use HTTP with the SSL or TLS protocols to secure transmissions to and from the web server. To find out if HTTP Secure (HTTPS) is being used in IE11, look for https and a padlock icon in the browser address box. Click the padlock to get information about the site security (see Figure 9-2).

9

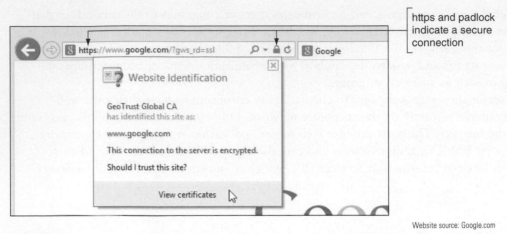

Website source: Google.com

Figure 9-2 A secure connection from browser to web server ensures all transmissions are encrypted

▲ *Repair or disable.* If you have a problem with IE11, use the same tools as you would for any Windows component to fix the problem, such as installing Windows updates, applying a restore point, or refreshing Windows 8. If you want to use a different browser, you can disable IE11. Open the **Programs and Features** window in Control Panel and click **Turn Windows features on or off**. In the Windows Features box, uncheck **Internet Explorer 11** and click **OK**.

▲ *Internet Options box.* Use the Internet Options box to manage Internet Explorer settings. To open the box, click the **Tools** icon on the right side of the IE title bar and click **Internet options**. Another method is to press **Alt**, which causes the menu bar to appear; then click **Tools, Internet options**. A third method is to click **Internet Options** in the Classic view of Control Panel. The Internet Options box appears. Whenever you make changes in the box, click **Apply** to apply these changes without closing the box. Alternately, you can click **OK** to save your changes and close the box.

> 🖉 **Notes** If you open the Internet Options box through Control Panel, the box is titled *Internet Properties* and the menus and options vary slightly.

Now let's see how to use each tab in the Internet Options box.

> ★ **A+ Exam Tip** The A+ 220-902 exam expects you to know how to use the General, Security, Privacy, Connections, Programs, and Advanced tabs on the Internet Options box.

GENERAL TAB

The General tab on the Internet Options box is shown on the left side of Figure 9-3.

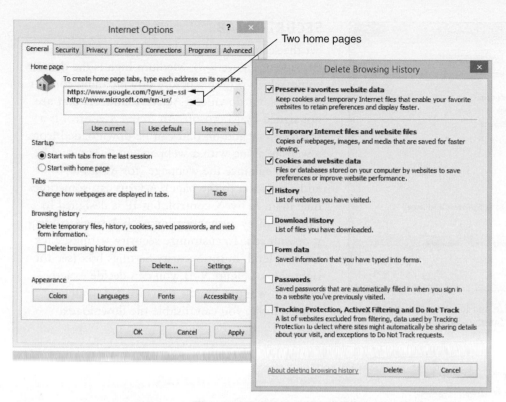

Figure 9-3 Use the General tab of the Internet Options box to delete your browsing history

Here's what you can do using the General tab:

▲ Change the home page or add a second home page tab. To add a second home page tab, insert the URL on a second line in the Home page area, as shown on the left side of Figure 9-3.

▲ To protect your identity and surfing records, it's a good idea to delete all your browsing history each time you use IE on a computer that is not your own. To delete this history, click **Delete**. In the Delete Browsing History box (see the right side of Figure 9-3), notice the item at the top. When you leave this item checked, any cookies used by websites in your Favorites list are *not* deleted. Select the items to delete and click **Delete**.

▲ If you want to delete your browsing history each time you close Internet Explorer, check **Delete browsing history on exit** on the General tab.

▲ Internet Explorer holds a cache containing previously downloaded content in case it is requested again. The cache is stored in several folders named Temporary Internet Files. To manage the IE cache, click **Settings** under Browsing history. The Website Data Settings box (called the Temporary Internet Files and History Settings box in Windows 7) appears, as shown in Figure 9-4. Use this box to change the maximum allowed space used for temporary Internet files and to control the location of these files.

Figure 9-4   Control the size and location of temporary files used by Internet Explorer

SECURITY TAB

Set the security level on the Security tab (see the left side of Figure 9-5). Medium-high is the default value, which prompts before downloading content and does not download ActiveX controls that are not signed by Microsoft. An ActiveX control is a small app or add-on that can be downloaded from a website along with a webpage and is executed by IE to enhance the webpage (for example, to add animation to the page). A virus can sometimes hide in an ActiveX control, but IE is designed to catch them by authenticating each ActiveX control it downloads. To customize security settings, click **Custom level**. In the Security Settings box (see the right side of Figure 9-5), you can decide exactly how you want to handle downloaded content. For example, you can disable file downloads.

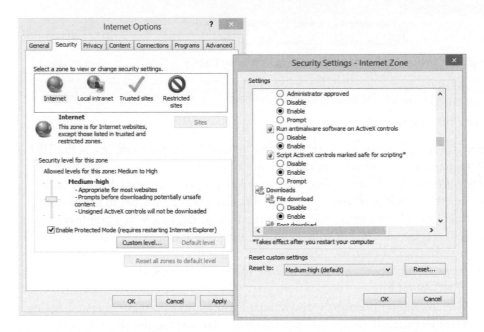

Figure 9-5   Use the Security tab to control what type of content is downloaded and how it is managed

PRIVACY TAB AND CONTENT TAB

Use the Privacy tab (see the left side of Figure 9-6) to block cookies that might invade your privacy or steal your identity. You can also use this tab to control the Pop-up Blocker, which prevents annoying pop-ups as you surf the web. To allow a pop-up from a particular website, click **Settings** and enter the URL of the website in the Pop-up Blocker Settings box (see the right side of Figure 9-6). Some pop-ups are useful, such as when you're trying to download a file from a website and the site asks permission to complete the download.

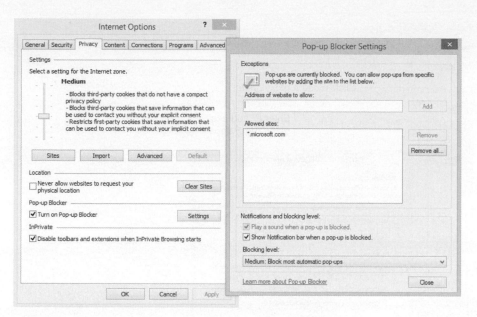

Figure 9-6   Use the Privacy tab to control pop-ups and cookies

The Content tab contains settings for Family Safety, certificates used by websites, and how AutoComplete and Feeds are handled.

CONNECTIONS TAB AND PROXY SETTINGS

The Connections tab allows you to configure proxy server settings and create a VPN connection. Many large corporations and ISPs use proxy servers to speed up Internet access. A web browser does not have to be aware that a proxy server is in use. However, one reason you might need to configure Internet Explorer to be aware of and use a proxy server is when you are on a corporate network and are having a problem connecting to a secured website (one using HTTP over SSL or another encryption protocol). The problem might be caused by Windows trying to connect using the wrong proxy server on the network. Check with your network administrator to find out if a specific proxy server should be used to manage secure website connections.

★ **A+ Exam Tip**   The A+ 220-902 exam expects you to know how to configure proxy settings on a client desktop.

If you need to configure Internet Explorer to use a specific proxy server, on the Connections tab, click **LAN settings**. In the settings box, check **Use a proxy server for your LAN** and enter the IP address of the proxy server (see Figure 9-7). If your organization uses more than one proxy server, click **Advanced** and enter IP addresses for each type of proxy server on your network (see Figure 9-8). You can also enter a port address for each server. If you are trying to solve a problem of connecting to a server using HTTP over SSL or another secured protocol, enter the IP address of the proxy server that is used to manage secure connections in the Secure field of this box.

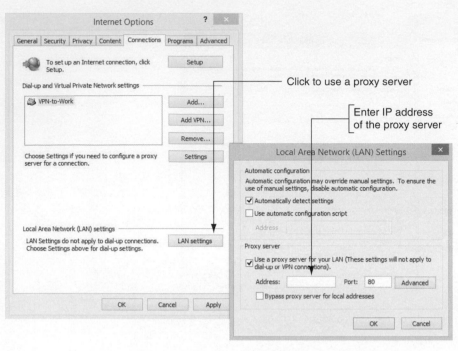

Figure 9-7   Configure Internet Explorer to use one or more proxy servers

Figure 9-8   Enter the IP addresses of all proxy servers on your corporate network

Also notice on the Connections tab of the Internet Options box that you can create a VPN connection. To do so, click **Add VPN** (refer back to the left side of Figure 9-7) and follow the steps of the connection wizard. Recall from the chapter, "Connecting To and Setting Up a Network," that you can also create a VPN connection using the Network and Sharing Center.

PROGRAMS TAB

Add-ons, also called plug-ins, are small apps that help Internet Explorer to display multimedia content, manage email, translate text, or other actions. The Programs tab (see Figure 9-9) is used to manage add-ons.

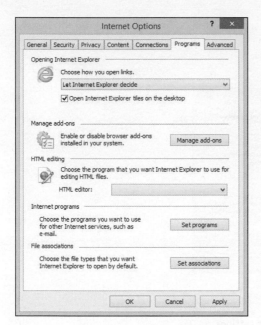

Figure 9-9   Use the Programs tab to manage add-ons and default applications used for Internet services

Click **Manage add-ons** to open the Manage Add-ons box (see Figure 9-10a). In the left pane under Show, you can display All add-ons, Currently loaded add-ons (default view), Run without permission, and Downloaded controls. Click an add-on to select it and see information about it in the lower pane. To disable an add-on, click **Disable**. To enable a disabled one, click **Enable**.

Downloaded ActiveX controls can be uninstalled using this window. To delete a selected ActiveX control, click **More information**. In the More Information box (see Figure 9-10b), click **Remove**. To see only the add-ons you can delete, select **Downloaded controls** in the Show dropdown list of the Manage Add-ons window. You can delete other add-ons using the Programs and Features window in Control Panel.

> **Notes** If you use Control Panel to open the Internet Properties box and open the Manage Add-ons box from there, the *Currently loaded add-ons* option is missing in the dropdown list under Show.

9

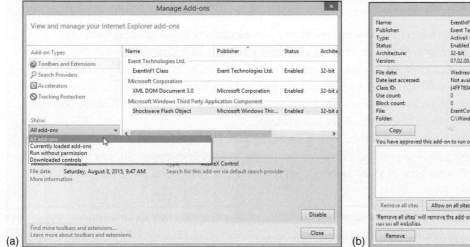
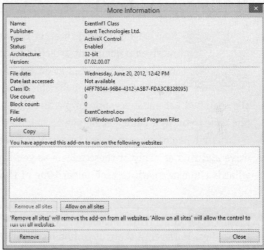

(a)   (b)

Figure 9-10   (a) Manage Internet Explorer add-ons, and (b) delete downloaded ActiveX controls

ADVANCED TAB

The Advanced tab (see the left side of Figure 9-11) contains several miscellaneous settings used to control Internet Explorer. If you suspect problems are caused by wrong settings, click **Reset** to return IE to all default settings. In the Reset Internet Explorer Settings box shown on the right side of Figure 9-11, make your decision about how to handle personal settings and then click **Reset**.

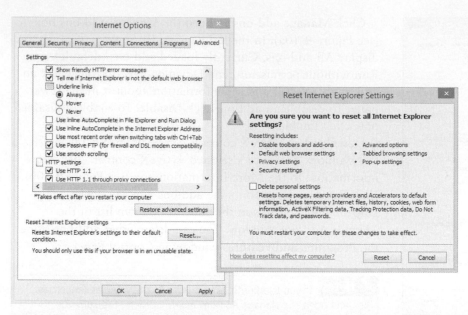

Figure 9-11 Solve problems with Internet Explorer by resetting it to default settings

Hands-On | Project 9-1 Find Lost Downloaded Files

A+
220-902
1.5, 1.6

Your friend is using Internet Explorer to send and receive email using her Hotmail account. She received a document attached to an email message from a business associate. She double-clicked the Word document listed as an attachment and spent a couple of hours editing it, saving the document as she worked. Then she closed the document. But where's the document? When she later needed it, she searched her email account online and the Documents folder on her hard drive, but could not find the document. She called you in a panic asking you to help her find her lost document.

Internet Explorer keeps downloaded files in several folders named Temporary Internet Files. Search your hard drive and find as many of these folders as you can. How many Temporary Internet Files folders did you find and what is the exact path to each folder? One of these folders is certain to contain a lost downloaded document.

> ✎ **Notes** As an IT technician, it's helpful to be familiar with the locations of temporary folders that might contain lost files. However, a shortcut to finding a lost Word document is to open Word, click **FILE**, click **Open**, and then search through the Recent Documents list.

Hands-On | Project 9-2 Use Google Chrome

Internet Explorer is not the only browser available, and many users prefer others such as Mozilla Firefox (*mozilla.org*) or Google Chrome (*google.com*). Go to the Google website and download and install Google Chrome. Use it to browse the web. How does it compare with Internet Explorer? What do you like better about it? What do you not like as well? When might you recommend that someone use Chrome rather than Internet Explorer? What security features does Google Chrome offer? What are the steps to import your favorites list from IE into Chrome?

REMOTE DESKTOP CONNECTION (RDC)

A+
220-902
1.4, 1.5,
1.6

Remote Desktop Connection (RDC), commonly called Remote Desktop, gives a user access to a Windows desktop from anywhere on the Internet. As a software developer, I find Remote Desktop extremely useful when I work from a remote location (my home office) and need to access a corporate network to support software on that network. Using the Internet, I can access a file server on these secured networks to make my software changes. Remote Desktop is easy to use and relatively safe for the corporate network. To use Remote Desktop, the computer you want to remotely access (the server) must be running business or professional editions of Windows 8/7/Vista, but the computer you're using to access it (the client) can be running any version of Windows.

★ **A+ Exam Tip** The A+ 220-902 exam expects you to know how to use Remote Desktop.

APPLYING | CONCEPTS CONFIGURE REMOTE DESKTOP ON TWO COMPUTERS

A+
220-902
1.4, 1.5,
1.6

In this section, you see how to set up Remote Desktop for first use, and then you learn how to use it.

How to Set Up Remote Desktop for First Use

The host or server computer is the computer that is serving up Remote Desktop to client computers that can remote in to the server. To prepare your host computer, you need to configure the computer for static IP addressing and also configure the Remote Desktop service. Here are the steps needed:

1. Configure the computer for static IP addressing. How to assign a static IP address is covered in the chapter, "Connecting To and Setting Up a Network."

2. If your computer is behind a firewall, configure the router for port forwarding and allow incoming traffic on port 3389. Forward that traffic to the IP address of your desktop computer. You learned how to set up port forwarding in the chapter, "Connecting To and Setting Up a Network."

3. To turn on the Remote Desktop service, open the System window and click **Remote settings** in the left pane. The System Properties box appears with the Remote tab selected (see the middle of Figure 9-12). In this window, you can control settings for Remote Assistance and Remote Desktop. In the Remote Desktop area,

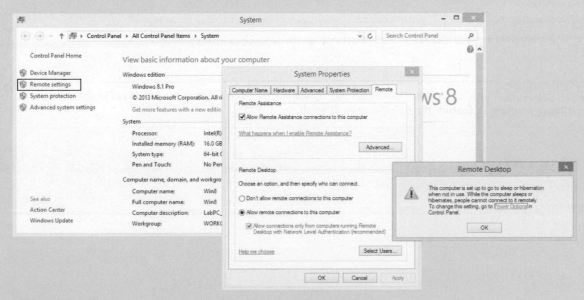

Figure 9-12 Configure a computer to run the Remote Desktop service

(continues)

check **Allow remote connections to this computer**. If a warning box appears about changing the power options in Control Panel (see the right side of Figure 9-12), click **OK** to close the box. Leave the box checked that says *Allow connections only from computers running Remote Desktop with Network Level Authentication (recommended)*.

◇ OS Differences To enable Remote Desktop on a Windows 7 computer, in the Remote Desktop area of the Remote tab in the System Properties box, check **Allow connections from computers running any version of Remote Desktop (less secure).**

4. Users who have administrative privileges are allowed to use Remote Desktop by default, but other users need to be added. If you need to add a user, click **Select Users** and follow the directions on screen. Then close all windows.

5. Verify that Windows Firewall is set to allow Remote Desktop activity to this computer. To do that, open **Control Panel** in Classic view and click **Windows Firewall**. The Windows Firewall window appears (see Figure 9-13). In the left pane, click **Allow an app or feature through Windows Firewall**.

Figure 9-13   Windows Firewall can block or allow activity on the network to your computer

◇ OS Differences To allow Remote Desktop activity on a Windows 7 computer, in the Windows Firewall window, click **Allow a program or feature through Windows Firewall.**

6. The Allowed apps window appears. Scroll down to Remote Desktop and adjust the settings as needed (see Figure 9-14). Click **OK** to apply any changes.

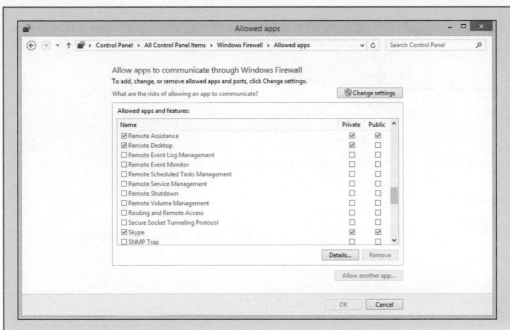

Figure 9-14   Allow Remote Desktop communication through Windows Firewall on your local computer

You are now ready to test Remote Desktop.

How to Use Remote Desktop

Try to use Remote Desktop from another computer somewhere on your local network and make sure that works before testing the Remote Desktop connection from the Internet. On the client computer, you can start Remote Desktop to remote in to your host computer by using the command mstsc (which stands for Microsoft Terminal Services Client). Follow these steps to use Remote Desktop:

1. Enter the **mstsc** command in the Windows 8 Run box or the Windows 7 Search box. The Remote Desktop Connection box opens (see Figure 9-15).

2. Enter the IP address or the host name of the computer to which you want to connect. If you decide to use a host name, begin the host name with two backslashes, as in *CompanyFileServer*.

Figure 9-15   The IP address of the remote computer can be used to connect to it

> **Notes**   If you have trouble using the host name to make a Remote Desktop connection on a local network, try entering the host name and IP address of the remote computer in the hosts file in the C:\Windows\System32\drivers\etc folder of the client computer.

3. If you plan to transfer files from one computer to the other, click **Show Options** for Windows 8 or **Options** for Windows 7, and then click the **Local Resources** tab, as shown on the left side of Figure 9-16. Click **More**. The box on the right side of Figure 9-16 appears. Check **Drives**. Click **OK**. Click **Connect** to make the connection. If a warning box appears, click **Connect** again. If another warning box appears, click **Yes**.

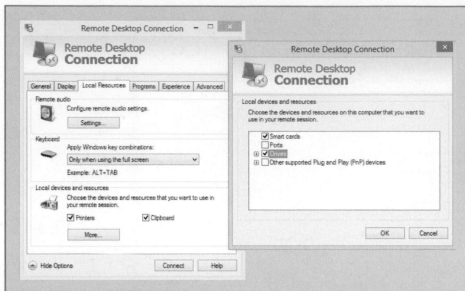

Figure 9-16   Allow drives and other devices to be shared using the Remote Desktop Connection

> 📝 **Notes** Server applications such as Remote Desktop listen for network activity from clients. If you want these server applications to be available at all times, you can set your network adapter properties to Wake-on-LAN, which you learned about in the chapter, "Connecting To and Setting Up a Network."

4. A Windows security box appears, which is displayed by the remote computer (see Figure 9-17). Sign in with a user name and password for the remote computer. If a warning box appears saying the remote computer might not be secure, click **Yes** to continue the connection.

5. The desktop of the remote computer appears with a toolbar at the top of the screen, as shown in Figure 9-18. Click **Restore Down** to show both the remote desktop and the local desktop on the same screen, as shown in Figure 9-19.

Figure 9-17   Enter your user name and password on the remote computer

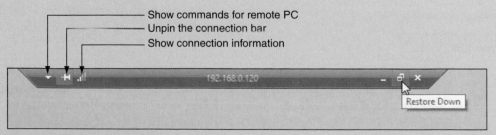

Show commands for remote PC
Unpin the connection bar
Show connection information

Figure 9-18   The RDC connection bar is pinned to the top of the window showing the remote computer's screen

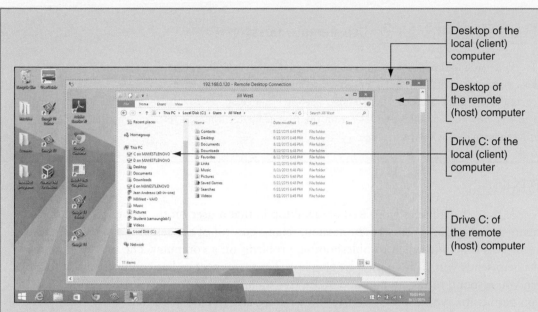

Figure 9-19   The desktop of the remote computer is available on your local computer

9

6. When you click in the remote desktop's window, you can work with the remote computer just as if you were sitting in front of it, except response time is slower. To move files back and forth between computers, use File Explorer or Windows Explorer on the remote computer. Files on your local computer and on the remote computer will appear in the Explorer window on the remote computer in the Windows 8 This PC group or the Windows 7 Computer group. For example, in Figure 9-19, you can see drive C: on each computer labeled in the figure. To close the connection to the remote computer, sign out from the remote computer or close the desktop window.

🖊 **Notes**   Even though Windows normally allows more than one user to be signed in at the same time, this is not the case with Remote Desktop. When a Remote Desktop session is opened, all local users on the remote computer must sign out after receiving a warning, as shown in Figure 9-20.

Figure 9-20   Local users must sign out before a Remote Desktop Connection can happen

Is your host computer as safe as it was before you set it to serve up Remote Desktop and enabled port forwarding to it? Actually, no, because a port has been opened, so take this into account when you decide to use Remote Desktop. In a project at the end of this chapter, you learn how you can take further steps to protect the security of your computer when using Remote Desktop. Alternately, you can consider using software that does not require you to open ports. Examples of this type of software, some of which are free, are TeamViewer (*teamviewer.com*), GoToMyPC by Citrix (*gotomypc.com*), and LogMeIn (*logmein.com*).

Hands-On | Project 9-3 Use Remote Desktop

**A+
220-902
1.4, 1.5,
1.6**

To use Remote Desktop, you need two networked computers. The computer you will configure as the host computer must be running a business or professional edition of Windows 8/7. Configure one computer to be the Remote Desktop host. Use the other computer to remote in to the host computer. Can you view and edit files and folders on the host computer from the remote computer? Try to copy a file from your local computer to the host.

REMOTE ASSISTANCE

**A+
220-902
1.5, 1.6**

Remote Assistance differs from Remote Desktop in that a user on the server computer can remain signed in during the remote session, retains control of the session, and can see the screen. This is helpful when troubleshooting problems on a computer. The user who needs your help sends you an invitation by email or chat to connect to her computer using Remote Assistance. When you respond to the invitation, you can see the user's desktop just as she sees it. And, if the user gives you permission, you can take control of her computer to change settings or do whatever else is needed to fix her problem or show her how to perform a task. Think of Remote Assistance as a way to provide virtual desk-side support.

There are several ways to initiate a Remote Assistance session:

◢ The user saves an invitation file and then sends that file to the technician. The file can be sent by any method, including email, chat, or posting to a shared folder on the network.
◢ The user can send an automated email through the Remote Assistance app. This option only works if the system is configured with a compatible email program.
◢ The user can use Easy Connect, which is the easiest method to start a Remote Assistance connection but only works if both computers used for the connection support the Easy Connect feature. Easy Connect requires Windows 8/7. Also know that some routers don't support the Peer Name Resolution Protocol (PNRP), which is the protocol Easy Connect uses to establish a Remote Assistance connection.
◢ The technician can initiate a session. This method is the most difficult to use, requiring that Group Policies be applied on the technician's computer.

To initiate a Remote Assistance connection from the host computer using Easy Connect, complete the following steps:

1. Open the **System** window and click **Remote settings** in the left pane. The System Properties box appears with the Remote tab selected (refer back to Figure 9-12).

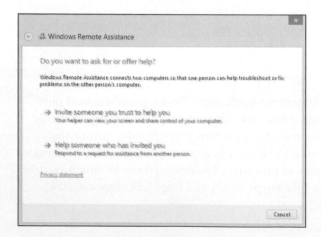

2. In the Remote Assistance area, check **Allow Remote Assistance connections to this computer**, and then click **OK**.

3. Open **Control Panel** in Category view. Click **System and Security**. Under System, click **Launch remote assistance**. (Alternately, you can press **Win+S** to open search and type **Invite**, then click **Invite someone to connect to your PC and help you**.) The Windows Remote Assistance box in Figure 9-21 appears.

> **◇ OS Differences** To launch Remote Assistance in Windows 7, click **Start**, type **Remote Assistance** in the Search box, and then click **Windows Remote Assistance**.

Figure 9-21 Create or respond to an invitation to connect

4. Click **Invite someone you trust to help you**, then click **Use Easy Connect**. Remote Assistance provides a password for the user to give the technician in order to create the connection, as shown in Figure 9-22. If needed, the user can also create an invitation file using this window.

Figure 9-22 The Easy Connect password validates the connection

Figure 9-23 Enter the 12-character password created by Easy Connect on the other computer

The technician can respond to the Easy Connect invitation by entering the password into Remote Assistance, as follows:

1. Launch Remote Assistance, as described in Step 3 above.

2. In the Windows Remote Assistance window (shown in Figure 9-21), click **Help someone who has invited you**, then click **Use Easy Connect**.

3. Enter the 12-character password (see Figure 9-23), which is not case sensitive, and click **OK**.

4. The user's computer generates a warning box requesting permission for the technician's computer to connect. The user clicks **Yes** to allow the connection. The user's desktop turns black and the Remote Assistance management window appears. The technician's computer opens the Windows Remote Assistance window, as shown in Figure 9-24, with a live feed from the user's computer.

9

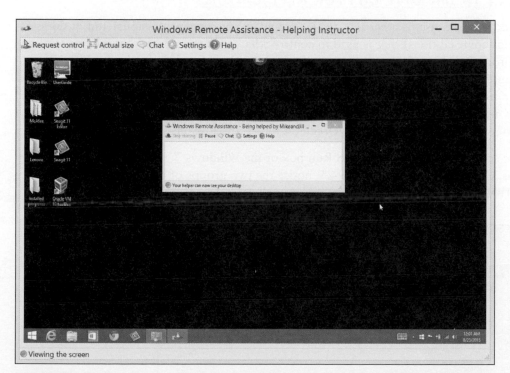

Figure 9-24 The size of the screen can be adjusted by using the toolbar options at the top

Here are some things you can do during a Remote Assistance session:

▲ To open a chat session with the user, click the **Chat** icon. A chat pane appears in the Remote Assistance window on both desktops.

▲ To ask the user if you can take control of her desktop, click **Request control** in the Remote Assistance control window. When the user accepts the request, you can control her computer. The user can stop sharing control by clicking **Stop sharing**.

▲ The user can hide her desktop from you at any time by clicking **Pause** in the control window.

▲ Either of you can disconnect the session by closing the control window.

▲ A log file is kept of every Remote Assistance session in the C:\Users*username*\Documents\Remote Assistance Logs folder. The file includes the chat session. If you type instructions during the chat session that will later help the user, she can use the log file to remind her of what was said and done.

▲ If an invitation created by a user is not used within six hours, the invitation expires. This time frame can be changed by clicking **Advanced** in the Remote Assistance section on the Remote tab of the System Properties dialog box.

If you have problems making the connection, do the following:

1. Windows Firewall on the user's computer might be blocking Remote Assistance. Verify that Remote Assistance is checked as an exception to blocked apps in the Windows Firewall window.

2. If you are outside the user's local network, the hardware firewall protecting her network might be blocking Remote Assistance. Verify that port forwarding on that hardware firewall is enabled for Remote Assistance. Remote Assistance uses port 3389, the same port used by Remote Desktop.

USE GROUP POLICY TO IMPROVE QoS FOR APPLICATIONS

Group Policy (gpedit.msc) is a console available only in Windows professional and business editions (not home editions) that is used to control what users can do and how the system can be used. Group Policy works by making entries in the registry; applying scripts to Windows startup, shutdown, and sign-in processes; and affecting security settings. Policies can be applied to the computer or to a user. Computer-based policies are applied just before the sign-in screen appears, and user-based policies are applied after sign in.

Follow these steps to use Group Policy to set the QoS level for an application:

1. Enter the **gpedit.msc** command in the Windows 8 Run box or the Windows 7 Search box. The Group Policy console opens. On the left side of Figure 9-25, notice the two groups of policies are Computer Configuration and User Configuration. To apply a policy to all users, create it under Computer

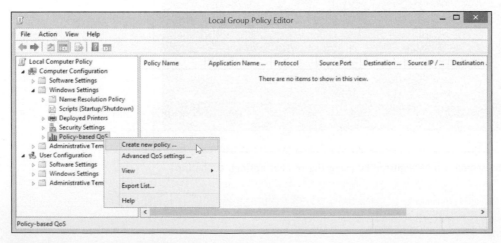

Figure 9-25   Use Group Policy to create a new QoS policy

Configuration. Also notice at the top of the list is Local Computer Policy, which means all policies apply only to the local computer.

2. In the Computer Configuration group, expand the Windows Settings group. Right-click **Policy-based QoS** and click **Create new policy,** as shown in Figure 9-25. A wizard opens to step you through the options for the policy (see Figure 9-26).

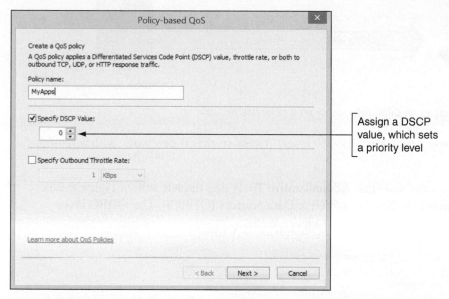

Figure 9-26   Name the QoS policy and enter a DSCP value that determines the priority level of the program(s) to which the policy applies

When creating a policy, here are important options that appear on different screens as you step through the wizard, but know you only need to use the ones that apply to your situation:

- ◢ The priority level is determined by a DSCP (Differentiated Services Code Point) value, which is a number from 0 to 63. The higher the number, the higher the priority.
- ◢ Outbound traffic can be throttled to limit the bandwidth assigned to an application.
- ◢ The policy can apply to all applications or a specific program. (The program name must have an .exe file extension.)
- ◢ You can specify the source IP address and/or destination IP address.
- ◢ You can select the protocol (TCP or UDP) and port numbers for the policy.
- ◢ When the wizard is finished, you are returned to the Group Policy console. Close the console. To apply the new policy, you can restart the computer or enter **gpupdate.exe** at a command prompt.

To get the most out of QoS, configure each router and computer on the network to use QoS.

ODBC DATA SOURCES

A+
220-902
1.4
As an IT technician, you might be called on to help set up a local computer on a corporate network to connect to a remote database stored on a company database server. For example, suppose Microsoft Access is installed on the local computer and you want to configure it to connect to a Microsoft SQL Server database on the server. Open Database Connectivity (ODBC) is the technology used to create the data source, which provides access to the database and includes the drivers required to interface between Access and the data (see Figure 9-27). Drivers for Microsoft SQL Server must be installed on the local computer (Windows has SQL drivers installed by default). Then you can use the ODBC Data Sources tool in the Administrative Tools group of Control Panel to configure the data source.

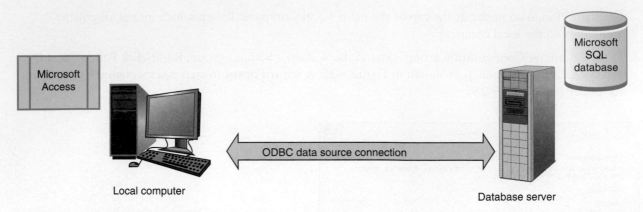

Figure 9-27   Microsoft Access connects to an ODBC data source on a corporate network

Do the following to create a new data source for Microsoft Access so that it can work with a remote Microsoft SQL Server database:

1. Open Control Panel in Classic view and click **Administrative Tools** (see the left side of Figure 9-28). Double-click **ODBC Data Sources** (in Windows 7, click **Data Sources (ODBC)**). The ODBC Data Source Administrator box opens (see the middle of Figure 9-28).

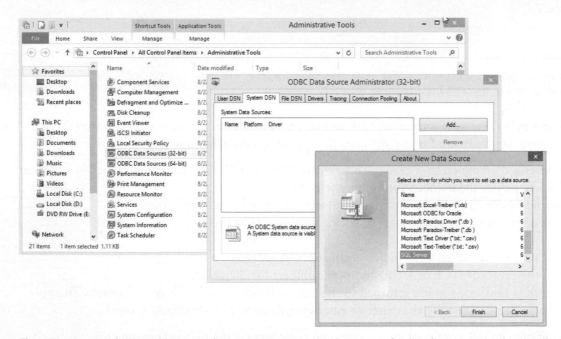

Figure 9-28   Use the Data Sources tool to create a connection between a foreign data source and an application

> **Notes** On 64-bit Windows 8 systems, you're given the option of clicking ODBC for 32-bit applications or ODBC for 64-bit applications. Make your selection based upon the application. In this example, Microsoft Access is a 32-bit application. Therefore, you click **ODBC Data Sources (32-bit)**.

2. To make the data source apply to all users of the system, click the **System DSN** tab. (DSN stands for Data Source Name, and the **User DSN** tab applies only to the current user.) Click **Add**. The Create New Data Source box appears (see the right side of Figure 9-28). Scroll down to and select **SQL Server** and click **Finish**. Follow directions on screen to enter the name of the SQL Server computer on the network and the sign-in ID and password to SQL Server. The database administrator in your organization can supply this information.

> ✎ **Notes** If you don't see the driver you need in the Create New Data Source box, close all windows and use Explorer to locate the C:\Windows\SysWOW64\Odbcad32.exe program file. When you double-click this file, the ODBC Data Source Administrator box appears and you can then access all ODBC drivers installed on the local computer.

Now let's turn our attention to managing another resource on the network: folders and files.

CONTROLLING ACCESS TO FOLDERS AND FILES

A+
220-902
1.2, 1.3,
1.4, 1.5,
1.6, 3.2,
3.3, 3.4

Responsibility for a small network can include controlling access to folders and files for users of a local computer and for remote users accessing shared resources over the network. Managing shared resources is accomplished by (1) assigning rights to user accounts and (2) assigning permissions to folders and files.

> ✎ **Notes** In Windows, the two terms, rights and permissions, have different meanings. Rights (also called privileges) refer to the tasks an account is allowed to do in the system (for example, installing software or changing the system date and time). Permissions refer to which user accounts or user groups are allowed access to data files and folders. Rights are assigned to an account, and permissions are assigned to data files and folders.

Let's first look at the strategies used for controlling rights to user accounts and controlling permissions to folders and files. Then you learn the procedures in Windows for assigning these rights and permissions.

CLASSIFY USER ACCOUNTS AND USER GROUPS

A+
220-902
1.3, 1.4,
3.2, 3.3,
3.4

Computer users should be classified to determine the rights they need to do their jobs. For example, some users need the right to sign in to a system remotely and others do not. Other rights granted to users might include the right to install software or hardware, change the system date and time, change Windows Firewall settings, and so forth. Generally, when a new employee begins work, that employee's supervisor determines what rights the employee needs to perform his job. You, as the support technician, will be responsible to make sure the user account assigned to the employee has these rights and no more. This approach is called the principle of least privilege.

In Windows, the rights or privileges assigned to an account are established when you first create a user account, which is when you decide the account type. You can later change these rights by changing the user groups to which the account belongs. User accounts can be created from Control Panel (using any edition of Windows) or by using the Computer Management console (using business and professional editions of Windows). User accounts can be assigned to different user groups using the Computer Management console (using business and professional editions of Windows). (Home editions of Windows, therefore, cannot be used to manage user groups.)

TYPE OF USER ACCOUNT

Recall from the chapter, "Survey of Windows Features and Support Tools," that when you use Control Panel to manage user accounts, you can choose between two account types: Administrator or Standard. When you use Computer Management to create an account, the account type is automatically a standard user account. To create a user account using Computer Management, first open the Computer Management console (compmgmt.msc). Then right-click **Users** under **Local Users and Groups** and select

New User in the shortcut menu. (Windows Home editions don't include the Local Users and Groups option in the Computer Management console.) Enter information for the new user a nd click **Create** (see Figure 9-29).

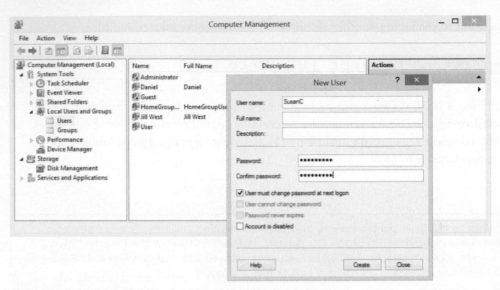

Figure 9-29	Create a new user

> ★ **A+ Exam Tip**	The A+ 220-902 exam expects you to know about groups and the administrator, standard user, power user, and guest accounts.

BUILT-IN USER GROUPS

A user account can belong to one or more user groups. Windows offers several built-in user groups and you can create your own. Here are important built-in user groups:

▲ *Administrators and Users groups.* By default, administrator accounts belong to the Administrators group, and standard user accounts belong to the Users group. If you want to give administrator rights to a standard user account, use the Computer Management console to add the account to the Administrators group.

▲ *Guests group.* The Guests group has limited rights on the system and is given a temporary profile that is deleted when the user signs out. Windows automatically creates one account in the Guests group named the Guest account, which is disabled by default.

▲ *Backup Operators group.* An account in the Backup Operators group can back up and restore any files on the system regardless of its access permissions to these files.

▲ *Power Users group.* Windows XP has a Power Users group that can read from and write to parts of the system other than its own user profile folders, install applications, and perform limited administrative tasks. Windows 8/7/Vista offers a Power Users group only for backward compatibility with XP to be used with legacy applications that were designed to work in XP.

To view user groups installed on a system, open the Computer Management console and click **Groups** under Local Users and Groups (see Figure 9-30).

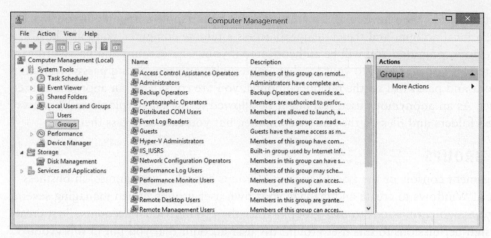

Figure 9-30 Users groups installed on a system

To change the groups a user account is in, click **Users**. The list of user accounts appears in the right pane of the console window (see the left side of Figure 9-31). Right-click the user account and select **Properties** in the shortcut menu. On the user account Properties box, click the **Member Of** tab (see the middle of Figure 9-31). Click **Add** and enter the user group name. You must type the user group name exactly as it appears in the list of user groups that you saw earlier in the list of groups (see Figure 9-30). (Alternately, you can click **Advanced**, click **Find Now**, and select the group name from the list of groups that appears.) Click **OK** twice to close both boxes.

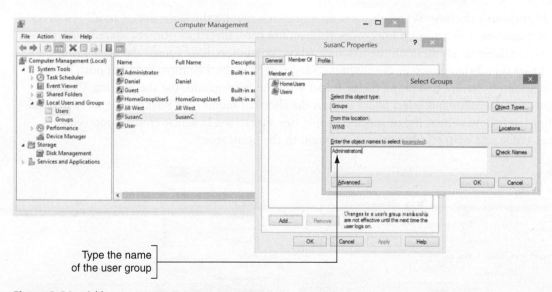

Type the name of the user group

Figure 9-31 Add a user account to a user group

In addition to the groups you can assign to an account, Windows might automatically assign one of these built-in user groups to an account when it is determining permissions assigned to a file or folder:

- The Authenticated Users group includes all user accounts that can access the system except the Guest account. These accounts include domain accounts (used to sign in to the domain) and local accounts (used to sign in to the local computer). The accounts might or might not require a password. When you create a folder or file that is not part of your user profile, by default, Windows gives access to all Authenticated Users.
- The Everyone group includes the Authenticated Users group as well as the Guest account. When you share a file or folder on the network or to a homegroup, by default, Windows gives access to the Everyone group.

◢ Anonymous users are those users who have not been authenticated on a remote computer. If you sign in to a computer using a local account and then attempt to access a remote computer, you must be authenticated on the remote computer. You will be authenticated if your user account and password match on both computers. If you signed in to your local computer with an account and password that do not match an account and password on the remote computer, you are considered an anonymous user on the remote computer. As an anonymous user, you might be allowed to use File Explorer or Windows Explorer to view shared folders and files on the remote computer, but you cannot access them.

CUSTOMIZED USER GROUPS

Use the Computer Management console or the Local Users and Groups console (lusrmgr.msc) in business and professional editions of Windows to create and manage your own user groups. When managing several user accounts, it's easier to assign permissions to user groups rather than to individual accounts. First create a user group and then assign permissions to this user group. Any user account that you put in this group then acquires these permissions.

User groups work especially well when several users need the same permissions. For example, you can set up an Accounting group and a Medical Records group for a small office. Users in the Accounting department and users in the Medical Records department go into their respective user groups. Then you only need to manage the permissions for two groups rather than multiple user accounts.

METHODS TO ASSIGN PERMISSIONS TO FOLDERS AND FILES

A+
220-902
3.2, 3.3

There are three general strategies for managing shared files and folders, also called directories, in Windows:

◢ *Homegroup sharing.* When all users on a network require the same access to all resources, you can use a Windows homegroup. Folders, libraries, files, and printers shared with the homegroup are available to all users on the network whose computers have joined the homegroup. You learned how to set up a homegroup in the chapter, "Survey of Windows Features and Support Tools." After the homegroup is set up, to share a file or folder with the homegroup, use the Sharing Wizard. To do so, right-click the item and select **Share with** in the shortcut menu. The wizard lists three general options for sharing followed by a list of specific people (see Figure 9-32). Click **Homegroup (view)** or **Homegroup (view and edit)** to assign this permission to the homegroup.

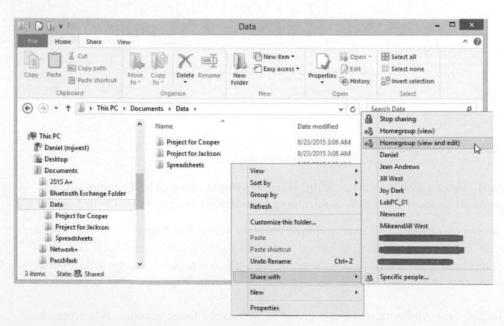

Figure 9-32   Share a folder with the homegroup

To verify the item is shared, select the folder or file in Explorer and look for the two-person shared icon in the status bar (see Figure 9-33). Notice in the status bar the item is assigned to the Homegroup group.

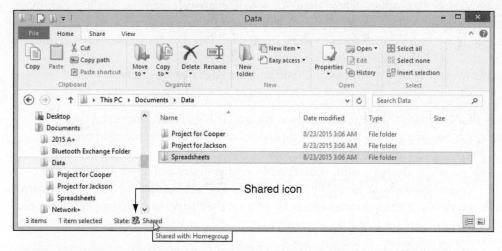

Figure 9-33   A folder shared with the homegroup shows the two-person Shared icon in the status bar of File Explorer

9

> **✎ Notes**   If the Sharing Wizard is disabled, the four sharing options shown in Figure 9-32 will not appear when you click *Share with*. To enable the Sharing Wizard, using Control Panel, open the Folder Options box and, on the View tab, select Use Sharing Wizard (Recommended). See Figure 9-34. If the Sharing Wizard is not used, you must use advanced sharing methods covered later in the chapter.

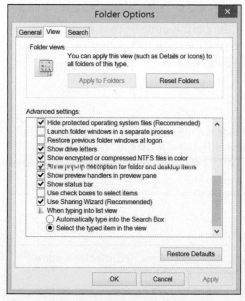

Figure 9-34   The Folder Options box shows the Sharing Wizard is enabled

> **★ A+ Exam Tip**   The A+ 220-902 exam expects you to know how to use the Folder Options box to enable or disable the Sharing Wizard.

▲ *Workgroup sharing.* For better security than a homegroup, use workgroup sharing. With this method, you decide which users on the network have access to which shared folder and the type of access they have. All rights and permissions are set up on each local computer so that each computer manages access to its files, folders, and printers shared on this peer-to-peer network.

▲ *Domain controlling.* If a Windows computer belongs to a domain instead of a workgroup or homegroup, all security is managed by the network administrator for the entire network.

In this chapter, we focus on workgroup sharing, which might use a file server. Here are some tips on which folders to use to hold shared data on a file server or personal computer:

▲ Private data for individual users is best kept in the C:\Users folder for that user. User accounts with limited or standard privileges cannot normally access these folders belonging to another user account. However, accounts with administrative rights do have access.

▲ The C:\Users\Public folder is intended to be used for folders and files that all users share. It is not recommended you use this folder for controlled access to data.

◢ For best security, create a folder not in the C:\Users folder and assign permissions to that folder and its subfolders. You can allow all users access or only certain users or user groups.

Some applications can be shared with others on the network. If you share a folder that has a program file in it, a user on another computer can double-click the program file and execute it remotely on his or her desktop. This is a handy way for several users to share an application that is installed on a single computer. However, know that not all applications are designed to work this way.

Using workgroup sharing, Windows offers two methods to share a folder over the network:

◢ **Share permissions.** Share permissions grant permissions only to network users and these permissions do not apply to local users of a computer. Share permissions work on NTFS, FAT32, and exFAT volumes and are configured using the Sharing tab on a folder's Properties box. Share permissions apply to a folder and its contents, but not to individual files.

◢ **NTFS permissions.** NTFS permissions apply to local users and network users and apply to both folders and individual files. NTFS permissions work on NTFS volumes only and are configured using the Security tab on a file or folder Properties box. (The Security tab is missing on the Properties box of a folder or file on a FAT volume.)

Here are some tips when implementing share permissions and NTFS permissions:

◢ If you use both share permissions and NTFS permissions on a folder, the most restrictive permission applies. For NTFS volumes, use only NTFS permissions because they can be customized better. For FAT volumes, your only option is share permissions.

◢ If NTFS permissions are conflicting, for example, when a user account has been given one permission and the user group to which this user belongs has been given a different permission, the more liberal permission applies.

◢ Permission propagation is when permissions are passed from parent to child. Inherited permissions are permissions that are attained from a parent object. For example, when you create a file or folder in a folder, the new object takes on the permissions of the parent folder.

◢ When you move or copy an object to a folder, the object takes on the permissions of that folder. The exception to this rule is when you move (not copy) an object from one location to another on the same volume. In this case, the object retains its permissions from the original folder.

✎ Notes You can use the xcopy or robocopy command with parameters to change the rules for how inherited permissions are managed when copying and moving files. For more information, see the Microsoft Knowledge Base Article cc733145 at *https://technet.microsoft.com/en-us/library/cc733145*. Also check out the article at *http://social.technet.microsoft .com/wiki/contents/articles/1073.robocopy-and-a-few-examples.aspx*.

★ A+ Exam Tip The A+ 220-902 exam expects you to know about NTFS and share permissions, including how allow and deny conflicts are resolved and what happens to permissions when you move or copy a file or folder.

HOW TO SHARE FOLDERS AND FILES

A+
220-902
1.5, 1.6,
3.2, 3.3

Now that you know about the concepts and strategies for sharing folders and files, let's look at the details of how to use Windows to manage user rights and file and folder permissions.

APPLYING | CONCEPTS   CREATE USER ACCOUNTS WITH DATA ACCESS

**A+
220-902
1.5, 1.6,
3.2, 3.3**

Nicole is responsible for a peer-to-peer network for a medical doctor's office. Four computers are connected to the small company network; one of these computers acts as the file server for the network. Nicole has created two classifications of data, Financial and Medical. Two workers (Nancy and Adam) require access to the Medical data, and two workers (Linda and Carlos) require access to the Financial folder. In addition, the doctor, Lucas, requires access to both categories of data. Here is what Nicole must do to set up the users and data:

1. Create folders named Financial and Medical on the file server. Create five user accounts, one each for Lucas, Nancy, Adam, Linda, and Carlos. All the accounts belong to the Windows standard user group. Create two user groups, Financial and Medical.

2. Using NTFS permissions, set the permissions on the Financial and Medical folders so that only the members of the appropriate group can access each folder.

3. Test access to both folders using test data and then copy all real data into the two folders and subfolders. Set up a backup plan for the two folders as you learned to do in the chapter, "Maintaining Windows."

Let's look at how each of these three steps is done.

Step 1: Create Folders, User Accounts, and User Groups

Follow these steps to create the folders, user accounts, and user groups on the file server computer that is using Windows 8/7 Professional:

1. Sign in to the system as an administrator.

2. Using an NTFS volume, create these two folders: **C:\Medical** and **C:\Financial**.

3. Open the Computer Management console or the Local Users and Groups console and create user accounts for **Lucas**, **Nancy**, **Adam**, **Linda**, and **Carlos**. The account types are automatically standard user accounts.

4. To create the Medical user group, right-click **Groups** under Local Users and Groups and select **New Group** in the shortcut menu. The New Group box appears. Enter the name of the group (**Medical**) and its description (**Users have access to the Medical folder**), as shown in Figure 9-35.

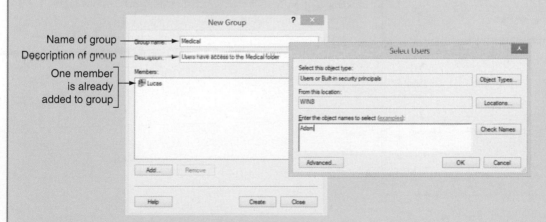

Name of group
Description of group
One member
is already
added to group

Figure 9-35   Setting up a new user group

5. Add all the users that need access to medical data (Lucas, Adam, and Nancy). To add members to the Medical group, click **Add**. The Select Users box opens, as shown on the right side of Figure 9-35. Under *Enter the object names to select*, enter the name of a user and click **OK**. As each user is added, his or her name appears

(continues)

9

under Members in the New Group box, as shown in Figure 9-35. To create the group, click **Create** in the New Group box.

6. In the same way, create the Financial group and add Lucas, Linda, and Carlos to the group. Later, you can use the Computer Management console to add or remove users from either group.

7. Close the Computer Management console.

> ★ **A+ Exam Tip** The A+ 220-902 exam expects you to be able to set up a user account or group and know how to change the group to which an account is assigned.

Step 2: Set NTFS Folder Permissions for User Groups

Follow these steps to set the NTFS permissions for the two folders:

1. Open File Explorer or Windows Explorer, right-click the **Medical** folder, and select **Properties** in the shortcut menu. The Properties box for the folder appears.

2. Click the **Security** tab (see Figure 9-36). Notice in the box that Authenticated Users, SYSTEM, Administrators, and Users all have access to the C:\Medical folder. When you select a user group, the type of permissions assigned to that group appears in the *Permissions* area. Table 9-1 gives an explanation of the more significant types of permission. Note that the Administrators group has full control of the folder. Also notice the checks under Allow are dimmed. These permissions are dimmed because they have been inherited from the parent object. In this case, the parent object is Windows default settings.

Figure 9-36 Permissions assigned to the Medical folder

> 📝 **Notes** For a thorough discussion of how permissions work, see the Microsoft Knowledge Base article cc783530 at *https://technet.microsoft.com/en-us/library/Cc783530(v=WS.10).aspx*.

> ★ **A+ Exam Tip** The A+ 220-902 exam expects you to know that NTFS permissions can customize permissions better than share permissions.

Permission Level	Description
Full control	Can read, change, delete, and create files and subfolders, read file and folder attributes, read and change permissions, and take ownership of a file or folder.
Modify	Can read, change, and create existing files and subfolders. Can delete the folder or file, but cannot delete subfolders and their files. Can read and change attributes. Can view permissions but not change them. Cannot take ownership.
Read & execute	Can read folders and contents and run programs in a folder. (Applies to both files and folders.)
List folder contents	Can read folders and contents and run programs in a folder. (Applies only to folders.)
Read	Can read folders and contents.
Write	Can create a folder or file and change attributes, but cannot read data. This permission is used for a drop folder where users can drop confidential files that can only be read by a manager. For example, an instructor can receive student homework in a drop folder.

Table 9-1   Permission levels for files and folders

3. To remove the inherited status from these permissions so you can change them, click **Advanced**. The Advanced Security Settings box appears (see the left side of Figure 9-37). Click **Disable inheritance**. The Block Inheritance box appears (see the right side of Figure 9-37). To keep the current permissions, but remove the inherited status placed on them, click **Convert inherited permissions into explicit permissions on this object**. Click **Apply**.

Figure 9-37   Remove the inherited status from the current permissions

◯ OS Differences To remove the inherited status of folder permissions in Windows 7, in the Advanced Security Settings box, click **Change Permissions**. In the new Advanced Security Settings box, you can now uncheck **Include inheritable permissions from this object's parent**. A Windows Security warning box appears. To keep the current permissions, but remove the inherited status placed on them, click **Add**.

(continues)

4. Close the Advanced Security Settings box.

5. In the Medical Properties box, notice the permissions are now checked in black, indicating they are no longer inherited permissions and can be changed. Click **Edit** to change these permissions.

6. The Permissions box opens (see Figure 9-38). Select the **Authenticated Users** group and click **Remove**. Also remove the **Users** group. Don't remove the SYSTEM group, which gives Windows the access it needs. Also, don't remove the Administrators group. You need to leave that group as is so that administrators can access the data.

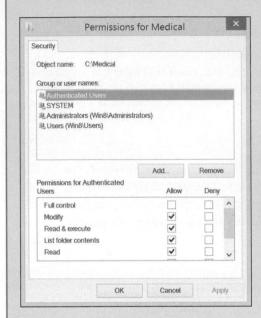

Figure 9-38   Change the permissions to a folder

Figure 9-39   Add a user or group to shared permissions

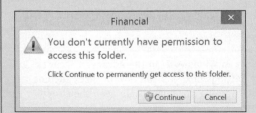

Figure 9-40   Access to a folder is controlled

7. To add a new group, click **Add**. The Select Users or Groups box opens. Under *Enter the object names to select*, type **Medical**, as shown in Figure 9-39, and click **OK**. The Medical group is added to the list of groups and users for this folder.

8. Using the check box under Permissions for Medical, check **Allow** under *Full control* to give that permission to this user group. Click **OK** twice to close the Properties box.

9. Change the permissions of the C:\Financial folder so that Authenticated Users and Users are not allowed access and the Financial group is allowed full control.

Step 3: Test, Set Share Permissions, and Go Live

It's now time to test your security measures. Do the following to test the NTFS permissions and implement your shared folders:

1. Test a user account in each user group to make sure the user can read, write, and delete in the folder he needs but cannot access the other folder. Put some test data in each folder. Then sign in to the system using an account you want to test and try to access each folder. Figure 9-40 shows the box that appears when an unauthorized user attempts to access a local folder. When you click **Continue**, entering an administrator password in the resulting UAC box gives you access.

2. Now that NTFS permissions are set correctly for each local and network user, you are ready to allow access over the network. To do that, both NTFS and share permissions must allow network access. (Share permissions apply only to network access, not local access.) Best practice is to allow full access using share permissions and restrictive access using NTFS permissions. The most restrictive permissions apply. To allow full access using share permissions, click the **Sharing** tab of each folder's properties box, and click **Advanced Sharing**.

3. In the Advanced Sharing box, if it is not already checked, check **Share this folder**. Then click **Permissions**. To add a new group, click **Add**. The Select Users or Groups box

opens. Under *Enter the object names to select*, type **Everyone** and click **OK**. The Everyone group is added to the list of groups and users for this folder.

4. With **Everyone** selected, check **Allow** under *Full control* to give that permission to the Everyone user group. Click **OK** twice and then close the Properties box.

5. Now that you have the security settings in place for one computer, go to each computer on the network and create the user accounts that will be using this computer. Then test the security and make sure each user can access or cannot access the \Financial and \Medical folders as you intend. Figure 9-41 shows the error message that appears when an unauthorized user attempts to access a network resource.

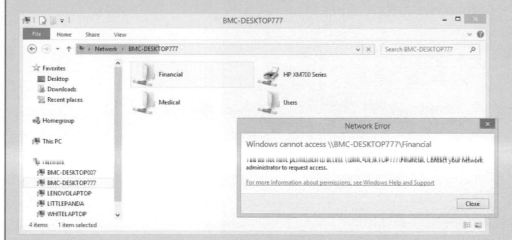

Figure 9-41 When a user is denied access to a network resource, there is no opportunity to provide access from this screen

6. To access shared folders, you can drill down into the Network group in File Explorer or Windows Explorer. Another method is to type the computer name—as in \\Win8—in the address bar of the Explorer window (see Figure 9-42).

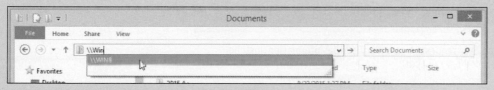

Figure 9-42 Use the computer name to access shared folders on that computer

7. After you are convinced the security works as you want it to, copy all the company data to subfolders in these folders. Check a few subfolders and files to verify that each has the permissions that you expect. And don't forget to put in place on the file server the backup procedures you learned about in the chapter, "Maintaining Windows."

9

USER AND GROUP INFORMATION WITH THE GPRESULT COMMAND

You can pull a list of all the groups a user belongs to with the gpresult command. This information can be helpful when troubleshooting user group issues or Group Policy problems. To retrieve information on a user other than the one signed in, open an elevated command prompt window and enter the command **gpresult /scope user /user** *username* **/r**. Figure 9-43 shows output for the user Adam and you can verify he belongs to the Medical group.

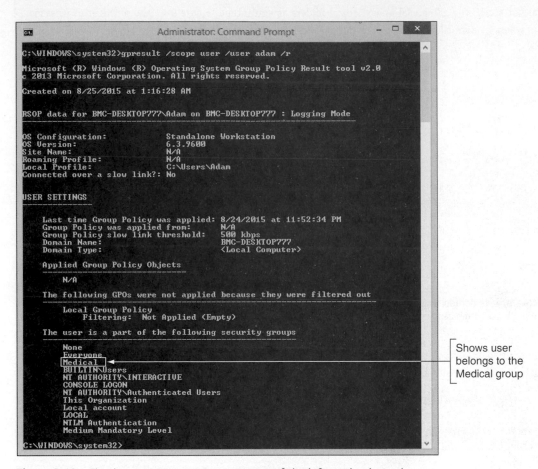

Figure 9-43   The /r parameter requests a summary of the information instead of more verbose (/v) output

To retrieve a summary of information for the computer rather than for a user, enter the command **gpresult /scope computer /r**, as shown in Figure 9-44. To learn more about gpresult, see the Microsoft Knowledge Base Article Bb490915 at *technet.microsoft.com*.

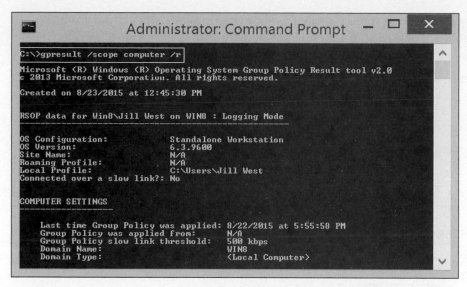

Figure 9-44 Setting the scope as *computer* requests information on computer-wide policies

HOW TO USE SHARE PERMISSIONS

Although you can mix NTFS permissions and share permissions on the same system, life is simpler if you use one or the other. For NTFS volumes, NTFS permissions are the way to go because they can be customized better than share permissions. However, you must use share permissions on FAT volumes. To do so, follow these steps:

1. Open the Properties box for the folder (*Personnel* in this case). Notice in Figure 9-45 the Security tab is missing because the folder is on a FAT volume. Select the **Sharing** tab and click **Advanced Sharing**. The Advanced Sharing box opens (see the right side of Figure 9-45).

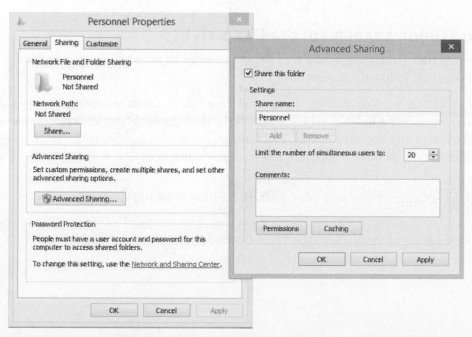

Figure 9-45 Use the Sharing tab of a folder Properties box to set up share permissions on a FAT volume

2. Check **Share this folder**. Then click **Permissions**. The Permissions box opens (see the left side of Figure 9-46). Initially, the folder is shared with Everyone. Also notice that share permissions offer only three permission levels, Full Control, Change, and Read.

3. Click **Add**. The Select Users or Groups box appears (see the right side of Figure 9-46). Enter a user account or user group and click **OK**.

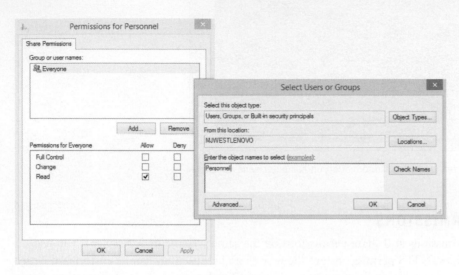

Figure 9-46   Add a user or user group to assign share permissions

4. To delete the Everyone group, select it in the Permissions box and click **Remove**. Click **OK** to close each open box in turn.

SUPPORT AND TROUBLESHOOT SHARED FOLDERS AND FILES

You have just seen how to set up user groups and folder permissions assigned to these groups. If you have problems accessing a shared resource, follow these steps:

1. Windows might be able to solve the problem for you. In Control Panel, click **Troubleshooting**. The Troubleshooting window presents a list of troubleshooters for addressing problems in the categories of Programs, Hardware and Sound, Network and Internet, or System and Security. Click **Access shared files and folders on other computers** and walk through the Shared Folders troubleshooter.

2. Open the Network and Sharing Center. Make sure your network location is set to Private (Home or Work for Windows 7).

3. In the left pane, click **Change advanced sharing settings**. The Advanced sharing settings window opens (see Figure 9-47).

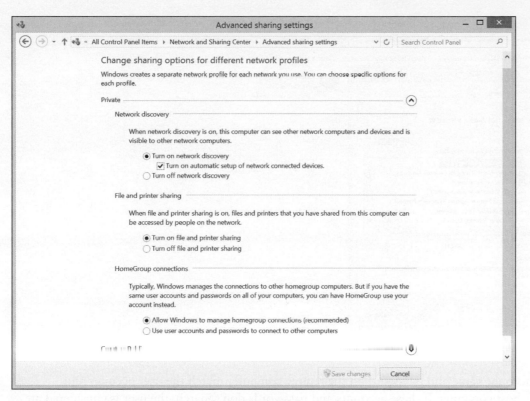

Figure 9-47 Use the Advanced sharing settings window to verify Windows is set to share resources

4. Verify the settings here are the default settings for a Private network profile:

  ◢ Select **Turn on network discovery** with **Turn on automatic setup of network connected devices** also checked.

  ◢ Select **Turn on file and printer sharing**.

★ **A+ Exam Tip** The A+ 220-902 exam expects you to know the difference between a shared printer and a network printer. A printer installed locally on a computer can be shared with other computers. This is different than a network printer, which is accessed by each networked computer directly through the network.

  ◢ If you want Windows to handle access to Homegroup resources, under HomeGroup connections, select **Allow Windows to manage homegroup connections (recommended)**.

✎ **Notes** If you are using NTFS permissions along with less restrictive share permissions to share resources on a network, disable homegroup sharing, which can cause conflicts.

  ◢ If you want to share the Public folder to the network, under All Networks, in the Public folder sharing section, select **Turn on sharing so anyone with network access can read and write files in the Public folders**.

  ◢ If you want the added protection of requiring that all users on the network must have a valid user account and password on this computer, select **Turn on password protected sharing**.

After you have made your changes, click **Save changes** at the bottom of the window.

5. In the Network and Sharing Center, click **Change adapter settings**. Right-click the network connection icon, and select **Properties** in the shortcut menu. In the Properties box, verify that **File and Printer Sharing for Microsoft Networks** is checked (see Figure 9-48).

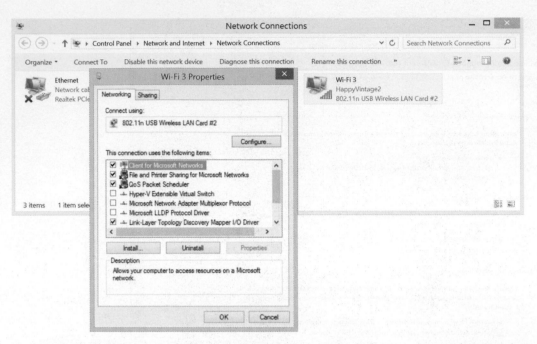

Figure 9-48   Verify the properties for the network connection are set for sharing resources over the connection

6. Verify the user account name and password on the remote computer match the user account and password on the host computer. If these accounts and passwords don't match, the user is considered an anonymous user and is denied access to resources shared on the remote computer.

Here are a few tips about managing shared folders and files:

◢ *Use advanced permissions settings.* If you need further control of the permissions assigned a user or group, click **Advanced** on the Security tab of a folder's Properties box. The Advanced Security Settings box appears (see Figure 9-49a). You can see that the Medical user group was given full control. To change these permission details, double-click the user group. In this example, the Medical group is being edited. The Permission Entry box opens. On Windows 8 systems only, click **Show advanced permissions** (see Figure 9-49b).

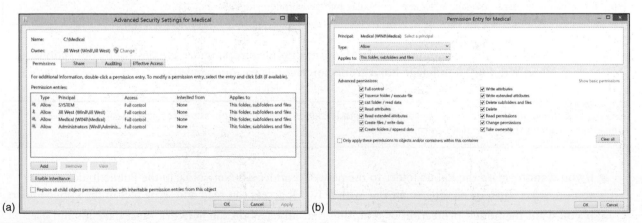

Figure 9-49   Advanced permissions settings

Detailed permissions can now be changed. Notice that the right to delete subfolders and files has been set to Deny, and the right to delete the folder itself has been set to Deny. Click **OK** to close each box. The resulting change means that users of the Medical group cannot delete or move a file or folder. (They can, however, copy the file or folder.)

▲ *Manage permissions using the parent folder.* When a subfolder is created, it is assigned the permissions of the parent folder. Recall that these inherited permissions appear dimmed, indicating they are inherited permissions. The best way to change inherited permissions is to change the permissions of the parent object. In other words, to change the permissions of the C:\Financial\ QuickBooks folder, change the permission of the C:\Financial folder. Changing permissions of a parent folder affects all subfolders in that folder.

▲ *Check the effective permissions.* Permissions manually set for a subfolder or file can override inherited permissions. Permissions that are manually set are called explicit permissions. When a folder or file has inherited an explicit permission set, it might be confusing as to exactly which permissions are in effect. To know exactly which permissions for a file or folder are in effect, see the Advanced Security Settings box. (Look back at Figure 9-49a.) NTFS permissions are reported on the Permissions tab and share permissions are reported on the Share tab. Use the Effective Access tab (for Windows 7, the tab is called Effective Permissions) to get a detailed report of resources available to a particular user.

▲ *Take ownership of a folder.* The owner of a folder always has full permissions for the folder. If you are having a problem changing permissions and you are not the folder owner, try taking ownership of the folder. To do that, click **Advanced** on the Security tab of the folder's Properties box. The Advanced Security Settings box appears. Next to the name of the owner, click **Change**. The name of the new owner can then be entered (see Figure 9-50). Click **Check Names** to confirm the name is entered correctly and click **OK** twice.

9

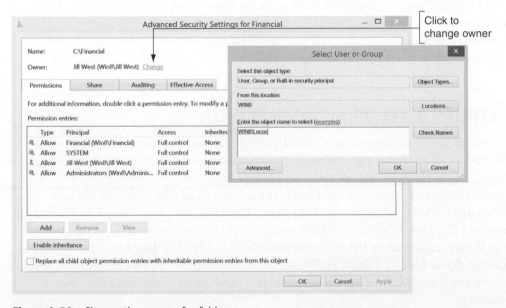

Figure 9-50 Change the owner of a folder

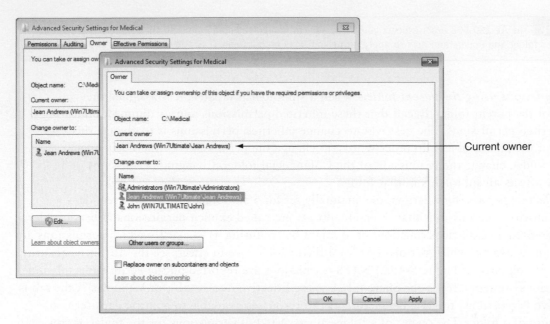

Figure 9-51   Change the owner of a folder in Windows 7

▲ *Use only one workgroup.* It is not necessary that all computers belong to the same workgroup in order to share resources. However, performance improves when they are all in the same workgroup.

▲ *Require passwords for all user accounts.* Don't forget that for best security, each user account needs a password. How to use Group Policy to require that all accounts have passwords is covered in the chapter, "Security Strategies."

▲ *Use a mapped network drive.* For the convenience of remote users, map network drives for shared folders that are heavily used. How to do that is coming up next.

HOW TO MAP A NETWORK DRIVE OR NETWORK PRINTER

A+
220-902
1.2, 1.6

A network share is one of the most powerful and versatile methods of communicating over a network. A network share makes one computer (the client) appear to have a new hard drive, such as drive E, that is really hard drive space on another host computer (the server). The client computer creates and saves a shortcut associated with a drive letter that points to the host computer's shared folder or drive. This is called mapping the drive. This client/server arrangement is managed by a Windows component, the Network File System (NFS), which makes it possible for files on the network to be accessed as easily as if they are stored on the local computer. NFS is a type of distributed file system (DFS), which is a system that shares files on a network. Even if the host computer uses a different OS, such as UNIX, the network share still functions. In addition to mapping a network drive, you can also map a network printer to a computer.

> ✎ **Notes**   A network-attached storage (NAS) device provides hard drive storage for computers on a network. Computers on the network can access this storage using a mapped network drive.

APPLYING | CONCEPTS — MAP A NETWORK DRIVE AND NETWORK PRINTER

A+ 220-902 1.6

To set up a network drive, follow these steps:

1. On the host computer, share the folder or entire volume to which you want others to have access.

2. On the remote computer that will use the network drive, open File Explorer. In the left pane, click **This PC**. At the top of the window, click the **Computer** tab and click **Map network drive**.

> **◇ OS Differences** On a remote computer running Windows 7, open Windows Explorer and press **Alt** to display the menu bar. Click the **Tools** menu and select **Map network drive**.

3. The Map Network Drive dialog box opens, as shown on the left side of Figure 9-52. Select a drive letter from the dropdown list.

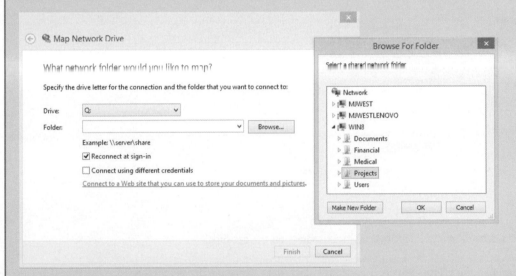

Figure 9-52 Mapping a network drive to a host computer

4. Click the **Browse** button and locate the shared folder or drive on the host computer (see the right side of Figure 9-52). Click **OK** to close the Browse For Folder dialog box, and click **Finish** to map the drive. The folder on the host computer now appears as one more drive in Explorer on your computer.

> **✎ Notes** When mapping a network drive, you can type the path to the host computer rather than clicking the Browse button to navigate to the host. To enter the path, in the Map Network Drive dialog box, use two backslashes, followed by the name of the host computer, followed by a backslash and the drive or folder to access on the host computer. For example, to access the Projects folder on the computer named Win8, enter **\\Win8\Projects** and then click **Finish**.

If a network drive does not work, go to the Network and Sharing Center, and verify that the network connection is good. You can also use the net use command to solve problems with mapped network drives.

> **✎ Notes** A host computer might be in sleep mode or powered down when a remote computer attempts to make a mapped drive connection at startup. To solve this problem, configure the host computer for Wake-on-LAN.

(continues)

Recall from the chapter, "Optimizing Windows," that you can connect a network printer to a server and the server can share the printer on the network. The Print Management console can be used to manage all shared printers on the network from a single workstation. You can also map a network printer directly to your computer, eliminating a print server or printer sharing from the process. Here's how:

1. Open **Control Panel** in Classic view and click **Devices and Printers**. Click **Add a printer** and select the printer available on the network (see Figure 9-53). Make sure you select a printer that shows its IP address; otherwise, you are connecting to a computer that has shared the printer to the network. If the printer doesn't show in the list, click **The printer that I want isn't listed**, and enter the name of the printer or its IP address, and click **Next**.

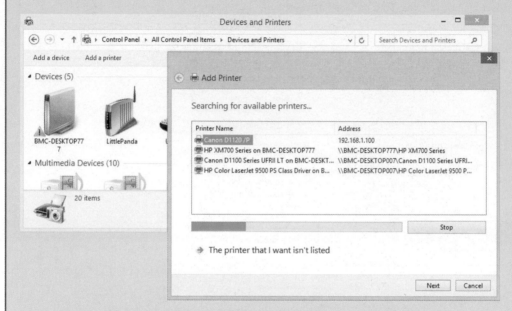

Figure 9-53 Select a network printer identified by its IP address on the network

2. Select and download the printer drivers if necessary. Click **Next**. You can choose whether to make this your default printer, then click **Finish**.

If you have problems mapping to a network printer, download the printer drivers from the website of the printer manufacturer and follow the manufacturer's directions to install the printer.

HIDDEN NETWORK RESOURCES AND ADMINISTRATIVE SHARES

A+
220-902
1.6, 3.3

Sometimes your goal is to ensure that a folder or file is not accessible from the network or by other users, or is secretly shared on the network. When you need to protect confidential data from users on the network, you can do the following:

◢ *Disable File and Printer Sharing*. If no resources on the computer are shared, use the Network and Sharing Center to disable File and Printer Sharing for Microsoft Networks.

◢ *Hide a shared folder.* If you want to share a folder, but don't want others to see the shared folder in File Explorer or Windows Explorer, add a $ to the end of the share name in the Advanced Sharing box, as shown in Figure 9-54a. This shared and hidden folder is called a hidden share. Others on the network can access the folder only when they know its name. For example, if a folder's share name is Projects$ on the computer named Fileserver, in order to access the folder, a user must enter *Fileserver*\Projects$

in the Search box (see Figure 9-54b) on the remote computer and press **Enter**. The user on the remote computer can also search for the hidden share's location through the File Explorer or Windows Explorer Search box.

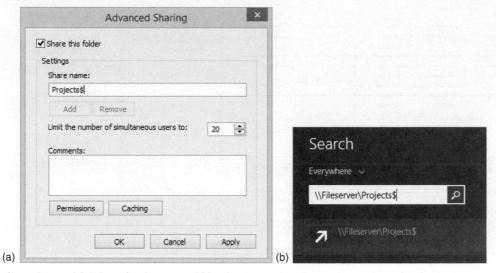

(a)   (b)

Figure 9-54 (a) A $ on the share name hides the share unless the exact name is used to locate it; (b) access a hidden, shared folder on the network by searching for its exact name

So far in this chapter, you have learned about folders and files on a computer that are shared with others on the network using local user accounts. These shares are called local shares. For computers that belong to a domain, you need to be aware of another way folders are shared, called administrative shares. Administrative shares are the folders that are shared by default that administrator accounts at the domain level can access. You don't need to manually share these folders because Windows automatically does so by default. Two types of administrative shares are:

▲ *The %systemroot% folder.* Enter the path *computername*\admin$ to access the *%systemroot%* folder (most likely the C:\Windows folder) on a remote computer in order to work with that computer's system folders and files. For example, in Figure 9-55, the entry in the Explorer address bar is *MJWestLenovo*\ *admin$*. Windows requests that the user authenticate with an administrator account to access this administrative share. The admin$ administrative share is called the Remote Admin share.

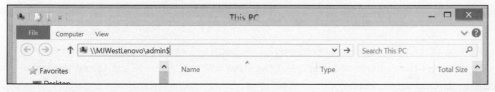

Figure 9-55 Access an administrative share on a domain

▲ *Any volume or drive.* To access the root level of any volume or drive on the network, enter the computer name and drive letter followed by a $, for example, \\MJWestLenovo\C$.

⭐ **A+ Exam Tip** The A+ 220-902 exam expects you to understand the difference between administrative shares and local shares.

✎ **Notes** To see a list of all shares on a computer, open the **Computer Management** console and drill down to **System Tools**, **Shared Folders**, **Shares** (see Figure 9-56).

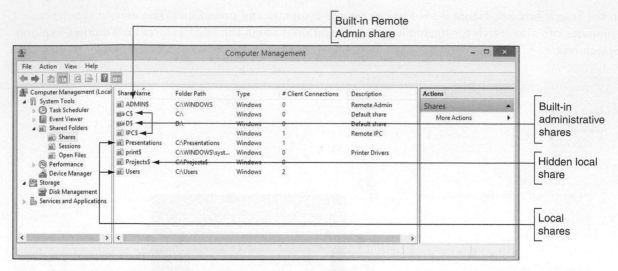

Figure 9-56   Use the Computer Management console to view all shares

---

⚡ **Caution**   When supporting a workgroup, you might be tempted to share all the drives on all computers so that you can have easy access remotely. However, to use local shares in this way is not a good security practice. Don't share the \ Windows folder or an entire drive or volume on the network. These local shares appear in everyone's Explorer window. You don't want your system files and folders exposed like this.

Hands-On | Project 9-4   Share and Secure a Folder

A+
220-902
3.2, 3.3,
3.4

Using two computers networked together, do the following to practice sharing and securing folders using Windows:

1. Create a user account on Computer 1 named **User1**. In the My Documents folder for that account, create a folder named **Folder1**. Create a text file in the folder named **File1**. Edit the file and add the text **Golden Egg**.

2. On Computer 2, create a user account named **User2**. Try to read the Golden Egg text in File1 on Computer 1. What is the result?

3. Configure the computers so that User1 signed in to Computer2 can open File1 and edit the text Golden Egg, but User2 cannot view or access the contents of Folder1. List the steps you took to share and secure the folder and to test this scenario to make sure it works.

4. Now make the folder private so that it cannot be seen from Computer2 in File Explorer or Windows Explorer but it can be accessed if User1 knows the folder name. Describe how you did that.

CLOUD COMPUTING

A+
220-902
2.3

At the beginning of this chapter, you learned about server resources available on a network, and throughout this chapter, you learned some ways of managing those resources. Not all of a network's resources reside on the local network. Cloud computing is when a third-party service or vendor makes computer resources available to its customers over the Internet. You've already learned about cloud storage services such as Dropbox, OneDrive, iCloud Drive, and Google Drive. Cloud computing can also provide many other types of resources, including applications, network services, websites, database servers, specialized developer applications, or even entire operating systems.

Regardless of the service provided, all cloud computing service models incorporate the following elements:

▲ *Service at any time.* On-demand service is available to users at any time. Cloud computing vendors often advertise uptime of their services, which is the percentage of time in any given year when their services were available online without disruption.

▲ *Elastic services and storage.* Rapid elasticity refers to the service's ability to be scaled up or down as the need level changes for a particular customer without requiring hardware changes that could be costly for the customer. Layers of services, such as applications, storage space, or number of users, can be added or removed upon request or automatically, depending upon the options made available by the service vendor.

▲ *Support for multiple client platforms.* Platform refers to the operating system, the runtime libraries or modules the OS provides to applications, and the hardware on which the OS runs. Cloud resources are made available to clients through standardized access methods that can be used with a variety of platforms, such as Windows, Linux, or Mac OS X, on any number of devices, such as desktops, laptops, tablets, and smart phones from various manufacturers.

▲ *Resource pooling and consolidation.* With resource pooling, services to multiple customers are hosted on shared physical resources, which are dynamically allocated to meet customer demand. Customers generally are not aware of where the physical devices providing cloud services are located geographically, which is called location independence.

▲ *Measured service.* Resources offered by a cloud computing vendor, such as storage, applications, bandwidth, and other services, are measured, or metered, for billing purposes and/or for the purpose of limiting any particular customer's use of that resource according to the service agreement. These measured services have reporting policies in place to ensure transparency between vendors and customers.

CLOUD COMPUTING CATEGORIES

A+ 220-902 2.3

Cloud computing service models are categorized by the types of services they provide. The National Institute of Standards and Technology (NIST) has developed a standard definition for each category, which varies by the division of labor implemented. For example, as shown on the left side of Figure 9-57, an organization is traditionally responsible for their entire network, top to bottom. In this arrangement, the organization has its own network infrastructure devices, manages its own network services and data storage, and purchases licenses for its own operating systems and applications. The other three cloud computing service models illustrated in Figure 9-57 incrementally increase the amount of management responsibilities outsourced to cloud computing vendors. The following list describes these service models:

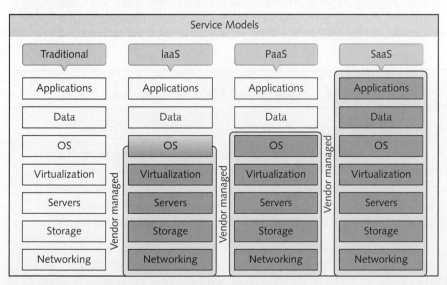

Figure 9-57 At each progressive level, the vendor takes over more computing responsibility for the customer

▲ *IaaS (Infrastructure as a Service).* With IaaS (Infrastructure as a Service), the customer rents hardware, including servers, storage, and networking, and can use these hardware services virtually. Customers are responsible for their own application installations, data management, and backup. In most situations, customers are also responsible for their own operating systems. For example, customers might install an OS on each virtual server provided by the vendor and use these servers to store data and host websites, email, DNS, or DHCP services, or install productivity software such as Microsoft Office for its employees. IaaS is ideal for fast-changing applications or to test software, or for startup businesses looking to save money by not having to invest in hardware. Examples of IaaS providers are Amazon Web Services (*aws.amazon.com*), Windows Azure (*azure.windows.com*), and Google Compute Engine (*cloud.google.com*).

▲ *PaaS (Platform as a Service).* With PaaS (Platform as a Service), a customer rents hardware, operating systems, and some applications that might support other applications the customer may install. PaaS is popular with software developers who require access to multiple platforms during the development process. A developer can build and test an application on a PaaS virtual machine made available over the web and then throw out the machine and start over with a new one with a few clicks in his browser window. Applications a PaaS vendor might provide to a developer are tailored to the specific needs of the project, such as an application to manage a database of test data. Examples of PaaS services include Google Cloud Platform and Microsoft Azure.

▲ *SaaS (Software as a Service).* With SaaS (Software as a Service), customers rent hardware, operating systems, and applications specific to the customer's needs. Applications are provided through an online user interface and are compatible with a multitude of devices and operating systems. Online email services, such as Gmail and Yahoo!, are good examples of SaaS. Google offers an entire suite of virtual software applications through Google Drive and their other embedded products. Except for the interface itself (the device and whatever browser software is required to access the website), the vendor provides every level of support from network infrastructure through data storage and application implementation.

▲ *XaaS (Anything as a Service or Everything as a Service).* In the XaaS (Anything as a Service or Everything as a Service) model, the "X" represents an unknown, just as it does in algebra. Here, the cloud can provide any combination of functions depending on a customer's exact needs.

Another SaaS implementation that doesn't quite fit the official definition of SaaS is rentable software, or software by subscription. Many companies are moving toward this subscription model, such as Adobe and Microsoft. When you buy an annual subscription to Office 365, for example, you must still install the software on your own computer, which means you must provide your own hardware, including a functioning OS. However, the downloadable software is available in formats that are compatible with multiple OSs, and the license provides for installation on multiple devices. This particular SaaS also includes built-in data storage, if desired by the user, by connecting the licensed account with OneDrive, a virtual data storage service.

Hands-On | Project 9-5   Use the Google Cloud Platform Service

A+
220-902
2.3

Google Cloud Platform is an example of PaaS. To use the service, do the following:

1. Go to **cloud.google.com** and click **Free Trial**. You will need to sign in using a Google account. If you don't have an account, you can create one with any valid email address. When you first set up an account, you must enter payment information, which Google promises not to use during your free trial period.

2. In the Developers Console, create a new project. Then drill down into **Compute**, **Compute Engine**, and **VM instances**. Create a VM instance of a Windows Server 2012 VM. Then wait several minutes for Google to create the instance.

3. Click the VM instances listed in your project. Buttons appear at the top of the window to manage the instance. Also note the External IP assigned to the VM instance. Click **Create or reset Windows password** and assign a

user name to your VM instance. Google Cloud assigns a password, which displays on screen (grayed out at the top of Figure 9-58).

4. Use the **mstsc** command to open Remote Desktop and remote in to your VM using its IP address, user name, and password. The lower window in Figure 9-58 shows the VM in a Remote Desktop Connection window. This Windows Server setup screen is the first screen that appears immediately after the first restart after installing Windows Server 2012.

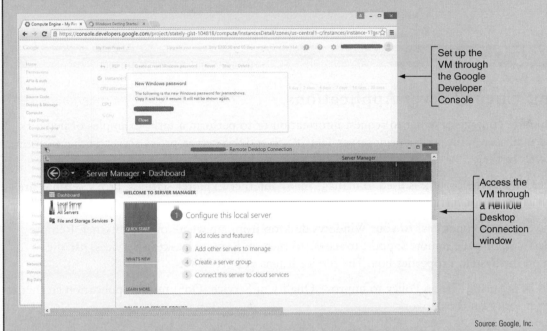

Set up the VM through the Google Developer Console

Access the VM through a Remote Desktop Connection window

Source: Google, Inc.

Figure 9-58   Google Cloud Platform serves up a VM that has Windows Server 2012 installed

> ✎ **Notes**   You will use the Google Cloud Platform Service for another project in the chapter, "Virtualization, Linux, and Mac OS X." Do not disable your Google Cloud Platform account until after you have completed that project.

DEPLOYMENT MODELS FOR CLOUD COMPUTING

**A+
220-902
2.3**

Cloud computing services are delivered by a variety of deployment models, depending on who manages the cloud and who has access to it. The main deployment models you are likely to encounter are:

▲ *Public cloud*. In a public cloud, services are provided over the Internet to the general public. Google or Yahoo! email services are examples of public cloud deployment.

▲ *Private cloud*. In a private cloud, services are established on an organization's own servers, or established virtually for a single organization's private use. For example, an insurance company might have a centralized data center that provides cloud services in a private cloud to branch offices throughout the United States.

▲ *Community cloud*. In a community cloud, services are shared between multiple organizations, but not available publicly. Organizations with common interests, such as government regulatory requirements, might share resources in this way. For example, a medical database might be made accessible to all hospitals in a geographic area. In that case, the community cloud could be hosted internally by one or more of the organizations involved, or hosted by a third-party provider.

◢ *Hybrid cloud.* A hybrid cloud is a combination of public, private, and community clouds used by the same organization. For example, a company might store data in a private cloud, but use a public cloud email service.

In today's world, cloud computing is deeply integrated into nearly every user's experience of productivity or entertainment technology. With all its strengths and flexibility, privacy and security continue to be high-priority concerns when using cloud computing resources. You'll learn more about how to address security concerns in the chapter "Security Strategies."

>> CHAPTER SUMMARY

Supporting Client/Server Applications

◢ A client computer contacts a server to request information or to perform a task. Examples of network servers are a mail server, file server, print server, DHCP server, DNS server, proxy server, authentication server, and web server.

◢ The Internet Options dialog box is used to manage many Internet Explorer settings. Proxy settings are managed using the Connections tab, and add-ons are managed using the Programs tab.

◢ Remote Desktop gives you access to your Windows desktop from anywhere on the Internet. Remote Assistance lets you provide remote support to users. To turn on Remote Desktop Services, use the Remote tab on the System Properties box. The service listens at port 3389.

◢ A policy can be set using Group Policy to improve Quality of Service (QoS) for an application so that it gets a higher priority on the network.

◢ Open Database Connectivity (ODBC) can create a data source, which provides a remote database and its drivers to a client computer.

Controlling Access to Folders and Files

◢ Controlling access to folders and files on a network is done by assigning rights to user accounts and assigning permission to folders and files.

◢ Apply the principle of least privilege when assigning rights to users. You can change the rights an account has by adding it to or removing it from a user group.

◢ Customized user groups that you create make it easier to manage rights to multiple user accounts.

◢ Three ways to share files and folders on the network are to use homegroup sharing, workgroup sharing, and domain controllers. With workgroup sharing, you can use share permissions and/or NTFS permissions.

◢ A mapped network drive makes it easier for users to access drives and folders on the network.

◢ Peer-to-peer networks use local shares, and a Windows domain supports administrative shares. You can also hide network resources so that a user must know the name of the resource to access it.

Cloud Computing

◢ Cloud computing is providing computing resources over the Internet to customers.

◢ Cloud computing service models, including IaaS, PaaS, SaaS, and XaaS, are categorized by the types of services they provide and the degree that a third-party service or vendor is responsible for the resources.

◢ A public cloud service is available to the public, and a private cloud service is kept on an organization's own servers or made available by a vendor only for a single organization's private use. A community cloud is shared between multiple organizations, and a hybrid cloud is any combination of these service models.

>> KEY TERMS

For explanations of key terms, see the Glossary for this text.

ActiveX control	hidden share	network share	public cloud
administrative share	hybrid cloud	NTFS permissions	rapid elasticity
Administrators group	IaaS (Infrastructure as a Service)	on-demand	Remote Admin share
anonymous users		Open Database Connectivity (ODBC)	Remote Assistance
Authenticated Users group	inherited permissions		Remote Desktop Connection (RDC)
authentication server	Internet Options	PaaS (Platform as a Service)	
Backup Operators group	local share		resource pooling
cloud computing	Local Users and Groups	permission propagation	SaaS (Software as a Service)
community cloud	location independence	permissions	
data source	mapping	platform	share permissions
Everyone group	measured service	Power Users group	subscription model
file server	mstsc (Microsoft Terminal Services Client)	principle of least privilege	Users group
gpresult		print server	XaaS (Anything as a Service or Everything as a Service)
Group Policy	name resolution	private cloud	
Guests group	Network File System (NFS)	proxy server	

>> REVIEWING THE BASICS

1. If a computer is having trouble navigating to a website when you enter the URL into the browser's address box, but is able to access the site when you enter the web server's IP address, which server available to your network should you make sure is functioning correctly?

2. Which type of server can function as a firewall?

3. Which editions of Windows can be used to serve up Remote Desktop?

4. What is the listening port for Remote Desktop?

5. What type of file can a user send a technician in order to get help remotely, when using Remote Assistance?

6. What is the command to open the Group Policy console?

7. What folder in Windows is intended to be used for folders and files that all users of a computer share?

8. When using Control Panel to manage user accounts, what two types of user accounts can be configured?

9. What is the command to launch the Local Users and Groups Manager console?

10. Which type of user group provides backward compatibility with Windows XP?

11. Why doesn't the Properties box for a file have a Sharing tab?

12. When you view the Properties box for a folder, why might the Security tab be missing?

13. What type of permissions does a folder receive from its parent folder?

14. What type of permissions must be used on a FAT volume?

15. If a folder has 10 subfolders, what is the easiest way to change the permissions for all 10 folders?

16. If you are having a problem changing the permissions of a folder that was created by another user, what can you do to help solve the problem?

17. A shared folder whose share name ends with a $ is called a(n)_____.

18. What command do you enter in the Explorer Search box to access the Remote Admin share on the computer named Fin?

19. What five elements define cloud computing services?

20. Gmail is an example of what type of cloud computing service model?

>> THINKING CRITICALLY

1. Your organization has set up three levels of data classification accessed by users on a small network:

   ◢ Low security: Data in the C:\Public folder.

   ◢ Medium security: Data in a shared folder that some, but not all, user groups can access.

   ◢ High security: Data in a shared and encrypted folder that requires a password to access. The folder is shared only to one user group.

   Classify each of the sets of data:

   a. Directions to the company Fourth of July party

   b. Details of an invention made by the company president that has not yet been patented

   c. Résumés presented by several people applying for a job with the company

   d. Payroll spreadsheets

   e. Job openings at the company

2. You work in the Accounting Department and have been using a network drive to post Excel workbook files to your file server as you complete them. When you attempt to save a workbook file to the drive, you see the error message: "You do not have access to the folder 'J:\'. See your administrator for access to this folder." What should you do first? Second? Explain the reasoning behind your choices.

   a. Ask your network administrator to give you permission to access the folder.

   b. Check File Explorer to verify that you can connect to the network.

   c. Save the workbook file to your hard drive.

   d. Using File Explorer, remap the network drive.

   e. Reboot your computer.

>> REAL PROBLEMS, REAL SOLUTIONS

REAL PROBLEM 9-1 Implementing More Security for Remote Desktop

When Jacob travels on company business, he finds it's a great help to be able to access his office computer from anywhere on the road using Remote Desktop. However, he wants to make sure his office computer as well as the entire corporate network are as safe as possible. One way you can help Jacob add more security is to change the port that Remote Desktop uses. Knowledgeable hackers know that Remote Desktop uses port 3389, but if you change this port to a secret port, hackers are less likely to find the open port. Search the Microsoft Knowledge Base articles (*support.microsoft.com* and *technet. microsoft.com*) for a way to change the port that Remote Desktop uses. Practice implementing this change by doing the following:

1. Set up Remote Desktop on a computer using Windows 8 Professional or Windows 7 Professional or Ultimate. This computer is your host computer. Use another computer (the client computer) to create a Remote Desktop session to the host computer. Verify the session works by transferring files in both directions.

2. Next, change the port that Remote Desktop uses on the host computer to a secret port. Print a screen shot showing how you made the change. Use the client computer to create a Remote Desktop session to the host computer using the secret port. Print a screen shot showing how you made the connection using the secret port. Verify the session works by transferring files in both directions.

3. What secret port did you use? What two or more Microsoft Knowledge Base Articles gave you the information you needed?

REAL PROBLEM 9-2 Using Chrome Remote Desktop

Chrome Remote Desktop by Google lets users sign in to remote computers through a Chrome browser. This blend of cloud computing technology and remote desktop access can be handy when you need to support computers that use operating systems other than Windows. Complete the following steps to install and use Chrome Remote Desktop:

1. On Computer 1, download and install Google Chrome, and sign in. Then add the Chrome Remote Desktop add-in.

2. Configure Chrome Remote Desktop to allow access to your computer over the Internet. Run the Chrome Remote Desktop Host Installer after it is downloaded. Be sure to record your PIN in a safe place.

3. On Computer 2, download and install Google Chrome, and sign in. Then add the Chrome Remote Desktop add-in.

4. Configure Chrome Remote Desktop to allow access to your computer over the Internet. Run the Chrome Remote Desktop Host Installer after it is downloaded. Be sure to record your PIN in a safe place.

5. Use Chrome Remote Desktop to create a remote connection to Computer 2. Can you use the utility to view the desktop of Computer 2? Can you control Computer 2 from Computer 1? Can you control Computer 2 directly from its own desktop? What options are available from the Remote Desktop menu on Computer 1?

6. What other operating systems will Chrome Remote Desktop work with?

7. List three reasons why a user might find Chrome Remote Desktop useful. Be sure to consider the advantages of using it with Google Cloud Platform.

Security Strategies

After completing this chapter, you will be able to:

- Secure a Windows personal computer

- Secure a mobile device

- Implement additional security techniques to protect a computer or SOHO network and its resources

- Recognize, remove, and protect personal computers against malicious software

- Recognize, remove, and protect mobile devices against malicious software

- Follow company policies to address issues of software copyright infringement and violations of prohibited content or activities

I n the chapter, "Windows Resources on a Network," you learned the concepts and principles of classifying users and data and protecting that data by applying appropriate permissions to the data so that only the authorized users can access it. In this chapter, you learn about additional tools and techniques to secure the resources on a personal computer, mobile device, and small network. You also learn how to recognize that a personal computer or mobile device is infected with malware and how to clean an infected system and keep it clean. Finally, you learn about how your employer might expect you to deal with issues of software copyright infringement and when company policies are violated regarding prohibited content and activities.

This chapter gives you the basics of securing a personal computer, mobile device, or small network. Later in your career as a support technician, you can build on the skills of this chapter to implement even more security such as controlling how Windows stores its passwords. However, keep in mind that even the best security will eventually fail. As a thief once said, "Locks are for honest people," and a thief will eventually find a way to break through. Security experts tell us that security measures basically make it more difficult and time consuming for a thief to break through so that she gets discouraged and moves on to easier targets.

SECURING A WINDOWS PERSONAL COMPUTER

A+
220-902
1.1, 1.4,
1.5, 1.6,
3.2, 3.3,
3.4

When you have a choice in the security measures that you use, keep in mind two goals, which are sometimes in conflict. One goal is to protect resources, and the other goal is to not interfere with the functions of the system. A computer or network can be so protected that no one can use it, or so accessible that anyone can do whatever they want with it. The trick is to provide enough security to protect resources while still allowing users to work unhindered (Figure 10-1). Also, too much security can sometimes force workers to find insecure alternatives. For example, if you require users to change their passwords weekly, more of them might start writing their passwords down to help remember them.

> **✎ Notes** The best protection against attacks is layered protection. If one security method fails, the next might stop an attacker. When securing a workstation, use as many layers of protection as is reasonable for the situation and are justified by the value of the resources you are protecting.

© Phil Marden/Getty Images

Figure 10-1   Security measures should protect resources without hindering how users work

USE WINDOWS TO AUTHENTICATE USERS

A+
220-902
3.4

Recall from the chapter, "Windows Resources on a Network," that controlling access to computer resources is done by authenticating and authorizing a user or process. A user is authenticated when he proves he is who he says he is. Recall that when a computer is on a Windows domain, the domain is responsible for authentication. For a peer-to-peer network, authentication must happen at the local computer. Normally, Windows authenticates a user with a Windows password.

As an administrator, when you first create an account, be sure to assign a password to that account. It's best to give the user the ability to change the password at any time. As an administrator, you can control how a user signs in, require a workstation be locked when the user steps away, disable the guest account, and reset a password if a user forgets it. Now let's see how to do all these chores to bring added security to a Windows computer.

REQUIRE SECURE SIGN-IN

Normally, when a computer is first booted or comes back from a sleep state, Windows displays a lock screen that can be dismissed by pressing a key on the keyboard or clicking anywhere on the screen, which then takes the user to the sign-in screen showing all active user accounts (see Figure 10-2). From here, a user clicks his account name and enters his password. Malware can sometimes display a false sign-in screen to trick users into providing user account passwords. A more secure method of sign in, called secure sign in or secure logon, requires the user to press **Ctrl+Alt+Delete** to get to a sign-in screen.

Figure 10-2 Windows 8 sign-in screen

The User Accounts utility (netplwiz.exe), also called the Network Places Wizard, can be used to change the way Windows sign-in works:

1. Enter the **netplwiz** command in the Windows 8 Run box or the Windows 7 Search box and respond to the UAC box. On the Users tab (see Figure 10-3a), you can add and remove users, change the user groups a user is in, and reset a password.

2. Click the **Advanced** tab (see Figure 10-3b). Check **Require users to press Ctrl+Alt+Delete**. Click **Apply** and close the box.

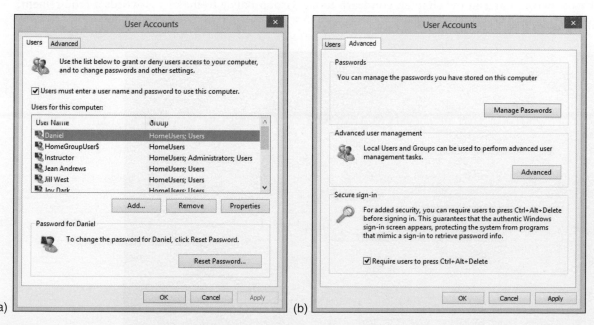

Figure 10-3 Change the way users sign in to Windows

When Ctrl+Alt+Delete is required, the lock screen looks like that shown in Figure 10-4. When a user presses Ctrl+Alt+Delete, the Windows sign-in screen that appears has not been known to be intercepted by malware.

Figure 10-4   Windows 8 lock screen after the boot or returning from sleep state

LOCK A WORKSTATION

To keep a system secure, users need to practice the habit of locking down their workstation each time they step away from their desks. The quickest way to do this is to press **Win+L**. Another method is to press **Ctrl+Alt+Delete**. If the user is already signed in when she presses these keys, the security screen in Figure 10-5 appears. When the user clicks **Lock** (*Lock this computer* in Windows 7), Windows locks down. To unlock Windows, the user must enter her password. For this method to be effective, all user accounts need a password. Later in the chapter, you learn to use Group Policy to make passwords a requirement.

Figure 10-5   Screen that appears when a signed-in user presses Ctrl+Alt+Delete

APPLYING | CONCEPTS REQUIRE A PASSWORD TO WAKE A COMPUTER

A+
220-902
3.4

An unauthorized user might get access to a system when you step away from your workstation and forget to lock it. To better secure the workstation, you can activate the screen saver (turn off the display) after a short period of inactivity and require a password be used to turn on the display and wake up the computer. Follow these steps:

1. In Control Panel, click **Power Options**.

2. In the Power Options window (see Figure 10-6), set the power options so that the computer goes to sleep after a short period of inactivity. Also, in the Power Options window, click **Require a password on wakeup**.

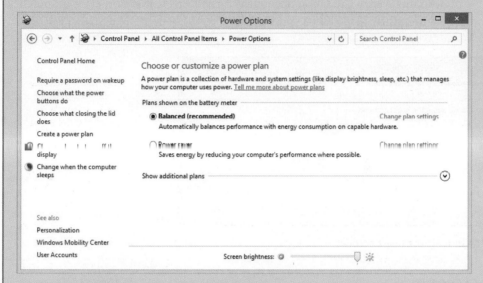

Figure 10-6 Windows power options available on the Power Options window to help lock down a workstation

3. In the System Settings window that appears, make sure **Require a password (recommended)** is selected (see Figure 10-7). If you need to change this setting, first click **Change settings that are currently unavailable**. Save your changes and close all windows.

Figure 10-7 Require a password when the computer wakes up

10

> **✎ Notes** A user might forget a password and, as an administrator, you can reset the password. However, know that resetting a password locks the user out from encrypted files, email, or personal certificates saved on the computer and from using Internet or network passwords stored on the computer. For business editions of Windows, use the Local Users and Groups (lusrmgr.msc) utility to reset a password. For all editions of Windows, use the **netplwiz** command or Control Panel.

DISABLE THE GUEST ACCOUNT

The Guest account is disabled by default and should remain disabled. If you want to set up an account for visitors, create a standard account and name it Visitor. To make sure the Guest account is disabled, open **Control Panel** in Classic view, click **User Accounts,** and then click **Manage another account.** Respond to the UAC if necessary. In the list of accounts, verify the Guest account is turned off. If it is not, click it and click **Turn off the guest account** (see Figure 10-8).

Figure 10-8　For best security, turn off the Guest account

CREATE STRONG PASSWORDS

A password needs to be a strong password, which means it should not be easy to guess either by humans or by computer programs using various methods, including a simple brute force attack, which tries every single combination of characters until it discovers your password.

A strong password, such as *y*3Q1693pEWJaTz1!*, meets all of the following criteria:

- ◢ Use 16 or more characters, which is the best protection against a password attack.
- ◢ Combine uppercase and lowercase letters, numbers, and symbols.
- ◢ Use at least one symbol in your password.
- ◢ Don't use consecutive letters or numbers, such as "abcdefg" or "12345."
- ◢ Don't use adjacent keys on your keyboard, such as "qwerty."
- ◢ Don't use your sign-in name in the password.
- ◢ Don't use words in any language. Don't even use numbers or symbols for letters (as in "p@ssw0rd") because programs can easily guess those as well.
- ◢ Don't use the same password for more than one system.

Studies have proven that the most secure technique of those listed above is the length of the password. Passwords of 16 characters or more that use letters, numbers, and symbols are the most difficult to crack.

> **✎ Notes** How secure is your password? Go to *howsecureismypassword.net* and find out how long it will take a computer to crack your password.

In some situations, a blank Windows password might be more secure than an easy-to-guess password such as "1234." That's because you cannot authenticate to a Windows computer from a remote computer unless the user account has a password. A criminal might be able to guess an easy password and authenticate remotely. For this reason, if your computer is always sitting in a protected room such as your home office and you don't intend to access it remotely, you might choose to use no password. However, if you travel with a laptop, always use a strong password.

Although it's not recommended you write your password down, if you do write it down, keep it in as safe a place as you would the data you are protecting. Don't send your passwords over email or chat. Change your passwords regularly, and don't type your passwords on a public computer. For example, computers in hotel lobbies or Internet cafés should only be used for web browsing—not for signing in to your email account or online banking account. These computers might be running keystroke-logging software put there by criminals to record each keystroke. Several years ago, while on vacation, I entered credit card information on a computer in a hotel lobby in a foreign country. Months later, I was still protesting $2 or $3 charges to my credit card from that country. Trust me. Don't do it—I speak from experience.

Hands-On | Project 10-1 Explore Password Management Software

Password management software, also called password vault software, such as KeePass (*keepass.info*), LastPass (*lastpass.com*), and Dashlane (*dashlane.com*), can hold your passwords safely so that you don't forget them or have to write them down. Choose two of these programs and a third of your own selection that interests you, then answer the following questions about each one:

1. Which platforms are supported?

2. Which web browsers are supported?

3. From how many competitors can the program import passwords?

4. What types of authentication are supported (e.g., master password, fingerprint, etc.)?

5. Where are the passwords stored? Are they synced across devices? How is the information protected?

6. What are some of the differences between the free edition of each program and the paid versions?

7. What happens to the user's account if the user dies or is otherwise incapacitated?

FILE AND FOLDER ENCRYPTION

**A+
220-902
3.3**

In Windows, files and folders can be encrypted using the Windows Encrypted File System (EFS). This encryption works only with the NTFS file system and business and professional editions of Windows. If a folder is marked for encryption, every file created in the folder or copied to the folder will be encrypted. An encrypted file remains encrypted if you move it from an encrypted folder to an unencrypted folder on the same or another NTFS volume. To encrypt a folder or file, right-click it and open its Properties box (see Figure 10-9). On the General tab, click **Advanced**. In the Advanced Attributes box, check **Encrypt contents to secure data** and click **OK**. In File Explorer or Windows Explorer, encrypted file and folder names are displayed in green.

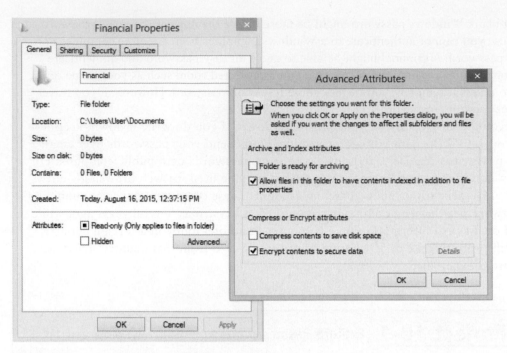

Figure 10-9   Encrypt a folder and all its contents

WINDOWS FIREWALL SETTINGS

A+
220-902
1.1, 1.5,
1.6, 3.2,
3.4

Recall from the chapter, "Connecting To and Setting Up a Network," that a SOHO router can serve as a hardware firewall to protect its network from attack over the Internet. Recall that the best protection from attack is layered protection (see Figure 10-10). In addition to a network hardware firewall, a large corporation might use a software firewall, also called a corporate firewall, installed on a computer that stands between the Internet and the network to protect the network. This computer has two network cards installed, and the installed software firewall filters the traffic between the two cards.

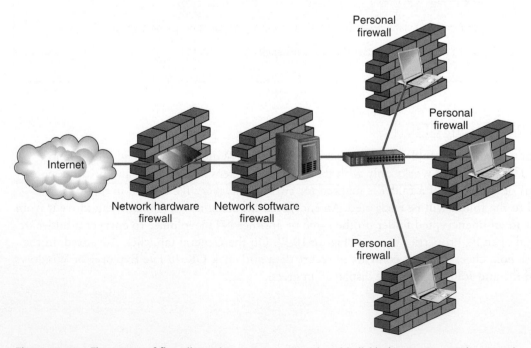

Figure 10-10   Three types of firewalls used to protect a network and individual computers on the network

A personal firewall, also called a host firewall or application firewall, is software installed on a personal computer to protect this computer. A personal firewall provides redundant protection from attacks over the Internet and also filters inbound traffic to protect a computer from attack from other computers on the same network and filters outbound traffic to prevent attacks on other computers on the same network. When setting up a SOHO network or a personal computer, configure a personal firewall on each computer.

Windows Firewall is a personal firewall that protects a computer from intrusion and from attacking other computers, and is automatically configured when you set up your security level for a new network connection. (Recall that, for Windows 8, the options are private and public security, and for Windows 7, the options are home, work, and public security.) However, you might want to customize these settings. For example, recall from the chapter, "Windows Resources on a Network," that you customized Windows Firewall to allow access through Remote Desktop connections.

APPLYING | CONCEPTS   CONFIGURE WINDOWS FIREWALL

A+
220-902
1.1, 1.5,
1.6, 3.2,
3.4

Follow these steps to find out how to configure Windows Firewall:

1. Use one of these methods to open Windows Firewall:
   ◢ Open the **Network and Sharing Center** and in the lower part of the left pane, click **Windows Firewall**.
   ◢ In Control Panel in Classic view, click **Windows Firewall**.
   The Windows Firewall window is shown in Figure 10-11.

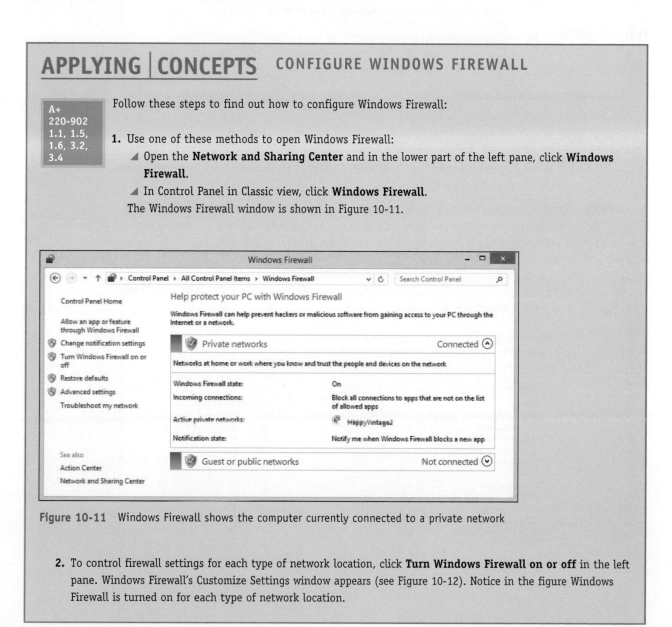

Figure 10-11   Windows Firewall shows the computer currently connected to a private network

2. To control firewall settings for each type of network location, click **Turn Windows Firewall on or off** in the left pane. Windows Firewall's Customize Settings window appears (see Figure 10-12). Notice in the figure Windows Firewall is turned on for each type of network location.

(continues)

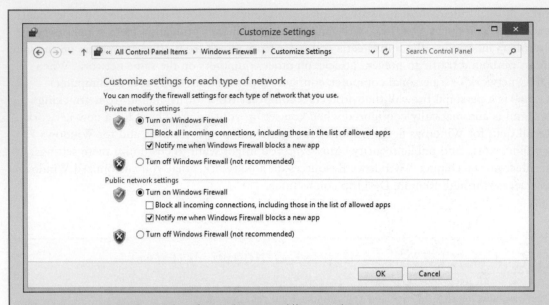

Figure 10-12 Customize settings for a private or public network

3. To allow no exceptions through the firewall on a private network (such as a home or work network) or public network, check **Block all incoming connections, including those in the list of allowed apps**. After you have made your changes, click **OK**.

4. You can allow an exception to your firewall rules. To change the programs allowed through the firewall, in the Windows Firewall window shown in Figure 10-11, click **Allow an app or feature through Windows Firewall**. The Allowed apps window appears (see Figure 10-13).

Figure 10-13 Allow programs to communicate through Windows Firewall

5. Find the program you want to allow to initiate a connection from a remote computer to this computer. In the right side of the window, click either **Private** or **Public** to indicate which type of network location the program is allowed to use. If you don't see your program in the list, click **Allow another app** to see more programs or to add your own. (If the option is gray, click **Change settings** to enable it.) When you are finished making changes, click **OK** to return to the Windows Firewall window.

6. For even more control over firewall settings, in the Windows Firewall window (refer back to Figure 10-11), click **Advanced settings**. The Windows Firewall with Advanced Security window opens. In the left pane, select Inbound Rules or Outbound Rules. A list of programs appears. Right-click a program and select **Properties** from the shortcut menu. Using the Properties box, you have full control of how exceptions work to get through the firewall, including which users, protocols, ports, and remote computers can use it (see Figure 10-14).

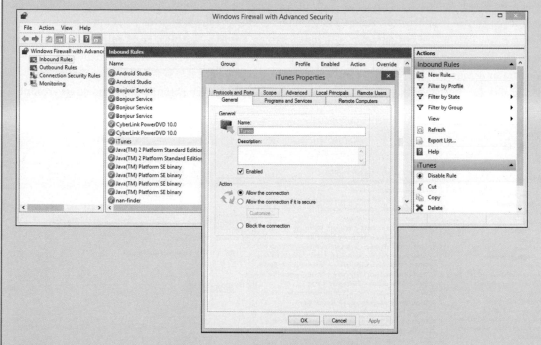

Figure 10-14   Use advanced settings to control exactly how a program can get through Windows Firewall

◇ OS Differences   In Vista, you can allow exceptions to Windows Firewall only by program name or port number.

LOCAL SECURITY POLICIES USING GROUP POLICY

**A+
220-902
1.4, 3.4**

Recall from the chapter, "Windows Resources on a Network," that the Group Policy utility controls what users can do with a system and how the system is used and is available with business and professional editions of Windows. Using Group Policy, you can set security policies to help secure a workstation. For example, you can set policies to require all users to have passwords and to rename default user accounts.

APPLYING | CONCEPTS   APPLY LOCAL SECURITY POLICIES

A+
220-902
1.4, 3.4

Follow these steps to set a few important security policies on the local computer:

1. Sign in to Windows using an administrator account on a system using Windows 8/8.1 Professional or Enterprise, or Windows 7 Professional, Ultimate, or Enterprise.

2. To start Group Policy, use the **gpedit.msc** command in the Windows 8 Run box or in the Windows 7 Search box. The Local Group Policy Editor console opens.

3. To change a policy, first use the left pane to drill down into the appropriate policy group and then use the right pane to view and edit a policy. Here are important security policies you might want to change:

   ◢ *Change default user names.* A hacker is less likely to hack into the built-in Administrator account or Guest account if you change the names of these default accounts. To change the name of the Administrator account, drill down in the **Computer Configuration**, **Windows Settings**, **Security Settings**, **Local Policies**, **Security Options** group (see the left side of Figure 10-15). In the right pane, double-click **Accounts: Rename administrator account**. In the Properties box for this policy (see the right side of Figure 10-15), change the name and click **OK**. To change the name of the Guest account, use the policy **Accounts: Rename guest account**.

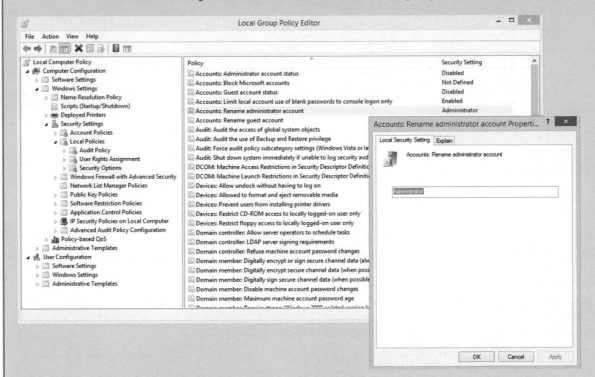

Figure 10-15   Use Group Policy to rename a default user account

> ✎ **Notes**   The Properties box for many policies offers the Explain tab. Use this tab to read more about a policy and how it works.

   ◢ *Require user passwords.* To require that all user accounts have passwords, drill down to the **Computer Configuration**, **Windows Settings**, **Security Settings**, **Account Policies**, **Password Policy** group (see the left side of Figure 10-16). Use the **Minimum password length** policy and set the minimum length to six or eight characters (see the right side of Figure 10-16). Additionally, reduce the password expiration time frame so users must create new passwords frequently. Use the **Maximum password age** policy to require users to reset their password every 60 days. (Best practice is to set the Maximum password age in the range of 30 to 90 days.)

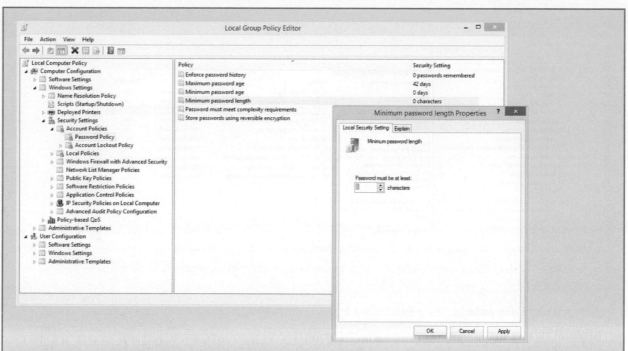

Figure 10-16 Require that each user account have a password by setting the minimum password length policy

▲ **Set failed logon restrictions.** Windows can be configured to lock a user account if too many incorrect logons are attempted. Drill down to the **Computer Configuration**, **Windows Settings**, **Security Settings**, **Account Policies**, **Account Lockout Policy** group. Use the **Account lockout threshold** to set the number of invalid logon attempts. When the number is exceeded, the account will be locked.

▲ **Restrict logon hours.** In many cases, users should only be allowed access to a workstation during specific hours, such as during office hours. Preventing access at other times of the day and throughout the weekend can increase a workstation's security. The schedule for a user's or group's logon hours is set through Active Directory, but individual workstations can be configured to respond differently once a user's logon hours have expired. To configure a workstation's response to the expiration of a user's logon hours, drill down to the **User Configuration**, **Administrative Templates**, **Windows Components**, **Windows Logon Options** group. Use the **Set action to take when logon hours expire** policy to choose Lock, Disconnect, or Logoff. If this policy is not enabled, the user's session will continue, but the user will not be able to log on outside of the assigned logon hours once the current session has been terminated.

▲ **Disable Microsoft account resources.** Recall that a Microsoft account is a single sign-on (SSO) account, which means it provides authentication to multiple services and resources. When a user signs in to a Windows 8 computer with a Microsoft account, she has access to online resources such as OneDrive and OneNote and can sync settings on this computer with other computers that use this same Microsoft account. Settings include Start screen tiles, desktop personalization, installed apps and app settings, web browser favorites, and passwords to apps, websites, and networks. (To see the settings you can sync when using a Microsoft account, in the charms bar, click **Settings**, click **Change PC settings**, click **OneDrive**, and click **Sync settings**.) Depending on your company's policy, you might need to restrict access to online resources and syncing settings that are linked to a user's Microsoft account. To disable OneDrive, for example, drill down to **Computer Configuration**, **Administrative Templates**, **Windows Components**, **OneDrive** group. Use the **Prevent the usage of OneDrive for file storage** policy. Enable this policy to prevent users and programs from accessing OneDrive. Additionally, in the **Windows Components** submenu, click the **Sync your settings** group and use these policies to disable syncing apps, app settings, passwords, and other Windows settings (see Figure 10-17).

10

(continues)

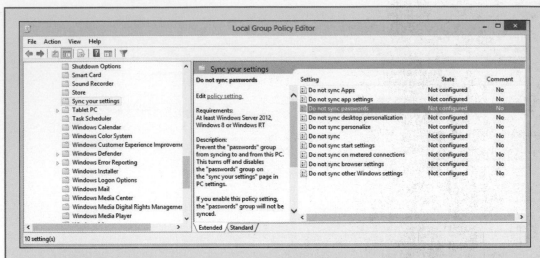

Figure 10-17 Restrict SSO authentication to online resources associated with a Microsoft account

▲ *Audit logon failures.* Group Policy offers several auditing policies that monitor and log security events. These Security logs can then be viewed using Event Viewer. For example, to set an audit policy to monitor a failed logon event, drill down to the **Computer Configuration**, **Windows Settings**, **Security Settings**, **Local Policies**, **Audit Policy** group. Use the **Audit logon events** policy. You can audit logon successes and failures. To keep the log from getting too big, you can select **Failure** to only log these events.

▲ *Disable logon and shutdown scripts.* Policies can run scripts for the computer or user during logon or shutdown. These scripts can contain programs, which might contain malware. To manage logon scripts, in the Computer Configuration or User Configuration group, drill down to the **Administrative Templates**, **System**, **Logon** group. Use the **Run these programs at user logon** policy. To manage shutdown scripts, drill down to the **Administrative Templates**, **System**, **Scripts** group. For a list of folders where Group Policy stores these scripts, see the appendix, "Entry Points for Windows Startup Processes."

▲ *Disable AutoRun and AutoPlay.* When attaching a USB flash drive or external hard drive, or inserting a disc in the optical drive, Windows automatically accesses the storage media and then requests instructions on what to do next. Media files can be played automatically, which is called AutoPlay. Executable files can be run automatically, which is called AutoRun. You can disable both of these features to add yet another layer of security protection. To disable AutoPlay, drill down to **Computer Configuration**, **Administrative Templates**, **Windows Components**, **AutoPlay Policies** group. Enable the **Turn off Autoplay** policy. To disable AutoRun, enable the **Set the default behavior for AutoRun** and use the **Disabled** option.

4. When you finish setting your local security policies, close the Local Group Policy Editor console. To put into effect the changes you have made, reboot the system or enter the command **gpupdate.exe** in a command prompt window. The gpupdate command refreshes local group policies as well as group policies set in Active Directory on a Windows domain.

> **✎ Notes** Sometimes policies overlap or conflict. To find out the resulting policies for the computer or user that are currently applied to the system, you can use the gpresult command in a command prompt window with parameters. To find out more about this command, search the *technet.microsoft.com* website.

> **★A+ Exam Tip** The A+ 220-902 exam expects you to know about the Local Security Policy snap-in, which is one of the Administrative Tools snap-ins in Control Panel. In Group Policy, the group of policies in the Local Computer Policy, Computer Configuration, Windows Settings, Security Settings group can also be edited from Control Panel. In Control Panel, open **Administrative Tools** and double-click **Local Security Policy**.

Hands-On | Project 10-2 Use Group Policy to Secure a Workstation

Using Windows 8.1/8 Professional or Enterprise, or Windows 7 Professional, Ultimate, or Enterprise, set local security policies to require a password for each account, to audit failed logon events, and to create a logon script that displays the message, "The Golden Pineapple Was Here!" when anyone signs in to the system. Test your policies by verifying a password is required, your script executes when you sign in, and a failed sign-in event using an invalid password is logged and can be viewed in Event Viewer. Answer the following questions:

1. Which policies did you set and what setting was applied to each policy?

2. What software did you use to create your script? What is the exact path and file name (including the file extension) to your script?

3. Which log in Event Viewer shows the logon failure event?

4. List three more policies you find in Group Policy not discussed in this chapter that can make a workstation more secure.

USE BITLOCKER ENCRYPTION

10

A+
220-902
1.1, 3.3

BitLocker Drive Encryption in Windows professional and business editions locks down a hard drive by encrypting the entire Windows volume and any other volume on the drive. A similar feature, BitLocker To Go, encrypts data on a USB flash drive and restricts access by requiring a password. You need to be aware of the restrictions and possible risks before you decide to use BitLocker. It's intended to work in partnership with file and folder encryption to provide data security.

> ★ **A+ Exam Tip** The A+ 220–902 exam expects you to know about the features, benefits, and drawbacks of BitLocker Drive Encryption and BitLocker To Go.

The three ways you can use BitLocker Drive Encryption depend on the type of protection you need and the computer hardware available:

▲ *Computer authentication.* Many laptop computers have a chip on the motherboard called the TPM (Trusted Platform Module) chip. The TPM chip holds the BitLocker encryption key (also called the startup key). If the hard drive is stolen from the laptop and installed in another computer, the data would be safe because BitLocker would not allow access without the startup key stored on the TPM chip. Therefore, this method authenticates the computer. However, if the motherboard fails and is replaced, you'll need a backup copy of the startup key to access data on the hard drive. (You cannot move the TPM chip from one motherboard to another.)

▲ *User authentication.* For computers that don't have TPM, the startup key can be stored on a USB flash drive (or other storage device the computer reads before the OS is loaded), and the flash drive must be installed before the computer boots. This method authenticates the user. For this method to be the most secure, the user must never leave the flash drive stored with the computer. (Instead, the user might keep the USB startup key on his key ring.)

▲ *Computer and user authentication.* For *best* security, a password can be required at every startup in addition to TPM. Using this method, both the computer and the user are authenticated. This practice is an example of multifactor authentication (MFA), which uses more than one method to authenticate.

BitLocker Drive Encryption provides great security, but security comes with a price. For instance, you risk the chance your TPM will fail or you will lose all copies of the startup key. In these events, recovering the data can be messy. Therefore, use BitLocker only if the risks of BitLocker giving problems outweigh the risks of stolen data. And, if you decide to use BitLocker, be sure to make extra copies of the startup key and/or password and keep them in a safe location.

For detailed instructions on how to set up BitLocker Drive Encryption, see the Microsoft Knowledge Base "BitLocker Overview" article hh831713 at *technet.microsoft.com*.

USE UEFI/BIOS FEATURES TO PROTECT THE SYSTEM

A+
220-902
3.4

Many motherboards for desktop and laptop computers offer several UEFI/BIOS security features, including UEFI secure boot, power-on passwords, support for intrusion-detection devices, and support for a TPM chip. Power-on passwords include a supervisor password (required to change UEFI/BIOS setup), user password (required to use the system or view UEFI/BIOS setup), and a drive lock password (required to access the hard drive). The drive lock password does not require a TPM chip and is stored on the hard drive so that it will still control access to the drive in the event the drive is removed from the computer and installed on another system. Figure 10-18 shows one BIOS setup Security screen where you can set the hard drive password. This screen can also be used to set the supervisor and user passwords to the system.

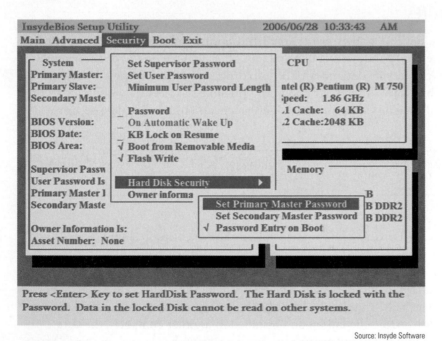

Source: Insyde Software

Figure 10-18   Submenu shows how to set a hard drive password that will be written on the drive

Some laptops contain the LoJack technology on the motherboard to support the laptop-tracking software Absolute LoJack® by Absolute Software (*absolute.com*). If you install the software on your laptop and the laptop is stolen, Absolute can lock down your hard drive and track down the laptop.

Now that you know about securing personal computers, let's turn our attention to securing mobile devices.

SECURING A MOBILE DEVICE

Smart phones and tablets are with us everywhere, and most of us keep much personal and professional information on our smart phones. In the chapter, "Supporting Mobile Operating Systems," you learned about a lot of the features on smart phones and tablets that make the data on them more accessible. In this chapter, you learn how to make that information more secure. Here's a list of what might be stored on a smart phone or tablet that would be at risk if the device is lost, stolen, or damaged:

- Data kept by apps can reveal much about our lives. Consider data kept on these iPhone and Android apps: Email, calendar, call logs, voice mail, text messages, Dropbox, iCloud Drive, Google Maps, Hangouts, Gmail, QuickMemo, YouTube, Amazon, Facebook, Videos, Photos, Notes, Contacts, and web browsers (bookmarks and browsing history).
- Videos and photos we have taken might reveal private information and be tagged with date and time stamps and GPS locations.
- Network connection settings, including Wi-Fi security keys, email configuration settings, user names, and email addresses.
- Purchasing patterns and history as well as credit card information might be stored—or at least accessible for use—in mobile payment apps, apps developed by our favorite retailers, or through membership card databases.

To keep your data safe, consider controlling access to your devices and consider what apps you can use to protect the data. These methods are discussed in this part of the chapter along with BYOD (Bring Your Own Device) policies that might be used in an enterprise environment to secure corporate data stored on a device.

DEVICE ACCESS CONTROLS

Because smart phones and tablets are so mobile, they get stolen more often than other types of computers. Therefore, protecting data on a mobile device is especially important. Consider the following lock methods to control access to the device:

- *Android screen lock*. A screen lock requires the correct input to unlock the device. Android devices provide a variety of options, as shown in Figure 10-19a. As the complexity of a lock code increases, so does the security of the device:
  - *Swipe*. Swipe your finger across the screen to unlock the device (not very secure but will prevent a pocket dial).
  - *Knock code*. Requires a pattern of taps on the screen.
  - *Pattern*. Requires a pattern to be drawn along dots on the screen (see Figure 10-19b).
  - *PIN*. Requires a numerical code, which is similar to iOS's passcode.
  - *Password*. Requires an alphanumeric code with letters and/or numbers.
  - *Face lock*. Uses the device's camera to perform facial recognition (this option is not available on the device shown in Figure 10-19a).

Some devices have different features that can still be accessed from the lock screen, such as emergency calls, weather information, a virtual assistant, or the camera app. A device might even let you post contact info, such as a friend's phone number, on the lock screen in case the device is lost and someone tries to return it. Thankfully, not everyone is a bad guy. Don't include the person's name with their phone number. Make sure they're informed and you have their permission to use their phone number for this purpose.

10

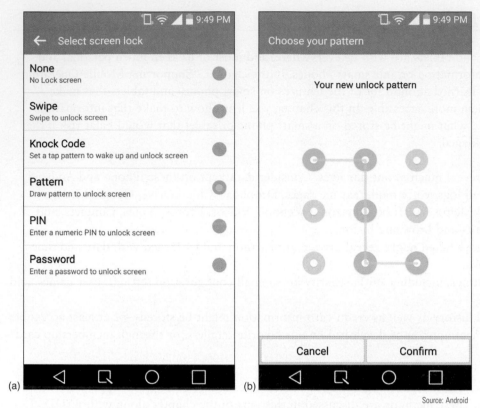

Source: Android

Figure 10-19   (a) Screen lock options, and (b) an unlock pattern follows dots on the screen

◢ *iOS screen lock.* Both iPhones and iPads offer a numerical passcode lock, and later models offer Touch ID, a fingerprint lock. The Home button on the iPhone and iPad acts as a fingerprint reader for this feature. Figure 10-20a shows the Touch ID & Passcode menu in the Settings app where these features can be enabled and configured.

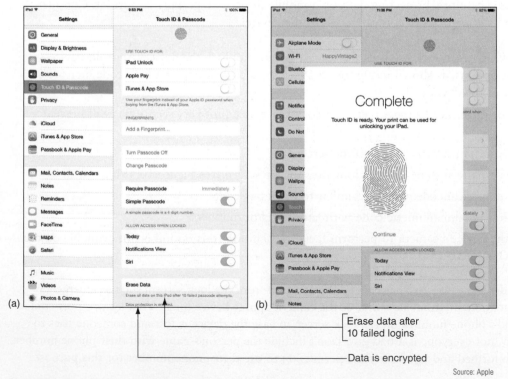

Source: Apple

Figure 10-20   (a) Use a numerical passcode to unlock an iPad, or (b) use your fingerprint to unlock

For best security, on the Touch ID & Passcode screen, turn off **Simple Passcode** so you can enter a strong password for your device and set **Require Passcode** to **Immediately**. Yes, both these features are annoying, but necessary for best security.

> ✎ **Notes** In the chapter, "Supporting Mobile Operating Systems," you learned how to recover from a system lockout when the screen lock prevents access to your device.

▲ *Biometric authentication.* A biometric device is an input device that collects biological data about a person, which can identify a person's fingerprints, handprints, face, voice, retinal, iris, and handwritten signatures. Touch ID on an iPhone is one example of biometric authentication (see Figure 10-20b), as is the face lock on an Android phone. Iris scanners and voice recognition are other options for some devices.

> ✎ **Notes** In some states, you cannot legally be forced to give your phone's password to investigators. But you are required to give your fingerprint.

▲ *Full device encryption.* Encrypting a device's data makes the data essentially useless to a thief. However, encryption might slow down device performance and the data is only as safe as the strength of the password keeping the data encrypted. Both Android and iOS devices offer full device encryption. With iOS, data is automatically encrypted when you set a screen lock password. To verify encryption, open the **Settings** app, tap **Passcode**, and then enter your passcode. At the bottom of the screen, verify *Data protection is enabled*, as shown in Figure 10-20a.

▲ *Restrict iOS failed login attempts.* When you set a screen lock, you can specify that data be erased after so many failed login attempts. For example, look back at Figure 10-20a to see near the bottom of the screen that if Erase Data is turned on, 10 failed login attempts causes all data on the device to be erased.

> ⚡ **Caution** If you have Erase Data turned on, be sure to keep backups of your data and other content. A small child can pick up your smart phone and with a little finger tapping accidentally erase all your data.

After five failed logins, the system locks down temporarily, and 10 failed logins results in the system locking down completely. The only way to access the system is to connect the device to iTunes where the device has already been synced to that installation of iTunes. You'll need to restore the device through iTunes using the latest backup, which you learned how to do in the chapter, "Supporting Mobile Operating Systems."

▲ *Restrict Android failed login attempts.* For Android, five failed logins causes the system to temporarily lock down. To restore functionality, some Android devices offer the option to sign in with the device owner's Google account credentials. For other devices, you can use Android Device Manager (*google.com/android/devicemanager*) to access a locked system, such as when the password has been forgotten.

▲ *Multifactor authentication.* Smart phones themselves can be used to authenticate to services and networks (for example, email, cloud services, corporate network accounts, VPNs, or even Facebook), as one of the two or more authentication techniques required for multifactor authentication. For example, you might first enter a password on a computer as the first authentication and then a code is sent as a text message to your smart phone and you must then enter the code in the computer as the second authentication. In another example, you enter a code in a computer that is at a certain location and the system you're signing in to checks the GPS location of your smart phone to make sure it is near the computer. In addition, authenticator apps, such as Google Authenticator for Android or iOS, Microsoft Authenticator for Windows Phone, or an independent competitor like Authy, can be installed on your smart phone and configured to provide multifactor authentication support for a huge variety of account types.

SOFTWARE SECURITY

In addition to controlling access to a device, you can use software to secure the data. Most of the methods discussed here require the user understand the importance of the security measure and how to use it:

▲ *OS updates and patches.* Android automatically pushes updates to many of its devices, but iOS devices and other mobile devices require manual updates. You learned how to update mobile device operating systems in the chapter, "Supporting Mobile Operating Systems."

▲ *Antivirus/anti-malware.* Because Apple closely protects iOS and iOS apps, it's unlikely an Apple device will need anti-malware software unless the device has been jailbroken. The Android OS and apps are not so closely guarded because apps can be downloaded from sources other than Google Play. Before installing an Android anti-malware app, be sure to read reviews about it. Most of the major anti-malware software companies provide Android anti-malware apps.

▲ *Trusted sources.* iOS devices are limited to installing apps only from Apple's App Store. Android and Windows devices can download and install apps from other sources, only some of which are trustworthy. Trusted sources generally include well-known app stores, such as Amazon Appstore for Android (*amazon.com*) or Slide ME (*slideme.org*). Look for lots of reviewer feedback as one measure of safety. Other trusted sources might include your bank's website, your employer, or your school, although often these apps are posted in Google Play (*play.google.com*) as well.

Android allows you to limit app sources to only the Google Play Store, which can help reduce the threat of untrusted sources for apps. In the **Settings** app, tap **Security** and make sure that **Unknown sources** is unchecked, as shown in Figure 10-21a. If you do decide to use third-party app sources, be sure you already have a good anti-malware program and a firewall running on your device.

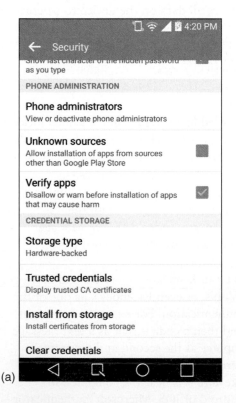

Source: Android

Figure 10-21   (a) Android security settings, and (b) a firewall app on an Android smart phone

▲ *Firewalls*. As with Windows computers, a firewall on a mobile device helps control what connections can be made by which programs or services. When you install an app, you're required to agree to the permissions it requests in order to get the app. A firewall gives you more control over what network access an app can have. For example, a firewall can prevent the Facebook app from sending SMS messages. Facebook's app might legitimately use SMS for two-factor authentication, but a firewall lets you decide if you're comfortable with the app having that level of access in exchange for being able to use that feature. Most firewall apps for mobile devices use VPN technology to mimic a VPN connection, which forces all network communication to be routed through that connection so the app can emulate firewall-type protection on the device. Figure 10-21b shows an example of one firewall app on an Android smart phone.

▲ *Android locator application and remote wipe*. You can use Android Device Manager (ADM at *google.com/android/devicemanager*) to locate your phone on a map, force it to ring at its highest volume, change the device password, or remotely erase all data from the device to protect your privacy, which is called a remote wipe. All of these features are built in to Android and are available if location access services are turned on. Third-party locator applications are also available in the Play Store.

To turn on location access services on an Android smart phone, do the following:

1. On the home screen, tap the **Apps Launcher**. Find and tap **Google Settings**. Note that this is not the same thing as the **Settings** app. The Google Settings app opens, as shown in Figure 10-22a.

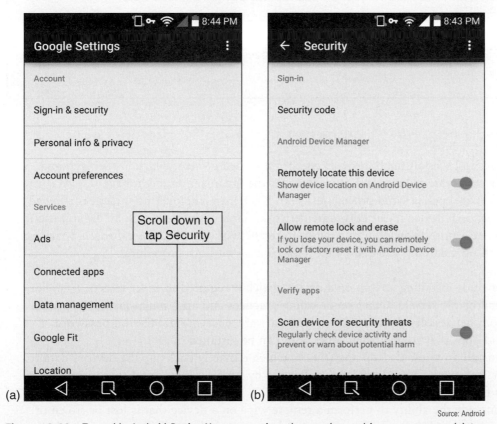

Source: Android

Figure 10-22 To enable Android Device Manager services that can be used in an emergency, (a) tap Security in Google Settings, and (b) turn on Android Device Manager features

2. Scroll down and tap **Security**. On the Security screen, under Android Device Manager, make sure *Remotely locate this device* and *Allow remote lock and erase* sliders are turned **on**, as shown in Figure 10-22b.

▲ *iOS locator application and remote wipe*. Similar to Android Device Manager, iCloud offers the ability to locate a lost iOS device if the feature is already enabled on the device. On an iPad or iPhone, turn on Find My iPhone or Find My iPad in the Settings app. How to do that is covered in the chapter, "Supporting

Mobile Operating Systems." Besides using a browser on a computer to find your device, you can also download the free app, Find My iPhone or Find My iPad, to another Apple device and use it to locate your lost device. If you have given up on finding your device, you can use iCloud to perform a remote wipe.

Hands-On | Project 10-3   Practice Locating Your iOS or Android Device

A+
220-902
3.5

Whether you have an Android device or an iOS device, knowing how to locate it when it gets lost or stolen or how to perform a remote wipe can be crucial skills in an emergency. Do the following to find out how these tasks work:

1. If you have an iOS device, go to **iCloud.com/#find**. If you have an Android device, go to **google.com/android/devicemanager**.

2. Sign in, and make sure the correct device is selected. Was the website able to locate your device? If not, check your device settings and make any adjustments necessary until the website successfully locates the device.

3. Explore the site to see how to make the device ring, how to lock the device by changing the passcode, and how to erase the device. What are the names of the three buttons that perform these tasks?

One potential snag in finding or remotely wiping your device would be relying on passwords stored in your device to access your Google or iCloud account. Be sure to store your sign-in information for these accounts in password vault software or memorize the information.

MOBILE SECURITY IN CORPORATE ENVIRONMENTS

A+
220-902
3.5

Corporations and schools might provide corporate-owned devices, which are secured and managed by corporate policies and procedures, or the organization might have BYOD (Bring Your Own Device) policies and procedures. With BYOD, an employee or student is allowed to connect his own device to the corporate network. For security purposes, an organization configures a person's device before allowing it to connect to the network in a process called on-boarding. The reverse process is call off-boarding. Here are important facts about both procedures:

◢ On-boarding might include installing an app on a device, which is required in order to access network resources such as email or file servers. Other on-boarding practices and apps might include apps that prevent the device from being jailbroken or rooted, anti-malware, encryption, PIN and password enforcement apps, and apps that control what other apps can be installed.

◢ On-boarding might install a remote backup application, which remotely backs up the device's data to a company file server. For example, Canopy Remote Backup by Atos (*canopy-cloud.com*) provides cloud-based backups for laptops, tablets, and smart phones.

◢ Off-boarding might include the ability to perform a remote wipe on a device that is lost or stolen or when an employee is abruptly dismissed. The process might even include the ability to completely disable the device and make it unusable for any network access at all.

◢ Two examples of software that support on-boarding and off-boarding, including remote locks and wipes, are Microsoft Exchange Server and Google Apps Mobile Management software.

Regardless of who owns a device, any device allowed to connect to a secured corporate network must meet certain security configuration requirements, including encryption, firewalls, anti-malware measures, or use of VPN connections. These profile security requirements must be clearly outlined, and users must be educated on how to ensure their devices continue to meet the baseline requirements.

Hands-On | Project 10-4   Learn About Google Apps Mobile Management

Google has posted several videos to *Youtube.com* that you can use to learn about its products and services. Search *Youtube.com* for videos about Google Apps Mobile Management by Google. (To know if a video is by Google, look for *Uploaded by GoogleApps* on the *Youtube.com* webpage below the video.) Answer the following questions:

1. What app should a user install on his device to use some of the features of Google Apps Mobile Management? What is the price of the software?

2. Can an administrator use the software to require that mobile devices must use a passcode? To lock a device remotely? To find a device when it is lost?

3. Which of the following mobile operating systems other than Android can work with Google Apps Mobile Management: iOS, Blackberry, Windows Phone?

4. Is it possible for a user to perform a remote wipe, or must it always be performed by an administrator?

ADDITIONAL METHODS TO PROTECT RESOURCES

A+
220-902
2.4, 3.1,
3.2, 3.4, 3.6

Securing data and other computer resources might seem like a never-ending task. Come to think of it, that's probably true. In this part of the chapter, you learn even more ways to securely authenticate users on a large network, physically protect computer resources, destroy data before you toss out a storage device, and educate users to not unintentionally compromise the security measures you've put in place.

AUTHENTICATE USERS FOR LARGE NETWORKS

A+
220-902
3.2

Normally, Windows authenticates a user with a Windows password. However, the best authentication happens when a user (1) knows something (such as a Windows password) and (2) possesses something, which is called a security token (such as a smart card or a fingerprint scan). In this part of the chapter, you learn about smart cards and biometric data used with multifactor authentication. One warning to keep in mind is a smart card or biometric data should be used in addition to, and not as a replacement for, a Windows password.

SECURITY TOKENS AND SMART CARDS

A security token provides an additional method of authentication in multifactor authentication scenarios or can serve as a replacement for a password. The most popular type of token used to authenticate a user is a smart card, which is typically a business-card sized card with embedded circuitry and contact points, although smart card technology can also be integrated into other security token form factors. (You also need to know that some people don't consider a card to be a smart card unless it has an embedded microprocessor.)

The information on the smart card can be typed on a sign-in window by a user, read by a smart card reader (when the device is inserted into the reader), or transmitted wirelessly. See Figure 10-23. At the same time, some smart cards can receive information from the reader to confirm that the reader is authentic. This is called mutual authentication, which occurs any time authentication goes in both directions at the same time as both entities confirm the identity of the other.

© antos777/Shutterstock.com

Figure 10-23 Smart card is read by a smart card reader

Here are some variations of security tokens:

▲ *Key fob.* A key fob is a security token that fits conveniently on a keychain, such as the one shown in Figure 10-24. The number on the key fob changes every 60 seconds. When a user signs in to the network, she must enter the number on the key fob, which is synchronized with the network authentication service. Entering the number proves that the user has the key fob in hand. Because the device doesn't actually make physical contact with the system, it is called a contactless token or disconnected token.

iStockphoto.com/David Clark

Figure 10-24 A security token such as this key fob is used to authenticate a user gaining access to a secured network

▲ *Wireless token.* Another type of contactless token uses wireless technology to transmit information kept by the token to the computer system. A Radio Frequency Identification (RFID) token transmits authentication to the system when the token gets in range of a query device. For example, an RFID badge worn by an employee can allow the employee entrance into a locked area of a building.

◢ *Memory stripe card.* An example of a contact token is an employee ID badge or other smart card with a magnetic stripe that can be read by a smart card reader (see Figure 10-25a). Because these cards don't contain a microchip, they are sometimes called memory cards. Some keyboards have an embedded smart card reader, and Figure 10-25b shows a reader that connects to a computer via a USB port. Used in this way, a memory stripe card is part of the authentication process into a network. The magnetic stripe can contain information about the user to indicate her rights on the system. The major disadvantage of this type of smart card is that each computer used for authentication must have one of these smart card reader machines installed. Also, in the industry, because a card with a magnetic stripe does not contain a microchip, some in the industry don't consider it to fit into the category of a smart card, but rather simply call it a magnetic stripe card.

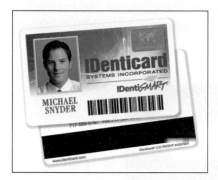

Courtesy of IDenticard Systems/ © Cousin_Avi/Shutterstock.com

Figure 10-25   (a) A smart card with a magnetic stripe can be used inside or outside a computer network, and (b) a USB reader for a magnetic stripe card

iStockphoto.com/viiwee

Figure 10-26   This access control device accepts typed code, fingerprint, or smart card input

◢ *Cell phone with token.* An app installed on a cell phone can hold the user's token, which includes a digital signature or digital certificate. A digital certificate is assigned by a Certification Authority (CA) (for example, VeriSign—*www.verisign.com*) and is used to prove you are who you say you are. The authentication can be sent to the network via a USB connection, text message, phone call, or Bluetooth connection. This method is sometimes used when an employee authenticates to a VPN connection to the corporate network.

BIOMETRIC DATA

As part of the authentication process, some systems use biometric data to validate the person's physical body, which, in effect, becomes the token. Figure 10-26 shows a biometric input device, a fingerprint scanner. Many mobile devices, such as iPads and some laptops, have fingerprint scanners built in. Other forms of biometric data include retinal scans (scans parts of the eye), handprints, face recognition, and voice recognition.

10

PHYSICAL SECURITY METHODS AND DEVICES

**A+
220-902
2.4, 3.2,
3.6**

Physically protecting a computer's resources is often seen by security experts as more important than digital security. Here are some best practices for physical security:

▲ *If the data is really private, keep it behind a locked door or under lock and key.* You can use all kinds of security methods to encrypt, password protect, and hide data, but if it really is that important, one obvious thing you can do is to keep the computer behind a locked door. You can also store the data on a removable storage device such as an external hard drive and, when you're not using the data, put the drive in a fireproof safe. And, of course, keep two copies. Sounds simple, but it works. Don't forget that printouts of sensitive documents should also be kept under lock and key as well as any passwords you might have written down.

▲ *Lock down the computer case.* Some computer cases allow you to add a lock so that you can physically prevent others from opening the case (see Figure 10-27a). Some motherboards have a UEFI/BIOS feature that alerts you when an intrusion has been detected.

(a)

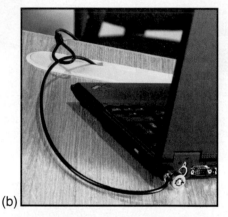
(b)

Figure 10-27   To physically secure a computer, (a) use a computer case lock and key for a desktop to prevent intrusion, or (b) use a cable lock system for a laptop to prevent theft

▲ *Use a lock and chain.* You can also use a lock and chain to physically tie a computer to a desk or other permanent fixture so someone can't walk away with it. Figure 10-27b shows a cable lock system for a laptop. Most laptops have a security slot on the case to connect the cable lock.

▲ *Use privacy filters.* To keep other people from viewing a monitor screen, you can install a privacy filter that fits over the screen to prevent it from being read from a wide angle.

▲ *Install a theft-prevention plate.* As an added precaution, physically mark a computer case or laptop so it can be identified if it is later stolen. You embed a theft-prevention plate into the case or engrave your ID information into it. The numbers or bar code identify you, the owner, and can also clearly establish to police that the laptop has been stolen. Two sources of theft-prevention plates and cable locks are Computer Security Products, Inc., (*computersecurity.com*) and Flexguard Security System (*flexguard .com*). To further help you identify stolen equipment, record serial numbers and model numbers in a safe place separate from the equipment.

▲ *Use a mantrap and security guard.* The ultimate in physical security is a mantrap, which consists of two doors on either end of a small entryway where the first door must close before the second door can open. A separate form of identification might be required for each door, such as a badge for the first door and a fingerprint scan for the second door. A security guard might also maintain an entry control roster, which is a list of people allowed into the restricted area and a log of any approved visitors.

DIGITAL SECURITY METHODS AND RESOURCES

A+
220-902
3.2

Windows Firewall is one example of digital-based security. Software can make up a significant portion of your defense resources. Following are some additional software security measures:

▲ *VPN (virtual private network)*. Recall from the chapter, "Connecting To and Setting Up a Network," that a VPN protects data by encrypting it over a remote connection to a private network.

▲ *Email filtering*. Email providers often offer email filtering to filter out suspicious email messages based on databases of known scams and spammers. Corporations might route incoming and outgoing email through a proxy server for filtering. Incoming email is inspected for scams or spam to protect against social engineering that might trick an employee into introducing malware into the corporate network.

Outgoing email from employees might be filtered for inappropriate content. This lawful interception is intended to verify that an employee is complying with privacy laws (for example, laws that apply to confidential medical records) and is not accidentally or intentionally leaking corporate data and secrets. Email filtering software used in this way is an example of data loss prevention (DLP) software, which helps protect against leaking corporate data.

▲ *Trusted software sources*. It's important to download software only from trusted publishers *and* providers. Even software from a trusted publisher can be filled with destructive extras if the software is obtained from an untrusted provider. Be careful which sites you use for software downloads even when you know the software is trusted.

▲ *Access control lists*. An access control list (ACL) determines what user, device, or program has access to a particular resource, whether that's a printer, folder, file, or other resource on a corporate network, server, or workstation. Corporate networks manage ACLs through Active Directory on a Windows domain, but a single workstation can also be protected with properly configured permissions. In the chapter, "Windows Resources on a Network," you learned to assign NTFS permissions and share permissions to user accounts in order to secure a workstation on a peer-to-peer network.

10

UNIFIED THREAT MANAGEMENT (UTM) APPLIANCE

A+
220-902
2.4

In the chapter, "Connecting To and Setting Up a Network," you learned that a router stands between the Internet and a private network to route traffic between the two networks and can also serve as a firewall to protect the network. A next-generation firewall (NGFW) combines firewall software with antivirus/anti-malware software. In addition, a NGFW device can offer comprehensive Unified Threat Management (UTM) services. A UTM appliance, also called a security appliance, network appliance, or Internet appliance, stands between the Internet and a private network, as does a router, and protects the network (see Figure 10-28).

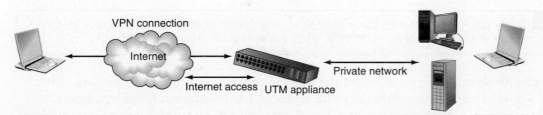

Figure 10-28 A UTM appliance is considered a next-generation firewall that can protect a private network

⭐ **A+ Exam Tip** The A+ 220-902 exam expects you to be able to summarize the purposes of services provided by a UTM Internet appliance, including an IDS and IPS.

A UTM appliance might offer these types of protections and services:

⬤ **Firewall.** The firewall software filters incoming and outgoing network traffic according to IP addresses, ports, the type of messages the traffic contains, and how the message was initiated.

⬤ **Antivirus and anti-malware software.** This software is usually much more advanced than what might be installed on a server or workstation.

⬤ **Identity-based access control lists.** These lists control access of users or user groups and can log and report activity of these users and groups to reveal misuse, data leaks, or unauthorized access to resources. The company can use this feature to satisfy legal auditing requirements to detect and control data leaks.

⬤ **Intrusion detection system.** An intrusion detection system (IDS) monitors all network traffic and creates alerts when suspicious activity happens. IDS software can run on a UTM appliance, router, server, or workstation.

⬤ **Intrusion prevention system.** An intrusion prevention system (IPS) not only monitors and logs suspicious activity, but it can also prevent the threatening traffic from burrowing into the system.

⬤ **VPN.** The appliance can provide a VPN to remote users of the network.

Figure 10-29 shows a UTM appliance by NETGEAR.

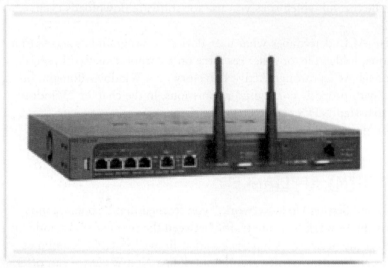

Source: netgear.com

Figure 10-29   ProSECURE UTM appliance by NETGEAR

DATA DESTRUCTION AND DISPOSAL

A+
220-902
3.6

On the flip side of protecting valuable data is safely destroying data that is no longer needed. Don't throw out a hard drive, CD, DVD, tape, or other media that might have personal or corporate data on it unless you know the data can't be stolen off the device. Trying to wipe a drive clean by deleting files or even by using Windows to format the drive does not completely destroy the data. Here are some ways to destroy printed documents and sanitize storage devices:

⬤ **Use a paper shredder.** Use a paper shredder to destroy all documents that contain sensitive data.

> ★ **A+ Exam Tip**   The A+ 220-902 exam expects you to know about data-destruction techniques, including a low-level format, drive wipe, shredder, degausser, incineration, and drill, which can do physical damage to a hard drive.

⬤ **Overwrite data on the drive.** To wipe a drive clean so that you can use it again, you can perform a low-level format of a drive, which overwrites the data with zeroes. (A low-level format is different from a standard Windows format. A device receives a low-level format at the factory, which writes sector markings on the drive.) You can also use a zero-fill utility that also overwrites all data on the drive with zeroes. You can download a low-level format utility or zero-fill utility from many hard drive manufacturers.

Either method works for most low-security situations, but professional thieves know how to break through this type of destruction. If you use one of these utilities, run it multiple times to write zeroes on top of zeroes. Data recovery has been known to reach 14 levels of overwrites because each bit is slightly offset from the one under it.

▲ *Physically destroy the storage media.* Use a drill to drill many holes through the drive housing all the way through to the other side of the housing. Break CDs and DVDs in half and do similar physical damage with a hammer to flash drives or tapes, even to the point of setting them on fire to incinerate them. Again, expert thieves can still recover some of the data.

▲ *For magnetic devices, use a degausser.* A degausser exposes a storage device to a strong electromagnetic field to completely erase the data on a magnetic hard drive or tape drive (see Figure 10-30). A degaussed drive can't be reused, but for the best destruction, use the degausser and also physically destroy the drive. Degaussing does not erase data on a solid-state hard drive or other flash media because these devices don't use a magnetic surface to hold data.

Figure 10-30   Use a degausser to sanitize a magnetic hard drive or tape

▲ *For solid-state devices, use a Secure Erase utility.* As required by government regulations for personal data privacy, the American National Standards Institute (ANSI) developed the ATA Secure Erase standards to wipe clean a solid-state device such as a USB flash drive or SSD drive. You can download a Secure Erase utility from the manufacturer of the device and run it to securely erase all data on the device and then reuse the drive.

▲ *Use a secure data-destruction service.* For the very best data destruction, consider a secure data-destruction service. To find a service, search the web for "secure data destruction." However, don't use a service unless you have thoroughly checked its references and guarantees of legal compliance that your organization is required to meet. The service should provide you with a digital certificate of destruction, which verifies that the data has been destroyed beyond recovery. Paper certificates can be forged, but digital certificates produced by the software performing the destruction will provide auditable results of the destruction process.

EDUCATE USERS

A+
220-902
3.1, 3.2,
3.4

Generally speaking, the weakest link in setting up security in a computer environment is people. That's because people can often be tricked into giving out private information. Even with all the news and hype about identity theft and criminal websites, it's amazing how well these techniques still work. Many users naively download a funny screen saver, open an email attachment, or enter credit card information on a website without regard to security. In the computer arena, social engineering is the practice of tricking people into giving out private information or allowing unsafe programs into the network or computer.

A good support technician is aware of the criminal practices used, and is able to teach users how to recognize and avoid this mischief. A document that can help educate users is an acceptable use policy (AUP), which explains what users can and cannot do on the corporate network or with company data, and the penalties for violations. The AUP might also describe how these measures help protect the network's security. Here is a list of important security measures that users need to follow to protect passwords and the computer system:

⊿ Never give out your passwords to anyone, not even a supervisor or tech support person who calls and asks for it.

⊿ Don't store your passwords on a computer unless you use company-approved password vault software (for example, KeePass). Some organizations even forbid employees from writing down their passwords.

⊿ Don't use the same password on more than one system (computer, network, application, or website).

⊿ Be aware of shoulder surfing, when other people secretly peek at your monitor screen as you work. A privacy filter can help.

⊿ Lock down your workstation each time you step away from your desk.

⊿ Users need to be on the alert for tailgating, which is when someone who is unauthorized follows the employee through a secured entrance to a room or building. Another form of tailgating is when a user steps away from her computer and another person continues to use the Windows session when the system is not properly locked.

Beware of online social engineering techniques. For example, don't be fooled by scam email or an email hoax such as the one shown in Figure 10-31. When the user who received this email scanned the attached file using antivirus software, the software reported the file contained malware.

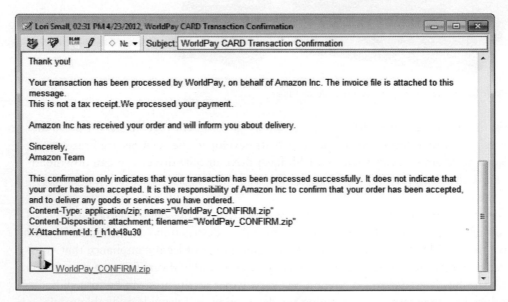

Figure 10-31   This phishing technique using an email message with an attached file is an example of social engineering

★ **A+ Exam Tip**   The A+ 220-902 exam expects you to be aware of social engineering situations such as tailgating, phishing, and shoulder surfing that might compromise security.

Here are some good sites to help you debunk a virus hoax or email hoax:

⊿ *snopes.com* by Barbara and David Mikkelson
⊿ *securelist.com* by Kaspersky Lab
⊿ *virusbtn.com* by Virus Bulletin, Ltd

Don't forward an email hoax. When you get a hoax, if you know the person who sent it to you, do us all a favor and send that person some of these links!

Here are some other types of online social engineering situations:

▲ Phishing (pronounced "fishing") is a type of identity theft in which the sender of an email message scams you into responding with personal data about yourself. Even more plausible is spear phishing, where the email appears to come from companies you already do business with. The scam artist baits you by asking you to verify personal data on your bank account, ISP account, credit card account, or something of that nature. Often you are tricked into clicking a link in the email message, which takes you to an official-looking site complete with corporate or bank logos, where you are asked to enter your user ID and password to enter the site. This tactic is called spoofing, which means the scam artist makes both the email and website look like the real thing.

▲ An email message might contain a link that leads to a malicious script. If you think an email is legitimate, to be on the safe side, still don't click the link. To keep a script from running, type the website's home page into your browser address bar and navigate to the relevant page on the website.

A study by Dell showed that 65 percent of business travelers have not secured the corporate data on their hard drives, and 42 percent don't back up that data. Here are some commonsense rules to help protect a laptop when traveling:

▲ When traveling, always know where your laptop is. If you're standing at an airport counter, tuck your laptop case securely between your ankles. At security checkpoints, pay attention to your belongings; tell yourself to stay focused. When flying, never check your laptop as baggage, and don't store it in airplane overhead bins; keep it at your feet.

▲ Never leave a laptop in an unlocked car. If you leave your laptop in a hotel room, use a laptop cable lock to secure it to a table.

▲ When at work, lock your laptop in a secure place or use a laptop cable lock to secure it to your desk.

An IT support technician will most certainly be called on to help a user rid a system of malware. Let's turn our attention to how to deal with that problem.

DEALING WITH MALICIOUS SOFTWARE ON PERSONAL COMPUTERS

A+
220-902
1.1, 1.5,
3.1, 3.2,
4.2

Malicious software, also called malware, or a computer infestation, is any unwanted program that means you harm and is transmitted to your computer without your knowledge. Grayware is any annoying and unwanted program that might or might not mean you harm, for example adware that produces all those unwanted pop-up ads. In this part of the chapter, you learn about the different types of malware and grayware, what to do to clean up an infected system, and how to protect a system from infection.

WHAT ARE WE UP AGAINST?

A+
220-902
3.1, 4.2

You need to know your enemy! Different categories of malicious software and scamming techniques are listed next:

▲ *Viruses.* A virus is a program that replicates by attaching itself to other programs. The infected program must be executed for a virus to run. The program might be an application, a macro in a document, a Windows system file, or a boot loader program.

▲ *Spyware.* Spyware spies on you to collect personal information about you that it transmits over the Internet to web-hosting sites. An example of spyware is a keylogger that tracks all your keystrokes and can be used to steal a person's identity, credit card numbers, Social Security number, bank information, passwords, email addresses, and so forth.

▲ *Worms.* A worm is a program that copies itself throughout a network or the Internet without a host program. A worm creates problems by overloading the network as it replicates and can even hijack or install a server program such as a web server.

▲ *Trojans.* A Trojan does not need a host program to work; rather, it substitutes itself for a legitimate program. In most cases, a user launches it thinking she is launching a legitimate program. A Trojan is often embedded in the files of legitimate software that is downloaded from an untrustworthy website, or a user is tricked into opening an email attachment (refer back to Figure 10-31).

▲ *Rootkits.* A rootkit loads itself before the OS boot is complete. It can hide in boot managers, boot loader programs, or kernel mode device drivers. UEFI secure boot is especially designed to catch rootkits that launch during the boot. Because it is already loaded when most anti-malware software loads, it is sometimes overlooked by the software. A rootkit can hide folders that contain software it has installed, cause Task Manager to display a different name for its process, hide registry keys, and can operate in user mode or kernel mode. This last trick helps it remain undetected (see Figure 10-32).

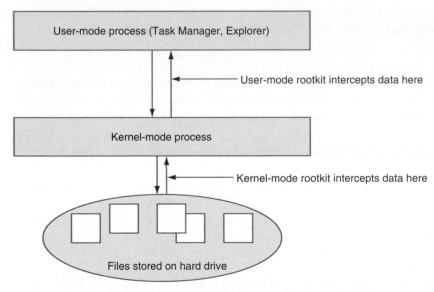

Figure 10-32   A rootkit can run in user mode or kernel mode

A rootkit running in user mode intercepts the API calls between the time when the API retrieves the data and when it is displayed in a window. A rootkit running in kernel mode actually interferes with the Windows kernel and substitutes its own information in place of the raw data read by the Windows kernel. Because most anti-malware software to one degree or another relies on Windows tools and components to work, the rootkit is not detected or cannot be deleted if the Windows tools themselves are infected.

> **⚡ Caution**   If anti-malware software reports a rootkit is present, but cannot delete it, the best solution is to immediately disconnect the computer from the network (if you have not already done so), back up your important data, format your hard drive, and reinstall Windows.

▲ *Ransomware.* Ransomware holds your computer system hostage until you pay money. For example, the CryptoLocker Trojan program that did damage in 2014 was embedded in email attachments and was known to work on Windows, Android, and even some iOS systems. When the user clicked the attachment, the program encrypted the computer's personal files. If the user didn't pay within a 24-hour period, all the files were lost. Many users who did not have backups of their data chose to pay the ransom.

◢ ***Zero-day attack.*** A zero-day attack can happen when a hacker discovers a security hole in software that is unknown to the developer of the software. The race is on for the vendor to provide a patch to the software before hackers have even one day to use the hole to infect systems and steal user data. Microsoft normally publishes security patches on the second and fourth Tuesday of each month (known as patch Tuesday), but sometimes releases patches off schedule so that hackers have zero days to attack customers.

◢ ***Man-in-the-middle attack.*** In a man-in-the-middle attack, the attacker intercepts communication between two parties and reads and/or alters the content of messages. The attacker can pretend to be a legitimate website, network, FTP site, or person in a chat session. For example, a user might connect to an "evil twin" Wi-Fi hotspot, thinking it's a legitimate hotspot, and attempt to start a chat session with a business associate. The attacker pretends to be the business associate and continues the chat with the intention of obtaining private information. The best protection against man-in-the-middle attacks is to use digital certificates to identify a person or service before transmitting sensitive information.

◢ ***Zombies and botnets.*** A zombie is a computer that has been hacked, and the hacker is using the computer to run repetitive software in the background without the knowledge of its user. For example, the zombie might be email spamming or performing denial-of-service attacks (attacks from multiple computers that overwhelm a server with requests until new connections can no longer be accepted). A hacker might build an entire network of zombies, which is called a botnet (a network of robots). The CryptoLocker Trojan program was distributed by a botnet and ultimately isolated when the botnet was taken down.

◢ ***Dictionary attack.*** A dictionary attack can be used to crack a password by trying words in a dictionary. Password cracker software might combine a brute force attack with a dictionary attack to use smarter guessing to guess the password.

> ★ **A+ Exam Tip** The A+ 220-902 exam expects you to be able to compare and contrast viruses, Trojans, worms, spyware, ransomware, and rootkits. You also need to know about zero-day attacks, man-in-the-middle attacks, zombies, botnets, dictionary attacks, brute force attacks, and noncompliant systems.

◢ ***Non compliant systems and violations of security best practices.*** Administrators who remotely manage many servers or workstations on a large network might use configuration management software, such as Microsoft System Center, to remotely configure computers and monitor these configurations. Agents are installed on each computer to be monitored that routinely report the configuration back to the management software. The administrator routinely receives and reviews these reports, comparing the reported configurations with the established configuration baseline. For security purposes, she specifically looks for non compliant systems that violate security best practices, such as out-of-date anti-malware software or no anti-malware software installed.

STEP-BY-STEP ATTACK PLAN

This section is a step-by-step attack plan to clean up an infected system. We use anti-malware software, also called antivirus software, to remove all types of general malware, including viruses, spyware, worms, and rootkits. Then we'll use some Windows tools to check out the system to make sure all remnants of malware have been removed and the system is in tip-top order.

> ⚡ **Caution** If a system is highly infected and will later hold sensitive data, a fresh start might be in order. In fact, Microsoft recommends reinstalling Windows as the safest way to deal with highly infected systems.
> For Windows 8, a refresh can be an excellent option if you have a custom refresh image and current backups of user data. For Windows 7, consider using a system image to reinstall Windows and then restore data from recent backups.

10

STEP 1: IDENTIFY MALWARE SYMPTOMS

An IT support technician needs to know how to recognize that a system is infected with malware and how to clean an infected system. Here are some warnings that suggest malicious software is at work:

▲ *Pop-up ads and browser redirection.* Basically, a user is losing control of his system. For example, Figure 10-33 shows the desktop immediately after a user signed in. Pop-up ads are randomly appearing and the browser home page has changed. A browser might also have an uninvited toolbar.

Source: Ruiware, LLC

Figure 10-33 A hijacked home page, security alerts, and pop-up ads indicate an infected system

▲ *Rogue antivirus software.* When the user above tried to run Windows Defender (anti-malware software embedded in Windows 8), it refused to run. She opened the Action Center to find that Defender had been disabled because other antivirus software she did not install was running. See Figure 10-34.

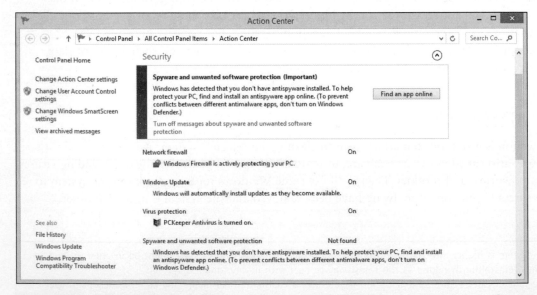

Figure 10-34 Action Center reports Windows Defender has been disabled and rogue antivirus software is running

Windows allows only one anti-malware product to run at a time. You can use Task Manager to stop the rogue antivirus software and then start Windows Defender.

◢ *Slow performance or lockups.* Generally, the system works much slower than it used to. Programs take longer than normal to load. Strange or bizarre error messages appear. Programs that once worked now give errors. Task Manager shows unfamiliar processes running. The system might even lock up.

◢ *Internet connectivity issues, application crashes, and OS updates fail.* These types of problems seem to plague the system with no reasonable explanation that is specific to the network, application, or Windows update. Remember that Event Viewer can be used to view logs of system crashes, application crashes, and failed OS updates.

◢ *Problems with files.* File names now have weird characters or their file sizes seem excessively large. Executable files have changed size or file extensions change without reason. Files mysteriously disappear or appear. Windows system files are renamed. Files constantly become corrupted. Files you could once access now give access denied messages, and file permissions change.

◢ *Email problems.* You receive email messages telling you that you have sent someone spam or an infected message, or you receive automated replies indicating you sent email you didn't know about. This type of attack indicates your email address or email client software on your computer has been hijacked.

◢ *Problems updating your anti-malware software.* Even though you can browse to other websites, you cannot access anti-malware software sites such as *www.symantec.com* or *www.mcafee.com*, and you cannot update your anti-malware software.

◢ *Invalid digital certificates.* An OS is responsible for validating certificates used to secure communication. For Windows, Microsoft maintains a database of trusted root certificates issued by Certification Authorities (CAs). (A root certificate is the original certificate issued by the CA.) When a Windows system opens a secure email or visits a secure website and encounters a new digital certificate, it requests the trusted root certificate from Microsoft, which is downloaded to the computer. The download happens seamlessly without the user's knowledge unless there's a problem. If Windows cannot obtain the root certificate to validate the email or website, it displays an error (see Figure 10-35). Don't trust websites or email whose certificates have expired or been revoked.

10

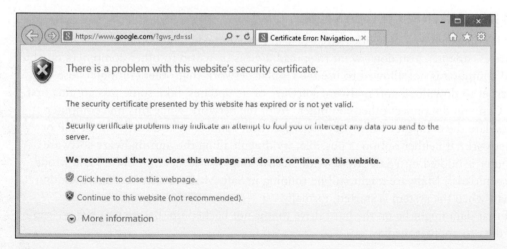

Figure 10-35   Windows reports a problem with a digital certificate

✎ **Notes**   If a computer gives invalid certificate errors, check that the Windows date is correct. A wrong Windows date before the certificate was issued can cause the problem.

You can use the Certificate Manager (certmgr.msc) to view and delete root certificates (see Figure 10-36). For example, the Superfish virus injects a rogue root certificate into the Microsoft store of trusted certificates on the local computer so that it can perform a man-in-the-middle attack to display adware on secure websites a user visits. If you see a Superfish certificate listed among trusted root certificates, be sure to delete it.

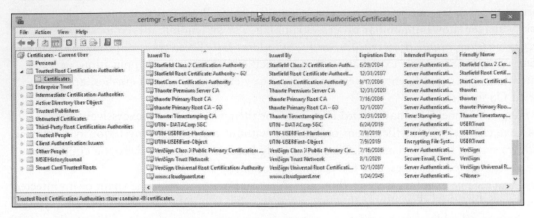

Figure 10-36   Windows Certificate Manager can be used to view and delete root certificates kept in the store of trusted certificates

> ★ **A+ Exam Tip**   The A+ 220-902 exam expects you to know about the common symptoms of malware listed previously and how to quarantine and remediate an infected system.

> ✎ **Notes**   Malicious software is designed to do varying degrees of damage to data and software, although it does not damage computer hardware. However, when partition table information is destroyed on a hard drive, the hard drive can appear to be physically damaged.

STEP 2: QUARANTINE AN INFECTED SYSTEM

If an infected computer is connected to a network (wired or wireless), immediately disconnect the network cable or turn off the wireless adapter. You don't want to spread a virus or worm to other computers on your network. A quarantined computer is not allowed to use the regular network that other computers use. If you need to use the Internet to download anti-malware software or its updates, take some precautions first. Consider your options. Can you disconnect other computers from the network while this one computer is connected? Can you isolate the computer from your local network, connecting it directly to the ISP or a special quarantined network? If neither option is possible, try downloading the anti-malware software updates while the computer is booted into Safe Mode with Networking or after a clean boot. (Safe Mode doesn't always allow downloads.) Malware might still be running in Safe Mode or after a clean boot, but is less likely to do so than when the system is started normally.

Always keep in mind that data might be on the hard drive that is not backed up. Before you begin cleaning up the system, back up data to another media.

STEP 3: DISABLE SYSTEM RESTORE

In Windows, some malware hides its program files in restore points stored in the System Volume Information folder maintained by System Protection. If System Protection is on, anti-malware software can't clean this protected folder. To get rid of that malware, turn off System Protection so that anti-malware can clean the System Volume Information folder (see Figure 10-37). Realize that when you turn off System Protection, all your restore points are lost. To turn off System Protection, open the System window and click **System protection**. Later, when you are sure the system is clean, turn System Protection back on and create a new restore point that you can use in the future if problems arise.

Source: McAfee VirusScan

Figure 10-37 Malware found in a restore point

> **⚡ Caution** Some highly infected systems will not allow anti-malware software to run. In this situation, you can boot the computer into Safe Mode and use System Restore to apply a restore point that was taken before the infection. Applying a restore point cannot be counted on to completely remove an infection, but it might remove startup entries the malware is using, making it possible to run the anti-malware software from the normal Windows desktop or run the software in Safe Mode. Consider that you might need to apply a restore point before you disable System Protection, which deletes all your restore points.

STEP 4: REMEDIATE THE INFECTED SYSTEM

Table 10-1 lists popular anti-malware software for personal computers and websites that also provide information about malware. Before selecting a product, be sure to read some reviews about it and check out some reliable websites that rate anti-malware software.

> **⚡ Caution** Beware of websites that appear as sponsored links at the top of search results for anti-malware software. These sites might make you think they are the home site for the software, but are really trying to lure you into downloading adware or spyware.

Anti-Malware Software	Website
Security Software by Trend Micro (for home use)	*trendmicro.com*
Intelligent Antivirus and Anti-malware by AVAST Software (home edition is free)	*avast.com*
AVG Antivirus Protection by AVG Technologies	*avg.com*
Bitdefender Antivirus	*bitdefender.com*
CLAMWIN Free Antivirus by ClamWin (open source and free)	*clamwin.com*
F-Secure Anti-Virus by F-Secure Corp	*f-secure.com*
Kaspersky Antivirus and Internet Security	*kaspersky.com*
Malwarebytes Anti-Malware (free version available)	*malwarebytes.org*
McAfee Total Protection	*mcafee.com*
Symantec Endpoint Protection	*symantec.com*
Panda Internet Security	*pandasecurity.com*
SUPERAntiSpyware	*superantispyware.com*
Microsoft Security Essentials (free)	*windows.microsoft.com*

Table 10-1 Anti-malware software and websites

> **↻ OS Differences** Windows Defender anti-malware software is embedded in Windows 8 and can be accessed through Control Panel. Windows 7 includes Windows Defender, but the Windows 7 version finds only spyware, not viruses and other malware. For Windows 7, you can download and install Microsoft Security Essentials, which is free anti-malware software.

10

Now let's look at different situations you might encounter when attempting to run anti-malware software.

When an Infected Computer Will Not Boot

If an infected computer will not boot, it might be that the boot manager, boot loaders, or kernel mode drivers launched at startup are infected or damaged. Launch the computer into Windows Recovery Environment (Windows RE) and use the Startup Repair process to repair the system. The chapter, "Troubleshooting Windows Startup," gives more information about solving boot problems. You can also install the hard drive as a second drive in another system and use that system to scan the drive for malware.

Update and Run Anti-Malware Software Already Installed

If anti-malware software is already installed and you suspect an infection, update the software and perform a full scan on the system. Do the following:

1. Make sure the anti-malware software is up to date. These updates download the latest malware definitions, also called malware signatures, which the software uses to define or detect new malware as it gets into the wild.

2. Use the anti-malware software to perform a full scan of the system. As it scans, the software might ask you what to do with an infected program or it might log this event in an event viewer or history log it keeps. For example, Windows Defender reports a threat, as shown in Figure 10-38. When you click **Clean PC**, you can decide what to do with the threat. In most situations, select **Remove** to delete the program.

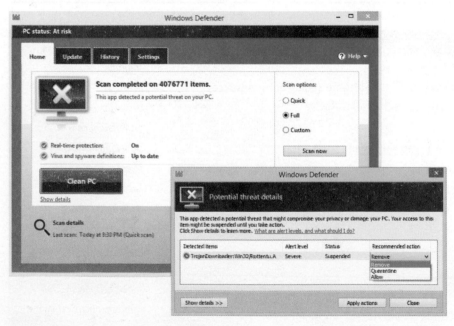

Figure 10-38   Decide what to do with a program that Windows Defender has identified as a severe threat to the system

3. After the scan is complete and you have decided what to do with each suspicious file, reboot the system and allow the software to update itself again and then scan the system again. Most likely, some new malware will be discovered. Keep rebooting and rescanning until a scan comes up clean.

> ✎ **Notes** If you ever encounter a virus that your updated anti-malware software did not find, be sure to let the manufacturer of the software know so they can research the problem.

Run Anti-Malware Software from a Networked Computer

If anti-malware software is not already installed, the most effective way to clean the computer is to run the software from another computer. Follow these steps:

1. Make sure the remote computer has its software firewall set for maximum protection and its installed anti-malware software is up to date and running.

2. Network the two computers and share drive C: on the infected computer. (Don't connect the infected computer to the entire network. If necessary, you can connect the two computers using a crossover cable or using a small switch and network cables.)

3. To make your work easier, you can map a network drive from the remote computer to drive C: on the infected computer.

4. Perform an anti-malware scan on the remote computer, pointing the scan to drive C: on the infected computer.

Install and Run Anti-Malware Software on the Infected Computer

If you don't have another computer available on the network to scan the infected computer, you can use another computer to purchase and download the anti-malware software and copy the downloaded files to a CD or flash drive that you can insert in the infected computer. Don't make the mistake of using the infected computer to purchase and download anti-malware software because keyloggers might be spying and collecting credit card information. During the installation process, the anti-malware software updates itself and performs a scan. You can also run free online anti-malware software without downloading and installing it, but be careful to use only reputable websites.

Install and Run Anti-Malware Software in Safe Mode

Some malware prevents anti-malware software from installing or running. In this situation, try booting the system in Safe Mode or performing a clean boot and installing the anti-malware software. Some viruses still load in Safe Mode or after a clean boot, and some anti-malware programs will not install in Safe Mode.

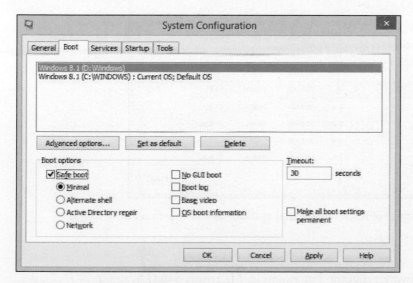

Recall that to launch Windows in Safe Mode, enter the **msconfig** command in the Windows 8 Run box or Windows 7 Search box. In the System Configuration box, on the Boot tab, check **Safe boot** (see Figure 10-39). To launch Safe Mode with Networking so that you can update your anti-malware software, select **Network** in the list of options. Then restart the system.

Figure 10-39 Use the Safe boot option to boot the system in Safe Mode to prevent malware from launching at startup

10

> **Notes** If viruses are launched even after you boot in Safe Mode and you cannot get the anti-malware software to work, try searching for suspicious entries in the Windows registry subkeys under HKLM\System\CurrentControlSet\Control\SafeBoot. Subkeys under this key control what is launched when you boot into Safe Mode. How to edit the registry is covered in the chapter, "Optimizing Windows."

RUN THE ANTI-MALWARE SOFTWARE FROM A BOOTABLE RESCUE CD OR FLASH DRIVE

Some anti-malware products, such as the AVG Rescue CD software, offer the option to create a bootable USB flash drive or CD. You can then use this device to boot the system and run the anti-malware software from the device in this preinstallation environment. Most of the products listed earlier in Table 10-1 offer the option on their website to download software to create a bootable CD or flash drive. Be sure to use a healthy computer to create the rescue CD or flash drive. In addition, you might need to create a 32-bit version to scan a 32-bit Windows system or a 64-bit version to scan a 64-bit system. When selecting a product to create a bootable device, find one that can store the latest updates on the CD or flash drive so you don't need Internet access when you scan the infected system.

RUN MORE THAN ONE SCAN OF ANTI-MALWARE

After you've scanned the system using one of the methods just discussed, reboot and install anti-malware software on the hard drive. Update the software, and then keep scanning and rebooting until the scan report is clean.

If a second or third scan doesn't remove all symptoms of malware, consider installing and running a second anti-malware program. What one anti-malware program cannot detect or remove, another one might. For example, Windows Defender on one system removed malware it detected, but did not detect or remove the downloader dnsatlantic.exe, which hijacks a browser and is still running in the background (see Figure 10-40).

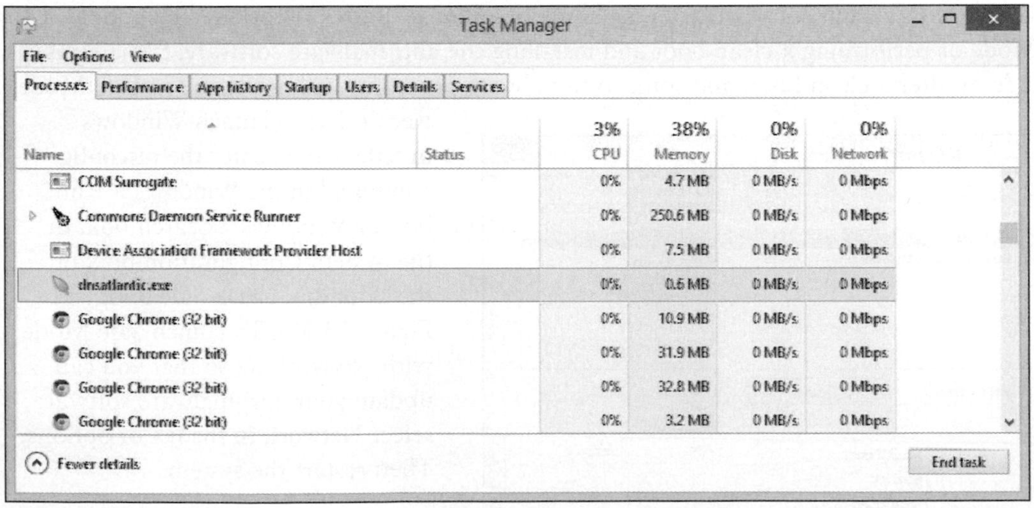

Figure 10-40 The malware downloader dnsatlantic.exe is still running after multiple scans of anti-malware software

In this situation, try another anti-malware program. For example, Microsoft Safety Scanner (*microsoft.com/security/scanner*) is not designed for on going malware prevention but can sometimes remove malware that Windows Defender did not find.

CLEAN UP WHAT'S LEFT OVER

Next, you'll need to clean up anything the anti-malware software left behind. Sometimes anti-malware software tells you it is not able to delete a file, or it deletes an infected file but leaves behind an orphaned entry in the registry or startup folders. If the anti-malware software tells you it was not able to delete or clean a file, first check the anti-malware software website for any instructions you might find to manually clean things up. Here are some general actions you can take to clean up what the software left behind:

1. *Respond to any startup errors.* On the first boot after anti-malware software has declared a system clean, you might still find some startup errors caused by incomplete removal of the malware. Use System Configuration and/or Task Manager to find out how a startup program is launched. If the program is launched from the registry, you can back up and delete the registry key. If the program is launched from a startup folder, you can move or delete the shortcut or program in the folder. See the chapter, "Optimizing Windows," for the details of how to remove unwanted startup programs.

2. *Research malware types and program files.* Your anti-malware software might alert you to a suspicious program file that it quarantines, and then ask you to decide if you want to delete it. Also, Task Manager and other tools might find processes you suspect are malware. The web is your best tool to use when making your decision about a program. Here are some websites that offer malware encyclopedias that are reliable and give you symptoms and solutions for malware:

   ◢ Process Library by Uniblue Systems Limited at *www.processlibrary.com*
   ◢ DLL Library by Uniblue Systems Limited at *www.liutilities.com*
   ◢ All the anti-malware software sites listed earlier in the chapter in Table 10-1

Beware of using other sites! Much information on the web is written by people who are just guessing, and some of the information is put there to purposefully deceive. Check things out carefully, and learn which sites you can rely on.

3. *Delete files.* For each program file the anti-malware software told you it could not delete, delete the program file yourself following these steps:

   a. First try File Explorer or Windows Explorer to locate a file and delete it. For peace of mind, don't forget to empty the Recycle Bin when you're done.

   b. If the file is hidden or access is denied, open an elevated command prompt window and use the commands listed in Table 10-2 to take control of a file so you can delete it. If the commands don't work using an elevated command prompt window, use the commands in a command prompt window in Windows RE.

Command	Description
`attrib -r -s filename.ext`	Remove the read-only and system attributes to a file.
`tasklist |more` `taskkill /f /pid:9999`	To stop a running process, first use the tasklist command to find out the process ID for the process. Then use the taskkill command to forcefully kill the process with the given process ID.
`takeown /f filename.ext`	Take ownership of a file.
`icacls filename.ext /GRANT ADMINISTRATORS:F`	Take full access of a file.

Table 10-2 Commands used to take control of a malware file so you can delete it

   c. To get rid of other malware files, delete all Internet Explorer temporary Internet files. To do so, use the Disk Cleanup process in the Drive C: properties box, or delete the browsing history using the Internet Options box.

   d. Delete all subfolders and files in the C:\Windows\Temp folder. Figure 10-41 shows where Windows Defender lists potentially unwanted programs (PuPs) that a Trojan downloader put in this folder.

10

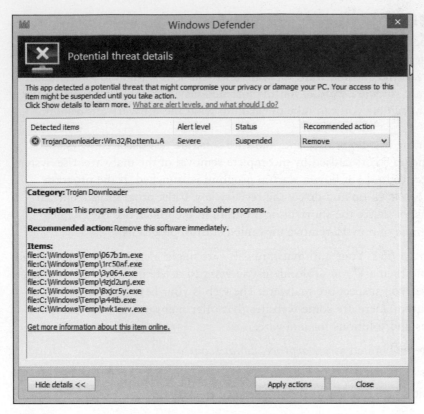

Figure 10-41   A Trojan downloader put programs in the C:/Windows/Temp folder, which must be manually deleted

4. *Clean the registry.* The appendix, "Entry Points for Windows Startup Processes," lists registry keys that can affect startup. You can search these keys and delete entries you don't want. After you have finished cleaning the registry, don't forget to restart the system to make sure all is well before you move on.

5. *Clean up Internet Explorer and uninstall unwanted programs.* Adware and spyware might install add-ons to Internet Explorer (including toolbars you didn't ask for), install cookie trackers, and change your Internet Explorer security settings. Anti-malware software might have found all these items, but as a good defense, take a few minutes to find out for yourself. The chapter, "Windows Resources on a Network," covers how to use the Internet

Options box to search for unwanted add-ons and delete ActiveX controls. You can uninstall unwanted toolbars, plug-ins, and other software using the Programs and Features window (see Figure 10-42).

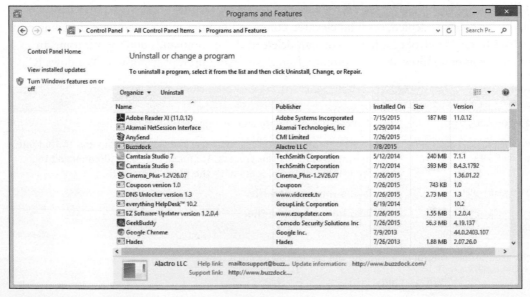

Figure 10-42   A Trojan downloader on this computer installed several unwanted programs, which must be uninstalled

STEP 5: PROTECT THE SYSTEM WITH SCHEDULED SCANS AND UPDATES

Once your system is clean, you'll certainly want to keep it that way. The three best practices you need to follow to protect a system against malware are:

▲ *Use anti-malware software.* Install and run anti-malware software and keep it current. Configure the software so that it (1) runs in the background in real time to alert users of malware that attempts to run or install, (2) automatically scans incoming email attachments, and (3) performs scheduled scans of the system and automatically downloads updates to the software. To find out what anti-malware software is installed and turned on, open the Action Center.

▲ *Always use a software firewall.* Never, ever connect your computer to an unprotected network without using a firewall. Windows Firewall is turned on by default. Recall that you can configure Windows Firewall to allow no uninvited communication in or to allow in the exceptions that you specify.

▲ *Keep Windows updates current.* Windows updates are continually being released to plug up vulnerable entrances in Windows where malware might attack and to update Windows Defender and Microsoft Security Essentials. Recall you can verify Windows Update settings by clicking **Windows Update** in the System window.

STEP 6: ENABLE SYSTEM PROTECTION AND CREATE A RESTORE POINT

Now that the system is clean, if System Protection is still turned off, turn it back on and create a restore point.

STEP 7: EDUCATE THE END USER

Now would be a good time to go over with the user some tips presented earlier in the chapter to keep the system free from malware. Sometimes the most overlooked step in preventing malware infections is to educate the user. Even with all your security measures in place, a user can still download and execute a Trojan, which can install more malware in the system.

> ★ **A+ Exam Tip** The A+ 220-902 exam expects you to know about the seven steps to remove malware. Memorize these seven steps and know how to use them.

Hands-On | Project 10-5 Create and Use an Anti-Malware Software Rescue Disc

A+ 220-902 4.2 When an infected computer does not have anti-malware software installed, one method to clean the infection is to create and use an anti-malware rescue disc. Select anti-malware software that offers a free download to create a bootable USB flash drive or CD. For example, Windows Defender Offline or F-Secure Rescue CD can be used. Create a bootable USB flash drive or CD and use it to scan a computer. Answer the following questions:

1. What is the URL where you found the download to create a rescue disc or drive?

2. List the files in the root directory of the USB flash drive or CD that the software created.

3. Describe the menu or screen that appears when you booted from the rescue media.

Hands-On | Project 10-6 Download and Use Anti-Malware Software

A+
220-902
4.2

A free trial of AVG Protection software is available on the AVG site at *www.avg.com*. Do the following to download, install, and run the software:

1. Download the free trial version of AVG Protection software from the *www.avg.com* site and install the software.

2. Update the software with the latest malware signatures.

3. Perform a complete scan of the system. Were any suspicious programs found?

4. Set the software to scan the system daily.

5. Set the software to scan incoming email.

Hands-On | Project 10-7 Use the Web to Learn About Malware

One source of information about malware on the web is F-Secure Corporation. Go to the website *www.f-secure.com*, and find information about the latest malware threats. Answer the following questions:

1. Name and describe a recent Trojan downloader. How does the Trojan install and what is its payload (the harm it does)?

2. Name and describe a recent rootkit. How does the rootkit install and what is its payload?

3. Name a recent worm. How does it get into the network and what is its payload?

DEALING WITH MALICIOUS SOFTWARE ON MOBILE DEVICES

A+
220-902
4.4

In this part of the chapter, you learn how to deal with malicious software on mobile devices. We begin with how to recognize a device might be infected.

COMMON MOBILE DEVICE MALWARE SYMPTOMS

A+
220-902
4.4

Android and Windows Phone devices are more susceptible to malware than iOS devices because apps can be downloaded from other sites than Google or Microsoft. With iOS devices, apps can be obtained only from the Apple App Store and, therefore, are more strictly vetted. However, for any mobile device, malware can be introduced by a Trojan that a user accepts as an email attachment or by some other means or by macros embedded in shared documents.

Here are some symptoms that malware might be at work on an Android, iOS, or Windows Phone device:

▲ *Battery drain, slow speeds, leaked data, strange text messages, and data transmission over limits.* Battery power draining faster than normal or slow data upload or download speeds can indicate that apps are running in the background. For example, when the XAgent malware app installs on an Apple device with iOS version 7 or below, the app icon is hidden, and the app runs in the background. When you close the app, it restarts. The malware not only uses resources, it steals personal data and makes screen shots and sends them to a remote command-and-control (C&C) server. A C&C server might send coded text messages to your phone. If you receive strange text messages, suspect malware. Another indication of malware at work is a spike in your data usage charges on your phone bill.

▲ *Dropped phone calls or weak signal.* Dropped phone calls can happen when malware is interfering and trying to eavesdrop on your conversations or is performing other background activities.

▲ *Unintended Wi-Fi and Bluetooth connections.* Malicious Wi-Fi hotspots and Bluetooth devices can hijack a device or inject it with malware. When your mobile device connects to a malicious Wi-Fi hotspot, the device can receive a malicious script that repeatedly reboots your device, which prevents you from using the device. To prevent this type of attack, avoid the free Wi-Fi hotspots. To prevent your device from pairing with a malicious Bluetooth device, turn off Bluetooth when you're not using it.

▲ *Unauthorized account access.* A malicious app can steal passwords and data from other apps and can pretend to be a different app to get access to online accounts. If you suspect an online account has been hacked, consider malware might be on your mobile device that uses this account.

▲ *Unauthorized location tracking.* Spyware apps installed on a mobile device can report its location to a C&C server.

▲ *Unauthorized use of camera or microphone.* Unauthorized surveillance is a sure sign of malware. Stalker spyware apps have been known to take photos and send them to a C&C server; send a text alert to a hacker and then add the hacker to a live call; use the microphone to record live conversations and then send the recording to a C&C server; report Facebook, Skype, Viber, and iMessage activity, including passwords and location data; and upload all photos, videos, and text messages to a C&C server.

▲ *Unauthorized root access.* Malware is more likely to install on a jailbroken iOS device or rooted Android or Windows Phone device. Here's what you need to know:

　▲ *Jailbroken iOS device.* To find out if an iOS device has been jailbroken, look for an unusual app icon on the home screen, for example, the Installer app, Cydia app, or Icy app. If any of these apps is present, the device has been jailbroken. If you have any app icon on your home screen that is not available in the App Store, the app is most likely a jailbreak app or other malware. A jailbroken device can download apps from sources other than the Apple App Store. When you update iOS using iTunes, the jailbreak will be removed.

　▲ *Rooted Android device.* One way to find out if an Android device has been rooted is to download and run the Root Checker Basic free app. Figure 10-43 shows the report you get when Root Checker Basic reports a device is not rooted.

　　Another way to tell if a device is rooted is to download a terminal window app. (A terminal window in Linux is similar to a command prompt window in Windows.) When you open the app, look at the command prompt. If the prompt is a #, the device is rooted. If the prompt is a $, the device is likely not rooted. With the $ prompt showing, try the sudo su root command, which in Linux allows you root access. If the prompt changes to #, the device is rooted.

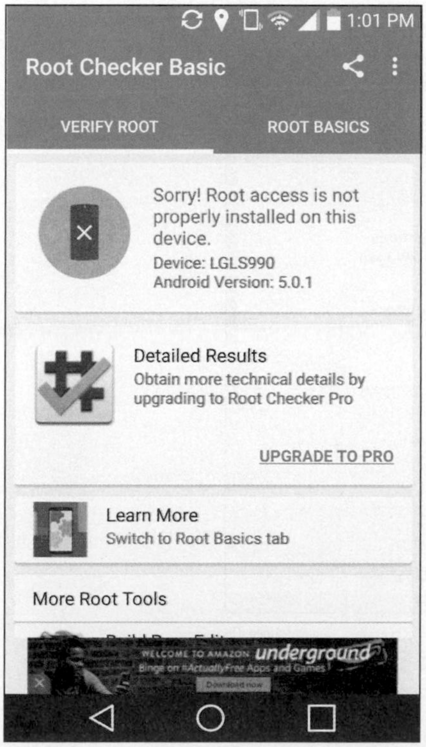

Source: Android

Figure 10-43 Root Checker Basic reports an Android device is not rooted

> **✎ Notes** In Linux, the # command prompt displays when a user has root access and the $ command prompt displays when a user does not have root access.

　▲ *Rooted Windows Phone.* Although it was possible to root Windows Phone 7, as of this writing, there is currently no way to root Windows Phone 8.1.

MOBILE DEVICE TOOLS AND MALWARE REMOVAL

A+
220-902
4.4

Here are general steps for removing malware from a mobile device, listed from least to most invasive:

▲ *Uninstall the offending app.* If you can identify the malware app, uninstall it. If the app won't uninstall, force stop it and try to uninstall again. Recall you can force stop Android apps using the Settings app. Tap **Apps**, swipe to the left to see running apps, and tap a running app to force stop it.

▲ *Update the OS.* For an iOS device, use iTunes on your computer to perform the update rather than updating the iOS directly from the device. For other devices, use the methods you learned about in the chapter, "Supporting Mobile Operating Systems."

▲ *Remove root access to the device.* An Android device that has been rooted cannot receive an Android OS update. To unroot the device so you can update it, use one of these methods:

   ▲ *Unroot with the app that was used to root the device.* For example, if you find the SuperSU app installed on the device, most likely it was used to root the device. Open the app and tap **Full unroot** to unroot the device.

   ▲ *Download a root removal app.* Search online for reviews about root removal apps before you select one. One example is the Universal Unroot app–download and install it to remove root access from the device.

▲ *Perform a factory reset.* The most sure fire way to remove malware is to back up your data and other content, reset your device to its factory default state, which is also called a clean install, and then restore your content from backup. Here are the steps for an iPhone:

1. Using iTunes on your computer, make sure iTunes is using the latest updates. Then connect your iPhone to your computer.

2. Use iTunes to back up your iPhone to the computer. In the Backups group, select **This computer** and click **Back Up Now** (see Figure 10-44). To verify the backup is made, click **Edit, Preferences, Device** and look for the backup listed.

Source: Apple iOS

Figure 10-44   Use the Backups section in the iTunes window to manage backups to this computer

3. If you have made purchases on the iPhone that have not yet been backed up to the computer, you can click **File, Devices,** and **Transfer Purchased from "iPhone".**

4. Click **Restore iPhone** to restore the device, which deletes all data and content and restores the device firmware to factory settings. After the restore, the device restarts and you are given the opportunity to select a previous backup to restore data and content. Select the backup you just made.

After you have removed malware on a mobile device, you will want to keep it clean. Here are a few tips:

◢ Don't jailbreak or root a device and keep OS updates current.

◢ Educate users about the importance of privacy settings (for example, disable cookies and turn off Bluetooth when it's not in use) and of not opening email attachments or downloading shared files from untrusted sources.

◢ Consider installing an anti-malware app. Apple claims that an iOS device cannot be infected with malware and does not make anti-malware apps available in the App Store. However, you can get an app from the App Store that monitors your device and scans for malware that might be in stored files, but not installed. For Android and Windows Phone devices, search online reviews and consider the features offered before deciding on an anti-malware app. An anti-malware app can scan apps and files for malware, scan for unauthorized surveillance, monitor security and privacy settings, find the device when it's lost and lock and remote wipe it, and maintain automatic updates.

In an enterprise environment, Wi-Fi analyzers and cellular network analyzers might be used to protect the network against intrusion. Next is a brief introduction to these tools.

WI-FI ANALYZERS

When you're responsible for a Wi-Fi network, you might want to consider monitoring it for rogue devices that could be attempting to hack transmissions. Wi-Fi analyzer software and hardware can be used to detect devices not authorized to use the network, identify attempts made by connected devices to hack transmissions, and even identify their physical location. Wi-Fi analyzers can also detect performance vulnerabilities and identify bottlenecks. They can detect security vulnerabilities, which allow a device to connect to the wireless network using a configuration the network is not set up to use (for example, an authorized channel or nonencrypted transmissions). An example of a Wi-Fi analyzer device is the OptiView tablet by Fluke Networks (*flukenetworks.com*), shown in Figure 10-45. This tablet computer comes preinstalled with AirMagnet WiFi Analyzer software, also by Fluke Networks. Figure 10-46 shows a demo window of the software.

10

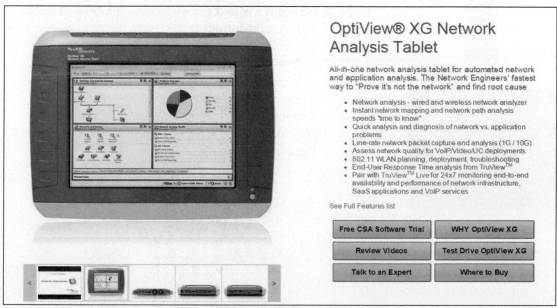

Figure 10-45   Wi-Fi analyzer tablet by Fluke Networks designed for monitoring enterprise-level wireless networks

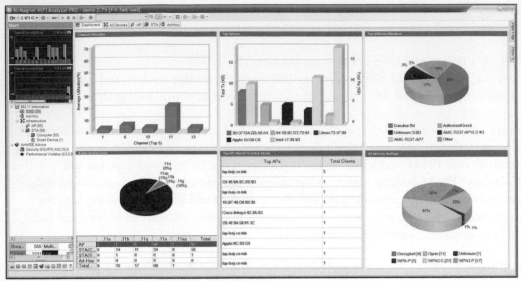

Source: flukenetworks.com

Figure 10-46   AirMagnet WiFi Analyzer PRO demo screen by Fluke Networks

CELLULAR NETWORK ANALYZERS

Large organizations that require cellular and Wi-Fi coverage over a large area (for example, a shopping mall or large hospital) might implement a distributed antenna system (DAS). Small antennas are installed over the facility to act as repeaters for cell tower and Wi-Fi access point (AP) coverage. In addition, with the trend toward BYOD (bring your own device), some organizations have found it necessary to closely monitor cellular connections to private networks to identify hackers performing tasks that appear malicious.

Source: Fluke Networks

Figure 10-47   AirMagnet RF spectrum analyzer by Fluke Networks connects to a computer via a USB port

Cellular network analyzer software and hardware can be used to monitor cellular networks for signal strength of cell towers, WAPs, and repeaters, which can help technicians better position antennas in a DAS. The software can also monitor for interference, performance, and voice and data transmissions. Voice and data transmissions can be analyzed for how the network is used, with the intent of identifying malicious activity. An example of cellular network analyzer hardware is the RF spectrum analyzer shown in Figure 10-47. Data from the spectrum analyzer is input to the AirMagnet Spectrum ES software for analysis. A demo screen of the software is shown in Figure 10-48.

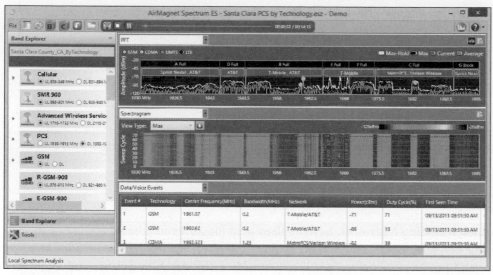

Source: Fluke Networks

Figure 10-48   AirMagnet Spectrum software analyzes cellular networks

SOFTWARE LICENSING AND PROHIBITED CONTENT OR ACTIVITY

10

**A+
220-902
5.3**

Many organizations have documented a code of conduct in policies that apply to their employees and/or customers. As an employee, you need to be aware of these codes of conduct and the procedures to follow when you believe these company policies have been broken. Examples of prohibited content or activity might be when an employee saves pornographic photos to company computers, uses company computers and time for personal shopping, or installs pirated software on these computers.

SOFTWARE LICENSING

**A+
220-902
5.3**

As an IT support technician, you need to be especially aware of the issues surrounding software licensing. As you have learned, open source software can be freely distributed and installed, but closed source software is owned by a vendor and a license is required to use the software. When someone purchases software from a software vendor, that person or organization has only purchased a commercial license for the software, which is the right to use it. The buyer does not legally *own* the software and, therefore, does not have the right to distribute it. The right to copy the work, called a copyright, belongs to the creator of the work or others to whom the creator transfers this right. Copyrights are intended to legally protect the intellectual property rights of organizations or individuals to creative works, which include books, images, and software. Your rights to use or copy the software are clearly stated in the End User License Agreement (EULA) that you agree to when you install the software (see Figure 10-49).

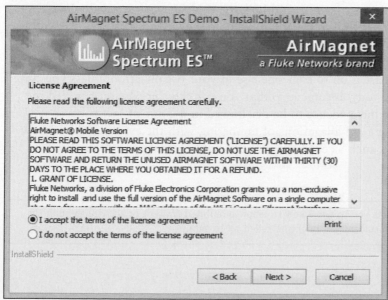

Source: Fluke Networks

Figure 10-49   Agreeing to the EULA is required before software installs

Making unauthorized copies of original software violates the Federal Copyright Act of 1976 and is called software piracy or, more officially, software copyright infringement. (This act allows for one backup copy of software to be made.) Making a copy of software and then selling it or giving it away is a violation of the law. Normally, only the employee who violated the copyright law is liable for infringement; however, in some cases, an employer or supervisor is also held responsible, even when the copies were made without the employer's knowledge.

> ✎ **Notes** When an individual or organization purchases the right to install one instance of software, the license is called a personal license. By purchasing a site license, also called an enterprise license, a company can obtain the right to multiple installations of software.

Many software companies, including Microsoft, have implemented measures to control the use of their software, which is called digital rights management (DRM). For example, the retail release of Windows 8.1 must be activated with a valid product key before it will run and Microsoft carefully verifies and monitors that this product key is used only in one installation.

CORPORATE POLICIES FOR DEALING WITH PROHIBITED CONTENT OR ACTIVITY

> A+
> 220-902
> 5.3

When you start a new job, find out from your employer how to deal with prohibited content or activity so that you can follow corporate policies and security best practices. Here are some things you need to know:

▲ When you identify what you believe to be an infringement of the law or the company's code of conduct, where do you turn to report the issue? Make sure you go only through proper channels; don't spread rumors or accusations with those who are not in these channels.

▲ What data or device should you immediately preserve as evidence for what you believe has happened? For example, if you believe you have witnessed a customer or employee using a company computer for a crime, should you remove and secure the hard drive from the computer, or should you remove and secure the entire computer?

▲ Proper documentation surrounding the evidence of a crime is crucial to a criminal investigation. What documentation are you expected to submit and to whom is it submitted? This documentation might track the chain of custody for the evidence, which includes exactly what, when, and from whom evidence was collected; the condition of this evidence; and how the evidence was secured while it was in your possession. It also includes a paper trail of exactly to whom the evidence has been passed on and when. For example, suppose you suspect that a criminal act has happened and you hold a CD that you believe contains evidence of this crime. You need to carefully document exactly when and how you received the CD. Also, don't pass it on to someone else in your organization unless you have this person's signature on a chain-of-custody document so that you can later prove you handled the evidence appropriately. You don't want the evidence to be disallowed in a court of law because you have been accused of misconduct or there are allegations of tampering with the evidence. Also know that more information than a signature, such as copy of a driver's license, might be required to identify persons in the chain of custody.

> ★ **A+ Exam Tip** The A+ 220-902 exam expects you to know how to report prohibited content or activity through the proper channels and about a chain-of-custody document you might be called on to sign.

>> *CHAPTER SUMMARY*

Securing a Windows Personal Computer

◢ The netplwiz command can be used to require the user to press Ctrl+Alt+Delete to sign in to Windows.

◢ Windows power settings can be used to lock down a computer after a short period of inactivity and to require a password to unlock the computer.

◢ A strong password is not easy to guess and contains uppercase and lowercase letters, numbers, and symbols. Using long passwords is the best protection against attack.

◢ The Encrypted File System (EFS) is used with an NTFS volume for Windows business and professional editions.

◢ Windows Firewall can block all communication initiated outside the computer and can allow exceptions for certain programs, protocols, ports, and remote computers.

◢ Local Security Policies in Group Policy are used in Windows professional and business editions to set policies that can secure the local computer.

◢ BitLocker Encryption with Windows professional or business editions can lock down the entire hard drive. It can be set to authenticate the computer, authenticate the user, or authenticate both the computer and the user.

◢ UEFI/BIOS security features include passwords, drive lock passwords, UEFI secure boot, and support for a TPM chip and an intrusion-detection device.

Securing a Mobile Device

◢ Controlling access to a mobile device can be accomplished by a screen lock, biometric authentication (for example, fingerprint or voice recognition), full device encryption, system lock after failed login attempts, and multifactor authentication.

◢ Software used to secure a mobile device includes OS updates and patches, anti-malware, downloading software from only trusted sources, firewalls, and locator and remote wipe apps.

◢ In a corporate environment, on-boarding and off-boarding company policies for BYOD might include remote backup apps, remote wipes, encryption, firewalls, VPN connections, anti-malware, and apps that prevent jailbreaking and rooting.

Additional Methods to Protect Resources

◢ Large networks might use a security token or smart card in addition to a Windows password to authenticate a user in multifactor and/or mutual authentication.

◢ Security tokens include a smart card (key fob, wireless token, RFID badge, or cell phone with token) and biometric data (iris scan, retinal scan, or fingerprint scan).

◢ Physical security can include a locked door, lock and chain, privacy filter, theft-prevention plate, and mantrap.

◢ A UTM appliance might include a firewall, anti-malware, access control lists, intrusion detection and prevention systems, and a VPN.

◢ Data can be partly or completely destroyed using a paper shredder, low-level format, zero-fill utility, drill, degausser, or Secure Erase utility.

◢ Security methods include educating users against social engineering and how to best protect a laptop when traveling.

10

Dealing with Malicious Software on Personal Computers

▲ Malware includes a virus, spyware, keylogger, worm, Trojan, rootkit, ransomware, zero-day attack, man-in-the-middle attack, zombies, botnets, and dictionary attacks.

▲ Symptoms that malware is present include pop-up ads, slow performance, error messages, file errors, spam, and strange processes running.

▲ To protect against malware, (1) know how to identify common malware symptoms, (2) quarantine the infected system, (3) disable System Restore, (4) remediate the system, (5) protect the system with scheduled scans and updates, (6) enable System Protection and create a restore point, and (7) educate the end user. Some systems become so highly infected that the only solution is to reinstall Windows.

Dealing with Malicious Software on Mobile Devices

▲ Symptoms of malware on mobile devices include battery drain, slow speeds, leaked data, dropped calls, unintended Wi-Fi and Bluetooth connections, location tracking, unauthorized use of camera or microphone, and root access.

▲ To remediate an infected device, uninstall the offending app, update the OS, factory reset the device, and/or restore data from backup.

▲ Wi-Fi and cellular network analyzers can help an organization monitor and protect Wi-Fi and cellular networks.

Software Licensing and Prohibited Content or Activity

▲ Commercial licensing of software can be a personal license or enterprise license. Terms of the licensing agreement are found in the EULA.

▲ A chain-of-custody document provides a paper trail of the evidence in a criminal case and includes how, when, where, and by whom evidence was preserved and secured.

>> KEY TERMS

For explanations of key terms, see the Glossary for this text.

acceptable use policy (AUP)	computer infestation	intrusion detection system (IDS)	Network Places Wizard
access control list (ACL)	copyright	intrusion prevention system (IPS)	next-generation firewall (NGFW)
anti-malware software	data loss prevention (DLP)	key fob	noncompliant system
antivirus software	degausser	keylogger	personal license
ATA Secure Erase	dictionary attack	Local Security Policy	phishing
biometric authentication	digital certificate	Local Users and Groups	privacy filter
biometric device	digital rights management (DRM)	LoJack	quarantined computer
BitLocker Drive Encryption	email filtering	malicious software	ransomware
BitLocker To Go	email hoax	malware	remote backup application
botnet	Encrypted File System (EFS)	malware definition	remote wipe
brute force attack	End User License Agreement (EULA)	malware encyclopedia	RFID badge
BYOD (Bring Your Own Device)	enterprise license	malware signature	root certificate
cellular network analyzer	entry control roster	man-in-the-middle attack	rootkit
certificate of destruction	gpresult	mantrap	security token
Certification Authority (CA)	gpupdate	multifactor authentication (MFA)	shoulder surfing
chain of custody	grayware	mutual authentication	site license
commercial license			

smart card
smart card reader
social engineering
software piracy
spear phishing
spoofing

spyware
strong password
tailgating
TPM (Trusted Platform
 Module)
Trojan

Unified Threat
 Management (UTM)
User Accounts
virus
Wi-Fi analyzer
Windows Defender

Windows Firewall
worm
zero-day attack
zombie

>> REVIEWING THE BASICS

1. Why is it more secure to require a user press Ctrl+Alt+Delete to sign in rather than displaying the Windows sign-in screen?

2. Which window available from Control Panel is used to require a Windows password to wake up a sleeping computer?

3. What command launches the User Accounts or Network Places Wizard, which can be used to manage users and their passwords?

4. Why is PINE963$&apple not a strong password?

5. What is the policy in Group Policy that can be set to audit failed logon events? Give the full path to the policy.

6. What hardware component is needed to set up BitLocker Encryption so that you can authenticate the computer?

7. What command can you use to refresh local group policies without having to reboot the system?

8. What type of employee badge does not have to be swiped by a card reader in order to allow the employee through a door?

9. What technique can be used so that sensitive company data on an employee's personal mobile device is not stolen when the device is stolen?

10. How can an Apple iOS device install an app that is downloaded from a source other than the Apple App Store?

11. What tool is best to use when destroying data on an SSD drive? Where can you get this tool?

12. What device can be installed on a laptop to prevent shoulder surfing?

13. Define and explain the differences between a virus, worm, and Trojan.

14. What is the best way to determine if an email message warning about a virus is a hoax?

15. What is the first thing you should do when you discover a computer is infected with malware?

16. What does anti-malware software look for to determine that a program or a process is a virus?

17. Which anti-malware software is embedded in Windows 8?

18. What registry key keeps information about services that run when a computer is booted into Safe Mode?

19. What folder is used by Windows to hold restore points?

20. What must you do to allow anti-malware software to scan and delete malware it might find in the data storage area where restore points are kept?

10

>> THINKING CRITICALLY

1. In which policy group of Group Policy is the policy that requires a smart card be used to authenticate a user to Windows?

   a. Computer Configuration, Windows Settings, Security Settings, Local Policies, Biometrics

   b. Computer Configuration, Administrative Templates, System, Logon

   c. Computer Configuration, Windows Settings, Security Settings, Local Policies, Security Options

   d. User Configuration, Administrative Templates, System, Logon

2. You open a folder Properties box to encrypt the folder, click Advanced, and discover *Encrypt contents to secure data* is dimmed. What is the most likely problem?

   a. Encryption has not been enabled. Use the Computer Management console to enable it.

   b. You are not using an edition of Windows that supports encryption.

   c. Most likely a virus has attacked the system and is disabling encryption.

   d. Encryption applies only to files, not folders.

3. A virus has attacked your hard drive and now when you start up Windows, instead of seeing the Windows Start screen, the system freezes and you see a blue screen of death. You have extremely important document files on the drive that you cannot afford to lose. What do you do first? Explain why this is your first choice.

   a. Try a data-recovery service even though it is very expensive.

   b. Remove the hard drive from the computer case and install it in another computer.

   c. Try GetDataBack by Runtime Software (*www.runtime.org*) to recover the data.

   d. Use Windows utilities to attempt to fix the Windows boot problem.

   e. Run antivirus software to remove the virus.

4. You sign in to your personal computer with your Microsoft account and then you want to verify your computer is a trusted device to make changes to the account settings. Microsoft sends a code to your cell phone in a text message. You enter the code on a Windows screen. This type of authentication is called:

   a. Multifactor authentication

   b. Mutual authentication

   c. Biometric authentication

   d. None of the above

>> REAL PROBLEMS, REAL SOLUTIONS

REAL PROBLEM 10-1 Recovering a Windows Password

You can use freeware to discover a forgotten Windows password, and hackers can use the software to steal a password. The stronger the password, the more difficult it is to discover. Follow these steps to learn more:

1. Create three user accounts on a system and assign the accounts an easy password (use only lowercase letters), a moderately easy password (use lowercase letters and numbers, but no symbols), and a strong password (see the rules given earlier in the chapter for strong passwords).

2. Go to **ophcrack.sourceforge.net** by Geeknet, Inc., and download the free ISO file that contains ophcrack Vista/7 LiveCD. (The software works in Windows 8/7/Vista.) Use the ISO file to burn the ISO image to a CD-R. Label the CD.

3. Boot from the CD. As it boots, it automatically searches for and lists the user accounts and passwords on the system. Answer the following questions:

   a. What is the name of the operating system the ophcrack software uses on the CD?

   b. Which user account passwords did ophcrack discover?

   c. If ophcrack did not discover a password, perhaps another freeware utility can. List three other password-cracking products that receive positive online reviews.

Keep the ophcrack LiveCD in your computer repair toolkit in case a client in the field asks you to help recover a forgotten Windows password.

REAL PROBLEM 10-2 Researching a Laptop with a TPM Chip

Many laptops sold today have a TPM chip, and some have encryption-enabled hard drives that don't require encryption software such as BitLocker. Research the web for a laptop that offers a TPM chip and answer these questions:

1. What is the brand and model laptop that has the TPM chip? Print the webpage listing the laptop specifications showing the chip.

2. Is the chip optional? If so, what is the cost of including the chip?

3. Does the laptop have an encryption-enabled hard drive?

4. Does the laptop come bundled with encryption software? If so, what is the name of the software?

5. Does the laptop offer a drive lock password?

6. What is the cost of the laptop, including the TPM chip?

10

CHAPTER 11

Virtualization, Linux, and Mac OS X

After completing this chapter, you will be able to:

• Implement and configure virtual machines and hypervisors

• Use various Linux commands to support applications and users

• Identify important features of Mac OS X

Throughout this course, you have practiced many of your new skills in virtual machines. In this chapter, you get a look behind the scenes at how virtualization works. Then you learn about two more operating systems for desktops and laptops other than Windows: Linux and OS X. As you will see in this chapter, understanding Windows gives you a solid foundation to approach learning and supporting other operating systems. IT technicians are expected to be familiar with a variety of operating systems and operating environments, and this chapter equips you for these skills.

VIRTUALIZATION BASICS

Virtualization is when one physical machine hosts multiple activities that are normally done on multiple machines. Two general types of virtualization are server-side virtualization and client-side virtualization. The basic difference between the two is where the virtualizing takes place. Let's see how each can be implemented.

SERVER-SIDE VIRTUALIZATION

Server-side virtualization provides a virtual desktop for users on multiple client machines. Most, if not all, processing is done on the server, which provides to the client the Virtual Desktop Infrastructure (VDI). See Figure 11-1.

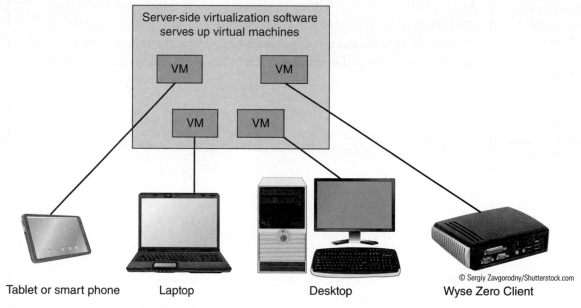

Server-side virtualization software serves up virtual machines

VM　VM

VM　VM

Tablet or smart phone　　Laptop　　　　　Desktop　　　Wyse Zero Client

© Sergiy Zavgorodny/Shutterstock.com

Figure 11-1 Server-side virtualization provides a virtual desktop to each user

With server-side virtualization, three categories of clients might be used, based on the computing power of the client:

◢ **Thick client or fat client.** The client computer can be a regular desktop computer or laptop. In this case, the client is called a thick client or fat client. The main advantage of using thick clients is the personal computer can be used for other purposes than server-side virtualization.

◢ **Thin client.** Because the client does little or no processing with server-side virtualization, a thin client can be used. A thin client is a computer that has an operating system, but has little computing power and might only need to support a browser used to communicate with the server. The main advantage of using thin clients is the reduced cost of the client machine. A decent tablet can serve as a thin client.

◢ **Zero client.** To even further reduce the cost of the client machine, a zero client, also called a dumb terminal or ultra-thin client, can be used. A zero client, such as a Wyse Zero Client, does not have an operating system and merely provides an interface between the user and the server. A zero client might contain little more than a keyboard, mouse, monitor, and network connection.

CLIENT-SIDE VIRTUALIZATION

Using client-side virtualization, a personal computer provides multiple virtual environments for applications. Client-side virtualization can be implemented using several methods, including these three, which are presented from the least amount of computing done on the client machine to the most computing done on the client machine:

▲ *Presentation virtualization.* Using presentation virtualization, a remote application running on a server is controlled by a local computer. Presentation virtualization is a form of SaaS cloud computing. The user remotely controls the application running on the server and the application data is also stored on the server (see Figure 11-2).

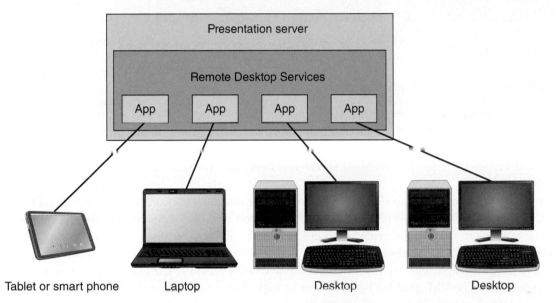

Figure 11-2 Microsoft Remote Desktop Services presents applications to the user at a local computer

▲ *Application virtualization.* Using application virtualization, an application can be made available to users without having to install the application on the user's computer. For example, Application Virtualization (App-V) by Microsoft manages applications so they don't install in Windows on the client computer. The App-V software is installed on the client computer. When a user selects an application from a list provided by App-V, App-V creates a virtual environment in memory for the application to install itself. The application doesn't make changes to the Windows registry or install components on the hard drive; the entire installation happens in memory. An application managed by App-V can be permanently stored on the local hard drive or on an application server.

▲ *Client-side desktop virtualization.* Using client-side desktop virtualization, software installed on a desktop or laptop manages virtual machines. Each VM has its own operating system installed. In the chapter, "Installing Windows," you learned that Oracle VirtualBox and VMware Player are two examples of freeware that can be installed on a computer and used to manage virtual machines. This type of software is called a hypervisor or virtual machine manager (VMM).

VIRTUAL MACHINES AND HYPERVISORS

Let's look at the different types of hypervisors, the hardware requirements needed for client-side virtualization, and how to secure a virtual machine.

TYPE 1 AND TYPE 2 HYPERVISORS

Hypervisor software can be a Type 1 or Type 2 hypervisor. The differences are diagrammed in Figure 11-3.

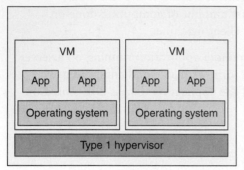
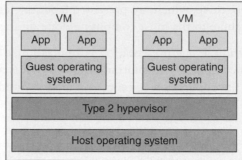

Figure 11-3 Type 1 and Type 2 hypervisors

Here is an explanation of the two types of hypervisors:

▲ A Type 1 hypervisor installs on a computer before any operating system, and is, therefore, called a bare-metal hypervisor. After it installs, it partitions the hardware computing power into multiple VMs. An OS is installed in each VM. Examples of Type 1 hypervisors are XenServer by Citrix, ESXi by VMware, and Hyper-V by Microsoft. Most server-side desktop virtualization is done using a Type 1 hypervisor.

Some Type 1 hypervisors are designed for client-side desktop virtualization on personal computers. For example, XenClient by Citrix installs on a personal computer and then you can install Windows or other operating systems in the VMs provided by XenClient. One major advantage of a local computer running a Type 1 hypervisor is added security because each OS and its applications are isolated from the others. For example, employees can install one OS in a VM for business use and another OS in a VM for personal use. The VM used for business can be locked down for secured VPN connections, and the personal VM does not require so much security.

> 🖊 **Notes** To see some interesting videos of how XenClient by Citrix works and what it can do, go to *citrix.com/xenclient*.

▲ A Type 2 hypervisor installs in a host operating system as an application. Client Hyper-V, VirtualBox, and VMware Player are examples of Type 2 hypervisors. A Type 2 hypervisor is not as powerful as a Type 1 hypervisor because it is dependent on the host OS to allot its computing power. A VM in a Type 2 hypervisor is not as secure or as fast as a VM in a Type 1 hypervisor. Type 2 hypervisors are typically used on desktops and laptops when performance and security are not significant issues. Here are some ways that virtual machines provided by Type 2 hypervisors might be used:

  ▲ Developers often use VMs to test applications. If you save a copy of a virtual hard drive (VHD) that has a fresh installation of Windows installed, you can easily build a new and fresh VM to test an application.

  ▲ Help-desk technicians use VMs so they can easily switch from one OS to another when a user asks for help with a particular OS.

  ▲ Honeypots are single computers or a network of computers that lure hackers to them so as to protect the real network. Virtual machines can be used to give the impression to a hacker that he has found a computer or entire network of computers. Administrators can monitor the honeypot for unauthorized activity.

  ▲ Students use VMs to install and practice using and supporting different operating systems.

HARDWARE REQUIREMENTS

When preparing to install a hypervisor and virtual machines, you need to be aware of the hardware requirements:

◢ *The motherboard UEFI/BIOS*. The motherboard UEFI/BIOS and the processor should support hardware-assisted virtualization (HAV). For Intel processors, this feature is called IntelVT. For AMD processors, the technology is called AMD-V. Most of today's motherboards support the feature, and it must be enabled in UEFI/BIOS setup. Figure 11-4 shows the UEFI setup screen for one motherboard where the feature is called Intel® Virtualization Technology. When you enable the feature, also verify that all subcategories under the main category for hardware virtualization are enabled.

Source: Intel

Figure 11-4 UEFI/BIOS setup screen to enable hardware virtualization

◢ *Hard drive space*. See the requirements provided by the hypervisor manufacturer for hard drive space for the hypervisor. Each VM has its own virtual hard drive (VHD), which is a file stored on the physical hard drive and acts like a hard drive complete with its own boot sectors and file systems. You can configure this VHD to be a fixed size or dynamically expanding. The fixed size takes up hard drive space whether the VM uses the space or not. An expanding VHD increases in capacity as the VM uses the space. Remember that about 20 GB is required for a Windows installation. Therefore, you'll need at least 20 GB for each VM.

◢ *Processor and memory*. Most processors sold today support hardware-assisted virtualization. Plan on using at least a dual-core processor or better. A system needs lots of RAM when running multiple virtual machines. Some hypervisors tie up all the memory you have configured for a VM from the time the VM is opened until the VM is closed. Other hypervisors support dynamic memory, which ties up only the memory the VM is actually using.

> ✎ **Notes** To see a list of Intel processors that support Intel VT, go to *ark.intel.com/Products/VirtualizationTechnology*.

When setting up a virtual machine, know that an emulator might be required. A hypervisor emulates hardware and presents this virtual hardware to each VM, which can include a virtual processor, memory, motherboard, hard drive, optical drive, keyboard, mouse, monitor, network adapter, SD card, USB device, smart phone, printer, and other components and peripherals. For example, recall from the chapter, "Supporting Mobile Operating Systems," you used Visual Studio and Client Hyper-V to create a Windows Phone emulator (see Figure 11-5). The emulator not only includes the Windows Phone OS, but also emulates the hardware of a smart phone.

Figure 11-5   Visual Studio and Client Hyper-V work together to emulate Windows Phone installed on a smart phone

A hypervisor offers a way to configure each VM, including which virtual hardware is installed. For example, when you launch VirtualBox, the VirtualBox Manager window shown on the left side of Figure 11-6 appears. To configure a VM, select the VM in the left pane and click **Settings**. The Settings box appears. Click the **Storage** menu, shown on the right side of Figure 11-6, to install and uninstall virtual hard drives in the VM.

Notice in the Settings box in Figure 11-6 that this VM has three hard drives installed. JumpWin8.1 is connected to SATA port 0 and contains the Windows 8.1 installation. NewDisk1 and NewDisk2 are smaller and are connected through SATA ports 1 and 2, respectively. The VM also has one optical drive with an .iso file mounted to it. Recall that an ISO file holds the image of a CD or DVD and can be used to hold Windows installation files. When you mount this file to the VM, you can install Windows in the VM from this virtual DVD, although many hypervisor programs will perform this step for you during setup of a new VM.

Click the **System** menu (see Figure 11-7) to configure motherboard settings, such as boot order and memory. Also consider network requirements for the VM. A VM can have one or more virtual network adapters. Click **Network** (see Figure 11-8) to change adapter settings. A VM connects to a local network the same as other computers and can share and use shared resources on the network. On the right side of the Settings box, you can control the number and type of installed network adapters up to four adapters.

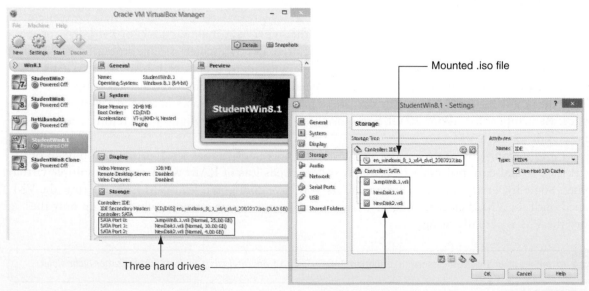

Source: Oracle VirtualBox

Figure 11-6   Emulated (virtual) hard drives are installed in a VM under VirtualBox

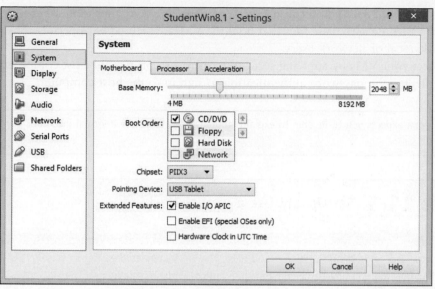

Source: Oracle VirtualBox

Figure 11-7 Configure motherboard settings in the VM to change the boot order

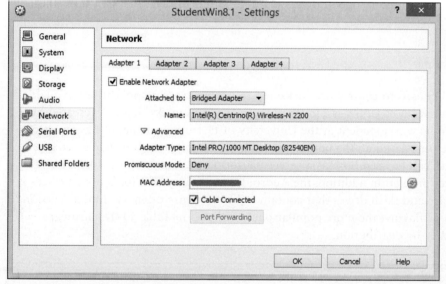

Source: Oracle VirtualBox

Figure 11-8 Configure up to four network adapters for a VM using Oracle VirtualBox

SECURE A VIRTUAL MACHINE

A virtual machine is susceptible to hackers and malware just as is a physical machine. When supporting a VM that holds sensitive data and has network and Internet connectivity or is located in a public area, keep these points in mind for securing the resources in the VM:

◢ *Secure the VM within the VM.* Using Windows installed in the VM, follow all the security measures you have learned throughout this text. For example, be sure to configure Windows Firewall in the VM, keep Windows updates current, install and run anti-malware software, require passwords for all user accounts in the VM, and encrypt data folders.

◢ *VMs should be isolated for best security.* One major advantage of using VMs on a desktop computer is that VMs running under a Type 1 hypervisor are isolated from each other. If one VM gets infected, the other VMs will not be affected.

◢ *Secure permissions to the files that hold a* VM. You can move a VM from one computer to another by moving the files that contain the VM. Be sure these files that hold the VM are secured with permissions that allow access only to specific local or network users.

◢ *Secure the host computer.* Protect your VMs by applying security measures to protect the host computer that holds the VMs. For example, require password authentication to sign in to the host computer.

> ★ **A+ Exam Tip**   The A+ 220-902 exam expects you to be able to explain methods used to secure a virtual machine installed on a client computer.

Hands-On | Project 11-1   Set Up and Use a Virtual Machine

> **A+**
> **220-902**
> **2.2**
>
> In the "Installing Windows" chapter, you installed VirtualBox and used it to create a VM and install Windows 8. Install VirtualBox on a second computer and move the VM you created earlier to this second computer. What files did you have to move? How did you configure VirtualBox on the second computer to find and use the VM?

Next you'll create a VM running a different operating system: Linux. But first, let's learn a little about how Linux works.

LINUX OPERATING SYSTEM

> **A+**
> **220-902**
> **1.2, 2.1,**
> **4.1**

UNIX is a popular OS used to control networks and to support server applications available on the Internet. A variation of UNIX is Linux (pronounced "Lih-nucks"), an OS created by Linus Torvalds when he was a student at the University of Helsinki in Finland. Basic versions of this OS are open source, and all the underlying programming instructions (called source code) are freely distributed. Linux can be used both as a server platform and a desktop platform, but its greatest popularity is in the server market. In addition, the Android operating system for mobile devices is based on Linux, and bootable CDs and flash drives that contain utility software often use Linux. Versions of Linux are called distributions or flavors; the more popular ones are listed in Table 11-1. Hardware requirements for Linux vary widely by distribution.

> ✎ **Notes**   For more information on Linux, see *linux.org* as well as the websites of the different Linux distributors.

Name	Comments	Website
Debian	This distribution specifically targets software enthusiasts. Debian is truly open source and maintained by developers of free software. It's slow to be updated with new features, which makes it a very stable OS.	*debian.org*
Fedora	Fedora is considered a cutting-edge distribution of Linux. If you're always wanting the latest and greatest of Linux, this distribution might be your first choice.	*getfedora.org*
Linux Mint	Linux Mint is based on Ubuntu with several features added.	*linuxmint.com*
Red Hat Enterprise Linux	Designed for enterprise use for servers and workstations, this commercial distribution is stable and comes with long-term support. The free version of Red Hat Enterprise is CentOS, which comes with no support.	*redhat.com*
Ubuntu	Ubuntu is probably the most popular distribution of Linux for desktops and servers with tons of online tutorials and help.	*ubuntu.com*

Table 11-1   Popular Linux distributions

Linux is popular because it's inexpensive, very stable (it seldom crashes), and is well suited to support various types of servers, such as a web server or email server. Linux itself is not a complete operating system, but is only the kernel for the OS. You also need a shell for user and application interfaces, and Linux shells vary widely by distributions. Many distributions of Linux include a GUI shell or desktop, which is called a windows manager. For example, Figure 11-9 shows the desktop or windows manager for Ubuntu Desktop.

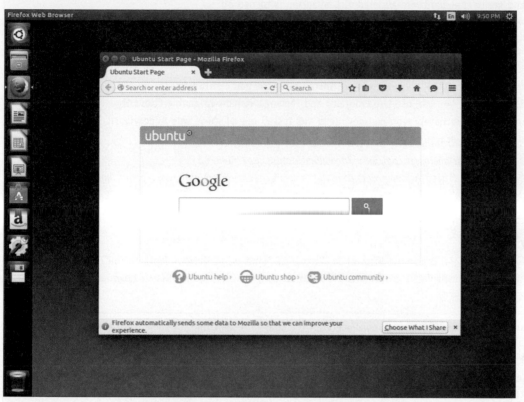

Source: Canonical Ltd.

Figure 11-9   Ubuntu Desktop with the Mozilla Firefox browser window open

Some distributions of Linux don't have a windows manager. For example, Ubuntu Server installs with only a command line interface. In Linux, the terminal refers to the command-line interface for the OS and the default shell for the terminal is the Bash shell. The name stands for "Bourne Again Shell" and takes the best features from two previous shells, the Bourne and the Korn shells. In this chapter, we use Ubuntu Server and its default Bash shell. In Linux, a command prompt in the terminal is called a shell prompt.

📝 **Notes** To find out what shell you're using, at a Linux shell prompt, enter the echo $SHELL command.

As an IT support technician, you should know a little about Linux, including a few basic commands, which are covered in this chapter. You will learn about root and user accounts, file structure, some common commands, and how to use the vi text editor. As you work, be aware that the organization of files and directories and the way each command works might be slightly different with the distribution and version of Linux you are using.

Hands-On | Project 11-2   Install Ubuntu Server in a VM

A+
220-902
2.1

To practice Linux skills covered in this chapter, you need an installation of Ubuntu Server. Follow these steps to install Ubuntu Server in a VM on a Windows computer:

1. On a Windows computer that has a 64-bit version of Windows installed, go into UEFI/BIOS setup and verify that hardware-assisted virtualization is turned on.

> **Notes** Ubuntu Server is only available as a 64-bit OS. To install a 64-bit guest OS in a VM, the host OS must also be 64-bit.

2. If you don't already have a hypervisor installed, install one that you can use to manage VMs. For example, in 64-bit Windows 8.1 Pro, you can use the Programs and Features window to enable Client Hyper-V, which comes embedded in the OS. Alternately, you can download and install one of these free hypervisors:

   ◢ Oracle VirtualBox at *virtualbox.org/wiki/Downloads*
   ◢ Windows Virtual PC at *microsoft.com/en-us/download/details.aspx?id=3702*
   ◢ VMware Workstation Player at *my.vmware.com/web/vmware/free#desktop_end_user_computing/vmware_workstation_player/12_0*

3. Go to **ubuntu.com/download/server** and download the Ubuntu Server OS to your hard drive. The file that downloads is an .iso file.

4. Open the Hyper-V Manager, Oracle VM VirtualBox, Virtual PC Manager, or VMware Workstation Player manager and create a new VM named VM50. Mount the ISO file that contains the Ubuntu Server download to a virtual DVD in your VM.

> **Notes** If you need help learning to use your hypervisor of choice, try searching for some tutorial videos at *youtube.com* or on the hypervisor manufacturer's website.

5. Start up the VM and install Ubuntu Server, accepting all default settings. Be sure to write down your Ubuntu host name, Ubuntu user name, and password. When given the option, decline to install any extra software bundled with the OS. If needed, the software can be installed later.

6. During the installation, you might be asked whether you want to install the GRUB boot loader in the Master Boot Record on the hard drive (see Figure 11-10). GRUB (GR and Unified Bootloader) is a boot loader used

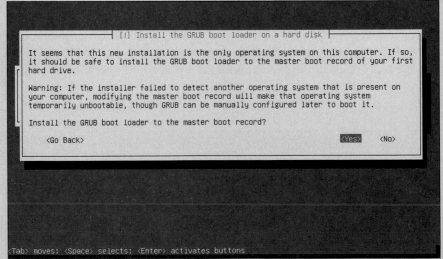

Source: Canonical Ltd.

Figure 11-10   Install GRUB to manage a dual boot with Ubuntu Server

to manage dual-boot systems and should not be installed if another OS is managing the dual boot. You can, however, choose to install it because Ubuntu Server is the only OS in your VM.

7. After the VM restarts, Ubuntu Server launches, and you should see the terminal shell, as shown in Figure 11-11.

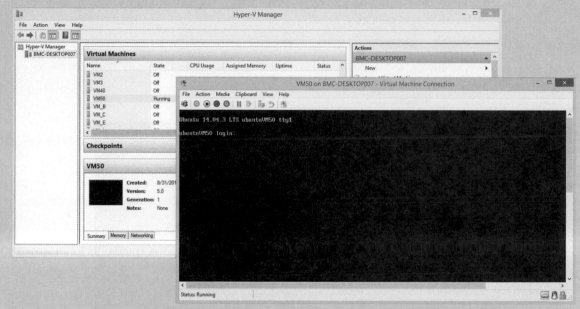

Source: Canonical Ltd.

Figure 11-11 Ubuntu Server is installed in a VM in Windows 8.1 Client Hyper-V

8. Enter your user name and password and you're logged in to Ubuntu Server. In the figure, the logged-in user is jean.

As you read along in the chapter learning about Linux commands, you can use your Ubuntu VM to practice these commands.

✎ Notes As you learn to use Ubuntu, know that the *help.ubuntu.com* website contains a wealth of information about Ubuntu and links to even more help.

DIRECTORY AND FILE LAYOUT

A+
220-902
2.1
Normally, the shell prompt includes the user name, host name, and the current directory, followed by a $. For example, in Figure 11-11, the first shell prompt shows the user name is jean, the host name is VM50, and the ~ character indicates the user's home directory, which for the jean account is /home/jean. When you first log in to Linux, the current directory is always the home directory of the logged-in user. (In Linux, directories in a path are separated with forward slashes, in contrast to the backward slashes used by Windows.)

APPLYING | CONCEPTS EXPLORE DIRECTORIES AND FILES

A+
220-902
2.1

Let's explore a few directories and files. As shown in Figure 11-12, use these commands:

1. Use the **pwd** command (print working directory) to display the full path to the current directory, which is /home/jean in the figure.

2. Use the **cd ..** command to move up one directory to /home.

3. Use the **ls** command to display the list of files and subdirectories in the /home directory. Notice in the figure, the one subdirectory in the /home directory is jean.

```
jean@ubuntuVM50:~$ cd ..
jean@ubuntuVM50:/home$ ls
jean
jean@ubuntuVM50:/home$ ls -l
total 4
drwxr-xr-x 3 jean jean 4096 Aug 31 14:07 jean
jean@ubuntuVM50:/home$ cd ..
jean@ubuntuVM50:/$ ls -l
total 81
drwxr-xr-x  2 root root  4096 Aug 31 13:28 bin
drwxr-xr-x  4 root root  1024 Aug 31 13:38 boot
drwxr-xr-x 15 root root  4120 Aug 31 14:05 dev
drwxr-xr-x 90 root root  4096 Aug 31 14:05 etc
drwxr-xr-x  3 root root  4096 Aug 31 14:03 home
lrwxrwxrwx  1 root root    33 Aug 31 13:21 initrd.img -> boot/initrd.img-3.19.0-25-generic
drwxr-xr-x 21 root root  4096 Aug 31 13:28 lib
drwxr-xr-x  2 root root  4096 Aug 31 13:20 lib64
drwx------  2 root root 16384 Aug 31 13:20 lost+found
drwxr-xr-x  4 root root  4096 Aug 31 13:20 media
drwxr-xr-x  2 root root  4096 Apr 10  2014 mnt
drwxr-xr-x  2 root root  4096 Aug  5 01:11 opt
dr-xr-xr-x 99 root root     0 Aug 31 07:05 proc
drwx------  2 root root  4096 Aug 31 13:20 root
drwxr-xr-x 17 root root   580 Aug 31 14:07 run
drwxr-xr-x  2 root root 12288 Aug 31 14:04 sbin
drwxr-xr-x  2 root root  4096 Aug  5 01:11 srv
dr-xr-xr-x 13 root root     0 Aug 31 14:19 sys
drwxrwxrwt  2 root root  4096 Aug 31 14:17 tmp
drwxr-xr-x 10 root root  4096 Aug 31 13:20 usr
drwxr-xr-x 12 root root  4096 Aug 31 13:35 var
lrwxrwxrwx  1 root root    30 Aug 31 13:21 vmlinuz -> boot/vmlinuz-3.19.0-25-generic
jean@ubuntuVM50:/$
```

Source: Canonical Ltd.

Figure 11-12 Directories in the root

4. Use the **ls -l** command to display the results using the long format. (A space must precede the −l parameter.)

Here is an explanation of the types of information in the list:

▲ **Attributes.** The first 10 characters define the file or directory attributes. The first character identifies the type of item: A d is a directory; a − is a regular file, and an l indicates the item is a link to another location. The other nine characters define the read, write, and execute permissions assigned to the file or directory.

▲ **Links.** The second column lists the number of links the item has. In Linux, a link is similar to a Windows shortcut to a file or directory.

▲ **Owners.** The third column lists the user owner and the fourth column lists the group that owns the file or directory. In Figure 11-12, the owner is jean and the owner group is also jean.

▲ **Size, date, and name.** The last columns list the size of the file or directory in bytes, the date the item was last modified, and the name of the file or directory.

5. When you use the **cd ..** command again, you move up to the main directory in Linux, called the root directory, which is indicated with a forward slash. The **ls -l** command lists the files and subdirectories in the root.

Table 11-2 lists some important directories that are created in the root during a typical Linux installation. (Some distributions of Linux modify the directory structure.) Not all directories in the root are listed in the table.

Directory	Description
/bin	Contains programs and commands necessary to boot the system and perform other system tasks not reserved for the administrator, such as shutdown and reboot.
/boot	Consists of components needed for the boot process, such as boot loaders.
/dev	Holds device names, which consist of the type of device and a number identifying the device. Actual device drivers are located in the /lib/modules /[kernel version]/ directory.
/etc	Contains system configuration data, including configuration files and settings and their subdirectories. These files are used for tasks such as configuring a user account, changing system settings, and configuring a domain name resolution service.
/home	Contains user data. Every user on the system has a directory in the /home directory, such as /home/jean or /home/scott, and when a user logs in, that directory becomes the current working directory.
/lib	Stores common libraries used by applications so that more than one application can use the same library at one time. An example is the library of C programming code, without which only the kernel of the Linux system could run.
/lost+found	Stores data that is lost when files are truncated or when an attempt to fix system errors is unsuccessful.
/opt	Contains installations of third-party applications such as web browsers that do not come with the Linux OS distribution.
/root	The home directory for the root user; contains only files specific to the root user. Don't confuse this directory with the root, which contains all the directories listed in this table.
/sbin	Stores commands required for system administration.
/tmp	Stores temporary files, such as the ones that applications use during installation and operation.
/usr	Constitutes the major section of the Linux file system and contains read-only data.
/var	Holds variable data such as logs, email, news, print spools, and administrative files.

Table 11-2   Important directories in a typical Linux root directory

ROOT ACCOUNT AND USER ACCOUNTS

A+
220-902
2.1

For a Linux server, the system administrator is the person who installs updates to the OS (called patches), manages backup processes, supports the installation of software and hardware, sets up user accounts, resets passwords, and generally supports users. The system administrator has root privileges, which means that he or she can access all the functions of the OS; the principal user account is called the root account. Notice in Figure 11-12 that all the directories and files in the root directory belong to the root account.

When logged in to the root account, the administrator is called the superuser. By default, Ubuntu disables login to the root account. Later in the chapter, you learn how to use the sudo command to execute any command that requires root access when you are logged in to the system with a regular user account that has root privileges.

✎ **Notes**   The Linux command prompt for the root user is different from the command prompt for ordinary users. The root command prompt is #, and other users have the $ command prompt. See Figure 11-13. In the figure, the su command is used to change the currently logged-in user from root to jean.

11

```
root@VM50:/home# su jean
jean@VM50:/home$ _
```

Source: Canonical Ltd.

Figure 11-13   The user account, host name, and current directory appear in the shell
prompt along with a # or $ to indicate root account or other account

LINUX COMMANDS

A+
220-902
2.1

Table 11-3 describes some basic Linux commands, together with simple examples of how some
are used. As you read along, be aware that all commands entered in Linux are case sensitive,
meaning that uppercase and lowercase matter.

Command	Description
adduser	Adds a user to a system: `adduser <username>`
apt-get	Used to install and remove packages in Linux. When you first install Linux, it installs with only a bare-bones set of commands and utilities and includes a library of packages that you can install as needed. For example, to install the SSH (Secure Shell) package so you can remote in to your Linux server, use this command: `sudo apt-get install ssh` The `apt-get` command requires root access, which means you must precede the command with `sudo`. See `sudo` later in this table.
cat	Lets you view the contents of a file. Many Linux commands can use the redirection symbol > to redirect the output of the command. For example, use the redirection symbol with the `cat` command to copy a file: `cat /etc/shells > newfile` The contents of the shells file are written to newfile.
cd	Changes the directory. For example: To change the directory to /etc: `cd /etc` To move up one level in the directory tree: `cd ..` To go to the root: `cd /`
chmod	Changes modes (or permissions) for a file or directory. You'll see several examples of this command later in the chapter.
chown	Changes the owner of a file or directory.
clear	Clears the screen. This command is useful when the screen has become cluttered with commands and data that you no longer need to view.
cp	Copies a file: `cp <source> <destination>`
dd	Copies and converts files, directories, partitions, and even entire DVDs or hard drives. It's a powerful command with many practical uses and parameters, and only a superuser can use it. The basic format of the command is: `dd if=<source> of=<destination>` For example, use this command to create an ISO file from the contents of a CD: `dd if=/dev/cdrom of=/tmp/cdimage.iso`

deluser	Removes a user from a system:
	`deluser <username>`
	Remove the user and his home directory:
	`deluser -remove-home <username>`

df	Stands for *disk filesystem* and displays the amount of free space on the hard drive. To see the file system the drive is using: `df -T`

Table 11-3   Some common Linux commands

Command	Description
echo	Displays information on the screen. For example, to display which shell is currently being used, enter this command: `echo $SHELL`
exit	Logs out; the login shell prompt appears, where you can log in again.
grep	Searches for a specific pattern in a file or in multiple files: `grep <pattern> <file>`

ifconfig	Used to troubleshoot problems with network connections under TCP/IP. This command can disable and enable network adapters and assign a static IP address to an adapter. For example, to show all configuration information:
	`ifconfig -a`
	To enable or disable an adapter, use the up or down parameter. For example, to enable eth0, the first Ethernet interface:
	`sudo ifconfig eth0 up`
	To assign a static IP address to the eth0 interface: `ifconfig eth0 192.168.1.90`

iwconfig	Works similarly to `ifconfig`, but applies only to wireless networks. Use it to display information about the wireless adapter's configuration or to change that configuration. Two examples: To set the wireless NIC to Ad-Hoc mode so that other devices within range can connect directly to it, use this command, where wlan0 identifies the wireless adapter: `iwconfig wlan0 mode Ad-Hoc` To force the NIC to use channel 3: `iwconfig wlan0 channel 3`
kill	Kills a process instead of waiting for the process to terminate. Use the `ps` command to list process IDs. To end a process, use the `kill` command followed by the PID. For example, to kill the process with PID of 984: `kill 984` The command sends a signal to the process to end itself orderly. If the process doesn't die peacefully, you can get the kernel involved to forcefully end the process: `kill -kill 984`
ls	Functions similarly to the DOS Dir command, which displays a list of directories and files. For example: To list files in the /etc directory, using the long parameter for a complete listing: `ls -l /etc` To include hidden files in the list: `ls -la /etc` (In Linux, hidden files begin with a . period.)
man	Displays the online help manual, called man pages. For example, to get information about the echo command: `man echo` The manual program displays information about the command. To exit the manual program, type `q`.
mkdir	Makes a new directory: `mkdir <directory>`
mv	Moves a file or renames it, if the source and destination are the same directory: `mv <source> <destination>`
parted	Manages partitions on a hard drive and works with MBR and GPT drives.
passwd	Changes your password. When a user enters the command, she is asked for the old password and then can change the password. The superuser can change the password for any account and does not need to enter the account's old password, making it possible to reset a forgotten password.
ping	Used to test network connections by sending a request packet to a host. If a connection is successful, the host will return a response packet. For example: `ping 192.168.1.100` The `ping` results continue until you manually stop the process. Press Ctrl+C to break out of the process. To specify the number of pings: `ping 192.168.1.100 -c 4`
ps	Stands for *process status* and displays the process table so that you can identify process IDs for currently running processes (once you know the process ID, you can use the `kill` command to terminate a process): To list processes of current user: `ps` To list processes owned by all users: `ps aux`

Table 11-3 Some common Linux commands (continues)

11

Command	Description
pwd	Shows the name of the current working directory: pwd When you first log in to Linux, the directory is /home/*username*.
rm	Removes or deletes the file or files that are specified: rm <file>
rmdir	Removes or deletes an empty directory: rmdir <directory>
shutdown	Automated shut down to the system. Here are options: To halt or shut down now: sudo shutdown –h now To warn users and then shut down: sudo shutdown –h +10 "Everyone log out now. The system will shut down in 10 minutes for maintenance." To reboot now: sudo shutdown –r now
su	Stands for *substitute user* and opens a new terminal shell for a different user account. When switching to superuser, add sudo to the command. To switch to the root account: sudo su root To switch back to the jean account: su jean
sudo	Stands for *substitute user to do the command* and is pronounced "sue-doe" or "sue-doo". When logged in as a normal user with an account that has the right to use root commands, you can start a command with sudo to run the command as the superuser. User password is required. For example: sudo shutdown –h now
touch	Creates a blank file in the current directory. For example: touch myfile
vi	Launches a full-screen editor that can be used to edit a file: vi <file>
who	Displays a list of users currently logged in: who

Table 11-3 Some common Linux commands (continued)

★ A+ Exam Tip The A+ 220-902 exam expects you to be familiar with these Linux commands: ls, grep, cd, shutdown, pwd, passwd, mv, cp, rm, mkdir, chmod, iwconfig, ifconfig, ps, q, su, sudo, apt-get, vi, and dd.

Here are a few tips when using commands at a shell prompt:

◢ *Retrieve previous commands*. Press the arrow-up key to retrieve previously entered commands and then edit a command that appears.

◢ *Use wildcard characters*. Linux can use the * and ? wildcard characters in command lines, similar to Windows. For example, the **ls *.???** command lists all items with any file name and the file extension must have three characters. In addition, Linux provides a third wildcard: Brackets can give a choice of characters. For example, the **ls *.[abc]*** command lists all files whose file extension begins with a, b, or c.

◢ *Redirect output*. Normally output from a command displays on the screen. To redirect that output to a file, use the redirection symbol >. For example, to redirect output of ifconfig to myfile, use this command: **ifconfig >myfile**

◢ *Page the output*. Append |more to the end of a command line to display the results of the command on the screen one page at a time. For example, to page the ls command: **ls -l |more**

◢ *Use Ctrl+C*. To break out of a command or process, press **Ctrl+C**. Use it to recover after entering a wrong command or to stop a command that requires a manual halt.

Hands-On | Project 11-3 Practice Linux Commands

**A+
220-902
2.1**

Practice using Linux commands listed in Table 11-4 using the Ubuntu Server you created earlier. As you do so, you'll examine the directory structure, create a new directory, and put a blank file in it.

Task	Command	Description
1	ls -l	Lists files and directories in the current directory. In Linux, a directory is treated more like a file than a Windows directory.
2	pwd	Displays the full path to the current directory. When you first log in to a system, that directory is /home/*username*.
3	mkdir mydir	Creates a directory named mydir. The directory is created in the current directory.
4	cd mydir	Goes to the directory you just created in the /home/*username* directory.
5	touch myfile	Creates a blank file named myfile in the current directory.
6	ls	Lists current directory contents.
7	cd ..	Moves up one level in the directory tree.
8	cd /etc	Changes directory to the /etc directory, where text files are kept for configuring installed programs.
9	ls	Examines the contents of the /etc directory.
10	cd /home	Changes directory to the /home directory.
11	ping 127.0.0.1	Pings the loopback address. Pinging continues until you stop it by pressing Ctrl+C.
12	ifconfig	Displays TCP/IP configuration data.
13	man ifconfig	Displays the page from the Linux Manual about the ifconfig command. Press q to exit.
14	df -T	Displays free space on the hard drive and the file system used.
15	exit	Logs out; the login shell prompt appears, where you can log in again.

Table 11-4 Practice using Linux commands

Notes The current Linux file system is ext4 (fourth extended file system), which replaced the ext3 file system. The ext3 file system was the first file system to support journaling, which is a technique that tracks and stores changes to the hard drive and helps prevent file system corruption.

11

THE VI EDITOR

**A+
220-902
2.1**

The vi editor (visual editor) is a text editor that works in command mode (to enter commands) or in insert mode (to edit text). In this section, you learn how to create a text file in the vi editor, edit text, and save your changes. All vi commands are case sensitive.

Let's create and work with a file called mymemo:

1. If you are not already in your home directory, use the cd command to go there, for example: **cd /home/jean**

2. To open the vi editor and create the new file, enter the command **vi mymemo**. The vi editor screen appears and the file name is shown at the bottom of the screen.

3. When you first open the vi editor, you are in command mode. Type **i** to switch to Insert mode. When you are in Insert mode, the word INSERT is shown at the bottom of the screen.

4. Type the three sentences of Step 3 as the text for your memo (see Figure 11-14). Use your arrow keys to move over the text to edit it. You can also use the Insert key to switch between inserting text and overwriting text.

Source: Canonical Ltd.

Figure 11-14　The vi text editor in Insert mode

5. To switch back to command mode, first press the **Esc** key. Your pointer goes to the bottom of the screen. Type **:wq** to save the file and exit the editor.

Here is a list of enough vi commands to get you started with the editor. You can find other commands online:

:w　　　Save your changes and don't exit the editor

:q　　　Exit the editor after you have just saved your changes with the :w command

:wq　　Save your changes and exit the editor

:q!　　　Quit without saving your changes

Hands-On | Project 11-4　Install FTP Server in Ubuntu

In this project, you set up an FTP server in Ubuntu. Follow these steps:

1. Using the same VM you created earlier, log in to Ubuntu Server with your user name and password.

2. To install the FTP program named vsftpd, enter this command:

```
sudo apt-get install vsftpd
```

3. Respond to the prompts and then wait for the package to install.

4. Now you need to configure the FTP program by editing the /etc/vsftpd.conf text file. But before you edit the file, go to the /etc directory and make a backup copy of the file just in case you need it later. The sudo command is needed because files in the /etc directory belong to root:

```
cd /etc

sudo cp vsftpd.conf vsftpd.backup
```

5. Use the vi editor to edit the FTP configuration file: `sudo vi vsftpd.conf`

6. Verify and/or change three lines in the file to create the settings listed. Part of the file, including the three lines, is shown in Figure 11-15.

`anonymous_enable=NO`	Disable anonymous logins.
`local_enable=YES`	If necessary, remove the # to uncomment the line and allow local users to log in.
`write_enable=YES`	If necessary, remove the # to uncomment the line and allow users to write to a directory.

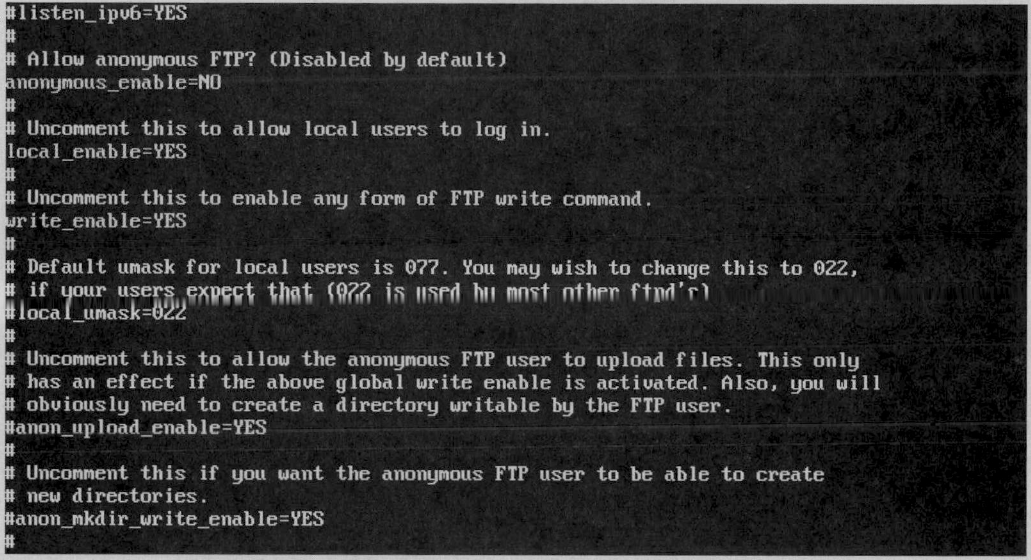

```
#listen_ipv6=YES
#
# Allow anonymous FTP? (Disabled by default)
anonymous_enable=NO
#
# Uncomment this to allow local users to log in.
local_enable=YES
#
# Uncomment this to enable any form of FTP write command.
write_enable=YES
#
# Default umask for local users is 077. You may wish to change this to 022,
# if your users expect that (022 is used by most other ftpd's)
#local_umask=022
#
# Uncomment this to allow the anonymous FTP user to upload files. This only
# has an effect if the above global write enable is activated. Also, you will
# obviously need to create a directory writable by the FTP user.
#anon_upload_enable=YES
#
# Uncomment this if you want the anonymous FTP user to be able to create
# new directories.
#anon_mkdir_write_enable=YES
#
```

Source: Canonical Ltd.

Figure 11-15   Part of the vsftpd.conf text file

7. Exit the vi editor, saving your changes. Restart the FTP service using this command: `sudo restart vsftpd`

8. To test your FTP server using the local machine, enter `ftp 127.0.0.1`. Then enter your user name and password. The ftp> prompt appears. Next use the `dir` command to see a list of directories and files. You should see the mydir directory and the mymemo file that you created in your /home/username directory earlier.

9. If you want to transfer files with FTP commands, use the `get` and `put` commands. To download the mymemo file, use the command `get mymemo`. Type `bye` to disconnect from the FTP server.

10. To find out the IP address of the server, type `ifconfig`.

11. Go to another computer on your local network, connect to your FTP server using the IP address of the server, and download the mymemo file to the local machine. See Figure 11-16. Your IP address might be different from the one shown in the figure.

12. Return to Ubuntu Server and examine the FTP log file /var/log/vsftpd.log. Because the file is short, you can use the `cat` command to display the entire log. The `sudo` command is required because /var files belong to root: `sudo cat /var/log/vsftpd.log`

(continues)

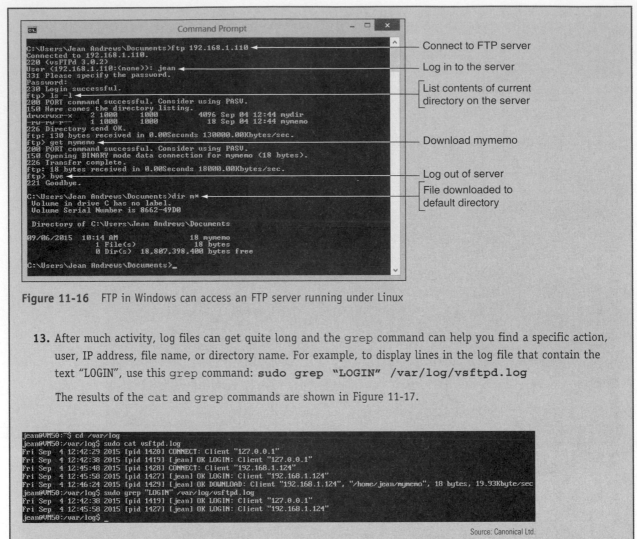

Figure 11-16   FTP in Windows can access an FTP server running under Linux

13. After much activity, log files can get quite long and the grep command can help you find a specific action, user, IP address, file name, or directory name. For example, to display lines in the log file that contain the text "LOGIN", use this grep command: **sudo grep "LOGIN" /var/log/vsftpd.log**

The results of the cat and grep commands are shown in Figure 11-17.

```
jean@VM50:~$ cd /var/log
jean@VM50:/var/log$ sudo cat vsftpd.log
Fri Sep  4 12:42:29 2015 [pid 1420] CONNECT: Client "127.0.0.1"
Fri Sep  4 12:42:38 2015 [pid 1419] [jean] OK LOGIN: Client "127.0.0.1"
Fri Sep  4 12:45:48 2015 [pid 1428] CONNECT: Client "192.168.1.124"
Fri Sep  4 12:45:58 2015 [pid 1427] [jean] OK LOGIN: Client "192.168.1.124"
Fri Sep  4 12:46:24 2015 [pid 1429] [jean] OK DOWNLOAD: Client "192.168.1.124", "/home/jean/mymemo", 18 bytes, 19.93Kbyte/sec
jean@VM50:/var/log$ sudo grep "LOGIN" /var/log/vsftpd.log
Fri Sep  4 12:42:38 2015 [pid 1419] [jean] OK LOGIN: Client "127.0.0.1"
Fri Sep  4 12:45:58 2015 [pid 1427] [jean] OK LOGIN: Client "192.168.1.124"
jean@VM50:/var/log$ _
```

Figure 11-17   The grep command can be used to search for specific text in log files

ASSIGNING PERMISSIONS TO FILES OR DIRECTORIES

> A+
> 220-902
> 2.1

A file or directory can have read, write, and/or execute permissions assigned to it. Permissions can be assigned to (a) the owner, (b) other users in the same group as the owner, and (c) all users. The chmod command is used to manage permissions for files and directories. To see current permissions, examine the 10 characters in the left column that display when you use the ls –l command. Here is the explanation of these characters:

◢ The first character identifies the type of item (d is a directory; - is a regular file).

◢ Characters 2–4 show the permissions assigned the owner (for example, rwx says the owner has read, write, and execute permissions).

◢ Characters 5–7 show the permissions assigned the group (for example, r-x says the group has read and execute permissions, but not write permission).

◢ Characters 8–10 show the permissions for others (for example, --- says others don't have read, write, or execute permission).

The chmod command changes these permissions. For example, suppose the output for the ls –l command on the /home/jean directory is that shown in Figure 11-18.

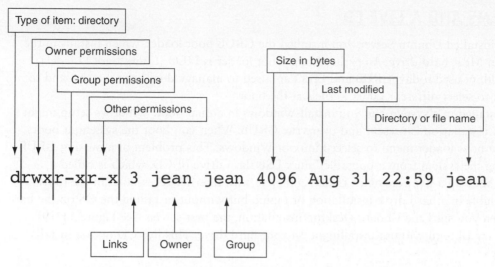

Type of item: directory

Owner permissions

Group permissions

Other permissions

Size in bytes

Last modified

Directory or file name

```
drwxr-xr-x 3 jean jean 4096 Aug 31 22:59 jean
```

Links   Owner   Group

Figure 11-18   Information about the jean directory displayed by `ls-l`

As labeled in the figure, the permissions for jean as owner is rwx (read, write, and execute). The permissions for the jean group are r-x (read and execute, but not write), and the permissions for others are also r-x. If the user jean wants to give read, write, and execute permissions to everyone (group and other), she can use this command:

```
chmod go+rwx /home/jean
```

The **g** assigns permission to the group and the **o** assigns permissions to others. (**u** can assign permissions to the owner.) A plus (+) gives permissions and a minus (−) removes permissions.

11

Hands-On | Project 11-5   Change Permissions for a Directory

**A+
220-902
2.1**

Follow these steps to change permissions for your home directory and then create a new user account to test these permissions:

1. Create a new user account named charlie. Log in to Ubuntu Server as charlie and try to copy a file to your own home directory. For example, you can use this command to make a new copy of the mymemo file you created earlier:

```
cp mymemo mymemo.charlie
```

When you do so, permission is denied.

2. Log back in to Ubuntu Server with your own account.

3. To install the chmod command, use this command:

```
sudo apt-get install coreutils
```

4. Use the chmod command to give full read, write, and execute permissions to everyone for your home directory.

5. Log out and log back in to the system as charlie and verify that the user charlie can now copy a file to your home directory.

DUAL-BOOT SYSTEMS AND A LIVE CD

When you installed Ubuntu Server, you installed the GRUB boot loader, which installs in the MBR for an MBR hard drive. An earlier Linux boot loader is LILO (LInux boot LOader), which is seldom used today. GRUB and LILO are used to manage dual-boot systems and to allow users to select different Linux kernels at the boot.

If Linux is already installed in a system and you install Windows in a dual boot, Windows setup might not recognize the Linux installation is present and overwrite GRUB. When you boot the system, it boots into Windows without a boot loader menu to select Linux or Windows. This problem of a missing GRUB can be solved by booting the system from a bootable Linux USB flash drive or CD, which is called a live CD. A live CD can boot up a live version of Linux, complete with Internet access and all the tools you normally have available in a hard drive installation of Linux, but without installing the OS on the hard drive. For example, when you start the Ubuntu Desktop installation, the first screen (see Figure 11-19) gives you the option to try Ubuntu without installing it on your hard drive. This live CD option installs Ubuntu only in memory.

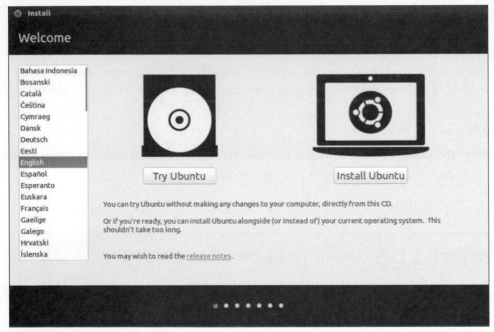

Source: Canonical Ltd.

Figure 11-19   Use a live CD to try Ubuntu Desktop without installing it on your hard drive

After booting from a live CD, you can reinstall GRUB and configure GRUB to manage the dual boot with Linux and Windows. The details of how to do that are beyond the scope of this chapter.

> ★ **A+ Exam Tip**   The A+ 220-902 exam expects you to know about GRUB and LILO and the problem of a missing GRUB.

> ✎ **Notes**   In a dual boot with Windows and Linux, you might want to access files in either volume from either OS. Know that Linux can access the NTFS file system on the Windows volume, but Windows cannot access the ext4 file system on the Linux volume. You can, however, install in Windows third-party software, such as Paragon ExtFS for Windows (*paragon-software.com*), to access the ext4 volume.

Hands-On | Project 11-6 Install Ubuntu Desktop in a VM

**A+
220-902
2.1, 2.2**

Follow these steps to install Ubuntu Desktop in a VM:

1. Go to **ubuntu.com/download/desktop** and download the free Ubuntu Desktop OS to your hard drive. The file that downloads is an ISO file.

2. Open the Hyper-V Manager, Oracle VM VirtualBox, Virtual PC Manager, or VMware Workstation Player manager and create a new VM named VM60. Mount the ISO file that contains the Ubuntu Desktop download to a virtual DVD in your VM.

3. Start up the VM and install Ubuntu Desktop in the VM, accepting all default settings. Be sure to write down your Ubuntu host name, Ubuntu user name, and password. When given the option, decline to install any extra software bundled with the OS. If needed, the software can be installed later.

4. When asked to restart the VM, first dismount (remove) the ISO file from the optical drive so that the VM boots to the hard drive. After Ubuntu Desktop launches, log in with your user name and password. Figure 11-20 shows the desktop with the System Settings window open and the System menu displayed.

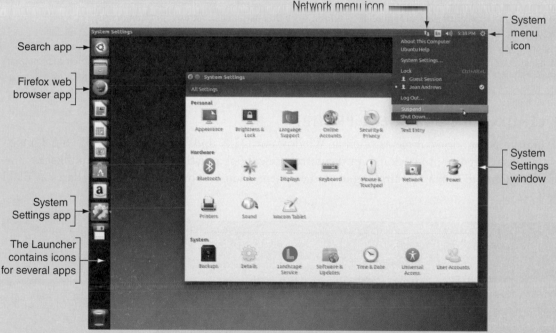

Sources: Canonical Ltd. and Mozilla Foundation

Figure 11-20 Ubuntu Desktop with the System Settings window and the Mozilla Firefox browser window open

5. Take a few minutes to poke around the desktop. For example, to open a Terminal window where you can enter Linux commands, click the **Search** icon to open the Search app and type **terminal**. Then click **Terminal** in the Applications group.

6. To shut down Ubuntu Desktop, click the **System** (cog) icon in the upper-right corner of the screen and click **Shut Down** in the System menu that appears.

To learn more about using Ubuntu Desktop, an excellent source of information is the Ubuntu Desktop Guide at *help.ubuntu.com/stable/ubuntu-help/*.

BACKUPS AND UPDATES

When supporting a Linux system, an IT technician needs to know how to create and maintain scheduled backups and system updates. For Ubuntu, the tools you use depend on whether you plan to do these chores from the shell prompt in Ubuntu Server or the graphical user interface in Ubuntu Desktop.

Here is what you need to know to get you started with making backups:

◢ *What is a dump and clone?* In Linux, a dump is a collection of data that is copied to backup media. For example, when Linux encounters a kernel panic (an error from which it cannot recover), it dumps an image of memory to a disk file for later examination. The image is called a core dump. You can dump the entire Linux volume to an external hard drive or dump a data folder to a location on the network. The first dump is called the initial dump and subsequent incremental dumps are called appended dumps or incremental dumps. A clone is an image of the entire partition on which Linux is installed.

◢ *Which backup program should I use?* Before choosing a shell prompt command or graphical program for the desktop, research the program to find out what others are saying about it and how it works. Compare several programs to find the one right for you. Examples of backup programs include the dump and TAR commands used at a shell prompt and the graphical SimpleBackupSuite that works from the desktop.

> 🖉 **Notes** For an overview of backup programs for Ubuntu, visit this page: *help.ubuntu.com/community/ BackupYourSystem%20*.
>
> Also, the cron and crontab commands can be used to schedule any shell command in Linux, including cp commands for making backups to another media. The crontab (cron table) command is used to schedule jobs and the cron command executes these jobs.

UPDATE LINUX FROM THE SHELL PROMPT

In general, Linux updates don't come as often as Windows or OS X updates. The creator of your Linux distribution publishes updates to packages in the current release of a distribution and also publishes new releases of a distribution. When you first log in to the system, Linux reports the package updates available (see Figure 11-21).

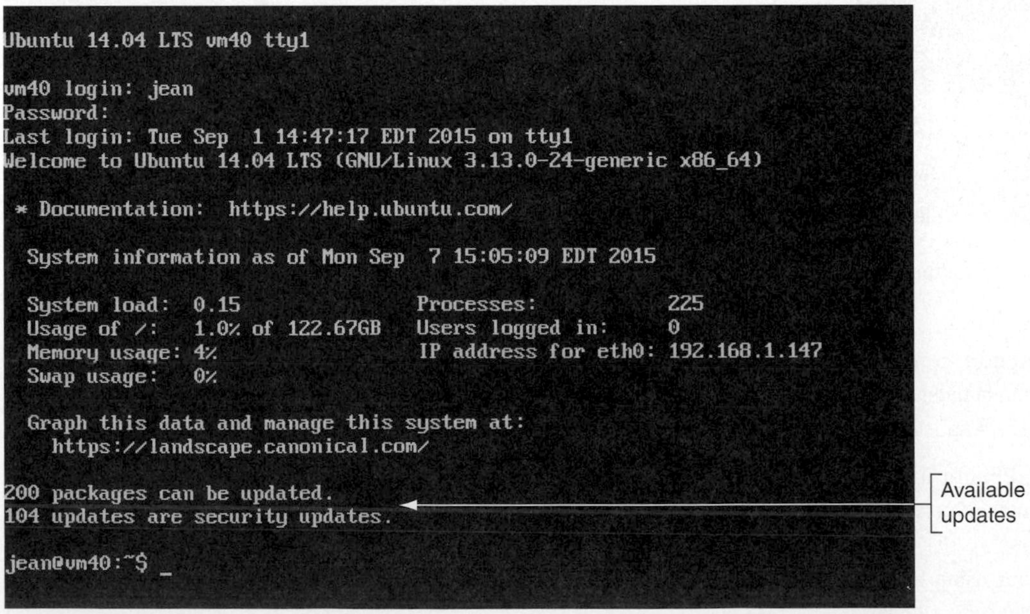

```
Ubuntu 14.04 LTS vm40 tty1

vm40 login: jean
Password:
Last login: Tue Sep  1 14:47:17 EDT 2015 on tty1
Welcome to Ubuntu 14.04 LTS (GNU/Linux 3.13.0-24-generic x86_64)

 * Documentation:  https://help.ubuntu.com/

  System information as of Mon Sep  7 15:05:09 EDT 2015

  System load:  0.15             Processes:           225
  Usage of /:   1.0% of 122.67GB  Users logged in:     0
  Memory usage: 4%               IP address for eth0: 192.168.1.147
  Swap usage:   0%

  Graph this data and manage this system at:
    https://landscape.canonical.com/

200 packages can be updated.
104 updates are security updates.

jean@vm40:~$ _
```

Available updates

Source: Canonical Ltd.

Figure 11-21   Available Ubuntu package updates

At a shell prompt, use these commands to update the packages previously installed in your system:

1. To refresh the list of all available updates:

```
sudo apt-get update
```

2. To update only the installed packages:

```
sudo apt-get upgrade
```

A new release of a distribution contains all updates since the last release. As a Linux administrator, you need to stay aware of the latest release of the distribution you are using and decide when or if it's appropriate to upgrade to that release.

Before you upgrade to a new release, be sure you have backups of your data and a clone of the entire Linux partition. Here's how to upgrade to a new release for Ubuntu Server:

1. Follow the previous steps to update all packages installed in the system.

2. To make sure the latest update manager program is installed:

```
sudo apt-get install update-manager-core
```

3. To install the latest release of Ubuntu Server:

```
sudo do-release-upgrade
```

If a new release is **available,** the last command reports it and you can follow directions to install it.

UPDATE UBUNTU DESKTOP

In Ubuntu Desktop, the Software Updater app manages updates to packages and new releases of Ubuntu Desktop. To open the updater, click the **Search** app and type **updater** in the Search box. Then click **Software Updater** (see Figure 11-22).

Source: Canonical Ltd.

Figure 11-22   Find and launch Software Updater

The updater searches for updates. In the box that appears, click **Details of updates** to see a list of updates (see the left side of Figure 11-23). To install updates, select your updates and click **Install Now.** To change update settings, click **Settings.** In the Software & Updates box (see the right side of Figure 11-23), you can decide how updates are managed.

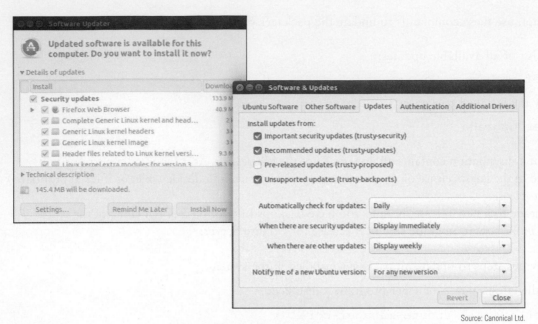

Source: Canonical Ltd.

Figure 11-23   Use the Software Updater to manage updates to Ubuntu Desktop

Now that you're familiar with Linux, let's move on to OS X.

MAC OS X OPERATING SYSTEM

A+
220-902
1.2, 2.1,
4.1, 4.2

OS X is the latest version of the proprietary operating system only available for Macintosh computers by Apple Inc. (*apple.com*). Like Linux, OS X is built on a UNIX foundation. The first Mac OS was released in 1984, and the final "classic" Mac OS, called Mac OS 9, was released in 1999. The first iteration of the desktop version of Mac OS X, dubbed "Cheetah," became available in 2001. From that point forward, the operating system continued to be called OS X (pronounced "O-S-ten") and received a version number to track its progress. The most recent release at the time of this writing, Yosemite, is version 10.10. Version 10.11, El Capitan, is already available in beta and is expected to be released as a free upgrade by the end of 2015.

USE THE MAC

A+
220-902
2.1, 4.2

Let's begin with a look at some major features of the Mac interface and how to use a Mac. In this section, you'll learn about the OS X desktop, Apple menu, multiple desktops, Finder, iCloud Drive, Keychain, System Preferences, Sharing, and Terminal.

GET TO KNOW THE OS X DESKTOP

The OS X desktop, with its major components labeled, is shown in Figure 11-24. The Finder application, which can help you find applications and data files, is open and active. Because Finder is the currently active application, the menu bar for the Finder window is displayed at the top of the screen. The menu bar provides drop-down menus that contain options for working with applications, files, and the interface.

By default, the dock appears at the bottom of the desktop. It contains shortcut icons to access frequently used applications. To open an application from its icon in the dock, click it once. The icons in the dock that represent open applications have a small, black dot underneath them. The OS X desktop can also include shortcuts that provide quick access to files, folders, and applications.

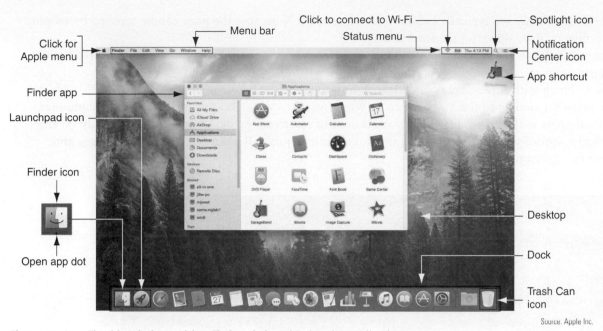

Figure 11-24   The OS X desktop with a Finder window showing the Applications screen

When a window is open, three circles at the upper-left corner (see Figure 11-25a) let you manipulate the window. The red circle closes the window, the yellow circle minimizes the window to the dock in the lower-right corner of the screen (see Figure 11-25b), and the green circle maximizes the window to full-screen size. (To restore a maximized window, move your pointer to the top of the screen. The circle icons appear. Click the green circle.)

11

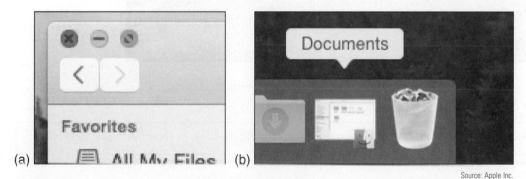

Figure 11-25   (a) Close, minimize, or expand a window; (b) this Finder window has been minimized, but the app is still running and is easily accessible in the dock

> ✎ **Notes**   Closing an app's window does not close the app. To quit an app, secondary-click (tap two fingers on the trackpad or right-click the mouse) the app's icon in the dock and click **Quit** in the menu that appears above the dock. Alternately, when the app's window is active on the desktop, click the name of the app in the menu bar and click **Quit** at the bottom of the drop-down menu.

Navigating OS X is made easier with a few, simple gestures, or finger movements, on the trackpad. Later in this chapter, you learn how to change the trackpad settings. In the meantime, here are a few of the most important default gestures:

▲ *Secondary click.* A secondary click is similar in function to a right-click in Windows. To secondary click, tap the lower-right corner of the trackpad with one finger or right-click the mouse. (You can also configure a secondary click to tap the trackpad with two fingers.)

▲ *Scroll.* Scroll bars are typically hidden from view in OS X because the page can be scrolled by swiping two fingers up or down on the trackpad.

▲ *Zoom.* Similar to zoom on a mobile device, pinch two fingers together to zoom out and spread two fingers apart to zoom in.

▲ *Pinch.* Pinch with three fingers and your thumb to show the Launchpad (see Figure 11-26), which is somewhat similar to the Start screen in Windows and shows all apps installed on the computer. Spread apart with three fingers and your thumb to return to the desktop. If you're already on the desktop, spread apart three fingers and your thumb to push all open windows to the edges and clear the desktop.

Source: Apple Inc.

Figure 11-26 When more apps are installed, Launchpad creates additional screens to the side

> ✎ **Notes** You can also open the Launchpad by clicking the Launchpad icon in the dock, as shown in Figure 11-24.

▲ *Swipe.* The number of fingers, direction of the swipe, and location of the swipe can all cause different results. Some of the most useful are:

   ▲ Swiping left or right with two fingers scrolls horizontally within an app (such as when scrolling through photos in the Photos app), and swiping left or right with three fingers switches between full-screen apps.

   ▲ Swipe two fingers from the right edge of the trackpad to reveal the Notification Center, as shown in Figure 11-27.

   ▲ Swipe up with three fingers to see Mission Control (see Figure 11-28), which gives an overview of all open windows and a thumbnail of Dashboard and the desktop. Dashboard (see Figure 11-29) contains widgets, such as a calendar, a calculator, a clock, and a weather report. Alternately, you can press F3 to access Mission Control.

Source: Apple Inc.

Figure 11-27 Click Edit at the bottom of the screen to customize the Notification Center

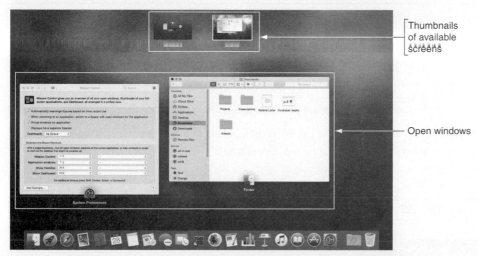

Thumbnails of available screens

Open windows

Source: Apple Inc.

Figure 11-28 Mission Control shows the open windows on the currently selected screen, which is the desktop

Click to change which widgets appear on Dashboard

Click to return to the desktop

Source: Apple Inc.

Figure 11-29 Dashboard has four default widgets, and several apps include a widget view option

11

Spotlight is Mac's search app, and can be configured to search the local computer, Wikipedia, iTunes, the Maps app, the web, and more. Click the Spotlight icon at the upper right of the screen to open the Spotlight Search box (see Figure 11-30), or press the Apple Command key (⌘) + spacebar.

Source: Apple Inc.

Figure 11-30   Spotlight searches the local computer and online resources

Hands-On | Project 11-7   Practice Using the OS X Desktop

A+
220-902
2.1

If you're not used to a Mac, the OS X desktop might feel strange compared with Windows. But with a little practice, you'll find all of the essential functions right at your fingertips. Complete the following steps to explore the OS X desktop:

1. *Confirm that you have a Wi-Fi connection.* Look for the Wi-Fi icon in the upper-right corner of the screen. If there is no connection, the icon will look like an empty upside-down triangle (see Figure 11-31). Click the Wi-Fi icon, turn on Wi-Fi if necessary, and connect to the network.

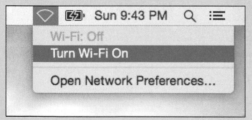

Source: Apple Inc.

Figure 11-31   Click to turn on Wi-Fi or click Open Network Preferences to set other options

2. *Install an app from the App Store.* Click the App Store icon in the dock; sign in if necessary. Select a free app and install it. A good one to try is Evernote. After installation is complete, leave the App Store window open. Use Finder to open the app.

3. *Switch between windows with Exposé.* Open two more windows, such as Safari and Maps. On a laptop, swipe down with three fingers to open Exposé. On a desktop, press **control + down arrow**. In Exposé, press **tab** to switch between windows. Press **esc** to return to the desktop.

4. *See all open windows with Mission Control.* On a laptop, swipe up with three fingers to open Mission Control. On a desktop, to open **Mission Control**, press **control + up arrow** or the **F3 Mission Control** key. Click a window to go to that window on the desktop.

5. *Uninstall the app.* Close all open windows on the desktop. You might need to use the Evernote menu on the menu bar to close it, if that is the app that you installed. Next, open Launchpad. On a laptop, use a trackpad gesture; on a desktop, press the **F4 Launchpad** key. In Launchpad, locate the icon for the app you installed. Press and hold the icon. All the icons jiggle. Some apps, such as Mission Control, are embedded in OS X and cannot be uninstalled; others that can be uninstalled have an x on the icon (see Figure 11-32). Click the **x** on the app you want to uninstall, then click **Delete** in the message bubble that appears, as shown in the figure. Click an open space on the screen to make the icons stop jiggling. Click the open space again to return to the desktop.

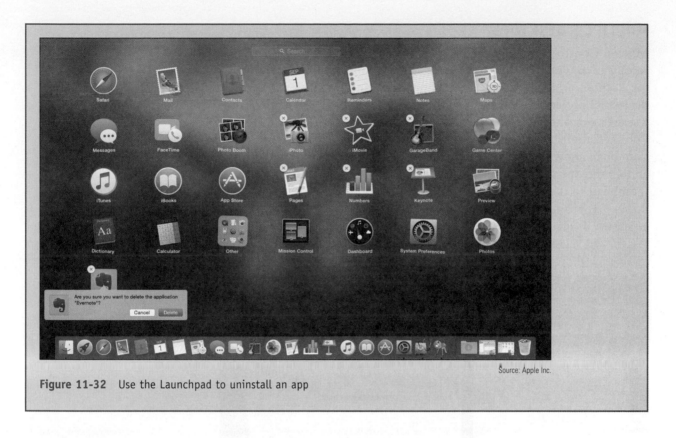

Figure 11-32   Use the Launchpad to uninstall an app

11

APPLE MENU

The menu at the top of the OS X screen changes with each application that is active except for the Apple icon, which is always shown at the far left of the menu bar. The Apple menu (see Figure 11-33) opens when you click the Apple icon and is similar to the Microsoft Windows Start menu in that it is constantly accessible no matter what folder, window, or application you are using. Use the Apple menu to put the computer to sleep, log out, restart, or shut down the system.

The Apple menu also provides access to system information, system preferences settings, the App Store, recent items, and the Force Quit option. When you click Force Quit, the Force Quit Applications window opens (see Figure 11-34). Similar to ending a task from Task Manager in Windows, to force quit an app, select it and click **Force Quit**. The application closes. You can also access the Force Quit Applications window by pressing ⌘ + option + esc.

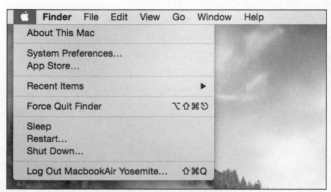

Figure 11-33   The Apple menu is always available no matter which application is active

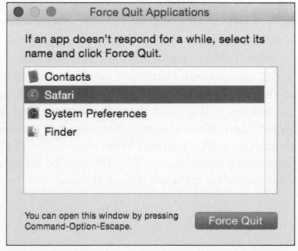

Figure 11-34   Force Quit can be used to close an app that is not responding

MULTIPLE DESKTOPS

Mission Control includes a feature called multiple desktops, which, as its name says, is several desktop screens each with its own collection of open windows. Suppose you're working with several windows for a school project, and you have a few more windows open for a project at work. You can place the school project windows on one desktop, called a Space, and place the work project windows on a separate desktop or Space.

To accomplish this feat, first open Mission Control as described above. By default, a single desktop thumbnail shows at the top of the screen beside the Dashboard thumbnail (refer back to Figure 11-28), and all the open windows show in this one desktop. To create a second desktop, drag a window's thumbnail to the right side of the default desktop thumbnail, and drop the window. A second desktop appears to hold that window. Repeat with another window for a third and fourth desktops, as shown in Figure 11-35.

Drag an open window here to create a new desktop

Source: Apple Inc.

Figure 11-35   Mission Control allows you to create multiple desktops to contain windows

Switch between desktops by clicking the desktop you want in Mission Control. Alternately, you can press **control + left arrow** or **control + right arrow** to switch between desktop screens. When an app is in full-screen mode, it acts as a separate Space and will show up in the list of Spaces as do the multiple desktops. Desktop configurations remain in place even when the computer is rebooted.

You can customize each desktop with a different wallpaper and with different apps that appear only on that desktop or in all desktops. To set a desktop's wallpaper, go to that desktop and secondary-click the desktop background, then click **Change Desktop Background** (see Figure 11-36a). The Desktop & Screen Saver window opens. (This window is one of the tools in System Preferences, which you learn about later in this chapter.) Select your wallpaper and close the window. Wallpaper settings in other, pre-existing desktops won't be affected. To assign an app to a specific desktop, go to that desktop and secondary-click the app's icon in the dock (see Figure 11-36b). Select **Options** then click **This Desktop**.

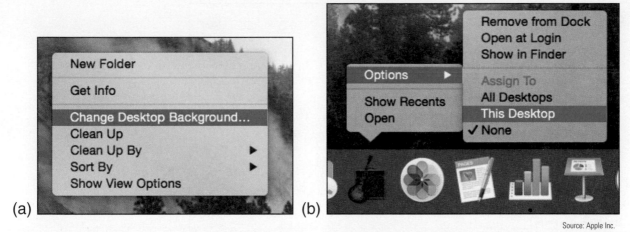

Source: Apple Inc.

Figure 11-36   (a) Set a different background for each desktop, and (b) assign different apps in the dock of each desktop

FINDER

The Mac's Finder window, shown earlier in Figure 11-24 and again here in Figure 11-37, functions something like File Explorer in Windows; use it to find and access Mac's files and applications. To open apps, click **Applications**, scroll to the app, and click it. To open files and folders, click **Documents** or some other location, such as iCloud Drive or Downloads. Double-click a folder to drill down into it, and double-click a document file to open it.

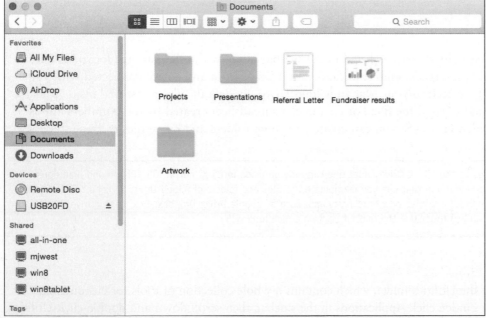

Source: Apple Inc.

Figure 11-37   The Finder window showing the Documents folder contents

> ✎ **Notes**   If you use an app frequently, such as GarageBand, you can add it to the dock. Click **Applications**, and then click and drag the app's icon to the dock.

SPOTLIGHT

If you're having a problem locating a file or folder, Spotlight can search for it. Open Spotlight and type the name of the file, folder, or text you want to find. For example, type **Projects** and Spotlight lists a folder named Projects as the Top Hit (see Figure 11-38).

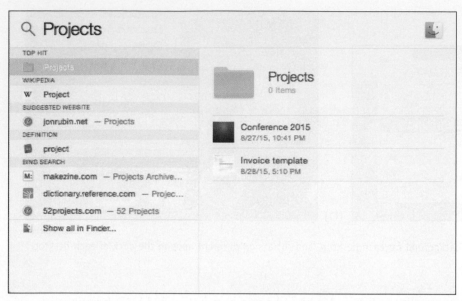

Source: Apple Inc.

Figure 11-38   Use Spotlight to search for files and folders

> ✎ **Notes** When you no longer need a file or folder, drag its icon to the Trash Can until the Trash Can is highlighted, and release. Note that this is the only way you can delete icons from the Finder window. When an item is in the Trash Can, you can recover it: Click **Trash Can** to open it and drag an item in the Trash Can to another location.

iCLOUD DRIVE

Notice in Figure 11-37 that iCloud Drive is listed in the sidebar along with other storage locations like Desktop, Documents, and Downloads. Files stored in iCloud Drive from any device connected with your Apple ID are automatically synced to your Mac in iCloud Drive. By default, files are stored inside folders titled by the application that created the file. For example, a spreadsheet created by the Numbers app is stored in the Numbers folder. However, you can create your own folders and move files to these folders.

> ↻ **OS Differences** Changes to the iCloud Drive folder tree can only be made in OS X, not in iOS. iPhone and iPad don't have an iCloud Drive app or a Finder app that lets you manipulate the files and folders of iCloud Drive. So keep this limitation in mind when choosing between iCloud Drive or a third-party app, such as Google Drive, Dropbox, Box, or OneDrive. These mobile apps all give you the ability to change the folder tree from a mobile device.

KEYCHAIN

Finder also gives access to the Utilities folder, which contains a whole collection of tools for customizing other features of OS X. In Finder, click **Applications** in the sidebar, then scroll down and double-click **Utilities**. Figure 11-39 shows the contents of the Utilities folder.

You'll learn about several of these utilities through the rest of this chapter. For now, let's look at Keychain, which is OS X's built-in password manager utility. To open Keychain, double-click **Keychain Access**. From the Keychain Access window (see the left side of Figure 11-40), you can view, edit, and remove accounts for applications, websites, servers, and other accounts that you've added, such as credit card numbers and bank accounts.

If you have problems with Keychain, verify or repair the Keychain configuration. In the **Keychain Access** menu, click **Keychain First Aid**. In the Keychain First Aid window (see the right side of Figure 11-40), make sure **Verify** is selected, then click **Start**. If the verification process reports a problem, select **Repair** and click **Start**.

Source: Apple Inc.

Figure 11-39 In Finder, use the Utilities folder to open useful tools to support the Mac

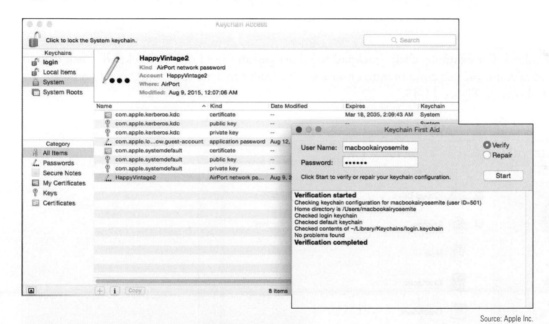

Source: Apple Inc.

Figure 11-40 The data stored in Keychain is encrypted

11

SYSTEM PREFERENCES

System Preferences can be opened from the Apple menu (refer back to Figure 11-33), or from the System Preferences icon in the dock (see Figure 11-41). The System Preferences window is shown in Figure 11-42 and contains options for customizing the Mac interface.

System Preferences contains several useful tools, including the Desktop & Screen Saver window you saw earlier, Mission Control settings, Security & Privacy, Energy Saver, Time Machine, iCloud settings,

Source: Apple Inc.

Figure 11-41 System Preferences icon in the dock shows the app is open

Click at any time
to return to this
screen in System
Preferences

Source: Apple Inc.

Figure 11-42   The System Preferences window is used to customize the Mac interface

and Printers & Scanners. For example, click **Trackpad** to adjust gestures used on the trackpad. Click **iCloud** to set up an iCloud account on this computer, to choose what content to sync to iCloud, and to adjust account details, as shown in Figure 11-43.

Source: Apple Inc.

Figure 11-43   Choose what content to sync with iCloud

As an IT technician, the most important tools for you in System Preferences are accessed through Time Machine, Users & Groups, and Sharing. You'll learn more about Time Machine and Users & Groups later in this chapter. For now, let's see how Sharing works.

SHARING

In System Preferences, click **Sharing** to open the Sharing window where you can set up file and folder sharing on the network, printer sharing, remote access, and screen sharing. Screen Sharing (see Figure 11-44) works similarly to Remote Assistance in Windows. When you turn on Screen Sharing, you can then use the Messages app to remotely view and control another Mac computer.

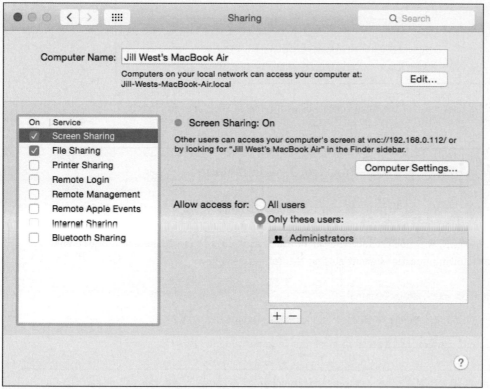

Source: Apple Inc.

Figure 11-44 Screen Sharing makes it easier to collaborate on projects or to help other users with their computers

If your Mac has an optical drive, the Sharing window includes the option *DVD or CD Sharing*. This feature, called Remote Disc, gives other Mac computers on the network access to this computer's optical drive. Remote Disc is especially useful when you need to install software or drivers from a disc on a Mac that doesn't have an optical drive. After you turn on *DVD or CD Sharing* on the Mac that has an optical drive, go to the Mac that doesn't have an optical drive and open Finder. In Finder, click **Remote Disc** in the sidebar under Devices (refer back to Figure 11-37).

> **◇ OS Differences** You can enable remote disc sharing on a Windows computer. To share a Windows computer's optical drive with Macs on your network, download and install **DVD or CD Sharing Update 1.0 for Windows**, available at the following website: *support.apple.com/kb/DL112?locale=en_US*.

TERMINAL

Terminal in OS X works much the same way as does a terminal shell in Linux. This is because both operating systems are based on UNIX. To open Terminal, first open **Finder**, click **Applications** in the sidebar, then scroll down and double-click the **Utilities** folder. Scroll down and double-click **Terminal**. (Alternately, press ⌘ + **spacebar** to open Spotlight, type **Terminal**, and press **return**.) The Terminal window opens, as shown in Figure 11-45.

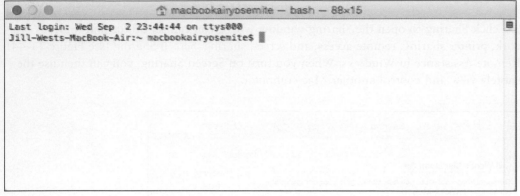

Source: Apple, Inc.

Figure 11-45 Terminal in OS X uses most of the same commands as a terminal shell does in Linux

---

Hands-On | Project 11-8 Practice OS X Commands

A+
220-902
2.1

To practice using Terminal, repeat the steps in Hands-On Project 11-3 using the OS X Terminal window. (For the df -T command, don't use the -T parameter.) In OS X, the final command of that project, exit, will not produce the same results as it does in Linux. Research online and answer the following questions about closing the Terminal window:

1. What does the command exit do in Terminal?

2. How can you adjust Terminal settings so that exit closes the Terminal window?

3. What keyboard shortcut can you use instead to close the Terminal window?

Notes Even if you don't have a Mac computer to use for completing this project, you can still research the answers to the questions above. The information is readily available online.

Hands-On | Project 11-9 Kill a Process

A+
220-902
2.1, 4.2

Terminal is a powerful tool and can be used to kill a hung process or to kill a process you suspect to be malware. First, try to use force quit to end the process. If that doesn't work, use Terminal to end the process. Follow these general directions to practice this skill:

1. Once again, install the Evernote app, but don't launch it.

2. Open **Terminal**. Use this command to list all running processes (the x option displays all processes, even those not started in this shell): **ps x**.

3. Leave Terminal open. Launch the Evernote app. Return to the Terminal window and list all running processes again. What are the Evernote app process IDs? Of the two process IDs, which one represents the application itself, and which one represents a login item?

4. The pgrep command combines the functionality of ps and grep. Research online to find the Apple man page for pgrep. What do the -f and -l options do?

5. Confirm the Evernote app's process IDs with the command `pgrep -f -l Evernote`. (Be sure to capitalize the *E* in Evernote.) Do the process IDs match the information you found earlier?

6. Use Terminal to kill the Evernote app (not the login item).

7. Return to the desktop and uninstall Evernote.

MAINTAIN AND SUPPORT A MAC

A+
220-902
2.1 In addition to working with files and applications, you will also need to know how to support and maintain OS X, including updates, backups, and hard drive maintenance. This section does not give you all you need to know to service Mac computers; it is simply intended to show you some important tools for working with the system. For more information specific to working with Macs, study books devoted specifically to the Mac, documentation and manuals that come with your system or its components, and the Apple website (*support.apple.com*).

> ⚡ **Caution**   Many Apple computers are covered by an Apple Care warranty, which provides excellent coverage for Mac computers. Always be absolutely certain a Mac is not covered by Apple Care before opening the case or doing anything else that might void the warranty.

UPDATE OS X, DRIVERS, AND FIRMWARE

Just like Windows, OS X needs regular updates. Updates often address zero-day vulnerabilities, which makes these updates important to maintaining a healthy system. However, sometimes the updates themselves introduce bugs, which is why many Mac experts advise against setting OS X updates to install automatically. Instead, waiting a few days after an OS X update's release before manually installing the update gives you a chance to see if the update introduces any significant issues.

OS X updates come from the App Store. To manually update OS X, click the **App Store** icon in the dock, then click **Updates** in the toolbar. Any available updates will show near the top of the screen, as shown in Figure 11-46. Additional updates to apps might also be available in this window, depending on whether you've configured the computer to automatically install app updates.

Source: Apple Inc.

Figure 11-46   The Updates window shows available updates and recently installed updates

11

> **Notes** Printer, scanner, and graphics driver updates are usually included in the OS X updates. Other devices that require drivers, if not included in OS X, can be downloaded from the manufacturer's website and installed. These drivers will not be updated through OS X updates. If any problems are encountered with that device, you'll need to check the manufacturer's website for updates.

To change the settings for automatic updates, open **System Preferences** and click **App Store** (see Figure 11-47). Here is an explanation of each option presented:

◢ *Automatically check for updates.* This option must be checked for any of its sub options to be available.

◢ *Download newly available updates in the background.* This option downloads updates without installing them.

◢ *Install app updates.* This option installs all updates to App Store applications without first requiring user approval.

◢ *Install OS X updates.* This option installs all updates to the operating system without first requiring user approval.

◢ *Install system data files and security updates.* This option installs critical system patches that address known vulnerabilities.

◢ *Automatically download apps purchased on other Macs.* This option installs apps purchased through the App Store on other Mac computers using the same Apple ID.

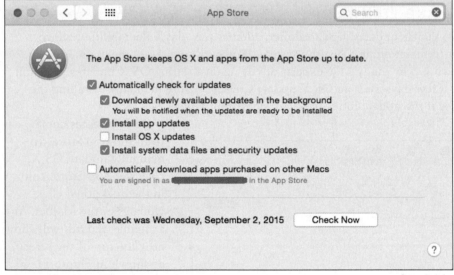

Source: Apple Inc.

Figure 11-47   Click Check Now to check for requested updates

Usually any needed firmware updates are included in the OS X update. Occasionally, however, Apple has released a firmware update as a stand-alone installer. You can find a list of available firmware updates in the Apple Knowledge Base Article at *support.apple.com/en-us/HT201518*.

To determine whether a Mac computer needs a firmware update, first check the current firmware version on the computer. This and a great deal more information is available in the System Information app. Open **Finder**, navigate to the **Utilities** folder, and double-click **System Information**. In the System Information window (see Figure 11-48), select Hardware in the sidebar and look under Hardware Overview for the *Model Identifier*, *Boot ROM Version*, and *SMC Version (system)*, as labeled in Figure 11-48. Compare the information in the System Information window with the information for the latest firmware update available on the *support.apple.com* website. Install a firmware update only if the version listed on Apple's website is newer than what is currently installed on the computer.

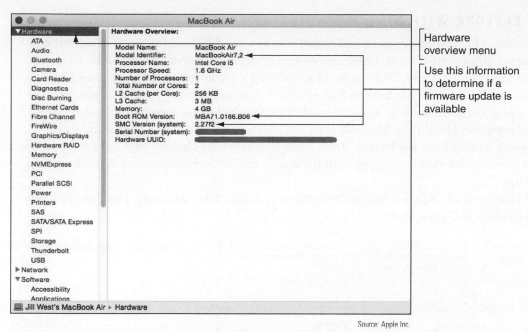

Hardware overview menu

Use this information to determine if a firmware update is available

Source: Apple Inc.

Figure 11-48 The System Information window gives detailed information about the computer

> **Notes** The System Information app can also be opened from the Apple menu. Click the Apple icon, then click **About This Mac**, which gives an overview of the computer's system information, as shown in Figure 11-49. Then click **System Report** to open the System Information window that you saw in Figure 11-48.

11

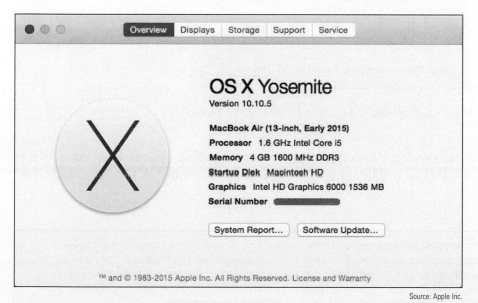

Source: Apple Inc.

Figure 11-49 Click System Report to go to the System Information window for more detailed information

> **Notes** Many experts believe that antivirus/anti-malware software is not required on a Mac computer. Whether this is true or not is still hotly debated. If you do choose to use anti-malware, however, be sure to keep it updated. One example of anti-malware for a Mac is AdwareMedic (*adwaremedic.com*) by Malwarebytes, which works well to remove adware that has infected a system.

BACK UP AND RESTORE WITH TIME MACHINE

Like iOS mobile devices, Mac computers can use iCloud Drive to store files and folders in the cloud and sync this content across all of your devices. Unlike the mobile devices you learned about in the chapter, "Supporting Mobile Operating Systems," iCloud is not sufficient for backing up a Mac. For this purpose, OS X includes Time Machine, which is a built-in backup utility that automatically backs up user-created data, applications, and system files onto an external hard drive attached either directly to the computer or through the local network. Once Time Machine is set up, backups are updated in the background. Depending on the space available on the backup drive, Time Machine keeps hourly backups for 24 hours, daily backups for a month, and weekly backups until the disk is full. Oldest backups are deleted to make space for new backups.

To set up Time Machine in OS X, open **System Preferences** and click **Time Machine**. The Time Machine window appears, as shown in Figure 11-50.

Source: Apple Inc.

Figure 11-50   Click Options to choose which content to include in a Time Machine backup

Follow the on-screen directions to select a backup disk and configure backup options. Everything on the disk will be erased. The original backup will be at least 20 GB, includes the entire OS X volume, and takes some time to complete.

> **✎ Notes** When your Mac OS X computer is not connected to the backup disk, Time Machine stores backup copies, called local snapshots, of created, modified, or deleted files on the startup drive. When you reconnect the computer to the backup disk, the local snapshots are copied to the backup disk. Local snapshots stay on the startup drive as long as they don't take up too much space, and can be restored from the startup drive if needed. Time Machine saves one daily snapshot each day and one weekly snapshot each week while the backup disk is disconnected.

To recover a file or folder from Time Machine, open **Finder**. In the **Applications** group, double-click **Time Machine**. The timeline and available backups in Finder appear (see Figure 11-51). Use the Finder window to locate the file or folder. Then go back though time to find the version of the file or folder you want to restore. To move through time, you can use the timeline on the right, the arrow buttons, or click a Finder window in the stack of available windows. Select the item and click **Restore**.

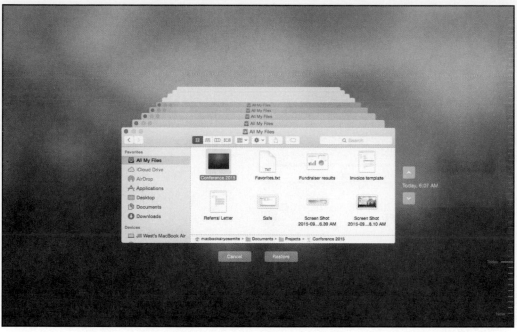

Source: Apple Inc.

Figure 11-51 Locate an item and then go back through time to find the version to restore

Later in this chapter, you learn how to use Time Machine to restore the entire OS X volume.

CLONE THE STARTUP DISK

The startup disk is the entire volume on which OS X is installed. In addition to a Time Machine backup of the entire startup disk, you can also clone the startup disk. The clone is a disk image and is stored in a DMG file.

> **Notes** A DMG file is a disk image file for a Mac and is similar to WIM or ISO files in Windows. In addition to storing clones, they're often used to hold app installers, as are EXE files in Windows.

To create a clone in OS X, follow these steps:

1. Boot into the Recovery System, which boots from a hidden volume on the startup disk. To do this, restart the computer and hold down ⌘ + r until the Apple logo appears.

2. When the OS X Utilities window appears (see Figure 11-52), click **Disk Utility** and click **Continue**.

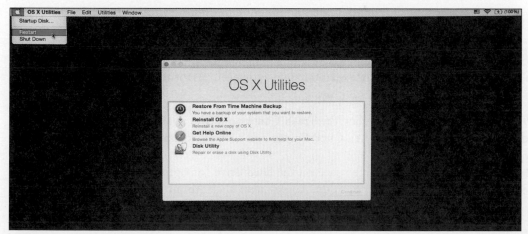

Source: Apple Inc.

Figure 11-52 Press ⌘ + r during the boot to access the Recovery System and the OS X Utilities window

3. The Disk Utility window opens, as shown in Figure 11-53. In the sidebar, select the partition to be copied, and then click **New Image** at the top of the window. Give the image a name and select a location to save the DMG file, and then click **Save**.

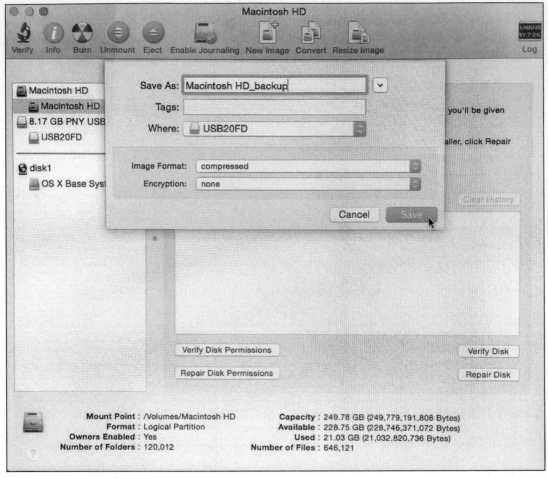

Figure 11-53   When creating a clone, choose an encryption type to increase the security of the disk image

4. To exit the Recovery System and return to a normal boot, click **Restart** on the Apple menu.

Later in this chapter, you learn how to use a clone to restore the OS X volume.

DRIVE MAINTENANCE TOOLS

Hard drives in Mac computers require very little maintenance. However, performing a few simple tasks on a regular basis can help keep things running smoothly:

▲ *Empty the trash.* To empty the Trash Can, click the Trash Can icon in the dock. Trash Can contents appear in a Finder window (see Figure 11-54). Click **Empty** and then click **Empty Trash** in the warning box. Items are permanently deleted.

▲ *Free up space.* Maintain at least 15–20% free space on the hard drive for optimal performance. To see how much free space is available on the drive, in the Apple menu click **About This Mac,** and then click the **Storage** tab, as shown in Figure 11-55.

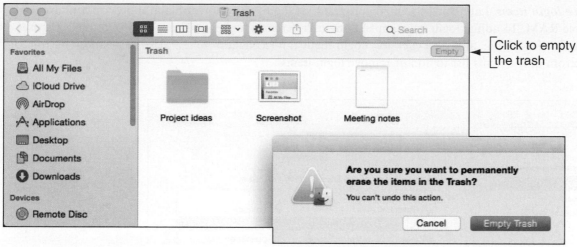

Source: Apple Inc.

Figure 11-54   Check the contents of the Trash Can before emptying it

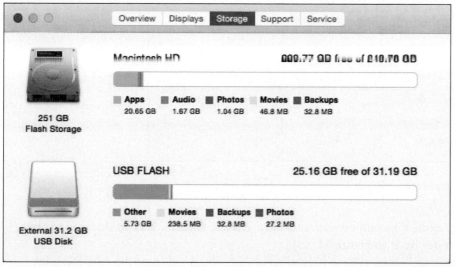

Source: Apple Inc.

Figure 11-55   Maintain at least 15% free space on the hard drive

▲ *Install updates*. Regularly check for and install OS X and app updates, which you learned how to do earlier in this chapter.

▲ *Verify no startup items*. Programs that automatically launch at startup are called startup items and programs that automatically launch after a user logs in are called login items. Apple discourages the use of startup items because they slow down the startup process and items in the startup folder might be malware. You can verify the system doesn't have startup items by looking in two directories that can contain startup items: /Library/StartupItems and /System/Library/StartupItems. Open Terminal and navigate to these directories, which you should find empty (see Figure 11-56).

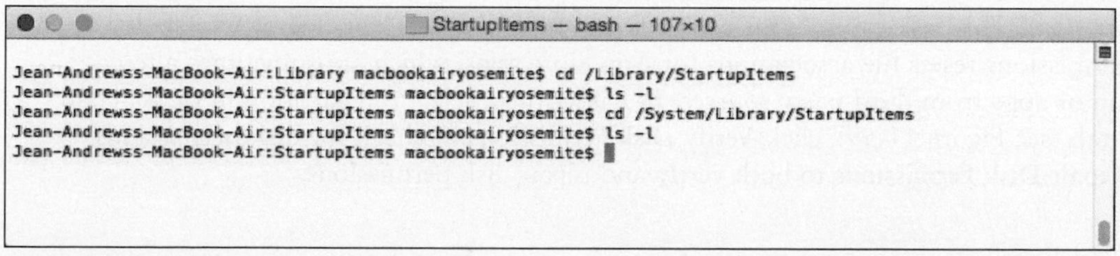

```
● ● ●                    🖿 StartupItems — bash — 107×10

Jean-Andrewss-MacBook-Air:Library macbookairyosemite$ cd /Library/StartupItems
Jean-Andrewss-MacBook-Air:StartupItems macbookairyosemite$ ls -l
Jean-Andrewss-MacBook-Air:StartupItems macbookairyosemite$ cd /System/Library/StartupItems
Jean-Andrewss-MacBook-Air:StartupItems macbookairyosemite$ ls -l
Jean-Andrewss-MacBook-Air:StartupItems macbookairyosemite$ █
```

Source: Apple Inc.

Figure 11-56   Two directories can contain startup items and both directories are empty

11

▲ *Remove login items.* Launching too many programs at login slows down the boot process and uses up valuable RAM. To adjust login items, open **System Preferences** and click **Users & Groups**. Select a user account in the sidebar, and then click the **Login Items** tab (see Figure 11-57). Use the + and – buttons at the bottom of the items list to add or remove login items.

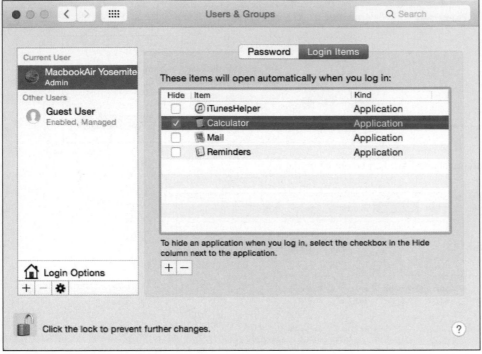

Source: Apple Inc.

Figure 11-57   List of login items applies to each user

▲ *Restart the computer.* Power cycle the computer at least once a week. A quick way to do so is to click **Restart** in the Apple menu (refer back to Figure 11-33).

▲ *Uninstall unneeded apps.* Uninstall apps you no longer need. Apps obtained from the App Store are uninstalled from Launchpad. For apps installed from other sources besides the App Store, locate the app in Finder and drag the app to the Trash Can. Empty the trash to complete the uninstallation.

REPAIRS USING THE DISK UTILITY APP

The Disk Utility app can be used to repair disk permissions and to repair hard drive corruptions. To open Disk Utility, open **Finder** and navigate to the **Utilities** folder. Double-click **Disk Utility**. The sidebar of the Disk Utility window (see Figure 11-58) shows attached drives with partitions listed below each drive. In Figure 11-58, the hard drive has a single partition, which can be changed on the Partition tab, and a USB flash drive is connected to the computer. Two disk maintenance tasks you can perform from Disk Utility include the following:

▲ *Repair disk permissions.* This task can prevent problems if you've recently installed or uninstalled apps. Repairing disk permissions resets file associations for App Store apps, which are sometimes altered during installation of apps from third-party sources. In Disk Utility, select the partition in the sidebar. On the **First Aid** tab (see Figure 11-59), click **Verify Disk Permissions** to check for disk permissions issues, or click **Repair Disk Permissions** to both verify and repair disk permissions.

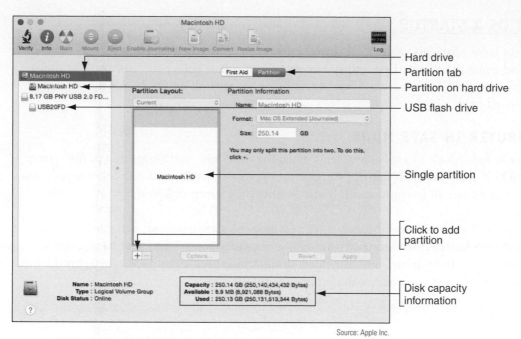

Source: Apple Inc.

Figure 11-58   Manage partitions from the Disk Utility app

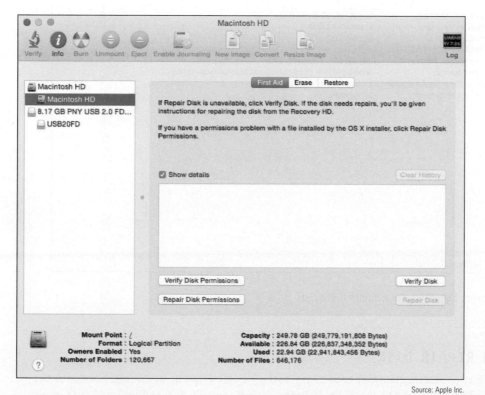

Source: Apple Inc.

Figure 11-59   The Erase and Restore tabs provide additional options for working with a disk

▲ *Verify disk.* Repair Disk checks the hard drive for minor problems, such as corrupted directory entries, and repairs them if necessary. This is especially important to perform if the system has recently frozen or experienced a sudden power loss. Notice in Figure 11-59 that Verify Disk is available, but Repair Disk is grayed out. This is because the disk cannot be repaired if the system is currently booted from that disk. Click **Verify Disk**. If the process finds errors, it will tell you to repair the disk using the Recovery System.

TROUBLESHOOT OS X STARTUP

A+
220-902
1.2, 2.1,
4.1

When you have problems with OS X startup, you can try booting the computer in Safe Mode and using the Repair Disk utility. If neither tool solves your problem, you can move on to recovering the system from a backup or clone or reinstalling OS X. All these solutions are discussed next.

START THE COMPUTER IN SAFE MODE

Starting the computer in Safe Mode can solve problems when the computer won't start due to file system errors. Safe Mode in OS X loads essential kernel components, prevents startup items and login items from launching, and loads a minimum of user processes. It also verifies the startup disk and repairs any file system errors it finds.

To boot the computer in Safe Mode, immediately after you hear the startup sound, press and hold the **shift** key. The boot will take longer than normal. To verify the computer booted into Safe Mode, open **System Information**. In the Software group, look for Boot Mode, which should say Safe (see Figure 11-60). Restart the computer normally and see whether the problem is solved.

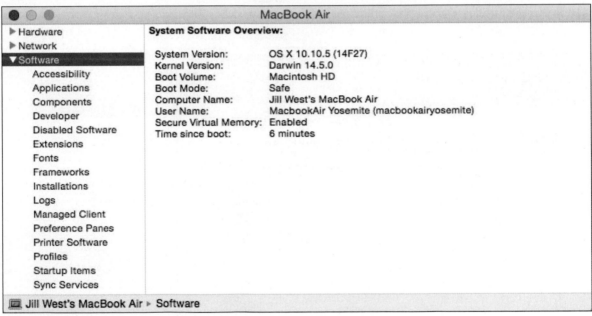

Source: Apple Inc.

Figure 11-60   Boot Mode indicates the computer is booted into Safe Mode

OS X RECOVERY AND REPAIR DISK

If Safe Mode didn't solve your problem, the next tool to try is the Repair Disk utility. First, boot into the Recovery System, then open **Disk Utility**. On the First Aid tab, click **Repair Disk** (see Figure 11-61), then restart into normal mode.

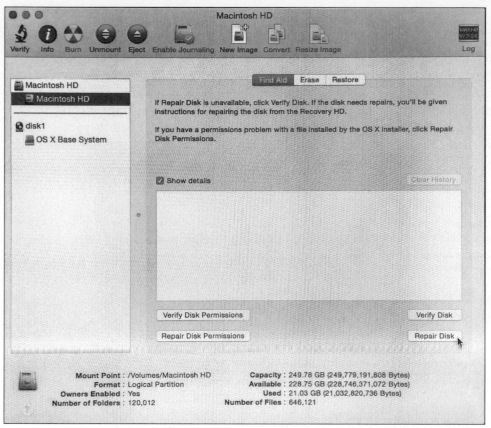

Source: Apple Inc.

Figure 11-61 Repair Disk repairs a corrupted OS X installation

RECOVERY FROM A TIME MACHINE BACKUP

If you have made a Time Machine backup of your system, you can use it to recover the startup disk. If the hard drive has failed, replace the hard drive and then connect your Time Machine backup device, for example, connect an external hard drive. Boot into the Recovery System. On the OS X Utilities window (refer back to Figure 11-52), select **Restore From a Time Machine Backup** and click **Continue**. Point to the backup device and follow directions on screen.

OS X RECOVERY WITH A CLONE OR THE INTERNET

You can also boot the system from a previously made clone. Any drive holding a clone DMG file can be used as a startup disk. Connect the drive to the computer, press and hold the **option** key during boot, and then select the drive that holds the clone DMG file to run the boot from that drive.

It's also possible to store the clone DMG file on a server on the network and, using a technology called NetBoot, the clone can be used to boot a Mac on the network or deploy OS X to multiple machines.

The image recovery process can also be performed over the Internet. If the Mac computer doesn't find a recovery image and is connected to the Internet, it will download and install OS X from the Apple website. However, obviously this will not be a customized image with your apps and settings already configured. You'll be starting from scratch. The version of OS X that came originally installed on your Mac will be installed.

> **Notes** Many of these same steps can also help when troubleshooting kernel panics. A kernel panic is similar to a BSOD in Windows. It might be caused by something simple, like a crashed app or a network communication issue, or it might result from a corrupted OS X installation. OS X restarts automatically when experiencing a kernel panic. If the kernel panic continues to prompt restarts, OS X will stop trying after five attempts and shut down the computer.

BOOT CAMP

A+
220-902
2.1

One more hard drive option you should be aware of is made possible by Boot Camp, a utility in OS X that allows you to install and run Windows on a Mac computer. You saw earlier in Figure 11-58 where the Macintosh HD in the figure held one partition. Boot Camp can split the partition and install Windows in the new partition for a dual boot. Access the Boot Camp Assistant through the Utilities folder; Figure 11-62 shows the first screen with options in the process of installing Windows on a Mac. After Windows is installed, you can choose which OS to use as your default for the computer, or press and hold the **option** key when starting the computer to reach the Startup Manager, which lets you choose from the installed operating systems.

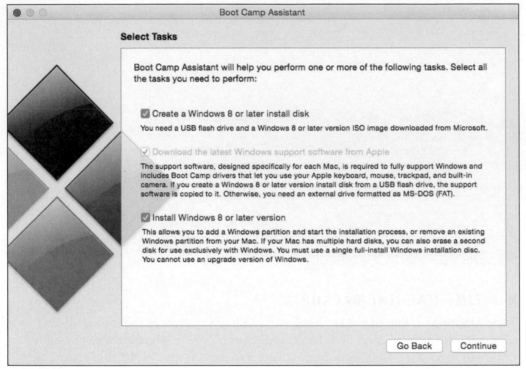

Source: Apple Inc.

Figure 11-62   Manage Windows installations from Boot Camp Assistant

>> CHAPTER SUMMARY

Virtualization Basics

◢ Server-side virtualization happens on the server, and client-side virtualization happens on the client machine.

◢ Three ways to implement client-side virtualization include presentation virtualization, application virtualization, and client-side desktop virtualization.

◢ Virtualization is done by creating multiple virtual machines on a physical machine using a hypervisor.

◢ A Type 1 hypervisor installs before any OS is installed and is called a bare-metal hypervisor. A Type 2 hypervisor is an application that installs in an OS. A Type 1 hypervisor is faster and more secure than a Type 2 hypervisor.

Linux Operating System

◢ Distributions of Linux provide a shell prompt in the Linux terminal and might also provide a desktop with a GUI. The default command-line shell for Linux is the Bash shell.

◢ The root account in Linux has access to all features of the OS. When logged in to the root account, the user is called the superuser.

◢ Important Linux commands include ls, grep, cd, shutdown, pwd, passwd, mv, cp, rm, mkdir, chmod, iwconfig, ifconfig, ps, q, su, sudo, apt-get, vi, and dd.

◢ A missing GRUB sometimes happens after installing Windows in a dual boot when Linux has been previously installed.

◢ Linux can access NTFS volumes created by Windows, but Windows cannot access ext4 volumes created by Linux unless third-party software is installed.

Mac OS X Operating System

◢ OS X is the latest version of the proprietary operating system available only for Macintosh computers by Apple Inc. Like Linux, OS X is built on a UNIX foundation.

◢ The dock appears at the bottom of the desktop. The icons in the dock that represent open applications have a small, black circle underneath them.

◢ Spotlight is Mac's search app, and can be configured to search the local computer, Wikipedia, iTunes, the Maps app, the web, and more.

◢ For IT technicians, the most important tools in System Preferences are accessed through Time Machine, Users & Groups, and Sharing. Screen Sharing, one of the Sharing tools, works similarly to Remote Assistance in Windows.

◢ OS X updates often address zero-day vulnerabilities, which makes these updates important to maintaining a healthy system.

◢ Time Machine is a built-in backup utility that automatically backs up user-created data, applications, and system files onto an external hard drive attached either directly to the computer or through the local network.

◢ Disk Utility can be used to repair disk permissions and to repair hard drive corruptions.

◢ A kernel panic is similar to a BSOD in Windows. It might be caused by something simple, like a crashed app or a network communication issue, or it might result from a corrupted OS X installation.

◢ Boot Camp is an OS X utility that allows you to install Windows on a Mac computer in a dual boot with OS X.

11

>> KEY TERMS

For explanations of key terms, see the Glossary for this text.

Apple menu	dd	hardware-assisted	NetBoot
application	DMG file	virtualization (HAV)	OS X
virtualization	dock	hypervisor	presentation
Application Virtualization	dumb terminal	ifconfig	virtualization
(App-V)	dump	iwconfig	Recovery System
apt-get	emulator	kernel panic	Remote Disc
Bash shell	ext3	Keychain	root account
Boot Camp	ext4	Launchpad	Screen Sharing
chmod	fat client	LILO (LInux boot LOader)	secondary click
chown	Finder	Linux	server-side virtualization
client-side desktop	force quit	live CD	shell prompt
virtualization	gestures	local snapshot	Space
client-side virtualization	grep	login item	Spotlight
clone	GRUB (GRand	Mission Control	startup disk
Dashboard	Unified Bootloader)	multiple desktops	startup item

su	thick client	ultra-thin client	virtual machine
sudo	thin client	vi editor	manager (VMM)
superuser	Time Machine	Virtual Desktop	virtualization
System Preferences	Type 1 hypervisor	Infrastructure	zero client
terminal	Type 2 hypervisor	(VDI)	

>> REVIEWING THE BASICS

1. Which type of client-side virtualization creates a virtual environment in memory for an application to run on a client machine?

2. In Question 1, what Microsoft software can be used to create this environment?

3. List two types of hypervisors and describe their fundamental differences.

4. What are the four main ways to secure a VM?

5. What is the Linux command to find out which shell you are using?

6. What is the name of the current Linux boot loader that is used to manage a dual boot?

7. What is the full path to the home directory of the user account lucio in Linux?

8. In which directory are you likely to find logs created by applications running in Linux?

9. In Linux, when logged in as a normal user with root privileges, which command must precede the apt-get command in the command line in order to install a program?

10. Which file system does Linux currently use for the volume on which Linux is installed?

11. Which Linux file system was the first to implement journaling?

12. What symbol displays in the shell prompt to indicate the logged-in user is root in Linux?

13. What is the Linux vi editor command to save your changes and exit the editor?

14. Why is the scroll bar typically hidden from view in OS X?

15. Which app manages multiple desktop screens in OS X?

16. Which app provides tools for customizing the Mac interface?

17. List the steps to open Terminal in OS X.

18. How can you install printer, scanner, and graphics driver updates in OS X?

19. How often does Time Machine create new backups, and how long are these backups kept?

20. What file format is used for OS X disk images?

>> THINKING CRITICALLY

1. You are managing an FTP server installed in Ubuntu Server. The server has created a very large log file, vsftpd.log. Which command is appropriate to search the log file for activity of the user charlie?

    a. `sudo cat /var/log/vsftpd.log`

    b. `grep "charlie" /var/log/vsftpd.log`

    c. `sudo grep "charlie" /var/log/vsftpd.log`

    d. `cat /var/log/vsftpd.log`

2. You need to use Repair Disk to repair the hard drive of a Mac computer. How should you reboot the computer?

   a. Open the Apple menu, then hold the shift key while clicking Restart.

   b. Reboot the computer. Press and hold the ⌘ + r keys during boot.

   c. Reboot the computer. Immediately after you hear the startup sound, press and hold the shift key.

   d. Reboot the computer. Press and hold the option key during boot.

3. Explain why most Linux commands work about the same on a Mac computer as they do on a Linux system. Research online and find three examples of Linux commands other than the ones presented in this chapter that also work in OS X Yosemite.

>> REAL PROBLEMS, REAL SOLUTIONS

REAL PROBLEM 11-1 Using the Google Cloud Platform to Create a Ubuntu VM

Recall that Google Cloud Platform is an example of PaaS that you can use to learn a new operating system or develop apps. To use the service to create an Ubuntu VM, do the following:

1. Go to **cloud.google.com** and click **Free Trial**. You will need to sign in using a Google account. If you don't have an account, you can create one with any valid email address.

2. In the Developers Console, create a new project. Then drill down into **Compute, Compute Engine**, and **VM instances**. Create a VM instance with Ubuntu 15.04 installed as the OS. Then wait several minutes for Google to create the instance.

3. Click the VM instances listed in your project. Buttons appear at the top of the window to manage the instance. Also note the External IP assigned to the VM instance. Click **SSH** and remote in to your VM using the SSH utility. The VM opens in a separate window where you can use Ubuntu commands (see Figure 11-63).

11

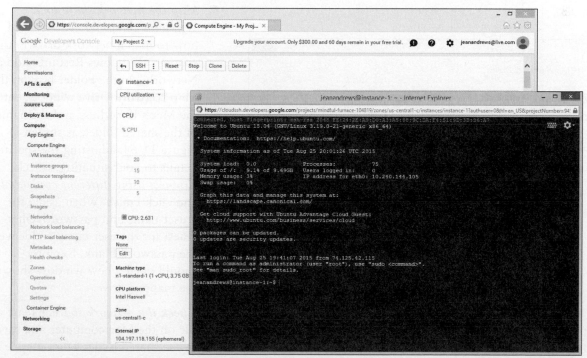

Source: Google and Canonical Ltd.

Figure 11-63 Google Cloud Platform serves up an instance of Ubuntu VM

> ✏️ **Notes** When you set up your Google Cloud account, your credit card information was required. If you're now done with your Google Cloud 60-day free trial, close your billing account so that your credit card will not be accidentally charged at the end of your free trial period. To do that, in the Developers Console, click the **Settings** cog icon and click **Billing**. Then click **Close billing account.**

REAL PROBLEM 11-2 Sharing a Folder on the Network from a Mac Computer and Mapping the Drive on a Windows Computer

In the chapter, "Windows Resources on a Network," you shared a folder on the network and mapped a network drive. These tasks can also be done in OS X, which makes it easier to share files between computers of various operating systems. Complete the following steps to set up a network share from a Mac computer:

1. *Create a folder to share.* Use Finder to create a subfolder in the Documents folder, and name the new folder **MeetingMinutes**.

2. *Set sharing options.* Open **System Preferences** and click **Sharing**. Select **File Sharing** in the sidebar and make sure it's turned on. Click the **Options** button and make sure that *Share files and folders using SMB* is checked. Under Windows File Sharing, check the box to turn on file sharing with Windows computers. Enter the Mac's user account password if necessary. Click **Done**.

3. *Share the folder.* Under Shared Folders, click the **+** button. Double-click the **MeetingMinutes** folder. Under Users, make sure the **Everyone** group is set to **Read Only**. Return to the System Preferences main window.

4. *Enable shared folders for the guest account.* Click **Users & Groups**. Click the lock icon in the lower-left corner of the window so you can make changes to user settings, and sign in. Click the **Guest User** account in the sidebar. Check *Allow guest users to connect to shared folders* and return to the main System Preferences window.

5. *Set a static IP address.* Click **Network**, and then click **Advanced**. Click the **TCP/IP** tab. Configure the IPv4 address with a manual address as directed by your instructor. Click **OK**.

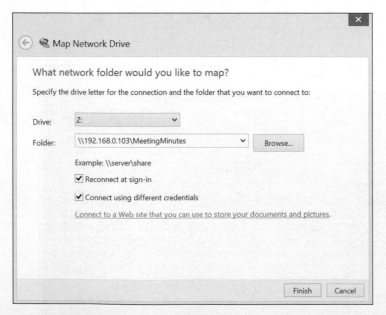

6. *Map the network share on a Windows computer.* You learned how to map a network drive in the chapter, "Windows Resources on a Network." In the Folder box on the Map Network Drive window, enter the Mac's IP address and the name of the shared folder, as shown in Figure 11-64, adjusting the specific details to your situation. Check *Connect using different credentials*, and click **Finish**. When asked for a user name and password, enter **Guest** for the user name and leave the password blank. Explorer should open a new window showing the mapped drive.

7. *Check the network share.* Create a file on the Mac computer and save it to the shared folder. Does it appear in the mapped network drive on the

Figure 11-64 Folder information includes the IP address of the remote computer and folder name

Windows computer? If not, troubleshoot and fix the problem. Create a file on the Windows computer and save it to the shared folder. Does the file appear in the shared folder on the Mac computer? What do you think went wrong? What setting do you need to change so you can add files to the shared folder from the Windows computer? Did it work? If not, troubleshoot and fix the problem.

8. *Change share permissions*. Currently the folder is shared with anyone on the network. This is fine in certain situations, but it's not a best practice for most corporate networks. What changes can you make to restrict the shared folder to a single user? To a group of users?

9. *Create a new user and a new group*. List the steps to create a new user and a new user group on the Mac computer. What types of user accounts are available? What did you name the new user account and the new user group? Add both the new user and your own user account to the new group. Change the share settings on the MeetingMinutes folder so that the new user group has read and write privileges, and the Everyone group has Read Only privileges.

10. *Take a screen shot and share it*. With the Sharing window showing these new settings, take a screen shot. To do this, press ⌘ + shift + 4, then press the spacebar. Click the Sharing window to capture a screen shot of the window. Drag the screen shot file from the desktop to the shared folder. Email this screen shot to your instructor.

11

APPENDIX A

Safety Procedures and Environmental Concerns

T his appendix covers how to stay safe and protect the equipment and the environment as you perform the duties of an IT support technician. We begin by understanding the properties and dangers of electricity.

MEASURES AND PROPERTIES OF ELECTRICITY

A+
220-902
5.1, 5.2
In our modern world, we take electricity for granted, and we miss it terribly when it's cut off. Nearly everyone depends on it, but few really understand it. A successful hardware technician is not one who tends to encounter failed processors, fried motherboards, smoking monitors, or frizzed hair. To avoid these excitements, you need to understand how to measure electricity and how to protect computer equipment from its damaging power.

Let's start with the basics. To most people, volts, ohms, joules, watts, and amps are vague terms that simply mean electricity. All these terms can be used to measure some characteristic of electricity, as listed in Table A-1.

Unit	Definition	Computer Example
Volt (for example, 115 V)	A measure of electrical force measured in volts. The symbol for volts is V.	A power supply steps down the voltage from the 115 V house current to 3.3, 5, and 12 V that computer components can use.
Amp or ampere (for example, 1.5 A)	An amp is a measure of electrical current. The symbol for amps is A.	An LCD monitor requires about 5 A to operate. A small laser printer uses about 2 A. An optical drive uses about 1 A.
Ohm (for example, 20 Ω)	An ohm is a measure of resistance to electricity. The symbol for ohm is Ω.	Current can flow in typical computer cables and wires with a resistance of near zero Ω (ohm).
Joule (for example, 500 J)	A measure of work or energy. One joule (pronounced "jewel") is the work required to push an electrical current of 1 A through a resistance of 1 Ω. The symbol for joule is J.	A surge suppressor (see Figure A-1) is rated in joules—the higher the better. The rating determines how much work it can expend before it can no longer protect the circuit from a power surge.
Watt (for example, 20 W)	A measure of electrical power. One watt is one joule per second and measures the total electrical power needed to operate a device. Watts can be calculated by multiplying volts by amps. The symbol for watts is W.	The power consumption of an LCD computer monitor is rated at about 14 W. A DVD burner uses about 25 W when burning a DVD.

Table A-1   Measures of electricity

Rating is 720 joules

Figure A-1   A surge suppressor protects electrical equipment from power surges and is rated in joules

> ✎ **Notes** To learn more about how volts, amps, ohms, joules, and watts measure the properties of electricity, see the content "Electricity and Multimeters" in the online content that accompanies this text at *cengagebrain.com*. To find out how to access this content, see the Preface to this text.

Now let's look at how electricity gets from one place to another and how it is used in house circuits and computers.

AC AND DC

Electricity can be either AC, alternating current, or DC, direct current. Alternating current (AC) goes back and forth, or oscillates, rather than traveling in only one direction. House current in the United States is AC and oscillates 60 times in one second (60 hertz). Voltage in the system is constantly alternating from positive to negative, which causes the electricity to flow first in one direction and then in the other. Voltage alternates from +115 V to 115 V. AC is the most economical way to transmit electricity to our homes and workplaces. By decreasing current and increasing voltage, we can force alternating current to travel great distances. When alternating current reaches its destination, it is made more suitable for driving our electrical devices by decreasing voltage and increasing current.

Direct current (DC) travels in only one direction and is the type of current that most electronic devices require, including computers. A rectifier is a device that converts AC to DC, and an inverter is a device that converts DC to AC. A transformer is a device that changes the ratio of voltage to current. The power supply used in computers is both a rectifier and a transformer.

Large transformers reduce the high voltage on power lines coming to your neighborhood to a lower voltage before the current enters your home. The transformer does not change the amount of power in this closed system; if it decreases voltage, it increases current. The overall power stays constant, but the ratio of voltage to current changes, as illustrated in Figure A-2.

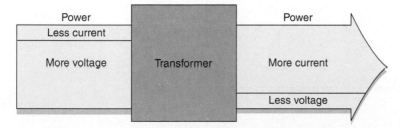

Figure A-2 A transformer keeps power constant but changes the ratio of current to voltage

Direct current flows in only one direction. Think of electrical current like a current of water that flows from a state of high pressure to a state of low pressure or rest. Electrical current flows from a high-pressure state (called hot) to a state of rest (called ground or neutral). For a power supply, a power line may be either +5 or -5 volts in one circuit, or +12 or -12 volts in another circuit. The positive or negative value is determined by how the circuit is oriented, either on one side of the power output or the other. Several circuits coming from the power supply accommodate different devices with different power requirements.

HOT, NEUTRAL, AND GROUND

AC travels on a hot line from the power station to a building and returns to the power station on a neutral line. When the two lines reach the building and enter an electrical device, such as a lamp, the device controls the flow of electricity between the hot and neutral lines. If an easier path (one with less resistance) is available, the electricity follows that path. This can cause a

A

short, a sudden increase in flow that can also create a sudden increase in temperature—enough to start a fire and injure both people and equipment. Never put yourself in a position where you are the path of least resistance between the hot line and ground!

> ⚡ **Caution**   It's very important that PC components be properly grounded. Never connect a PC to an outlet or use an extension cord that doesn't have the third ground plug. The third line can prevent a short from causing extreme damage. In addition, the bond between the neutral and ground helps eliminate electrical noise (stray electrical signals) within the PC that is sometimes caused by other electrical equipment sitting very close to the computer.

To prevent uncontrolled electricity in a short, the neutral line is grounded. Grounding a line means that the line is connected directly to the earth, so that, in the event of a short, the electricity flows into the earth and not back to the power station. Grounding serves as an escape route for out-of-control electricity because the earth is always capable of accepting a flow of current. With computers, a surge suppressor can be used to protect a computer and its components against power surges.

> ⚡ **Caution**   Beware of the different uses of black wire. In desktop computers and in DC circuits, black is used for ground, but in home wiring and in AC circuits, black is used for hot!

The neutral line to your house is grounded many times along its way (in fact, at each electrical pole) and is also grounded at the breaker box where the electricity enters your house. You can look at a three-prong plug and see the three lines: hot, neutral, and ground (see Figure A-3).

Neutral

Hot

Ground

Figure A-3   A polarized plug showing hot and neutral, and a three-prong plug showing hot, neutral, and ground

Notes House AC voltage in the United States is about 110–120 V, but know that in other countries, this is not always the case. In many other countries, the standard is 220 V. Outlet styles also vary from one country to the next.

Now that you know about electricity, let's turn our attention to protecting yourself against the dangers of electricity and other factors that might harm you as you work around computers.

PROTECTING YOURSELF

A+
220-902
5.1, 5.2

To protect yourself against electrical shock, when working with any electrical device, including computers, printers, scanners, and network devices, disconnect the power if you notice a dangerous situation that might lead to electrical shock or fire. When you disconnect the power, do so by pulling on the plug at the AC outlet. To protect the power cord, don't pull on the cord itself. Also, don't just turn off the on/off switch on the device; you need to actually disconnect the power. Note that any of the following can indicate a potential danger:

- The power cord is frayed or otherwise damaged in any way.
- Water or other liquid is on the floor around the device or spilled on it.
- The device has been exposed to excess moisture.
- The device has been dropped or you notice physical damage.
- You smell a strong electronics odor.
- The power supply or fans are making a whining noise.
- You notice smoke coming from the computer case or the case feels unusually warm.

SAFELY WORK INSIDE COMPUTERS, PRINTERS, AND OTHER ELECTRICAL DEVICES

A+
220-902
5.1, 5.2

To personally stay safe, always do the following, before working inside computers, printers, and other electrical devices:

- *Remove jewelry.* Remove your jewelry that might come in contact with components. Jewelry is made of metal and might conduct electricity if it touches a component. It can also get caught in cables and cords inside computer cases.
- *Power down the system and unplug it.* For a computer, unplug the power, monitor, mouse, and keyboard cables, and any other peripherals or cables attached and move them out of your way.
- *For a computer, press and hold down the power button for a moment.* After you unplug the computer, press the power button for about three seconds to completely drain the power supply. Sometimes when you do so, you'll hear the fans quickly start and go off as residual power is drained. Only then is it safe to work inside the case.

ELECTRICAL FIRE SAFETY

A+
220-902
5.1

Never use water to put out a fire fueled by electricity because water is a conductor and you might get a severe electrical shock. A computer lab needs a fire extinguisher that is rated to put out electrical fires. Fire extinguishers are rated by the type of fires they put out:

- Class A extinguishers can use water to put out fires caused by wood, paper, and other combustibles.
- Class B extinguishers can put out fires caused by liquids such as gasoline, kerosene, and oil.
- Class C fire extinguishers use nonconductive chemicals to put out a fire caused by electricity. See Figure A-4.

A

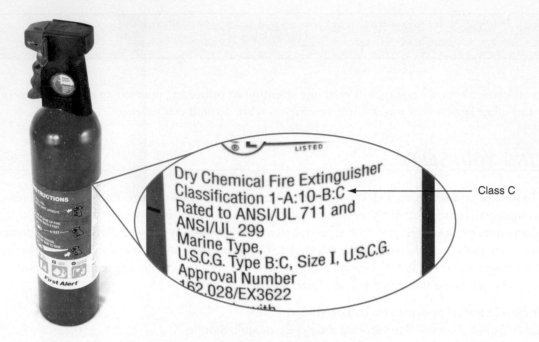

Class C

Figure A-4   A Class C fire extinguisher is rated to put out electrical fires

PROPER USE OF CLEANING PADS AND SOLUTIONS

A+
220-902
5.1, 5.2

As a support technician, you'll find yourself collecting different cleaning solutions and cleaning pads to clean a variety of devices, including the mouse and keyboard, CDs, DVDs, Blu-ray discs and their drives, tapes and tape drives, and monitors. Figure A-5 shows a few of these products. For example, the contact cleaner in the figure is used to clean the contacts on the edge connectors of expansion cards; the cleaning can solve a problem with a faulty connection.

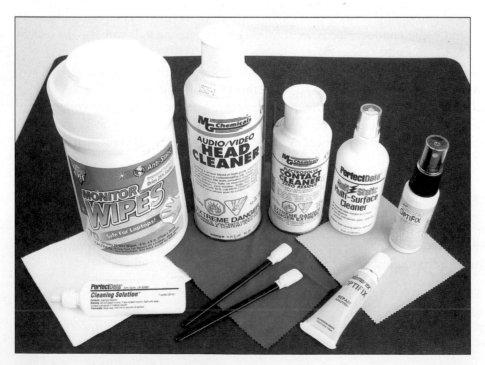

Figure A-5   Cleaning solutions and pads

Most of these cleaning solutions contain flammable and poisonous materials. Take care when using them so that they don't get on your skin or in your eyes. To find out what to do if you are accidentally exposed to a dangerous solution, look on the instructions printed on the can or check out the material safety data sheet (see Figure A-6). A material safety data sheet (MSDS) explains how to properly handle substances such as chemical solvents and how to dispose of them.

An MSDS includes information such as physical data, toxicity, health effects, first aid, storage, shipping, disposal, and spill procedures. It comes packaged with the chemical; you can order one from the manufacturer, or you can find one on the Internet (see *www.ilpi.com/msds*).

★ **A+ Exam Tip** The A+ 220-901 exam expects you to know how to use MSDS documentation to find out how to dispose of chemicals so as to help protect the environment. You also need to know that you must follow all local government regulations when disposing of chemicals and other materials dangerous to the environment.

If you have an accident with these or other dangerous products, your company or organization might require you to report the accident to your company and/or fill out an incident report. Check with your organization to find out how to handle reporting these types of incidents.

Figure A-6 Each chemical you use should have a material safety data sheet available

MANAGING CABLES

A+
220-902
5.1

People can trip over cables or cords left on the floor, so be careful that cables are in a safe place. If you must run a cable across a path or where someone sits, use a cable or cord cover that can be nailed or screwed to the floor. Don't leave loose cables or cords in a traffic area where people can trip over them (called a trip hazard).

LIFTING HEAVY OBJECTS

A+
220-902
5.1

Back injury, caused by lifting heavy objects, is one of the most common injuries that happen at work. Whenever possible, put heavy objects, such as a large laser printer, on a cart to move them. If you do need to lift a heavy object, follow these guidelines to keep from injuring your back:

1. Looking at the object, decide which side of the object to face so that the load is the most balanced.

2. Stand close to the object with your feet apart.

3. Keeping your back straight, bend your knees and grip the load.

4. Lift with your legs, arms, and shoulders, and not with your back or stomach.

5. Keep the load close to your body and avoid twisting your body while you're holding it.

6. To put the object down, keep your back as straight as you can and lower the object by bending your knees.

Don't try to lift an object that is too heavy for you. Because there are no exact guidelines for when heavy is too heavy, use your best judgment as to when to ask for help.

SAFETY GOGGLES AND AIR FILTER MASK

If you are required to work in an environment such as a factory where flying fragments, chips, or other particles are about, your employer might require you wear safety goggles to protect your eyes. In addition, if the air is filled with dust or other contaminants, your employer might require you to wear an air-purifying respirator, commonly called an air filter mask, which filters the dust and other contaminants from the air you breathe. If safety goggles or a mask is required, your employer is responsible for providing you one that is appropriate for the environment in which you are working.

PROTECTING THE EQUIPMENT

As you learn to troubleshoot and solve computer problems, you gradually begin to realize that many problems you face could have been avoided by good computer maintenance that includes protecting the computer against environmental factors such as humidity, dust, and out-of-control electricity.

PROTECT THE EQUIPMENT AGAINST STATIC ELECTRICITY OR ESD

Suppose you come indoors on a cold day, pick up a comb, and touch your hair. Sparks fly! What happened? Static electricity caused the sparks. Electrostatic discharge (ESD), commonly known as static electricity, is an electrical charge at rest. When you came indoors, this charge built up on your hair and had no place to go. An ungrounded conductor (such as wire that is not touching another wire) or a nonconductive surface (such as your hair) holds a charge until the charge is released. When two objects with dissimilar electrical charges touch, electricity passes between them until the dissimilar charges become equal.

To see static charges equalizing, turn off the lights in a room, scuff your feet on the carpet, and touch another person. Occasionally, you can see and feel the charge in your fingers. If you can feel the charge, you discharged at least 1500 volts of static electricity. If you hear the discharge, you released at least 6000 volts. If you see the discharge, you released at least 8000 volts of ESD. A charge of only 10 volts can damage electronic components! *You can touch a chip on an expansion card or motherboard, damage the chip with ESD, and never feel, hear, or see the electrical discharge.*

ESD can cause two types of damage in an electronic component: catastrophic failure and upset failure. A catastrophic failure destroys the component beyond use. An upset failure damages the component so that it does not perform well, even though it may still function to some degree. Upset failures are more difficult to detect because they are not consistent and not easily observed. Both types of failures permanently affect the device. Components are easily damaged by ESD, but because the damage might not show up for weeks or months, a technician is likely to get careless and not realize the damage he or she is doing.

> ⚡ **Caution**   Unless you are measuring power levels with a multimeter or power supply tester, never, ever touch a component or cable inside a computer case while the power is on. The electrical voltage is not enough to seriously hurt you but more than enough to permanently damage the component.

Before touching or handling a component (for example, a hard drive, motherboard, expansion card, processor, or memory modules), to protect it against ESD, always ground yourself first. You can ground yourself and the computer parts by using one or more of the following static control devices or methods:

▲ ***ESD strap.*** An ESD strap, also called a ground bracelet, antistatic wrist strap, or ESD bracelet, is a strap you wear around your wrist. The strap has a cord attached with an alligator clip on the end. Attach the clip to the computer case you're working on, as shown in Figure A-7. Any static electricity between you and the case is now discharged. Therefore, as you work inside the case, you will not damage the components with static electricity. The bracelet also contains a resistor that prevents electricity from harming you.

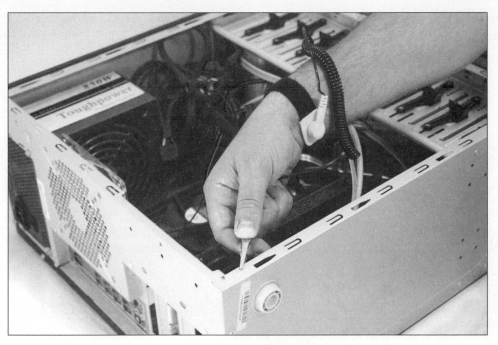

Figure A-7   A ground bracelet, which protects computer components from ESD, can clip to the side of the computer case and eliminate ESD between you and the case

> **⚡ Caution**   When working on a laser printer, *don't* wear the ESD strap because you don't want to be the ground for these high-voltage devices.

A

◢ ***Ground mats.*** A ground mat, also called an ESD mat, dissipates ESD and is commonly used by bench technicians (also called depot technicians) who repair and assemble computers at their workbenches or in an assembly line. Ground mats have a connector in one corner that you can use to connect the mat to the ground (see Figure A-8). If you lift a component off the mat, it is no longer grounded and is susceptible to ESD, so it's important to use an ESD strap with a ground mat.

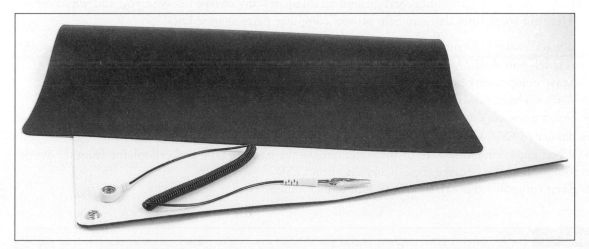

Figure A-8   An ESD mat dissipates ESD and should be connected to the ground

◢ ***Static shielding bags.*** New components come shipped in static shielding bags, also called antistatic bags. These bags are a type of Faraday cage, named after Michael Faraday, who built the first cage in 1836. A Faraday cage is any device that protects against an electromagnetic field. Save the bags to store other devices that are not currently installed in a computer. As you work on a computer, know that a device is not protected from ESD if you place it on top of the bag; the protection is inside the bag (see Figure A-9).

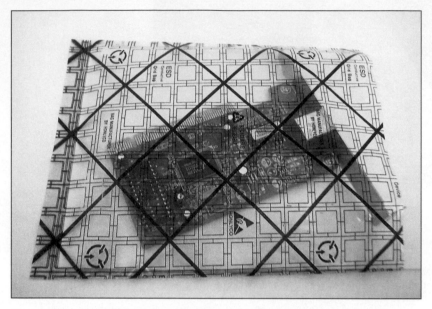

Figure A-9   An antistatic bag help protect components from ESD

> ⚡ **Caution**   A CRT monitor can also damage components with ESD. Don't place or store expansion cards on top of or next to a CRT monitor, which can discharge as much as 29,000 volts onto the screen.

The best way to guard against ESD is to use an ESD strap together with a ground mat. Consider an ESD strap essential equipment when working on a computer. However, if you are in a situation in which you must work without one, touch the computer case or the power supply before you touch a component in the case, which is called self-grounding. Self-grounding dissipates any charge between you and whatever you touch. Here are some rules that can help protect computer parts against ESD:

◢ *Rule 1:* When passing a circuit board, memory module, or other sensitive component to another person, ground yourself and then touch the other person before you pass the component.
◢ *Rule 2:* Leave components inside their protective bags until you are ready to use them.
◢ *Rule 3:* Work on hard floors, not carpet, or use antistatic spray on the carpets.
◢ *Rule 4:* Don't work on a computer if you or the computer have just come in from the cold because there is more danger of ESD when the atmosphere is cold and dry.
◢ *Rule 5:* When unpacking hardware or software, remove the packing tape and cellophane from the work area as soon as possible because these materials attract ESD.
◢ *Rule 6:* Keep components away from your hair and clothing.

> ★ **A+ Exam Tip**   The A+ 220-901 exam emphasizes that you should know how to protect computer equipment as you work on it, including how to protect components against damage from ESD.

Hands-On | Project A-1 Practice Handling Computer Components

Working with a partner, you'll need some computer parts and the antistatic tools you learned about in this part of the chapter. Practice touching, picking up, and passing the parts between you. As you do so, follow the rules to protect the parts against ESD. Have a third person watch as you work and point out any ways you might have exposed a part to ESD. As you work, be careful to not touch components on circuit boards or the gold fingers on the edge connector of an expansion card. When you are finished, store the parts in antistatic bags.

PHYSICALLY PROTECT YOUR EQUIPMENT FROM THE ENVIRONMENT

**A+
220-902
5.2**

When you protect equipment from ongoing problems with the environment, you are likely to have fewer problems later, and the less troubleshooting and repair you will have to do. Here is how you can physically protect a computer:

▲ *Protect a computer against dust and other airborne particles.* When a computer must sit in a dusty environment, around those who smoke, or where pets might leave hair, you can:

▲ Use a plastic keyboard cover to protect the keyboard. When the computer is turned off, cover the entire system with a protective cover or enclosure.

▲ Install air filters over the front or side vents of the case where air flows into the case. Put your hand over the case of a running computer to feel where the air flows in. For most systems, air flows in from the front vents or vents on the side of the case that is near the processor cooler. The air filter shown in Figure A-10 has magnets that hold the filter to the case when screw holes are not available.

A

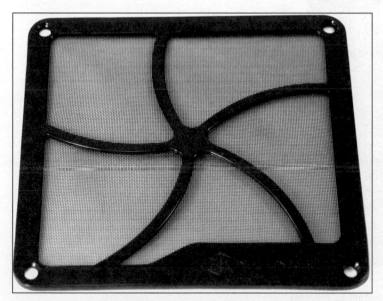

Figure A-10   This air filter is designed to fit over a case fan, power supply fan, or panel vent on the case

▲ Whenever you have the case cover open, be sure to use compressed air or an antistatic vacuum (see Figure A-11) to remove dust from inside the case. Figure A-12 shows a case fan that jammed because of dust and caused a system to overheat. And while you're cleaning up dust, don't forget to blow or vacuum out the keyboard.

> ✎ **Notes**   When working at a customer site, be sure to clean up any mess you created by blowing dust out of a computer case or keyboard.

Figure A-11   An antistatic vacuum designed to work inside sensitive electronic equipment such as computers and printers

Figure A-12   This dust-jammed case fan caused a system to overheat

◢ *Allow for good ventilation inside and outside the system.* Proper air circulation is essential to keeping a system cool. Don't block air vents on the front and rear of the computer case or on the monitor. Inside the case, make sure cables are tied up and out of the way so as to allow for airflow and not obstruct fans from turning. Put covers on expansion slot openings on the rear of the case and put faceplates over empty bays on the front of the case. Don't set a tower case directly on thick carpet because the air vent on the bottom front of the case can be blocked. If you are concerned about overheating, monitor temperatures inside and outside the case.

⭐ **A+ Exam Tip** The A+ 220–901 exam expects you to know how to keep computers and monitors well ventilated and to use protective enclosures and air filters to protect the equipment from airborne particles.

◢ *High temperatures and humidity can be dangerous for hard drives.* I once worked in a basement with PCs, and hard drives failed much too often. After we installed dehumidifiers, the hard drives became more reliable. If you suspect a problem with humidity, you can use a hygrometer to monitor the humidity in a room. High temperatures can also damage computer equipment, and you should take precautions to not allow a computer to overheat.

✎ **Notes** A server room where computers stay and people generally don't stay for long hours is set to balance what is good for the equipment and to conserve energy. Low temperature and moderate humidity are best for the equipment, although no set standards exist for either. Temperatures might be set from 65 to 70 degrees F, and humidity between 30 percent and 50 percent, although some companies keep their server rooms at 80 degrees F to conserve energy. A data center where both computers and people stay is usually kept at a comfortable temperature and humidity for humans.

◢ *Protect electrical equipment from power surges.* Lightning and other electrical power surges can destroy computers and other electrical equipment. If the house or office building does not have surge protection equipment installed at the breaker box, be sure to install a protective device at each computer. The least expensive device is a power strip that is also a surge suppressor, although you might want to use a UPS for added protection.

Lightning can also get to your equipment across network cabling coming in through an Internet connection. To protect against lightning, use a surge suppressor such as the one shown in Figure A-13 in line between the ISP device (for example, a DSL modem or cable modem) and the computer or home router to protect it from spikes across the network cables. Notice the cord on the surge suppressor, which connects it to ground.

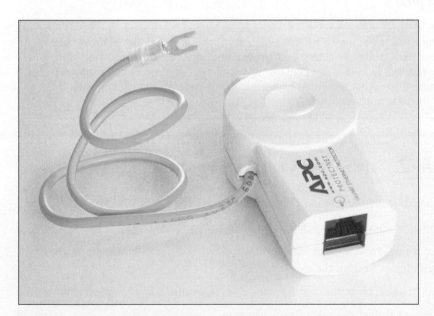

Figure A-13 Surge protector by APC for Ethernet lines

An uninterruptible power supply (UPS) is a device that raises the voltage when it drops during brownouts or sags (temporary voltage reductions). A UPS also does double-duty as a surge suppressor to protect the system against power surges or spikes. In addition, a UPS can serve as a battery backup to provide power for a brief time during a total blackout long enough for you to save your work and shut down the system.

A

A UPS is not as essential for a laptop computer as it is for a desktop because a laptop has a battery that can sustain it during a blackout.

A common UPS device is a rather heavy box that plugs into an AC outlet and provides one or more outlets for the computer and the monitor (see Figure A-14). It has an on/off switch, requires no maintenance, and is very simple to install. Use it to provide uninterruptible power to your desktop computer and monitor. It's best not to connect it to nonessential devices such as a laser printer or scanner.

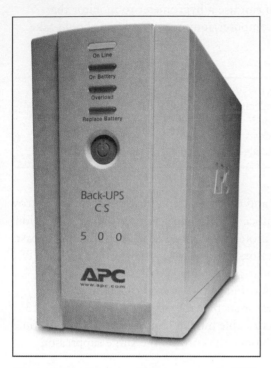 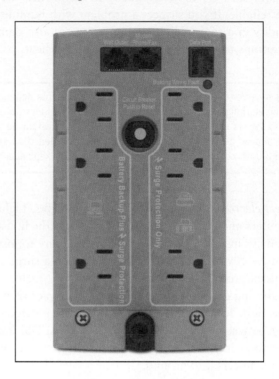

Figure A-14   Uninterruptible power supply (UPS)

✎ Notes   Whenever a power outage occurs, unless you have a reliable power conditioner installed at the breaker box in your house or building, unplug all power cords to the computers, printers, monitors, and the like. Sometimes when the power returns, sudden spikes are accompanied by another brief outage. You don't want to subject your equipment to these surges. When buying a surge suppressor, look for those that guarantee against damage from lightning and that reimburse for equipment destroyed while the surge suppressor is in use.

Hands-On | Project A-2   Safely Clean Computer Equipment

Practice some preventive maintenance tasks by following these steps to clean a computer:

1. Shut down the computer and unplug it. Press the power button to drain power.

2. Clean the keyboard, monitor, and mouse. For a wheel mouse, remove the ball and clean the wheels. Clean the outside of the computer case. Don't forget to clean the mouse pad.

3. Open the case and using a ground bracelet, clean the dust from the case. Make sure all fans move freely.

4. Verify the cables are out of the way of airflow. Use cable ties as necessary.

5. Check that each expansion card and memory module is securely seated in its slot.

6. Power up the system and make sure all is working.

7. Clean up around your work area. If you left dust on the floor as you blew it out of the computer case, be sure to clean it up.

PROTECTING THE ENVIRONMENT

A+
220-902
5.1, 5.2

IT support technicians need to be aware that we can do damage to the environment if we carelessly dispose of used computer equipment improperly. As a support technician, one day you're sure to face an assortment of useless equipment and consumables (see Figure A-15).

Before you decide to trash it all, take a moment and ask yourself if some of the equipment can be donated or at least recycled. Think about fixing up an old computer and donating it to a needy middle school student. If you don't have the time for that, consider donating to the local computer repair class. The class can fix the computers up as a class project and donate them to young students.

Figure A-15 Keep, trash, recycle, or donate?

When disposing of any type of equipment or consumables, make sure to comply with local government environmental regulations. Table A-2 lists some items and how to dispose of them.

Part	How to Dispose
Alkaline batteries, including AAA, AA, A, C, D, and 9-volt	Dispose of these batteries in the regular trash. First check to see if there are recycling facilities in your area.
Button batteries used in digital cameras and other small equipment; battery packs used in notebooks	These batteries can contain silver oxide, mercury, lithium, or cadmium and are considered toxic waste that require special toxic waste handling. Dispose of them by returning them to the original dealer or by taking them to a recycling center. To recycle, pack them separately from other items. If you don't have a recycling center nearby, contact your county for local regulations for disposal.
Laser printer toner cartridges	Return these to the manufacturer or dealer to be recycled.
Ink-jet printer cartridges, computer cases, power supplies, and other computer parts, monitors, chemical solvents, and their containers	Check with local county or environmental officials for laws and regulations in your area for proper disposal of these items. The county might have a recycling center that will receive them. Discharge a CRT monitor before disposing of it. See the MSDS documents for chemicals to know how to dispose of them.
Storage media such as hard drives, CDs, DVDs, and BDs	Do physical damage to the device so it is not possible for sensitive data to be stolen. Then the device can be recycled or put in the trash. Your organization might be required to meet legal requirements to destroy data. If so, make sure you understand these requirements and how to comply with them.

Table A-2 Computer parts and how to dispose of them

> ★ **A+ Exam Tip** The A+ 220–901 exam expects you to know to follow environmental guidelines to dispose of batteries, laser printer toner, and CRT monitors, chemical solvents, and containers. If you're not certain how to dispose of a product, see its MSDS document.

Be sure a CRT monitor is discharged before you dispose of it. Most CRT monitors are designed to discharge after sitting unplugged for 60 minutes. It can be manually discharged by using a high-voltage probe with the monitor case opened. Ask a technician trained to service monitors to do this for you.

> 🖉 **Notes** Go to *www.youtube.com* and search on "discharge a CRT monitor" to see some interesting videos that demonstrate the charge inside a monitor long after the monitor is turned off and unplugged. As for proper procedures, I'm not endorsing all these videos; just watch for fun.

Hands-On | Project A-3   Research Disposal Rules

Research the laws and regulations in your community concerning the disposal of batteries and old computer parts. Answer these questions regarding your community:

1. How do you properly dispose of a monitor?

2. How do you properly dispose of a battery pack used by a notebook computer?

3. How do you properly dispose of a large box of assorted computer parts, including hard drives, optical drives, computer cases, and circuit boards?

>> KEY TERMS

For explanations of key terms, see the Glossary for this text.

air filter mask	direct current (DC)	joule	static electricity
alternating current (AC)	electrostatic	material safety data	surge suppressor
amp	discharge (ESD)	sheet (MSDS)	transformer
antistatic bag	ESD mat	ohm	trip hazard
antistatic wrist strap	ESD strap	rectifier	uninterruptible power
brownout	ground bracelet	safety goggles	supply (UPS)
Class C fire	ground mat	sag	volt
extinguisher	inverter	self-grounding	watt

APPENDIX B

Entry Points for Startup Processes

This appendix contains a summary of the entry points that can affect Windows 8/7/Vista startup. The entry points include startup folders, Group Policy folders, the Scheduled Tasks folder, and registry keys.

Programs and shortcuts to programs are stored in these startup folders:

- C:\Users*username*\AppData\Roaming\Microsoft\Windows\Start\Menu\Programs\Startup
- C:\ProgramData\Microsoft\Windows\Start Menu\Programs\Startup

Startup and shutdown scripts used by Group Policy are stored in these folders:

- C:\Windows\System32\GroupPolicy\Machine\Scripts\Startup
- C:\Windows\System32\GroupPolicy\Machine\Scripts\Shutdown
- C:\Windows\System32\GroupPolicy\User\Scripts\Logon
- C:\Windows\System32\GroupPolicy\User\Scripts\Logoff

Scheduled tasks are stored in this folder:

- C:\Windows\System32\Tasks

To see a list of scheduled tasks, enter the **schtasks** command in a command prompt window. These keys cause an entry to run once and only once at startup:

- HKLM\Software\Microsoft\Windows\CurrentVersion\RunOnce
- HKLM\Software\Microsoft\Windows\CurrentVersion\RunServiceOnce
- HKLM\Software\Microsoft\Windows\CurrentVersion\RunServicesOnce
- HKCU\Software\Microsoft\Windows\CurrentVersion\RunOnce

Group Policy places entries in the following keys to affect startup:

- HKCU\Software\Microsoft\Windows\CurrentVersion\Policies\Explorer\Run
- HKLM\Software\Microsoft\Windows\CurrentVersion\Policies\Explorer\Run

Windows loads many DLL programs from the following key, which is sometimes used by malicious software. Don't delete one unless you know it's causing a problem:

- HKLM\Software\Microsoft\Windows\CurrentVersion\ShellServiceObjectDelayLoad

Entries in the keys listed next apply to all users and hold legitimate startup entries. Don't delete an entry unless you suspect it to be bad:

- HKLM\Software\Microsoft\Windows\CurrentVersion\Run
- HKCU\Software\Microsoft\Windows NT\CurrentVersion\Windows
- HKCU\Software\Microsoft\Windows NT\CurrentVersion\Windows\Run
- HKCU\Software\Microsoft\Windows\CurrentVersion\Run

These keys and their subkeys contain entries that pertain to background services that are sometimes launched at startup:

- HKLM\Software\Microsoft\Windows\CurrentVersion\RunService
- HKLM\Software\Microsoft\Windows\CurrentVersion\RunServices

The following key contains a value named BootExecute, which is normally set to autochk. It causes the system to run a type of Chkdsk program to check for hard drive integrity when it was previously shut down improperly. Sometimes another program adds itself to this value, causing a problem. For more information about this situation, see the Microsoft Knowledge Base article 151376, "How to Disable Autochk If It Stops Responding During Reboot," at *support.microsoft.com*.

- HKLM\System\CurrentControlSet\Control\Session Manager

Here is an assorted list of registry keys that have all been known to cause various problems at startup. Remember, before you delete a program entry from one of these keys, research the program file name so that you won't accidentally delete something you want to keep:

- HKCU\Software\Microsoft\Command
- HKCU\Software\Microsoft\Command Processor\AutoRun
- HKCU\Software\Microsoft\Windows\CurrentVersion\RunOnce\Setup
- HKCU\Software\Microsoft\Windows NT\CurrentVersion\Windows\load
- HKLM\Software\Microsoft\Windows NT\CurrentVersion\Windows\AppInit_DLLs
- HKLM\Software\Microsoft\Windows NT\CurrentVersion\Winlogon\System
- HKLM\Software\Microsoft\Windows NT\CurrentVersion\Winlogon\Us
- HKCR\batfile\shell\open\command
- HKCR\comfile\shell\open\command
- HKCR\exefile\shell\open\command
- HKCR\htafile\shell\open\command
- HKCR\piffile\shell\open\command
- HKCR\scrfile\shell\open\command

Finally, check out the subkeys in the following key, which apply to 32-bit programs installed in a 64-bit version of Windows:

- HKLM\Software\Wow6432Node

Other ways in which processes can be launched at startup:

- Services can be set to launch at startup. To manage services, use the Services Console (services.msc).
- Device drivers are launched at startup. For a listing of installed devices, use Device Manager (devmgmt.msc) or the System Information Utility (msinfo32.exe).

B

CompTIA A+ Acronyms

CompTIA provides a list of acronyms that you need to know before you sit for the A+ exams. You can download the list from the CompTIA website at *www.comptia.org*. The list is included here for your convenience. However, CompTIA occasionally updates the list, so be sure to check the CompTIA website for the latest version.

Acronym	Spelled Out
AC	alternating current
ACL	access control list
ACPI	advanced configuration power interface
ACT	activity
ADSL	asymmetrical digital subscriber line
AGP	accelerated graphics port
AHCI	Advanced host controller interface
AP	Access point
APIPA	automatic private internet protocol addressing
APM	advanced power management
ARP	address resolution protocol
ASR	automated system recovery
ATA	advanced technology attachment
ATAPI	advanced technology attachment packet interface
ATM	asynchronous transfer mode
ATX	advanced technology extended
AUP	Acceptable Use Policy
A/V	Audio Video
BIOS	basic input/output system
BNC	Bayonet-Neill-Concelman or British Naval Connector
BTX	balanced technology extended
CAPTCHA	Completely Automated Public Turing Test To Tell Computers and Humans Apart
CCFL	Cold Cathode Fluorescent Lamp
CD	compact disc
CD-ROM	compact disc-read-only memory
CD-RW	compact disc-rewritable
CDFS	compact disc file system
CFS	Central File System, Common File System, Command File System
CIFS	Common Internet File System
CMOS	complementary metal-oxide semiconductor
CNR	Communications and Networking Riser
COMx	communication port (x=port number)
CPU	central processing unit
CRT	cathode-ray tube
DAC	discretionary access control
DB-25	serial communications D-shell connector, 25 pins
DB-9	9 pin D shell connector
DC	direct current
DDOS	distributed denial of service
DDR	double data-rate
DDR RAM	double data-rate random access memory
DDR SDRAM	double data-rate synchronous dynamic random access memory

Acronym	Spelled Out
DFS	distributed file system
DHCP	dynamic host configuration protocol
DIMM	dual inline memory module
DIN	Deutsche Industrie Norm
DLT	digital linear tape
DLP	digital light processing
DMA	direct memory access
DMZ	demilitarized zone
DNS	domain name service or domain name server
DOS	denial of service
DRAM	dynamic random access memory
DRM	Digital Rights Management
DSL	digital subscriber line
DVD	digital video disc or digital versatile disc
DVD-RAM	digital video disc-random access memory
DVD-ROM	digital video disc-read only memory
DVD-R	digital video disc-recordable
DVD-RW	digital video disc-rewritable
DVI	digital visual interface
ECC	error correcting code/error checking and correction
ECP	extended capabilities port
EEPROM	electrically erasable programmable read-only memory
EFS	encrypting file system
EIDE	enhanced integrated drive electronics
EMI	electromagnetic interference
EMP	electromagnetic pulse
EPROM	erasable programmable read-only memory
EPP	enhanced parallel port
ERD	emergency repair disk
ESD	electrostatic discharge
EULA	End User License Agreement
EVGA	extended video graphics adapter/array
EVDO	evolution data optimized or evolution data only
FAT	file allocation table
FAT12	12-bit file allocation table
FAT16	16-bit file allocation table
FAT32	32-bit file allocation table
FDD	floppy disk drive
Fn	Function (referring to the function key on a laptop)
FPM	fast page-mode
FRU	field replaceable unit
FSB	Front Side Bus

C

Acronym	Spelled Out
FTP	file transfer protocol
FQDN	fully qualified domain name
Gb	gigabit
GB	gigabyte
GDI	graphics device interface
GHz	gigahertz
GUI	graphical user interface
GPS	global positioning system
GSM	global system for mobile communications
HAL	hardware abstraction layer
HAV	Hardware Assisted Virtualization
HCL	hardware compatibility list
HDD	hard disk drive
HDMI	high definition media interface
HPFS	high performance file system
HTML	hypertext markup language
HTPC	home theater PC
HTTP	hypertext transfer protocol
HTTPS	hypertext transfer protocol over secure sockets layer
I/O	input/output
ICMP	internet control message protocol
ICR	intelligent character recognition
IDE	integrated drive electronics
IDS	Intrusion Detection System
IEEE	Institute of Electrical and Electronics Engineers
IIS	Internet Information Services
IMAP	internet mail access protocol
IMEI	International Mobile Equipment Identity
IMSI	International Mobile Subscriber Identity
IP	internet protocol
IPCONFIG	internet protocol configuration
IPP	internet printing protocol
IPS	In-plane Switching
IPSEC	Internet Protocol Security
IR	Infrared
IrDA	Infrared Data Association
IRP	Incident Response Plan
IRQ	Interrupt Request
ISDN	Integrated Services Digital Network
ISO	International Organization for Standardization/Industry Standards Organization
ISP	Internet Service Provider
JBOD	Just a Bunch of Disks

Acronym	Spelled Out
Kb	Kilobit
KB	Kilobyte or Knowledge Base
LAN	Local Area Network
LBA	Logical Block Addressing
LC	Lucent Connector
LCD	liquid Crystal Display
LDAP	lightweight directory access protocol
LED	light emitting diode
Li-on	lithium-ion
LPD/LPR	line printer daemon / line printer remote
LPT	line printer terminal
LVD	low voltage differential
MAC	media access control / mandatory access control
MAPI	messaging application programming interface
MAU	media access unit, media attachment unit
Mb	megabit
MB	megabyte
MBR	master boot record
MBSA	Microsoft Baseline Security Analyzer
MFD	multi-function device
MFP	multi-function product
MHz	megahertz
MicroDIMM	micro dual inline memory module
MIDI	musical instrument digital interface
MIME	multipurpose internet mail extension
MIMO	Multiple Input Multiple Output
MMC	Microsoft management console
MP3	Moving Picture Experts Group Layer 3 Audio
MP4	Moving Picture Experts Group Layer 4
MPEG	Moving Picture Experts Group
MSCONFIG	Microsoft configuration
MSDS	material safety data sheet
MUI	multilingual user interface
NAC	network access control
NAS	network-attached storage
NAT	network address translation
NetBIOS	networked basic input/output system
NetBEUI	networked basic input/output system extended user interface
NFS	network file system
NIC	network interface card
NiCd	nickel cadmium
NiMH	nickel metal hydride

C

Acronym	Spelled Out
NLX	new low-profile extended
NNTP	network news transfer protocol
NTFS	new technology file system
NTLDR	new technology loader
NTP	Network Time Protocol
OCR	optical character recognition
OEM	original equipment manufacturer
OLED	Organic Light Emitting Diode
OS	operating system
PAN	personal area network
PATA	parallel advanced technology attachment
PC	personal computer
PCI	peripheral component interconnect
PCIe	peripheral component interconnect express
PCIX	peripheral component interconnect extended
PCL	printer control language
PCMCIA	Personal Computer Memory Card International Association
PE	Preinstallation Environment
PGA	pin grid array
PGA2	pin grid array 2
PII	Personally Identifiable Information
PIN	personal identification number
PKI	public key infrastructure
PnP	plug and play
POP3	post office protocol 3
PoS	Point of Sale
POST	power-on self test
POTS	plain old telephone service
PPP	point-to-point protocol
PPTP	point-to-point tunneling protocol
PRI	primary rate interface
PROM	programmable read-only memory
PS/2	personal system/2 connector
PSTN	public switched telephone network
PSU	power supply unit
PVC	permanent virtual circuit
PXE	preboot execution environment
QoS	quality of service
RAID	redundant array of independent (or inexpensive) discs
RAM	random access memory
RAS	remote access service
RDP	Remote Desktop Protocol

Acronym	Spelled Out
RF	radio frequency
RFI	radio frequency interference
RGB	red green blue
RIP	routing information protocol
RIS	remote installation service
RISC	reduced instruction set computer
RJ-11	registered jack function 11
RJ-45	registered jack function 45
RMA	returned materials authorization
ROM	read only memory
RTC	real-time clock
SAN	storage area network
SAS	Serial Attached SCSI
SATA	serial advanced technology attachment
SC	subscription channel
SCP	secure copy protection
SCSI	small computer system interface
SCSI ID	small computer system interface identifier
SD card	secure digital card
SDRAM	synchronous dynamic random access memory
SEC	single edge connector
SFC	system file checker
SFF	Small Form Factor
SLI	scalable link interface or system level integration or scanline interleave mode
S.M.A.R.T.	self-monitoring, analysis, and reporting technology
SMB	server message block or small to midsize business
SMTP	simple mail transfer protocol
SNMP	simple network management protocol
SoDIMM	small outline dual inline memory module
SOHO	small office/home office
SP	service pack
SPDIF	Sony-Philips digital interface format
SPGA	staggered pin grid array
SRAM	static random access memory
SSH	secure shell
SSID	service set identifier
SSL	secure sockets layer
ST	straight tip
STP	shielded twisted pair
SXGA	super extended graphics array
TB	terabyte
TCP	transmission control protocol

C

Acronym	Spelled Out
TCP/IP	transmission control protocol/internet protocol
TDR	time domain reflectometer
TFTP	trivial file transfer protocol
TKIP	Temporal Key Integrity Protocol
TPM	trusted platform module
UAC	user account control
UDF	user defined functions or universal disk format or universal data format
UDP	user datagram protocol
UEFI	Unified Extensible Firmware Interface
UNC	universal naming convention
UPS	uninterruptible power supply
URL	uniform resource locator
USB	universal serial bus
USMT	user state migration tool
UTP	unshielded twisted pair
UXGA	ultra extended graphics array
VESA	Video Electronics Standards Association
VFAT	virtual file allocation table
VGA	video graphics array
VM	Virtual Machine
VoIP	voice over internet protocol
VPN	virtual private network
VRAM	video random access memory
WAN	wide area network
WAP	wireless access protocol/wireless access point
WEP	wired equivalent privacy
WIFI	wireless fidelity
WINS	windows internet name service
WLAN	wireless local area network
WPA	wireless protected access
WPS	WiFi Protected Setup
WUXGA	wide ultra extended graphics array
XGA	extended graphics array
ZIF	zero-insertion-force
ZIP	zigzag inline package

GLOSSARY

Software Key Terms

32-bit operating system Type of operating system that processes 32 bits at a time.

64-bit operating system Type of operating system that processes 64 bits at a time.

802.11 a/b/g/n/ac The collective name for the IEEE 802.11 standards for local wireless networking, which is the technical name for Wi-Fi.

A+ Certification A certification awarded by CompTIA (The Computer Technology Industry Association) that measures an IT technician's knowledge and skills.

accelerometer A type of gyroscope used in mobile devices to sense the physical position of the device.

acceptable use policy (AUP) A document that explains to users what they can and cannot do on the corporate network or with company data, and the penalties for violations.

access control list (ACL) A record or list of the resources (for example, a printer, folder, or file) that a user, device, or program has access to on a corporate network, server, or workstation.

Action bar On an Android device, an area at the bottom of the screen that can contain up to five custom software buttons, called Home touch buttons. The three default buttons are back, home, and overview.

Action Center A tool in Windows 8/7 that lists errors and issues that need attention.

Active Directory A Windows server directory database and service that is used in managing a domain to allow for a single point of administration for all shared resources on a network, including files, peripheral devices, databases, websites, users, and services.

active partition For Master Boot Record (MBR) hard drives, the primary partition on the drive that boots the OS. Windows calls the active partition the system partition.

active recovery image In Windows 8, the custom refresh image of the Windows volume that will be used when a refresh of the Windows installation is performed. *Also see* custom refresh image.

ActiveX control A small app or add-on that can be downloaded from a website along with a webpage and is executed by a browser to enhance the webpage.

adapter address *See* MAC (Media Access Control) address.

address reservation When a DHCP server assigns a static IP address to a DHCP client. For example, a network printer might require a static IP address so that computers on the network can find the printer.

administrative share The folders that are shared by default on a network domain that administrator accounts can access.

Administrative Tools A group of tools accessed through the Control Panel that you can use to manage the local computer or other computers on the network.

administrator account In Windows, a user account that grants to the administrator(s) rights and privileges to all hardware and software resources, such as the right to add, delete, and change accounts and to change hardware configurations. *Compare with* standard account.

Administrators group A type of user group. When a user account is assigned to this group, the account is granted rights that are assigned to an administrator account.

Advanced Boot Options menu A Windows 7/ Vista menu that appears when you press F8 when Windows starts. The menu can be used to troubleshoot problems when loading Windows.

Aero user interface The Windows 7/Vista 3D user interface that gives a glassy appearance. *Also called* Aero glass.

AES (Advanced Encryption Standard) An encryption standard used by WPA2 and is currently the strongest encryption standard used by Wi-Fi.

AFP (Apple Filing Protocol) An outdated file access protocol used by early editions of the Mac operating system by Apple and is one protocol in the suite of AppleTalk networking protocols.

AirDrop A feature of iOS whereby iPhones and iPads can transfer files between nearby devices. The devices use Bluetooth to detect nearby devices and Wi-Fi to establish connectivity and transfer files.

air filter mask A mask that filters the dust and other contaminants from the air for breathing safety. *Also called* air-purifying respirator.

airplane mode A setting within a mobile device that disables the cellular, Wi-Fi, and Bluetooth antennas so the device cannot transmit signals.

alternate IP address When configuring TCP/IP in Windows, the static IP address that Windows uses if it cannot lease an IP address from a DHCP server.

alternating current (AC) Current that cycles back and forth rather than traveling in only one direction. In the United States, the AC voltage from a standard wall outlet is normally between 110 and 115 V. In Europe, the standard AC voltage from a wall outlet is 220 V.

amp (A) A measure of electrical current.

Android An operating system used on mobile devices that is based on the Linux OS and supported by Google.

anonymous users User accounts that have not been authenticated on a remote computer.

ANSI (American National Standards Institute) A nonprofit organization dedicated to creating trade and communications standards.

answer file A text file (.bat) that contains information that Windows requires in order to do an unattended installation.

anti-malware software Utility software that can prevent infection, scan a system, and detect and remove all types of general malware, including viruses, spyware, worms, and rootkits.

antistatic bag Static shielding bags that new computer components are shipped in.

antistatic wrist strap *See* ESD strap.

antivirus software Utility software that can prevent infection, scan a system, and detect and remove viruses.

anycast address Using TCP/IP version 6, a type of IP address used by routers and identifies multiple destinations. Packets are delivered to the closest destination.

APK (Android Application Package) The format used by Android apps for distributing the app in a package of files wrapped into one file with an .apk file extension.

App Store The app on an Apple device (iPad, iPhone, or iPod touch) that can be used to download content from the iTunes Store website (*itunes.apple.com*).

Apple ID A user account that uses a valid email address and password and is associated with a credit card number that allows you to download iOS updates and patches, apps, and multimedia content.

Apple menu In OS X, the menu that appears when the user clicks the Apple icon in the upper-left corner of the screen.

AppleTalk An outdated suite of networking protocols used by early editions of the Apple Mac OS, and has been replaced by the TCP/IP suite of protocols.

application virtualization Using this virtualization, a virtual environment is created in memory for an application to virtually install itself.

Application Virtualization (App-V) Software by Microsoft used for application virtualization.

Apps Drawer An Android app that lists and manages all apps installed on the device. By default, this app's icon is in the Favorites tray on an Android screen.

apt-get A Linux and OS X command to install and remove software packages and install OS updates.

ATAPI (Advanced Technology Attachment Packet Interface) An interface standard, part of the IDE/ATA standards, that allows tape drives, optical drives, and other drives to be treated like an IDE hard drive by the system.

ATA Secure Erase Standards developed by the American National Standards Institute (ANSI) that dictate how to securely erase data from solid-state devices such as a USB flash drive or SSD drive in order to protect personal privacy.

Authenticated Users group   All user accounts that have been authenticated to access the system except the Guest account. *Compare with* anonymous users.

authentication server   A server responsible for authenticating users or computers to the network so they can access network resources.

Automatic Private IP Address (APIPA)   In TCP/IP Version 4, IP address in the address range 169.254.x.y, used by a computer when it cannot successfully lease an IP address from a DHCP server.

Backup and Restore   The Windows 7/Vista utility used to create and update scheduled backups of user data and the system image.

Backup Operators group   A type of Windows user account group. When a user account belongs to this group, it can back up and restore any files on the system regardless of its having access to there files.

Bash shell   The default shell used by the terminal for many distributions of Linux.

basic disk   The term Windows uses that applies to a hard drive when the drive is a stand-alone drive in the system. *Compare with* dynamic disk.

batch file   A text file containing a series of OS commands. Autoexec.bat is a batch file.

bcdedit   A Windows command used to manually edit the BCD (Boot Configuration Data).

beamforming   A technique supported by IEEE 802.11ac Wi-Fi standard that can detect the location of connected devices and increase signal strength in that direction.

Berg power connector   A type of power connector used by a power cord to provide power to a floppy disk drive.

best-effort protocol   *See* connectionless protocol.

biometric authentication   To authenticate to a network, computer, or other computing device by means of biometric data, such as a fingerprint or retinal data. Touch ID on an iPhone or face lock on an Android device can perform biometric authentication.

biometric device   An input device that inputs biological data about a person; the data can identify a person's fingerprints, handprints, face, voice, eyes, and handwriting.

BIOS (basic input/output system)   Firmware that can control much of a computer's input/output functions, such as communication with the keyboard and the monitor. *Compare with* UEFI.

BitLocker Drive Encryption   A utility in Windows 8/7/Vista that is used to lock down a hard drive by encrypting the entire Windows volume and any other volume on the drive.

BitLocker To Go   A Windows utility that can encrypt data on a USB flash drive and restrict access by requiring a password.

blue screen error   *See* blue screen of death (BSOD).

blue screen of death (BSOD)   A Windows error that occurs in kernel mode, is displayed against a blue screen, and causes the system to halt. The error might be caused by problems with devices, device drivers, or a corrupted Windows installation. Also called a stop error.

Bluetooth PIN code   A code that may be required to complete the Bluetooth connection in a pairing process.

Boot Camp   A utility in OS X that allows you to install and run Windows on a Mac computer.

Boot Configuration Data (BCD) store   A small Windows database structured the same as a registry file and contains configuration information about how Windows is started. The BCD file replaces the Boot.ini file used in Windows 2000/XP.

boot loader menu   A startup menu that gives the user the choice of which operating system to load, such as Windows 8 or Windows 7, when both are installed on the same system, creating a dual boot.

boot partition   The hard drive partition where the Windows OS is stored. The system partition and the boot partition may be different partitions.

booting   The process of starting up a computer and loading an operating system.

BootMgr   In Windows 8/7/Vista, the boot manager program responsible for loading Windows.

bootrec   A Windows command used to repair the BCD (Boot Configuration Data) and boot sectors.

bootsect   A Windows command used to repair a dual-boot system.

botnet   A network of zombies or robots.

brownout   Temporary reductions in voltage, which can sometimes cause data loss. *Also called* sags.

brute force attack   A method to hack or discover a password by trying every single combination of characters.

G

BYOD (Bring Your Own Device)   A corporate policy that allows employees or students to connect their own devices to the corporate network.

call tracking software   A system that tracks the dates, times, and transactions of help-desk or on-site IT support calls, including the problem presented, the issues addressed, who did what, and when and how each call was resolved.

Category view   Default view in Windows Control Panel that presents utilities grouped by category. *Compare with* Classic view.

cd (change directory)   The Windows command to change the current default directory.

CDFS (Compact Disc File System)   The 32-bit file system for CD discs and some CD-R and CD-RW discs. *Also see* Universal Disk Format (UDF).

CDMA (Code Division Multiple Access)   A protocol standard used by cellular WANs and cell phones for transmitting digital data over cellular networks.

cellular network analyzer   Software and hardware that can monitor cellular networks for signal strength of cell towers, wireless access points (WAPs), and repeaters, which can help technicians better position antennas in a distributed antenna system (DAS).

chmod   A Linux and OS X command to change modes (or permissions) for a file or directory.

chown   A Linux and OS X command to change the owner of a file or directory.

CPU   *See* central processing unit (CPU).

Certificate of Authenticity   A sticker that contains the Windows product key.

certificate of destruction   Digital or paper documentation, which assures that data has been destroyed beyond recovery.

Certification Authority (CA)   An organization, such as VeriSign, that assigns digital certificates or digital signatures to individuals or organizations.

chain of custody   Documentation that tracks evidence used in an investigation and includes exactly what, when, and from whom the evidence was collected, the condition of the evidence, and how the evidence was secured while in possession of a responsible party.

channel   A specific radio frequency within a broader frequency.

charm   A shortcut that appears in the charms bar.

charms bar   A menu that appears on the right side of any Windows 8 screen when you move your pointer to a right corner.

child directory   *See* subdirectory.

chkdsk (check disk)   A Windows command to verify the hard drive does not have bad sectors that can corrupt the file system.

chkdsk /r   A Windows command to check the hard drive for errors and repair the file system.

CIDR notation   A shorthand notation (pronounced "*cider notation*") for expressing an IPv4 address and subnet mask with the IP address followed by a / slash and the number of bits in the IP address that identifies the network. For example, 15.50.35.10/20.

CIFS (Common Internet File System)   A file access protocol and the cross-platform version of SMB used between Windows, Linux, Mac OS, and other operating systems. *Also called* SMB2.

Class C fire extinguisher   A fire extinguisher rated to put out electrical fires.

Classic view   View in Windows Control Panel that presents utilities in small or large icons and are not grouped. *Compare with* Category view.

clean boot   A process of starting Windows with a basic set of drivers and startup programs that can be useful when software does not install properly.

clean install   Used to overwrite the existing operating system and applications when installing Windows on a hard drive.

client/server   Two computers communicating using a local network or the Internet. One computer (the client) makes requests to the other computer (the server), which answers the request.

client-side desktop virtualization   Using this virtualization, software installed on a desktop or laptop manages virtual machines used by the local user.

client-side virtualization   Using this virtualization, a personal computer provides multiple virtual environments for applications.

clone   In Linux and OS X, an image of the entire partition on which the OS is installed.

closed source   Software owned by a vendor that requires a commercial license to install and use the software. *Also called* vendor-specific or commercial license software.

cloud computing   A service where server-side virtualization is delegated to a third-party service, and the Internet is used to connect server and client machines.

cluster   On a magnetic hard drive, one or more sectors that constitute the smallest unit of space on the drive for storing data (also referred to as a file allocation unit). Files are written to a drive as groups of whole clusters.

cold boot   *See* hard boot.

commercial license   As applied to software, the rights to use the software, which have been assigned to the user by the software vendor.

community cloud   Online resources and services that are shared between multiple organizations, but not available publicly.

compatibility mode   A group of settings that can be applied to older drivers or applications that might cause them to work using a newer version of Windows than the one the programs were designed to use.

Complete PC Backup   A Vista utility that can make a backup of the entire volume on which Vista is installed and can also back up other volumes. *Compare with* system image.

Component Services (COM+)   A Microsoft Management Console snap-in that can be used to register components used by installed applications.

compressed (zipped) folder   A folder with a .zip extension that contains compressed files. When files are put in the folder, they are compressed. When files are moved to a regular folder, the files are decompressed.

computer infestation   *See* malicious software.

Computer Management   A Windows console (compmgmt.msc) that contains several administrative tools used by support technicians to manage the local computer or other computers on the network.

computer name   *See* host name.

connectionless protocol   A TCP/IP protocol such as UDP that works at the OSI Transport layer and does not guarantee delivery by first connecting and checking where data is received. It might be used for broadcasting, such as streaming video or sound over the web, where guaranteed delivery is not as important as fast transmission. *Also called* a best-effort protocol. *Also see* UDP (User Datagram Protocol).

connection-oriented protocol   In networking, a TCP/IP protocol that confirms a good connection has been made before transmitting data to the other end, verifies data was received, and resends it if it is not. An example of a connection-oriented protocol is TCP.

console   A window that consolidates several Windows administrative tools.

Control Panel   A window containing several small Windows utility programs called applets that are used to manage hardware, software, users, and the system.

copy   The Windows command to copy a single file, group of files, or folder and its contents.

copyright   The right to copy the work that belongs to the creators of the works or others to whom the creator transfers this right.

custom installation   In the Windows setup program, the option used to overwrite the existing operating system and applications, producing a clean installation of the OS. The main advantage is that problems with the old OS are not carried forward.

custom refresh image   In Windows 8, an image of the entire Windows volume including the Windows installation. The image can be applied during a Windows 8 refresh operation.

Dashboard   In OS X, a screen that contains widgets, such as a calendar, a calculator, a clock, and a weather report.

data loss prevention (DLP)   Methods that protect corporate data from being exposed or stolen; for example, software that filters employee email to verify privacy laws are not accidentally or intentionally being violated.

data source   A resource on a network that includes a database and the drivers required to interface between a remote computer and the data.

Data Sources   A tool in the Administrative Tools group of Control Panel that is used to allow data files to be connected to applications they normally would not use.

Date and Time applet   Accessed through Control Panel, used to set the date and time in Windows.

G

dd A Linux and OS X command to copy and convert files, directories, partitions, and entire DVDs or hard drives. You must be logged in as a superuser to use the command.

default gateway The gateway a computer on a network uses to access another network unless it knows to specifically use another gateway for quicker access to that network.

default program A program associated with a file extension that is used to open the file.

defrag The Windows command that examines a magnetic hard drive for fragmented files and rewrites these files to the drive in contiguous clusters.

defragment A drive maintenance procedure that rearranges fragments or parts of files on a magnetic hard drive so each file is stored on the drive in contiguous clusters.

defragmentation tool A utility or command to rewrite a file to a disk in one contiguous chain of clusters, thus speeding up data retrieval.

degausser A machine that exposes a magnetic storage device such as a hard drive or tape drive to a strong magnetic field to completely erase the data on the storage device.

del The Windows command to delete a file or group of files. *Also called* the erase command.

deployment strategy A procedure to install Windows, device drivers, and applications on a computer, and can include the process to transfer user settings, application settings, and user data files from an old installation to the new installation.

Destination Network Address Translation (DNAT) When a firewall using network address translation (NAT) allows uninitated communication to a computer behind the firewall through a port that is normally closed. *Also see* port forwarding.

device driver Small program stored on the hard drive and installed in Windows that tell Windows how to communicate with a specific hardware device such as a printer, network, port on the motherboard, or scanner.

Device Manager Primary Windows tool (devmgmt.msc) for managing hardware.

DHCP (Dynamic Host Configuration Protocol) A protocol used by a server to assign a dynamic IP address to a computer when it first attempts to initiate a connection to the network and requests an IP address.

DHCP client A computer or other device (such as a network printer) that requests an IP address from a DHCP server.

DHCPv6 server A DHCP server that serves up IPv6 addresses.

dictionary attack A method to discover or crack a password by trying words in a dictionary.

digital certificate A code used to authenticate the source of a file or document or to identify and authenticate a person or organization sending data over a network. The code is assigned by a certificate authority such as VeriSign and includes a public key for encryption. Also called digital ID or digital signature.

digital rights management (DRM) Software and hardware security limitations meant to protect digital content and prevent piracy.

dir The Windows command to list files and directories.

direct current (DC) Current that travels in only one direction (the type of electricity provided by batteries). Computer power supplies transform AC to low DC.

DirectX A Microsoft software development tool that software developers can use to write multimedia applications such as games, video-editing software, and computer-aided design software.

disc image *See* ISO image.

Disk Cleanup A Windows utility to delete temporary files to free up space on a drive.

disk cloning *See* drive imaging.

disk imaging *See* drive imaging.

diskpart A Windows command to manage hard drives, partitions, and volumes.

distribution server A file server holding Windows setup files used to install Windows on computers networked to the server.

distribution share The collective files in the installation that include Windows, device drivers, and applications. The package of files is served up by a distribution server.

DMG file In Mac OS X, a disk image file similar to WIM or ISO files in Windows.

DMZ (demilitarized zone) Refers to removing firewall protection from a computer or network within an organization of protected computers and networks.

DNS (Domain Name System or Domain Name Service) A distributed pool of information (called the name space) that keeps track of assigned host names and domain names and their corresponding IP addresses. DNS also refers to the system that allows a host to locate information in the pool and the protocol the system uses.

DNS client When Windows queries the DNS server for a name resolution, which means to find an IP address for a computer when the fully qualified domain name is known.

DNS server A Doman Name Service server that uses a DNS protocol to find an IP address for a computer when the fully qualified domain name is known. An Internet Service Provider is responsible for providing access to one or more DNS servers as part of the service it provides for Internet access.

dock (1) For an Android device, the area at the bottom of the Android screen where up to four apps can be pinned. (2) For a Mac computer, a bar that appears by default at the bottom of the screen and contains program icons and shortcuts to files and folders.

domain In Windows, a logical group of networked computers, such as those on a college campus, that share a centralized directory database of user account information and security for the entire domain.

domain account *See* global account.

domain name A name that identifies a network and appears before the period in a website address such as *microsoft.com.* A fully qualified domain name is sometimes loosely called a domain name. *Also see* fully qualified domain name.

drive imaging Making an exact image of a hard drive, including partition information, boot sectors, operating system installation, and application software to replicate the hard drive on another system or recover from a hard drive crash. *Also called* disk cloning or disk imaging.

dual boot The ability to boot using either of two different OSs, such as Windows 8 and Windows 7. *Also called* multiboot.

dumb terminal *See* zero client.

dump In Linux, a collection of data that is copied to a backup media.

dxdiag.exe A Windows command used to display information about hardware and diagnose problems with DirectX.

dynamic disk A way to partition one or more hard drives so that the drives can work together to store data in order to increase space for data or to provide fault tolerance or improved performance. *Also see* RAID. *Compare with* basic disk.

dynamic IP address An IP address assigned by a DHCP server for the current session only, and is leased when the computer first connects to a network. When the session is terminated, the IP address is returned to the list of available addresses. *Compare with* static IP address.

dynamic volume A volume type used with dynamic disks by which you can create a single volume that uses space on multiple hard drives.

EFI System Partition (ESP) For a GPT hard drive, the bootable partition used to boot the OS and contains the boot manager program for the OS.

electrostatic discharge (ESD) Another name for static electricity, which can damage chips and destroy motherboards, even though it might not be felt or seen with the naked eye.

elevated command prompt window A Windows command prompt window that allows commands that require administrator privileges.

email filtering To search incoming or outgoing email messages for matches kept in databases, searching for known scams and spammers to protect against social engineering.

email hoax An email message that is trying to tempt you to give out personal information or trying to scam you.

emergency notifications Government alerts, such as AMBER alerts, that are sent to mobile devices in an emergency.

emulator A virtual machine that emulates hardware, such as the hardware buttons on a smart phone.

Encrypted File System (EFS) A way to use a key to encode a file or folder on an NTFS volume to protect sensitive data. Because it is an integrated system service, EFS is transparent to users and applications.

End User License Agreement (EULA) A digital or printed statement of your rights to use or copy software, which you agree to when the software is installed.

enterprise license A license to use software that allows an organization to install multiple instances of the software. *Also called* site license.

entry control roster A list of people allowed into a restricted area and a log of any approved visitors that is used and maintained by security guards.

erase *See* del.

escalate Assigning a problem to someone higher in the support chain of an organization. This action is normally recorded in call tracking software.

ESD mat A mat that dissipates electrostatic discharge (ESD) and is commonly used by technicians who repair and assemble computers at their workbenches or in an assembly line. *Also called* ground mat.

ESD strap A strap you wear around your wrist that is attached to the computer case, ground mat, or another ground so that electrostatic discharge (ESD) is discharged from your body before you touch sensitive components inside a computer. *Also called* antistatic wrist strap *or* ground bracelet.

Event Viewer A Windows tool (eventvwr.msc) useful for troubleshooting problems with Windows, applications, and hardware. It displays logs of significant events such as a hardware or network failure, OS failure, OS error messages, a device or service that has failed to start, or General Protection Faults.

Everyone group In Windows, the Authenticated Users group as well as the Guest account. When you share a file or folder on the network, Windows, by default, gives access to the Everyone group.

executive services In Windows, a group of components running in kernel mode that interfaces between the subsystems in user mode and the HAL (hardware abstraction layer).

expand The Windows command that extracts files from compressed distribution files, which are often used to distribute files for software installation.

expert system Software that uses a database of known facts and rules to simulate a human expert's reasoning and decision-making processes.

ext3 The Linux file system that was the first to support journaling, which is a technique that tracks and stores changes to the hard drive and helps prevent file system corruption.

ext4 The current Linux file system, which replaced the ext3 file system. Stands for "fourth extended file system."

extended partition On an MBR hard drive, the only partition on the drive that can contain more than one logical drive. In Windows, a hard drive can have only a single extended partition. *Compare with* primary partition.

factory default To restore a mobile device or other computer to its state at the time of purchase. The operating system is reinstalled and all user data and settings are lost.

Fast Startup A Windows 8 feature to speed up startup by performing a partial hibernation at shutdown. At shutdown, Windows saves the drivers and kernel state in the Windows hibernate file, hiberfil.sys, and then reads from this file on the next cold boot.

FAT (file allocation table) A table on a hard drive, USB flash drive, or floppy disk used by the FAT file system that tracks the clusters used to contain a file.

fat client *See* thick client.

Favorites tray On Android devices, the area above the Action bar that contains up to seven apps or groups of apps. These apps stay put as you move from home screen to home screen.

file allocation unit *See* cluster.

file association The association between a data file and an application to open the file that is determined by the file extension.

file attributes The properties assigned to a file. Examples of file attributes are read-only and hidden status.

File Explorer The Windows 8 utility used to view and manage files and folders.

file extension A portion of the name of a file that indicates how the file is organized or formatted, the type of content in the file, and what program uses the file. In command lines, the file extension follows the filename and is separated from it by a period, for example, Msd.exe, where exe is the file extension.

File History In Windows 8, the utility that can schedule and maintain backups of data. It can also create a system image for backward compatibility with Windows 7.

file name The first part of the name assigned to a file, which does not include the file extension. In DOS, the file name can be no more than eight characters long and is followed by the file extension. In Windows, a file name can be up to 255 characters.

file server A computer dedicated to storing and serving up data files and folders.

file system The overall structure that an OS uses to name, store, and organize files on a disk. Examples of file systems are NTFS and FAT32. Windows is always installed on a volume that uses the NTFS file system.

Finder An app embedded in Mac OS X that functions similar to File Explorer in Windows; use it to find and access files and applications in OS X.

firewall Hardware and/or software that blocks unwanted traffic initiated from the Internet into a private network and can restrict Internet access for local computers behind the firewall.

fixboot A Windows 7/Vista command that repairs the boot sector of the system partition.

fixmbr A Windows 7/Vista command to repair the MBR (Master Boot Record).

floppy disk drive (FDD) A drive that can hold either a 5½ inch or 3¼ inch floppy disk. *Also called* floppy drive.

folder *See* subdirectory.

Folder Options applet Accessed through the Control Panel, manages how files and folders are displayed in File Explorer or Windows Explorer.

force stop To abruptly end an app without allowing the app to go through its close process.

force quit In OS X, to abruptly end an app without allowing the app to go through its close process.

format The Windows command to prepare a hard drive volume, logical drive, or USB flash drive for use by placing tracks and sectors on its surface to store information (for example, format d:). This process erases all data on the device.

formatting *See* format.

fragmented file A file that has been written to different portions of the disk so that it is not in contiguous clusters.

FTP (File Transfer Protocol) A TCP/IP protocol and application that uses the Internet to transfer files between two computers.

FTP server A server using the FTP or Secure FTP protocol that downloads or uploads files to remote computers.

full duplex Communication that happens in two directions at the same time.

fully qualified domain name (FQDN) Identifies a computer and the network to which it belongs and includes the computer name and domain name. For example, *jsmith.amazon.com*. Sometimes loosely referred to as a domain name.

gadget A mini-app that appears on the Windows 7 desktop or Vista sidebar.

gateway Any device or computer that network traffic can use to leave one network and go to a different network.

geotracking A mobile device routinely reports its position to Apple, Google, or Microsoft at least twice a day, which makes it possible for these companies to track your device's whereabouts.

gestures In OS X, finger movements on the trackpad of a Mac laptop.

global account An account is used at the domain level, created by an administrator, and stored in the SAM (security accounts manager) database on a Windows domain controller. *Also called* domain account *or* network ID. *Compare with* local account.

global address *See* global unicast address.

global unicast address In TCP/IP Version 6, an IP address that can be routed on the Internet. *Also called* global address.

Globally Unique Identifier Partition Table (GUID or GPT) A partitioning system installed on a hard drive that can support 128 partitions and is recommended for drives larger than 2 TB.

Gmail An email service provided by Google at *mail.google.com*.

Google account A user account, which is a valid email address, that is registered on the Google Play website (*play.google.com*) and is used to download content to an Android device.

Google Play The official source for Android apps, also called the Android marketplace, at *play.google.com*.

gpresult The Windows command to find out group policies that are currently applied to a system for the computer or user.

G

gpupdate   The Windows command to refresh local group policies as well as group policies set in Active Directory on a Windows domain.

GPS (Global Positioning System)   A receiver that uses the system of 24 or more satellites orbiting the earth. The receiver locates four or more of these satellites, and from these four locations, calculates its own position in a process called triangulation.

graphical user interface (GUI)   An interface that uses graphics as compared to a command-driven interface.

grayware   A program that is potentially harmful or potentially unwanted.

grep   A Linux and OS X command to search for and display a specific pattern of characters in a file or in multiple files.

ground bracelet   *See* ESD strap.

ground mat   *See* ESD mat.

Group Policy   A console (gpedit.msc) available only in Windows professional and business editions that is used to control what users can do and how the system can be used.

GRUB (GRand Unified Bootloader)   The current Linux boot loader, which can handle dual boots with another OS installed on the system.

GSM (Global System for Mobile Communications)   An open standard for cellular networks and cell phones that uses digital communication of data and is accepted and used worldwide.

Guests group   A type of user group in Windows. User accounts that belong to this group have limited rights to the system and are given a temporary profile that is deleted after the user logs off.

gyroscope   A device that contains a disc that is free to move and can respond to gravity as the device is moved.

HAL (hardware abstraction layer)   The low-level part of Windows, written specifically for each CPU technology, so that only the HAL must change when platform components change.

half duplex   Communication between two devices whereby transmission takes place in only one direction at a time.

Handoff   A technique of devices and computers made by Apple that lets you start a task on one device, such as an iPad, then pick up that task on another device, such as a Mac desktop or laptop.

hard boot   Restart the computer by turning off the power or by pressing the Reset button. *Also called* a cold boot.

hard-link migration   A method used by USMT (User State Migration Tool) that does not copy user files and settings when the source computer and destination computer are the same.

hard reset   (1) For Android devices, a factory reset, which erases all data and settings and restores the device to its original factory default state. (2) For iOS devices, a forced restart similar to a full shutdown followed by a full clean boot of the device.

hardware address   *See* MAC (Media Access Control) address.

hardware RAID   One of two ways to implement RAID. Hardware RAID is more reliable and better performing than software RAID, and is implemented using UEFI/BIOS on the motherboard or a RAID controller card.

hardware-assisted virtualization (HAV)   A feature of a processor whereby it can provide enhanced support for hypervisor software to run virtual machines on a system. The feature must be enabled in UEFI/BIOS setup.

help   The Windows command to get help about another command.

hibernation   A power-saving state that saves all work to the hard drive and powers down the system.

hidden share   A folder whose folder name ends with a $ symbol. When you share the folder, it does not appear in the File Explorer or Windows Explorer window of remote computers on the network.

high-level formatting   A process performed by the Windows Format program (for example, FORMAT C:/S), the Windows installation program, or the Disk Management utility. The process creates the boot record, file system, and root directory on a hard drive volume or logical drive, a floppy disk, or USB flash drive. Also called formatting, OS formatting, or operating system formatting. *Compare with* low-level formatting.

high-touch using a standard image   A strategy to install Windows that uses a standard image for the installation. A technician must perform the installation on the local computer. *Also see* standard image.

high-touch with retail media   A strategy to install Windows where all the work is done by a technician sitting at the computer using Windows setup files. The technician also installs drivers and applications after the Windows installation is finished.

HKEY_CLASSES_ROOT (HKCR)   A Windows registry key that stores information to determine which application is opened when the user double-clicks a file.

HKEY_CURRENT_CONFIG (HKCC)   A Windows registry key that contains information about the hardware configuration that is used by the computer at startup.

HKEY_CURRENT_USER (HKCU)   A Windows registry key that contains data about the current user. The key is built when a user signs in using data kept in the HKEY_USERS key and data kept in the Ntuser.dat file of the current user.

HKEY_LOCAL_MACHINE (HKLM)   An important Windows registry key that contains hardware, software, and security data. The key is built using data taken from the SAM hive, the Security hive, the Software hive, and the System hive and from data collected at startup about the hardware.

HKEY_USERS (HKU)   A Windows registry key that contains data about all users and is taken from the Default hive.

homegroup   A type of peer-to-peer network where each computer shares files, folders, libraries, and printers with other computers in the homegroup. Access to the homegroup is secured using a homegroup password.

host name   A name that identifies a computer, printer, or other device on a network, which can be used instead of the computer's IP address to address the computer on the network. The host name together with the domain name is called the fully qualified domain name. *Also called* computer name.

Hosts file   A file in the C:\Windows\System32\ drivers\etc folder that contains computer names and their associated IP addresses on the local network. The file has no file extension.

hot-plugging   Plugging in a device while the computer is turned on. The computer will sense the device and configure it without rebooting. In addition, the device can be unplugged without an OS error. *Also called* hot-swapping.

hotspot   A small area that offers connectivity to a wireless network, such as a Wi-Fi network.

hot-swappable   The ability to plug or unplug devices without first powering down the system. USB devices are hot-swappable.

HTTP (Hypertext Transfer Protocol)   The TCP/IP protocol used for the World Wide Web and used by web browsers and web servers to communicate.

HTTPS (HTTP secure)   The HTTP protocol working with a security protocol such as Secure Sockets Layer (SSL) or Transport Layer Security (TLS), which is better than SSL, to create a secured socket that includes data encryption.

hybrid cloud   A combination of public, private, and community clouds used by the same organization. For example, a company might store data in a private cloud, but use a public cloud email service.

hypervisor   Software that creates and manages virtual machines on a server or on a local computer. *Also called* virtual machine manager (VMM).

IaaS (Infrastructure as a Service)   A cloud computing service that provides only the hardware, which can include servers, storage devices, and networks.

iCloud   A website by Apple (*www.icloud.com*) used to sync content on Apple devices in order to provide a backup of the content.

iCloud Backup   A feature of an iPhone, iPad, or iPod touch whereby the device's content is backed up to the cloud at *icloud.com*.

iCloud Drive   Storage space at *icloud.com* that can be synced with files stored on any Apple mobile device or any personal computer, including an OS X or Windows computer.

IDE (Intergrated Drive Electronics or Integrated Device Electronics)   A hard drive whose disk controller is integrated into the drive, eliminating the need for a controller cable and thus increasing speed, as well as reducing price.

IEEE 802.11ac   The latest Wi-Fi standard that supports up to 7 Gbps (actual speeds are currently about 1300 Mbps) and uses 5.0 GHz radio frequency and beamforming.

IEEE 802.11n   A Wi-Fi standard that supports up to 600 Mbps and uses 5.0 GHz or 2.4 GHz radio frequency and supports MIMO.

ifconfig (interface configuration)   A Linux and OS X command similar to the Windows ipconfig command that displays details about network interfaces and can enable and disable an interface. When affecting the interface, the command requires root privileges.

image deployment   Installing a standard image on a computer.

IMAP4 (Internet Message Access Protocol, version 4)   A protocol used by an email server and client that allows the client to manage email stored on the server without downloading the email. *Compare with* POP3.

IMEI (International Mobile Equipment Identity)   A unique number that identifies a mobile phone or tablet device worldwide. The number can usually be found imprinted on the device or reported in the About menu of the OS.

IMSI (International Mobile Subscriber Identity)   A unique number that identifies a cellular subscription for a device or subscriber, along with its home country and mobile network. Some carriers store the number on a SIM card installed in the device.

inherited permissions   Permissions assigned by Windows that are attained from a parent object.

initialization files   Text files that keep hardware and software configuration information, user preferences, and application settings and are used by the OS when first loaded and when needed by hardware, applications, and users.

in-place upgrade   A Windows installation that is launched from the Windows desktop. The installation carries forward user settings and installed applications from the old OS to the new one. A Windows OS is already in place before the installation begins.

interface   In TCP/IP Version 6, a node's attachment to a link. The attachment can be a physical attachment (for example, when using a network adapter) or a logical attachment (for example, when using a tunneling protocol). Each interface is assigned an IP address.

interface ID   In TCP/IP Version 6, the last 64 bits or 4 blocks of an IP address that identify the interface.

Internet Options   A dialog box used to manage Internet Explorer settings.

Internet Protocol version 4 (IPv4)   A group of TCP/IP standards that uses IP addresses that have 32 bits.

Internet Protocol version 6 (IPv6)   A group of TCP/IP standards that uses IP addresses that have 128 bits.

intranet   Any private network that uses TCP/IP protocols. A large enterprise might support an intranet that is made up of several local networks.

intrusion detection system (IDS)   Software that can run on a UTM (Unified Threat Management) appliance, router, server, or workstation to monitor all network traffic and create alerts when suspicious activity happens.

intrusion prevention system (IPS)   Software that can run on a UTM (Unified Threat Management) appliance, router, server, or workstation to monitor all network traffic, create alerts, and prevent the threatening traffic from burrowing into the system.

inverter   An electrical device that converts DC to AC.

iOS   The operating system owned and developed by Apple and used for their various mobile devices.

iPad   A handheld tablet developed by Apple.

IP address   A 32-bit or 128-bit address used to uniquely identify a device or interface on a network that uses TCP/IP protocols. Generally, the first numbers identify the network; the last numbers identify a host. An example of a 32-bit IP address is 206.96.103.114. An example of a 128-bit IP address is 2001:0000:B80::D3:9C5A:CC.

ipconfig (IP configuration)   A Windows command that displays TCP/IP configuration information and can refresh TCP/IP assignments to a connection including its IP address.

iPhone   A smart phone developed by Apple.

iPod touch   A multimedia recorder and player developed by Apple.

ISATAP   In TCP/IP Version 6, a tunneling protocol that has been developed for IPv6 packets to travel over an IPv4 network and stands for Intra-Site Automatic Tunnel Addressing Protocol.

ISO file   *See* ISO image.

ISO image   A file format that has an .iso file extension and holds an image of all the data, including the file system that is stored on an optical disc. ISO stands for International Organization for Standardization. *Also called* disc image.

iTunes Store   The Apple website at *itunes.apple.com* where apps, music, TV shows, movies, books, podcasts, and iTunes U content can be purchased and downloaded to Apple devices.

iTunes U   Content at the iTunes Store website (*itunes.apple.com*) that contains lectures and even complete courses from many schools, colleges, and universities.

iwconfig   A Linux and OS X command similar to ifconfig, but applies only to wireless networks. Use it to display information about a wireless interface and configure a wireless adapter.

jailbreaking   A process to break through the restrictions that only allow apps to an iOS device to be downloaded from the iTunes Store at *itunes.apple.com*. Gives the user root or administrator privileges to the operating system and the entire file system and complete access to all commands and features. Note that jailbreaking voids any manufacturer warranty on the device, violates the End User License Agreement (EULA) with Apple, and might violate BYOD (Bring Your Own Device) policies in an enterprise environment.

joule   A measure of work or energy. One joule of energy produces one watt of power for one second.

kernel   The portion of an OS that is responsible for interacting with the hardware.

kernel mode   A Windows "privileged" processing mode that has access to hardware components.

kernel panic   A Linux or OS X error from which it cannot recover, similar to a blue screen of death in Windows.

Keychain   In OS X, a built-in password manager utility.

key fob   A device, such as a type of smart card, that can fit conveniently on a key chain.

keylogger   A type of spyware that tracks your keystrokes, including passwords, chat room sessions, email messages, documents, online purchases, and anything else you type on your computer. Text is logged to a text file and transmitted over the Internet without your knowledge.

Last Known Good Configuration   In Windows 7/Vista, registry settings and device drivers that were in effect when the computer last booted successfully. These settings are saved and can be restored during the startup process to recover from errors during the last boot. Windows 8 does not save the Last Known Good Configuration.

launcher   The Android graphical user interface (GUI) that includes multiple home screens, and supports windows, panes, and 3D graphics.

Launchpad   In OS X, the screen that shows all apps installed on the computer, similar to the Windows 8 Start screen.

library   In Windows 7, a collection of one or more folders that can be stored on different local drives or on the network.

Lightweight Directory Access Protocol (LDAP)   A protocol used by various client applications when the application needs to query a database.

LILO (LInux boot LOader)   The outdated Linux boot loader that could handle a dual boot and has been replaced by GRUB.

link (local link)   In TCP/IP version 6, a local area network or wide area network bounded by routers. *Also called* local link.

link-local address   *See* link-local unicast address.

link-local unicast address   In TCP/IP Version 6, an IP address used for communicating among nodes in the same link and is not allowed on the Internet. *Also called* local address *and* link-local address.

Linux   An OS based on Unix that was created by Linus Torvalds of Finland. Basic versions of this OS are open source, and all the underlying programming instructions are freely distributed.

lite-touch, high-volume deployment   A strategy that uses a deployment server on the network to serve up a Windows installation after a technician starts the process at the local computer.

live CD   In Linux, a CD, DVD, or flash drive that can boot up a live version of Linux, complete with Internet access and all the tools you normally have available in a hard drive installation of Linux, but without installing the OS on the hard drive.

live sign in   Sign in to Windows 8 using a Microsoft account.

live tiles   On the Windows 8 Start screen, some apps use live tiles, which offer continuous real-time updates.

loadstate   A command used by the User State Migration Tool (USMT) to copy user settings and data temporarily stored at a safe location to a new computer. *Also see* scanstate.

local account   A Windows user account that applies only to the local computer and cannot be used to access resources from other computers on the network. *Compare with* global account.

G

local area network (LAN) A network bound by routers or other gateway devices.

local link *See* link.

Local Security Policy A Windows Administrative Tools snap-in in Control Panel that can manage the group of policies in the Local Computer Policy, Computer Configuration, Windows Settings, Security Settings group of Group Policy.

local share Folders on a computer that are shared with others on the network by using a folder's Properties box. Local shares are used with a workgroup and not with a domain.

local snapshot In OS X, the temporary backups that Time Machine creates when the Mac is not connected to the backup media. When the media is later available, local snapshots are copied to the media.

Local Users and Groups For business and professional editions of Windows, a Windows utility console (lusrmgr.msc) that can be used to manage user accounts and user groups.

location data Data that a device can routinely report to a website, which can be used to locate the device on a map.

location independence A function of cloud computing whereby customers generally are not aware of where the physical devices providing cloud services are located geographically.

logical drive On an MBR hard drive, a portion or all of a hard drive extended partition that is treated by the operating system as though it were a physical drive or volume. Each logical drive is assigned a drive letter, such as drive F, and contains a file system. *Compare with* volume.

logical topology The logical way computers connect on a network.

login item In OS X, programs that are automatically launched after a user logs in. Login items are managed in the Users & Groups utility in System Preferences.

LoJack A technology by Absolute Software used to track the whereabouts of a laptop computer and, if the computer is stolen, lock down access to the computer or erase data on it. The technology is embedded in the UEFI/BIOS of many laptops.

Long Term Evolution (LTE) The latest standard used to transmit both voice and digital data over cellular networks and is expected to eventually replace CDMA and GSM.

loopback address An IP address that indicates your own computer and is used to test TCP/IP configuration on the computer.

low-level formatting A process (usually performed at the factory) that electronically creates the hard drive tracks and sectors, and tests for bad spots on the disk surface. *Compare with* high-level formatting.

LPT (Line Printer Terminal) Assignments of system resources that are made to a parallel port and that are used to manage a print job. Two possible LPT configurations are referred to as LPT1: and LPT2:.

MAC (Media Access Control) address A 48-bit (6-byte) hardware address unique to each network interface card (NIC) or onboard network controller that is assigned by the manufacturer at the factory and embedded on the device. The address is often printed on the adapter as hexadecimal numbers. An example is 00 00 0C 08 2F 35. *Also called* a physical address, an adapter address, or a hardware address.

MAC address filtering A technique used by a router or wireless access point to allow access to a private network to only certain computers or devices identified by their MAC addresses.

malicious software Any unwanted program that is transmitted to a computer without the user's knowledge and that is designed to do varying degrees of damage to data and software. Types of infestations include viruses, Trojan horses, worms, adware, spyware, keyloggers, browser hijackers, dialers, and downloaders. *Also called* malware, infestation, or computer infestation.

malware *See* malicious software.

malware definition Information about malware that allows anti-malware software to detect and define malware. *Also called* a malware signature.

malware encyclopedia Lists of malware, including symptoms and solutions, often maintained by manufacturers of anti-malware and made available on their websites.

malware signature *See* malware definition.

man-in-the-middle attack An attack that pretends to be a legitimate website, network, FTP site, or person in a chat session in order to obtain private information.

mantrap A physical security technique of using two doors on either end of a small entryway where the first door must close before the second door can open. A separate form of identification might be required for each door, such as a badge for the first door and a fingerprint scan for the second door. In addition, a security guard might monitor people as they come and go.

mapping   The client computer creates and saves a shortcut, called a network drive, to a folder or drive shared by a remote computer on the network. The network drive has a drive letter associated with it, which points to the network share.

Master Boot Record (MBR)   On an MBR hard drive, the first sector on the drive, which contains the partition table and a program BIOS uses to boot an OS from the drive.

master file table (MFT)   The database used by the NTFS file system to track the contents of a volume or logical drive.

Material Safety Data Sheet (MSDS)   A document that explains how to properly handle substances such as chemical solvents; it includes information such as physical data, toxicity, health effects, first aid, storage, disposal, and spill procedures.

md (make directory)   The Windows command to create a directory.

measured service   When a cloud computing vendor offers services that are metered for billing purposes or to ensure transparency between vendors and customers.

Memory Diagnostics   A Windows 8/7/Vista utility (mdsched.exe) used to test memory.

Metro User Interface (Metro UI)   See modern interface.

Microsoft account   For Windows 8 and above, an email address and password that allows access to several types of online accounts including Microsoft OneDrive, Facebook, LinkedIn, Twitter, Skype, Outlook, and others.

Microsoft Assessment and Planning (MAP) Toolkit   Software that can be used by a system administrator from a network location to query hundreds of computers in a single scan to determine if a computer qualifies for a Windows upgrade.

Microsoft Exchange   A server application that can handle email, contacts, and calendars and is a popular application used by large corporations for employee email, contacts, and calendars.

Microsoft Management Console (MMC)   A Windows utility to build customized consoles. These consoles can be saved to a file with an .msc file extension.

Microsoft Store   The official source for Windows apps at *microsoftstore.com*.

MIMO   *See* multiple input/multiple output (MIMO).

Miracast   A wireless display-mirroring technology that requires a Miracast-capable screen or dongle in order to mirror a smart phone's display to a TV, a wireless monitor, or a wireless projector.

Mission Control   In OS X, a utility and screen that gives an overview of all open windows and thumbnails of the Dashboard and desktops.

mobile payment service   An app that allows you to use your smart phone or other mobile device to pay for merchandise or services at a retail checkout counter.

modern interface   An interface that presents the Start screen to the user. *Also called* Windows 8 interface, *formerly called* Metro User Interface *or* Metro UI.

mount point   A folder that is used as a shortcut to space on another volume, which effectively increases the size of the folder to the size of the other volume. *Also see* mounted drive.

mounted drive   A volume that can be accessed by way of a folder on another volume so that the folder has more available space. *Also see* mount point.

mstsc (Microsoft Terminal Services Client)   A Windows command that allows you to start Remote Desktop Connection to remote in to your host computer using Remote Desktop.

multiboot   *See* dual boot.

multicast address   In TCP/IP version 6, an IP address used when packets are delivered to a group of nodes on a network.

multicasting   In TCP/IP version 6, one host sends messages to multiple hosts, such as when the host transmits a video conference over the Internet.

multifactor authentication (MFA)   To use more than one method to authenticate access to a computer, network, or other resource.

multimonitor taskbar   The Windows 8 option to extend the desktop taskbar across multiple monitors. Use the taskbar properties box to adjust the taskbar.

G

multiple desktops   A feature of Mission Control in OS X, where several desktop screens, each with its own collection of open windows, are available to the user.

multiple input/multiple output (MIMO)   A feature of the IEEE 802.11n/ac standards for wireless networking whereby two or more antennas are used at both ends of transmissions to improve performance.

multiple monitor misalignment   When the display is staggered across multiple monitors, making the display difficult to read. Fix the problem by adjusting the display in the Windows Screen Resolution window.

multiple monitor orientation   When the display does not accurately represent the relative positions of multiple monitors. Use the Windows Screen Resolution window to move the display for each monitor so they are oriented correctly.

multitouch   A touch screen on a computer or mobile device that can handle a two-finger pinch.

mutual authentication   To authenticate in both directions at the same time, as both entities confirm the identity of the other.

name resolution   The process of associating a character-based name with an IP address.

NAT (Network Address Translation)   A technique that substitutes the public IP address of the router for the private IP address of computer on a private network when these computers need to communicate on the Internet. *See also* Destination Network Address Translation (DNAT).

native resolution   The actual (and fixed) number of pixels built into an LCD monitor. For the clearest display, always set the resolution to the native resolution.

navigation pane   In File Explorer, Windows Explorer, or the Computer window, pane on the left side of the window where devices, drives, and folders are listed. Double-click an item to drill down into the item.

neighbors   In TCP/IP version 6, two or more nodes on the same link.

NetBIOS   A legacy suite of protocols used by Windows before TCP/IP.

NetBIOS over TCP/IP   A feature of Server Message Block (SMB) protocols that allows legacy NetBIOS applications to communicate on a TCP/IP network.

NetBoot   A technology that allows a Mac to boot from the network and then install OS X on the machine from a clone DMG file stored on the server.

network adapter   *See* network interface card (NIC).

Network and Sharing Center   The primary Windows 8/7/Vista utility used to manage network connections.

Network Attached Storage (NAS)   A device that provides multiple bays for hard drives and an Ethernet port to connect to the network. The device is likely to support RAID.

network drive map   Mounting a drive to a computer, such as drive E:, that is actually hard drive space on another host computer on the network.

Network File System (NFS)   A Windows component that is a distributed file system used to manage shared files on a network.

network ID   *See* global account.

network interface card (NIC)   An expansion card that plugs into a computer's motherboard and provides a port on the back of the card to connect a computer to a network. *Also called* a network adapter.

Network Places Wizard   *See* User Accounts.

network share   One computer (the client) on the network appears to have a hard drive, such as drive E:, that is actually hard drive space on another host computer (the server). *Also see* mapping.

next-generation firewall (NGFW)   A firewall that combines firewall software with anti-malware software and other software that protects resources on a network.

node   Any device that connects to the network, such as a computer, printer, or router.

non-compliant system   A system that violates security best practices, such as out-of-date anti-malware software or no anti-malware software installed.

nonvolatile RAM (NVRAM)   Flash memory on the motherboard that UEFI firmware uses to store device drivers and information about Secure Boot. Contents of NVRAM are not lost when the system is powered down.

Notepad   A Windows text editing program.

notification area   An area to the right of the taskbar that holds the icons for running services; these services include the volume control and network connectivity. *Also called* the system tray *or* systray.

notifications Alerts and related information about apps and social media sent to mobile devices.

NTFS permissions A method to share a folder or file over a network and can apply to local users and network users. The folder or file must be on an NTFS volume. *Compare with* share permissions.

octet In TCP/IP version 4, each of the four numbers that are separated by periods and make up a 32-bit IP address. One octet is 8 bits.

Offline Files A utility that allows users to work with files in the folder when the computer is not connected to the corporate network. When the computer is later connected, Windows syncs up the offline files and folders with those on the network.

ohm (Ω) The standard unit of measurement for electrical resistance. Resistors are rated in ohms.

onboard NIC A network port embedded on the motherboard.

on-demand A service that is available to users at any time. On-demand cloud computing means the service is always available.

OneDrive Microsoft cloud service that allows users with a Microsoft account to store, sync, and share files with other people and devices.

Open Database Connectivity (ODBC) A technology that allows a client computer to create a data source so that the client can interface with a database stored on a remote (host) computer on the network. *Also see* data source.

open source Source code for an operating system or other software whereby the source code is available for free and anyone can modify and redistribute the source code.

operating system (OS) Software that controls a computer. An OS controls how system resources are used and provides a user interface, a way of managing hardware and software, and ways to work with files.

Original Equipment Manufacturer (OEM) license A software license that only manufacturers or builders of personal computers can purchase to be installed only on a computer intended for sale.

OS X The latest version of the proprietary operating system only available for Macintosh computers by Apple Inc. (*apple.com*). OS X was originally based on Unix.

OSI Model A model for understanding and developing computer-to-computer communication, it divides networking functions among seven layers: Physical, Data Link, Network, Transport, Session, Presentation, and Application.

PaaS (Platform as a Service) A cloud computing service that provides the hardware and the operating system and is responsible for updating and maintaining both.

packet A message sent over a network as a unit that contains the data and information at the beginning that identifies the type of data, where it came from, and where it's going. *Also called* data packet or datagram.

pagefile.sys The Windows swap file that is used to hold the virtual memory that is used to enhance physical memory installed in a system.

pairing The process of two Bluetooth devices establishing connectivity.

parallel ATA (PATA) An older IDE cabling method that uses a 40-pin flat or round data cable or an 80-conductor cable and a 40-pin IDE connector. *Also see* serial ATA.

partition A division of a hard drive that can hold a volume. MBR drives can support up to four partitions on one hard drive. In Windows, GPT drives can have up to 128 partitions.

partition table A table that contains information about each partition on the drive. For MBR drives, the partition table is contained in the Master Boot Record. For GPT drives, the partition table is stored in the GPT header and a backup of the table is stored at the end of the drive.

patch A minor update to software that corrects an error, adds a feature, or addresses security issues. *Also called* an update. *Compare with* service pack.

path A drive and list of directories pointing to a file such as C:\Windows\System32.

PC Card A card that uses a PC Card slot on a laptop, and provides a port for peripheral devices or adds memory to the laptop. A PC Card is about the size of a credit card, but thicker.

PCL (Printer Control Language) A printer language developed by Hewlett-Packard that communicates to a printer how to print a page.

peer-to-peer (P2P) As applied to networking, a network of computers that are all equals, or peers. Each computer has the same amount of authority, and each can act as a server to the other computers.

G

Performance Monitor   A Microsoft Management Console snap-in that can track activity by hardware and software to measure performance.

permission propagation   When Windows passes permissions from parent objects to child objects.

permissions   Varying degrees of access assigned to a folder or file and given to a user account or user group. Access can include full control, write, delete, or read-only.

personal license   A license to use software that gives the right to install one instance of the software.

phishing   Sending an email message with the intent of getting the user to reveal private information that can be used for identify theft. *Also see* spear phishing *and* spoofing.

physical address   *See* MAC (Media Access Control) address.

physical topology   The physical arrangement of connections between computers.

pinning   To make a frequently used application more accessible, add its icon to the taskbar on the desktop.

platform   The hardware, operating system, runtime libraries, and modules on which an application runs.

POP or POP3 (Post Office Protocol, version 3)   The protocol that an email server and client use when the client requests the downloading of email messages. The most recent version is POP version 3. *Compare with* IMAP4.

port   (1) As applied to services running on a computer, a number assigned to a process on a computer so that the process can be found by TCP/IP. *Also called* a port address *or* port number. (2) A physical connector, usually at the back of a computer, that allows a cable from a peripheral device, such as a printer, mouse, or modem, to be attached.

port address   *See* port.

port filtering   To open or close certain ports so they can or cannot be used. A firewall uses port filtering to protect a network from unwanted communication.

port forwarding   A technique that allows a computer on the Internet to reach a computer on a private network using a certain port when the private network is protected by NAT and a firewall that controls the use of ports. *Also called* port mapping.

port mapping   *See* port forwarding.

port number   *See* port.

port triggering   When a firewall opens a port because a computer behind the firewall initiates communication on another port.

POST (power-on self test)   A self-diagnostic program used to perform a simple test of the CPU, RAM, and various I/O devices. The POST is performed by startup UEFI/BIOS when the computer is first turned on.

PostScript   A printer language developed by Adobe Systems that tells a printer how to print a page.

Power Options applet   Accessed through the Control Panel, manages power settings to conserve power.

Power Users group   A type of user account group. Accounts assigned to this group can read from and write to parts of the system other than their own user profile folders, install applications, and perform limited administrative tasks.

Preboot eXecution Environment (PXE)   Programming contained in the UEFI/BIOS code on the motherboard used to start up the computer and search for a server on the network to provide a bootable operating system. *Also called* Pre-Execution Environment (PXE).

presentation virtualization   Using this virtualization, a remote application running on a server is controlled by a local computer.

primary partition   A hard disk partition that can be designated as the active partition. An MBR drive can have up to three primary partitions. In Windows, a GPT drive can have up to 128 primary patitions. *Compare with* extended partition.

principle of least privilege   An approach where computer users are classified and the rights assigned are the minimum rights required to do their job.

Print Management   A utility located in the Administrative Tools group in Windows 8/7/Vista professional and business editions that allows you to monitor and manage printer queues for all printers on the network.

print server   Hardware or software that manages the print jobs sent to one or more printers on a network.

print spooler   A queue for print jobs.

privacy filter A device that fits over a monitor screen to prevent other people from viewing the monitor from a wide angle.

private cloud Services on the Internet that an organization provides on its own servers or established virtually for a single organization's private use.

private IP address In TCP/IP version 4, an IP address that is used on a private network that is isolated from the Internet.

PRL (Preferred Roaming List) A list of preferred service providers or radio frequencies your carrier wants a mobile device to use and is stored on a Removable User Identify Module (R-UIM) card installed in the device.

process A program that is running under the authority of the shell, together with the system resources assigned to it.

product activation The process that Microsoft uses to prevent software piracy. For example, once Windows 8 is activated for a particular computer, it cannot be legally installed on another computer.

Product Release Instructions (PRI) Information published by the manufacturer of an operating system that describes what to expect from a published update to the OS.

Programs and Features A window within Control Panel that lists the programs installed on a computer, where you can uninstall, change, or repair programs.

protocol A set of rules and standards that two entities use for communication. For example, TCP/IP is a suite or group of protocols that define many types of communication on a TCP/IP network.

proxy server A computer that intercepts requests that a client (for example, a browser) makes of a server (for example, a web server) and can serve up the request from a cache it maintains to improve performance or can filter requests to secure a large network.

public cloud Cloud computing services provided over the Internet to the general public. Google or Yahoo! email services are examples of public cloud deployment.

public IP address In TCP/IP version 4, an IP address available to the Internet.

pull automation A Windows installation that requires the local user to start the process. *Compare with* push automation.

push automation An installation where a server automatically pushes the installation to a computer when a user is not likely to be sitting at the computer. *Compare with* pull automation.

Quality of Service (QoS) A feature used by Windows and network hardware devices to improve network performance for an application that is not getting the best network performance. VoIP (Voice over IP) requires a high QoS.

quarantined computer A computer that is suspected of infection and is not allowed to use the network, is put on a different network dedicated to quarantined computers, or is allowed to access only certain network resources.

quick format A format procedure, used to format a hard drive volume or other drive, that doesn't scan the volume or drive for bad sectors; use it only when a drive has been previously formatted and is in healthy condition.

Quick Launch menu The menu that appears when the Windows Start button is right-clicked.

radio frequency (RF) The frequency of waves generated by a radio signal, which are electromagnetic frequencies above audio and below light. For example, Wi-Fi 802.11n transmits using a radio frequency of 5 GHz and 2.4 GHz.

RAID (redundant array of inexpensive disks or redundant array of independent disks) Several methods of configuring multiple hard drives to store data to increase logical volume size and improve performance, or to ensure that if one hard drive fails, the data is still available from another hard drive.

RAID 0 Using space from two or more physical disks to increase the disk space available for a single volume. Performance improves because data is written evenly across all disks. Windows calls RAID 0 a striped volume. *Also called* striping *or* striped volume.

ransomware Malware that holds your computer system hostage with encryption techniques until you pay money or a time period expires when the encrypted content is destroyed.

rapid elasticity A cloud computing service that is cabable of scaling up or down as a customer's need level changes.

raw data Data sent to a printer without any formatting or processing.

G

rd (remove directory)   The Windows command to delete a directory (folder) or group of directories (folders).

ReadyBoost   A Windows utility that uses a flash drive or secure digital (SD) memory card to boost hard drive performance.

ReadyDrive   The Windows 7/Vista technology that supports a hybrid hard drive.

recover   The Windows command that can recover a file when part of the file is corrupted.

recovery drive   A Windows 8 bootable USB flash drive that can be used to recover the system when startup fails and can be created using the Recovery applet in Control Panel.

recovery image   A backup of the Windows volume.

recovery partition   A partition on a hard drive that contains a recovery utility and installation files.

Recovery System   In OS X, a lean operating system that boots from a hidden volume on the OS X startup disk and is used to troubleshoot OS X when startup errors occur.

rectifier   An electrical device that converts AC to DC. A computer power supply contains a rectifier.

Recycle Bin   In Windows, location on the hard drive where deleted files are stored.

refresh   A Windows 8 technique to recover from a corrupted Windows installation and can recover using a custom refresh image, a recovery partition, or the Windows setup DVD. Depending on the health of the system, user settings, data, and Windows 8 apps might be restored from backup near the end of the refresh operation.

refresh rate   As applied to monitors, the number of times in one second the monitor can fill the screen with lines from top to bottom. *Also called* vertical scan rate.

registry   A database that Windows uses to store hardware and software configuration information, user preferences, and setup information.

Registry Editor   The Windows utility (regedit.exe) used to edit the Windows registry.

Regsvr32   A utility that is used to register component services used by an installed application.

Reliability and Performance Monitor   A Vista utility (perfmon.msc) that collects, records, and displays events, called Data Collector Sets, that can help track the performance and reliability of Windows.

Reliability Monitor   A Windows 8/7 utility that provides information about problems and errors that happen over time.

Remote Admin share   Gives an administrator access to the Windows folder on a remote computer in a Windows domain.

remote application   An application that is installed and executed on a server and is presented to a user working at a client computer.

Remote Assistance   A Windows tool that allows a technician to remote in to a user's computer while the user remains signed, retains control of the session, and can see the screen. This is helpful when a technician is troubleshooting problems on a computer.

remote backup application   A cloud backup service on the Internet that backs up data to the cloud and is often used for laptops, tablets, and smart phones.

Remote Desktop Connection (RDC)   A Windows tool that gives a user access to a Windows desktop from anywhere on the Internet.

Remote Desktop Protocol (RDP)   The Windows protocol used by Remote Desktop and Remote Assistance utilities to connect to and control a remote computer.

Remote Disc   A feature of OS X that gives other computers on the network access to the Mac's optical drive.

remote network installation   An automated installation where no user intervention is required.

remote wipe   Remotely erases all contacts, email, photos, and other data from a device to protect your privacy.

ren (rename)   The Windows command to rename a file or group of files.

repair installation   A reinstallation of Windows using the recovery utilty and installation files stored on the recovery partition.

reset   Restore a Window 8 installation to factory state or to the state after a clean install of Windows. The hard drive is formatted and all user data and settings are lost.

resiliency   In Windows 8 Storage Spaces, the term refers to the degree the configuration can resist or recover from drive failure.

Resilient File System (ReFS)   A file system that offers excellent fault tolerance and compatibility with virtualization and data redundancy in a RAID system.

resolution   The number of pixels on a monitor screen that are addressable by software (example: 1024 × 768 pixels).

Resource Monitor   A Windows tool that monitors the performance of the processor, memory, hard drive, and network.

resource pooling   Cloud computing services to multiple customers that are hosted on shared physical resources and dynamically allocated to meet customer demand.

restore point   A snapshot of the Windows system, usually made before installation of new hardware or applications. Restore points are created by the System Protection utility.

retinal scanning   As part of the authentication process, some systems use biometric data by scanning the blood vessels on the back of the eye and is considered the most reliable of all biometric data scanning.

RFID badge   A badge worn by an employee and is used to gain entrance into a locked area of a building. A Radio Frequency Identification token transmits authentication to the system when the token gets in range of a query device.

RJ-45   A port that looks like a large phone jack and is used by twisted-pair cable to connect to a wired network adapter or other hardware device. RJ stands for registered jack. *Also called* Ethernet port.

robocopy (robust file copy)   A Windows command that is similar to and more powerful than the xcopy command, used to copy files and folders.

root account   In Linux and OS X, the account that gives the user access to all the functions of the OS; the principal user account.

root certificate   The original digitate certificate issued by a Certification Authority.

root directory   The main directory, at the top of the top-down hierarchical structure of subdirectories, created when a hard drive or disk is first formatted. In Linux, it's indicated by a forward slash. In DOS and Windows, it's indicated by a backward slash.

rooting   The process of obtaining root or administrator privileges to an Android device which then gives you complete access to the entire file system and all commands and features. Note that rooting may void any manufacturer warranty on the device and might violate BYOD (Bring Your Own Device) policies in an enterprise environment.

rootkit   A type of malicious software that loads itself before the OS boot is complete and can hijack internal Windows components so that it masks information Windows provides to user-mode utilities such as File Explorer or Task Manager.

router   A device that manages traffic between two or more networks and can help find the best path for traffic to get from one network to another.

RSA tokens   A type of smart card that contains authentication information.

S/MIME (Secure/Multipurpose Internet Mail Extensions)   A protocol that encrypts an outgoing email message and includes a digital signature and is more secure than SMTP, which does not use encryption.

S1 state   On the UEFI/BIOS power screen, one of the five S states used by ACPI power-saving mode to indicate different levels of power-savings functions. In the S1 state, the hard drive and monitor are turned off and everything else runs normally.

S2 state   On the UEFI/BIOS power screen, one of the five S states used by ACPI power-saving mode to indicate different levels of power-savings functions. In S2 state, the hard drive and monitor are turned off and everything else runs normally. In addition, the processor is also turned off.

S3 state   On the UEFI/BIOS power screen, one of the five S states used by ACPI power-saving mode to indicate different levels of power-savings functions. In S3 state, everything is shut down except RAM and enough of the system to respond to a wake-up. S3 is sleep mode.

S4 state   On the UEFI/BIOS power screen, one of the five S states used by ACPI power-saving mode to indicate different levels of power-savings functions. In S4 state, everything in RAM is copied to a file on the hard drive and the system is shut down. When the system is turned on, the file is used to restore the system to its state before shut down. S4 is hibernation.

S5 state   On the UEFI/BIOS power screen, one of the five S states used by ACPI power-saving mode to indicate different levels of power-savings functions. S5 state is the power off state after a normal shutdown.

SaaS (Software as a Service)   A cloud computing service whereby the service is responsible for the hardware, the operating systems, and the applications installed.

G

Safe Mode The technique of launching Windows with a minimum configuration, eliminating third-party software and reducing Windows startup to only essential processes. The technique can sometimes launch Windows when a normal Windows startup is corrupted.

safety googles Eye googles worn while working in an unsafe environment such as a factory where fragments, chips, or other particles might injure eyes.

sag *See* brownout.

SCSI (Small Computer System Interface) An interface between a host adapter and the CPU that can daisy chain as many as 7 or 15 devices on a single bus.

scanstate A command used by the User State Migration Tool (USMT) to copy user settings and data from an old computer to a safe location such as a server or removable media. *Also see* loadstate.

screen orientation The layout or orientation of the screen that is either portrait or landscape.

screen resolution The number of dots or pixels on the monitor screen expressed as two numbers such as 1680 x 1050.

Screen Sharing In OS X, a utility to remotely view and control a Mac and is similar to Remote Assistance in Windows.

SDK (Software Development Kit) A group of tools that developers use to write apps. For example, Android Studio is a free SDK that is released as open source.

secondary click In OS X, right-click the mouse or tap the bottom-right corner of the trackpad on a Mac laptop.

secondary logon Using administrator privileges to perform an operation when you are not logged on with an account that has these privileges.

sector On a hard disk drive or SSD, the smallest unit of bytes addressable by the operating system and UEFI/BIOS. On hard disk drives, one sector usually equals 512 bytes; SSD drives might use larger sectors.

Secure Boot A UEFI feature that prevents a system from booting up with drivers or an OS that are not digitally signed and trusted by the motherboard or computer manufacturer.

Secure FTP (SFTP) A TCP/IP protocol used to transfer files from an FTP server to an FTP client using encryption.

Secure Shell (SSH) A protocol that is used to pass login information to a remote computer and control that computer over a network using encryption.

Security Center A center in Vista where you can confirm Windows Firewall, Windows Update, anti-malware settings, including that of Windows Defender, and other security settings.

security token A smart card or other device that is one factor in multifactor authentication or can serve as a replacement for a password.

self-grounding A method to safeguard against ESD that involves touching the computer case or power supply before touching a component in the computer case.

Server Message Block (SMB) A protocol used by Windows to share files and printers on a network.

Service Set Identifier (SSID) The name of a wireless access point and wireless network.

server-side virtualization Using this virtualization, a server provides a virtual desktop or application for users on multiple client machines.

service A program that runs in the background to support or serve Windows or an application.

service pack A collection of several patches or updates that is installed as a single update to an OS or application.

Services console A console used by Windows to stop, start, and manage background services used by Windows and applications.

setup UEFI/BIOS Used to change motherboard settings. For example, you can use it to enable or disable a device on the motherboard, change the date and time that is later passed to the OS, and select the order of boot devices for startup UEFI/BIOS to search when looking for an operating system to load.

shadow copy A copy of open files made so that open files are included in a backup.

share permissions A method to share a folder (not individual files) to remote users on the network, including assigning varying degrees of access to specific user accounts and user groups. Does not apply to local users of a computer and can be used on an NTFS or FAT volume. *Compare with* NTFS permissions.

shell The portion of an OS that relates to the user and to applications.

shell prompt In Linux and OS X, the command prompt in the terminal.

Short Message Service (SMS) A technology that allows users to send a test message using a cell phone.

shoulder surfing As you work, other people secretly peek at your monitor screen to gain valuable information.

shutdown The Windows command to shut down the local computer or a remote computer.

sidebar Located on the right side of the Vista desktop and displays Vista gadgets.

side-by-side apps In Windows 8, an application or page can be snapped to the left or right side of the screen so a second page can share the screen.

SIM (Subscriber Identity Module) card A small flash memory card that contains all the information a device needs to connect to a GSM or LTE cellular network, including a password and other authentication information needed to access the network, encryption standards used, and the services that a subscription includes.

Simple Network Management Protocol (SNMP) A TCP/IP protocol used to monitor network traffic.

simple volume A type of volume used on a single hard drive. *Compare with* dynamic volume.

single sign-on (SSO) An account that accesses multiple, independent resources, systems, or applications after signing in one time to one account. An example is a Microsoft account.

site license A license that allows a company to install multiple copies of software, or to allow multiple employees to execute the software from a file server. *Also called* enterprise license.

slack Wasted space on a hard drive caused by not using all available space at the end of a cluster.

sleep mode A power-saving state for a computer used to save power when not using the computer. *Also see* S3 state.

sleep timer The number of minutes of inactivity before a computer goes into a power-saving state such as sleep mode.

smart card Any small device that contains authentication information that can be keyed into a sign-in window or read by a reader to authenticate a user on a network.

smart card reader A device that can read a smart card used to authenticate a person onto a network.

SMB2 *See* CIFS (Common Internet File System).

SMTP (Simple Mail Transfer Protocol) A TCP/IP protocol used by email clients to send email messages to an email server and on to the recipient's email server. *Also see* POP and IMAP.

SMTP AUTH (SMTP Authentication) An improved version of SMTP and used to authenticate a user to an email server when the email client first tries to connect to the email server to send email. The protocol is based on the Simple Authentication and Security Layer (SASL) protocol.

snap-in A Windows utility that can be installed in a console window by Microsoft Management Console.

social engineering The practice of tricking people into giving out private information or allowing unsafe programs into the network or computer.

socket An established connection between a client and a server, such as the connection between a browser and web server.

soft boot To restart a computer without turning off the power, for example, in Windows 8, press Win+X, point to Shut down or sign out, and click Restart. *Also called* warm boot.

soft reset (1) For Android, to forecefully reboot the device (full shut down and cold boot) by pressing and holding the power button. (2) For iOS, to put the device in hibernation and not clear memory by pressing the Wake/sleep button.

Software Explorer A Vista tool used to control startup programs.

software piracy The act of making unauthorized copies of original software, which violates the Federal Copyright Act of 1976.

software RAID Using Windows to implement RAID. The setup is done using the Disk Management utility.

solid-state drive (SSD) A hard drive that has no moving parts. *Also see* solid state device (SSD).

Sound applet Accessed through the Control Panel, used to select a default speaker and microphone and adjust how Windows handles sounds.

Space In OS X, one desktop screen is called a Space. Multiple desktops or Spaces can be open and available to users.

spear phishing A form of phishing where an email message appears to come from a company you already do business with. *See also* phishing.

G

spoofing   A phishing technique where you are tricked into clicking a link in an email message, which takes you to an official-looking website where you are asked to enter your user ID and password to enter the site. *See also* phishing.

spooling   Placing print jobs in a print queue so that an application can be released from the printing process before printing is completed. Spooling is an acronym for simultaneous peripheral operations online.

Spotlight   In OS X, the search app that can be configured to search the local computer, Wikipedia, iTunes, the Maps app, the web, and more.

spyware   Malicious software that installs itself on your computer or mobile device to spy on you. It collects personal information about you that it transmits over the Internet to web-hosting sites that intend to use your personal data for harm.

standard account   The Windows 8/7/Vista user account type that can use software and hardware and make some system changes, but cannot make changes that affect the security of the system or other users. *Compare with* administrator account.

standard image   An image that includes Windows, drivers, and applications that are standard to all the computers that might use the image.

Start screen   Introduced in Windows 8, the Start screen contains tiles that represent lean apps, which use few system resources and are designed for social media, social networking, and the novice end user.

startup disk   In OS X, the entire volume on which OS X is installed.

startup items   In OS X, programs that automatically launch at startup. Apple discourages the use of startup items, which are stored in two directories: /Library/StartupItems and /System/Library/StartupItems. Normally, both directories are empty.

startup UEFI/BIOS   Part of UEFI or BIOS firmware on the motherboard that is responsible for controlling the computer when it is first turned on. Startup UEFI/BIOS gives control over to the OS once the OS is loaded.

startup repair   A Windows 8/7/Vista utility that restores many of the Windows files needed for a successful boot.

static electricity   *See* electrostatic discharge (ESD).

static IP address   A permanent IP address that is manually assigned to a computer.

Storage Spaces   A Windows 8 utility that can create a storage pool using any number of internal or external backup drives. The utility is expected to replace Windows software RAID.

striping   *See* RAID 0.

strong password   A password that is not easy to guess.

su   A Linux and OS X command to open a new terminal shell for a different user account. Stands for "substitute user".

subdirectory   A directory or folder contained in another directory or folder. *Also called* a child directory *or* folder.

subnet   A group of local networks when several networks are tied together in a subsystem of the larger intranet. In TCP/IP Version 6, one or more links that have the same 16 bits in the subnet ID of the IP address. *See* subnet ID.

subnet ID   In TCP/IP Version 6, the last block (16 bits) in the 64-bit prefix of an IP address. The subnet is identified using some or all of these 16 bits.

subnet mask   In TCP/IP Version 4, 32 bits that include a series of ones followed by zeroes. For example, 11111111.11111111.11110000.00000000, which can be written as 255.255.240.0. The 1s identify the network portion of an IP address, and the 0s identify the host portion of an IP address. The subnet mask tells Windows if a remote computer is on the same or different network.

subscription model   A method of licensing software with a paid annual subscription where the software is installed on your local computer. For example, Office 365 uses a subscription model.

sudo   A Linux and OS X command to execute another command as a superuser when logged in as a normal user with an account that has the right to use root commands. Stands for "substitute user to do the command."

superuser   Refers to a Linux or Mac OS X user who is logged in to the root account.

surge supressor   A device designed to protect against voltage spikes by blocking or grounding excessive voltage.

suspend mode   *See* sleep mode.

switch   A device used to connect nodes on a network in a star network topology. When it receives a packet, it uses its table of MAC addresses to decide where to send the packet.

system UEFI/BIOS   UEFI (Unified Extensible Firmware Interface) or BIOS (basic input/output system) firmware on the motherboard that is used to control essential devices before the OS is loaded.

System Configuration   A Windows utility (msconfig.exe) that can identify what processes are launched at startup and can temporarily disable a process from loading.

System File Checker (SFC)   A Windows utility that verifies and, if necessary, refreshes a Windows system file, replacing it with one kept in a cache of current system files.

system image   The backup of the entire Windows 8/7 volume and can also include backups of other volumes. The backup is made using the Windows 8 File History or Windows 7 Backup and Restore utility.

System Information   A Windows tool (msinfo32.exe) that provides details about a system, including installed hardware and software, the current system configuration, and currently running programs.

system partition   The active partition of the hard drive containing the boot loader or boot manager program and the specific files required to start the Windows launch.

System Preferences   In OS X, a utility to customize the OS X interface and is available on the Apple menu.

System Protection   A Windows utility that automatically backs up system files and stores them in restore points on the hard drive at regular intervals and just before you install software or hardware.

system repair disc   A disc you can create using Windows 7 that can be used to launch Windows RE. The disc is not available in Windows 8.

System Restore   A Windows utility used to restore the system to a restore point.

system state data   In Windows, files that are necessary for a successful load of the operating system.

system tray   *See* notification area.

System window   A window that displays brief and important information about installed hardware and software and gives access to important Windows tools needed to support the system.

systray   *See* notification area.

tailgating   When someone who is unauthorized follows an employee through a secured entrance to a room or building.

Task Manager   A Windows utility (taskmgr.exe) that lets you view the applications and processes running on your computer as well as information about process and memory performance, network activity, and user activity.

Task Scheduler   A Windows tool that can set a task or program to launch at a future time, including at startup.

taskbar   A bar normally located at the bottom of the Windows desktop, displaying information about open programs and providing quick access to others.

taskkill   A Windows command that uses the process PID to kill a process.

tasklist   A Windows command that returns the process identifier (PID), which is a number that identifies each running process.

TCP (Transmission Control Protocol)   The protocol in the TCP/IP suite of protocols that works at the OSI Transport layer and establishes a session or connection between parties and guarantees packet delivery.

TCP/IP (Transmission Control Protocol/Internet Protocol)   The group or suite of protocols used for almost all networks, including the Internet. Fundamentally, TCP is responsible for error checking transmissions, and IP is responsible for routing.

technical documentation   The technical reference manuals, included with software packages and hardware, that provide directions for installation, usage, and troubleshooting. The information extends beyond that given in user manuals.

Telnet   A TCP/IP protocol used by the Telnet client/server applications to allow an administrator or other user to control a computer remotely.

Teredo   In TCP/IP Version 6, a tunneling protocol to transmit TCP/IPv6 packets over a TCP/IPv4 network, named after the Teredo worm that bores holes in wood. Teredo IP addresses begin with 2001, and the prefix is written as 2001::/32.

terminal   In Linux and OS X, the command-line interface.

tether   To connect a mobile device with a cellular connection to the Internet to a computer so that the computer can access the Internet by way of the mobile device.

G

thick client   A regular desktop computer or laptop that is sometimes used as a client by a virtualization server. *Also called* fat client.

thin client   A computer that has an operating system, but has little computing power and might only need to support a browser used to communicate with a virtualization server.

thin provisioning   A technique used by Storage Spaces in Windows whereby virtual storage free space can be configured as if it has more virtual storage than the physical storage allotted to it. When the virtual storage free space is close to depletion, the administrator is prompted to install more physical storage.

third-party driver   Drivers that are not included in UEFI/BIOS or Windows and must come from the manufacturer.

thread   Each process that the processor is aware of; a single task that is part of a longer task or request from a program.

ticket   An entry in a call-tracking system made by whoever receives a call for help and used to track and document actions taken. The ticket stays open until the issue is resolved.

Time Machine   In OS X, a built-in backup utility that can be configured to automatically back up user-created data, applications, and system files onto an external hard drive attached either directly to the computer or through the local network.

TKIP (Temporal Key Integrity Protocol)   A type of encryption protocol used by WPA to secure a wireless Wi-Fi network. *Also see* WPA (WiFi Protected Access).

TPM (Trusted Platform Module)   A chip on a motherboard that holds an encryption key required at startup to access encrypted data on the hard drive. Windows 8/7/Vista BitLocker Encryption can use the TPM chip.

track   One of many concentric circles on the surface of a hard disk drive.

transformer   An electrical device that changes the ratio of current to voltage. A computer power supply is basically a transformer and a rectifier.

trip hazard   Loose cables or cords in a traffic area where people can trip over them.

Trojan   A type of malware that tricks you into downloading and/or opening it by substituting itself for a legitimate program.

Type 1 hypervisor   Software to manage virtual machines that is installed before any operating system is installed.

Type 2 hypervisor   Software to manage virtual machines that is installed as an application in an operating system.

UDF (Universal Disk Format)   A file system for optical media used by all DVD discs and some CD-R and CD-RW discs. *Also see* CDFS (Compact Disc File System).

UDP (User Datagram Protocol)   A connectionless TCP/IP protocol that works at the OSI Transport layer and does not require a connection to send a packet or guarantee that the packet arrives at its destination. The protocol is commonly used for broadcasting to multiple nodes on a network or the Internet. *Compare with* TCP (Transmission Control Protocol).

UEFI CSM (Compatibility Support Module) mode   Legacy BIOS in UEFI firmware.

ultra-thin client   *See* zero client.

unattended installation   A Windows installation that is done by storing the answers to installation questions in a text file or script that Windows calls an answer file so that the answers do not have to be typed in during the installation.

Unified Threat Management (UTM)   A computer, security appliance, network appliance, or Internet appliance that stands between the Internet and a private network and runs firewall, anti-malware, and other software to protect the network.

unicast address   Using TCP/IP version 6, an IP address assigned to a single node on a network.

Unified Extensible Firmware Interface (UEFI)   An interface between firmware on the motherboard and the operating system that improves on legacy BIOS processes for booting, handing over the boot to the OS, and loading device drivers and applications before the OS loads. UEFI also manages motherboard settings and secures the boot to ensure that no rogue operating system hijacks the system.

uninterruptible power supply (UPS)   A device that raises the voltage when it drops during brownouts.

unique local address (ULA)   In TCP/IP Version 6, an address used to identify a specific site within a large organization. It can work on multiple links within the same organization. The address is a hybrid between a global unicast address that works on the Internet and a link-local unicast address that works on only one link.

Universal Plug and Play (UPnP) An unsecure method a router can use to allow unfiltered communication between nodes on a private network. Hackers sometimes are able to exploit UPnP, so use with caution.

Upgrade Advisor *See* Upgrade Assistant.

Upgrade Assistant Software used to find out if a system can be upgraded to Windows 8.1.

upgrade path A qualifying OS required by Microsoft in order to perform an in-place upgrade.

USB 3.0 B-Male connector A USB connector used by SuperSpeed USB 3.0 devices such as printers or scanners.

User Account Control (UAC) dialog box A Windows security feature that displays a dialog box when an event requiring administrative privileges is about to happen.

User Accounts A Windows utility (netplwiz.exe) that can be used to change the way Windows sign-in works and to manage user accounts, including changing passwords and changing the group membership of an account. *Also called* Network Places Wizard.

Users group A type of Windows user account group. An account in this group is a standard user account, which does not have as many rights as an administrator account.

user mode In Windows, a mode that provides an interface between an application and the OS, and only has access to hardware resources through the code running in kernel mode.

user profile A collection of files and settings about a user account that enables the user's personal data, desktop settings, and other operating parameters to be retained from one session to another.

user profile namespace The group of folders and subfolders in the C:\Users folder that belong to a specific user account and contain the user profile.

User State Migration Tool (USMT) A Windows utility that helps you migrate user files and preferences from one computer to another to help a user make a smooth transition from one computer to another.

usmtutils A command used by the User State Migration Tool (USMT) that provides encryption options and hard-link management.

vi editor A Linux and OS X text editor that works in command mode (to enter commands) or in insert mode (to edit text).

virtual assistant A mobile device app that responds to a user's voice commands with a personable, conversational interaction to perform tasks and retrieve information. *Also called* a personal assistant.

Virtual Desktop Infrastructure (VDI) A presentation of a virtual desktop made to a client computer by a server that is serving up a virtual machine.

virtual machine (VM) Software that simulates the hardware of a physical computer, creating one or more logical machines within one physical machine.

virtual machine manager (VMM) *See* hypervisor.

virtual memory A method whereby the OS uses the hard drive as though it were RAM. *Also see* pagefile.sys.

virtual private network (VPN) A security technique that uses encrypted data packets between a private network and a computer somewhere on the Internet.

virtualization When one physical machine hosts multiple activities that are normally done on multiple machines.

virtual XP mode The term used by CompTIA for Windows XP mode. *See* Windows XP mode.

virus A program that often has an incubation period, is infectious, and is intended to cause damage. A virus program might destroy data and programs.

Voice over LTE (VoLTE) A technology used on cellular networks for LTE to support voice communication.

VoIP (Voice over Internet Protocol) A TCP/IP protocol and an application that provides voice communication over a TCP/IP network. *Also called* Internet telephone.

volume A primary partition that has been assigned a drive letter and can be formatted with a file system such as NTFS. *Compare with* logical drive.

volt (V) A measure of potential difference or electrical force in an electrical circuit. A computer ATX power supply usually provides five separate voltages: 112 V, 212 V, 15 V, 25 V, and 13.3 V.

Wake-on-LAN Configuring a computer so that it will respond to network activity when the computer is in a sleep state.

G

warm boot *See* soft boot.

watt (W) The unit of electricity used to measure power. A typical computer may use a power supply that provides 500W.

WEP (Wired Equivalent Privacy) An encryption protocol used to secure transmissions on a Wi-Fi wireless network; however, it is no longer considered secure because the key used for encryption is static (it doesn't change).

Wi-Fi (Wireless Fidelity) The common name for standards for a local wireless network as defined by IEEE 802.11. *Also see* 802.11 a/b/g/n/ac.

Wi-Fi analyzer Hardware and/or software that monitors a Wi-Fi network to detect devices not authorized to use the network, identify attempts to hack transmissions, or detect performance and security vulnerabilities.

Wi-Fi calling On mobile devices, voice calls that use VoIP over a Wi-Fi connection to the Internet.

Wi-Fi Protected Setup (WPS) A method to make it easier for users to connect their computers to a secured wireless network when a hard-to-remember SSID and security key are used, and is considered a security risk that should be used with caution.

wildcard An * or ? character used in a command line that represents a character or group of characters in a file name or extension.

Windows 7 Windows 7 editions include Windows 7 Starter, Windows 7 Home Basic, Windows 7 Home Premium, Windows 7 Professional, Windows 7 Enterprise, and Windows 7 Ultimate. Each edition comes at a different price with different features and capabilities.

Windows 8.1 A free update or release of the Windows 8 operating system. The edition of choice for a laptop or desktop computer used in a home or small office. This edition supports homegroups, but it doesn't support joining a domain or BitLocker Encryption.

Windows 8.1 Enterprise A Windows 8 edition that allows for volume licensing in a large, corporate environment.

Windows 8.1 Pro for Students A version of Windows 8 that includes all the same features as Windows 8 Pro, but at a lower price, available only to students, faculty, and staff at eligible institutions.

Windows 8.1 Professional (Windows 8.1 Pro) A version of Windows 8 that includes additional features at a higher price. Windows 8.1 Pro supports homegroups, joining a domain, BitLocker, Client Hyper-V, Remote Desktop, and Group Policy.

Windows Assessment and Deployment Kit (ADK) The Windows ADK for Windows 8 contains a group of tools used to deploy Windows 8 in a large organization and contains the User State Migration Tool (USMT).

Windows Automated Installation Kit (AIK) The Windows AIK for Windows 7 contains a group of tools used to deploy Windows 7 in a large organization and contains the User State Migration Tool (USMT).

Windows Boot Loader One of two programs that manage the loading of Windows 8/7/ Vista. The program file (winload.exe or winload.efi) is stored in C:\ Windows\System32, and it loads and starts essential Windows processes.

Windows Boot Manager (BootMgr) The Windows 8/7/Vista program that manages the initial startup of Windows. For a BIOS system, the program is bootmgr; for a UEFI system, the program is bootmgfw.efi. The program file is stored in the root of the system partition.

Windows Defender Anti-malware software embedded in Windows 8 that can detect, prevent, and clean up a system infected with viruses and other malware. Antispyware utility included in Windows 8/7/Vista.

Windows Easy Transfer A Windows tool used to transfer Windows 8/7/Vista user data and preferences to the Windows 8/7/Vista installation on another computer.

Windows Experience Index A Windows 7/Vista feature that gives a summary index designed to measure the overall performance of a system on a scale from 1.0 to 7.9.

Windows Explorer The Windows 7/Vista utility used to view and manage files and folders.

Windows Firewall A personal firewall that protects a computer from intrusion and is automatically configured when you set your network location in the Network and Sharing Center.

Windows Phone (WP) An operating system by Microsoft (*microsoft.com*) that is based on Windows and is used on various smart phones (not on tablets).

Windows Powershell A command-line interface (CLI) that processes objects, called cmdlets, which are pre-built programs built on the .NET Framework, rather than processing text in a command line.

Windows Preinstallation Environment (Windows PE) A minimum operating system used to start the Windows installation.

Windows Pro Pack An upgrade available to Windows 8 that adds the functionality of Windows 8.1 Pro to the more basic edition.

Windows Recovery Environment (Windows RE) A lean operating system installed on the Windows 8/7/Vista setup DVD and also on the Windows 8/7 volume that can be used to troubleshoot problems when Windows refuses to start.

Windows RT A Windows 8 edition that is a lighter version, designed for tablets, netbooks, and other mobile devices.

Windows Store Access to purchase and download apps that use the Windows 8 interface.

Windows Vista Windows Vista editions include Windows Vista Starter, Windows Vista Home Basic, Windows Vista Home Premium, Windows Vista Business, Windows Vista Enterprise, and Windows Vista Ultimate. Each edition comes at a different price with different features and capabilities.

Windows XP Mode A Windows XP environment installed in Windows 8/7 that can be used to support older applications.

Windows.old folder When using an unformatted hard drive for a clean installation, this folder is created to store the previous operating system settings and user profiles.

wireless access point (WAP) A wireless device that is used to create and manage a wireless network.

wireless LAN (WLAN) A type of LAN that does not use wires or cables to create connections, but instead transmits data over radio or infrared waves.

wireless locator A tool that can locate a Wi-Fi hotspot and tell you the strength of the RF signal.

wireless wide area network (WWAN) A wireless broadband network for computers and mobile devices that uses cellular towers for communication. *Also called* a cellular network.

workgroup In Windows, a logical group of computers and users in which administration, resources, and security are distributed throughout the network, without centralized management or security.

worm An infestation designed to copy itself repeatedly to memory, on drive space, or on a network, until little memory, disk space, or network bandwidth remains.

WPA (WiFi Protected Access) A data encryption method for wireless networks that use the TKIP (Temporal Key Integrity Protocol) encryption method and the encryption keys are changed at set intervals while the wireless LAN is in use. WPA is stronger than WEP.

WPA2 (WiFi Protected Access 2) A data encryption standard compliant with the IEEE802.11i standard that uses the AES (Advanced Encryption Standard) protocol. WPA2 is currently the strongest wireless encryption standard.

XaaS (Anything as a Service or Everything as a Service) An open-ended cloud computing service that can provide any combination of functions depending on a customer's exact needs.

xcopy A Windows command more powerful than the copy command that is used to copy files and folders.

zero client A client computer that does not have an operating system and merely provides an interface between the user and the server. *Also called* dumb terminal.

zero-day attack When a hacker discovers and exploits a security hole in software before the developer of the software can develop and provide a protective patch to close the hole.

zero-fill utility A hard drive utility that fills every sector on the drive with zeroes.

zero-touch, high volume deployment An installation strategy that does not require the user to start the process. Instead a server pushes the installation to a computer when a user is not likely to be sitting at it.

zombie A computer that has been hacked, and the hacker is using the computer to run repetitive software in the background without the knowledge of its user. *Also see* botnet.

G

INDEX

I

I

I

I